A History of the Moghuls of Central Asia

A History of the Moghuls of Central Asia

The Tarikh-I-Rashidi of Mirza Muhammad Haidar, Dughlat

By

N. ELIAS

TRANSLATED BY

E. DENISON ROSS

GYAN

Published by

Gyan Publishing House
5, Ansari Road
Daryaganj, New Delhi-110002
Phone: 011-47034999, 9811692060
E-mail: books@gyanbooks.com

Distribution Network
gyanbooks.com
India, USA, Canada, UK, Australia, France

ISBN : 978-81-212-6615-4 (PB)
First Published, 1895

2nd Impression 2022

Printed at: Gyan Press, Delhi.

A History of the Moghuls of Central Asia
Author: E. DENISON ROSS

THE

TARIKH-I-RASHIDI

OF

MIRZA MUHAMMAD HAIDAR, DUGHLÁT

A HISTORY OF THE MOGHULS OF CENTRAL ASIA

AN ENGLISH VERSION

Edited, with Commentary, Notes, and Map

BY

N. ELIAS

H.M. CONSUL-GENERAL FOR KHORASAN AND SISTAN;

GOLD MEDALLIST OF THE ROYAL GEOGRAPHICAL SOCIETY; CORRESPONDING MEMBER OF THE GEOGRAPHICAL SOCIETY, BERLIN

THE TRANSLATION

BY

E. DENISON ROSS

DIPLOMÉ DE L'ÉCOLE DES LANGUES ORIENTALES VIVANTES, PARIS;
OUSELEY SCHOLAR

1895

We'll lead you to the stately tent of war,
Where you shall hear the Scythian Tamburlaine
Threatening the world with high astounding terms.

—*Marlowe.*

PREFACE.

ALTHOUGH this is the first time that a translation of the *Tarikh-i-Rashidi*, into English, has been presented to the public, it is necessary to explain that translators and historians have already used the book, to some extent, as a source from which to draw facts for their writings. Not only has its scope and its general purport, as a history of the Moghuls, been familiar to Orientalists for some fifty years, but much of its contents has also been made known, in a more or less scattered way, while its name is frequently found quoted in support of one historical passage or another. And if this is the case in English writings, it is the same when we refer to the works of Continental authors who have occupied themselves with the annals of Central Asia. Yet, though the value of the book has been acknowledged in this indirect manner, no complete translation into any European language has hitherto been made.

The nearest approach to an adequate translation, so far as I am able to ascertain, was that made by the late Mr. W. Erskine of the E. I. Company's service, more than half a century ago, and some fourteen years after the publication of the *Memoirs of Baber*. Mr. Erskine's work, however, has never been put into print, and seems, indeed, to be very little known outside the MS. department of the British Museum. It appears to have been taken in hand in 1840, after his retirement from the Company's service, and to have been completed at the beginning of the next year.[1] It consists of 221 folio pages closely written, and, in one form or another, includes the greater part of the *Tarikh-i-Rashidi*. But the work varies greatly in character; in some places the author has set himself to translate fully and accurately from the text, and has been at pains to produce a rendering that would seem to be intended for publication; in other places lengthy passages—sometimes whole folios—are

[1] From a note in the margin, it appears that he finished it on the 4th of January, 1841. The MS. is numbered at the British Museum, *Add.* 26,612.

summarised more or less briefly; and in others, again, mere memoranda, or headings, are given to show the drift of the author's narrative; while, finally, considerable sections of the book, at various places, are omitted altogether.

The document, therefore, valuable though it is, can scarcely be regarded as a translation of the *Tarikh-i-Rashidi*. Rather, it appears to me, after a close acquaintance with it, to have been prepared less with a view to producing a complete English version of Mirza Haidar's history, than for some other and more special purpose. Whether Mr. Erskine ever contemplated publishing the *Tarikh-i-Rashidi* in an English dress, there is nothing to indicate, but there are several circumstances connected with the MS. at the British Museum, which lead me to conjecture that it was intended rather as a preparatory study for the compilation of his second important work—*The History of India under the Moghuls*—of which the first and second volumes (the only ones ever completed) appeared in 1854. In the first place, the passages, or sections, of the *Tarikh-i-Rashidi* devoted to the dynastic history of the Moghul Khans and their transactions, are usually those which are translated in full in the manuscript. Secondly, the *Tarikh-i-Rashidi* is not only frequently cited in the two volumes of the history, but, in many parts of them, passages from the MS. are found transcribed word for word, while the author mentions, in his preface, that he has based his knowledge of the Moghuls and their chronicles chiefly on Mirza Haidar's evidence. Indeed, the greater part of Mr. Erskine's introduction is a summary of the Moghul annals as put forward by Mirza Haidar, and by Mirza Haidar alone, for no other Asiatic author deals with the subject in any but a merely incidental way. A third circumstance pointing to the same conclusion is, that bound up in the same volume of MSS. with the fragmentary translation of the *Tarikh-i-Rashidi*, we find a second document, which consists of a similar condensed translation, in Mr. Erskine's handwriting, of the third volume of the *Ikbál Náma Jahángiri* of Mutamad Khan, a work that seems to have been studied with a view to another—probably the fourth—volume of the History of India. Thus it seems very likely that the *précis* (if it may be so called) of the *Tarikh-i-Rashidi*, was drawn up as a preliminary study for the historical works the author was at that time planning; and if this is the case, no better proof could be offered of the care and thoroughness he devoted to the task, for this document alone seems to have needed nearly a year of labour, while the *Tarikh-i-Rashidi* is only one among many Oriental authorities whom Mr. Erskine studied, in the original, and made use of—a fact to which the footnotes of his History clearly testify.

Besides serving the purpose of its own author, the *précis* translation has also been made to contribute much that is valuable to the works of Sir H. Howorth, whom little escapes that is authentic and original, however difficult of access. In his *History of the Mongols* more especially, Sir H. Howorth gathered much information regarding the tribes of Central Asia and the genealogy of Moghul Khans, and was able to throw light on some of the most obscure chapters of Asiatic history, from Mirza Haidar's data, as found in this document. Had it only been more complete, and had the geography and ethnography of Central Asia been known in Mr. Erskine's day as well as they are known now, the *History of the Mongols* would no doubt have contained all the essential parts of the *Tarikh-i-Rashidi*, and little would have been left to occupy the editor of the present translation. But it is precisely during the last fifty years that much has been learned on these subjects, so that a great deal of what was unintelligible to Mr. Erskine, and consequently left untranslated or in obscurity, is now easily filled in, by the light of more modern knowledge.

The only English writer besides Mr. Erskine who has made any extensive use of the *Tarikh-i-Rashidi*, in the original Persian, is the late Surg.-Gen. W. H. Bellew. In 1873 Dr. Bellew accompanied Sir D. Forsyth's mission to Kashgar, and compiled, as a contribution to the official report of the mission, a history of Eastern Turkistan, which is largely drawn from Mirza Haidar's data, for the period covered by the latter's narrative. Dr. Bellew had not set himself the task of translating the *Tarikh-i-Rashidi*, nor was he concerned with any part of it that did not bear directly on the country to which the mission report had reference. His history, therefore, is a compilation, only, from certain portions of Mirza Haidar's work, and though in some places it contains much detail, it cannot be compared, even as a *précis* of the book, with Mr. Erskine's MS. at the British Museum. In some respects—as for instance, the names of places and geographical notices—it is, perhaps, more valuable than that document, for the writer's local knowledge, and opportunities for deriving information from the natives of the country, gave him a distinct advantage over the earlier translator.

In the same way, Mr. R. B. Shaw, while on duty in Yarkand and Kashgar, took up a section of the book and translated some passages from it, which were published in the *Geographical Society's Journal* for 1876. These do not touch on the history, but relate exclusively to the geography of Eastern Turkistan and its neighbouring regions on the south and south-west. They contain translated extracts from Mirza Haidar's opinions, which are fully and accurately elucidated by Mr. Shaw, according to modern knowledge of the subject and local information.

Another short section of the *Tarikh-i-Rashidi* is found in Elliot's *History of India told by its Own Authors*—a work that consists of extracts (by various translators) from Asiatic writers, only when these relate to the history of India. The translation, in this instance, is by Professor Dowson, and comprises the one episode of the battle of Kanauj in 1540, when the Afghans, under Shir Shah, won for a time the so-called Moghul Empire of Hindustan. But even this has not been given in full: only the actual account of the battle being thought necessary, by the editor, as an illustration of the events of the period, while some rather lengthy passages, containing the author's views of the policy to be adopted by the Moghuls at that critical moment, have been omitted.

Whether Moorcroft used the book, is not clear from the posthumous narrative of his travels which has come down to us, through Professor H. H. Wilson. He mentions Mirza Haidar's name on one occasion only, and ascribes a statement to him connected with Kashmir, without directly citing his work. If, however, Moorcroft did know the *Tarikh-i-Rashidi*, he would be, probably, the first Englishman to become acquainted with it, for his reference to it dates from 1822.

In Russia, I believe Professor Grigorieff used the *Tarikh-i-Rashidi* in editing the Russian version of Ritter's *Erdkunde*, and it may be that other Orientalists in that country have also reproduced portions of it in their own language; but in French and German Oriental literature, I do not know that the book is more than referred to, and even that very rarely. I make this statement, however, with reserve, for it is quite possible that extracts may have been published, though I have not met with them.

As regards texts in the original Persian (for Mirza Haidar

wrote in Persian), though not particularly rare in Europe, they are seldom to be obtained, as far as my experience goes, in any Asiatic country. In England, there are three copies at the British Museum, one in the possession of Professor Cowell, at Cambridge, and it would appear that three or four more, at least, are in the hands of private persons. But these are not all of equal value: one, at any rate, of those in the British Museum being a modern Indian copy, marred by many corruptions, while another is not quite complete. The British and Foreign Bible Society own two partial translations into Turki, which they were good enough to place at the disposal of the British Museum, to be used for purposes of collation in preparing the present English version. Neither of these, however, is complete; one of them consists of the Second Part only, and the other of merely a portion of that Part. In the public libraries on the Continent, I am informed that examples are often to be met with, but whether in the original or in Turki, I am not aware.

It appears, in any case, that European collectors have, in a great measure, exhausted the supply that might be thought to be available in one part of Asia or another. In India, I believe that copies exist in some of the libraries of Calcutta and perhaps elsewhere, but a search among the native booksellers, which was made for me in 1891, resulted in finding nothing. In Persia and Afghan Turkistan I have never been able to hear of the *Tarikh-i-Rashidi*, while in the country to which it chiefly refers, and where it would be most likely to be in request, there is reason to think that scarcely any examples are now left; at any rate, all the inquiries that I was able to make from 1880 to 1885, at Yarkand and Kashgar, produced only the Turki fragment alluded to above, as consisting of a portion of the Second Part of the book. In Kashmir, no copy was ever procurable by native inquirers, who endeavoured, at different times, to obtain one for me; yet it seems probable that the more perfect Turki copy in the Bible Society's library, may have been acquired, some twenty or twenty-five years ago, by a civil officer in Kashmir.

For the present translation, Mr. Ross made use, chiefly, of the Persian text numbered *Add.* 24,090, of the British Museum Catalogue, and with this he collated the one marked *Or.* 157, that of Professor Cowell (who very kindly lent it for the purpose) and, in the Second Part, the more perfect of the two

Turki versions belonging to the Bible Society. This last proved a valuable aid in clearing up obscure passages, and in deciphering ill-spelled and badly written names of places and tribes. It is the work of an intelligent man, who knew the countries his author wrote about, and who read what he translated with judgment and discrimination. He constantly interpolates a word or two, or a sentence, in order to make the meaning clearer, and frequently spells the names of places in Turki-speaking countries, with vowel points, and in so clear a way that they can be recognised, if not identified. This is a service few Asiatic translators, or copyists, are able to render to the modern European reader; and the only pity is that the anonymous scholar was unable to do for the Tibetan names, what he accomplished for the Turki ones. He nowhere gives his name, but the end of his work is subscribed by a line as follows: "I completed this translation in the year 1263, Jamád II. 22nd, in the town of Khotan"—*i.e.*, in the year 1845 A.D.

A few words may be necessary to explain how this English version has come to see the light, and how it is that it should have been undertaken by one who has not enough Persian to be his own translator. My attention was first called to the *Tarikh-i-Rashidi* as far back as 1877, by my friend the late Mr. R. B. Shaw, who had used portions of it when he himself was living and travelling in the countries it describes. He was enthusiastic in his admiration of the author's intelligence, and of the value of the work as a "guide book" to Eastern Turkistan and the surrounding regions. He had intended, as I always understood, to take up the translation of it after completing his Turki vocabulary; but in June 1879 he died, while on service in Burma, leaving the vocabulary only just finished.[1]

For some years after this, I endeavoured to find a copy,

[1] I may remark here, that since completing the present version, and indeed, within the last few weeks, I have been favoured by Capt. F. E. Younghusband, and others of Mr. Shaw's friends, with an opportunity of examining some of the papers which he left. Among these are several unpublished extracts from the *Tarikh-i-Rashidi*, as well as some more complete sections of a rare Turki work called the *Tazkira-i-Khwájagán* ('The Memoirs of the Khwâjas') which forms—from a chronological point of view—a continuation of Mirza Haidar's history. The translations from the latter work were evidently intended, by Mr. Shaw, for early publication, but the fragments from the *Tarikh-i-Rashidi* appear only to have been preliminary studies destined to serve, at some future time, as a groundwork for a more complete translation.

believing that, with the help of native Munshis, my small knowledge of Persian might be sufficient to produce a practical, working, English version, though by no means a scholarly translation. But where, and when, I could avail myself of native assistance, no text was forthcoming, and it was only on returning to England in 1893, that I became acquainted with Mr. Erskine's partial translation among the MSS. of the British Museum. My first impression was that by filling up the gaps in this document, and rectifying the names, etc., a version might be obtained, which would be sufficiently complete to publish under Mr. Erskine's name. It soon became apparent, however, that the bulk of the MS. was only a summary of the text, and in some places was so brief, that the word "translation" could in no way be made to apply to it. It was also found that in addition to many other omissions—some long, some short—the whole of the lengthy extracts from the *Zafar-Náma* of Sharaf-ud-Din Ali, Yazdi, which the author embodies in the First Part of the *Tarikh-i-Rashidi*, to tell the story of Timur's times, had been left untouched; while certain marginal notes showed that Mr. Erskine had, in many passages, been uncertain of the author's meaning. In these circumstances, there seemed no course open but to make a new translation. Accordingly I sought advice in the only quarter where a knowledge of Mirza Haidar's original work was to be found. Dr. Charles Rieu, in compiling his catalogue of the Oriental MSS. in the British Museum, had thoroughly examined the *Tarikh-i-Rashidi*, and had described its contents; he knew its difficulties and saw, also, how imperfect would be the result of trying to expand and piece together Mr. Erskine's document. It was owing to his advice therefore, and through his good offices, that I obtained the assistance of his former pupil, Mr. Ross, to undertake a new translation; and I believe that although Mr. Ross holds a diploma for Persian from the Ecole des Langues Orientales Vivantes of Paris, and has won the Ouseley scholarship, no better guarantee for his proficiency is needed than Dr. Rieu's recommendation. It need hardly be added that in the new translation Mr. Erskine's *précis* was extensively used, and that Mr. Ross derived from it much light and assistance.

The work of translation was begun with the year 1894 and took seven months to finish. The method followed was for Mr. Ross to put sections of about five folios at a time into English, generally leaving out obscure or uncertain passages.

Each of these sections was then gone through, in company with Mr. Ross and, usually, with one of the texts at hand. The uncertain passages were then discussed and filled in, or marked off for further investigation; but the revision of the English, and the addition of footnotes, together with the solution of the puzzles in which the book abounds, were subjects left for me to take up at a later opportunity. In editing the English version, my object has been to render the language fairly clear and readable, without so changing the translation as to alter the author's meaning. But this has proved to be not always an easy task, for numerous passages occur where the translation will only bear slight amendments, without impairing its accuracy. As a rule, indeed, the latitude that could be allowed was small, so that it has been necessary to leave many sentences and paragraphs standing in rather awkward phraseology, which it would have been easy—and was even tempting—to improve, had the author's words permitted the license.

As regards the spelling of proper names, it was at first intended that all should be reproduced according to the system in use at the British Museum—*i.e.*, an exact transliteration, where each Persian and Arabic letter which has no single equivalent in English, is distinguished by some accent or diacritical sign. This design, however, could not be followed out for various reasons. Indeed, the work of translation was scarcely finished, when Mr. Ross left England to pursue his Oriental studies on the Continent, and the task of attempting to harmonise the spelling fell to me. I found it impossible, with the time at my disposal, to carry out the original intention, seeing that many of the names would have had to be searched out, afresh, in the vernacular texts—an undertaking that would have involved frequent attendance at the British Museum. I decided, therefore, to write all according to the simple method of Sir W. Jones, or that adopted by the Government of India in their official documents and publications. This system may be, to a certain extent, imperfect, for it does not, in every instance, show exactly what was the Persian or Arabic spelling of the word represented, and therefore is not a complete guide to re-conversion; but it gives, as nearly as possible, the correct pronunciation, while it secures a degree of accuracy sufficient for practical purposes.[1] It has moreover the advantage of

[1] It may be said to consist of accentuating the *a*, in order to give the sound of that letter in *father;* while other vowels are expressed (as Mr. H. G. Keene has tersely put it) "by the English sounds in '*r*u*m*i*na*nt' and '*o*bey'"

simplicity, and avoids that air of pedantry which readers who do not occupy themselves with Oriental languages, usually discern in the more perfect system, and which they find repellant. On the other hand, those who are proficient in the languages concerned, do not require to be informed how the great majority of names are written by the original authors. A small number of new and unfamiliar place-names form the only exception to this proposition, but these are usually so carelessly and incompletely written in the original texts, that a critical transliteration can have no great value, even when it is possible to give one.

In endeavouring to throw light on the narrative, and to illustrate the author's statements on subjects connected with the people or the geography of the countries he speaks of, I have used, as far as possible, the authority of writers whose information may be cited, and verified, from works already before the public. Though I am personally acquainted, more or less, with all the tribes and races Mirza Haidar introduces, and with most of the localities, the reader will probably find it more satisfactory to be referred to a published authority, than to rely on the editor's own reminiscences. This remark, however, only applies to a portion of the footnotes and of the Introduction. For all historical matters, reference to acknowledged authorities would, in any case, be needed.

It may be observed that in reproducing Mirza Haidar's lengthy extracts from the *Zafar-Náma*, at the beginning of the book, his transcription was not relied upon. Mr. Ross translated these sections directly from the texts of the work in the British Museum, and only added the Mirza's interpolation (which is repeated in several places) that the country called "Jatah," by the author of the *Zafar-Náma*, was one and the same with "Moghulistan." Neither was the very free version of the *Zafar-Náma*, by Pétis de la Croix, used for any purpose beyond the comparison of names, and Mr. Ross's translation will be found, I believe, to be much more perfect than the French one of two hundred years ago. It has been embodied in the

(*Orient. Biogr. Dict.*, p. vii.). It may be added that ordinarily used and well-known names have been spelled, in the Introduction and footnotes, as they are commonly met with in English writings; though in the text they stand as the author has written them. Thus in the text will be found, for instance, *Babar*, *Dehli*, *Gang*, etc.; while elsewhere these names occur as *Baber*, *Delhi*, *Ganges*, etc.

text without any break in the numbering of the chapters, as Mirza Haidar embodies it in his original manuscript, but it has been printed in somewhat smaller type than the rest of the text, in order to distinguish the difference of authorship.

A few words, only, are needed in explanation of the map. In the first place, its object is to show all the places mentioned in the *Tarikh-i-Rashidi*, which can surely be identified, and the positions of which can be established. In the second place, it was obviously necessary to lay down all the localities alluded to, on a basis of the best data available, regarding the physical geography of the region concerned. But a map containing only the names mentioned by Mirza Haidar would have had little significance. As a guide to their whereabouts, easily recognised points of some kind were needed, and for this purpose a number of the most ordinarily known, and least irrelevant, names in modern geography, have been used. They are marked at fairly wide intervals all over the included region, and may be regarded, for the most part, as mere "signposts" for pointing to the places spoken of by the author.

It might appear, at first sight, that the map would have been more useful, if the designations of the tribes had been inserted, and marked in such a way as to show the regions they inhabited; also that the boundaries, or approximate limits, of the various countries and kingdoms should have been indicated. But information of this kind it is impossible to give on a single sheet, intended to serve for a period of over two centuries in duration. The whole burden of the history to be illustrated is "mutability"; and a series of maps, instead of one, would be requisite to show the boundaries that existed from time to time, or the moves that occurred among the tribes. It has been found expedient, therefore, to omit all information of a transitional nature from the face of the map, and rather to make it exclusively geographical.

For the rest, everything has been done to render it plain and easy to refer to; and with this end in view, all needless details, both in the matter of names and of physical features, have been avoided. It will be found, I believe, to be the only map which contains most of the names used in historical works relating to Central Asia during the Middle Ages. The original drawing is by Mr. H. Scharbau, and is clear and excellent of its kind.

It is with pleasure that I take this opportunity to acknowledge my indebtedness to several gentlemen who have been so good as to lend me a helping hand, at various stages of my task. To no one am I more grateful than to Sir Henry Howorth, whose interest in the book, from first to last, has been manifested in so many practical ways, that it is perhaps doubtful whether, in its absence, the manuscript would ever have reached the printer. Dr. Rieu's good offices I have already alluded to; but I herewith offer him my thanks for the grace and patience with which he rendered them, in part to myself, and in part to Mr. Ross in connection with the technicalities of the translation. My gratitude is also due to Mr. Stephen Wheeler for the valuable advice he has accorded me, and for many references to books and other documents which his extensive reading—perhaps unsurpassed on most Asiatic subjects—enabled him, with great generosity, to place at my disposal. In tendering my acknowledgments to Dr. L. A. Waddell for the favour he has done the reader in adding some notes to Mirza Haidar's chapters on Tibet, I have only to refer to his able and original work on 'Lamaism in Tibet,' to guarantee appreciation of his remarks. I gladly avail myself of this occasion, also, to express my sense of obligation to Her Majesty's Secretary of State for India, for the material assistance so liberally accorded by him, towards securing the publication of the volume.

Finally, I must echo the author's words when he tells his readers that he knows his book to be full of mistakes. The subject on which I have chiefly to beg the indulgence of the critical is that of the spelling of Asiatic names, though there may be other errors and omissions, due to a want of those minute and repeated revisions of the proofs, that a book of this kind requires. My time on furlough, however, is limited, and as it has been necessary to complete the revisions before leaving England to return to Khorasán, some hurry has been inevitable.

Mirza Haidar also tells his readers that no one but a Moghul can be interested in this history. Let us hope that he may not be entirely right in his forecast. Some few who are not Moghuls may regard the preservation of his work as an advantage, and may find some attraction in it, even in an English dress; but how far these will bear with an editor who knows but little of his author's language, is another question. It may be thought that a scholarly knowledge of the language of a book is essential in one who undertakes to elucidate it, in order that he may realise the true significance of its scope, and properly understand its design. This may occasionally be the case; but if there be any virtue in the words of the German poet—

> Wer den Dichter will verstehen,
> Muss in Dichter's Lande gehen,

I would plead that the present is an instance in which something besides language may help lead to a right interpretation of the author, and to an appreciation of his theme.

N. E.

Oriental Club,
25*th March*, 1895.

TABLE OF CONTENTS.

PART I.

THE TARIKH-I-RASHIDI.

PART II.

PAGE

APPENDICES.

GENEALOGICAL TABLES.

NOTE.

The First Part of the Tarikh-i-Rashidi *is called, by the Author, the* Tarikh-i-Asl, *or 'Real History.' The Second Part he styles* Mukhtasar, *or 'Epitome.'*

The First Part was written after the Second Part had been completed. This accounts for the Author remarking, in several places in Part I., that he has written *certain passages in Part II.; while in Part II. he* promises to make *certain statements in Part I.*

The system adopted in spelling proper names has been explained in the Preface, pp. x. and xi., which see.

It has also been noticed in the Preface (p. xii.) that the extracts from the Zafar-Náma *are printed in smaller type than the rest of the text. No difference in type, however, has been made for the extracts from the* Tarikh-i-Jahán Kushai. *Those from the former work (with the exception of the very brief one in Chapter XCIX. of Part II.) were translated from original texts; while those from the latter (though collated with a copy of the* Jahán Kushai) *were translated from the* Tarikh-i-Rashidi, *as Mirza Haidar gives them.*

The ordinary, or curved, parentheses in the text, are the Author's. The light *angular brackets enclose words inserted by the translator or the editor, in order to render a passage complete in English, or to make sense. The* heavy *angular brackets contain words, or sentences, interpolated by the Turki translator, or substituted from his version, and are the outcome of the collation of the Turki text with the Persian. They appear first at page* 177 *and continue, at intervals, to the end of the book.*

The foot-notes to the text, referring to the translation, and signed R., *are those of Mr. Ross. Those in Section IV. of the Introduction, when signed* H. H., *are by Sir Henry Howorth. Those in Chapters LXXXIX. to XCI. added by Dr. L. A. Waddell on certain Tibetan subjects, are signed with his initials. The rest of the notes are editorial.*

TARIKH-I-RASHIDI.

INTRODUCTION.

SECTION I.

THE AUTHOR AND HIS BOOK.

> The Poet wandering on, through Arabie
> And Persia, and the wild Carmanian waste,
> And o'er the aërial mountains which pour down
> Indus and Oxus from their icy caves,
> In joy and exultation held his way;
> Till in the vale of Cashmire, ...
> . . . . he stretched
> His languid limbs.
>
> —*Alastor.*

THE object of the *Tarikh-i-Rashidi*, as the author tells his readers, is to preserve the memory of the Moghuls and their Khans, which, at the time he wrote, stood in danger of being altogether lost through the want of a chronicler. It was a race that he knew to be not only declining, but speedily approaching an end: its power was a dream of the past; its numbers were dwindling at a rapid rate, chiefly through absorption into the neighbouring tribes then rising to influence; while he himself had been a witness of the events and an actor in the scenes, which had resulted in the remnant of his people being ousted from their own country, to find an asylum in a strange land. In short, the Moghuls of Moghulistan—the eastern branch of the Chaghatai—had been nearly blotted from existence, while their Khans, through a long course of intermarriage with other races, had ceased to be Moghuls in anything but the name. Mirza Haidar foresaw, therefore, that there might soon be nobody left to tell the story of a people who, only a few generations earlier, had regarded themselves with pride as the descendants of Chingiz's conquering hordes, who made themselves feared if not respected, by their neighbours, and who gloried in the independence of the wide steppe-land which was their home. All this had been changed when our author—himself an exile and serving a foreign monarch—had to constitute himself the historian of their fall. Whether he was able to appreciate the changes that were taking place around him, where they did more than affect his own people, is perhaps doubtful. It may be supposed that he was regarding events from too close a standpoint to be able to judge of their true proportions; but it has become evident to later observers that he had, for the period of his history, a time of gradual but extensive change, which brought results of the greatest importance to the future of a large section of Asia. Mr. Erskine, the historian of the rise of the Moghul dynasty in India, has pointed to this period, as that which gave Transoxiana to the Uzbegs, Moghulistan to the Kirghiz, and India to the Moghuls—but to the descendants of a branch of the Moghuls quite separate from that of Moghulistan.[1]

In Central Asia it was a period full of incident: wars were on foot on every side: states were being overrun and cities besieged, while rulers arose or went down, almost from day to day, according to their fortune in war or intrigue. The princes and the descendants of exiled ruling families, together with most of the Khans and Begs of the various tribes, found themselves forced to take a side, either in support of their house or their relations, or in self-defence; and in many cases they seem to have changed sides with as little consideration for the rights and wrongs of the cause, as when they first took a part in the quarrel. When they were strong they attacked a neighbour with or without reason; if successful, they enjoyed, usually, a short period of bloody revenge and debauchery, but soon had again to "mount"—as the phrase was—for a new campaign; if beaten, they fled to some other neighbour, and if not put to death by him, waited, in exile, till a turn of fortune's wheel should afford a fresh chance of aggrandizement or plunder. "In the space of about 120 years," writes Sir H. Yule, "no less than thirty descendants or kinsmen of Chaghatai are counted

[1] It will be seen, lower down, that Mirza Haidar invariably speaks of the ruling house which we know as "the Moghuls of India," by the name of *Chaghatai*, which is, of course, strictly correct. He reserves the name of *Moghul* to denote his own race—*i.e.*, the descendants of the Moghuls (or Mongols) of Moghulistan. The subject will be explained farther on in this Introduction.

to have occupied his throne; and indeed revolutions, depositions, murders, and usurpations seem to have succeeded each other with a frequency unusual even in Asiatic governments."[1]

Here, then, were times that could hardly fail to make a historian of any soldier of fortune, who happened to have a taste for recording the events of his own life. Baber, the first of the Moghuls of India, and our author's cousin, especially answered to this description, and left behind him a picture of his age which is almost, if not quite, unique among the works of Asiatic authors. He has been represented as at once a soldier, a historian, and an autobiographer; and his kinsman, Mirza Haidar, may justly be described in the same way. Baber, however, was a better autobiographer than Mirza Haidar, and he was incomparably a greater soldier, as history proves. But, on the other hand, his cousin may be fairly acknowledged the better historian. While Baber made history incidental to his own memoirs, the reverse was the case with Mirza Haidar. The Mirza wrote the history of his race and family with a definite purpose; and when he came to his own days, he wove in his personal adventures as those of an actor and participator in the events he was recording—making the one illustrate the other; so that it may, with truth, be said that his life belongs to his history.

Though they differed in remote origin, Mirza Haidar was, to all intents and purposes, of the same nation and country as Baber; yet he wrote in Persian, while the latter wrote in the Chaghatai Turki (as the modern name is), current then, as now, all over Central Asia. Baber was a descendant of Amir Timur (or Tamerlane), and was, consequently, on one side of his family, more a Turk than a Moghul, for Timur belonged to the Barlás, a Turki tribe of distinguished lineage. Following the common usage of the day, however, Mirza Haidar would have called Baber a "Chaghatai," while the latter would have spoken of his cousin as a "Moghul." Mirza Haidar came of the Dughlát tribe—a sub-division, or sept, of the true Moghuls of Chaghatai's line—and one that was accounted about equal, in point of nobility, to the Barlás. By the end of the fifteenth century the members of all the Moghul and Chaghatai ruling families had become much scattered, and mixed in blood, through frequent intermarriages with aliens. Many of them had, for several generations, lived in Turki countries, where they had become

Turks in manners and language. So much was this the case with Baber and his kindred, that he had come to look upon himself as more of a Turk than a Moghul, and in his Memoirs mentions, more than once, his aversion and contempt for the Moghul race.[1] The Dughlát had remained more distinctively Moghul, though among its members, also, much intermixture with Turki tribes appears to have taken place. Thus the Turki in which Baber wrote his Memoirs, must have been the natural language of Mirza Haidar also, who probably knew little or nothing of the Moghul tongue, and in his capacity of Musulman, would have despised it as something appertaining to infidels and barbarians. But however this may be, when he wrote in Persian, he was certainly using a foreign language, and it is for this reason, perhaps, that his style is wanting in the simplicity which (it is said) characterises that of Turki writers—a simplicity that Baber loved, and impressed upon his son, Humayun, as an accomplishment to be cultivated.[2]

That the *Tarikh-i-Rashidi* was not written for effect, or for the indulgence of a taste for literature, need hardly be remarked after what has been said above. The work is an earnest one, and the author, no doubt intended that it should be, before everything else, a clear and complete exposition of the times he had set himself to chronicle. On the whole he has been successful, and has produced a record that, in point of usefulness, will bear comparison (as far as can be judged from translations) with most of those of Asiatic authors who have occupied themselves in the same field, from the thirteenth century to the seventeenth.[3] His task was not an easy one, for much of the history of the times is complicated and obscure, and would require infinite care and method to present it to the reader with perfect clearness. All was change and disorder. Princes and members of

[1] He sums up his sentiments regarding them in some verses, which are translated, as follows:—

> If the Moghul race were a race of Angels, it is a bad race;
> And were the name Moghul written in gold, it would be odious.
> Take care not to pluck one ear of corn from a Moghul's harvest.
> The Moghul seed is such that whatever is sowed with it is execrable.
> —(*Memoirs*, p. 93.)

[2] "You certainly do not excel in letter writing, and fail chiefly because you have a great desire to show your acquirements. For the future you should write unaffectedly, with clearness, using plain words, which would cost less trouble both to the writer and the reader."—(*Ib.*, p. 392.)

[3] Mr. Erskine has remarked that it forms a "valuable accompaniment to the Commentaries of Baber, which it illustrates in every page."—(*Hist. of India*, i., p. 193.)

reigning families wandered and married in every direction, and their houses dovetailed into one another in a manner almost calculated to set at defiance any method of narration, however systematic: the limits of countries were nowhere fixed, while, unlike in any other part of the world, many of the nations dealt with were nomads, who sometimes migrated *en masse* from one region to another, or sometimes were found divided in their political subordination, as well as in their abodes. Even the names of the countries were not defined; and in some cases the tribe and the region it occupied, were confused under one name. In others, the country and the chief town were not distinguished; while in some, again, a place or a people might be known by different names to different neighbouring nations. The author who could construct from these confused materials an intelligible and fairly consecutive narrative, can scarcely be blamed if his reader should occasionally be perplexed in linking the various incidents together, or in distinguishing between some of the actors who took part in them. More especially should he be treated with leniency, when it is considered that what was clear to him at the time, and on the spot, must necessarily bear an entirely different complexion when viewed by the Western reader, after a lapse of more than three hundred years, and after all the changes that have taken place in the interval. It may be said that the art of the historian consists in overcoming these difficulties, and in leaving behind him a narrative that will be clear for all time; but this would be too much to expect from an Asiatic author, even though he might be an experienced writer, and not, as in Mirza Haidar's case, a roving adventurer or soldier of fortune, exposed to all the vicissitudes of the times. To the most practised among them, systematic arrangement and clearness of statement, as we understand the terms, are unknown, and even if they thought it worth while to consider the convenience of the readers they knew of, they could hardly have contemplated their works being studied by foreigners, from countries of which they had scarcely heard even the names.

Still, after making every allowance, it must be admitted that Mirza Haidar's book has its shortcomings, when viewed as a practical history. His flights of unmeaning rhetoric are, unfortunately, frequent, if scarcely so extravagant as those of most Persian writers. He constantly breaks out into verse, also, though he usually indulges in this form of ornament parenthetically—by way of declamation—and thus only interrupts the course of the narrative, while not marring its sense. His sentences, again, are often involved and his meaning not always apparent. This is more especially the case where he uses the *ratio obliqua*, and where he puts speeches into the mouths of his characters; but when he confines himself to the direct relation of an event, such as the siege of Yangi-Hisar or the battle of Kanauj, his descriptive power is excellent, and the picture he presents is all that can be desired. On the whole, it may be said that for an author who takes credit to himself (as the Mirza does in his prologue) for being a past master in the art of making verses and in the "epistolary style," his writing is not obscure as Asiatic writings go; and though rather tedious repetitions are found in some of the historical sections, this is a fault on the right side, and causes less embarrassment than when gaps occur in the narrative.

These points relate more particularly to the author's style, but the chief imperfections in the work lie deeper. Perhaps those most to be deplored, are the weakness of the chronology and the looseness with which numbers and measurements are used. The former is a serious blemish, but as it is most marked in the early parts of the history, where the faults can be, to some extent rectified, by references to Chinese and other annals, it is not of vital consequence. A great part of his information having reached him by means of verbal tradition, passed down through three or four generations, the dates, above all, would tend to suffer; while, generally, it may be supposed that Mirza Haidar had scarcely realised, as did Sir Walter Scott, that "tradition is as frequently an inventor of fiction, as a preserver of truth." The second defect is greatly to be regretted, as many interesting passages relating to military operations, the tribes, cities, ruins and curiosities are greatly diminished in value, from the want of accuracy in the figures recorded. The tendency, generally, it to exaggerate freely. A third, but less important deficiency, is the one partially alluded to above —*i.e.*, the want of systematic arrangement into divisions, or sections, the absence of which is the cause of the frequent repetitions that occur, and the involution of one subject with another.

The scope and character of the *Tarikh-i-Rashidi* may be briefly summarised in much the same way as Dr. Charles Rieu, the learned Keeper of the Oriental Manuscripts at the British

Museum, has described it in his official catalogue.[1] It may be regarded as the history of that branch of the Moghul Khans who separated themselves, about the year 1321, from the main stem of the Chaghatai, which was then the ruling dynasty in Transoxiana; and it is the only history known to exist of this branch of the Moghuls. The original, or western line—that of Transoxiana—was at that time declining in power, and through internal dissensions and administrative decay, was rapidly approaching a final dissolution. The princes of the branch then thrown off, became masters of Moghulistan (or Jatah, as it was called at that period) and of all Eastern Turkistan, and continued as a ruling dynasty for more than two and a half centuries. The book is divided into two parts, called *Daftar*, the first of which is entirely historical, while the second contains reminiscences of the author's life and notices of Chaghatai, Uzbeg and other princes, with whom he was acquainted.

The first Part, or history proper, was written in Kashmir in 1544 and 1545, and was completed about February, 1546, or five years after his installation as regent of that country. It includes, however, a later addition, in which 953 of the Hajra (4th March, 1546, to 21st February, 1547) is mentioned as the current year. For the earlier periods it deals with, it is based on the traditions handed down to the author chiefly by his older relatives, combined with the statements of Sharaf-ud-Din, Yazdi in the prolegomena of the *Zafar-Náma*; and, for the later periods, on his personal recollections. It contains a record of two distinct and parallel dynasties: (1) that of the Khans of Moghulistan, beginning with Tughluk Timur, who reigned from 1347 to 1362, and whose father, Isán Bugha, was the first to separate from the main Chaghatai stem; and (2) of their vassals, the Dughlát Amirs of Eastern Turkistan, one of the earliest of whom, Amir Bulaji, the author's ancestor, had raised Tughluk Timur to the Khanship. In the second period, the family of the Khans divided into two branches, one of which, superseding the Amirs of Kashghar (or Eastern Turkistan), continued to rule over Moghulistan proper and Eastern Turkistan, with their capital at Kashghar, while the other became rulers of the provinces eastward of Aksu (known as Uighuristan), and had their seat of government usually at

[1] Catalogue of the Persian MSS. in the British Museum, by Ch. Rieu, Ph.D., 1879, vol. i., p. 167. But I have only partially followed Dr. Rieu's analysis of the *Turikh-i-Rashidi*.

Turfán. The author concludes his account of each with a short sketch of their reigning representatives, at the time of writing.

The second Part, which has more than twice the extent of the first, and contains Mirza Haidar's record of his life and times, was the first in point of date. The author wrote it in 1541–42, and, as he states in the *Prologue*, with a view to preparing himself for the more arduous task of historical composition.[1] It begins with his birth and concludes with an account of his second invasion of Kashmir, when, by a battle fought on the 2nd August, 1541, he became master of the country. This Part includes also some rules of conduct for kings, drawn up at the request of the author, by his spiritual guide, Maulána Muhammad Kázi, whose death, in 1515, is recorded in the preceding passage; while another moral treatise by a holy Shaikh, Shaháb-ud-Din Mahmud, styled Khwája Nura, is inserted in full.[2]

The author is usually known as Mirza Haidar, and in this way he styles himself, though his full name and designation would be Mirza Muhammad Haidar, Dughlát, Kurkán. By some European writers, his usual appellation has been reversed, and he has become Haidar Mirza. In some parts of Asia the distinction would be a wide one; for when "Mirza" is placed before a name, it means merely "Mr." or "Esq.," and has about the same signification as the word "Khan," when used by Persians of the better class, and by Hindustani Musulmans of all classes, at the present day. When placed after a name, it is equivalent to "Prince," and is so used only by persons belonging to a reigning family. In the case of our author either would be suitable, seeing that he was a prince of the branch of Moghul Khans who were, at that time, rulers of the Kashghar province. But his grandfather, who had been one of these rulers, had borne the same names, and seems always to have been styled with the word Mirza at the end—Muhammad Haidar Mirza. It may be as well, therefore, to draw as clear a distinction as possible between him and his grandson. The latter tells us, too, that he was known to his associates by the

[1] This should be borne in mind in reading the text, for in Part I. the author frequently alludes to what he *has written* in Part II.; while in Part II. he *promises to* make mention of certain events in Part I.

[2] As these two documents do not properly belong to the history, they have not been included in the translation.

style of ***Mirza Haidar***, and as he himself uses it, the words may safely be placed in that order.

In recording his own descent, Mirza Haidar describes himself as the son of Muhammad Husain Kurkán, son of Muhammad Haidar Kurkán, son of Amir-i-Kabir Said Ali, son of Amir Ahmad, son of Khudaidad, son of Amir Bulaji. He was born in the year of the Hajra 905 (1499–1500 A.D.)[1] at Tashkand, the capital of the province then known as Shásh, where his father, Husain, had been made governor some six years before, by Mahmud, the titular Khan of Moghulistan and Kashghar. The others named in the pedigree were all Amirs of Kashghar, while the earliest of them, Bulaji of the Dughlát tribe, is remembered as being the first of the line to become a Musulman. It was on the side of his mother, Khub Nigár Khánim, that our author was related to the Emperor Baber. She was a daughter of Yunus, Khan of the Moghuls, and a younger sister of Kutlugh Nigár Khánim, the mother of Baber.[2]

Mirza Haidar began his life in the midst of strife and adventures. His father—a treacherous and intriguing man—had been convicted of a mischievous plot against Baber at Kabul, but had been pardoned on account of his blood relationship. Shortly afterwards he had fallen into the hands of Shahi Beg Khan (otherwise Shaibani Khan), the Uzbeg leader, and had incurred that chief's suspicion also; but once more he was permitted to escape, and repaired to Herat, then the capital of Khorasán. His intriguing nature, however, being thought by Shahi Beg to be dangerous even at a distance, he caused him to be put to death there, after a short time, by emissaries whom he sent for the purpose from Transoxiana. Muhammad Husain had taken with him into exile some members of his family, among whom was our author, then quite a child; and it appears that after his father's murder, some of the retainers of the family, believing the son to be doomed to a similar fate, had carried him off to Bokhara, and had placed him in concealment there. In 1508, when about nine years of age, he was taken in charge by one of these faithful friends, called Maulána Muhammad (formerly his father's *khálifa*, or religious guide) who determined to save the child from the death that awaited him at the hands of the relentless Uzbegs, and contrived to escape with him from the city. After a difficult and exciting

[1] The year 905 H. began 8th August, 1499.

[2] See the genealogical table of the house of Chaghatai facing p. **49**.

flight across the hill tracts of Khatlán and Kuláb, in the course of which they several times narrowly escaped falling into the hands of hostile Uzbegs, they succeeded in crossing the Oxus into Badakhshán. Here one Khan Mirza, a cousin and dependent of Baber, was at the time the reigning chief, with his capital at Kila Zafar on the Kokcha. He received the fugitives with kindness, and they remained a year with him, when Baber sent to summon them to Kabul. On their arrival, Mirza Haidar was made a member of the Emperor's household, and seems to have been treated with much consideration. Within a few months, however, Baber had to march northwards against the Uzbegs, whose main force was then at Hisar, and his young cousin accompanied the army. The next two years were stirring times, and Mirza Haidar, if not too young, must have learned much of warfare, as it was conducted in those days in Central Asia.

Baber's first two attempts on Hisar failed, but, on being joined by a large body of Persians from Khorasán, his third advance resulted in a victory which gained him the possession of Kunduz, Khatlán, and Khuzár. Taking advantage of the reputation they had established, and of the defeat and death of Shahi Beg, which had just then (1510) taken place in a battle with the Persians near Merv, the allies lost little time in making an attempt on Samarkand, the capital of Transoxiana. They marched first on Bokhara, where the inhabitants opened their gates to them, and afterwards to Samarkand, which they found undefended, the Uzbeg leaders having fled on their approach. Here Baber was received with enthusiasm by the people, and was virtually master, for a time, of the greater part of Central Asia. With his young guest in his following, he remained in Samarkand for some months, when a strong combination of Uzbeg tribes, compelled him and his Persian allies once more to take the field—though this time with very different results. They advanced against Bokhara, which had in the meantime been seized by the Uzbegs, but were repulsed, and shortly afterwards were disastrously defeated at the battle of Ghajdiwán, some distance to the north of the city. The alliance with the Persians came to an end and Baber retreated to Hisar, where he was surprised by an attack made by a body of Moghuls in the service of the Uzbegs, and again experienced a crushing defeat. He then retired to Kabul, but Mirza Haidar had now left him. After the retreat from Samarkand, his uncle,

Sultan Ahmad, the Khan of Moghulistan, having written several times to ask Baber's permission for the boy to be sent to him, at last obtained it, and Mirza Haidar, "led away by youthful impatience," as he himself writes, availed himself of the Emperor's consent, unwillingly given, and followed his uncle to Andiján, then the capital of Farghána.

It was about the beginning of the year 1514 that Mirza Haidar arrived at Andiján, and almost immediately afterwards entered the service of his kinsman Sultan Said Khan (the son of Sultan Ahmad), who had just then been conducting an expedition against the Uzbegs in Tashkand, but had returned to Andiján on the enemy evacuating their positions. During the following summer, however, the Uzbegs recovered themselves and marched with a large force to lay siege to the Farghána capital. Sultan Said convened a council of his chiefs, who were unanimously of opinion that they were unable, without allies, to contend against the power of the Uzbegs; they believed themselves to have a fairer chance of success by undertaking an invasion of Kashghar, and wresting that province from Mirza Abá Bakr, who then held it. This resolution was accordingly adopted, and before the Uzbegs had time to enter the country, the Khan with all his Amirs, their families and baggage, set out from Andiján and advanced towards Kashghar, by a route leading through Moghulistan. This Mirza Abá Bakr was of the line of Dughlát Amirs, and was regarded by the Khans of Moghulistan as a usurper. He was an active and able soldier, though a cruel tyrant, and during his long rule, had made himself master of nearly the whole of Eastern Turkistan, besides several of the neighbouring countries. In 1511 he had invaded Farghána, but had there received a check by coming into conflict with Sultan Said, from whose forces he experieneed a severe defeat at the battle of Tutluk, near Andiján. It was this victory over the usurper, that emboldened Sultan Said and his Amirs to attack him again in his own stronghold. Their enterprise resulted in a complete success: Kashghar was taken in 1514, while Yangi-Hisar, Yarkand, and the remainder of the cities of Eastern Turkistan fell shortly afterwards. Abá Bakr, driven an exile to Ladak, was murdered on the road, and the line of Moghul Khans was re-established in Moghulistan and Eastern Turkistan.

Mirza Haidar, though now only fifteen years of age, was raised by his cousin the Khan to a high position, and his life of activity may be said to have begun about this time. For the ensuing nineteen years, during which Sultan Said's reign lasted, the Mirza served him in various capacities, but chiefly as a soldier; and it was only after the Khan's death, which occurred while returning from an expedition against Ladak in 1533, that he abandoned Kashghar and transferred his services to the Chaghatais in India. He not only took part in Sultan Said's wars against the Kirghiz and Uzbegs in Moghulistan, and against other tribal enemies, but was entrusted with important commands on distant expeditions. The first of these was an invasion of the hill country, then known as Bilur, or Bolor, in 1527. The expedition was nominally under the command of the Khan's eldest son, Rashid Sultan, but seeing that our author acted as a sort of tutor, or governor, to this young prince, it seems that he had much to do with the conduct of the campaign. Bolor may be described, roughly, as all the small hill states lying south of the Hindu Kush, between Baltistan on the east and Afghanistan on the west—as the limits of these countries are now accepted. Thus it included Hunza, Gilgit, Chitral, and probably most of the petty states sometimes known as "Yághistan." There appears to have been no cause for the invasion, other than that the inhabitants were not Musulmans; but considerations of this kind did not weigh with the Central Asian Khans, and Sultan Said, as the author tells us, had always been ambitious of gaining glory by waging wars against "infidels." The Bolor states were accordingly overrun and plundered during a whole winter, and the expedition returned to Kashghar in the following spring.

In 1529-30 the Khan undertook, in person, a campaign against Badakhshán, but sent Mirza Haidar in advance to begin operations. The Mirza records that he laid waste the environs of the chief town, Kila Zafar, and when the Khan arrived, his men had only to carry off what little had been left. The object of this expedition was to gain possession of the districts on the Upper Oxus—Wakhán, Shighnán, etc.—which had been conquered by the late Mirza Abá Bakr, and which Sultan Said, in consequence, considered himself the heir to. But the chief of Badakhshán was a relation and nominee of Baber, who took a view of the matter entirely opposed to that of Sultan Said, and threatened to support the chief. As Baber had now recovered, in India, the influence he had lost in Transoxiana, a letter from him to the aggressive Sultan Said, seems to have been sufficient to cause the Kashghar forces to be withdrawn across the Pamirs.

But it was in 1531 that Mirza Haidar undertook his most important service for Sultan Said Khan. This was the invasion, first of Ladak, then of Kashmir and Baltistan, and afterwards of Tibet proper, or the country known to Europeans under that name[1]—an invasion as culpably aggressive as the raid into the Bolor states. There was much paganism, he tells us, in Tibet, and the Khan, always animated by a love of Islam and a desire to carry on holy wars, was led by his pious aspirations to conquer that infidel country. It was not the first time that Ladak had been wantonly overrun from the side of Turkistan. Mirza Abá Bakr, during his long reign, had once at least, carried his arms into Ladak, while it would appear, from what Mirza Haidar records, that several parties had been sent to plunder the country since the accession of his patron, Sultan Said, to the Khanate. Very little is known of these earlier invasions, beyond the mere mention of them by Mirza Haidar, and by the author of the *Haft Iklim*,[2] who, however, obviously derived his information from the *Tarikh-i-Rashidi*. That all were unprovoked and prompted by a mere craving for plunder, however disguised under the mask of religious zeal, may be assumed with moderate confidence. None of them, including that of Sultan Said and Mirza Haidar, appear to have prospered, or to have made much impression on the inhabitants, who have preserved their old religion and manners to the present day; and though they have, in modern times, fallen politically under the Hindu yoke of the Dogras, they still keep up their ancient connection with Lassa, in all matters concerning their Buddhism and social customs. As Mirza Haidar says little about the fighting in Ladak, it is probable that the inhabitants offered only a feeble military opposition to the invaders, but trusted rather to the rugged nature of their country, the severity of the climate, and to the weapon common to most of the yellow races—passive resistance—to free them eventually from their enemy. And they were indeed successful. After subduing Ladak, a rapid march was made into Kashmir, where, to begin

[1] Mirza Haidar, like all natives of Central Asia, used the name *Tibet* to signify Ladak, but he applies it also, on some occasions, to the territory ruled from Lassa, or Tibet proper, as understood in modern times. (See notes, pp. 135 and 136.)

[2] See Quatremère's extracts from this work, in the *Notices et Extraits des Manuscrits de la Biblioth.*

with, some easy victories were won, but treachery and discontent having appeared in the Moghul camp, Mirza Haidar had, after a few months' occupation, to fall back on Ladak, leaving Kashmir, to all intents and purposes, independent.

Sultan Said Khan, hoping to share in the glories of the "holy war," had followed his lieutenant into Ladak, but his constitution, undermined by excessive drinking, proved less vigorous than his religious zeal, and the attenuated air of the Ladak passes had nearly proved fatal to him on the journey across. He recovered, however, sufficiently to lead a portion of his force into Baltistan, while Mirza Haidar was engaged in Kashmir, but after passing a winter there, distracted by cold and hunger, he too had to retreat into Ladak, and very shortly afterwards, set out on his return to Kashghar with a portion of the army. This second journey across the heights, achieved for him what the first had so nearly accomplished. He died on the Suget Pass, from the malady known as "damgiri," or mountain sickness, and was at once succeeded by his eldest son, Abdur Rashid.

The death of the Khan in no way checked the course of the "holy war," for his second son, Iskandar Sultan, and many other Amirs, remained with Mirza Haidar, who now (July, 1533) started on an expedition to "earn merit" by destroying the great temple at Lassa—an exploit, he tells his readers, that had never been achieved by any King of Islám. He appears to have marched for about a month's journey towards the south-east, over some of the highest table-lands in Asia, to the region which gives rise to most of the great rivers of India, and to within a few days' journey of the Tibetan border of Nipal. His total force is nowhere stated in figures, and apparently it was divided into at least two, or perhaps three, columns. One of these was attacked by a force of "men armed with short swords," sent by "a Rai of Hind" to the assistance of the Tibetans—a statement that appears to point to a body of Nipali tribesmen, armed with their national weapon, the kukri. The inference is that the Moghuls were beaten in at least one fight with these people. Yet Mirza Haidar continued his march towards the capital, until he arrived at, and plundered, a place he calls Astábrak (or Astákbark), which was represented as being within eight days' journey of Lassa. No map or book of any date, now available, seems to contain this name or any variant of it, but if the estimate of eight marches from

Lassa be correct, and these marches are intended for the long Tibetan post-stages, the invaders would still have been some 300 miles, or more, distant from their goal. However this may be, the mortality among his horses, want of supplies, and the general distress caused by cold and the high elevation, obliged the Mirza to abandon his enterprise at this point, and to set out in retreat towards Ladak. His experience, indeed, was almost exactly that of the Dogra general Zoráwar Sing who, in 1841, made an attempt to conquer the western provinces of Tibet for his master, Rájah Guláb Sing of Kashmir. Of fighting there was little in either case, except against the climate and conditions of the country, and in both instances these adversaries proved victorious.

In the early months of 1534 Mirza Haidar returned defeated, and with a mere remnant of his force, to a position of safety in Ladak. Of those who were left even, many deserted him here to find their way back to their homes across the mountains. Yet, broken and almost helpless as he was, the chiefs of Upper Ladak received him and his men with hospitality, and even assisted him in getting together a force with which, the next year, he proceeded to attack and plunder the western districts of the country, known as Purik, Suru, and Zangskar. His success in all these forays was very doubtful. He seems to have been able to do little more, during the first year, than keep his men and animals from starving, while in the second year (1535) he had again, from sheer distress, to fall back on the neighbourhood of Leh and throw himself on the mercy of the strangely tolerant Ladak chiefs. His followers, under these conditions, became discontented if not mutinous, and began to desert him; while he received such evil tidings from Kashghar, that the "holy war" against the Tibetans at length came to an end.

Rashid Sultan (otherwise Abdur Rashid Khan) had begun his reign at Kashghar, by putting to death many of his own relations, and among them the author's uncle, Sayyid Muhammad Mirza, whom he suspected of plotting against him in favour of the late Khan's younger son, Iskandar. These events seem to have made a deep impression on Mirza Haidar's mind, for he alludes to them with bitterness, more than once in the course of his narrative. His uncle had served Sultan Said faithfully for many years, and had done much arduous work for him, while Mirza Haidar himself had been the chief agent in extending the Khan's kingdom and power. But besides this, he had been companion and instructor to two of the Khan's sons, and when the elder of these marked the commencement of his reign by acts of ingratitude and bloodshed, it is scarcely surprising that he should be deeply hurt, and should record his feelings, years afterwards, in his history.

Hence, fearing that he might meet with the same treatment as his uncle and others of his family, if he returned to Kashghar, he had to seek for a refuge. It was impossible to stay longer in Ladak, while all the direct roads to India and Kabul were in the hands of those whom he had lately been chastising and plundering, in the name of religion. With the daring of despair, he determined to try and reach Badakhshán with the handful of adherents that remained in his service, by turning off from the usual track between Ladak and Yarkand, at a point called Ak-Tagh, to the north of the Karakorum Pass; and after following the course of the Yarkand river for some distance, to gain Ráskám, the southern Pamirs, and Wakhán. This adventure—apparently almost hopeless under the conditions in which he attempted it—he accomplished successfully, accompanied by about twenty followers, though not without much hardship and suffering. The winter of 1536–7 he spent in Badakhshán, the following summer he repaired to Kabul, and shortly after to Lahore, where he was received by Baber's son, Kámrán Mirza, and found himself, as he tells us, raised from the depths of distress to honour and dignity.

Kámrán was at that time engaged in a struggle for territory with the Persians, and had, soon after our author's arrival, to proceed to the relief of Kandahar, which was being besieged by Sám Mirza and by Shah Tahmásp, the sons of Shah Ismail, the Safavi; but before setting out he appointed his guest to the governorship of those parts of India (the whole of the Punjab) which belonged to him, and in this capacity Mirza Haidar resided for over a year at Lahore, "collecting taxes, suppressing revolt, protecting the frontiers, and establishing Islám." It was shortly after Kámrán's return to the Punjab, (1538) that Humayun had sustained a severe defeat in Bengal at the hands of Shir Sháh Sur, the Afghán leader, who was now advancing towards Agra by the left bank of the Ganges. A large part of Humayun's army having accompanied him to Bengal, he made an appeal to Kámrán and his other brothers to send assistance to Agra, while he himself hurried northward. Kámrán, after some hesitation, consented, and moved first to Delhi and then to Agra, with an army of 20,000 men, and in company with our author. Here dissensions took place among the brothers; Kámrán repented of his decision to support the Emperor, and putting forward bad health as a reason, determined to return to Lahore, while Shir Shah was yet on the far side of the Ganges. He endeavoured to persuade Mirza Haidar to return with him, but the Mirza declined on patriotic grounds, and from that time forward (1539) became an adherent of Humayun, who treated him with great honour and called him "*brother*, after the Moghul fashion."

The disastrous battle of Kanauj soon followed.[1] Humayun's force numbered some 40,000, but was less an army than a huge undisciplined mass, commanded by Amirs who had no intention of fighting the Afghans. Mirza Haidar appears to have acted as a kind of general adviser or chief of the Emperor's staff, but he mentions incidentally that he also led the centre division.[2] The confusion and corruption that prevailed on the side of the Chaghatais he describes with much candour, and clearly shows that the battle was lost before it had been fought. Whatever his position in the army may have been, he seems to have done his best to advise and support his master, and finally joined him in his flight to Agra,[3] and thence to Lahore. His narrative gives, in a few words, a vivid picture of the crowd of refugees that were assembled at the Punjab capital, their state of panic, and the divided and interested counsels with which the Emperor was perplexed. Mirza Haidar advised that the Chaghatai Amirs should occupy separate positions along the lower hills, from Sirhind to the Salt Range, where the army might be reorganised in safety and, on a favourable opportunity presenting itself, might be used with effect to regain possession of India. He himself would undertake the reduction of Kashmir, a task he hoped to accomplish in so short a time that the Emperor

[1] 17th May, 1540, or 10 Muharam, 947 H.

[2] Abul Fazl (according to Price) implies that Humayun, in person, commanded the centre, while the right and left wings were led by a brother and a nephew, respectively. (*Muhamd. Hist.* iii., p. 781.)

[3] The historian Jauhar mentions that during a brief halt made at Fattehpur Sikri, Humayun, while sitting in a garden, was shot at by some unseen person, and that "two attendants" having been sent in pursuit of the would-be assassin, both returned wounded. Mr. Erskine (following apparently the *Akbar-Náma* of Abul Fazl) mentions that one of the wounded "attendants" was Mirza Haidar. (See Jauhar's *Tazkirát ul Wakiát*, trans. by Stewart,

and his brothers might send their families thither, and secure, for them at least, a refuge from all enemies. But the Mirza's advice was of no avail; for though Humayun seems to have been inclined to listen, he was overborne by other councillors.

While acting at Lahore as Kámrán's delegate, Mirza Haidar had been approached by certain chiefs of Kashmir who were at variance with the native prince then reigning in their country, and who, on being worsted by him, had found a refuge in the Punjab. They endeavoured to procure, through Mirza Haidar's influence, the assistance of a body of Kámrán's troops, to invade their own country and expel the obnoxious ruler. The scheme seems to have commended itself to the Mirza's judgment, and after some delay he was able to gather a respectable force, which he placed under the command of one Bába Chuchak, one of the most experienced officers in the service of Kámrán, with instructions to accompany the Kashmiri chiefs and restore them to the possession of their State. The Bába, however, found pretexts for evading the execution of these orders, and the expedition proved a failure. After the retreat of the Chaghatais from Kanauj to Lahore, these chiefs renewed their appeals for assistance, and it was during the discussions that took place there as to the general line of action to be adopted, that Mirza Haidar impressed on Humayun the advantage of seizing the opportunity to gain a footing in Kashmir. He had learned from his previous incursion into that country, while in the service of the Khan of Kashghar, the value of its position and resources, and calculated that, with a reasonable force, he would require only two months to subjugate it and make it a suitable asylum for the Emperor and his family, together, if necessary, with the remains of the Chaghatai army. Shir Shah, on the other hand, with the wheeled carriages and the artillery, on which his strength mainly depended, would not, the Mirza reckoned, be able to reach the outer hills in less than four months, and his troops would be exhausted by the effort.

Though these plans were not taken advantage of by Humayun (who continued his retreat to the Indus), he permitted them to be put into practice by Mirza Haidar. The Mirza was given a small body of troops, and was sent forward from Lahore to join the Kashmiri chiefs, in whose company he was to enter the hills of their country, and to be followed, at intervals, by two of Humayun's officers, called respectively Iskandar Tupchi and Khwája Kalán. When all had assembled above Jhilam, and the force had begun to ascend the passes leading to the valley of Kashmir, dissensions arose among the commanders. Khwája Kalán, with his men, first separated himself from the expedition, and the Tupchi shortly afterwards followed him, leaving Mirza Haidar to prosecute the undertaking with no more than a handful of retainers in his own pay, and a few more who had joined him on the personal authority of the Emperor. With this following he determined to advance, and on the 21st November, 1540, crossed the Punch pass and descended into the valley. His calculations proved correct: he met with no resistance from the chiefs or people, but obtained possession of the country without striking a blow.

It is curious how little our author relates about his invasion and administration of Kashmir, or of the affairs of that country during the eleven years that his regency lasted. He was to all intents and purposes king of the State; while the value of the territory and the importance of its position, from a military point of view, at the juncture when he found himself its ruler, were well known to him, for he had impressed them urgently on Humayun only a short time before. Yet all he has to say of the period is summed up in two short chapters at the end of his history; though he devotes much more space to the events that were happening at the time across the passes. It was in Kashghar and Yarkand that his nearest relatives and his friends were living—most of them in suffering and danger—and that his political enemies were ruling, on lines that he regarded as dangerous, and subversive of the power and prosperity that he had himself helped to build up. It seems evident, indeed, that to the end of his life, his mind was chiefly occupied with the affairs of what may be called his own country, and communications between his friends and himself seem to have been kept up to the last, while he felt himself to be more or less an exile in Kashmir. So meagre is his story of this period of his life, and so abruptly broken off, that from the year 1540 onwards, I have had to follow chiefly the accounts of Abul Fazl, the historian of Akbar, and of Firishta. Both of these authors wrote within an interval not very remote from that which they chronicle, so that the events they deal with must have been fresh in the memories of their informants.[1]

[1] See for Abul Fazl, Price's *Muham. Hist.* iii., pp. 787–862; Jarrett's *Ain-i-Akbari*, p. 390; Erskine's *Hist.* ii., pp. 364–68. For Firishta, Briggs, iv., pp. 497 *seq.*, and Mr. C. J. Rodgers' Extracts, in *J.A.S.B.*, 1885, pp. 98 *seq.*

Kashmir had, for some time previously, acknowledged no one supreme ruler, except those set up as mere nominal representatives of the old line of kings. Several native chiefs exercised the real authority, in various parts, and at that particular time were supporting, as a pageant, a prince whose title was Názuk Shah.[1] Whether Mirza Haidar began by joining issue with this personage we are not informed, but it appears rather, that he took him under his protection. It is related, however, that one Káchi Chak, the principal of those chiefs through whose representations Mirza Haidar had been originally induced to undertake the reduction of the State, very shortly deserted his benefactor. He perceived, says Abul Fazl, that his own schemes would be defeated by the establishment of Mirza Haidar's power, and "with the natural perfidy inherent in the character of the Kashmirians, suddenly withdrew from the country to seek the protection of Shir Khan"[2] [*i.e.* Shir Shah]; with the result that a force of 2,000 Afghans was immediately despatched by the Shah, to conduct the petitioner back to his country. A threat of invasion by Shir Shah and his Afghans was sufficient to deprive Mirza Haidar of all his Kashmiri allies, and he had to retire to an inaccessible part of the country, with a few of his own followers, where he led a precarious and unsettled life for about three months. At last, on the 2nd August, 1541 (8 Rabi II. 948 H.) he gave battle to his enemies, who were computed at 5,000 combatants (including natives and auxiliary Afghans), and defeated them with great loss, the Afghans retiring to Delhi, while the Kashmiri malcontents fled to the outer hills. By this victory, our author rendered himself undisputed master of the whole of Kashmir.

A period of tranquillity followed, but was destined to last only till the year 1543, when the fugitives beyond the borders, having combined their forces with those of some of their relatives, marched on Srinagar for the purpose of subverting Mirza Haidar's government. They were completely routed, however, and again took refuge in the outer hills. Not long afterwards, the Mirza himself took the offensive against Ladak, and is said to have reduced several of its districts to subjection. Only one of these is named by Firishta, who writes it "Looshoo"—a name impossible to identify, unless it can be regarded as a corruption

[1] The name appears in this form in the histories of both Abul Fazl and Firishta, but Mr. Rodgers informs us that all the coins bear *Nádir* in place of

of "Suru." During his absence on this expedition, an epidemic disease broke out, which carried off the three discontented chiefs who had, up to that time, been his most persistent opponents. Their removal afforded him again a period of peace, which lasted for about two years, when he proceeded to attack the province of Kishtawár. One Bandagán Koka was sent forward in command of a portion of the force, while Mirza Haidar followed at a distance. Bandagán Koka came up with the enemy on the banks of the Kishtawár river, and after two engagements, was defeated and killed, together with a number of his men. The remainder of his force fell back on the division of the Mirza, who, however, does not appear to have followed up his intention of subduing the province. The next year, 1548, he is reported to have turned his attention first towards Little Tibet (or Baltistan), then to Tibet (or Ladak) again, and subsequently to Rajaori and Pakhli. In all these provinces he is said to have succeeded in his objects, and to have added them, finally, to his Kashmir dominions.

In 1549 an occurrence is recorded, which nearly brought our author once more into conflict with the Afghans of Hindustan. In 1545 Shir Shah had been succeeded by his son, Islám Shah (otherwise known as Salim Khan), against whose rule the Niázi tribe of Afghans, then settled in the Punjab, rose in rebellion. After being worsted by Salim in the plains, they fled towards the hills and took refuge in the Kashmir province of Rajaori. Here they were received by the descendants of those Kashmiri chiefs, who had so persistently opposed Mirza Haidar's rule, up to a few years previously. Intrigues were entered into between these and the Niázi, but in the meantime Salim, pursuing the latter, arrived at the foot of the hills near Nau Shahra in Rajaori, while Mirza Haidar advanced to block the road from the side of Kashmir. According to Firishta, a peaceful arrangement was come to between the various parties; Salim was appeased on certain hostages being made over to him, and returned to Delhi, while the Kashmiri partisans, abandoning their plans, some joined Mirza Haidar, and others accompanied Salim to his capital. A different version of this affair (it may be noted) is given by Abdulla, the author of the *Tarikh-i-Daudi*, who records that a fight took place between the Niázi and a force sent by Mirza Haidar to prevent them from entering Kashmir, and the writer locates this encounter, not in Rajaori, but in the district of Banihál. The Kashmiri force is represented as gaining a complete victory, while Mirza Haidar is said to have propitiated Salim Khan, by sending him the heads of the slain Niázi as a peace-offering. Which of these two accounts is the more correct, it is not easy to judge, but it seems that Mirza Haidar had, about this time, some transactions with the Afghan Shah of Hindustan, and may possibly have felt it necessary to propitiate him. At any rate, Firishta relates that he sent ambassadors with presents to Delhi in 1550, and that Salim, in return, deputed an envoy with horses, muslins, etc., to Srinagar. What brought about this exchange of courtesies, or what came of it, the historian does not state.

In the same way, the events of the ensuing year, 1551, relating to Mirza Haidar's death, are to some extent at variance. The only two historians (as far as I am aware) who record them in any detail are Abul Fazl and Firishta; but, as the former seems somewhat uncertain of his facts, the account of the latter may perhaps be more advantageously followed.

General Briggs' version of Firishta records, quite briefly, that Mirza Haidar had appointed one Kirán Bahádur, a commander of Moghul horse, to the government of the district of Bhirbal.[1] The measure gave great offence to the inhabitants, who resisted Kirán's authority, and eventually proceeded to attack him. Mirza Haidar, in order to support his officer, put himself at the head of his Moghuls, and marched towards the scene of the disturbance. On the road, a night attack was made upon his camp, the Moghuls were defeated, and he himself was killed by an arrow in the course of the fight. The exact date of the event in 1551 is nowhere recorded, but it would appear to have taken place on one of the last days of Rámzán, or about the beginning of October.[2] In Mr. Rodgers' version, the circumstances are related in much greater detail, but some of the particulars are not quite intelligible. The substance, however, is the same, and the account makes it appear that the locality where Mirza Haidar fell, must have been somewhere near Báramula on the Jhilam. It points also to his death having been caused through being accidentally struck by an arrow, discharged by one of his own men, in the darkness.

During the ten years (counting from the battle of 2nd August, 1541) over which Mirza Haidar's regency extended, he is said,

[1] These names are given elsewhere in Firishta as Kará Bahádur and Bhirpul. The latter stands probably for *Bhimber* below Nau Shahra.

[2] The Hajra year is 958, which began 9th January, 1551.

in the *Akbar-Náma*, to have devoted himself, when not actively engaged with his enemies, to the restoration of the province and the improvement of its resources. He found it in a state of ruin and desolation, and raised it to a land abounding in cultivation and flourishing towns; he extended the frontiers also, and ruled with moderation and justice. Yet the austere Abul Fazl takes him to task for devoting too much of his time and attention to music, and thereby becoming forgetful of the dangers that surrounded him. Still more he blames him for continuing the government of the State in the name of the puppet Prince, Názuk Shah. After his military successes, it was his duty, the historian considers, to read the prayers and strike the coins in the name of "his imperial benefactor then struggling with adversity;" while there was no necessity to cultivate the attachment of the native rulers. Yet he is obliged to admit that when Humayun had returned from exile in Persia, and had repossessed himself of Kabul, Mirza Haidar at once conceded to him the honours due to a sovereign.

How far Abul Fazl's estimate of Mirza Haidar's character is a just one, may be open to question. In the first place, it was not entirely to music that he devoted the interval of well-earned repose that he enjoyed in Kashmir. It was during these years that he wrote the *Tarikh-i-Rashidi*—a work which, strange to say, Abul Fazl makes no mention of. Yet it is evident, from incidental allusions to dates in the body of the book, that this task occupied no little of the Mirza's time. To judge by the number of authors he cites, or speaks of, in the course of his history, he must have collected a good number of books about him, and the study of these may perhaps have occupied more of his leisure than the lute or the zitára. Among them, it may be noted, was a copy of the "Memoirs" of his cousin Baber, which, in all probability, he had obtained while in India at the court either of Humayun or of Kámrán; and, no doubt, it was the first copy ever utilised for historical purposes. Secondly, as regards the imputed infidelity towards the Chaghatai Emperor, it should not be forgotten that the historian of Akbar was writing after events had seemed to justify his view. At the time when Mirza Haidar administered Kashmir in the name of Názuk Shah, Humayun was a refugee in Persia, dependent on the uncertain friendship of Shah Tahmásp, and it must have been quite a matter for speculation whether he would ever return, or if, indeed, any member of the house of Baber would again occupy the throne of Hindustan. After completely subjugating Kashmir, and defeating the troops that Shir Shah had sent against him, there seems to have been no reason, but loyalty to the Chaghatais, why the Mirza should not have set himself up as king of the State.

His action in recognising the native puppet may fairly be regarded as one of self-denial—a temporary measure, undertaken while waiting to see whether his patron might not return, and claim his own kingdom in India. As events fell out, he did return, though not till January 1555, or nearly four years after our author's death. Step by step, he made himself master of the principal districts of Afghanistan, regained Kunduz and Badakhshán, and disposed of Kámrán Mirza, together with other enemies of his house. But as early as 1545, when, with the aid of Shah Tahmásp, he had wrested only Kandahar and Kabul from his rebellious brother, and while still far beyond the limits of India, Mirza Haidar transferred to Humayun the nominal sovereignty with which he had invested Názuk Shah. He sent an envoy to Kabul, to inform his patron of these proceedings and to invite him to Kashmir. His letters were full of expressions of loyalty and attachment, and, in pressing his invitation, he pointed out that the country he had subdued would serve as an impregnable position, from which the Emperor might pour down his troops for the conquest of Hindustan—an enterprise which he urged him to attempt without delay.[1] He is recorded, moreover, by Abul Fazl himself, to have read the prayers and to have struck the coins in Humayun's name at about this period; while unanswerable evidence as regards the coinage is to be found, to this day, among the specimens of the money of Kashmir, which have come down to us. In the British Museum there is a silver coin of Kashmir, bearing the name of Humayun and dated 952 or 953 [2] of the Hajra (1545 or 1546). Mr. Rodgers also describes two coins of Humayun which were struck, in Kashmir, in the year 953, and another bearing a date subsequent to 950, but on which the third figure is illegible. This last one, however, contains in the field a letter *ha*, which Mr. Rodgers believes may stand for the initial letter of the name *Haidar*. In any case, the dates that are decipherable not

[1] Erskine, ii., pp. 366–7; on the authority of the *Akbar-Náma.*

[2] Probably the former date, but perhaps the latter; for there is some uncertainty about the third figure. See S. L. Poole, *Cat. Coins of Muham. States of India*, p. xlviii.

only fall within the period of Mirza Haidar's regency, but they are good evidence that he regarded Humayun as his sovereign, while at the height of his own power in Kashmir, although no coins are known which show that he so regarded him previous to his recovery of Kabul.[1] Neither the coins nor the documentary history of the period, however, are completely worked out, and until the tales that both have to tell are exhausted, it would perhaps be premature to conclude that, even prior to the subjugation of Afghanistan in 1545, Mirza Haidar may not have afforded testimony, in one form or another, that he regarded himself and his puppet king as, alike, dependants of the Chaghatai Emperor.

Thus, whatever faults the Mirza may have had, disloyalty to his chiefs can hardly be accounted one of them. He served his first master, Sultan Said Khan, with devotion till the end of the Khan's reign, and when forced by the barbarities of his successor, Rashid Sultan, to seek safety for his life with the Chaghatais in India, he served them likewise with good faith, as long as he lived.

Besides Abul Fazl's and Firishta's, the notices of Mirza Haidar's life, among the writings of Asiatic authors, appear to be few. Several quote his history, and even copy from it extensively, but only two, as far as I have been able to ascertain from translations, make any mention of his personality. Jauhar, in his *Memoirs of Humayun*,[2] does no more than briefly allude to his master's faithful lieutenant. The author of the *Tarikh-i-Daudi*, cited above, calls him "a youth of a magnanimous disposition," but vouchsafes no more.[3] Amin Ahmad Rázi, however, has devoted a few sentences to him in his geographical work, the *Haft Iklim*, an important extract from which was translated into French by Quatremère, and published in 1843.[4] Ahmad Rázi tells us that Mirza Haidar "was endowed with an excellent character and a rare talent for elegant composition in verse, as well as in prose. To these

[1] The date of Humayun's recovery of Kabul varies somewhat in the accounts of different native authors, but Mr. Erskine adopted that of 10 Ramzán 952, or 15th November, 1545 (*Hist.* ii., p. 325), so that it is possible that these coins may have been struck, as Mr. S. L. Poole suggests, to commemorate that event. (*Loc. cit.*)

[2] The *Tazkirát ul Wakiát*, trans. by Major Ch. Stewart, 1832, mentioned

gifts of nature, he added those of extreme valour, and all the qualities that constitute a great general. Having been sent into Kashmir by Sultan Abu Said Khan,[1] he penetrated into this province by the road of Kashghar and Tibet [Ladak] and entirely subdued it. He entered it also a second time from the side of India, and establishing his residence in Kashmir, formed it into an independent principality . . . . He was author of the historical work entitled the *Tarikh-i-Rashidi*, which was named in this way after Rashid Khan, sovereign of Kashghar. This book enjoys universal esteem." Ahmad Rázi then appends some verses of the Mirza's, as a specimen of his poetic genius.

Among Europeans, Mr. W. Erskine is perhaps the only original author who has touched on Mirza Haidar's personal characteristics or attainments; even he does so only very briefly, though in several passages he praises his work in the highest terms. He sums him up as "a man of worth, of talent, and of learning."[2] For his own part, he naively tells us that he had many accomplishments, and though most of those he names were of a more or less mechanical order, others, at least, show a taste for authorship, and make us picture him as a man of some imagination. Taking into consideration the life he led—his adventures, sufferings, discomfitures, and escapes—and the age and countries he lived in, he may be accounted also a man of learning. At any rate, he was a patron of the learned whom he came in contact with, and seems to have taken an interest in their teachings, as well as in the books he knew of; though it may be open to question, perhaps (from a European point of view), how far he used them to the best advantage for historical purposes. Yet, withal, he was a bigoted Musulman and a fanatical Sunni, as his remarks about the transactions of Baber with the Persian Shias, after the capture of Samarkand in 1511, clearly indicate. And his bigotry took many curious forms, as, for instance, his approval of the hypocritical proceedings of Sultan Said Khan, his refraining to trace his pedigree beyond the date of Amir Bulaji, because Bulaji's ancestors were not Musulmans, and his pious invocations on the Moghul Khan, whose religious zeal and enlightenment led him to drive horseshoe nails into the heads of his subjects, to induce them to become Musulmans. In short

[1] The Khan's name is occasionally written in this way, but it is incorrect. The word *Abu* is redundant.

[2] *Hist.* ii., p. 368.

he belonged to his times, and herein lies the chief value of all that he has left on record.

The reader, however, will form his own judgment of the author's character and worth. What may safely be said is that his history carries with it a conviction of honesty; while he himself, though a soldier of fortune, was, as shown by the advice he tendered to Humayun, and by his administration of Kashmir, no mere Dugald Dalgetty of the East.

SECTION II.

THE LINE OF CHAGHATAI.

Think, in this batter'd Caravanserai
Whose Doorways are alternate Night and Day,
How Sultán after Sultán with his Pomp
Abode his Hour or two, and went his way.
—*Omar Khayyám.*

THE story of the conquests of Chingiz Khan, and the partition of nearly the whole of Northern Asia among his descendants, has been so often told, that no useful purpose would be served by recounting it again in this Introduction. Only those phases need be briefly sketched, which form the basis of Mirza Haidar's history, or which help to elucidate the course of events immediately preceding it. Though the *Tarikh-i-Rashidi* embraces many wide regions and deals with many tribes and nations, its chief scenes are laid within the appanage of Chingiz's second son Chaghatai, and it is, before all things, a history of part of the Chaghatai branch of the Mongol dynasty. This is the branch, moreover, which hitherto has remained the most obscure of all those of the family of Chingiz Khan. The other divisions of the empire founded by the great conqueror, have all found abundant historians, not only in China and Mongolia, but among the Musulman writers of Western Asia and among Europeans. The great works of Deguignes, D'Ohsson, and Howorth, though designed to tell the story of all the Chingizi branches, have failed, as yet, to complete that of the house of Chaghatai. The two older authors frankly avow the want of materials, as their reason for leaving this section of their field almost untouched, while Sir H. Howorth, though he is understood to have completed his researches in it, has been prevented by other circumstances, from giving to the world his much desired volume on the Chaghatais.

Perhaps the nearest approaches to histories of the Chaghatais are to be found, (1) in an excellent paper entitled *The Chaghatai Mughals*, by Mr. E. E. Oliver, in the Journal of the Royal

Asiatic Society,[1] where the writer has summarised, in a consecutive manner, most of that which can be gathered on the subject, from European sources and from translations of Asiatic authors; and (2) in Erskine's *History of India under Baber and Humayun.* The learned translator of Baber's *Memoirs* had read widely among the Musulman authors, and compiled, in his last work, a more complete epitome of Chaghatai history, from original sources, than is to be found in any other European writings—unless possibly in those of Russian Orientalists, whose books, indeed, are sealed to most European readers. The source from which Mr. Erskine chiefly drew his information was the *Tarikh-i-Rashidi,* which he not only studied, but, as we have seen in the Preface, partially translated in a summarised form. The *Tarikh-i-Rashidi,* however, does not begin at the beginning of the Chaghatai history, but at an arbitrary point, dating nearly a hundred years after the allotment of his empire by Chingiz Khan, and at the period when the Khans of Moghulistan, having separated themselves from those of Mávará-un-Nahr, a distinct history of their branch became possible. In order, then, to furnish a foundation for Mirza Haidar's chronicle, it is necessary to fill in, however briefly, this gap of a hundred years, and, in doing so, to take a rapid glance at the two allotments which bordered on that of Chaghatai Khan—the one on the west and the other on the east—for the affairs of all three are, to some extent, interwoven at certain periods.

In assigning his dominions to his four sons, Chingiz Khan appears to have followed an ancient Mongol custom. The sons of a chief usually ruled, as their father's deputies, over certain nations or clans, and at his death each received, as an appanage, the section of the population which had been under his care. Thus the distribution was rather tribal than territorial, and the tribes, which were in most cases nomadic, sometimes shifted their abode, or were driven, by enemies, to migrate from one district to another. These movements, as a fact, do not seem to have occurred very frequently, nor to have altered the position of the main body of the people to any great extent. It will be more convenient, therefore, and far more intelligible, to state the distribution of Chingiz's dominions, as far as possible, in territorial terms.

Juji, or Tushi, the eldest son of Chingiz, died some months

before his father, and therefore, never became supreme Khákán[1] in the regions he governed; but they descended intact to his own son and successor, Batu, as an appanage direct from Chingiz. The centre of this dominion may be taken to be the plains of Kipchak, but it comprised all the country lying north of the lower course of the Sir Daria (the Sihun or Jaxartes) and of the Aral and Caspian seas—"wherever the hoofs of Mongol horses had tramped"; it included also the valleys of the Volga and the Don, and some wide-spread regions on the north shore of the Black Sea; while towards the north it extended beyond the Upper Yaik (or Ural River) into Western Siberia. On its southern and south-eastern confines, this appanage of the Juji line marched with that of Chingiz's second son, Chaghatai, whose central kingdom, Mávará-un-Nahr, or Transoxiana, was situated chiefly between the rivers Sir and Amu (the Jihun or Oxus), but included, in its extension towards the north-east, the hill ranges and steppes lying beyond the right bank of the Sir, east of the Kipchák plains, and west of lakes Issigh-Kul and Ala-Nor. Towards the east, the Chaghatai domain took in the greater part of the region now known as Chinese (or Eastern) Turkistan, Farghána (or Khokand) and Badakhshán; while towards the south it embraced Kunduz, Balkh, and, at the outset, Khorasán—a country which, at that time, spread eastward to beyond Herat and Ghazni, and southward to Mekrán. This was, perhaps, the most extensive appanage of all, and within its limits were to be found the greatest variety of races and tribes, and the greatest diversity of modes of life. It comprised, on the one hand, some of the richest agricultural districts, peopled by settled inhabitants, far advanced in Asiatic civilisation, and some of the most flourishing cities in Asia; while, on the other hand, some of the rudest hill tribes, or Hazáras as they were called then, had their homes in the

[1] As the word *Khákán* will often be met with in the *Tarikh-i-Rashidi*, it may be explained, here, that the difference between it and the simple form of *Khán* was one of degree. *Khákán* was a form of *Kaán* which was, originally, the peculiar title of the supreme sovereign of the Mongols, while the subordinate princes of the Chaghatai, and other Chingizi lines, were styled only *Khan*. After a time the higher title degenerated, and was used by many besides the sovereign, as will be observed in the course of the *Tarikh-i-Rashidi*. Marco Polo always wrote *Kaán*, and applied the title to Kublai, the Mongol Emperor of China. The meaning of *Khákán*, Sir H. Yule considered to be "*Khan of Khans*," or the equivalent of the modern *Khán-Khánán*. (See Marco Polo, Intro. pp. 9, 10; also Dr. Terrien de Lacouperie in *Babylonian and Oriental Record* for December, 1888.)

southern highlands, and large tracts of barren steppe-land were occupied by almost equally primitive nomads, who drove their flocks from hill to valley and valley to hill, in search of pasture, according to season.

Eastward, again, of this "middle dominion," as it was often termed, came that of Oktai (or Ogodai), the third son of Chingiz Khan. His allotment was the country of the original Mongols with that of the tribes immediately around it, while he was also heir to his father's capital, Karakorum, and to the supreme authority over the Mongol people. On its western confines his dominion bordered, at first, on that of Chaghatai, in the country since known as Jungar or Zungaria [1]—a region that, for want of more exact boundaries, may be roughly described as lying north of the Tian-Shan, from about Urumtsi on the east, to the river Chu on the west, and having for its middle line the upper course of the Ili river. This region became the subject of much contention among the descendants of Oktai and Chaghatai, in the latter half of the thirteenth century, and as the house of the former declined, the greater part of it, if not the whole, appears to have gradually merged into the territories of the Chaghatai Khans; while the clans that inhabited it, were dispersed among the tribes of Transoxiana and Kipchak, and their chiefs lived in obscurity under the Khans, or conquerors, for the time being.

Chaghatai himself appears to have been a just and energetic governor, though perhaps rough and uncouth, and addicted to the vice, common among the Mongols, of hard drinking. At any rate, he was animated by the soldier-like spirit of his father, and succeeded in keeping order among as heterogeneous a population, as a kingdom was ever composed of. In 1232, for instance, when sedition showed itself at Bokhara, he acted with promptitude, if with severity, and saved his country from a far-reaching calamity. He was, in all probability, an old-fashioned Mongol, for we read that he stood by the Yasák, or code of laws instituted by Chingiz Khan, and that he showed little favour to what was, at that time in his dominions, the comparatively new and rising religion of Islám. He must, however, have been fairly tolerant, for it is recorded that his minister for Transoxiana was a Musulman, called the Jumilat-ul-Mulk, and that mosques and colleges were founded during his reign. But if Chaghatai did not lean towards Islám, neither does it appear

[1] *I.e.*, the country of the Jungar, or Zungar—the *left-hand*—Kálmáks.

that he ever inclined towards Christianity, though that religion, as practised by the Nestorians, must have been familiar to him. It existed in his own dominions and in those of his brother Oktai, who seems to have been thoroughly tolerant, and to have encouraged at his capital, Karakorum, every form of worship, besides the enlistment in his service of men of all religions—a circumstance which had, as will be seen later, an important bearing on subsequent history.

Chaghatai's own capital was at Almáligh, in the valley of the Upper Ili, near the site of the present Kulja, and consequently in the extreme east of his dominion. His reason for fixing it in that remote position, instead of at Bokhara or Samarkand, was probably one of necessity. His Mongol tribesmen and followers—the mainstay of his power—were passionately fond of the life of the steppes: the only existence worthy of men and conquerors, was that passed in the felt tents of their ancestors, among the flocks and herds that they tended in time of peace, and led with them on their distant campaigns. The dwellers in houses and towns were, in their eyes, a degenerate and effeminate race;—the tillers of the soil, slaves who toiled like cattle, in order that their betters might pass their time in luxury. They would serve no Khan who did not pass a life worthy of free-born men and "gentlemen rovers"; and Chaghatai and his immediate successors probably saw, as his later descendants are described by Mirza Haidar to have seen, that the one way of retaining the allegiance of his own people, was to humour their desires in this respect, and live, with them, a nomad's life.

Chaghatai died in 1241, after a reign of about fourteen years, and within the same year the death of Oktai occurred at Karakorum. Thus two out of four of the chief divisions of the Mongol empire were suddenly deprived of their sovereigns, with the result that nearly the whole of the successors of Chingiz were set disputing for the succession. "Among the most violent as regards party spirit and warlike temper," writes Mr. Oliver in his summary of this period, "were some of the representatives of Chaghatai. For the time being, it ended in Turakina, Oktai's widow, being appointed regent; but there were set up lasting disputes among the rival claimants, and the seeds of much future mischief were sown. For long after, the disputes regarding the succession to the throne of the great Kaán became inextricably mixed up with the affairs, more especially of the eastern part, of Chaghatai's Khanate, and it is impossible to give an intelligible account of the latter without occasional references to the former."[1]

Little is known of the way in which Chaghatai disposed of his kingdom at his death, and there appears to be no mention, anywhere, of his having followed the ancestral custom of his house in distributing it among his descendants. He is recorded to have left a numerous family, but to have been succeeded by a grandson, and a minor, named Kara Hulaku, while his widow, Ebuskun, assumed the regency. This statement, however, seems to apply to Turkistan, Transoxiana, and the adjacent regions: at all events not to Kashghar, Yarkand, Khotan, Aksu, and the southern slopes of the Tian Shan mountains—or, in other words, to the province south of the line of the Tian Shan, which is called, in our times, Eastern Turkistan. As regards this province, Mirza Haidar tells us that it was given by Chaghatai, presumably at his death, to the clan or house of Dughlát, whose members were reckoned to be of the purest Mongol descent, and one of the noblest divisions of that people. We shall hear more of this clan and the province they ruled, farther on; but the important point to notice here, with reference to subsequent events, is that the Dughláts were made hereditary chiefs, or Amirs, of the various districts of Eastern Turkistan, as far back as the time of Chaghatai, for it is chiefly on this incident that hinges the permanent division of the Chaghatai realm into two branches, at a later date.

Ebuskun's sway was a short one, for as early as 1247 Almáligh was attacked by Kuyuk, the son and successor of Oktai, and she was deprived of her power. For a time, disorder prevailed throughout the Khanate; but Kuyuk seems to have had sufficient power to set up one Yasu (or Isu) Mangu, who, being himself a worthless debauchee, governed the country through the agency of a Musulman Wazir, called Khwája Bahá-ud-Din. Kuyuk died within three years of his accession, and was followed, as supreme Khakán, by Mangu, who, in 1252, restored Kara Hulaku and Ebuskun to their former dignities. Bahá-ud-Din and Yasu Mangu were now, in their turn, removed, the former being put to death at once. Kara Hulaku died within a few months of his restoration, and after his death we hear no more of Ebuskun. Hulaku's throne passed over to his own widow—one Orgánah Khatun—whose first act was to execute Yasu Mangu, under some compact, which appears to have been made for his riddance, between her predecessor and the Khakán Mangu.

Orgánah is described as possessing much beauty, wisdom, and influence, and as long as Mangu lived she was allowed to reign in peace. But he died in 1259, when a war of succession to the supreme Khakánate broke out between his brothers Irtukbuka and Kublai. In this strife, the Chaghatai princess appears to have taken no part, but she suffered nevertheless, for in 1261 she was driven from Almáligh by Algu (a great-grandson of Chingiz), who had been nominated by Irtukbuka to rule in her place, and to bring over the Chaghatai forces to assist him in his war with Kublai. Algu, however, betrayed his patron, who, abandoning Karakorum to his rival Kublai, marched against Almáligh, whence Algu had to fly for safety, first to Kashghar and Khotan, and finally to Samarkand. Irtukbuka spent the winter of 1263 in Almáligh, devastating the district and putting to death many of Algu's followers. By these excesses he weakened his own army and resources to so great a degree, that he had to submit to Kublai and make peace with Algu, stipulating to retain for himself a portion only, of the eastern part of the Chaghatai Khanate. These transactions brought about not only a reconciliation between Algu and Orgánah, but a marriage. Both, however, died within a few months, and Irtukbuka, having done homage to Kublai, by prostrating himself at the door of Kublai's tent, the latter remained supreme from Peking to Transoxiana, and acquired the title of Khakán. He was the "Great Kaán" of Marco Polo.

But a rival was beginning to show himself in the person of Kaidu, a grandson of Oktai. This prince was plotting, in western Kipchák, for the assistance of his uncle Batu, in asserting his claim to the province of Turkistan—the north-western division of the Chaghatai Khanate—and probably also for the region then becoming known as Moghulistan, which lay immediately to the eastward of Turkistan, and comprised the Zungar country, already alluded to. At the death of Algu, Kublai nominated Mubárak Shah, a son of Algu and Orgánah, to the Chaghatai succession, but immediately afterwards is said to have appointed, as his vice-regent, another great-grandson of Chaghatai, named Borák (or Barák), to support Mubárak Shah in resisting Kaidu. So far from assisting the young Khan, Borák drove him from the throne, made common cause with Kaidu, and for a time exercised joint sovereignty with the latter over Transoxiana. But jealousies were not long in showing themselves between the allies, and quarrels ensued which were only partially composed at a *kuriltai*, or conference of the chiefs of the tribes, held in Turkistan in 1269, when certain points were agreed on, the most important being "the implied recognition of Kaidu as the rightful Khakán of the Moghuls, which from this time was extended by the Chaghatai Khans both to him and his son Chapár."[1]

Borák now proceeded to indemnify himself by invading Khorasán, but his campaigns resulted in nothing but defeat, and eventually he retired to Bokhara, where he died, or was perhaps poisoned, in 1270. "His reign," says Mr. Oliver, "had extended only to some four years, but they were years of misery and destruction to some of the fairest lands and most prosperous cities on the Zaráfshán. His death delivered them from at least one cowardly tyrant and persecutor, though they still continued to suffer from the fratricidal wars that constantly raged between the rival chiefs of the lines of Oktai and Chaghatai, and the unhappy citizens had even more reason than Venice of old for invoking 'a plague on both their houses.'

"Borák's death left Kaidu sole master of the western portion of the Khanate. The dispossessed Mubárak Shah and other chiefs took the oath of allegiance to him, thus rendering him a still more dangerous rival of Kublai. In 1270 (668 H.), much to the indignation of the sons of Borák, he nominated Nikpai, a grandson of Chaghatai, chief of the tribe, but in less than two years Nikpai seems to have revolted, been killed, and succeeded by Tuka Timur, another scion of the house (*circa* 1271, or 670 H.), who, in less than two years more, was ousted by Davá, the son of Borák (*circa* 1273, or 672 H.). Davá had made up his quarrel with Kaidu, his claims having been constantly urged by the latter's son Chapár. His reign was the longest ever enjoyed by a descendant of Chaghatai, and the Khanate might have hoped for some peace from an alliance between the rival houses, but unfortunately a third firebrand appeared on the scene. Abáká, the Il-Khán of Persia, who had always acknowledged Kublai as the rightful Khakán in opposition to Kaidu, and who had never forgiven Borák's invasion of Khorasán, was only watching his opportunity, and his Wazir, Shams-ud-Din Juvaini,[2]

[1] Oliver, p. 96.

[2] This Wazir was brother of Ala-ud-Din Ata-Mulk, Javaini, the historian and author of the *Tarikh-i-Jahán Kushai*—a work that will be often alluded to farther on.

had only to draw his attention to a favourable omen, to start him for Bokhara, which he entered about 1274 (672 H.), plundering, burning, and murdering right and left." [1]

Davá reigned for some thirty-two years and was almost constantly at war. He possessed himself of Ghazni, and from that stronghold, as a base, made several expeditions into India, ravaging the Punjab and Sind, and sacking at different times between 1296 and 1301 Peshawar, Multan, Lahore, and Delhi. In the meantime, Kaidu had involved himself in wars of long duration with the Khakán Kublai, and as these took place shortly before the time of Marco Polo's travels through Central Asia and China, detailed accounts of some of them have been handed down to us in his narrative. These wars extended, from first to last, over a period of some thirty years, and were not even concluded in 1294, when Kublai died and was succeeded as Khakán by his grandson Uljaitu.[2] The credit indeed of finally overthrowing Kaidu is due rather to this prince, and moreover it was not Kaidu alone whom he subdued, but Davá also, for this last, on his return from a campaign in India in 1301, seems to have allied himself with Kaidu and to have assisted in the wars against the Khakán. Kaidu's death followed quickly on his final reverse, and must have occurred in 1302, about. His son Chapár, backed by the influence of Davá, obtained the recognition of his succession to the Khanate of the eastern division of the country, and both having sent envoys to Uljaitu bearing professions of submission, a period of peace should, it might appear, have been established. But this was not the case. Within a year of Kaidu's death, Davá and Chapár fell out, and the latter was defeated in a battle fought between Samarkand and Khojand. This engagement was followed by several others, victory falling sometimes to one side and sometimes to the other, until at length the Khakán Uljaitu routed Chapár and obliged him to submit to Davá.

The death of Davá occurred in 1306, and he was succeeded by his son Kuyuk, who lived only two years, and was in his turn followed by a descendant of Chaghatai named Taliku. This prince is said to have adopted the Musulman religion, and in consequence to have been put to death by his own officers, who raised in his place, one Kabak, a son of Davá. Kabak was

[1] Oliver, pp. 97, 98.

[2] Properly "Timur Uljaitu;" the Tie-mu-urh, or Ching Tsung, of the Chinese.

installed in 1309, and was at once attacked by Chapár, in alliance with several members of the house of Oktai. The allies were beaten in a number of fights, and eventually fled for refuge to the territory of the Khakán (now Kuluk,[1] a nephew of Uljaitu), while their dominions were appropriated by the house of Chaghatai, the clans who inhabited them becoming in part its subjects and in part those of the Kipcháks. "With Chapár," says Mr. Oliver, "the house of Oktai disappears, though representatives came to the front for a brief period again in the persons of Ali and of Dánishmanjah, while Timur (Tamerlane), after displacing the family of Chaghatai, selected his puppet khans from the Oktai stock."[2] Within a year of his installation, Kabak made way for an elder brother, who ascended the throne of the Chaghatai under the name of Isán Bugha, though his historical identity (in connection with this name at least) is somewhat uncertain. He provoked the Khakán into war, and was beaten almost at the outset of his rule; afterwards he invaded Khorasán with a like result, and was finally forced to fly from the country, before the combined forces of one of his brothers and of the seventh Il-Khán, or King of Persia. This occurred in 1321, when Kabak seems to have resumed the throne which he had abdicated twelve years previously.

It was about this time that a permanent division occurred in the realm of Chaghatai, the two parts being known by the general names of Mávará-un-Nahr (or Transoxiana) and Moghulistan (or Jatah), though there were other provinces attached to each section. The story of the Khans of the former branch, roughly sketched above need not be followed further, as the history of Mirza Haidar, which chiefly concerns us, belongs to the other or eastern division, and is told by him, a descendant of its princes, in full. It is only necessary to remark with regard to Mávará-un-Nahr, that from the time of this division forward, the fifty years that remained till the great Amir, Timur, made himself master of the land, confusion and discord prevailed. During those few years the names of fifteen Khans appear in the lists—some of them not even of the Chaghatai line—together with some periods of anarchy when no name occurs. The rise of Timur was the turning-point from decadence to power in Mávará-un-Nahr, but at the same time, the death-blow to the original line of Chaghatai. He reduced the country to order,

[1] Hai Shan, or Wu Tsung, in the Chinese annals.
[2] Oliver, p. 105.

and ruled with uncontrolled power, though he left to the Khans, whom he set up or pulled down at pleasure, certain dignities and privileges which were nothing more than nominal.

We have seen already, how near the empire of Chaghatai came to being divided during the wars of Kaidu. This Prince was, as far as can be gleaned, one of the ablest of the Oktai line, and an active and determined soldier. During his struggles for supremacy, he held a large tract of country carved chiefly out of the Chaghatai appanage, though taken partly from that of Oktai. It is not clear what were the limits of the territory he held thus temporarily, and indeed it is probable that no actual limits were ever acknowledged. In all likelihood his power extended chiefly over certain tribes who were nomads, or dwellers in tents, and thus in the habit of moving their abodes when expedient; such movements, too, may have been more frequent than usual about Kaidu's period, for the tribesmen must have been constantly entangled in the prevailing wars, and subject therefore, to the changes of fortune of those with or against whom they had to serve. His dominion, consequently, would have been more tribal than territorial in its extent. At any rate it would seem that during Kaidu's last days—the period when he was allied with Borák—his power reached from the Tálás River and Lake Bálkásh on the west, to Kara-Khoja (between Turfán and Hami) on the east, and that it thus included nearly the whole length of the Tian Shan mountains, together with the Zungar country on the north, and Kashghar, Yarkand, Aksu, etc., on the south of them. Although this wide tract never fell permanently to him or his race, his temporary hold over it seems to have assisted in marking it out as a self-contained eastern division of the Chaghatai realm, and the greater portion of it—all that lay to the north of the Tian Shan—acquired, about this time, the name of Moghulistan, or vulgarly "Jatah." It was, above all parts of that realm, the land of the purely nomad Moghul (or Mongol) tribes, as distinguished from the settled populations of Turkistan, Farghána, and Má-vará-un-Nahr on the one hand, and the mountaineers of Hisar, Karatigin, Badakhshán, etc., on the other. It was the land to or from which the tent-dwelling population could migrate, and carry with them their only wealth—their flocks and herds—when safety or other interests demanded a move; and it became, moreover, as Mirza Haidar's history will show, a sort of refuge for the defeated and discontented among those tribes and the neighbouring nations, and the country that the true Moghul loved to call his own.

Thus, at the beginning of the fourteenth century, when the Khans of Chaghatai were rapidly declining in power, and could scarcely maintain themselves in their central kingdom of Mávará-un-Nahr, this eastern division, or Moghulistan, appears scarcely to have felt their sway. The hereditary Dughlát Amirs who, as we have seen, had been set up by Chaghatai, governed in detail, with more or less power, in the different cities and districts of the region south of the Tian Shan (or Eastern Turkistan), and left scarcely a trace behind them in any history but that of one of their own clan—Mirza Haidar. They acted in the name of the Chaghatai Khan of the time, and though nominally hereditary, they seem in practice to have held office very much at the pleasure of the tribesmen whose affairs they administered; while the popularity of each one probably depended more on the degree of independence he was able to secure for the small section that regarded him as its chief, than on his hereditary rights. Still in the early days, the power of some of them must have been considerable, and it seems to have risen in degree, as that of the Chaghatai Khans declined. They fought among themselves as a matter of course, and the people suffered, no doubt, from the consequent disorder. It would be quite natural therefore that Isán Bugha, a Moghul by descent, when forced to retire from Mávará-un-Nahr, should turn his steps towards Moghulistan, and its companion province south of the mountains.

Just at this point the histories of the period are discordant. As remarked above, the identity of Isán Bugha is to some extent uncertain. He is known to have been a son of Davá Khan, and is believed to have had some brothers. Abul Gházi Khan, the historian King of Khwárizm of the seventeenth century, speaks of him as "Il Khwája, surnamed Isán Bugha." On the other hand, Khwándamir makes Isán Bugha continue to reign over the western branch of the Chaghatai until his death, and alludes to one Imil Khwája (apparently another son of Davá) as having established himself in Moghulistan.[1] It is possible that Imil, or Il, may denote one and the same person;[2]

[1] See Abul Ghází's *Hist. des Mongols*, transl. by Desmaisons, pp. 164–5, and Khwándamir's *Habib us Siyár*, transl. by Defrémery in *Journal Asiat.* 4me Série, tom xix., pp. 270 and 280.

[2] Erskine notes (*Hist.* i., p. 37) that in the *Tarikh-i-Rashidi* he is called *Ais* or *Isán Bugha;* in the *Shajrat*, p. 378, and by Price (*Muham. Hist.*,

but however this may be, if the usually accurate Abul Gházi be followed, we learn that: "As there remained no longer in Kashghar, Yarkand, Alah-Tágh or Uighuristan, any prince descended from Chaghatai Khan, whose authority was acknowledged, the Moghul Amirs held a council, at which it was decided to summon Isán Bugha from Bokhara; and they proclaimed him Khan of Kashghar, Yarkand, Alah-Tágh, and of Moghulistan."[1] This would make it appear that Isán Bugha was still reigning in Mávará-un-Nahr when summoned by the Dughlát Amirs; but the point is doubtful, for we have just been told that he had fled to Moghulistan. In any case, the dates of the two events agree, for the disappearance of Isán Bugha from Mávará-un-Nahr is recorded by one author to have taken place in 721 H. (1321 A.D.), and this is just the year when he is said, by the other, to have been summoned to Kashghar and made Khan of Moghulistan, with (it may be assumed) its dependencies.

Thus, although the chronology and even some of the events of the times are uncertain, the final division of the Chaghatai Khanate appears to have taken place in or about the year 1321, and it resulted in two separate lines of Khans being established which were never afterwards united. The western branch was, a little later, superseded by Timur, whose descendants, through Baber, gave the ruling house to India, which has gone, for three centuries, by the name of "Moghul"; though, as we shall see from Mirza Haidar's narrative, it was, in its early days, known—and perhaps more correctly—as the "Chaghatai." The history of the eastern branch—that of the true "Moghuls" of Central Asia—we may now leave to be told, in detail, by our author; but as this line was several times broken, or subdivided, and as the subject is a complicated one, it may aid the reader to give (immediately below), in the form of an epitomised statement, a general view of the succession of the Moghul Khans from the time of Isán Bugha onwards. It is extracted almost entirely from Erskine's *History of India*,[2] and was com-

vol. iii., p. 7), following the *Khulásat-ul-Akbar*, *Il*, or *Ail*, Khwája; by Sharaf-ud-Din (Pétis' transl. tom. i., p. 26), *Aimal*; and by Abul Ghází, "*Aimal Khwája*, who reigned in Mavara-un-Nahr under the title of Isán Bugha Khan." As regards the name *Ais*, however, there is some mistake due to a misreading of the text by Erskine. The name nowhere occurs in this form.

[1] Desmaisons, p. 165.

[2] Vol. i., Appendix B.

piled by him from the *Tarikh-i-Rashidi*; but it contains some emendations from the Chinese history of the Ming dynasty, as translated by Dr. Bretschneider, for the period immediately succeeding the reign of Khizir Khwája, and a few other alterations besides.

It is about this period that Mirza Haidar's chronicle is at its weakest; and it is also a period where some of the best of the Musulman authors fail us. The *Rauzat us Safá* of Mir Khwánd and the *Zafar-Náma* of Sharaf-ud-Din, both differ from the *Tarikh-i-Rashidi*, and the Ming history is at variance with all three. Thus between Khizir Khwája and Vais Khan, the *Rauzat us Safá* and the *Zafar-Náma* show two reigning Khans of Moghulistan, and the *Tarikh-i-Rashidi* also gives accounts of two only, though the names in the last-mentioned work are not the same as in the other two histories.[1] But the *Tarikh-i-Rashidi*, in another place, relates that six Khans, including Khizir Khwája and Vais, were raised to the throne by the Dughlát Amir, Khudáidád, thus placing four between them. These Khans are—

Shama-i-Jahán,
Nakhsh-i-Jahán,
Muhammad,
Shir Muhammad,

and the author states them in this order; so that the three which correspond with the names of those given in the Chinese histories, do not fall in the same succession. Again none of the Musulman authors supply the date of succession for any of the intermediate Khans whom they mention. The Chinese annals show three Khans for the period between Khizir Khwája and Vais, and furnish the year of succession for each of them, besides giving dates of other contemporary occurrences, which indicate that a particular Khan was reigning at a particular time. The annals chiefly refer to tributary missions and appeals for assistance addressed to the Chinese Emperor, but it is precisely such occurrences as these that the Chinese chroniclers record with care and exactness. Their dynastic histories are believed to be not always trustworthy, but they are, at any rate, compilations, more or less methodical, from State documents and are not based merely on tradition, as are most of the Musulman

[1] As the *Haft Iklim* copies from the *Tarikh-i-Rashidi*, and does not copy completely, it need not be referred to as an authority. (See *Not. et Extraits*, xiv., pp. 474 *seq.*)

histories. As mere records of events and dates, therefore, the Chinese accounts are likely to be the best guides; and I should be inclined to substitute their data, regarding this period, for those of Mirza Haidar. I have, however, shown both in amending Mr. Erskine's epitome, as will be seen (at p. 46). A full extract from Dr. Bretschneider's translation of the Chinese history is also appended immediately below.

The three lists just spoken of, stand as follows:—

(A.)—*The Rauzat us Safá*[1] *and the Zafar-Náma.*[2]

(1.)	Khizir Khwája	died 1399
(2.)	Muhammad Khán	No date
(3.)	Nakhsh-i-Jahán	„
(4.)	Vais Khán	„

(B.)—*The Chinese Annals of the Ming dynasty.*[3]

(1.)	Khizir Khwája	died 1399
(2.)	Shama-i-Jahán	„ 1408
(3.)	Muhammad Khán . . .	„ 1416
(4.)	Nakhsh-i-Jahán	„ 1418
(5.)	Vais Khán	„ 1428

(C.)—*The Tarikh-i-Rashidi.*

(1.)	Khizir Khwája	died 1420
(2.)	Shama-i-Jahán	No date
(3.)	Nakhsh-i-Jahán	„
(4.)	Muhammad Khán	„
(5.)	Shir Muhammad	„
(6.)	Vais Khán	died 1428–9

Of the two dates furnished by the *Tarikh-i-Rashidi*, the one indicating the year of Khizir Khwája's death is certainly incorrect, for there is evidence to show, in addition to the concurrence of the authorities named above, that this Khan did not reign up to the year 1420. The portion of the *Matla' Asaadin*, of Abdur Razzák, translated by Quatremère,[4] though it contains no list of these Khans, makes mention of ambassadors having been sent to Shah Rukh, of Mávará-un-Nahr, in

[1] Price's *Muham. Hist.*, iii., p. 300.
[2] Pétis de la Croix, *Hist. de Timur Bec*, iii., p. 213.
[3] Bretschneider, *Med. Res.*, ii., pp. 231, 239.
[4] *Notices et Extraits*, vol. xiv., p. 296.

819 H. (1416), by Nakhsh-i-Jahán, who is described as a son of Shama-i-Jahán of Moghulistan; thereby implying, it would seem, that Nakhsh-i-Jahán was reigning in that year in Moghulistan. This date accords with the Chinese indication for the accession of Nakhsh-i-Jahán—or the year when he would most probably have despatched envoys to his neighbours. The same work[1] mentions also that in 823 H. (1420) Shah Rukh's ambassadors, then on their way to China, learned that disorder prevailed in Moghulistan in consequence of Vais Khan, who was then reigning, having attacked Shir Muhammad Oghlán. This statement stands by itself; but it has some resemblance to that of Mirza Haidar, who relates that between Vais Khan and "Shir Muhammad Khan there arose great disputes." It also appears, from the *Matla' Asaadin,* that in 1425 Shir Muhammad held powers of some kind in Moghulistan, though he may not have been the reigning Khan. It is stated, at any rate, that in that year Mirza Ulugh Beg, who was ruling in Mávará-un-Nahr, undertook an expedition into Moghulistan and defeated Shir Muhammad. Yet, according to the Chinese, Vais Khan was then reigning, he having slain Nakhsh-i-Jahán in 1418. On the subject of Shir Muhammad, therefore, the *Matla' Asaadin* and the *Tarikh-i-Rashidi* would seem to be at one, in so far that they both name him as living at a period immediately previous to the accession of Vais, though neither states precisely that he was a reigning Khan of the dynasty.

As I have placed in juxtaposition above, the lists of reigning Khans, according to the various authorities, it may be useful also to show how they vary in their statements regarding the sons of Khizir Khwája, some of whom reigned, though some did not.

Thus the *Rauzat us Safá* has—

(1.) Shama-i-Jahán,
(2.) Shir Ali,
(3.) Shah Jahán Oghlán.

The *Zafar-Náma* gives:—

(1.) Shama-i-Jahán,
(2.) Muhammad Oghlán,
(3.) Shir Ali,
(4.) Shah Jahán,

[1] *Notices et Extraits*, p. 388.

while the *Tàrikh-i-Rashidi* mentions :—

(1.) Muhammad Khan,
(2.) Shama-i-Jahán,
(3.) Nakhsh-i-Jahán,
" } "and others."
"

The passage taken from Dr. Bretschneider's version of the Ming history runs thus [1] :—

"After Yung-lo acceded to the throne he sent an envoy with a letter and presents to the King of Bie-shi-ba-li.[2] But at that time Hei-di-rh-ho-djo had died,[3] and had been succeeded by his son *Sha-mi-cha-gan.* The latter sent in the next year an embassy to the emperor, offering as tribute a block of rude jade and fine horses. The envoy was well treated and rewarded. At that time it had happened that *An-ko Tie-mu-rh,* Prince of Hami, had been poisoned by *Gui-li-chi,* Khan of the Mongols, and Sha-mi-cha-gan made war on the latter. The emperor was thankful, and sent an envoy with presents to him, exhorting the King to be on good terms with *To-to,* the Prince of Hami.

"In 1406 Sha-mi-cha-gan sent tribute, and the emperor accordingly despatched *Liu Tie-mu-rh,* a high officer, with presents to Bie-shi-ba-li. In the year 1407 Sha-mi-cha-gan presented three times tribute. His envoys had been ordered to solicit the assistance of Chinese troops for reconquering Sa-ma-rh-han, which country, as they stated, had formerly belonged to Bie-shi-ba-li. The emperor sent his eunuchs, *Pa Tai* and *Li Ta,* together with Liu Tie-mu-rh, to Bie-shi-ba-li to inquire cautiously into the matter. The envoys presented silk stuffs to the King, and were well received. They returned home in the next year, and brought the intelligence that Sha-mi-cha-gan was deceased, and his younger brother, *Ma-ha-ma,* had succeeded him. The emperor then sent the same envoys once more to Bie-shi-ba-li, to offer a sacrifice in memory of the late King and bestow presents on Ma-ha-ma. When, in 1410, imperial envoys on their way to Sa-ma-rh-han passed through Bie-shi-ba-li, they were well treated by Ma-ha-ma, who in the next year despatched an embassy to the Chinese court, offering fine horses and a *wen pao* (leopard).

[1] *Med. Researches,* ii., pp. 239–42.

[2] Bishbálik: the Chinese name for Moghulistan, as will be seen lower down.—[Ed.]

[3] According to the *Zafer-nameh,* Khizir Khodja died in 1399. . . .

"When this embassy returned, they were accompanied by *An*, who carried gold embroidered silk stuffs for the King. At that time an envoy of the *Wa-la* (Oirats) complained that Ma-ha-ma was arming for making war on the Wa-la. The emperor sent to warn him. In 1413 Ma-ha-ma sent one of his generals with tribute to China. He reached Kan Su. Orders had been given to the civil and military authorities to receive him honourably.

"In the next year (1414) people returning from the *Si-yu* brought the intelligence that Ma-ha-ma's brother and another had both died in a short interval. The emperor sent again *An* to Bie-shi-ba-li, with a letter of condolence. When Ma-ha-ma died he left no son. His nephew, *Na-hei-shi-dji-han*, succeeded him, and in the spring of 1416 despatched an envoy to inform the emperor of his uncle's death. The emperor sent the eunuch Li Ta to offer a sacrifice in memory of the late King and confer the title of *wang* (King) on his successor. In 1417 Na-hei-shi-dji-han sent an embassy to inform the emperor that he was about to marry a princess from *Sa-ma-rh-han*,[1] and solicited in exchange for horses, a bride's trousseau. Then 500 pieces of variegated and 500 of plain white silk stuff were bestowed on the King of Bie-shi-ba-li as wedding presents.

"In 1418 an envoy, by name *Su-ko*, arrived from Bie-shi-ba-li, reporting that his sovereign (Na-hei-shi-dji-han) had been slain by his cousin, *Wai-sz*, who then had declared himself King. At the same time Wai-sz with his people had transferred their abode to the west, changing the former name of the empire (Bie-shi-ba-li) into *I-li-ba-li*. The emperor said that it was not his custom to meddle with the internal affairs of foreign countries. He bestowed upon Su-ko the rank of *tu tu ts'ien shi*, and at the same time sent the eunuch Yang Chung with a mission to Wai-sz, conferring on the King, as presents, an arrow, a sword, a suit of armour, and silk stuffs. The chieftain *Hu-dai-da*[2] and more than seventy other people of I-li-ba-li all received presents. Subsequently Wai-sz sent frequently tribute to the Chinese court,[3] as did also his mother, *So-lu-tan Ha-tun* (Sultan Khatun).

[1] The Mohammedan authors do not record this marriage.

[2] This seems to be the Amir *Khodaidád* of Kashgar, a man of great influence in Moghulistan. . . . The embassy of Shah Rok to China in 1420 met the Amir Khodaidad, who then enjoyed great authority in the country of Moghulistan.

[3] The embassy of Shah Rok saw an envoy of Awis Khan, by name *Batu Timur Anka*, in Peking, in 1421.

"In 1428 Wai-sz died, and was succeeded by his son, *Ye-sien bu-hua*,[1] who also sent repeatedly tribute to China. Tribute was also offered by *Bu-sai-in*, the son-in-law of the late King.

"*Ye-sien bu-hua* died in 1445, and was succeeded by *Ye-mi-li-hu-djo*.[2] The latter sent camels as tribute, and also a block of rude jade weighing 3800 *kin*, but not of the best quality. The Chinese government returned for every two *kin* of jade one piece of white silk.

"In 1457 a Chinese envoy was sent to *I-li-ba-li* with presents for the King, and in 1456 again.[3] It was then settled that I-li-ba-li was to send tribute every three or five years, and the number of the people in the suite of the envoy should not surpass ten men. Subsequently embassies from that country were seldom seen at the Chinese court."

Epitomised Account of the Khans of Moghulistan.
(*Chiefly from Erskine.*)

Isán Bugha Khán seems to have been called into Moghulistan about A.H. 721 (1321), and to have reigned till 730 (1330).

An Interregnum.

Tughluk Timur Khán, son of Isán Bugha, born about 730, began to reign 748 (1347), died 764 (1363).

Usurpation of Amir Kámar-ud-Din. It was against him that the expeditions of Timur into Moghulistan were directed —A.H. 768–94 (1367–1392).

Khizir Khwája Khán, son of Tughluk Timur, raised to the throne in 791, before Kámar-ud-Din's death. He reigned till 801 (1399), and was succeeded by his son,
Shama-i-Jahán, who was succeeded by his brother,
Nakhsh-i-Jahán, who was succeeded by his brother,
Muhammad Khán, who was succeeded by his son,
Shir Muhammad Khán, who was succeeded by his nephew,
Sultan Vais Khán, the son of Shir Ali Oghlán, the brother of Shir Muhammad. Sultan Vais was killed 832 (1428–9).[4]

[1] *Isan Buka* II. of the Mohammedan authors. . . .

[2] *Imil Khodja.* This Khan is not mentioned by the Mohammedan authors.

[3] The two dates should probably be reversed.—[Ed.]

[4] According to Chinese annals, the portion of the list bracketed above, should stand:—

Khizir Khwája	died 1399
Shama-i-Jahán	„ 1408
Muhammad Khán	„ 1416
Nakhsh-i-Jahán	„ 1418
Vais Khán	„ 1428

Each of these appears to have succeeded immediately on the death of his predecessor.

On the death of Vais there was a division among the Moghuls, some adhering to Yunus Khán, the eldest son of Vais, others to Isán Bugha II., the younger son.

West.

Yunus Khan, who was expelled 832 (1429), returned 860 (1456), and regained the western part of Moghulistan. Hostilities were maintained between the eastern and western Moghuls till the death of his grand-nephew, Kabak Sultan, when he reigned without a rival.

In the latter part of his life, the remoter tribes of the steppes, displeased with his fondness for towns, separated from him, and acknowledged his second son, Sultan Ahmad, or Alácha Khán, as their Khán—so that the kingdom was again divided into two during his lifetime. He died 892 H. (1487).

Sultan Mahmud Khan, Yunus' eldest son, succeeded his father in Tashkand and as chief of the western tribes. He was defeated by Shaibáni Khán in 908 (1502–3), lost Tashkand and Sairám, and was finally put to death by Shaibáni in 914 H. (1508–9).

East.

Isán Bugha II., raised to the throne in 832 H. (1429), and through life supported by the eastern Moghuls, died 866 (1462),[1] was succeeded by his son

Dust Muhammad Khán, who ruled in the eastern districts (Uighuristán, etc.), died 873 (1468-9).

Ḳabak Sultan Oghlán, his son, ruled for a time about Turfán, or Uighuristán, where he was murdered.

Sultan Ahmad Khán, second son of Yunus, governed the eastern Moghuls in Aksu and Uighuristán. He was generally known as Alácha Khán—"the slaughtering Khán." He was bent on making himself absolute ruler of the steppes, destroyed the chiefs, and curtailed the power of many of the tribes. Defeated by Shaibáni Khán in 908 (1502–3), he died of grief in 909 (1503–4).

The death of Sultan Ahmad was followed by many civil wars and much anarchy in Moghulistan. His elder brother, Sultan Mahmud, invaded his dominions from the west. Sultan Ahmad's numerous sons contended with one another. Several sections of the people, and among others the Kirghiz, separated from the main body. The anarchy and civil wars lasted some years. The country was overrun by Abá Bakr (a Dughlát) of Kashghar, by the Kalmáks and the Kazáks. The whole of the tribes of Moghulistan never again united under one head. Two Khanates and the confederation of the Kirghiz-Kazáks seem to have arisen out of the ruins of the Khanate of the Moghuls. Sultan Mansur, the eldest son of Sultan Ahmad,

[1] According to the Chinese accounts Isán Bugha II. died in 1445, and was succeeded by one Ye-mi-li-hu-jo (Im-il Khwája), a personage who does not appear to be mentioned by any of the Musulman historians.

established himself in Aksu, Turfán, etc., and a new Khanate arose in Kashghar and the western provinces.

West.	*East.*
Sultan Said Khan, third son of Sultan Ahmad, in Rajab 920 (Sept. 1514), or eleven years after his father's death, seized Kashghar, and expelled Abá Bakr Mirza. He died 16 Zilhajah 939 (9 July, 1533); and was succeeded by his son, Abdur Rashid Khan, who died 973 (1565–6); and was succeeded by his son, Abdul Karim.	Mansur Khan, Sultan Ahmad's eldest son, was acknowledged and ruled in Turfán and the eastern provinces—*i.e.*, Uighuristán. He died in 950 (1543–4), having reigned two years along with his father, and forty more by himself; he was succeeded by his son, Sháh Khán.

Meanwhile in the steppes of Moghulistan, the Kirghiz established themselves under Khans of their own, and in process of time, formed a kind of federative union with the Kazák Uzbegs, which has, in some degree, lasted to the present day, and has been called "the three hordes of Kirghiz."

Amirs of Kashghar, or Alti Shahr, who were contemporary with the Khans of Moghulistan.

Amir Tulik, *Ulusbegi* (or chief of the tribe) of the Moghul Khans, contemporary with Isán Bugha I., succeeded by

Amir Bulaji, his brother; raised Tughluk Timur to the throne; succeeded by his son,

Amir Khudáidád, who is said to have reigned about ninety years in Kashghar. He succeeded his father, probably soon after the year 748 H. (1347). In his time Amir Kamar-ud-Din, his uncle, usurped the Khanship of the Moghuls, and for a time also (it would appear) that of the greater part of Alti Shahr. The chronology of Amir Khudáidád's life is very uncertain. He was succeeded by

Amir Sayyid Ali, grandson of Khudáidád (by his son Amir Sayyid Ahmad). Sayyid Ali reigned about twenty-four years—838 to 861 H. (1435 to 1457)—and was succeeded by his sons,

Sániz Mirza, in Yarkand, who expelled his brother from Kashghar, and reigned seven years. He died 868 H. (1463–4).	Muhammad Haidar Mirza in Kashghar, whence he was expelled by his brother.

Muhammad Haidar Mirza, on his brother's death, succeeded. He is said to have reigned twenty-four years in all, or eight years with imperfect authority and sixteen years with full authority. In 885 H. (1480) he was expelled by his nephew and stepson, Abá Bakr.

Abá Bakr Mirza, son of Sániz, reigned in all forty-eight years. The years of his reign are probably reckoned from the date of his taking possession of Yarkand, about 873 H. (1468–9). He was finally defeated and expelled by Sultan Said Khan, the third son of Sultan Ahmad Khan (Alácha Khan), who changed the dynasty. *See Khans of Moghulistan, above.* Abá Bakr was murdered 920 H.

It may perhaps help to make matters clear as regards the dates, if I append here, a list of the western branch of the line of Chaghatai Khans (those of Mávará-un-Nahr or Transoxiana), extracted from Mr. Stanley Lane Poole's *Muhammadan Dynasties* (p. 242).

			A.H.		A.D.
1.	Chaghatai	Began to reign	624	=	1227
2.	Kara Huláku	,,	639	=	1242
3.	Isu Mangu	,,	645	=	1247
.	Kara Huláku (*restored*)	,,	650	=	1252
4.	Orgánah Khátun	,,	650	=	1252
5.	Algu	,,	659	=	1261
6.	Mubárak Shah	,,	664	=	1266
7.	Barák Khan	,,	664	=	1266
8.	Nikpai	,,	668	=	1270
9.	Tuka Timur	,,	670	=	1272
10.	Davá Khan	,,	c 672	=	c 1274
11.	Kunjuk Khan	,,	706	=	1306
12.	Taliku	,,	708	=	1308
13.	Kabak Khan	,,	709	=	1309
14.	Isán Bugha	,,	709	=	1309
.	Kabak Khan (*restored*)	,,	c 718	=	1318
15.	Ilchikadi	,,	721	=	1321
16.	Davá Timur	,,	721	=	1321
17.	Tarmashirin	,,	722	=	1322
.	Sanjar ?	,,	730–4 ?	=	1330–4 ?
18.	Jinkishai	,,	734	=	1334
19.	Buzun	,,	c 735	=	c 1335
20.	Isun Timur	,,	c 739	=	c 1339
.	Ali (of Oktai stock)	,,	c 741	=	c 1340
21.	Muhammad	,,	c 743	=	c 1342
22.	Kazán	,,	744	=	1343
.	Danishmanja (of Oktai stock)	,,	747	=	1346
23.	Buyan Kuli	,,	749	=	1348
			—760		—1358

Anarchy and rival chiefs until the supremacy of Timur in 771 A.H. = 1370 A.D.

GENEALOGICAL TABLE OF THE DUGHLAT AMIRS.

- BÁBDÁGHÁN
  - ⋮
    - Urtubu
      - An un-named Amir
        - Tulik
        - Bulaji
          - Khudaidád
            - Muhammad Shah
            - Sayyid Ahmad
              - Sayyid Ali
                - Sániz Mirza
                  - Omar Mirza
                  - Abá Bakr
                    - Jahángir
                    - Turángir
                    - Bustángir
                    - Sultán Muhamd.
                    - Others
                  - Sayyid Muhamd.
                - Muhamd. Haidar Mirza
                  - Muhamd. Husain
                    - Muhamd. Haidar (*The Author*)
                    - Abdulla Mirza
                    - Muhamd. Shah
            - Others
        - Kamar-ud-Din
        - Shams-ud-Din
        - Shaikh Daulat

GENEALOGICAL TABLE OF THE HOUSE OF CHAGHATAI.]

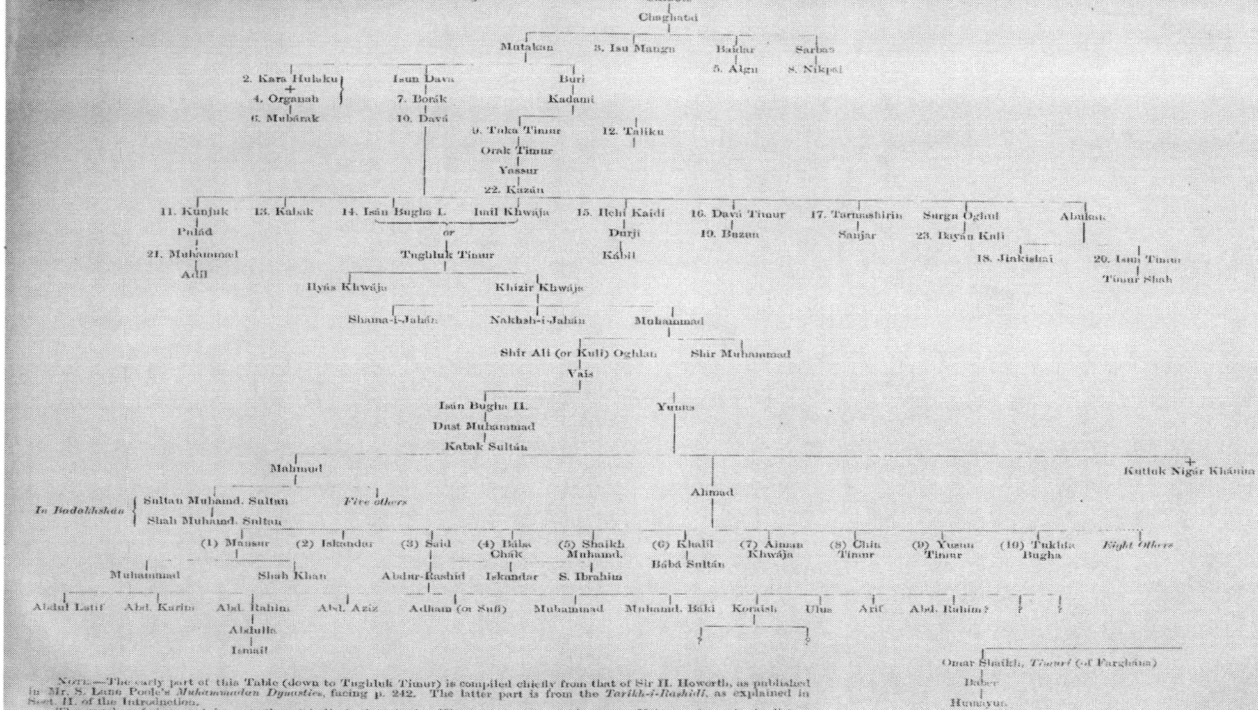

NOTE.—The early part of this Table (down to Tughluk Timur) is compiled chiefly from that of Sir H. Howorth, as published in Mr. S. Lane Poole's *Muhammadan Dynasties*, facing p. 242. The latter part is from the *Tarikh-i-Rashidi*, as explained in Sect. II. of the Introduction.

The numbers (where not in parentheses) indicate the reigning Khans of the line of Mávara-un-Nahr, as shown in the list at p. 49, Sect. II. of the Introduction.

GENEALOGICAL TABLE OF THE HOUSE OF TIMUR.

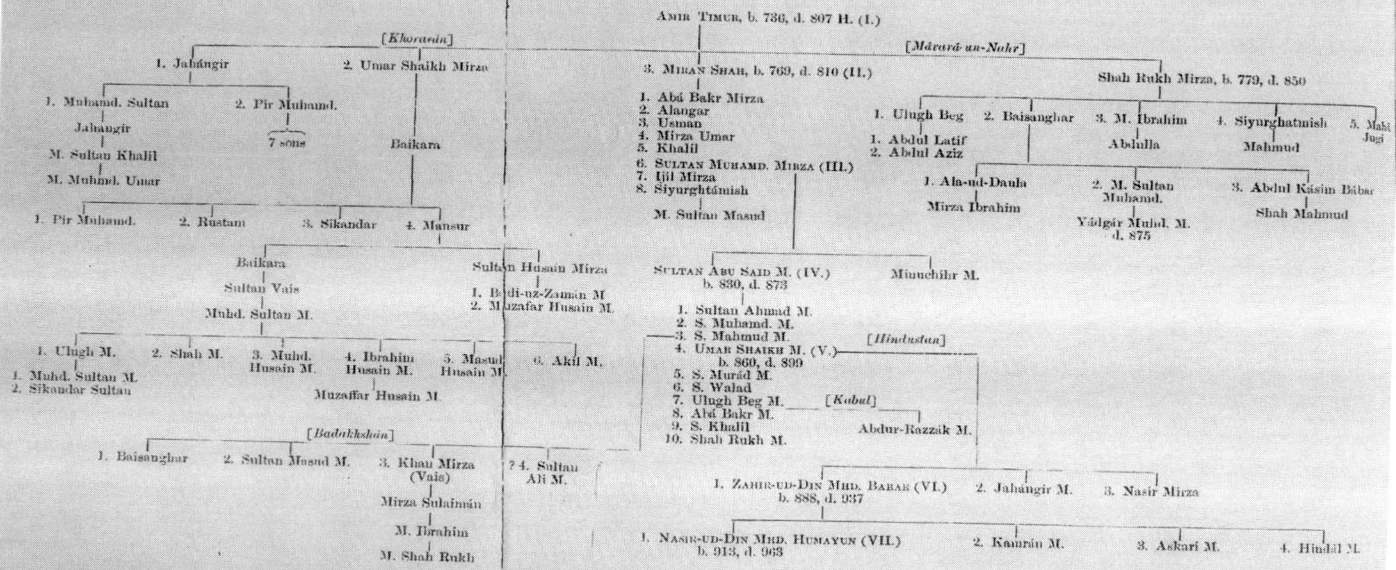

NOTE.—This Table is almost entirely from Prof. Blochmann's *Ain-i-Akbari*—but abridged.

To face p.50.

SECTION III.

THE LAND OF THE MOGHULS.

His eye might there command wherever stood
City of old or modern fame, the seat
Of mightiest Empire, from the destined walls
Of Cambalu, seat of Cathaian Can,
And Samarchand by Oxus, Temur's throne,
To Paquin of Sinæan Kings; and thence
To Agra and Lahor of great Mogul. . . . .
—*Paradise Lost*, Bk. XI.

THE area over which Mirza Haidar's history extends is a wide one. Expressed in the geographical terms of our times, it may be said to deal with Western Turkistan, Bokhara, Farghána, the Russian province of Semirechensk (or the seven rivers), the Chinese province of Ili (or Zungaria), Eastern Turkistan, Tibet, Ladak, Baltistan, Gilgit and the neighbouring states, Chitral, Wákhán, Badakhshán, Afghanistan, Kashmir, and Northern India; while references are frequently made to countries lying even beyond these regions. But it is a history, especially, of the eastern branch of the Chaghatais—*i.e.*, the Moghuls proper—and, therefore, the chief scene of action lies in and immediately around their home-land. The situation and extent of this region are not difficult to describe, but it is far from easy to give a name to it as a whole.

Its limits were not very clearly defined at any period, and were seldom the same for twenty years at a time, while even the names of "Jatah" and "Moghulistan," by which a portion of it was known, are now not only obsolete, but have hitherto been subject to some doubt regarding the exact locality to which they were applied. Moreover, there was at no time any one name in use, which served to designate the entire Khanate. Mirza Haidar usually speaks of 'Moghulistan' and 'Kashghar,' but it is not always clear whether, by 'Kashghar,' he means only the city and district of that name, or the entire province of *Alti-Shahr*—the Six Cities[1] of Eastern Turkistan—a

[1] The six cities were Kashghar, Yangi Hisar, Yarkand, Khotan, Ush-Turfán, and Aksu. Dr. Bellew informs us that Marálbashi was sometimes added to the list, when *Alti Shahr* became *Yati Shahr*, or seven cities. (*Yarkand Report*, p. 185.) The name is probably of Khokandi origin, and belongs to the present century.

region which, he tells us more than once, was, when combined with Farghána, termed *Mangalai Suyah* or "Facing the Sun."[1] This territory would almost exactly correspond to the provinces of Farghána and the Chinese Turkistan of modern times, less the districts of Karashahr, Turfán and Hami in the extreme east; or, in other words, to Farghána and Alti-Shahr. But even if we were to give the entire country the double name of "Moghulistan and Mangalai Suyah," there would still remain some difficulties of definition. At first sight it would appear that the author describes the limits very exactly; but this is not quite the case, and for two reasons. In the first place, he sets forth the provinces that composed it on several occasions, but does not always make them the same: the other is that, in common with all Asiatics who attempt to describe an area, he names a district or a geographical feature as a boundary, but does not mention whether it should be included or excluded—whether the limiting district, range or lake lay beyond or within the area he is describing. In addition to these uncertainties there is also the inconsistency that Farghána, as a whole, was seldom included within the actual possessions of the Khans of Moghulistan. They always regarded it as theirs by right, but they rarely held more than a few positions, or districts, within its limits, and even these they were usually unable to keep for any length of time. Practically, therefore, Farghána can scarcely be held to have formed a part of their dominions, although it may have been comprised in the geographical term "Mangalai Suyah." With this reservation, however, and in order to show what the author describes, it would seem as well that Farghána should be included nominally with Moghulistan and Alti-Shahr; so that, after making due allowance for the fluctuations that occurred at different periods, the following may be regarded (as nearly as possible) as a statement of the extent of the dominions of the Moghul Khans, from about the middle of the fourteenth century to the middle of the sixteenth.

There was no central division, but the province of Moghulistan proper—or Jatah, as it was also called during the early part of that period—being a "steppe" or pastoral country, and the homeland of the dominant tribe, was therefore the principal division. Its western boundary marched with the province of Shásh, the modern Táshkand, which seems to have contained

[1] For some remarks on this name, see note, p. 7.

the whole of the lowlands of the valley of the Sir, from a little above Khojand to about the Arys tributary, and included such towns as Sháhrukhia, Táshkand and Sairám. Immediately to the east of this level agricultural stretch, rise the hills which separate it from the valley of the Upper Tálás, and it was this line of hills, or uplands, which seems to have stood usually, and in a general way, for the boundary of the Moghuls. To the north of Shásh lay the province of Turkistan, with the Káratau hills between it and the Lower Tálás, and here again the hills appear to have been the western limit of the nomad tribes. Turning towards the north-west, a line drawn from the Káratau to the southern extremity of Lake Balkásh, and continued again from its other extremity to the Tárbágatai mountains, may be taken roughly to have been the frontier in that direction. We hear, at any rate, of no transactions of the Moghuls, as a tribe, anywhere to the north-west of the Balkásh; nor do we trace them anywhere to the north of the Imil river, which is fed from the Tárbágatai mountains, except when flying before Timur's avenging army in 1389 and 1390, they crossed the range into the valley of the Irtish. But this was an occasion when danger led them to seek refuge beyond the bounds of their own country. From the Tárbágatai range, the limiting line would probably bend south-eastward to some point at the northern foot of the Tian Shan, near the present Urumtsi; but this is somewhat uncertain. All that is clear is that the tract now known as "Zungaria" (or the land of the Zungár, or Jungár, Kalmáks) formed a part of the Moghul dominion, but how far precisely, "Zungária" extended towards the east, there is nothing to show. Probably it included Lakes Ebi Nor and Ayar Nor, and had for its central feature the upper course of the Ili river. On the south, the main range of the Tian Shan, as far west as about the head of the Nárin river, divided Moghulistan from Kuchar, Aksu, etc., while westward, again, the water-parting ranges between the Nárin and Lake Issigh-Kul, continued up to the heads of the Tálás, would seem, approximately, to have been the line of separation from Kashghar and Farghána.

The boundaries of Alti-Shahr were better defined by natural features than Moghulistan. It may be said, generally, to have embraced the whole of the system of the Tarim, together with some of the upper waters of the Sir. On the north it marched with the southern limit of Moghulistan, as described above. On the east it included the town and district of Kuchar (which was usually a dependency of Aksu), and probably the region of Lake Lob; while it excluded Karashahr—then known as Chálish—and all to the east of it, which constituted, as we shall see, a province that bore the ancient name of 'Uighuristán.' On the south, along the whole length of the country, the mountains forming the scarp of the Tibetan highlands—the Kuen-lun and the Altyn Tágh—shut it off from all beyond. Towards the west the Pamirs, generally speaking, constituted its extreme limit, till these abut northward on the southern confines of the valley of the river Sir; for these uplands, then as now, seem to have divided the Kashghar district from Farghána. What the precise limits in the Pamir region were, there is nothing to indicate, but in speaking of Sárigh-Kul, Mirza Haidar implies that that district, at least, lay within the province of Alti-Shahr, and for a time also, we find Wakhán and Shighnan described as territory dependent on Kashghar, though this was not usually the case.

But if these were approximately and usually the limits, it does not follow that they were, on the one hand, never overstepped, or on the other, that the area they included was always held intact. As a matter of fact, they varied considerably from time to time. Before the rise of Timur, for instance, invasions, by the Moghuls, of Shásh, Turkistan and even Mávará-un-Nahr were of common occurrence, while at times in their later history, they extended their sway over districts in the east which did not properly belong to Alti-Shahr. In the same way, when the affairs of their neighbours were in the hands of strong rulers, portions of Moghulistan were cut off for a time, and numbers of the inhabitants seem to have had no scruple in joining the service of the successful conqueror of the time being.

The section known as Moghulistan differed widely, in most respects, from its companion province on the south. It was a land of mountains, streams and lakes, of upland pastures and steppes, of wooded valleys and even forests; for while it lay north of the regions which can only become productive if reached by the monsoon from the southern seas, or if irrigated by the art of its inhabitants, it was yet far enough from the blighting snows and sunless days of Siberia, to be in most parts clothed with natural verdure of some kind. Its altitudes were moderate, and its climate, therefore, as Mirza Haidar describes it, cool and invigorating, though to Europeans, accustomed to live within the modifying influence of the sea, it would appear to be subject to extremes of temperature. Deserts in the proper sense of the word—sandy or stony wastes, with little or no vegetation or water—nowhere existed, except on the extreme north-western confines, and wherever the word 'desert' occurs in the text, when referring to Moghulistan, it is because the author has used the Persian or Turki equivalent, though the real meaning would be 'the open country,' or the 'country devoid of towns and cultivation'—the 'steppe'—a feature which no English word will describe.

However this may be, it was a land in every way suited to the habits and customs of a sparse population of nomadic graziers and shepherds, and it accordingly evolved, or at least attracted, a race whose requirements it fulfilled. But the peaceable pursuits of raising flocks and attending herds were not the only avocations of a people with the traditions of the Moghuls. Perhaps their chief requirement was a land whence they might raid on their settled and more wealthy neighbours, and whither, if beaten, they could retire and find a refuge—a land, in short, so inaccessible and unproductive to all but themselves, that it formed, at once, a base for their own description of warfare, a secure retreat, and an inhospitable waste for the pursuing enemy; for where they moved, the whole resources of the country—the food supplies, the transport, the shelter—moved with them, and were used to meet their wants alone. There could have been no forts or towns or immovable property, worthy of the name, for an invader to destroy, and no stationary population, left undefended, upon whom he might wreak his vengeance; for the women and children and the aged all formed part of the expedition, and were doubtless employed or disposed of, in much the same way while the tribe was on the march, as while at home in their own encampment. In times of peace—or rather of inactivity—they probably bred, besides the camels and sheep, which were their principal food-producers, large numbers of ponies, for it was on these that all depended, when wars or forays were on hand. Mobility must have been the quality they relied on more than any other, both in attack and retreat, and we find them baffling their enemies more by their movements than by their fighting power. Indeed, fighting in its proper sense must have been with them, as with most of their neighbours, a pursuit very sparingly indulged in. We read, it is true, of armies counted by hundreds of thousands, and of pitched battles when thousands were killed on either side, but apart from the facts that populations such as those in question could not have put such masses of fighting men in the field, and that numbers among Orientals are at all times used as mere figures of speech, it is remarkable that where a particular battle or other special incident is described in detail, there are usually indications that the numbers engaged were very small indeed.

This must have been more especially the case with the tribe of Moghuls and the other nomads who allied themselves with them, after the first quarter of the sixteenth century. During Amir Timur's reign, the Moghuls under Kamar-ud-Din, one of their best leaders, seem to have been always beaten when met by the Amir's troops, yet they were never thoroughly repressed until the great conqueror had put forth all his strength and resources in following them up, in separate bodies, to the farthest confines of their territory. His problem was not how to beat the Moghuls in battle or to invade their country, but how to catch their mobile forces in sufficient numbers, to make an impression on the nation at large; while, on their part, the Moghuls never seem to have attempted an incursion into Timur's dominions, except when he and his troops were engaged in prosecuting a war elsewhere. Later, the same difficulty occurred to Ulugh Beg Mirza, who only succeeded in dealing them a heavy blow, through the accident of a piece of treachery on the part of one of their own people, by which he was afforded an unlooked-for opportunity. And later again—within the sixteenth century—when the Kirghiz and Kazáks had to a great extent supplanted the Moghuls in what had been the latter's own land, and the nominal Khans of the country (Sultan Said and his successor) had their headquarters at Kashghar, it seems evident, though Mirza Haidar says little about it, that the tactics of the nomads left them practically masters of the situation. Yet even in those days, when brought to battle, they are said usually to have been beaten. Perhaps the only power which the Moghuls stood in fear of, after the days of Timur, was that of the Uzbegs, when these were first rising to power. Under Shaibáni Khan the confederated tribes of Uzbegs still possessed the characteristics and qualities of nomadic nations, and it is not a little remarkable that the Moghuls, so far from dealing with them as they were accustomed to do with others in the low countries, enlisted under Shaibáni in large numbers, and assisted him against the more civilised forces of Baber and the Khorasáni Mirzas. They seem to have feared to measure themselves with those who could use their own tactics against them, or fight them, indeed, with their own weapons.

In many places in Mirza Haidar's history, as well as in the *Zafar-Náma* and other books, mention is made of the 'cities' or 'towns' of Moghulistan; but as the same words must necessarily be used when speaking of the settled countries of Mávará-un-Nahr, Turkistan, and Alti-Shahr, they are somewhat misleading terms to apply to the *auls*, or encampments, of a nomadic people. One native writer, whose book dates from the first half of the fourteenth century, presents, in a few words, a telling picture of Moghulistan in his day—or part of Turkistan as it was then still called. "Since the region has been devastated by the arms of the Tatars," he writes, "it is inhabited only by a scanty population. According to what I have been assured by a man who has travelled through the country, there is nothing to be seen in Turkistan but ruins, and more or less obliterated remains. From a distance one sees a well-built village, the environs of which are covered with beautiful verdure; but on approaching, in the hope of meeting with some inhabitants, there are found only houses completely deserted. The population is composed entirely of nomads—that is, of shepherds and graziers who never occupy themselves with cultivating the land or sowing crops. There is no other verdure but that of the steppes, which grows naturally."[1] That towns, in the true sense of the word, had existed in the land is thus correct, but they had been built when others possessed and governed it, and before it had become the home of the Mongolian nomads. The Uighurs, a Turki tribe of considerable cultivation by comparison, had owned the greater part, if not the whole, of the country up to less than a century prior to the rise of the Mongols, and were probably the founders of several towns of more or less importance; while the whole of Moghulistan had, during the interval, been occupied by the Kara Khitai, whose people, although perhaps much mixed with nomad tribesmen, seem also to have been capable of building cities and carrying on cultivation. The advent of the Mon-

[1] See the *Masálak-al-Absár* of Shaháb-ud-Din, transl. by Quatremère in *Not. et Extr.* xiii., p. 257.

golian hordes, however, under Chingiz and his successors, put an end to all such practices, and from that time till the date when Mirza Haidar's history closes (and probably for long after also), the country reverted to a purely pastoral condition. When, therefore, we read of the cities of Taráz, Bálásaghun, Aimal, Bishbálik, Almáligh, etc., within the Moghul period, it can hardly be that Moghul cities are intended, but rather encampments—some of them, perhaps, central in situation and well inhabited—standing on or near the sites of the remains of these places.

In the more advanced of the countries conquered by the Mongolian armies—in Persia, Mávará-un-Nahr, Turkistan, etc. —no obliteration or even systematic destruction of towns (except in the course of the wars), and no reversion to a nomadic level, seems to have taken place; but the difference in the case of Moghulistan was that, in that country, the nomadic tribesmen of the steppes immediately to the eastward —the true Mongolia—pressed in, and appropriating the land for their own habitation, took root, while in the lower countries they settled as rulers only. Those of the Mongols who, after the first invasion, stayed in the conquered countries with their governing Khans or chiefs, probably intermarried, after a time, with the settled population, and were soon absorbed; while in what became known—and partly for this very reason—as 'Moghulistan,' or the 'land of the Mongols,' the invaders found a suitable home, and establishing themselves as one of the nations of the soil, became, for a time at least, the dominant one. As generations passed, they tended, no doubt, to lose their identity by intermarrying with other races already sparsely inhabiting the region, but in this instance their absorption would be a slow process, as compared with the few left among the overwhelming populations of the lower countries in the west. The *aul* was probably a tribal community, and the number of the Moghuls was perhaps greater than that of their neighbours, while the life of the steppes rendered a certain degree of isolation inevitable. All these circumstances would combine to retard a fusion of races, though it may not, as far as the evidence goes, have obviated it in the end.

Here, then, no cities sprang up, while those already in existence soon fell to ruin. But the Musulmán writers, who constantly confuse the words for 'city' and 'country,' and even 'nation,' would be unlikely to draw any distinction between a built and permanent town, and an encampment of felt tents—an *urdu* or an *aul*, as the Turki words are. In several cases Mirza Haidar mentions towns of Moghulistan as existing in the form of ruins only, and he is explicit on this point. But he nowhere describes one as an inhabited centre at his own time, though it is only reasonable to suppose that he would, at least, have made some mention of them had they existed, in the same way that he speaks of, and even describes, those of Alti-Shahr. The *aul*, or collection of felt tents, pitched without order or any view to permanency, near the banks of a stream, and in the centre of some district where pasture was near at hand, was probably the nearest approach to a town at the period our history belongs to. Here, possibly, a square or oblong shed of brown mud bricks, ornamented with yaks' tails, antelopes' heads, and rows of small, coloured flags, may have stood to represent the *urdu* proper, or reception-room and court-house of the chief; while round it were scattered the dome-shaped tents of willow laths, covered with sheets of felt—all grimy and greasy—and ready at any moment to be taken down by the women of the tribe, and packed, with the rest of their domestic belongings, on the backs of the camels. Of forts, walls, or streets there could have been no sign. In the daytime, the ground on which the encampment stood would have been black with the dried droppings of sheep, a foot in depth, which, whirled into the air by the west wind, would pervade, with its pungent smell, the valley for a mile round, and cover everything, even the surface of the river, with a film of black. By the evening, this unsavoury carpet would be overlaid by thousands of sheep, driven in from the neighbouring glens and packed close, in scarcely separated flocks, for the night, while outside these, long rows of camels would kneel at their tethering-ropes, and groups of shaggy ponies stand fastened to the doors of their masters' tents. Near at hand, it may be, some ruined walls or weather-worn mounds pointed to the remains of an Uighur town, or fort, destroyed hundreds of years ago, and having no more connection with the life of the people of the *aul* than have the ruins of an Elizabethan castle, or a Norman keep, with the inhabitants of a neighbouring county town in England at the present day.

Encampments such as these would not only leave no trace of where they stood, but even their names would be unlikely to endure in history. Such were, no doubt, At-Báshi, Kuchkar,

Jumgál, Jud Kuzi, and others, so often spoken of in the Second Part of the *Tarikh-i-Rashidi*, and several more that are mentioned in the *Zafar-Náma* and the *Tarikh-i-Jahán Kushai*, now impossible to identify. They were typical of the Moghuls as a race—of a nation devoid of constructive instincts, destined only to fallow the land and then make place for others.

The period subsequent to the conquest of Chingiz's successors was one when disorder and intolerance prevented European travellers, who might have left a description behind them, from traversing the country of the Moghuls; but a side-light is shed on the subject by a brief mention in Rubruk's narrative of his visit to Mangu Kaán (Chingiz's grandson) at Karakorum in the year 1253, and consequently only just at the outset of the establishment of the Mongols in the region in question. Karakorum was then the Mongol capital: it numbered among its inhabitants many Chinese, Uighurs, and other comparatively cultivated people, and was, presumably, if not the only permanent Mongolian town, at any rate by far the best of them. Yet the walls only measured about a mile in circumference, and Rubruk relates of it: "You must understand that if you set aside the Kaán's own palace, it is not as good as the borough of St. Dennis; and as for the palace, the abbey of St. Dennis is worth ten of it! There are two streets in the town, one of which is occupied by the Saracens, and in that is the market-place. The other street is occupied by the Cathayans, who are all craftsmen . . . . There are also twelve idol temples belonging to different nations, two Mahummeries, in which the law of Mahomet is preached, and one Church of the Christians at the extremity of the town. The town is enclosed by a mud wall and has four gates."[1] The Chinese travellers of the thirteenth century give no description of the inhabited centres of Moghulistan which they passed through, though one of them, Chang Té (who seems to have had an eye for irrigation) mentions briefly that at Almáligh there were reservoirs in the market-places, "connected by running water." Farther westward also, in the valley of the Chu, he remarks that the country was intersected in all directions by canals which irrigated the fields, while numerous ancient walls and other ruins were seen which he attributed to the days of the Kitan or the Kara Khitai.[2] But all these marks of civilisation had been swept away in Mirza Haidar's time, as he himself implies in his description of

[1] See Yule's *Marco Polo*, i., p. 228.
[2] See Bretschneider, i., pp. 127, 129.

the antiquities of that part of the Khanate which, he says, was formerly known as 'Kara Khitai.'

In attempting to make clear the condition of Moghulistan and the neighbouring regions of Central Asia, perhaps the chief perplexity is experienced in unravelling the nomenclature of places and people. The names of countries and towns not only changed with time, but different nations applied, frequently, a different designation to one and the same place. Thus, names often arose at a certain period, were employed by writers for a time, and again fell out of use. The Mongols, for instance, during their ascendency, gave names of their own to many places which, after the decline of their power, became obsolete. In the same way, the conquests of Timur seem to have given birth to names that are peculiar to that period alone, and were perhaps only in vogue among those connected with the conqueror's court or his armies. This circumstance, in addition to the habit of applying nicknames to tribes and nations, may account for many of the difficulties that surround the identification of names mentioned by various authors, and should act as a warning, in the case of the tribes, not to attach too readily a racial significance to every name that is met with.

To the Chaghatais of Mávará-un-Nahr and the west, Moghulistan was known, in the 13th and 14th centuries, by the name of *Jatah*, and though this was only a term of depreciation, or a nickname (as will be explained below), it is employed in the gravest way by several Persian authors of the Timuri period, whose works have become standards of historical reference. What is perhaps more curious to remark is, that the name of Bishbálik, which so often occurs in mediæval histories and travels, and in the Chinese historical annals, is that by which the Chinese knew the Khanate of Moghulistan, during the earlier part of the period over which Mirza Haidar's history extends. This name had originally no connection with the Moghuls or their dominion, but was a survival from the days when the region had belonged to the Uighurs. Properly it was the name of a city only, which had been built by the Uighurs, and, having become their capital, had lent its name to the whole kingdom. The meaning, in Turki, is 'Five Cities,' and seems, possibly, to have indicated the capital of the five divisions, or provinces, into which the country of the Uighurs, at that time, (about the middle of the ninth century) was divided; or otherwise, it may have meant that the tribe was divided into five sections, or the town (as one authority has it) into five quarters.[1] However this may be, the Chinese knew the country by its Turki name (which they sometimes translated into its Chinese equivalent—Wu-chêng), while they gave the city itself the Chinese style of Pei-ting, or 'Northern Court'; and subsequently (early in the fifteenth century) changed that of the whole country from 'Bishbálik' into 'Ili-bálik.'

The town of Bishbálik was situated on, or near, the site of the modern Urumtsi, and the country of which it was the chief place, extended to the westward and north-westward, as well as beyond the southern slopes of the Tian Shan. Like the rest of this part of Asia, it fell into the empire of Chingiz Khan, and, after his death, passed to his son Chaghatai. Later again, in the time of the Chinese Mings, the official historians of that dynasty described the limits of the region in such a way, as to leave no doubt that the country they termed Bishbálik was, indeed, Moghulistan. "Bie-shi-ba-li," says the *Ming Shi*,[2] "is a great empire in the Si Yü [countries of the west]. It is bordered on the south by Yü-tien [Khotan], on the north by the country of the Wa-la [the Oirát Kalmáks], on the west by Sa-ma-rh-han [Samarkand], and to the east it is contiguous with Huo-chou [Kara Khoja]. It is distant [probably the *urdu* of the Khan is meant] from Kia-Yü-Kuan in the south-east, 3700 li. It is believed that Bie-shi-ba-li occupies the same tracts as, in ancient times, Yenki or Kui-tsz."[3] As a description of the land and people, the Ming history adds:—"The country of Ili-ba-li is surrounded by deserts. It extends 3000 li from east to west and 2000 li from north to south. There are no cities or palace buildings. The people are nomads living in felt tents, and exchanging their abode, together with their herds, in accordance with the existence of water and pasture land. They are of a fierce appearance. Their common food is flesh and *kumis*. They are dressed in the same fashion as the Wa-la."

Many embassies are recorded in the *Ming Shi* as having

[1] See Bretschneider, i., p. 258. But Mr. Watters deriving his information, it seems, from Chinese sources, counts Bishbálik, or Urumtsi, as one of the "Five Cities," and mentions Yenki (now Karashahr) and Kuitze (the present Kuchar) as two of the others. The remaining two he does not specify. (*China Review*, xix., No. 2, pp. 108, 112.)

[2] Bretschneider, ii., pp. 225 *seq*.

[3] These were two ancient kingdoms, explained by Dr. Bretschneider to have existed before the Christian era, and to be generally identified, by the Chinese, with the modern Karashahr and Kuchar.

passed between Bishbálik, or Ili-bálik, and the Chinese capital, which make it appear that the Khans of Moghulistan and the Dughlát Amirs paid tribute to China. Whether the position of tributaries was imposed upon them by superior force, or whether, as is far more probable, the missions were sent to cultivate the friendship of a powerful neighbour, and to profit by an exchange of presents, is nowhere intimated; but the result remains, that from the time of Khizir Khwája, about the year 1391, down to the reign of Isan Bugha II. in 1456, each successive Khan (as we have seen in Section II.) sent one or more tribute-bearing missions to the Ming court. After the latter date, it appears to have been settled that 'Ili-bali' was to send tribute every three years, but no further mention is made of any special mission, and it is possible that not long afterwards, the growing weakness of the Mings caused the custom to fall into disuse.

It may be thought strange, perhaps, that Mirza Haidar's history nowhere speaks of intercourse with China, or mentions that the Moghul Khans performed these acts of homage to her Emperors. Whether he omitted any allusion to them, from a feeling that the payment of tribute was derogatory to his ancestors, or whether he thought the subject not worth recording, must remain a matter of conjecture. In all likelihood the latter was the reason, as we shall see, further on, when referring to similar missions from Uighuristán. The proceeding was, presumably, looked upon as a mere form, or indeed a farce, and therefore attracted no attention on the part of the historian. Still, his silence on the point cannot be taken to disprove the statements of the Chinese, for these are explicit and persistent, and can hardly be otherwise than correct as records of bare facts. What is remarkable, however, is that the same Khans and Amirs who were bowing the knee to China, whether in good faith or otherwise, had no hesitation in measuring their strength with so great a soldier as Timur. The fact that his power was near and visible did not inspire them with respect, or deter them from raiding into his territory and otherwise provoking his vengeance. But the Chinese, then as now, seem to have possessed the art of attracting the outward forms of submission from distant States, though they had no power to exact the reality.

Passing now across the mountains to the south-east, an entirely different land and people present themselves, in the province that may be most appropriately and correctly called *Alti-Shahr*, or the 'Six Cities' of Eastern Turkistan. Here the low ranges and open valleys of the steppes, are changed for gigantic mountains on the one hand, and sandy deserts on the other; the *aul* of felt tents for the town of brown mud-bricks and close-packed bazars; the grazing grounds and hill-side torrents for cultivated fields and irrigation canals; while, above all, the thriftless, irresponsible nomad is replaced by the cultivator and artisan, with all the elements of stability that their industry confers upon a people. Though the area is large, the culturable and habitable spots in it are, out of all proportion, small. One modern traveller describes it as a huge desert fringed by a few small patches of cultivation. Another tells us that a bird's-eye view of the country would show a huge bare desert, surrounded on three sides by barren mountains, along the bases of which would be seen some vivid green spots, showing out sharp and distinct like streaks of green paint on a sepia picture. At the western end, the cultivation is of greater extent and more continuous than in the eastern half, where the oases are small and separated from each other by stretches of desert, which increase in length as the traveller passes eastward; while the eastern extremity is desert pure and simple. The oases, however, are fertile enough in themselves, for every drop of the water brought down by the streams from the mountains, is drawn off into irrigating canals, and made to reach as far as possible toward the desert, for agricultural purposes.

All except the shifting sands of the central waste, appears to require only water to render the ground fertile; but water is precisely the boon that is withheld. Though the monsoon clouds roll in every summer across the mountain masses on the south, they seldom do more than tantalise the cultivator, who watches them in the hope of rain. Indeed, rain but rarely falls, and a Chinese traveller of ancient days[1] has recorded the incredulity of the people, when told that water for cultivation fell from heaven, onto the favoured soil of his country, and rendered it independent of melted snow from the mountains. They laughed, and cried: "How can heaven provide enough for all?"[1] Snow may be less of a rarity, but so dry is the atmosphere, that when a fall occurs, it evaporates after a few hours, and leaves the surface of the ground scarcely moistened.

That a land of this nature should support only a small population, and be too poor, as Mirza Haidar tells us, to maintain an army on its own produce, is not surprising. Whether

[1] Sung Yun, in 518 A.D. See Beal's *Si-Yü-Ki*, i., p. xc.

its weakness as a State is owing to this or to whatever other cause, it has always been an easy prey to invaders, and has seldom had a native ruler within historic times. Its population has been a Turki one for ages past, and the Uighur branch of that race may be regarded (as far as historic times are concerned) as the original owners of the soil, and the parent stock of the bulk of the present inhabitants.[1] That in later times, at least, they were not an aggressive race appears evident from the little we hear of them, and that they had some capacity for crafts and literature seems also to be established. No doubt the tendency of such a people would be to live peaceably under any government strong enough to repel external enemies; so that when Mirza Haidar tells us that Alti-Shahr was "free from the discord of men and the trampling of hoofs, and became an asylum for the contented and the prosperous," he is probably drawing a picture of the country not only true of his own time, but one that serves for several centuries both before and after it.

During the periods that the Dughlát Amirs and Moghul Khans held sway, we hear of expeditions being sent to overrun Badakhshán, Ladak, and other weak States, but these were evidently undertaken by foreign rulers with their foreign troops, and not by the people of the country; indeed, we come much more frequently upon records of invasions which they themselves underwent at the hands of various enemies, such as the Arabs, the Mongols, the Kara Khitai, and even the Kalmáks. In the raids of the Moghuls into Western Turkistan and Mávará-un-Nahr, in their wars with Timur and Ulugh Beg, and their long campaigns with the Uzbegs, it is probable that the natives of Alti-Shahr took little part, for they are never mentioned as combatants. They had, in short (and have still), all the attributes of a lowland and unwarlike people, whose wealth excites the cupidity of aggressive neighbours, but the nature of whose country and customs prevent them from becoming themselves aggressive.

It would be interesting to learn what the armies were composed of, that invaded, in the reigns of Abá Bakr and Sultan Said, Badakhshán, Chitral, etc., Ladak, Tibet and Kashmir. In all likelihood the numbers were very small—to be counted in some instances by hundreds rather than by thousands—while most of the men were probably mercenaries from countries

[1] Comp. Klaproth, in Timkowski's *Voy. à Peking*, i., p. 392, and Radloff in Petermann's *Mittheilungen*, 1866, Heft. iii., p. 97.

other than Alti-Shahr. Mirza Haidar nowhere specifies the races which furnished the rank and file of these forces. When entering on the conquest of Kashghar, in 1514, he gives an analysis of the chiefs of Sultan Said's army, nearly all of whom were Moghuls of various clans, or members of tribes who had long previously thrown in their lot with the Moghuls, and the number of tribal followers that each chief brought with him is specified in each case. If the figures given are correct—and as they are not mere round numbers, they appear as if intended to be exact—it is evident that the tribal following which each chief could muster was a mere handful, for the total of the tribesmen mentioned does not approach that of the entire army of 4700 men, as he states it.[1] The remainder must have been mercenaries and adventurers who were, no doubt, to be found in abundance all over Central Asia in those times, in the persons of Kipcháks, Turkomans, Afghans, Kárluks and what not. On this occasion, too, a great effort was being made and a prize worth winning was at stake; the army was raised, moreover, in Farghána and Moghulistan, and not in peaceful Alti-Shahr. Thus it was probably a much more numerous one than those afterwards employed on distant expeditions beyond the mountains, though it may be fairly conjectured that the composition was very similar in all cases. In the expedition of Sultan Said against Ladak, Kashmir and Tibet in 1532, the author puts the total of the army at the round figure of 5000 men, but in this instance he gives none of the minute particulars that he records with regard to the 4700 and their supports, who invaded Kashghar. The round number is likely, therefore, to be one of the many similar exaggerations in which his book abounds; for it is improbable that as large a force would have been thought necessary for this enterprise as for the wresting of Kashghar and the whole of Alti-Shahr from so formidable an enemy as Mirza Abá Bakr. He tells us, it is true, that Ladak was incapable of supporting the Khan's army, but this might have been the case with even half 5000 men and their complement of horses.

Perhaps the most noteworthy feature of this land of the Six Cities, and the one that has chiefly struck the imagination of

[1] This force was, however, only the army actually operating against Kashghar, Yangi Hisar, etc., for the author mentions other troops that were guarding the road from Moghulistan, and the baggage; though as regards the number of these, he gives no indication.

both ancient and modern writers, is the central desert with its moving sands and buried towns. It is referred to in Chinese writings of more than 2000 years old, by travellers who gave the region the name of *Liu Sha*, or 'Moving Sands,' from its chief characteristic and most obvious peculiarity;[1] and it was made known to Europeans through the graphic accounts of it which Marco Polo left on record. The phenomenon of the shifting sands could hardly have escaped Mirza Haidar, and the story he tells of the overwhelming of Katak, with its mosque and minaret, is one of the best pieces of description in his book. It is almost an exact counterpart of that told by Hiuen Tsang in the eighth century, of a town between Khotan and Pima (Pain?) which was said to have been overwhelmed by the same agency, some hundreds of years previously. In this case, neglect in the proper worship of a Buddhist idol was the cause, while in the later one the Musulmans detected the wrath of God. The earlier calamity too, is said to have been predicted by a pious Arhát seven days before it occurred. At first a great storm of wind arose, which carried sand and soil before it, while "on the seventh day," continues the narrative, "in the evening, just after the division of the night, it rained sand and earth and filled the city . . . . The town of Ho-lo-lo Kia is now a great sand mound. The kings of neighbouring countries, and persons in power from distant spots, have, many times, wished to excavate the mound and take away the precious things buried there; but as soon as they have arrived at the borders of the place, a furious wind has sprung up, dark clouds have gathered together from the four quarters of heaven, and they have become lost."[2]

Similar stories are in the mouth of nearly every native of the country down to the present time, and several have been recorded by Dr. Bellew and Sir Douglas Forsyth. These travellers themselves visited some of the sand-buried ruins in the neighbourhood of Yangi Hisár. One of them was the fort of a Uighur chief called Tokhta Rashid, which had been destroyed about the eleventh century by Arsalan Khan, and afterwards overwhelmed by the sand. Another was the Mazár, or shrine, of one Hazrat Begum, which had been first swallowed up, and again, at a later date, left free by the receding dunes. The neighbourhood of the latter ruin is described as "a perfect sea

[1] See Bretschneider, ii., pp. 18, 144.
[2] Beal's *Si-Yü-Ki*, ii., pp. 323–4.

of loose sand, advancing in regular wave lines from north-west to south-east. The sand dunes are mostly from ten to twenty feet high, but some are seen, like little hills, full a hundred feet high, and in some spots higher. They cover the plain, of which the hard clay is seen between their rows, with numberless chains of two or three or more together in a line, and follow in successive rows one behind the other, just like the marks left by wave ripples on a sandy beach, only on a large scale. Towards the south-east these sand dunes all present a steep bank in the shape of a crescent, the horns of which slope forwards and downwards, in points, to the ground . . . ." The process of submergence, Dr. Bellew found to be usually a very gradual one, until the symmetry of the dune, becoming broken by an obstructing object, its loose materials subside, and thus overwhelm the obstruction. In the instance of one of the buildings inspected, it was found that "a chain of three crescentic dunes, side by side, had advanced in line across the plain, till one of the outer crescents had struck the walls of the court of the tenement, and growing up, had, in time, overtopped, and thus overflowed and filled its area by its downfall; whilst the other two crescents at its side, continuing their unobstructed course, maintained their proper form uninjured."[1] The rate of progression the writer was unable to determine, as it depends on the varying force of the propelling power, the slope of the land, and the obstructions on its surface. The operation, however, is the same as in the well-known instance of Eccles church, on the coast of Norfolk, only on a larger scale. By 1839 the whole of the church, except a portion of the tower, had been buried; by 1862 the tower had nearly emerged again, while in 1892 the whole building rose free from the level of the strand, the dunes having passed to its landward side.

The phenomenon thus seen in operation, explains how the town of Katak, and others mentioned by Mirza Haidar, became engulfed, and confirms the stories still current in Eastern Turkistan of ruined towns, or buildings, now and then appearing for a while and being again submerged.[2] In the extreme east of the country, the sandy desert is found at its worst, and it is in connection with this quarter that most of the tales of weird horrors have their origin. How deeply the superstitious

[1] See *Journ. Rl. Geo. Socy.*, 1877, pp. 9–11.

[2] Mirza Haidar and the Chinese traveller, referred to above, attribute these calamities to the showers of fine sand that frequently fall after violent storms

mind of the Asiatic may be impressed by these wastes of moving sands, and how little reason there is to wonder at the stories of ghosts, demons, and visions with which he has invested the region, may be judged by General Prejevalski's vivid description of it. "The effect of these bare yellow hillocks," he writes, "is most dreary and depressing when you are among them, and can see nothing but the sky and the sand; not a plant, not an animal is visible, with the single exception of the yellowish-grey lizards (*Phrynocephalus Sp.*) which trail their bodies over the loose soil and mark it with the patterns of their tracks. A dull heaviness oppresses the senses in this inanimate sea of sand. No sounds are heard, not even the chirping of the grasshopper; the silence of the tomb surrounds you." [1]

Hiuen Tsang's description scarcely varies from that of the Russian traveller. "These sands," he says, "extend like a drifting flood for a great distance, piled up or scattered before the wind. There is no trace left behind by travellers, and oftentimes the way is lost, and so they wander hither and thither quite bewildered, without any guide or direction. So travellers pile up the bones of animals as beacons. There is neither water nor herbage to be found, and hot winds frequently blow. When these winds rise, both man and beast become confused and forgetful, and then they remain perfectly disabled. At times, sad and plaintive notes are heard and piteous cries, so that between the sights and sounds of this desert, men get confused and know not whither they go. Hence there are so many who perish on the journey. But it is all the work of demons and evil spirits." [2]

And if the superstition of the Asiatic is moved by the mystic scenes of the desert, his cupidity is also stirred by the legends of buried riches which the submerged cities are supposed to

---

of wind. It is, no doubt, a fact that a high wind carries quantities of impalpable dust into the air, and that much of this gradually falls to the ground again when the storm subsides. In this way the dust showers are formed which have been described by the Georgian traveller Danibeg, in 1795, and by Mr. W. H. Johnson, who visited Khotan in 1865. But these showers cannot be held to account for the disappearance of towns, or even buildings, in the sudden and calamitous manner described by Asiatic authors. Their action would be extremely gradual, and could only submerge a building after operating for centuries, while that of the sand-dunes can accomplish it in a few years. (See, for Danibeg, *Geogr. Mag.* 1876, p. 150. Johnson in *J. R. G. S.* 1867, p. 5. Also note, p. 11.)

[1] Prejevalski, *Kulja to Lake Lob*, pp. 163–4.

[2] Beal's *Si-Yü-Ki* ii., pp. 324–5.

contain. Traditions lose nothing from age or from being often repeated, and no doubt, the stories of hidden treasures are now —and, indeed, were in Mirza Haidar's time—ancient enough to acquire a very strong influence on numbers of the population. From time to time ornaments, vessels, images, and coins of great curiosity are unearthed, but their value to the finders, whose only interest lies in the worth of the metal they are made of, can scarcely be great. Perhaps the only systematic exploitation of the ancient sites, ever undertaken, is that of Mirza Abá Bakr, Amir of Kashghar, so fully described by our author. It may be dated about the end of the fifteenth and beginning of the sixteenth century, and we may infer that nearly everything of intrinsic value was brought to light, while much that was of antiquarian interest was destroyed, so that when, at some future time, civilised explorers come to investigate the ruins, and find little to reward their labours, they may feel themselves indebted to the cupidity of Mirza Abá Bakr for their disappointment. The tales which the author tells of the riches accumulated by the Mirza, may safely be regarded as, in a great measure, fabulous; but it is precisely tales such as these that have given rise to the inflated estimates of buried wealth so common in the country, even at the present day.

Here and there valuable records of the past may still be forthcoming from the submerged towns, like those obtained in 1874, by Sir D. Forsyth, who enumerates a figure of Buddha of the tenth century, a clay figure of the Hindu monkey-god Hanuman, and Hindu women's ornaments, all pointing to that close intercourse with India which we know, from other sources, to have existed in times before Muhammadanism prevailed and crushed it. He also obtained several Greek coins of great antiquity and interest. Among these is mentioned especially one of Antimachus, dating about 140 B.C., and another, of Menander, from about the year 126 B.C., while a third, an iron one of Hermæus, might, it was thought, prove even older than either of these. But it is not necessarily among the ruins buried by the shifting sands, that relics of remote ages will be found. Very ancient remains are known already to exist at various points along the southern spurs of the Tian Shan, though nothing has yet been ascertained as to the age they belong to. It was near the town of Kuchar—the ancient Kuitze of the Chinese—that Captain Bower found the famous birch-bark manuscript, written in Sanskrit and dating from the fifth century, while he also points to ruins of cities which, though buried beneath the present level of the country, have no connection with the shifting sands.[1]

But it is time to turn from the land of the man to the man of the land.

[1] See *Pros. R. A. S. B.*, Nov. 1890.

SECTION IV.

THE PEOPLE—MOGHUL, TURK, AND UIGHUR.[1]

Men from the regions near the Volga's mouth,
Mixed with the rude, black archers of the South;
. . . . . . Chiefs of the Uzbek race,
Waving their heron crests with martial grace;
Turkomans, countless as their flocks, led forth
From th' aromatic pastures of the North;
Wild warriors of the turquoise hills,—and those
Who dwell beyond the everlasting snows
Of Hindoo Kosh, in stormy freedom bred, ...
—*Veiled Prophet of Khorasan.*

In the foregoing Section, it has been found convenient to use the word *Moghulistan* for the region occupied by the descendants of the Mongols, subsequent to the time of Chaghatai Khan, though it has been necessary, when speaking of the people or their language from a racial point of view, to employ, occasionally, the terms *Mongol* and *Mongolian* rather than *Moghul.* The distinction may not be a very satisfactory one, and need not be carried farther than is absolutely needed to differentiate between the earlier racial attributes, and the later national, or political, aspects of the land and people. It is not easy, however, to distinguish, nominally, between the Mongols of Mongolia proper, before they spread to the westward under Chingiz Khan, and the same people when, at a later date, having separated from the land of their ancestors, they had come to close quarters with the Musulman inhabitants of the western states of Central Asia. These neighbours mispronounced the name of the new-comers' original nation and, afterwards becoming their historians, handed it down to posterity under what appears to be an altered form. Fortunately it was not greatly changed by either Persian or Turki writers, yet the slight modification they made has led, in modern times, to doubts whether the terms *Mongol* and *Moghul* were intended

[1] This section was read, in MS., by Sir H. Howorth, who had the kindness to add some marginal notes. These I have distinguished by subscribing his initials.

for the same word, and whether they denoted one people or two. We may be satisfied that the two forms, as also the *Mo-al* of some of the earlier transliterators from the Chinese, are intended for one and the same.[1]

With the name of the land it was somewhat different. The Mongols themselves have perhaps never had a general name for the whole of the countries inhabited by their tribes—that is, for the region known to Europeans as 'Mongolia' in its most extended sense. At the time of Chingiz Khan, probably whatever country was vaguely regarded by Turki and Persian writers as being in the original occupation of the Mongols, or Moghuls, was called simply *Moghulistan;* but later, when a specific region, bordering on some of the most advanced and thickly peopled countries of the Turks and Tájiks, became the home of Mongol tribesmen, who made their presence felt in a manner none too agreeable, they absorbed the attention of their neighbours and came to be spoken of as the *Moghuls* in a special sense, and their land as *Moghulistan.* The rest of the race fell out of sight: their territory was far away and probably seldom heard of, while taking into consideration the loose ideas prevalent among Asiatics on such subjects, it is not in the least unlikely that the smaller, but better known, region, should have acquired for itself the name which, by strict right, should have been applied to the whole.

That the original population of this smaller region was composed of various nations, previous to its becoming the home of Mongol tribesmen, we have seen already. Abul Ghází tells us that it was inhabited by many tribes—some that were of Mongol race and others that were not—and D'Ohsson and Howorth amply demonstrate the same thing. It contained Uighurs, who were a tribe of Turki descent; Kara Khitai, whose origin was chiefly Manchu (and therefore of a Tungusic root), though probably much mixed with Mongol blood; also Naimans and Karluks, and perhaps some original Kirghiz, all of Turki ancestry; and, moreover, there were Kalmáks, who must be regarded as a branch of the Mongol race.[2] But when, during

[1] At the present day, it takes a sharp ear to distinguish the exact pronunciation, when the word is spoken by a true Mongol—as, for instance, a Khalka or a Chakhar. It sounds as often *Mo-ghol* or *Mo-ol* as *Mongol;* and sometimes even *Monghol.* But always with the vowel sound of *o*, and never that of *ú*. The latter vowel is, no doubt, a foreign introduction.

[2] The name Kalmák is a difficulty. It is unknown among the so-called Kalmáks, who treat it as a term of opprobrium, and it has been suspected to

the time of the Mongol ascendency, large numbers of that people settled in the country and became, from a military point of view, the dominant race, it is scarcely surprising that the western foreigners should have given the whole of the region the name of *Moghulistan*,[1] just as they had previously, when the Kara Khitai were supreme there, called the same territory *Kara Khitai.* It was the name that the Mongols themselves affected and were (at that time, at any rate) proud of, while it was also that with which their fame and their most cherished traditions were associated. Their mode of procedure, and the result they unconsciously attained, are paralleled in European history by the instance of the Franks in Gaul. During the third century, the Franks were still a loose confederacy of Germanic tribes living beyond the right bank of the Rhine. By degrees, under the Merovingians, they began to invade the country on the left bank. As the Roman power declined, their own increased till, in the fifth century, they had extended it over the whole of northern Gaul. Here they adapted themselves to the conditions of their new territory, and gradually spread over the entire surface of what is now France. Their numbers were so small that they were overlaid by the large Gallic population, yet the new-comers succeeded eventually in imposing their name on the larger nation, and originated the names of *France* and *French*, which entirely displaced those of the ancient inhabitants.

But Moghulistan was not the only name the new land of the Mongols acquired, for in many books of the fourteenth and

---

be a corruption of Kalpák. Kara-kalpáks—black hats—will be remembered as an appellation. I am quite convinced that the Naimáns and Karlughs were a branch of the Uighurs. Naimán means "eight," and, by itself, is an impossible appellation. They were really called "Naimán-Uighurs," or the "Eight Uighurs." When the Mongol Empire broke up, the Naimáns joined the Kazák and Uzbeg confederacies, and the chief tribe of the Middle Horde is still called Naimán.—H. H.

[1] The late Professor Grigorief has explained that: "from the time of Timur the name Mongol, or Mogol, was given, by Musulman historians, not to the Mongols, but to the Turkish subjects of the Jaghatis who ruled in Zungaria and the western parts of what are now called the Kirghiz steppes." (See Schuyler's *Turkistan*, i., p. 375.) The word "western" is probably a misprint for "eastern;" but Professor Grigorief can hardly mean that the name of *Mongol*, or *Moghul*, was applied only to those who were Turks, and consequently not Mongols, by race. My impression is that the confusion he has fallen into, will be sufficiently cleared up by observing the non-ethnic way in which Asiatic writers use the word *Turk*, but which the Professor seems to have taken in a strictly ethnical sense. This subject will be explained farther on in the present Section.

fifteenth centuries, we find both country and people alluded to under the name of *Jatah*—a name that, in translating, has been made to assume several unnecessary forms. Thus Pétis de la Croix, who put the *Zafar-Náma* into French, as far back as the end of the seventeenth century, transliterated the word *Geta*, and many subsequent authors followed his example. From the name mis-spelled in this way, much speculation arose among European writers, some of whom were able to derive from it the designation of the *Jats* of India, and others to recognise the *Getæ*, or *Masagetæ*, of classical authors. It is fair to say that most modern Orientalists have hesitated to accept these speculative conjectures, though the meaning and origin of the name have been hidden from them. Mirza Haidar now (and he is the first to do so) clears the matter up by informing his readers, parenthetically, in a number of places, that *Moghulistan* and *Jatah* were one and the same country. In the passages from the *Zafar-Náma*, which he cites in the First Part of his history, he interpolates this definition repeatedly, while in the closing chapter of that Part, he adds the further explanation that the Chaghatais called the Moghuls *Jatah*, on account of their enmity towards them, and by way of depreciation. Thus it was merely a nick-name—a term of contempt or reproach—and when, with this clue, the word is sought in a Mongol dictionary, it is found to mean a 'worthless person,' a 'ne'er-do-well,' or 'rascal.'[1] It has therefore no racial significance, but like such names as Kazák, Kalmák, etc., was probably applied to the Moghuls by their more cultivated neighbours, on account of their barbarous manners, lawless character, and unsettled habits generally.[2] This being the sense, it need not be used except in translating from the texts; explained once for all, the Jatahs who have haunted the works of historians and commentators for two

[1] My attention has been called to a Mongol word *jété, chété*, or *chata*, having the meanings of 'margin,' 'border,' or 'a march;' but these are significations which could scarcely have been applied as a term of reproach or depreciation.

[2] Quatremère, though unaware of the meaning of the word, sagaciously inferred, from the numerous authors he had read, that it was employed to designate a nation composed of Mongol tribes and others, and was not in reality a race name. He tells us also that the term *Jatah* is of very recent origin. It is not to be found in the works of authors previous to the fifteenth century, and is about contemporaneous with the birth of such denominations as *Kazák, Sart, Sirr, Kalmák*, and others. On the other hand, the word could not be traced by Quatremère in any book subsequent to that of Abdur Razzák (the *Matla i Saadain*), who died 1482. (See *Not. et Extraits*, xiii., p. 231.)

hundred years, fall into their right place and need be heard of no more.

But the anomalies of nomenclature did not stop here, for our author further implies that the Moghuls retorted on the Chaghatais with the reproachful name of *Karáwánás.* Unfortunately he does not, in this instance, give any clue to the meaning of the word, and neither Turki dictionaries nor the transliterated Mongol dictionaries (as far as I am able to use them) throw any light upon it. Indeed, I know of nothing to point to the word being a term of depreciation, except the inference to be drawn from this one statement of Mirza Haidar's; but, taking into consideration the connection in which he introduces it, and the common practice over the greater part of Asia, of one nation calling another by a reproachful nickname, this single instance is probably sufficient. The name, under one variant or another, has been found by translators in several Oriental works, and appears in many cases to be applied to a tribe or community: thus Quatremère cites the *Tarikh-i-Wassáf* to the effect that the army of the "Karavenas" resembled monkeys rather than men, but that they were the bravest "among the Mongols"; also Mirkhwánd, who is represented as describing them in precisely the same way; Rashid-ud-Din, who also speaks of their bravery; and several others who, however, only make mention of the name. Not one of these authors assists us in assigning a meaning to the word, or in tracing the origin of its application to the Chaghatais as a people. None of them do more than represent the Karáwánás to have been a sub-tribe of Mongols who entered Khorasán and Persia under Hulaku, or very shortly after him.

It appears from Wassáf that there was, indeed, a tribe among the Mongols named *Kuránas*[1] towards the end of the twelfth century, though the name is not traceable in Rashid-ud-Din's lists, unless we are prepared to recognise it in that which Dr. Erdmann transliterates "*Ckaranut*" (where the final *t* is only the Mongol plural) or "*Ckurulás.*"[2] In any case, the form *Kuránas* is said to have afterwards become modified in Persia, into *Karáwanás*, which, but for the absence of an accent on the third *a*, is the same spelling as Mirza Haidar's. But the fact

[1] It occurs in a list of thirty-nine tribes furnished by Wassáf, who compiled his list from a book called the *Tarikh-i-Mogul.* This information reaches me from Khan Bahádur Maula Bakhsh, H.M.'s Attaché at the Consulate General in Khorasán. (See also App. B.)

[2] In Erdmann's *Temudschin de· Unerschütterliche*, p. 168.

that a tribe, or sub-tribe, bearing this name existed in the twelfth or thirteenth centuries, in no way accounts for its having been applied, as a general term of contempt, to the Chaghatais as a people: there must have been some other reason and origin. The name itself was found, by Quatremère, never to appear previous to the Mongol invasions of the west, or subsequent to the date of the *Zafar-Náma*—viz., 1424.[1] Marco Polo was one of the earliest to mention it, and he gives it the form *Caraonas.* He relates that he met with the *Caraonas* at Kirmán and, apparently also, at other places in Persia farther north, and describes them as a robber tribe who were "the sons of Indian mothers by Tartar fathers." Probably the word "Indian" may have been employed by him in a very broad sense, or it may, as Sir H. Yule has suggested, perhaps stand for Biluchi; but in any case, Marco Polo refers to them as a race of half-breeds, and states that the name of *Caraonas* had been given them on account of their mixed parentage.[2] Dr. Erdmann, again, alludes to the *Karawinah*, or *Karawinas*, stationed in Khorasán about the same period, and explains, on the authority of Wassáf, that they were the artillerists (Feuerwerker) of the Chaghatai army.[3] These are the only two instances known to me, where meanings for the term are suggested by original contemporary authors; but there seems no reason to suppose that the name was specially given to any such classes as half-caste robbers or artillerymen. It was imposed, Mirza Haidar tells us, on the Chaghatais generally, and therefore is far more likely to have had its origin in something quite unconnected with either the banditti of Kirmán or the gunners of the army in Khorasán, for both these classes may have inherited a right to the distinction with their Chaghatai relationship:[4] the lesser would be contained in the greater.

But under whatever name the Moghuls were known to their neighbours, one of the most noteworthy circumstances connected with them, during the period to which Mirza Haidar's history refers, was that they were rapidly declining in power and in numbers. With the introduction among them of the Musulman

[1] *Not. et Extr.* xiv. p. 282.

[2] Marco Polo, i., p. 99, and note.

[3] *Temudschin*, Introd. p. 183.

[4] It is not clear in what sense Marco Polo uses the word "Tartar," but it may, I think, be assumed that with him, as with most Western writers, the Chaghatais would have come under that denomination.

For some further remarks by Mr. Maula Bakhsh on the Karáwánás in Persia, see App. B.

religion, they seem to have tended gradually to lose their national characteristics and to merge more and more into the tribes or nations—for the most part of Turki descent—by whom they were surrounded. From the time of the Mongol conquests down to the first half of the sixteenth century, nearly three hundred years had elapsed. In so long a period, it is only reasonable to conclude that some changes may have taken place in a politically weak and unstable people like the Mongols, and who, in addition, were pressed upon from the west and south by alien nations much superior to themselves in numbers. It is not, however, necessary to assume, as some writers have done, that the mass of the Moghuls, even in the latest years of this period, were of Turki blood, or that they used the Turki language as their own.[1] The circumstances that appear rather to have given rise to this view are: (1) the glimpses that are occasionally obtained in history of the Moghul Khans and chiefs (almost the only persons ever noticed individually by historians) who had become to all intents and purposes Turks, at a period following pretty closely on that of the Mongol ascendency—a matter that affects only the Moghuls of Moghulistan; and (2) the use made by Musulmán authors of the word *Turk*, when designating, sometimes all nomad and steppe-dwelling, or pastoral, tribes, and sometimes a specific race. This dual use of the word *Turk* underlies the whole of the ethnography of Central Asia, as it has come down to us through the writings of Oriental authors. It has been my object to avoid, if possible, all discussion of this much-debated question, but in order that some of our author's statements may not be wrongly interpreted, it is necessary to make some brief remarks upon it.

One instance which touches phase (1) is that of the racial characteristics of the family of Baber, which gave to India the

[1] In making this remark I am not alluding to the origin of the Mongol tribes. How Mongol, Turk, and Tatar arose in remote ages, is a subject with which Mirza Haidar's book has no concern, and which, therefore, need not occupy us here. Dr. Erdmann, in his learned work just cited, has thoroughly sifted the matter, and has shown how the Mongol was originally connected with the Turk. Sir H. Howorth has come to similar conclusions with regard to the common origin of the two people. I am dealing, here, with only the long subsequent period when Mongols and Turks had come to differ from one another, in feature and in language, to as great an extent as the Scandinavian and Latin races in Europe. What does concern this history is that that section of the Mongols, best known to their Western neighbours as the inhabitants of Moghulistan, were at the period in question still Mongol, in fact, though perhaps gradually tending to become Turkish by fusion of language and blood.

so-called 'Moghul' line of kings. It will hardly be disputed that not alone Baber himself, but some of his more immediate ancestors, were to all intents and purposes Turks; and this was the case not only in the acquisition of language and manners, but by intermixture of blood; while his successors, whose portraits, painted in India, are extant at the present day, show no trace in their features of descent from a Mongoloid race. It is said that Baber's grandfather (Sultan Abu Said of Khorasan, 1452–67) was described by a Khivan contemporary, who visited him, as a very handsome man with a full beard and unlike a Moghul. Another, and perhaps more perfect, instance of the same thing is the description given in the *Tárikh-i-Rashidi* of the personal appearance of Yunus, Khan of Moghulistan, in 1456, or some two centuries only after the death of Chaghatai Khan—who was certainly a pure Mongol. Yunus is reported, by one who says that he expected to see a beardless man, "like any other Turk of the desert," to have had a full beard and Tájik (*i.e.*, Aryan) features;[1] and brief though this description is, it tells so significant a tale of a changed race, that it is probably as trustworthy a record, as a portrait painted by even a superior artist to those of Hindustan. In the case of the few families of the chiefs, there would be a tendency to change much more rapidly than in that of the bulk of the people. Their custom was to give their relations in marriage to the friendly rulers of foreign countries, and, in exchange, to take to wife a member of those rulers' families; if one Khan subjugated another, he usually demanded a daughter or a sister in marriage; while it was no doubt possible, and perhaps fashionable, for the governing classes to add foreign wives to their harems, in the same way that Musulmáns of means and position have loved to do at all periods and in most countries.

In these circumstances, the physical characteristics of the original race would soon pass away among the families of the chiefs, and with them would go the language and the customs. But with the mass of the tribes-people it would be otherwise. There appears to be no description of them indicating a resemblance to the Turks; on the contrary, the description of Yunus implies a difference between him and the mass of his people. Moreover, we may assume that the rank and file of the Moghuls would not have the same opportunities for rapidly connecting themselves in blood relationship with their neighbours; conse-

[1] See p. 97.

quently the distinctive features of their race would take longer to undermine. As already observed, the life of the steppes and the comparative isolation of the *aul,* would tend rather to preserve the purity of the race. It may not be possible to form an estimate of the length of time that would be needed to bring about a change of type by gradual intermarriage, but we know, at any rate, of one instance where this same Mongol people, from living in more or less isolated positions, and mixing with neighbouring races only to a very slight extent, have preserved all the physical characteristics of their original type, as well as the language, down to our own day—or some six and a half centuries from the date of their transplantation, during the era of the Mongol conquests. I refer to the Hazáras of Afghanistan, most of whom are still as unmistakably Mongol in feature and build as the inhabitants of Mongolia itself. According to the most trustworthy accounts of them, they descend from the remnants of the army of Nikudar Oghlán, a son of Hulaku,[1] who invaded the region in which they dwell now, about the latter half of the thirteenth century; while Professor von der Gabelentz has shown that, in spite of a slight mixture of Persian words, their language is still strictly Mongolian, or more particularly, West Mongolian—*i.e.,* Kalmák.[2]

On the general question of the rise and decay of languages, enough is known of the process which a nation has to go through before it can completely change its tongue, to justify the belief that a very long period is needed for the transfer to become finally accomplished. The first step is that the people should become bi-lingual—that the mass of them (not a few of the chiefs) should come to use both the old and the new language with equal facility—and this alone is a process requiring many generations. The next step is that the old language should fall into disuse and be forgotten. The second

[1] More exactly, seventh son of Hulaku, who, becoming converted to Islam, towards the end of the thirteenth century, took the name of Ahmad, and reigned as Sultan Ahmad, in succession to his brother Abáká. The name, however, instead of Nikudar, should perhaps read Takudar. (See Howorth, iii., pp. 310 and 680.

[2] See H. C. von der Gabelentz, "Uber die Sprache der Hazaras und Aimaks," in *Zeitschrift Deutsch. Morgenland. Gesell.* xx., pp. 326–35 (1866). According to Khanikoff, the Hazáras are the posterity of an army, or tribe, led into the hills they now inhabit, by Shah Rukh. (*Ibid,* p. 335.) If so, they must have been pure Mongols in type, while dwelling in the low countries, as late as the end of the fourteenth century; but the view given in the text above is the more probable. (See also Col. Jarrett's note in *Ain-i-Akbari,* ii., pp. 401–2, Calcutta, 1891.)

stage may, perhaps, take less time to work itself out than the first; but it must, nevertheless, require a period measured in generations. Thus, when we consider that a century (according to the usual computation) embraces only about three generations, it must be regarded as improbable that the tribes which were pure Mongols at the end of the thirteenth century should have become the pure Turks they are sometimes represented, at the period dealt with by our author. The Russian savant Gmelin, who travelled in Central Asia in the last century, is emphatic in stating his belief in the permanency of the Mongol race in general, as far as physical attributes are concerned. He affirms that, in spite of all mixtures of blood by their wars in distant countries, the Mongol tribes have not only preserved their characteristic type of features, but have even impressed it on other races with whom they have come in contact—such as the Kirghiz and others.[1] This statement perhaps hardly affords a proof on the subject in question, but it goes towards showing that the eradication of the Mongol type is not a simple matter, or one that is likely to have been accomplished in a space of barely two hundred years.

Amir Khusru, the poet of mediæval India, draws—or perhaps overdraws—a picture of the Moghuls who invaded Northern India towards the end of the thirteenth century, in a manner which leaves no doubt that he is attempting to describe a Mongoloid race. He had previously fallen into their hands as a prisoner, and, according to his own account, had been badly treated by them; as he was no doubt burning with dread and resentment, his description must be taken to be somewhat tinged by his feelings. However, omitting some offensive details, he writes thus: "There were more than a thousand Tatar infidels and warriors of other tribes, riding on camels, great commanders in battle, all with steel-like bodies clothed in cotton; with faces like fire, with caps of sheepskin, with heads shorn. Their eyes were so narrow and piercing that they might have bored a hole in a brazen vessel. . . . Their faces were set on their bodies as if they had no neck. Their cheeks resembled soft leathern bottles, full of wrinkles and knots. Their noses extended from cheek to cheek, and their mouths from cheek bone to cheek bone. . . . Their moustaches were of extravagant length. They had but scanty beards about their chins. . . . They looked like so many white demons, and the people fled from

[1] Découvertes Russes, vol. iii., p. 209.

them everywhere in affright."[1] Is it possible that a race which would call forth such a description as this, from even a terrified poet, could have become, in the mass, men like Yunus or Baber between the end of the thirteenth century and the latter half of the fifteenth?

Thus, although it might appear at first sight that, with the change taking place in the families of the Khans, with the advance of the Musulman religion and the growing use of the Turki language, it would be impossible to distinguish a true Moghul people, still evidence is not wanting to show that even up to the first half of the sixteenth century, the Moghuls of Moghulistan—the Moghul *Ulus* of Mirza Haidar—were in fact a separate people from the Turks. During the period 1514 to 1533, the Mirza constantly alludes to a distinct tribe or community of Moghuls—however reduced in numbers—in exactly the same terms as he refers to them at a period dating two hundred years before. They were neither Kirghiz, nor Uzbegs, nor Kalmáks, but were the natural enemies of all three; they were of the *Ulus* (or clan) of the Khans descended from Chaghatai; they preserved Mongol customs and, from occasional incidental references which he makes to Mongol terms and phrases, must have retained something, at least, of the original language of their nation, though they had no literature in which it could become fixed. This being the case, the bulk of them must have preserved their Mongol type to the last, and it may perhaps be fairly conjectured that whatever change they had undergone, was due less to the fusion of blood than to the conversion of the people to Islam. The spread of the Musulman religion tends always to the modification of manners and customs, and to the use of the Arabic, Turki or Persian language; but in spite of all, racial characteristics remain, until very gradually expunged by a course of inter-breeding, that must extend over many centuries. Several parallel cases (besides that of the Hazáras) might be cited among Asiatic nations; but one, having no relation to the Mongol tribes, will suffice. The Baltis of Baltistan, or Little Tibet, formed originally a section of the ordinary population of Tibet, were of the same religion, and used the same language. Some three centuries or more ago, they were converted to the Musulman faith, and began gradually to change their manners. At present the written language of Tibet is unknown among them, Persian having

[1] Elliot's *Hist. of India*, iii., pp. 528–9.

replaced it; their chiefs, through intermarriage with neighbouring Musulman peoples, have changed so greatly, even in type, that usually no trace of the Tibetan is left; but the mass of the nation, though practising Musulman social customs and wearing a Musulman costume, have not lost the Tibetan spoken language, and are, in feature and other personal attributes, as thoroughly Tibetan as ever they were. Had the Baltis occupied an open country, and been constantly engaged in wars and invasions, there might have been a greater and more rapid change. Their secluded mountainous home (like that of the Hazáras) has mitigated this, and has helped to preserve them as a race: but the principle is the same as with the Moghuls.

With regard to the misleading employment of the word *Turk*, alluded to above, it must be explained that, among Asiatic authors, it is constantly met with as the definition of a race or people distinguished from the Tartars and the Moghuls, on the one hand, and from Tájiks, or Táziks, on the other. But in the same writings, and often on the same page, it is used to denote all nomads and inhabitants of the steppes, irrespective of race or origin, and merely to distinguish such people from those who dwelt in towns, and who cultivated the settled districts —or from the Tájiks generally. The first may be regarded as its ethnological sense: the second as sociological only, and as about synonymous with the adopted English word *nomad*. In this second sense it included, as we shall see, all Mongoloid and Tartar races. In dictionaries we find among its many meanings those of *barbarian, robber, vagabond, wanderer*, etc. It is also, in poetry, applied to the planet Mars as "a *Wanderer* of the sky," and to the sun as "the Turk of China," that is of the East; or "the Turk of midday"—viz., the South; or "the Turk of the Spheres." All who lived in the steppes and ranges, outside the pale of what was regarded as civilisation, and led a pastoral or unsettled life, but who were not distinctively mountaineers, were deemed a separate class (irrespective of race) and required a separate name to denote them. To this class the name of *Turk* attached itself throughout Central Asia. In Europe and in India the word *Turk* was not used in this sense. By Europeans, and perhaps Western Asiatics also, the word *Tatar*, or *Tartar*, was usually in vogue, down to quite modern times, to indicate the nomadic nations of the interior of Asia, without reference to any racial considerations;[1] while in India the name ***Moghul*** came to be applied (in times subsequent to the rise of the Mongols, at any rate) in a very similar way, to these same races.

Abul Gházi, the historian Khan of Khiva, himself a Turk by nationality, though of remote Mongol descent, constantly uses the word *Turk* in its sociological sense, and applies it indiscriminately to all the nomad and steppe-dwelling tribes, when he requires a name for the whole of them; but, when referring to their descent or language, or when in any way particularising between them, I do not know of a single instance of his alluding to the Moghuls as connected by blood with the Turki tribes. In other words, although he employs the name *Turk* to describe certain nations—among them the Moghuls—for whom he knows no other general designation, he never applies it in the particular instances where a racial consideration is involved, except to those among them whom he regards as, in reality, Turks by race. He writes, for instance: "Of all the Turk tribes who inhabited those countries at that period, the Tatars were the most numerous . . . ."; and again: "We have . . . . recounted what we know of the other branches of the race of Turks. Now, we will speak of the branches of Mongol race."[2] It is in the same non-racial sense that Mirza Haidar uses the word *Turk*, when putting the remark (alluded to above) about Yunus Khan, into the mouth of Maulana Muhammad Kázi: "I had heard that Yunus Khan was a Moghul," says the Maulana, "and I concluded that he was a beardless man, with the ways and manners of any other Turk of the desert; but when I saw him, I found that he was a person of elegant deportment, with

[1] The name of Tatar, we are told by D'Ohsson, was applied to the Mongols by their Western neighbours, and became propagated, from nation to nation, to the extremities of Europe; although the Mongols themselves rejected it with disdain, as belonging to a hostile people whom they had exterminated. (*Hist. des Mongols*, i., p. 94.)

[2] *Hist. des Mongols, etc.*, Desmaisons' transl., pp. 34 and 52–3. Abul Gházi's evidence on this point is not particularly satisfactory, but it has some value, because he was one of the latest of the Musulman historians. His book was only completed about 1664; and he was therefore aware of all the changes that had taken place among the Moghuls down to that time. If they had become the pure Turks they are sometimes represented, we should probably find the fact noticed by him, though not by earlier authors. The history of Rashid-ud-Din is often spoken of as the best and fullest, and no doubt this is the case, but it is some 350 years earlier in date than that of Abul Gházi, and consequently previous to the decadence of the Moghuls. Moreover, the latter knew the contents of Rashid-ud-Din's book, for he tells his readers that he had it before him when compiling his own, together with seventeen other historical works.

a full beard and a Tájik face."[1] That is, the speaker knew that Yunus was a Moghul by descent, and expected to see a man with Mongolian features, but he classed him with other Turks of the steppes.

D'Ohsson became conscious, from the extensive use he had made of Asiatic historians, that these writers constantly employed the word *Turk* to signify the nomad and pastoral tribes, known in Europe as 'Tatars.' In one passage he writes: "The Mongols gave the name of Tájik, or Tázik, to the Muhammadans, and in the historical works of this period it will be found that they employed this word in opposition to that of 'Turk.' The first served to designate the Muhammadan inhabitants of towns and cultivated lands, whether they were of Turki, Persian, or Arab origin mattered not; while under the name of 'Turk' were comprised the nomad nations of Turki and Tatar race. It was in this general acceptation that Chingiz Khan and the Mongols styled themselves 'Turks'; they rejected, on the other hand, the name of 'Tatar.'"[2] In another passage, when speaking of the Tatars proper, previous to the rise of the Mongols, D'Ohsson quotes Rashid-ud-Din as follows: "They made themselves so powerful and formidable, that other nations of Turks passed themselves off as Tatars, and regarded the name as an honour."[3]

Again, Major Raverty, in his translation of the *Tabákát-i-Násiri*, notes the headings of the first four sections of Rashid-ud-Din's history, the second, third, and fourth of which contain the following:—"*2nd Section.* Account of the Turk tribes whom they designate by the name of Mughals, but every one of which, in ancient times, bore distinct and particular surnames. . . . *3rd Section.* Account of the Turk tribes, every one of which have had Badshahs and chiefs, but who bore no relationship to the tribes mentioned in the preceding sections. *4th Section.* Account of the tribes of Turks, whose surname, from time immemorial, was Mughal. . . ."[4] These brief extracts are sufficient to show the sense in which Rashid-ud-Din, one of the best of the Musulman authors of the Mongol period, used the work *Turk*, and how, though he was able to distinguish specifically between real Turks and other tribes,

[1] See p. 97 of the text.
[2] D'Ohsson's *Hist. des Mongols*, i., p. 217.
[3] *Ibid.*, p. 248.
[4] Raverty's *Tabákát-i-Násiri*, note, p. 891.

when ethnological considerations were in question, still used the word in a non-ethnic sense, to denote a group of tribes who had to be distinguished from the Tájiks.

Other Asiatic authors wrote on these subjects in the same way. Thus, Minháj-ud-Din, the author of the *Tabákát-i-Násiri*, frequently uses the word *Turk* to designate the nomadic group generally, and, like Rashid-ud-Din, even brings the name *Tatar* into the same category. The following is an instance taken from three consecutive paragraphs:—"In this same year the Chingiz Khan, the Mughal, rose up in the Kingdom of Chin and Tamghaj, and commenced to rebel; in all books it is written that the first signs of the end of time are the outbreak of the Turks. . . . The name of the father of this Chingiz Khan, the accursed, was the Tatar, Timurchi, and he was the mihtar [chief] of the Mughal tribes, and ruler over his people . . . . Among the tribes of the Mughal was another Turk of importance, a ruler and leader, and greatly venerated; and the whole of the tribes of the Mughals were under the rule of these two persons. . . . All the tracts of the Turk tribes, at the hand of their iniquity and sedition were reduced to misery. . . ."[1]

Juvaini, the author of the *Jahán Kushai*, applies to the Mongols the passage from the Koran: "Beware of provoking the Turks, for they are formidable."[2] Abul-feda quotes an Arab author to the effect that the Russians are a people of Turkish race,[3] when pointing to them as belonging to the group of non-Musulman and non-Tájik inhabitants of what were regarded as civilised countries. Ibn Haukal, touching on the question from a geographical point of view, writes: "Tiráz [Táráz] is on the extreme frontier between the country of the Turks and that of the Musulmans"[4]; yet the Musulmans, in this case, were, to a great degree, of Turki race. And, again, Minháj-ud-Din mentions an invasion of Tibet (from Upper Bengal apparently) and says: "All the people [of Tibet] were Turks, archers, and [furnished with] long bows."[5] Idrisi, also, in speaking of Tibet, says: "This is the country of the Tibetan Turks"; and afterwards: "This intervening space is covered with pastures, forests, and strong castles belonging to the

[1] *Tabákát-i-Násiri*, pp. 935–6.
[2] D'Ohsson, *Introd.* p. xxiii.
[3] Reinaud's *Abul-feda*, ii., pt. 1, p. 296.
[4] Thonnelier, *Dict. Geogr.*, p. 48.
[5] *Tabákát-i-Násiri*, p. 566.

Tibetan Turks." Further on again, he tells us: "There are Turks of very diverse races" (*de races très diverses*); and he proceeds to detail, among others, the Tibetans and the Kalmáks. The names of the remaining tribes he mentions in this passage, are spelled in so unintelligible a manner, that I can recognise none but the Kirghiz and Kipcháks, with whom he thus classes the Tibetans and the Kalmáks as, all alike, Turks![1]

The poet Khusru, in the passage cited above, calls the people he describes, by the name of *Tatar*, though a little lower down (on the same page) he says they were "Turks of Kai;" while elsewhere, he frequently speaks of the same people as Moghuls.[2] Further, the late Mr. R. B. Shaw has explained, with regard to the word *Tájik*, that it stands in opposition to *Turk*, just as *Arab* stands to *Ajam*,[3] and thus is not necessarily a race name.

Many other instances might be given of this non-ethnic use of the word *Turk*, and with them might be included also some relating to a similar employment of the term *Tatar*.[4] But the above will suffice to make it clear that, though the Moghuls of Moghulistan were often called Turks, during the period including the thirteenth to sixteenth centuries, it need

[1] Jaubert's *Idrisi*, pp. 494 and 498.

[2] His editor, Professor Dowson, in a foot-note, marvels that his author should "sometimes confound Turks and Mughals," while "in some passages he discriminates very accurately between them." Herein lies precisely the difficulty that has occurred to other translators and commentators. The solution, I venture to think, is as now pointed out.

[3] According to some authorities it might be said that *Turk* was used in opposition to *Sart*; but the application of the word *Sart* is subject to some variations. Mr. Shaw gives as a definition of *Sart*:—"A term applied by the nomads (Kirghiz, Kazzáks, etc.), to dwellers in settled habitations, whether Turks or Tájiks, *i.e.*, whether Turanians or Iranians." But, in some cases, the name *Sart* is used to denote only the settled Turks, and to differentiate them from the Tájiks. Moreover, in the works of Musulman authors referring to the period of the *Tarikh-i-Rashidi*, it is seldom found as an ordinary appellation, though Baber, it is true, employs it in describing Marghinán. In our own times it is not often heard in the eastern parts of Central Asia; though, to judge by Russian writings, it is perhaps more frequently used in Khiva and the adjoining regions of Russian Turkistan, etc. It is, however, an imperfect term to make comparisons with. (See Shaw, *Sketch of Turki Language*, Asiat. Socy., Bengal, pt. ii., 1880, pp. 61 and 116; Baber, p. 3; and Lerch in *Russische Revue*, 1872, Heft. i., p. 33. Also Shaw's *High Tartary*, p. 26, where he defines the Sarts as "a settled people, who include the Aryan Tajiks as well as the Tartar Oosbeks and others.")

[4] The Hiung Nu of Chinese historians have often been described as a Turki race, yet it is significant that Professor de Lacouperie, on investigating the point, came to the conclusion that the Hiung Nu "seem to have been a political, not a racial, unity." (See *Western Origin of Chinese Civilisation*, p. 223.)

not be assumed that they were actually of Turkish race, either by origin or by subsequent fusion of blood. There was, however, another and very important circumstance that complicated this question of nomenclature still further. It was, it seems, the desire of all the tribes and nations of Central Asia, to identify themselves with the race which happened to be in the ascendant at any particular time. They endeavoured to adopt its name, and to pass themselves off as members of the nation in supremacy, regardless of racial affinities. Rashid-ud-Din has laid special stress on this point in his great work on the Mongols, and has explained the matter in one place as follows: "They [the Tatars] made themselves so powerful and formidable, that the other nations of Turks passed themselves off as Tatars, and regarded as an honour this name, under which they had become famous; just as at the present day[1] the Jalair, Tatar, Uirát, Ungut, Karait, Naimán, Tangut, and others, find glory in the name of Mongol, made illustrious by that of Chingiz Khán and his descendants—a name which, at an earlier date, they would have disdained. The young people of all these nations believe, even now, that their ancestors have always borne the style of Mongol; but it was not so, for formerly the Mongols were only one of the nations of Turks. . . . This name has been extended to such a degree, that nowadays the people of Khitai (Northern China) and of Nan-gyass (Southern China), as well as the Churchi, the Uighur, the Kipchák, the Turkoman, and the Karluk; also the Captives and the Táziks (Muhammadans), who have been brought up among the Mongols are [all of them] called Mongols; and they are all interested in passing for Mongols, in order that they may gain consideration. Previous to this period it was the same with the Tatars, on account of their power, and this is the reason why the Mongols are still called Tatars in China and in India, by the Kirghiz, the Báshgirds, in the Kipchák country, in the north of Asia, in Arabia, in Syria, in Egypt, and in Africa."[2]

It has been observed above, that in India the word *Moghul* was employed, subsequent to the days of Chingiz, in the same way as the word *Turk* in Central Asia, and *Tatar* in Europe, and on this subject Mr. H. G. Keene has come to conclusions which coincide with the teachings of Rashid-ud-Din. It denoted, in the first place, the group of tribes or nations who

[1] *I.e.*, the early years of the fourteenth century.

[2] D'Ohsson, i., pp. 428–9.

composed the armies of the northern invaders, with little or no reference to their racial origin; and secondly, at the time of Baber, it was regarded as something scarcely better than a term of contempt. But later, when the so-called Moghul dynasty came to be looked up to as the supreme power, the name assumed a different and more respectful significance. Mr. Keene writes: "Under Akbar, when the empire had become a firm result of successful war, the word [Moghul] recovered its prestige and—like the name of 'Goth' in Spain—came to indicate 'a noble conqueror,' or the descendant of one"; [1] and in support of this view he cites a valuable passage from Kháfi Khan (for which he acknowledges his indebtedness to the late Professor Blochmann, who may be inferred to have translated it), which runs as follows: "The flourishing condition of Mugholistan commenced with Mughol Khan, who was a great king. Although from the time of Akbar the word Mughol has been applied to the Turks and Tajiks of Irán (Persia) to such an extent that even the Sayyids of Khorasán were called Mughols, yet in reality the word is the proper term for those Turks who belong to the descendants and house of Mughol Khan; and it was used in this sense in the time of the earlier (Moslem) kings of Delhi . . . ." Here Kháfi Khan uses *Turk* in the same sociological sense as Rashid-ud-Din, Minháj-ud-Din, Mirza Haidar, and the rest.[2]

Mr. Denzil Ibbetson, too, furnishes some instructive remarks, in his Report on the Punjab census, on the way the words *Turk* and *Moghul* have come to be used in modern times in the north of India. A Turk is there regarded as a native of Turkistan and a man of Mongolian race. "In the Delhi territory, indeed," writes Mr. Ibbetson, "the villagers, accustomed to describe the Mughals of the Empire as Turks, use the word as

[1] *Turks in India*, p. 24.

[2] I may take this opportunity of remarking that Mr. Keene must have referred to the old translation of the Swedish officers of Charles XII., when he states (p. 50) that Abul Gházi "is represented as saying that he wrote his book 'in the Moghul or Turki language.'" I cannot find such a passage in Desmaisons' version. At p. 36 the author is made to write:—Afin de mettre cette histoire à la portée de toutes les classes, je l'ai écrite en Turc;" and I believe this to be the only allusion he makes to the subject. It is an additional instance of the dual mode of using the word *Turk*, for here Abul Gházi employs it to denote the language of the Turks proper, in an ethnic sense. He in no way classes the two tongues as one. He was, himself, a Turk of Khiva, and Mr. Erskine, who remarked the inconsistency in the old version of Abul Gházi's history, has well said:—"No Moghul or Turk would have confounded these two languages." (*Hist.*, i., p. 536, App.)

synonymous with 'official'; and I have heard my Hindu clerks, of Kayath caste, described as Turks merely because they were in Government employ. On the Biloch frontier, also, the word Turk is commonly used as synonymous with Mughal."[1]

But though Oriental writers make use of the tribal name of *Turk* to denote a nomadic people, similar inconsistencies are not wanting in European languages. The way in which the French apply the word *Bohêmien* to the gipsies is a parallel instance. The gipsies, though in no way belonging to the same race as the natives of Bohemia, acquired their name in France, on account of certain social habits and customs which they were believed to have brought with them from Bohemia, and because they were known to wander into France from that country.[2] An almost similar instance, though not precisely parallel, was the use in English of the word *Indian,* during the seventeenth and eighteenth centuries, to define the aborigines of North America, the Caribbean, and many other islands. In this case it was not the social condition and proclivities of the inhabitants that caused the misapplication of name, but their colour, the climate and products of their countries, and other circumstances, which reminded those who came into contact with them, of the India of the East. The process and result, however, are much the same. But if we leave out of consideration the fact that *Turk* happened also to be a race-name, its employment to designate the pastoral tribes of unsettled abodes becomes no more anomalous than such appellations as *Kohistani, Baduin,* etc., in Asia, or the familiar *Mountaineer, Islander*, etc., in Europe.

Misapplication, or change in the application, of race-names is a practice so commonly met with, that it is almost superfluous to mention it here. It may, however, be briefly pointed out, in regard to the names we are dealing with, that the term *Tájik* has been made, in one instance, to take exactly the opposite meaning to that which it usually bears. Mr. A. G. Ellis, of the British Museum, informs me that while early Armenian writers applied it to the Arabs,[3] modern Armenians

[1] *Report on the Punjab Census for* 1881. Calcutta, 1883, vol. i., p. 276.

[2] It is curious that the name *Gypsey* is a corruption of *Egyptian.* They are always called Egyptians in our early Acts of Parliament, and it is probable that they came to England first from Egypt, whither they had gone from the country of the Golden Horde, where we first meet with them.—H. H.

[3] Whence it came about that the Arabs are referred to as *Ta-hi* in early Chinese accounts of the West.—H. H.

have imposed it on the Turks and the Turkish Empire, and even on Musulmans in general. In this case it seems that the word is used to imply a 'stranger,' or 'barbarian';[1] but it is a curious example of the length to which misapplication can go, for it constitutes an absolute reversal of the usual and original sense of the word. In the *Tarikh-i-Rashidi*, among other books, we find *Hazára* used for 'hill-men,' or 'mountaineers,' without reference to its original meaning or to any racial consideration, while in modern times the term has become the name of a specific race or people. *Hazára* meant simply "a thousand," and was the name, it appears, which was given to a particular section of cavalry or other troops, who were perhaps the original settlers in the hill districts in question.[2] What Mr. Ibbetson has told us above, of the employment of the words *Turk* and *Moghul* in the Punjab, is another instance of mere misapplication or irrelevent nomenclature; but we need hardly go far from home to find a telling example of the same thing. From Earle's *Philology of the English Tongue*[3] we learn, with regard to the Cymraeg, or British language now spoken in Wales, that "the Anglo-Saxons called it *Wylse*, and the people who spoke it they called *Walas*, which we have modernised into Wales and Welsh. So the Germans of the Continent called the Italians and their language *Welsch*. The word simply means *foreign* or *strange*. At various points on the frontiers of our race we find them affixing the name on the conterminous Romance-speaking people . . . . The French . . . . in the reign of Edward the Confessor, are called, by the contemporary [Anglo-Saxon] annalist, *tha Welisce* men, by which was meant 'the foreigners.'"[4]

Thus, the evidence on this subject (apart from that of nicknames or terms of contempt) points to three distinct conclusions. The first is that, in reading the histories of Musulman authors, the tribal names they use must not always be

[1] Professor Nöldeke has been good enough to inform Mr. Ross that *Tájik* (better *Táchik*) and *Tázi* are the same word, the former being merely the older form. *Chik* means "belonging to," and in this case "belonging to the tribe of *Tai*." In modern Persian *Chik* becomes *Zi*.

[2] It is quite possible that the name of the famous Turkish tribe of the *Khazars* is connected with the same word.—H. H.

[3] Page 23. I am indebted to Mr. Stephen Wheeler for this appropriate extract.

[4] In another way, the name of the specific tribe *Alemanni*, who lived nearest to Gaul of all the Germans, became the generic name of all Germany —Allemagne.—H. H.

taken to have a racial significance; or, in other words, it is necessary in every case where either the term *Turk* or *Tatar* occurs, to see whether the writer is applying it in its general and sociological acceptation, or in a specific and discriminating ethnic sense. The second conclusion is that the word *Moghul*, even where it is used in an ethnic sense, is frequently misapplied, and so extended, at certain periods in history, as to comprise many tribes of real Turki race (among others), until large numbers of people who were not of Moghul race came to be called Moghuls. This habit appears to have been prevalent first in the time of Chingiz and his immediate successors, and subsequently during the ascendency of the Chaghatai (or so-called Moghul) dynasty in India. The third conclusion is that the application and significance of all three names—Turk, Tatar, and Moghul—varied at different times and in different countries. It appears to me that a due appreciation of these three points will help to clear up much that has been regarded hitherto as inconsistent, and even contradictory, in the Musulman histories, and has occasioned no little controversy among European writers. That the ethnographic nomenclature of Persian, Turki, and Arabic writers is anomalous, cannot but be granted; but in Asiatic nomenclature what is there that is not anomalous? They had no knowledge of the scientific ethnology that guides the modern European commentator on their works, but merely followed the common speech of the time, and employed the terms that had grown into use among the people around them. In reading their books, therefore, it is futile to look for systematic nomenclature; but if they are read with a due regard to date, locality, and other circumstances, they will seldom be found, I think, to contain actual contradictions; for loose and inaccurate though Asiatics are in some respects—such as in figures, measurements, geographical details, etc.—they are usually remarkably clear on such subjects as blood relationship, family lineage, and racial descent.

But here we must leave the Moghuls, and glance briefly at those original Turks, or Uighurs, who may be regarded as the immediate ancestors of the population of Alti-Shahr (and indeed all Eastern Turkistan) and the main stock of their race. Who the Uighurs were in remote times, and what was their origin, are speculative questions which need not be investigated here. The best notices of them during early historic times point to their home-land as lying in north-western Mongolia;

but in the ninth century they are recorded, in the Chinese annals,[1] to have been displaced from that region and to have been driven southward by the Kirghiz,[2] who were themselves, at that time, beginning to rise to power, and tending, like other Turki tribes, to press towards the south and west. In early times there seem to have been at least two confederacies of Uighurs in the further east: one living in the region now known as Zungaria, and called the *Naimán Uighur*, or "Eight Uighurs," while the other inhabited the country watered by the Orkhon and the Tula, and were known as the *Toghuz Uighur*, or "Nine Uighurs."[3] When the latter were driven to the south and west, the former remained in their old country, where they are found at the time of Chingiz Khan. The Toghuz Uighur settled in the eastern ranges of the Tian Shan, and gradually built up a new kingdom, extending over all the eastern portion of that chain. Here one of their states seems to have been established on the south of the mountains, and subsequently another on the north. The first had for its chief town the representative of the modern Kara-Khoja (called at different periods Si-Chao, Ho-Chao, and Kao-Chang), and embraced, at some periods at least, the modern district of Kuchar, then known as Kui-tze; while the capital of the second was Bishbálik (the Five Towns), which stood on, or near, the site of the present Urumtsi. Very little is known of even these later Uighur kingdoms, although the date when they flourished is not a very remote one. It is chiefly from the Chinese chronicles that any knowledge of their history is to be gathered, but even these do not appear to have been compiled with completeness, nor to have embraced the entire Uighur nation, which must have been a large and influential one for a long period.

In addition to these Uighurs, always so named, and living in the Eastern Tian Shan, there was a third section of the race dwelling farther west. They are called sometimes the 'Karlughi,' and their seat of power was originally at Ili-bálik and on the head waters of the Chu. During the eleventh and twelfth centuries, they appear to have dominated Western Turkistan and perhaps the whole of Alti-Shahr, while one of

[1] See Bretschneider, i., p. 236 *seq.* Also Klaproth, *Tableaux Hist.*, p. 129.

[2] Or more properly, as Sir H. Howorth notes—"the people whom the Chinese call Hakas, and who are identified, in my paper on the Kerais, with the ancestors of that famous people—the subjects of Prester John—who, in the time of Chingiz, are found dominating the old Uighur country."

[3] I owe this definition to Sir H. Howorth.

their chief towns was Kashghar, then known as Urdu-Kand. Their rulers were the so-called 'Ilak-Khans,' or 'Kara-Khans,' whose history is more or less known through the works of Arab and Persian authors, since the conversion of one of the line—a certain Sátuk Kara Khan—to Islám, in the first half of the tenth century. That the state and dynasty of the Ilak Khans were in reality Uighur, there seems to be sufficient evidence to prove, although the name of *Uighur* was not used by Musulmán authors till a much later date. They seem to have been known by the name of *Ta-gaz-gaz*[1] until the thirteenth century, when they begin to appear under that of *Uighur* in Western annals, though the Ilak Khans were then no more. From these same Musulman historians we learn that, during parts of the tenth and eleventh centuries, the kingdom of the Ilak Khans extended from Khorasán to China, which is perhaps scarcely to be taken literally, but is only another way of saying that it extended a long way to the east; for the Chinese, in their chronicles of the same period, speak of transactions between their Emperors and the Khans of Kao-Chang and Bishbálik, as if these were independent chiefs.[2]

We come to surer ground about the year 1124, when Yeliu Taishi, the Gurkhán of the Kara Khitai, overran the whole of Eastern Turkistan and captured Balasághun, together with much of the country to the northward, which was then under the sway of the Ilak Khans. This invasion put an end to the kingdom of the Western Uighurs—the Kárluks, or Karakháni—while the Eastern Uighurs became tributary to the conquerors. But it was a conquest that probably had little influence on the people by whom the land was inhabited. It is uncertain what tribes the army of the Gurkhán was composed of; in all probability it was much mixed in race, while in any case, it was a mere army of invasion and by no means constituted the migration of a people. The dominion of the Kara Khitai, moreover,

[1] This word is, no doubt, an Arab corruption of some Turki term, or a mis-reading due to copyists. *Ta-gar-gar*, *Ba-gaz-gaz*, etc., are other variants of the same word; and all look as if they contained a corruption of *Uighur*, or possibly even of *Toghuz-Uighur*. In the geographical notices of the Arab, Yakuti (fifteenth century) the name occurs as *Taghaz-ghaz*—without any *alif*. He calls them a race of Turks. (*Not. et Extr.*, ii., p. 531.)

[2] I have purposely omitted to mention the separate Uighur state which is said to have been established near Kan-chou and Su-chou, on the borders of China, as that lay beyond the range of the provinces in question in the *Tarikh-i-Rashidi*, and was probably a mere isolated state or community of very small importance.

lasted for less than a hundred years, so that the Uighurs, as a nation, must have formed too solid a mass to have been in any degree changed in race by this conquest.

Thus, it may be said generally, that for several centuries previous to the rise of the Mongols, certain Turki-Uighur peoples (they may, in future, be called simply Uighurs), under whatever line of kings, had overspread the whole of the province of Alti-Shahr and the districts to the east of it, while at some periods they held sway in Zungaria and extended their dominion westward into Transoxiana. While exercising independent rule, and even subsequently, when allied with Chingiz Khan against the Kara Khitai and other enemies,[1] they appear to have shown warlike qualities, but at later dates the impression we receive of them is that of a peace-loving, cultivated race, of settled habits, and forming as great a contrast as possible to their Moghul neighbours. Their taste for literature must have been a strong one; in fact, they were the only literate people at that time in existence between China in the east, and Transoxiana in the west. They are credited with having been the first to reduce the Turki language to writing, by borrowing the Syriac written character from the Nestorian missions which, in the Middle Ages, were spread over Central Asia; while the writing, thus founded by the Uighurs, became, at a later period, the origin of the systems still in use among the Mongols and the Manchus.[2] Many books were written by them, and both Rashid-ud-Din and Abul Gházi point to their services being in request as administrators, accountants and writers of the Turki language. The latter author especially bears witness to their capabilities in these pursuits. He says: "During the reign of the grandsons of Chingiz Khan the accountants and chief officers of government in Mávará-un-Nahr, in Khorasán and in Irák, were all Uighurs. Similarly, it was the Uighurs who filled these posts in Khitai during the reign of the sons of Chingiz Khan. Oktai Kaán, son and successor of Chingiz Khan, entrusted Khorasán, Mazandarán and Gilán to a Uighur named Kurguz, who was well versed in keeping accounts and knew thoroughly how to levy, in these provinces, the taxes, which he remitted regularly, each year, to Oktai Kaán."[3] They occupied, indeed, a very similar position to that of the Bengali and

[1] They submitted voluntarily to Chingiz in 1209.
[2] Yule's *Cathay*, pp. 205 and 264–5. Also Bretschneider, i., p. 262.
[3] Pages 41–2.

Marathi Hindus in the administrations of the Chaghatai Emperors of India.

Though the Arabs, during their invasions of Eastern Turkistan in the eighth century, had done their best to impose the Musulman religion on the old Uighur population, it seems that they met only with very partial success, as far as the bulk of the people was concerned. They no doubt converted the Kara-Khani, as is shown by the coinage, and it is probable that from the eleventh century onwards, the population in the western districts was largely Muhammadan. In the central and eastern parts, however, the Uighurs continued to be Buddhists and belonged to the red sect of that religion; but Nestorian Christianity must also have been fairly prevalent among them. They are spoken of very generally as *Tarsi*, and according to some authorities, this should be taken to indicate that they were Christians; but as regards the exact meaning of the word *Tarsi*, there are differences of opinion. In many cases it was, no doubt, applied to the Nestorians in various parts of Asia, but it was also applied to the Buddhists, the Zoroastrians, and was even used to denote idolators.[1]

Strangely enough, the only two European accounts we have of the Uighurs in the Middle Ages (the thirteenth century) differ on this subject: Plano Carpini stating positively that they were Nestorian Christians, while William Rubruk, only eight years later, pronounces them, with equal certainty, to have been idolators, and he adds that they dwelt in towns together with Nestorians and others. It is possible that Rubruk may have regarded most of those he saw as Buddhists, and that he classed all Buddhists with idolators; if so, he would only have been following the practice of many of the Musulmán writers, who drew no very clear distinction between religions that were foreign to their own. But however uncertain this may be, the name of *Tarsi* frequently included the Nestorians, though it was ordinarily used, during the thirteenth and fourteenth centuries, to indicate the Uighurs as a nation—or more particularly the Uighurs of the eastern Tian Shan. It is in this latter sense that Friar John of Montecorvino, at the beginning of the fourteenth century, speaks of the *Tarsi* tongue, for he could not have meant a Buddhist tongue. About the same period, too, the Armenian author Hayton, Prince of Gorigos, in his account of the kingdoms of Asia, expressly applies the name of *Tarsi* to

[1] See note, p. 290.

the country of the "Yogurs" or Uighurs.[1] Mirza Haidar, writing in the sixteenth century, makes no mention of *Tarsi*, or even of Uighurs generally, as being the inhabitants of Eastern Turkistan,[2] and it may be inferred that, by his time, the bulk of the people having become Musulmans, had ceased to be distinguished by their race-name of *Uighur*. He speaks only of the 'Sárigh,' or 'Yellow,' Uighurs, who appear to have been a small community occupying a territory to the east, or north-east, of Khotan, and to have been, according to his view, idolators.[3] These may quite possibly have been merely a section of the original inhabitants who had retained their old religion—Christianity or Buddhism—and had found a refuge from the converting Musulmans in the secluded region bordering on the eastern desert. In this case they would have been Turks, like the rest of the population, in race and language.

Besides the Uighurs, the only people that are heard of in Alti-Shahr, at the period of the *Táríkh-i-Rashidi*, are the Kalmáks, as they had begun then to be called by Musulman writers.[4] To the Mongols and the Chinese they were known as *Oirat*, and this was probably their real name.[5] They must have been few in number, and were, of course, Mongolian, and not Turki, in race. Their home was among the eastern ranges of the Tian Shan, and therefore only partially within the limits of Alti-Shahr: thus they were more properly borderers of the "Eastern Khanate," or Uighuristán, and indeed occupied very much the same localities in which they are found at the present day. In this region, like in Moghulistan, there were no towns or cultivated districts: the people were tent-dwellers, and owners of flocks, and their religion was, no doubt, Buddhism then, as it is now. During the period of the Moghul Khans, they appear to have played but a small part in the history of the country, and to have exercised little influence over the course of its affairs; though after the dis-

[1] See Yule's *Cathay*, p. 205.

[2] He notices only certain persons as Uighurs, and in the one passage where he mentions the word *Tarsa*, he is citing the *Tarikh-i-Jahán Kusháí*. In his day the name was probably extinct.

[3] See p. 348, and note, p. 349.

[4] Professor Grigorief states that the name of *Kalmák* (or *Kal-imák*) only appears for the first time in the fifteenth century. (Schuyler, i., p. 369.)

[5] The Chinese corruption was *Wa-la*. They are the same people who became subsequently known as *Eleuth* or *Olöt*, and *Zungar* (Bretschneider, ii., p. 159); though it would perhaps be more correct to follow the Chinese traveller Chuan Yuan, of the last century, and say that the *Zungars* were a branch of the *Eleuths*. (See Gueluy, *Chine Occid.* in *Le Muséon*, 1887, p. 100.)

appearance of the Moghuls, and with the opening of the eighteenth century, they began to rise to very considerable power, and, in connection with the Tibetans of Lassa, entered into intrigues and wars that resulted in their own country, together with all Eastern Turkistan and the Ili region, falling into the possession of China.

In Alti-Shahr there could not have been many Moghuls, for with the exception of some few valleys among the southern slopes of the western Tian Shan, the country could, in no way, have been suited to their mode of life. When Sultan Said Khan conquered Kashghar in 1514, perhaps a certain proportion of them may have followed him, but at that date their numbers, even in Moghulistan, must have become much reduced from what they had previously been. Therefore, when a few years later (1525-6), he withdrew the remnant of them from their own country to the hills near Kashghar, in order to rescue them from the hostility of the Kirghiz, they would have formed too small a body to have been accounted part of the population of Alti-Shahr. By that date the Moghul *Ulus* had become a mere band of refugees; and though afterwards, for a short time, at fitful intervals, their Khans sallied forth from Kashghar and gained some successes over the Kirghiz, the middle of the sixteenth century may be said, approximately, to have seen their practical extinction as a nation.[1]

[1] See for some further remarks on this subject Sec. VI. of this Introduction.

SECTION V.

The Eastern Khanate, or Uighuristan.

Their inward thought is that their houses shall continue for ever, and their dwelling places to all generations; they call their lands after their own names. Nevertheless man being in honour abideth not; . . .—*Ps.* xlix., 11–12.

The province called by Mirza Haidar, 'Mangalai Suyah,' extended, as we have seen, from the western limit of Farghána as far east as the modern Kara Shahr, a town and district that, in his day, bore the name of Chálish, and more anciently that of 'Yanki' or 'Yen-Ki.' This district, and the larger one of Turfán, that lay beyond it to the eastward, formed, during the two centuries (or the greater part of them) that the *Tárikh-i-Rashidi* embraces, a Moghul principality which had an entirely separate government from that of the chief Moghul Khanate. During the latter half of the fourteenth century and the first quarter of the fifteenth, while the Dughlát Amirs were in power in the provinces of Kashghar, Aksu, Khotan, etc.—that is, in the whole of Alti-Shahr—there is nothing in the *Tárikh-i-Rashidi*, or in the work of any Musulman author that I am acquainted with, to indicate who were the rulers of these eastern districts, except Mirza Haidar's mention of their temporary conquest by Khizir Khwája. It seems probable, from what may be learned from the side of China, that the region was regarded as more or less under the power of the Moghul Khans, and the author of the *Zafar-Náma*, in narrating the wars between Timur and the Moghuls, seems also to imply that this was the case, as has been seen above. Later, again, towards the middle of the fifteenth century, when a division in the Moghul *Ulus* had taken place, Isán Bugha II., with the support of one section, set himself up in Chálish and Turfán, and there established a separate principality, or Khanate, which lasted down to, and even beyond, the date when Mirza Haidar's history closes.

Our author is fond, as will be found in the course of his narrative, of using copulate names, and therefore generally applies to this eastern Khanate, the form *Chálish-Turfán*, or

'*Chálish and Turfán,*' from its two central and principal districts. There were times, however, as he relates, when the province of Aksu also fell under the rule of the eastern Khan, though it belonged properly to Alti-Shahr. But on two occasions he mentions a country or province of *Uighuristán*, and in one passage, when describing the boundaries of 'Mangalai Suyah,' says that it marched, on the east, with the province of Uighuristán. It would appear, therefore, that the small eastern Khanate really bore that name down to the sixteenth century; and if this is the case, the survival is an interesting one.

Within the district of Turfán, and only some twenty-seven miles to the south-east of it, stands the little known, but ancient, town of Kara-Khoja, which has borne also, in the course of its history, several other names, the chief of them having come to us, through the Chinese, in the forms of *Kao-Chang* and *Ho-Chao*. The Chinese annals of the Sung and Yuan dynasties [1] mention this place frequently, and make it clear that from the ninth century to within the twelfth, Kao-Chang was the capital of a Uighur kingdom which bordered on the north with another Uighur state, called Bishbálik (the modern Urumtsi), and on the west with a third known, anciently, as Kui-tze, Kus, etc., and now as Kuchar.[2] These States, collectively, appear to have been the home and centre of the Uighur race, until a much later date than when, in the twelfth century, they lost their political independence and became subject to the Kara-Khitai. It would not be improbable, therefore, that the region having become known to neighbouring nations on the west as *Uighuristán*, when independent, should have retained that name long afterwards, though subject to foreign rulers.

On the partition of the empire of Chingiz Khan among his sons, we read of Uighuristán falling to the appanage of Chaghatai Khan, and we also learn, from Mirza Haidar, of Chaghatai having entrusted the province called 'Mangalai Suyah,' as far east as Chálish, to the care of the Dughláts, but not a word is said regarding the disposal of the districts to the eastward of Chálish. Referring to a later date—about 1320—Abul Ghâzi mentions Uighuristán as one of the countries, the inhabitants of

[1] As translated by Dr. Bretschneider, i., pp. 238–50; and ii., pp. 198–202.

[2] This is the Chinese acceptation, but it is perhaps more probable that Kuitze or Kuchar did not form a third state; it may have been included in Kao-Chang. At an earlier period (seventh century) Kuitze or Ku-tze is believed by Mr. Watters to have been one of the five divisions, or five cities, of Bishbálik. (See note, p. 62 of Introduction).

which, being without a Khan at that time, summoned Isán Bugha I. from Mávará-un-Nahr to reign over them. But although a region is often mentioned by this name subsequent to the time of Chingiz, no indication, as far as I am aware, is given of its situation, until we come to Mirza Haidar's incidental statement that it constituted the eastern neighbour of 'Mangalai Suyah,' and was, consequently, identical with the Khanate of 'Chálish and Turfán.' On the other hand, though the Khanate is mentioned by Erskine, he does not connect it with the Uighuristán of Asiatic authors, but speaks of it always as "the Eastern districts"—presumably of the Moghul Khanate in general.

Mirza Haidar, unfortunately, omits to apprise his readers of the extent of the Khanate of Uighuristán. At periods when Aksu was not comprised within its limits, it could not have been large. On the east it did not include Kumul (Hami) till as late as 1513, when Mansur Khan annexed that State and joined it on to Turfán,[1] as we learn from Chinese sources of information. On the south it may have stretched to a considerable distance, but if so it could have enclosed, in that direction, only the sands of the desert. Northward, among the ranges of the Tian Shan, and along the valley of the Yulduz river, the inhabitants in the sixteenth century, at all events, and probably long before, appear to have been the Oirát or Kalmáks, but whether the Khans of Uighuristán counted these people among their subjects is, from the *Tárikh-i-Rashidi*, not clear. It is possible that they may have done so at some periods, if not always, and in this case their State may have extended to the upper waters of the Yulduz and to the northern slopes of the Tian Shan. In the days of Khizir Khwája of Moghulistan (about 1383 to 1399), the country of the Kalmáks would appear to have formed part of that Khan's possessions, and, for this reason evidently, was invaded by Timur in his expedition of 1388.[2] According to Klaproth (who does not name his authorities in this instance) the region, thus limited, is almost exactly that which was occupied by the Uighurs at the latest period of their existence as a people, though this was long past the time when they had ceased to constitute self-contained or independent states. Indeed, he assigns to them

[1] Kumul remained dependent on Turfán till the year 1669, when it became Chinese.

[2] See Pétis de la Croix, *Hist. de Timur Bec*, ii., p. 46.

this position until beyond the date of Timur, or within the fifteenth century, and speaks of them as a group of small but not independent principalities.[1] In all probability the independence, or otherwise, of these Uighur communities, had no influence on the name which their country went by among neighbouring nations; it seems merely to have acquired the race-name of the inhabitants, as is often the case elsewhere, and (what chiefly concerns us here) to have preserved that name for some two hundred years, after a new and foreign principality had sprung up on its soil.

The only consecutive account of the history of Turfán, from the days of Chingiz and the Uighur chiefs onwards, would seem to be that contained in the Chinese chronicles of the Ming dynasty, and we are indebted to Dr. Bretschneider for an epitomised translation of them.[2] The companion province of Chálish is not mentioned in the epitome, and for this reason, we may assume that no notice of it is contained in the *Ming-Shi*. Possibly the Chinese annalists may have regarded it as part of Turfán, and if this was the case, their account of that province may be taken to embrace the whole of the eastern Khanate of Uighuristán. The Ming record begins very shortly after the opening dates of the *Tárikh-i-Rashidi*, by relating how the prince of *Tu-lu-fan* (or Turfán), having repeatedly plundered foreign embassies proceeding through his dominion towards China, the Emperor, in 1377, despatched an army to punish him and ravage his territory—a task that seems to have been accomplished with success. No name is mentioned for this prince. The date would correspond with the reign, in Moghulistan, of Kamar-ud-Din, but I know of nothing that points to Uighuristán forming a part of Kamar-ud-Din's territory, unless perhaps the fact that Timur, shortly after the date in question, when overruning Moghulistan in the course of a punitive expedition, sent one of his columns as far east as Kara-Khoja, which lay well within Uighuristán. On the other hand, a few years later, on the death of Khizir Khwája, Timur's army, under Mirza Iskandar, laid waste the country only as far east as Kuchar, and then (for what reason is not stated)

[1] *Tableaux Historiques*, pp. 121–5.

[2] Most, but apparently not all, of what Dr. Bretschneider has translated is contained in De Mailla's *Hist. de la Chine* (vol. x.), but it is there much scattered and involved with the history of Hami. Dr. Bretschneider's version is therefore the more useful of the two. (See his *Med. Researches*, ii., pp. 193 *seq.*)

drew off towards Khotan.[1] Yet Khizir Khwája is known, from Mirza Haidar's narrative, to have made at least a temporary conquest of Turfán and Kara-Khoja.

These events occurred during the best days of the Moghul power, when raiding and general lawlessness flourished, and it is to be inferred from what little we know of the history of those times, that even if Kamar-ud-Din sometimes held sway in Uighuristán, he was not necessarily the recognised chief of the State. But, whoever was the chief, he seems to have been subdued by the Ming army, for we read of Turfán, in 1406, sending a mission of homage to Peking, while two years after that date another is recorded to have been despatched by the ruling Khan, this time under the leadership of a Buddhist priest. In 1422 a chief of Turfán, whose name is given as *In-ghi-rh-cha*, is reported to have been expelled from his government by Vais Khan of Bishbálik (*i.e.*, Moghulistan), and to have personally carried his appeal for redress before the Emperor, who caused Vais Khan to restore In-ghi-rh-cha to his possessions. What means the Chinese Emperor took to compel the Moghul to perform this act of restitution is not stated, but the *Ming-Shi* goes on to relate that in 1425 and 1426 In-ghi-rh-cha appeared a second and third time at Peking, "at the head of his tribe," to present tribute. In 1428, shortly after his return home, he died.

The next reigning chief mentioned is one *Ba-la-ma-rh*, on whom the Ming Emperor bestowed presents in 1441, on the occasion of the Egyptian envoy passing through Turfán on his way homeward from Peking. It was about this time—the middle of the fifteenth century—that the Turfán chief, one *Ye-mi-li Huo-jo* (Imil Khwája?) took possession of Kara-Khoja and Lu-ko-tsin and assumed the title of *Wang*, or 'Prince.' Previous to this, says the Ming historian, Turfán was of little account, but it now became powerful, and appears to have extended its territory, for he incidentally mentions that it was bordered on one side by Moghulistan, and on another by Khotan. The rise in power of the Turfán chiefs did not prevent them from continuing to send tribute to China, and it was shortly afterwards (in 1465) settled that a mission should be despatched regularly once every five years.

The particulars of these missions, the demands they made at

[1] Pétis de la Croix, iii., pp. 216–17.

the Ming court, and the concessions granted from time to time by the Emperor, need not be followed here. One of them which appeared at Peking in 1469 reported that the Turfán chief had taken the title of 'Sultan,' and the name of this personage is recorded to have been *Ali*.[1] In the *Tárikh-i-Rashidi* no mention is made of the name of Ali, in connection with Uighuristán. The date points to Kabak Sultan, as well as the title; but as Ali is represented further on in the Chinese history to have been the father of Ahmad, we can hardly assume Kabak to be the Sultan indicated. The father of Ahmad was Yunus, who nowhere appears under the name of Ali, while Kabak was grand-nephew of Yunus. That Sultan Ahmad (or Aláchá Khan)—and no other Ahmad—is the personage pointed to by the Chinese annals, seems more than probable, seeing that the dates of his succession and death agree very nearly with those given in the *Tárikh-i-Rashidi*, and that he is said to be the father of Mansur. But this is not the only reason to suspect inaccuracy in this matter, on the part of the Chinese chroniclers. Even if Ahmad were to be regarded as chief of Turfán, in the sense of being suzerain over the local prince, he could scarcely have played the part they attribute to him, without Mirza Haidar making some mention of his deeds. They represent him, for example, as having proceeded in person against Hami in 1488, as having captured the town, and put to death the local chief[2]—a series of important events about which the *Tárikh-i-Rashidi* is silent. We find there only a brief statement that his son, Mansur, carried on several wars against Khitai, or China.

To proceed, however. In 1473 this Sultan Ali is said to have attacked and captured Hami, together with some tracts to the eastward, proceedings which called forth an expedition from China to recover these places from him. The Chinese had to retire unsuccessful; the Sultan retained Hami, but the tribute missions went on as before. About the same year that he annexed Hami, it appears that Sultan Ali also captured more than 10,000 of the tribe of Oirát, or Kalmáks, and in general he seems to have been a chief of warlike tendencies. He had in his hands the road by which all the tribute missions from the western

[1] Klaproth says that in 1490 a rebel arose in Turfán, who took the title of Sultan; and he appears to be using some Chinese history as his authority. (*Sprache u. Schrift d. Uiguren*, p. 47.)

[2] Bretschneider, ii., p. 196; De Mailla, x., pp. 255, 257.

countries were in the habit of coming and going, and he made the Emperor feel that it was well to be on good terms with him.

In 1478 Ali died, and his son *A-hei-ma* (Ahmad) succeeded him as Sultan of Turfán. He also was generally successful in holding Hami against the Chinese; if he lost it at one time, he regained it shortly afterwards, and he made the governor nominated by the Chinese, a prisoner. During the period 1478 to 1493 he was nearly always at war with the Chinese, yet he seems to have been ever ready with his tribute, and several missions, carrying lions and other presents, are recorded to have been despatched during these years. At length, however (in 1493) his mission, consisting of 172 men, was stopped and imprisoned near the Chinese border. This event, occurring at a time when the Kalmáks on his northern frontier were assuming a threatening attitude towards him,[1] decided Ahmad to abandon Hami, and finally peace was established with the Chinese in 1499. Five years later (1504) Ahmad died, and a struggle for the succession to the Khanate took place among his sons. The eldest, by name *Man-su-rh* (Mansur), got the upper hand, declared himself Sultan, and began at once to despatch tribute to Peking. In 1513 the subordinate Prince of Hami, *Bai-ya-dsi* by name, made over his province to Mansur, who soon afterwards began to make incursions on Chinese territory proper, by invading Su-chou and Kan-chou. Whether he obtained any but a mere temporary hold on these districts is not apparent, but he is related to have had dissensions with the Chinese, on subjects connected with Hami, till his death in 1545. He was succeeded by his son, *Sha—i.e.*, Shah Khan.

This is a brief outline of Dr. Bretschneider's epitome of the chapters in the Ming history which relate to Turfán, or Uighuristán. It shows, briefly, the course of the history of the province according to the Chinese view; but when we come to compare the names and dates with the same story as gathered from the *Tárikh-i-Rashidi*, the two accounts are found not to agree. In the summary, or discursive table, given in Section II. of this Introduction, some of the Khans of Uighuristán have been mentioned, with the dates of their reigns (as far as obtainable), from Mirza Haidar's statements. They may be placed here in

[1] De Mailla says the Oirát were perpetual enemies of the Musulmans of Turfán, and could put 50,000 men into the field. (*Hist.*, x., p. 302.)

juxtaposition with those of the *Ming-Shi*, for purposes of comparison, as follows :—

Ming-Shi.			*Tárikh-i-Rashidi.*		
1. In-ghi-rh-cha .	. died	1428	1. Vais Khan .	. died	1428
2. Manku Timur.	. .	?	2. Isán Bugha II.	. „	1462
3. Ba-la-ma-rh	was reigning	1442	3. Dust Muhamd.	. „	1468
4. Ye-mi-li Huo-jo	„	1450	4. Kabak Sultan	. .	?
5. Sultan Ali .	. died	1478	5. Ahmad . .	. died	1504
6. Ahmad . .	. „	1504	6. Mansur . .	. „	1543
7. Mansur .	. „	1545	7. Shah Khan .	was reigning at close of history.	
8. Shah Khan .	. „	1570			

From this, it appears that none of the rulers mentioned by the Chinese are the same as those given in the *Tárikh-i-Rashidi*, till the name of Ahmad Khan is reached, while the date of the death of his successor, Mansur Khan, differs by two years in the two accounts. The allusion to Vais Khan accords fairly satisfactorily as to date; but here all accordance ends. The first and third names on the Chinese list would appear to be of Mongol origin; the second is certainly Mongol, while the fourth and fifth, though Musulman, are in no way to be traced among the Moghul Khans whom we know of. It is, perhaps, possible that the earlier Moghul chiefs, while Islam had only partially spread among them, bore Mongol as well as Musulman names, and that the Chinese found it more convenient to use the former, in reducing them to their own phonetics; but against this conjecture for solving the difficulty, it must be considered that the number of Khans, previous to Ahmad, is too great, and that the dates do not correspond sufficiently to admit of the assumption that the Mongol names point to Khans of Moghulistan. A more probable explanation, perhaps, may be that during the reigns of Isán Bugha II. and Dust Muhammad, there were also Moghul Amirs who (like the Dughlát Amirs in Alti Shahr), if they did not reign, at all events held some kind of hereditary position as local chiefs, and that it was they who sent the tribute missions, and carried on intercourse, with the Chinese court. Thus, though not supreme in the Khanate, they might have been the chiefs best known to the Chinese. The possibility of this suggestion derives some support, I think, from the accounts the Chinese furnish of the towns of Kara-Khoja and Lu-ko-tsin (more anciently Liu-Chêng). During the first half of the fifteenth century, both these towns, though situated close to Turfán, were reckoned independent, and sent their own tribute, separately, to Peking; and it was only when Turfán became powerful, after the middle of the century, that they were annexed to their more important neighbour.[1] This would have been only very shortly before the commencement of the reign of Sultan Ahmad, or when we come to corresponding names and dates in the two lists. At this time, it may be, the custom was changed, and the reigning Khan may have begun to send the tribute missions in his own name; while the names—especially the non-Musulman ones—of the subordinate chiefs, would have tended soon to fall into oblivion and remain unnoticed by Muhammadan writers. This, however, is only a suggestion—a possible explanation of the discrepancies.

Unfortunately, it is not the only puzzle connected with this eastern Khanate. In his *Mémoires concernant les .... Chinois*,[2] Père Amyot has published several Chinese documents relating to Turfán, one of which is a rescript by the Emperor Shun-Chi (the first of the present dynasty), dated 1647, where notice is taken of the fact that Turfán had not sent to tender homage to China for more than 280 years—*i.e.*, since some date previous to the year 1367, or the commencement of the Ming epoch! So direct a contradiction is this of all that the Ming history has recorded, that it would appear almost hopeless to attempt to reconcile the two statements. It would be tempting to put the Tsing Emperor's direct assertion into the same side of the scales with Mirza Haidar's silence on the subject, and to suspect the veracity of the Ming chronicles; but my impression is that these records contain too much internal evidence of truth, and are too circumstantial in their facts, to admit of the matter being disposed of in so summary a manner. The Emperor Shun-Chi, it must be remembered, had only come to the throne in 1644. He was a mere child of nine years of age in 1647, while his elder relations, who were presumably his advisers, were Manchus, who had been deeply engaged in the wars which had won for him the Empire of China. They probably knew little of the affairs of the country, or of the history of the dynasty that had just been crushed by them and their people. The dynastic history of the Mings, moreover, was not written till many years later,[3] while events connected with an

[1] Bretschneider, ii., pp. 185, 187.

[2] Vol. xiv., p. 15.

[3] The order for the compilation of the *Ming Shí*, Dr. Terrien de Lacouperie informed me, was passed in 1679. Fifty-eight scholars were appointed to engage in the work, which was not finished till 1724.

insignificant Khanate in Central Asia would scarcely have been in the minds of the courtiers and secretaries, when the Emperor was made to pen, or to approve, the rescript in question; or if it was known to them that Turfán had sent tribute regularly—rather effusively—they probably sought to please him by concealing the fact from his knowledge. The rescript is obviously intended to convey the idea that Shun-Chi is flattered by the homage paid him by the Sultan of Turfán, whose predecessors had never rendered so great an honour to the Emperors of the late dynasty; indeed, the whole document appears to be, more than anything else, a display of exultation on the part of the Emperor, intended to reflect on his Chinese predecessors. The occasion which brought about its promulgation, was the arrival of an envoy from the Turfán Sultan of the time, who is therein called "Ablun-Mouhan"—a corruption not easy to identify with any Musulman name. "Le Sultan," runs the French translation, "qui règne aujourd'hui sur le Tourfan, descend en droit ligne de Tchahatai, un des fils de Tsinkiskan, fondateur de la dynastie des Yuen ou Mongoux. Ces prédécesseurs, depuis plus de deux cens quatre-vingts ans n'avaient point envoyé d'ambassade solemnelle pour rendre hommage à la Chine, et lui apporter le tribut. Le Sultan Ablun-Mouhan, ayant appris que j'étais sur le trône de l'Empire Chinois, m'envoie des ambassadeurs. . . . Une telle conduite mérite quelque attention de ma part. . . ." And the venerable Amyot adds significantly:—"Ten years afterwards, that is to say in the year 1657, the King of Tourfan again despatched ambassadors carrying tribute, which means in plain French, that he sent people to trade and to receive presents from the Emperor. Yet His Imperial Majesty was greatly flattered by this new mission."

A still more inexplicable statement is contained in a letter written by Amyot from Peking some time subsequently.[1] Referring to Turfán, he says the country was so broken up in the early part of the sixteenth century, that in the year 1533 there were seventy-five small independent States, all the chiefs of which called themselves king. Here, all that can be said is that Amyot must have fallen into some error. He was living at Peking as far back as the middle of the eighteenth century, and may be assumed to have had good sources of information on historical as well as other subjects, but on this occasion he does not mention the authority for the statement he makes. The

[1] *Mém. Con. les Chin.* xiv., p. 19. No date is traceable for this letter.

Ming-Shi, as we have just seen, refers to the two towns of Kara-Khoja and Lu-ko-tsin, as having been thought, by the Chinese, to be independent of Turfán, about a century before the date spoken of by Amyot, but during this interval the tendency of events in Uighuristán was towards consolidation of the kingdom, and centralisation of the power of the Khan. The date 1533 falls within the reign of Mansur Khan, who, we see from the histories of Mirza Haidar and that of the Ming dynasty, was the most powerful and prosperous ruler that the Khanate had had, and it cannot be regarded as likely that, during his reign, the country should have been split up into more independent divisions than there were towns in it, or perhaps into almost as many as there were villages. Had any disintegration been going on, Mirza Haidar could hardly have failed to notice it, and moreover, Sultan Said, then Khan of Moghulistan and Alti-Shahr (Mansur's brother) would scarcely have submitted (as Mirza Haidar reports him to have done in 1516) to a ruler whose kingdom had broken up into small States. In this instance it is far more likely that Père Amyot made use of some imperfect information, than that both the official history of the Ming dynasty and the independent one of our author, should be wrong. What we find from the latter to have been the case is, that after the death of Ahmad, and with the succession of Mansur, Uighuristán obtained a great increase of strength. Mansur had been chief of Aksu, which province had been invaded and conquered by Mirza Abá Bakr of Kashghar, and the chief had migrated to Turfán with the whole of his tribe and family. The number of the tribe is not stated, but the advent of a large body of Moghuls, together with the Khan, can hardly have failed to prove a source of increased strength to the Khanate, and would point rather to unification than the reverse.

Perhaps if any explanation of so curious a discrepancy may be hazarded, it might be found in the abuse of the tribute missions. As the Ming dynasty declined and approached its fall, the practice of encouraging counterfeit missions seems to have become common; and towards the end of the sixteenth century, and at the beginning of the seventeenth, they came much into vogue among the States bordering on the west of China. This fact stands out with special clearness in the narrative of Benedict Goës, who travelled from Lahore to China in the years 1603–1604, and who died at the frontier town of Suchou, in Kansu, after passing through Yarkand, Aksu, Turfán and

Kumul. The account of his journey is, indeed, a meagre one, for the greater part of his journal was lost at the time of his death. Some fragments, however, were recovered and passed into the hands of one of the ablest of the Jesuit missionaries then at Peking—Father Matthew Ricci—who compiled from them the story of Goës' adventures. In this way much of the narrative that has come down to us, is from the pen of a man specially well informed and qualified to expose the real state of affairs, on such a subject as the missions of homage from the west. He tell us that the tribute brought to the capital was merely nominal in value, but that the Emperor, considering it beneath his dignity to receive presents from foreigners without making a return, not only entertained the tribute-bearers on a handsome scale, but paid highly for the objects presented to him in the shape of return gifts, so that every man pocketed "a piece of gold daily, over and above his necessary expenses." For this reason, the privilege of carrying offerings to China was keenly competed for among merchants and others, who paid highly for a nomination to the post of tribute-bearer. When the time came for setting out, these so-called ambassadors, says Ricci, forged letters in the name of the kings they professed to represent, in which the Emperor of China was addressed in obsequious terms. "The Chinese," he continues, "receive embassies of a similar character from various other kingdoms, such as Cochin-China, Siam, Leu-Chieu, Corea, and some of the petty Tatar kings, the whole causing incredible charges on the public treasury. The Chinese themselves are quite aware of the imposture, but they allow their Emperor to be befooled in this manner, as if to persuade him that the whole world is tributary to the Chinese; the fact being, rather, that China pays tribute to those kingdoms." [1]

This account may be somewhat overdrawn in respect of the comparisons made with such States as Cochin-China, Siam, Korea, etc., for in these cases it is well known that there was no question of the Chinese winking at an imposture, and allowing themselves to be befooled. Tribute from these States meant political subjection; the exaction of it at regular periods was a serious affair, and one of the cardinal points of Chinese foreign policy. But where the small States of Central Asia were concerned, it was apparently not regarded as so important a matter, and there can be no doubt of the fact that, at the period in question, the custom of sending tribute-bearing missions to China had degenerated, in the Khanates of Eastern Turkistan, to mere trading adventures, and that the Chinese must have been aware of the abuse the custom had undergone.[1] Even one of the circumstances that gave rise to Goës' mission, hinged upon a fraudulent embassy of this kind. A Musulman merchant, on his return to Lahore from China, gave the Jesuits there, information regarding the road to 'Cathay,' which appears to have had much influence in deciding them to send forward Benedict Goës. The man, on appearing at Akbar's court, and on being asked by the Emperor how he obtained admission to the Chinese capital, replied with frankness, that he had gone in the character of an ambassador from the King of Kashghar.

It may, therefore, be possible that spurious tribute-missions arrived at Peking from so many petty chiefs, or governors of towns, that the Chinese had actually recorded as large a number as seventy-five for the Turfán region, at the time Père Amyot speaks of; though this would in no way demonstrate that the State of Turfán, or Uighuristán, had, in reality, been split up into small divisions.

Though a separate and self-contained State, the Khanate of Uighuristán was in no way disconnected, physically, from the rest of Eastern Turkistan, or Alti-Shahr. No range of mountains or great river divided the two States, and even their people, in race and language, must have been practically one. No doubt there were slight variations in type and dialect, as is the case at the present day, between the natives of Turfán and those of Kashghar and Khotan; but all were of the Uighur stock, and those of the eastern Khanate, occupying, as they did, one of the ancient seats of the nation, perhaps retained the characteristics of the race in greater purity than the communities of the more western provinces. They lived, as it were, on the ruins of ancient Uighuria, and were less accessible than the communities further west to foreign influences, except perhaps, to those emanating from China—which must, however, have been slight. Their land, placed as it is, in the very centre of Asia, is less known, even nowadays, than almost any other part of the continent; the few modern travellers who have visited

[1] Sir H. Yule cites Abel Rémusat to show that the same thing had happened in the days of the Sung Emperors—*i.e.* the last native Chinese dynasty prior to the Mings. (*Cathay*, p. 583.)

it having furnished only a meagre description of it. A Chinese author of the last century says that the whole population of the province, in his time, could be estimated at no more than 3000 families, and these were, for the greater part, so poor that they were scarcely able to provide for themselves. In the summer the heat was excessive, and the blaze of the sun on the barren ridges in the neighbourhood of the town, insupportable—wherefore the people had named them "the fire mountains."[1]

One of its distinctive features is the depression, to some 150 or 200 feet below the level of the sea, of the central districts of Turfán and Kara-Khoja. This is one of the driest as well as one of the hottest portions of Eastern Turkistan, and the one where the greatest ingenuity of the inhabitants, both ancient and modern, has been displayed in irrigating the land so as to render it habitable. Mirza Haidar relates the personal exertions of Vais Khan (though these were not particularly ingenious) to provide water for the cultivation of the land; but possibly the tradition regarding Vais Khan's manual labour is not intended to be taken literally. The attention of modern travellers has been attracted by the remains of aqueducts and systems of wells, showing how dependent the population was, and is, on artificial irrigation. Thus Dr. Regel mentions the reservoirs where water from the mountains is stored, and the underground canals that lead it to the town, and serve also as dwelling-places for the inhabitants, during the fierce heat of summer.[2] Captain F. E. Younghusband found the modern city of Turfán surrounded by lines of pits upwards of a hundred feet in depth—the lines extending for several miles into the desert.[3]

In contrast to the low-lying group of oases in the burning desert, and among the "fire hills," there rise immediately to the north, the eastern ranges of the Tian Shan, with summits reaching to 12,000 or 14,000 feet above the sea, and capped with eternal snow. One of these is the famous Bogdo-Ula of the Mongols and Kalmáks, or the Tengri-Tágh of the Kirghiz; a mountain that, for ages past, has been held sacred by the pastoral tribes that have inhabited the regions around, and whose people have venerated it, no doubt, because it is the

[1] Bretschneider ii., p. 202.
[2] Petermann's *Mittheilungen*, 1880, p. 205.
[3] *P. R. G. S.*, 1888, p. 498.

central and most commanding feature of their landscape, and the parent of many of the streams that bring them life.

Yet, in spite of its natural drawbacks of heat and drought, the country appears to have supported, at times during its history, a fairly large population, and to have been one of the chief centres of the Buddhists in the earlier centuries of the Middle Ages; for these communities have left many relics behind them, not only in the shape of buildings, but also of inscriptions and objects of art. The Russian traveller Grijmailo speaks of a place called Singim, lying to the south of Lu-ko-tsin (the old Liu-Chêng),[1] where "leaflets enclosed in horn and wooden boxes," and bearing ancient writings in a language now unknown, are still, from time to time, unearthed;[2] while Dr. Regel, again, tells us of vast ruins at a short distance to the south-east of modern Kara-Khoja (the Ho-Chao of the Chinese), to which he gives the name of 'Old Turfán,' but which are more likely to be those of ancient Kara-Khoja. These remains are described as covering a large tract of ground, with massive walls, gates and bastions, besides underground passages, vaulted and arched; the whole bearing witness to a high development of architectural knowledge. He mentions also other ruins of a similar kind, lying to the south of the town of Turfán.[3] From the Ming history too, we learn that to the east of Ho-Chao there stand the ruins of a city of the past, which are regarded as remains of the ancient Uighur capital, Kao-Chang, and with regard to the aspect of the place in the days of the Mings, the author adds that there were in Ho-Chao more Buddhist temples than dwelling-houses of the people.[4]

With the gradual break up of the power of the Moghuls towards the end of the sixteenth century, and the rise of the Manchu dynasty in China in the first half of the seventeenth, the Khanate of Uighuristán fell more and more under the influence of China. For a time, during the eighteenth century, the Kalmáks, with the help of the Tibetans, obtained a hold over it, but this was of short duration, and on their final subjugation by the Manchus, about 1755, the whole country

[1] In Dr. Regel's map this place is marked some thirty-six miles to the north-west of La-ko-tsin (Luktochin), an instance of how uncertain our information is regarding this region. (See map in Petermann, 1881, Band 27, No. X.)

[2] *P. R. G. S.*, 1891, p. 223.

[3] *Loc. cit.*, p. 207.

[4] Bretschneider, ii., p. 187.

became Chinese territory. In the intervals, however, several petty principalities arose within its limits, and some of these appear to have had for their chiefs, Musulman Khans who claimed descent from the Moghuls. It was probably to one of these that the Manchu emperor Shun-Chi alluded, when in his rescript of 1644 (mentioned above) he spoke of his tributary as a descendant of 'Cha-ha-tai.'

SECTION VI.

THE "TÁRIKH-I-RASHIDI" AND AFTER.

> Kingdoms are shrunk to provinces, and chains
> Clank over sceptred cities; nations melt
> From power's high pinnacle, when they have felt
> The sunshine for a while, and downward go,
> Like lauwine loosened from the mountain's belt.
>
> —*Childe Harold* iv., 12.

WHAT is chiefly wanting to throw light on Mirza Haidar's history, is the narrative of some judicious European traveller—a contemporary, or nearly so—who might have afforded an outside view of the state of Central Asia at the period in question, and thus have brought some of our author's statements into touch with Western aspects of history. The *Tárikh-i-Rashidi* refers, for the most part, to the darkest times in the annals of the inner Asiatic States: when strife and disorder prevailed, and no commanding personality or stable dynasty existed in any quarter, to check confusion and form a centre of security. In the days of Chingiz and his immediate successors, Mongol rule was supreme over the greater part of Central Asia and China. The Khans were in most respects uncouth and uncivilised, but their government was a vigorous and consistent one while it lasted. They had confidence in their strength, and were, for that reason probably, liberal and tolerant in their general policy, when dealing with the many foreign nations with whom they came in contact. They knew, also, how to ensure order in their own possessions, and thus attracted envoys, merchants, and missionaries, who have been the means (whatever it may be worth) of handing them down in history with perhaps their best side foremost.

The decay of Mongol authority and the rise of Musulman influence, changed all this in the more westerly regions, while, on the side of China, the accession of an unwarlike dynasty tended to weakness at the extremities of the empire, and laid open large tracts of the interior of the continent to the misrule of unstable and lawless tribes, whose chiefs, while unable to gain permanency for themselves, repelled all intercourse with civilised nations, and were the means only of intensifying the barbarism of their people. For a time, towards the end of the fourteenth century and the early part of the fifteenth, the ascendency of Timur and his immediate descendants proved, to some extent, an agency for the preservation of order, and perhaps prevented the tide of nomad misrule from overwhelming the whole of the best parts of Central Asia. Except for this check, it is probable that the relapse into barbarism would have been even more lasting than it was, and would have had more far-reaching results. But the times of Timur and Ulugh Beg were stormy ones, and had little of the steadying influences of those of the Mongols. Being Musulman rulers, the advance of Islám, and the intolerance that always goes hand in hand with that system of religion and government, was encouraged, so that as soon as the secular authority of the Timuri began to weaken, the religious element grew stronger and came to the front. Saints and religious pretenders increased in numbers, and nothing is more clear in Mirza Haidar's history than the influence they gained in all political affairs. Each Khan and Chief, besides many of the leading Amirs, he tells us, retained at their headquarters one or more of these advisers; and he shows how in his own case, and in that of his master, Said Khan, they gained an altogether inordinate degree of control over their patrons. Even such barbarous tyrants as Abá Bakr of Kashghar, and the most blood-thirsty of the Uzbeg chiefs, seem to have honoured them with superstitious reverence, and to have accepted their guidance. It was in deference, apparently, to the teachings of this class, and under the pretence of religious zeal, that all the worst deeds of these potentates were done—that plundering expeditions assumed the name of holy wars, that murders, prompted in reality by fear or revenge, were committed under priestly sanction, and that wholesale slavery was carried on as a meritorious measure of conversion from infidelity.

Under such conditions as these Central Asia must have been impenetrable to European travellers, whether missionaries or merchants, while it is impossible to imagine that any European monarch would depute envoys to such rulers as Shaibani Khan or Mirza Abá Bakr, as they had done to the Mongol Khákáns and to Timur. Even when these personages had disappeared, Uzbegs, Uzbeg-Kazáks, and Kirghiz, acting under chiefs whose names are scarcely known in history (but who were to the full as rude and lawless), were always at war with each other or with their neighbours. They kept the whole of the country north of the Sir and the Tian Shan in a state of tumult, and consequently closed to all foreign intercourse; whilst they were, besides, the means of weakening the governments—such as they were—of Khorasán, Transoxiana, and Alti-Shahr, and assisted in cutting them off from the West. In the days of the grandsons and early successors of Chingiz Khan, we find envoys like Plano Carpini and Rubruk traversing Asia with safety from the Ural to the northern confines of Mongolia, and there finding Europeans in the service of the Khákáns; the Polos could march backwards and forwards from the Mediterranean and the Persian Gulf, to China, and carry with them their wares in security; while preaching friars and missionaries, such as Odoric of Pordenone, John of Marignolli, William of Modena, and their companions, were tolerated not only as travellers, but as propagandists.

These are only a few among those whose names happen to have been preserved in documents which they, or their friends, left behind them, and which have survived till modern times. But for one who committed his experiences to writing, there must have been many of the same class who attempted nothing in the shape of a record, and as many more whose journals, letters, or what not, have been lost during the intervening ages, or which have not yet come to light. In short, all that we know of the early part of the Mongol period, or from the middle of the thirteenth century to nearly the middle of the fourteenth, points to order and security, and thus to a constant intercourse with the West and Europe. But for the whole of what may be called the authentic period of Mirza Haidar's history—*i.e.*, from the second half of the fourteenth century until it closes in the middle of the sixteenth—not a single instance can be mentioned of a European having visited any of the regions of Central Asia, east of Samarkand.

If any there were, no vestige of them has survived; indeed, the party of missionaries, twenty in number, with six lay companions, who had been sent forth from Avignon in 1333 under Friar Nicholas, as Bishop of Cambulu (Khan Báligh), can only be traced as far as Almáligh, and seems never to have been heard of later than 1338.[1] The latter date would fall within the reign of the Chaghatai Khan, Buzun, and at a time when no Khan was reigning in Moghulistan. As far as can be gathered from the imperfect chronology of those times, as furnished by Mirza Haidar's history, Isán Bugha, the first Moghul Khan, was already dead, and the second, Tughluk Timur, had not yet succeeded him. Probably Amir Bulaji, the Dughlát, was the *Ulusbegi*, or chief of the tribe, and he, as we are told, was a Musulman of very recent date. Whether the disappearance of the friars had any connection with the rise of Islam in the country at that time, or with the general disorder that prevailed, can only be a matter of conjecture. All that is certain is that no other European is heard of in Central Asia till the embassy of Ruy Gonzalez Clavijo from Henry III. of Spain to the Court of Timur, which reached Samarkand in 1404, or about a year before Timur's death. The narrative of this embassy, however, does not relate to the part of Central Asia now alluded to, but to the centre of the kingdoms, mentioned above, as forming a barrier against the misrule of the barbarous nomads farther east. Don Ruy's narrative therefore cannot be utilised to throw light on the obscurities of Mirza Haidar's history, for all that the *Tárikh-i-Rashidi* relates concerning Transoxiana is amply elucidated by other Musulman chronicles, and among them some of the best. More properly it should be said that from the middle of the fourteenth century no European is heard of in eastern Central Asia till some fifty and odd years after the death of Mirza Haidar, and when the kingdom of the Moghul Khans, having split up into a number of small States, was, to all intents and purposes, at the end of its existence.

And if there were no European spectators to review what was passing in eastern Central Asia, neither does there appear to have been any Musulman annalist contemporary, or even nearly so, with our author, who devoted attention to the Moghul Khanates during this dark period. At any rate, I have met with no writer, who has done more than allude to them casually. Perhaps the book which casts the most light on the country and the times, is the *Zafar-Náma* of Sharaf-ud-Din Ali, Yazdi. As one of the historians of Timur's reign, and the chronicler of his campaigns in Moghulistan, Sharaf-ud-Din has necessarily become an authority on the period ending with the date of Timur's death, although he had never set himself the special task of writing a history of Moghulistan and its

Khans. He merely speaks of those against whom his hero, Timur, carried on campaigns or had other direct dealings with, but he in no way professes to write the story of the Moghuls for any period. Thus, his narrative ends about a hundred and twenty years before Mirza Haidar was of an age to begin collecting the traditions, which constitute the groundwork of much of the early part of his own book; and for this interval, as well as for the subsequent quarter of a century (about) over which his life extended, it may be said, I think, that he is the sole Musulman authority for the history of the Moghuls. What the Chinese have recorded is brief and incidental only, as we have seen. Where, however, Sharaf-ud-Din occupied himself with Moghulistan and events connected with it in the neighbouring regions, Mirza Haidar has given no account of his own—he trusted entirely to the Yazdi author, and has simply copied his work. The brief period that falls between the opening date of the *Tárikh-i-Rashidi*, and the point where the *Zafar-Náma* takes up the narrative, is dealt with to some slight extent by other Musulman authors, though Mirza Haidar gives his own version of it as founded on the traditions of his ancestors.

It may be regarded, therefore, that his history is the only work we have, which deals with the period subsequent to the accounts furnished by the *Zafar-Náma*—or from the early years of the fifteenth century to the middle of the sixteenth; while for this epoch Mirza Haidar's evidence is unsupported by any European witness, and only very partially attested to by the Chinese annalists. This solitary, individual character of the book may perhaps enhance its value as a history, and render it indispensable as a reference, for the interval where it stands alone; but it must be admitted that it would have had a still higher value had it been illustrated by outside commentary, and had it been connected with Western countries and events by a link of foreign testimony. If, in other words, some European spectator, regarding matters from a different point of view from that of Mirza Haidar, had done for him what Plano Carpini and Rubruk chanced to do for the *Jahán Kushai* of Juvaini, or Marco Polo for the field covered by authors who treat of the various countries of Asia in the thirteenth and fourteenth centuries, the history of the times might have been worked out to better purpose than is the case now, and fewer doubtful points left unelucidated.

The sequel to the *Tárikh-i-Rashidi* is, perhaps, scarcely a subject which should encumber this Introduction, yet it may be worth while to sketch very briefly an outline of what took place in Moghulistan and Eastern Turkistan after the last pages of the book were written. At that time the author had been some six years regent of Kashmir, and had already been absent from the kingdom of the Moghuls for about fourteen years, but he continued, it would seem, to keep up communication with his friends in Kashghar till the end, and evidently took a deep interest in all that was happening there. So much was this the case, that in the last recorded chapters of his book,[1] though he omits much that might have been worthy of notice regarding the events that were passing around him in Kashmir, he gives some particulars of the course of affairs in what may be called his own country.

At the time when he left it, to conduct Said Khan's expedition into Ladak, Tibet and Kashmir, the Kirghiz and the Shaibán Uzbegs, who were the most inveterate enemies of his people, had been so far checked as to admit of the Khan turning his attention to other quarters. Still they were only checked and by no means subdued: in fact, their power was increasing as that of the Moghuls declined, and very shortly after Said Khan's eldest son, Rashid Sultan, came into possession of his father's kingdom, wars broke out afresh with the Kirghiz, and this time also with the Kazák Uzbegs. Again the Khan is said to have been victorious, and is described as defeating the Uzbegs in more than one great battle; but these victories, like the earlier ones, were mere checks to the enemy, and it seems evident that during Rashid's reign they gained in strength and became practically masters of the greater part, if not the whole, of Moghulistan; while the territory of the Khanate became almost entirely confined to the districts of Alti-Shahr.

This Rashid Sultan (otherwise Abdur Rashid Khan) succeeded his father in 1533, and long outlasted our author, for the length of his reign is given by Amin Ahmad Rázi, in the *Haft Iklim*,[2] as thirty-three *hajra* years, which would bring the date of his death to 973 H., or 1565–6 A.D. As Ahmad Rázi's account of the dynasty, though exceedingly brief, is the only one that approaches a consecutive story, it may be followed here.

He tells us that Rashid had thirteen sons, the eldest of whom was named Abdul Latif. This prince is extolled for his bravery, and is said to have been sent several times, by his father, into Moghulistan, to oppose the Kirghiz and the Kazáks, and that, though he was always victorious over his enemies, he lost his life during the wars.[1] His brother Abdul Karim, who was reigning in 1593, when Ahmad Rázi wrote, is also praised for his courage and accomplishments, after the manner of Asiatic writers. Abdul Rahim, the third son, is stated to have left the country without his father's consent and to have led an expedition into Tibet, where he was killed; while the fourth, named Abdul Aziz, died a natural death at the age of sixteen. The fifth son's name was Adham Sultan, but he was known as Sufi Sultan. He had been made governor of Kashghar, by his father, and retained the post for sixteen years, but he survived the latter only for a short time. He appears to have been succeeded at Kashghar by his brother, Muhammad Sultan, the sixth son of Rashid, who was governor of that place at the date of the completion of the *Haft Iklim.*[2] The seventh was called Muhammad Báki, but nothing is recorded of him. The eighth was Koraish Sultan, who had dissensions with his brother Abdul Karim, and retired to India, where he was received with every honour, presumably by the Chaghatais. He left two children, who were still alive when Ahmad Rázi wrote his history. Of the five remaining sons of Rashid Sultan nothing is related; the names of three only are

[1] Haidar Rázi, the author of the *Zabdat-ut-Tavárikh*, says that Abdul Latif was killed at the age of twenty-nine in a fight with "Tou Nazar Khan, sovereign of the Kazáks and Kirghiz." The date is quite uncertain; but for some years ending in 1580 the Kazák-Kirghiz (or White Horde) were ruled by one Ak Nazar, who is perhaps the personage intended by "Tou Nazar." (See *Not. et Extraits*, xiv., p. 511, and Howorth, ii., pp. 632–34.)

[2] Since completing this Introduction I have been favoured, through the good offices of Capt. F. E. Younghusband, with the loan of some valuable papers by the late Mr. R. B. Shaw, among which I find the following note referring evidently to this sixth son of Abdur Rashid, although called "Khan" and not "Sultan." It runs: "A *Yarligh*, or title-deed, is still in existence granted by Muhammad Khan, son of Abdul Rashid, as reigning sovereign, which confers the dignity of *Tarkhán* or 'franklin' on a certain Mhd. Fazl of 'Puski.' It is dated from Kashghar in H. 996 = A.D. 1587." The year 996, however, fell chiefly in 1588—*i.e.*, from Dec. 2, 1587, to Nov. 20, 1588.

Again, with reference to Abdul Rahim, the third son, Mr. Shaw has noted certain title-deeds which indicate that he was governor of Yarkand in 1011 H. (1602–3 A.D.), and of Kuchar in 1017 (1608–9). It also appears from these notes, that several grandsons of Abdur Rashid inherited power of some kind in the various districts of Eastern Turkistan, down to near the middle of the seventeenth century.

mentioned, as Ulus Sultan, Arif Sultan, and Adul Rahim Sultan.

From this meagre account, little can be gathered regarding the course of events during the forty-four years that followed on the close of Mirza Haidar's work.[1] The only two points that seem clear are, that there was much contention with the Kirghiz and a tendency towards subdivision of the Khanate. At length, however, we come to a ray of light (though, alas, too late to be of great value) shed by a European traveller; for the next glimpse we get of the Moghuls and their State is from the narrative of the Portuguese missionary Benedict Goës, which was mentioned, in the last chapter, as having been partially rescued from oblivion by Father Matthew Ricci of the Jesuit mission at Peking.

Goës, in seeking a road to China, from Agra and Lahore, passed through Afghanistan and over the Pamirs, and reached Yarkand towards the end of 1603. Here he remained for about a year, paying, during that interval, a brief visit to Khotan. After this he proceeded, with many delays, eastward, through Aksu, Chálish (the modern Karashahr) Turfán and Kamul, to Suchou on the western frontier of China, where he died in April 1607. He speaks of Yarkand as the capital of the kingdom of Kashghar, and it was there that resided "the king" whose name was Muhammad Khan. How far this Khan's authority extended is nowhere stated, but the pass with which he furnished Goës' party, for their journey eastward, seems to have been respected, at any rate, as far as Kuchar. Aksu is particularly mentioned as "a town of the kingdom of Cascar" (Kashghar), and the chief there is described as a nephew of the king's, and only twelve years of age; but he is not named. The territory of "Cialis" (Chálish) was governed by an illegitimate son of the king of Kashghar; but here again the traveller furnishes no name, and gives no indication of whether the territory was a dependency, or not, of Muhammad Khan's. Similarly, when mentioning Khotan, he merely alludes to "the prince of Quotan," but gives no name or other information regarding him. Thus the only personage whose name can be identified from Goës' narrative, is Muhammad Khan, who

[1] Dr. Bellew's memoranda derived from the *Tarikh-i-Khánán Chághatáya* (a book, however, which he says he had not seen), and from personal inquiries, are contradictory *inter se*, and altogether at variance, as to names, with the slight information afforded by Ahmad Rázi in the *Haft Iklim.*—*Yarkand Report*, pp. 174–5.

appears to be the 'Muhammad Sultan' of Ahmad Rázi's list, and the sixth son of Rashid Sultan. This, at any rate, seems possible as far as dates are concerned, though Ahmad Rázi states that Abdul Karim (the second son of Rashid) was the reigning Khan in 1593, and Muhammad Sultan only governor of Kashghar—meaning, presumably, the town and district of that name, but not the entire Khanate. Ten years, however, had passed between the date when Ahmad Rázi wrote and that of Goës' visit to the country. It is just possible, therefore, that Muhammad Sultan may have succeeded his elder brother during the interval, and in that case he would, according to the ordinary custom, have added the title of "Khan" to his name.

The only other name that occurs in the history of Eastern Turkistan as that of a ruler of Kashghar, is one Ismail Khan, who was apparently the last of all the Moghuls to fill that position, if indeed, he was a ruler, or 'Khan,' in the proper sense of the word. It would seem from Mr. Shaw's fragmentary papers, mentioned in note 2, p. 121, above, that he was a great-grandson of Rashid Sultan, and he is shown in this degree, in the genealogical table at the end of Section II. of this Introduction. He must have lived in the third quarter of the seventeenth century when the Khwájas held the real and practical authority in the State; while at a somewhat earlier date we hear of one Muhammad Khan as governor at Yarkand, Abdulla at Khotan, Khudabanda at Aksu, and a certain Abdur Rashid in the districts of Kuchar and Turfán.[1] But how these personages were descended we are not told. It is probable that all were grandsons or great-grandsons of Rashid Sultan, but it cannot be so said for certain.

Of the Eastern Khanate, or Uighuristán, nothing is to be gleaned from any Musulman author accessible to me, subsequent to the date of Mirza Haidar's history. A short fragment regarding the succession of the Khans, however, is to be found in Dr. Bretschneider's extracts from the Chinese history of the Mings. It is related there that on Mansur Khan's death, in 1545, he designated his eldest son, Sha (Shah Khan), to be his successor; but Sha's brother Ma-hei-ma (Muhammad) laid claim to the throne, and though he did not

[1] See Bellew, *Yarkand Report*, p. 175, and Vali-Khanoff in *Russians in C. Asia*, p. 169.

succeed in obtaining it, took possession of a part of Hami—a province which was included in his brother's dominions.[1] Afterwards he allied himself with the "Wa-la" (the Oirát or Kalmáks), and with their assistance attacked Shah Khan.

No date for this last event is given, nor is the result of the attack mentioned; it is not clear, therefore, whether he gained the throne by force, or by what means. All that is vouchsafed is that Shah Khan died in 1570, and was succeeded on "the throne of Tulufan" (Turfán) by Ma-hei-ma, when three other brothers revolted against him. One of these was named So-fei (Sufi), of whom it is recorded that he "aspired to the crown," called himself Su-tan (Sultan), and that he sent an embassy to China.[2]

As the Khans and their descendants tottered to their fall, the Kirghiz began to descend into the lowlands of Alti-Shahr and interfere, directly, in the affairs of their old opponents. They were, in some cases, the supporters of influential priests, or Khwájas, who were rapidly acquiring an influence that was to gain for them the sovereign power in the country; but without attempting here to follow all the gradual changes that brought about the establishment of these new rulers, it may be said generally, that before the middle of the seventeenth century, the priests and saintly teachers, spoken of above, had acquired so great an authority, that the governing power of the country was rapidly passing into their hands. Their ascendency was the direct result of the encouragement they had received, for some generations past, from the superstitious Khans and Amirs of all the surrounding countries, and it is hardly a matter for surprise that their power, as a class, should develop, or if, when the authority of the dynastic chiefs in Eastern Turkistan was decaying, they should take advantage of the situation to build up a government of their own. As Khwájas, or reputed descendants of the Prophet, their lineage was undeniable, and ranked, in the estimation of Musulman zealots, far in advance of that of any of the Khans or Sultans who held the secular power.

[1] Hami remained dependent on Turfan till the year 1696, when, according to the Chinese annals of the present dynasty, the chief of the province, named Beg Abdullah, acknowledged the supremacy of the Emperor Kang-hi (*Med. Researches*, ii., p. 182).

[2] *Ib.* ii., p. 198. If the dates are correct, this Sufi cannot be the personage of that name mentioned in the list of Ahmad Rázi, as fifth son of Rashid; for the Sufi of the list is reported to have died only a short time after his father —*i.e.*, shortly after 1566.

They had no special nationality, but formed a class or brotherhood of devotees, banded together in aim and design, though wandering or dwelling, separately, in all the countries of Central Asia. They became expounders of the Musulman law, and the executive authority (such as it was) dare not oppose them; they were also workers of miracles and healers of the sick, and in these capacities obtained a hold over the minds of the mass of the people. "Their tombs," Dr. Bellew tells us, "were converted into sacred shrines endowed with all sorts of munificent virtues. Rich grants of land were apportioned by successive Khans for the support of their establishments, whose presiding elders in return dispensed, in the name of their patron saint, endless favours and bounties to an illiterate and superstitious peasantry." [1]

The Khwájas, in short, were a class that had been evolved by all that had gone before, during the rule of the Moghul Khans—a rule that had begun with the raiding and lawlessness of irresponsible nomads, and had ended with the hypocrisy and fanaticism that usually mark a people incapable of attaining to any degree of civilisation. In the Khwájas they unconsciously raised up rivals who were to displace their house, while these, within little over a century, had, for much the same reasons as their predecessors, to quit the stage and make room for others. They had scarcely begun to wield the power that had fallen into their hands when, as is the case with most governments and dynasties of Asia, discord began to spring up among them, and their brotherhood was divided into two opposing camps. One of these was known as the party of the "White Mountain," and the other as that of the "Black Mountain"—the *Ak-tághlik* and the *Kara-tághlik.* Their feuds were at first based on religious dissensions, but this rendered them none the less bitter: they soon developed into political strife, which would speedily have brought about the end of their rule, but for the support that both parties obtained from the Kirghiz. The White mountaineers summoned the nomad clans from Moghulistan, while the Black mountaineers called in those from the Pamir region; and though the White party, under the leadership of the celebrated saint, Khwája Hidáyat Ullah (better known as Hazrat Afák) obtained the upper hand for a time towards the end of the seventeenth century, their perpetual contentions resulted in the entire country falling first into the hands of the Kalmáks, and finally passing to the rule of the Manchu Emperors of China.

Thus the Kirghiz were amply avenged on their ancient enemies, and began to form the great confederacies that have endured to the present day.

They and their kinsmen, the Kazáks, not only prospered in their own way, but multiplied, so that at the present time they represent a large section of the population in the Russian Asiatic dominions. Both families are found spread over the whole of the provinces of Central Asia, north of the Sir and the western Tian Shan, in large, if somewhat scattered, communities. Thus, of the Kirghiz proper (the 'Black,' or 'Hill,' Kirghiz of the Russians), the estimates compiled by Mr. P. Lerch in 1873, from various sources, show a total of about 176,000 persons,[1] while a good many more, for whom no numerical estimate is forthcoming, are known to exist in the Chinese provinces to the east of the Russian possessions, and in the hill tracts of Southern Farghána and the Pamirs. The Kazáks—the Uzbeg-Kazák of Mirza Haidar—are even more numerous. For those who are still nomadic in their mode of life, sufficiently ample statistics were available, about twenty years ago, to enable Mr. Lerch to sum up their total numbers, in Russian territory, as some 867,000 souls. But to this section also, some addition would have to be made for communities living in Chinese territory. Moreover, the figures furnished refer only to the nomads among both the Kazák and the so-called Kirghiz proper. There are, however, sections of settled Kazáks who are fairly numerous in the Zaráfshán valley, Kuráma, etc., but they are so much intermingled with the Uzbegs and Tájiks of those regions, that their strength was not (at the time Mr. Lerch wrote) to be ascertained with any degree of certainty.[2]

At the same time the other tribal enemies of the Moghuls—the Uzbegs proper—who had become established in Transoxiana since the early part of the sixteenth century, continued their sway under the dynasty then founded, down to a date about coeval with the break up of the Moghul kingdom; while, indirectly and after many vicissitudes, they gave rise to the line of Bokhara Khans now reigning. Mirza Haidar's own

[1] This figure does not include those dwelling in the Vernoye circle. For these no estimates were obtainable.

[2] See *Rüssische Revue*, 1872, Heft i., pp. 26–9 and 39.

successors in Kashmir are, for some thirty-five years subsequent to his time, to be found among the members of the families, to whose weakness and incapacity he owed his own successful regency of nearly eleven years—a term not often reached, about that period, by any of the native chiefs. After his death, the same internal strife and disorder prevailed, that had been habitual for many years before his government began, so that no less than eight kings are recorded to have reigned between the years 1551 and 1587, when Akbar stepped in and finally annexed the country to the dominions of the Chaghatais in India.

A small residue of the Moghuls still exists among the Turki inhabitants of Eastern Turkistan. The number is trifling indeed, and they are scattered chiefly among the northern towns, where, however, they form no separate communities; on the contrary, they are so much mixed in blood that no one but their immediate neighbours and associates are aware of any difference in their origin to that of the people around them. Still, a difference is so far acknowledged that they are called, and call themselves, Moghuls. In this capacity it must be said, according to the testimony of Dr. Bellew, that they enjoy very little respect: rather they are given over to the meanest modes of life, and are looked down upon as an inferior people.[1] It is possible that some may also exist in Western Turkistan, Farghána or Transoxiana, but I know of no mention of them in these countries. In the northern Hazára country, and on the Indian frontier of Afghanistan (among the divisions of the Afridis) we find sub-tribes still flourishing under the name of *Mongol* or *Mangal*, who, Sir H. Howorth believes, may very possibly be remnants of the Mongols, and may thus represent the Moghuls of a later date.[2] Just as the Hazáras still form a people apart, having descended from Mongol invaders of the country they now inhabit, it may also be that the Mangals are a relic of some other Mongolian army which overran Afghanistan in the days of Chingiz or one of his successors. But whether the features and language of the Mangals show any trace of such an origin, I have no information.

[1] *Yarkand Report*, pp. 81, 174.

[2] Dr. Bellew was of the same opinion. He mentions an early conquest of the Afridi country by "Turkish tribes;" and speaks of the Mangals as a "Mongol or Chaghatai-Turk clan," who became "settled about the Péivar, and the head waters of the Kurram river." (See *Races of Afghanistan*, pp. 78–9, and 102.

Perhaps it may be in India that Moghuls, of one variety or another, are more numerously represented than elsewhere at the present day. In the course of the operations connected with the compilation of the census of the Punjab, in 1881, Mr. Denzil Ibbetson found large numbers of people claiming the name of Moghul, many of whom, though perhaps descended from the tribesmen who entered India at the time of Baber or Humayun, can scarcely owe their origin to the Moghuls of Moghulistan—the true Moghul *Ulus* of Mirza Haidar. Such as they are, however, they are chiefly to be found in the neighbourhood of Delhi, in the Rawal Pindi division, and on the routes that cross the northern frontiers of the province. In these localities they are divided into numerous sub-tribes, but of real Moghuls among them, only those calling themselves Chaghatai and Barlás seem to be numerously represented. For the former, Mr. Ibbetson gives 23,593 as the total number, and of the latter 12,137.[1] But how far they have retained the characteristics of their race, or whether, in their changed condition, they would be recognised as the blood relations of the present Mongols of Mongolia, or even of the Hazáras of Afghanistan, there is nothing to show. Sill, something of the Mongoloid type must remain, it would seem, to support their individuality as a tribe.

On the frontiers of India, apparently, as in Eastern Turkistan, the descendants of the Moghuls do not bear a good name; but with the people of a tribe that has fallen from a position of supremacy, and one that at no time has had any very high qualities to recommend it, this is perhaps not surprising. The national character of a community would naturally degenerate with the loss of political and military power, and in the absence of a consciousness among its members, that they belonged to a ruling caste. The more remarkable circumstance is that the race, when transplanted to a foreign country as populous as India, should have endured at all, and that it should still show any signs of individuality. The fact that Moghuls of any variety should yet remain as a people, is one more piece of evidence which may be added to those mentioned in Section IV. above, that many hundreds of years are needed to eradicate the Mongol type, or to blot out its racial affinities, even when overlaid by the superior numbers of an alien nation.

PROLOGUE.

IN THE NAME OF GOD, THE MERCIFUL, THE CLEMENT!

It is fitting that the opening of a royal history, and the beginning of a book of victory and good fortune, should be the praise and glory of that Monarch, the length and breadth of whose kingdom, (according to the words: "Say—verily God is the holder of the Empire,") is defended and preserved from change and decay, and whose palace is securely guarded from the evil of destruction and ruin.

"He setteth upon the throne whomsoever He will," is a testimony to His glorious unity; "He deposes whomsoever He will," is a proof of the permanence of His kingdom.

[Verses]:

And all that is 'twixt earth and sky,
The sun and moon, the east and west;
From India to far Turkistan,
The mighty conquerors of the earth
Have girt the belt of service on,
Prepared to do their Lord's behest.

The splendour of His greatness is beyond the reach of the contentions of friends or adversaries, and the glory of His omnipotence is exempt from the pretentious claims of passionate and dissentient men.

The kings of the earth place the forehead of helplessness and impotence upon the dust of submission and humility, at the palace of His glory; and the Khákáns, powerful as the heavens, standing upon the threshold of the portal of His divinity, stretch forth the hand of humility, supplication and devotion.

"*Amma bád.*" Let it not be concealed from the minds of the wise that the Korán, which is the greatest of the miracles of Muhammad, is divided into three sections. The first contains the declaration of the Unity of God; the second the statutes of the Holy Law of Muhammad, and the third historical matter, such as the lives of the Prophets. Thus, we see, one-third of this book (none but the clean shall touch it) is intended to teach the history of past generations; and therein lies the clearest proof of the excellence of the science of history. Moreover, all are agreed concerning the utility of this science; and most nations, nay, all the peoples of the world, have studied it, and have collected and handed down traditions of their forefathers, of which they give ample proofs and upon which they rely.

For instance, the Turks, in their literary compositions and in their transaction of business, as well as in their ordinary intercourse, employ a speech based upon the traditions and chronicles of their ancestors.

Consequently I, the least of God's servants, Muhammad Haidar, son of Muhammad Husain Kurkán—known familiarly as Mirza Haidar—notwithstanding my ignorance and want of skill, felt it my duty to undertake this difficult task. For much time has already passed since the Khákáns of the Moghuls were driven from the towns of the civilised world, and have had to content themselves with dwellings in the desert. On this account they have written no history of themselves, but base their ancestral records upon oral tradition.

At this present date—951 [1544 A.D.]—there remains not one among them who knows these traditions, and my boldness in attempting this difficult work is due to the consideration that, did I not make the venture, the story of the Moghul Khákáns would be obliterated from the pages of the world's history. The more I considered the matter, the more conscious I became of my inability to write an elegant and ornate preface. [Verses.] . . . For this reason, and in order to give my book an auspicious opening, I transcribed the Prolegomena to the *Zafar-Náma* of Sharaf-ud-Din Ali Yazdi, as far as the "*Amma bád.*" This *Zafar-Náma* contains a history of the Moghuls and their Khákáns, from Chingiz Khán to Tughluk Timur Khán, but of the successors of this latter no mention is made, except where the context required it.

I began my history with the reign of Tughluk Timur Khán for three reasons. (1.) That which had happened before the time of Tughluk Timur Khán had been already recorded, but no account had been written of events which took place after his time, and which, not being contained in any history, ought to be written. But to write of the times preceding Tughluk Timur Khán, when we have already that other excellent history, the *Zafar-Náma*, would be like digging a well on the margin of the Euphrates. (2.) None of his successors have attained to so great a degree of pre-eminence, or acquired so extensive a dominion, as Tughluk Timur Khán. (3.) He was one of the Moghul Khákáns who were converted to Islám, and during his reign the Moghuls, having withdrawn their necks from the yoke of Unbelief, entered into that state of freedom in Islám enjoyed by all Musulmáns. For these reasons, this history is dedicated to his illustrious name and his most noble memory.

And for three chief reasons, out of many, I have called this book the *Táríkh-i-Rashidi!*

1. It was Mauláná Arshad-ud-Din who converted Tughluk Timur to Islám, as will be recounted hereafter.

2. Although before the time of Tughluk Timur, Barák Khán, and after Barák Khán, Kabak Khán, had become Musulmáns, neither these Khákáns nor the Moghul people had had a knowledge of the *Rushd*, or "True Road to Salvation," but their natures had remained base, and they had continued in the road that leads to Hell. But a full knowledge of the *Rushd* fell to the lot of the enlightened Tughluk Timur and his happy people. And inasmuch as the beginning of this history will deal with this matter, the suitability of the title *Rashidi* is evident.

3. Since at the present date, Abdur Rashid, the last of the Moghul Khákáns, is reigning, and since this book has been dedicated to, and written for, him, the reason for the title, *Táríkh-i-Rashidi* is [still more] apparent.

CONTENTS OF THIS BOOK.

It is divided into two Parts [*Daftar*].

Part I.—From the beginning of the reign of Tughluk Timur Khán to the time of Abdur Rashid, who is still reigning.

Part II.—Concerning myself and what I have seen and known of the Sultáns and Khákáns of the Uzbeg, the Chaghatái and others; and, in fact, everything that happened during my lifetime.

I thank God that He has, in His graciousness, made me absolutely independent of the Moghuls. For though the Khákáns of that tribe are of my own race, nay, are my own cousins, I received very bad treatment at their hands—a matter of which I shall speak in the Second Part.

[Verses.] . . . .

The ancestors of my mother and of my father's mother have, for several generations back, been related, on the paternal side, to the Khákáns. At the age of sixteen,[1] having just been left an orphan, I went to the court of Sultan Said Khán, who by his fatherly kindness, greatly alleviated my grief; he showed me so much attention and favour, that I became an object of envy to his brothers and sons. I passed twenty-four years at his court, living a life of luxury and splendour, and acquiring, under his instruction and guidance, many accomplishments and much learning. In the

[1] It was in 920 H., or 1514 A.D., that the author first joined Sultan Said Khán, of Káshghar.

arts of calligraphy, reading, making verses, epistolary style [*inshá*] painting and illuminating I became not only distinguished, but a past-master. Likewise in such crafts as seal-engraving, jeweller's and goldsmith's work, saddlery and armour making; also in the construction of arrows, spear-heads and knives, gilding and many other things which it would take too long to enumerate: in all of these, the masters of each could teach me no more. And this was the outcome of the care and attention of the Khán. Then again in the affairs of the State, in important transactions, in planning campaigns and forays [*Kazáki*], in archery, in hunting, in the training of falcons and in everything that is useful in the government of a kingdom, the Khán was my instructor and patron. Indeed, in most of the above-mentioned pursuits and studies he was my only instructor.

Although I have received from his sons the worst possible treatment, I will return them good for evil; and whether the Khán's son accept this small work or reject it, I will, all the same, dedicate it to him, in order that he may have a remembrance of me and that the world may have a remembrance of him. And the title of this book is derived from his illustrious name, which is: Khákán bin ulkhákán ussultán bin ussultán almutawakkil ala Ulláh al Malik Almumin abul muzaffar Abd-ur-Rashid Khán bin Sultán almabrur, wa Khákán almaghfur assaid ash-shahid abul Fath Sultán Said Khán. [Verses.] . . .

* * * * *

Here are omitted one or two Muhammadan legends such as are usually found in Musulman histories, and a quotation from the *Kashf-ul-Hujub*. They have no bearing on the author's history.

TARIKH-I-RASHIDI.

PART I.

CHAPTER I.

BEGINNING OF THE TARIKH-I-RASHIDI.

ONE day when Tughluk Timur Khán was feeding his dogs with swine's flesh, Shaikh Jamál-ud-Din was brought into his presence. The Khán said to the Shaikh: "Are you better than this dog or is the dog better than you?" The Shaikh replied: "If I have faith I am the better of the two, but if I have no faith this dog is better than I am." The Khán was much impressed by these words, and a great love for Islám took possession of his heart.

Tughluk Timur Khán was the son of Isán Bughá Khán, son of Davá, son of Barák Khán, son of Kará Isun, son of Mutukan, son of Chaghatái Khán, son of Chingiz Khán, son of Yusukái, son of Birtán, son of Kabal, son of Tumana, son of Báisanghar, son of Kaidu, son of Dutumanin, son of Buká, son of Burunjar Khán, son of Alánkuá Kurkluk (which means an immaculate woman). Of her the Prolegomena of the *Zafar-Náma* tells the following story: One day a brilliant light shone into her mouth, and thereupon she felt within her a kind of pregnancy—just in the way that Miriam, the daughter of Omrán, became pregnant by means of the breath of Gabriel. And neither of these things is beyond the power of God. [Verses.] . . .

The object of this book is not to tell such tales as these, but simply to point out that Burunjar Khán was born of his mother, without a father. All histories trace the genealogy of his mother, Alánkuá Kurkluk, back to Japhet son of Noah (upon them be peace), and detailed accounts of all her ancestors are given in these histories. But I have not accorded them a place in this one, for it would take too long; moreover, I have, in this work, limited my subject to events that took place after the conversion to Islám of the Moghuls, and have said nothing of their history previous to that time.

CHAPTER II.

THE EARLY HISTORY OF TUGHLUK TIMUR.

I HAVE heard from trustworthy Moghul sources (and my father and my uncle used also to relate) that Isán Bughá Khán,[1] the father of Tughluk Timur Khán, had for his favourite wife a certain Sátilmish Khátun; while he had also another wife whose name was Manlik. Now the Khán had no children, and Sátilmish Khátun was barren. The Khán, on a certain occasion, went on an expedition with his army. According to an old Moghul custom, the favourite wife has the allotment and disposal of a man's wives, keeping back or giving him whichever of them she pleases. Sátilmish Khátun learnt that Manlik was with child by the Khán, and, being envious, gave her in marriage to Dukhtui Sharáwal, who was one of the great Amirs. When the Khán returned from his expedition he asked after Manlik. Sátilmish Khátun replied: "I have given her away to some one." The Khán then said: "But she was with child by me," and he was very wroth; but as this was a usual practice among the Moghuls, he said nothing.

Soon after this, Isán Bughá Khán died, and there was no Khán left of the tribe of Moghul. Every man acted for himself, and ruin and disorder began to creep in among the people. Amir Buláji Dughlát,[2] an ancestor of the humble narrator, determined on discovering a Khán, and restoring order to the State; so he sent a certain Tásh Timur to find Dukhtui Sharáwal, and to obtain what information he could, concerning Manlik and her child; telling Tásh Timur that if it were a boy, he was to steal the child away and bring it back with him. Tásh Timur replied: "It is a very long and tedious expedition, and fitting preparations for the journey must be made. I beg of you to supply me with six hundred goats, that we may first drink their milk and then kill and eat them, one by one."

Amir Buláji complied with his wishes and supplied him with all that was necessary. Tásh Timur then set out. He journeyed

[1] The reign of Isán Bughá and the circumstances under which he became Khan of Moghulistan, have been discussed in Sec. II. of the Introduction. As far as the uncertain chronology of the times admits of its being stated, his reign lasted from about 721 to 730 A.H., or from 1321 to 1330 A.D.

[2] The name of this Dughlát Amir has been transliterated by some writers *Yulaji* and *Pulaji*, but though the initial letter is always found unpointed, and therefore capable of being read *B*, *Y*, or *P*, I have, throughout, adopted *Bulaji* as the more probable form. If (as is most likely) it is of Mongol origin, it may be the name met with in the narrative of the Chinese traveller, Chang Chun, where it has been transliterated (from the phonetics) by Dr. Bretschneider—*Bo-lu-dji*. (See *Med. Researches*, i., p. 82.)

for a long while in Moghulistan, and by the time he came upon the party of Dukhtui Sharáwal, there was but one goat remaining, and that was a brown one [*kabud*]. On his inquiring after Manlik[1] and her child, they replied that she had borne a son, and that she had a second son by Dukhtui Sharáwal;[2] the name of the Khán's son was Tughluk Timur, and the name of the son of Sharáwal was Inchumalik.[3] Finally Tásh Timur succeeded in carrying off Tughluk Timur, and returned to the Amir with him.

Buláji belonged to Aksu. When Chaghatái Khán apportioned his kingdom, he gave Mangalái Suyah to Urtubu, who was the grandfather of Amir Buláji. Mangalái Suyah is the equivalent of *Aftáb Ru*, or "sun-faced." It is bounded on the east by Kusan and Tárbugur; on the west by Sám, Gaz and Jakishmán, which are situated on the confines of Farghána; on the north by Issigh Kul, and on the south by Jorján and Sárigh-Uighur. This territory is called Mangalái Suyah, and it was subject to Amir Buláji. In his time it contained many large towns, the most important of which were Káshghar, Khotan, Yárkand, Kásán, Akhsiket, Andiján, Aksu, At-Bashi and Kusan.[4] From all these towns, Amir Buláji

[1] This name has been very variously read by different translators. Baron Desmaisons took it for *Mingli* in Abul Ghází's history. Mr. Erskine read his copy of the *Tarikh-i-Rashidi*, *Mánselik;* while Dr. Bellew, using the same work, made it *Minilik*. One of the texts used for this translation has *Miling*. Like many of the earlier names that occur in the *Tarikh-i-Rashidi*, it is probably Mongol, and therefore, being an unfamiliar one to Musulman writers, they would be very likely to distort it. (See Desmaisons' *Abul Gházi*, p. 165; Erskine's *History of India*, i. p. 39; Bellew, *Report on Mission to Yarkand*, p. 147.)

[2] Desmaisons has *Schiri-Oghul* for this name. (*Abul Ghází*, *loc. cit.*)

[3] Here Desmaisons reads *Timur Melik*. (*Ibid.*)

[4] The name the author makes use of here is to be found in no other book or document that I have any knowledge of. His description of the region to which he applies it, is fairly distinct, and his translation of the term into Persian leaves no uncertainty as to its mere verbal meaning. But he does not tell us what language the term belongs to, what country it originated in, or who were the people that he borrowed it from. The first word of the term, *Mangalai*, is perfectly good Turki, and means "forward, in advance, fronting, the forehead," etc., as for instance, the "*advance*" guard of an army, etc. It is written with some variants, such as *Mankalai*, *Mankali*, but the meaning is in every case the same. It may therefore well be *facing* or *fronting*, as he translates it into Persian.

The second word should thus have the signification of *Sun*. It may perhaps be subject to some uncertainty in the reading, for when unpointed, it may be taken for *Subah*—an Arabic word, very commonly employed in India and some other countries, in the sense of a *province* or *administrative division*. Indeed, the two words differ by only a dot in the Persian spelling. But there are two reasons for rejecting the reading of *subah*. The first is that Mirza Haidar translates the whole term *Aftáb Rui*, so that if *Mangalai* represents *Rui*, or *fronting*, there would be no word left as an equivalent for *Aftáb*. Secondly, in one of the texts used by Mr. Ross, the word is clearly pointed for *Suyah*. The *Haft Iklim*, whose author copied from Mirza Haidar, also makes the word *Suyah*.

But *Suyah* is neither Persian nor Turki: no such word seems to exist in either language, and no such proper name, as far as I am able to ascertain. If one word of the term is Turki, it is likely that the other would belong also to that language. But this is not quite certain, for a combination would not be impossible. It is probable, however, that *Suyah* should be sought in the language of some neighbouring nation, and for preference in that of the Mongols, though

selected Aksu as a residence, and it was in Aksu that Tásh Timur found him. As he still had with him the one brown [*kabud*] goat,

the Kara-Khitais, the Arabs, the Chinese, or even the Buddhists of India may have had a hand in inventing a name for the country in ancient times—if ancient the name is; but this last point is also one on which Mirza Haidar fails to enlighten us.

The late Dr. Terrien de Lacouperie, who did me the kindness to look into the term, with a view to finding a solution, suggested the similarity of a name variously written in the historical records of Szema Tsien—*Su Hiai, Sui Yeh*, and *Su Yep*, which was that of a state that has been identified with Yárkand. It lay, at any rate, to the east of Farghána, was not Kashghar, and was connected with *Ku She*, which was perhaps the modern Kuchar. My attention has also been directed towards the ancient Indian word *Suriya*, for the *sun*, but this could hardly have been combined with the common Turki word *Mangalai*, while it is unlikely that it could have been corrupted by losing its most distinctive letter. My impression is that Mirza Haidar's name is something comparatively modern, and is rather a laudatory term for the region in question, than a revival applying to any particular district or town.

In the seventh century the name of *Su-Yeh* (unconnected with *Mangalai* or any other word) was used by the Chinese pilgrim, Hiuen Tsang, according to Julien, Beal, and other commentators, for a town on the upper waters of the Chu, then the capital of certain Turki Khans; though Mr. Watters affirms that the name in Hiuen Tsang should be read, not *Su-Yeh*, but *Su-Sa* or *Su-She*. This place, as will be shown later (see note, pp. 361–3), was most probably the same as *Bálá-Sághun*. If so it was situated some distance to the north of Farghána, and would therefore not fall within the region described by Mirza Haidar as *Mangalai Suyah*. There is, moreover, a difference in date between Hiuen Tsang and Mirza Haidar of some nine hundred years, and the latter nowhere implies that he is employing an ancient term. *Su-Yeh* or *Su-Sa* was, in fact, applied by the Chinese writers to a different locality, though, strangely enough, in the syllable *Su* it has a certain degree of connection with a part of our author's province—that is, with Kashghar. *Su-li* was an ancient name for Kashghar,[1] and Hiuen Tsang tells us: "From the town of the *Su-Yeh* river as far [west] as the *Ki Shwang Na* country, the land is called *Su-li*, and the people are called by the same name" (Beal's *Si Yu Ki*). *Ki Shwang Na* is usually identified with *Kesh*, in Mávara-un-Nahr, and if that be correct it would mean that most of Western Turkistan and a great part of Mávara-un-Nahr went, in the seventh century, by the same name as the city (and perhaps district) of Kashghar, though the latter place stood altogether apart from the tract of country between the *Chu* and *Kesh*. Thus, whether it is in any way possible, that Hiuen Tsang's *Su-Yeh*, *Su-Sa*, or *Su-li* can be connected with Mirza Haidar's *Suyah* must remain extremely doubtful. If Mr. Watters' reading of *Su-Sa* instead of *Su-Yeh* is the right one, such a suggestion could not hold good. (See *China Rev.*, as below.)

A curious passage, it may be noted here, occurs in the *Geographical Dictionary* of the Arab author Yakut, as translated by Thonnelier. He writes: "Farghanah . . . . confinant avec le Turkestan du coté du district de Haïtal, lequel fait face au soleil levant, à droite du voyageur qui se rend au pays des Turks." This passage would be too obscure, in any case, to throw light on the question at issue. It is remarkable only as an instance, in this particular region, of regarding a certain tract, or province, as "facing the sun."

With regard to the limits given for *Mangalai Suyah*, the only boundary that the author defines by names that appear to be unknown at the present day, is the western one. *Sám*, *Gaz* (or the two may be read together as *Sámgaz*) and *Jákishmán* are indeed subject to some variants, but however read, I can find no place to answer to any of them on the western confines of Farghána, unless it be a small town, or village, marked on Ritter and Oetzel's map of 1841, as *Sam Seirak*, and placed on the *Angren*, tributary of the Syr, about midway between

[1] The Chinese, quite recently, have revived the ancient *Su-li*, and have applied it as the official name for Kashghar.

he received the surname [*lakab*] of Kuk Uchgu, which is now borne by all his descendants.

As they neared Aksu, they fell in with a party of merchants, and while they were crossing a pass, the Khán [Tughluk Timur] fell down a fissure in the ice. Tásh Timur, at this, raised a loud cry for help, but he could make no one hear him, for the caravan had crossed the pass and had arrived at a halting ground. Tásh Timur went to one of the merchants, whose name was Begjik, and told him what had befallen the Khán; the merchant communicated this to some of his companions, and several of them set out with Tásh Timur to the place where the Khán had disappeared. Begjik descended into the chasm and found the Khán uninjured, and then and there formed a friendly agreement with him. After that, by way of precaution, he said apologetically to the Khán: "If you go up first they will not pull me up at all; let me go first and they must perforce pull you up after." Again, proffering many apologies, he called out to them to throw down the rope, which they did, and he went up first, and afterwards they pulled up the Khán. All then went on to Aksu. Amir Buláji raised Tughluk Timur to the rank of Khákán, and in course of time he ruled not only the whole of Moghulistán, but also much of the country of Chaghatái, as shall be related hereafter.

Khojand and Tashkend. The exact situation of these places is of little importance, as the author sufficiently indicates that all Farghána was included, when he mentions the names of *Akhsiket* and *Kásán*. The first of these two does not exist nowadays, but it is known to have stood near the site of the present *Námangán*, while *Kásán* is again somewhat farther westward, and consequently not far from the western confines of the province. Among the other limits, none leave any doubt except in detail. *Kasan* and *Tárbuqur* on the east, are both well-known towns on the main road leading from Kashghar towards Karashahr and China, though called nowadays *Kuchar* and *Buqur* respectively. The position of *Jorján* is also readily recognised, under the modern spelling of *Chárchán*, or *Chárchand*; while the country of the *Sárigh Uighur* (or Yellow Uighur), though long forgotten, may be placed with moderate certainty to the eastward of *Chárchán*, or south and somewhat west of *Lake Lob*. Farther on in his history (pp. 348–9), Mirza Haidar alludes to this country again, as lying very much in this position. Dr. Bretschneider has some interesting notes on the subject of the Sárigh Uighur taken from Chinese sources, and places their country "somewhere north of Zaidam, on the southern verge of the stony desert." They would in any case have dwelt on, or beyond, the south-eastern confines of Eastern Turkistan. (For Hiuen Tsang, see Beal's *Si Yu Ki*, i., p. 26; Thonnelier, *Dict. de Géogr. de l'Asie Cent.*, p. 29; Bretschneider, *Mediæval Researches*, i., p. 263; Mr. T. Watters in *China Review*, xix., No. 2, 1890, p. 117.)

CHAPTER III.

THE CONVERSION OF TUGHLUK TIMUR KHÁN TO ISLÁM.

MAULÁNÁ KHWÁJA AHMAD (may God sanctify his soul) was descended from Mauláná Arshad-ud-Din. He was exceedingly pious and much esteemed and revered. He belonged to the sect of *Khwájás* (may God sanctify their spirits). For twenty years I was in his service, and worshipped at no other mosque than his. He led a retired life, devoting his time to religious contemplation, and he used to recite the traditions of his sect in a beautiful manner; so much so, that any stranger hearing him was sure to be much impressed.

From him I heard that it was written in the annals of his forefathers concerning Mauláná Shuja-ud-Din Mahmud, the brother of Háfiz-ud-Din, an elder of Bokhárá (who was the last of the Mujtahids, for after the death of Háfiz-ud-Din there was never another Mujtahid), that during his interregnum, Chingiz Khán assembled the Imáms of Bokhára, according to his custom, put Háfiz-ud-Din to death, and banished Mauláná Shuja'ud-Din Mahmud to Karákorum. [The ancestors of] Mauláná Khwája Ahmad also were sent there. At the time of a disaster in Karákorum,[1] their sons went to Lob Katak, which is one of the most important towns between Turfán and Khotan, and there they were held in much

[1] In this story (beginning after the word "forefathers") I have had, slightly, to alter the translation in order to make sense; the meaning intended, however, is, I believe, preserved. In the text there is some confusion, which renders the passage unintelligible.

The word *Mujtahid*, it may be remarked, means properly, a jurist who can deliver judgment without reference to past or present authorities; but it is usually employed, throughout Central Asia, to denote a high-priest or Musulmán Doctor of Divinity. It is in more common use among the Shiahs than among the Sunnis.

It is perhaps curious to read of Chingiz Khán deporting rebellious priests from Bokhara to his capital in Northern Mongolia, but it is quite a likely thing to have happened. The disaster in Karákorum here referred to by the author, is impossible to trace, for wanted some indication of a date. The place underwent many vicissitudes in the Middle Ages. From the time of Chingiz, it remained the capital of the Mongol Khákáns only till the year 1256, when Mangu transferred the seat of government to Kai-ping fu, in Southern Mongolia, and some distance north of Peking. Traces of Karákorum are still in existence; they were found in 1889 by Mr. N. Yadrintzeff, on the left bank of the Orkhon, about thirty miles south-east of Lake Ugei Nor; and in this position the site is marked on the map attached to this volume. The ancient city appears to have covered an area of six miles in circumference, and some portion of it may have existed contemporaneously with Lob, or Lob-Katak—a town, or towns, which have long since passed out of existence, and even the sites of which are only to be traced conjecturally. (See next note; also Introduction, Sec. III.; Yule's *Marco Polo*, i., pp. 228 *seq.*; Howorth's *Hist. of the Mongols*, i., pp. 182–6; *Pro. R. G. S.*, 1890, p. 424.)

honour and esteem. I was told many particulars concerning all of them, but I have forgotten them for the most part. The last of the sons was called Shaikh Jamál-ud-Din, an austere man who dwelt in Katak.

On a certain Friday, after the prayers, he preached to the people and said: "I have already, on many occasions, preached to you and given you good counsel, but no one of you has listened to me. It has now been revealed to me that God has sent down a great calamity on this town. A Divine ordinance permits me to escape and save myself from this disaster. This is the last sermon I shall preach to you. I take my leave of you, and remind you that our next meeting will be on the day of resurrection."

Having said this, the Shaikh came down from the pulpit. The *Muazzin* [crier to prayer] followed him and begged that he might be allowed to accompany him. The Shaikh said he might do so. When they had journeyed three *farsákhs* they halted, and the Muazzin asked permission to return to the town to attend to some business, saying he would come back again immediately. As he was passing the mosque, he said to himself: "For a last time, I will just go and call out the evening prayer." So he ascended the minaret and called the evening prayer. As he was doing so, he noticed that something was raining down from the sky; it was like snow, but dry. He finished his "call," and then stood praying for a while. Then he descended, but found that the door of the minaret was blocked, and he could not get out. So he again ascended and, looking round, discovered that it was raining sand, and to such a degree that the whole town was covered; after a little while he noticed that the ground was rising, and at last only a part of the minaret was left free. So, with fear and trembling, he threw himself from the tower on to the sand; and at midnight he rejoined the Shaikh, and told him his story. The Shaikh immediately set out on his road, saying: "It is better to keep at a distance from the wrath of God." They fled in great haste; and that city is, to this day, buried in sand. Sometimes a wind comes, and lays bare the minaret or the top of the dome. It often happens also, that a strong wind uncovers a house, and when any one enters it he finds everything in perfect order, though the master has become white bones. But no harm has come to the inanimate things.[1]

[1] Throughout this story, *Katak* is spoken of as a single town, and when, just above, the author brackets *Lob* and *Katak* together, he probably means to denote the district generally, in which the two places were situated. During the mission of Sir D. Forsyth to Eastern Turkistan in 1873-4, the question of these sand-buried cities was inquired into by himself and Dr. Bellew. As regards their positions, the opinion arrived at was that *Lob* must have stood a short distance to the south-west of the lake of that name, while *Katak* lay probably about three days farther towards the south, on the road leading to Chárchan and Khotan. Three years later General Prejevalski visited Lake Lob, and indeed spent the

In short, the Shaikh finally came to Bái Gul,[1] which is in the vicinity of Aksu. At that time Tughluk Timur Khán was in Aksu. When he had first been brought there he was sixteen years of age. He was eighteen when he first met the Shaikh, and he met him in the following way. The Khán had organised a hunting-party, and had promulgated an order that no one should absent himself from the hunt. It was, however, remarked that

---

winter of 1876–7 in its vicinity, with the modern village of Chárgalik (about one day's march to the south-west of the lake) for his headquarters. In this place there were the remains, in the shape of earthen walls and watch-towers, of an ancient town, which the natives called Ottogush-Shahr, or city of Ottogush, after a khan who was said to have ruled there. Two days' journey from Chárgalik, in the direction of Chárchan, the ruins of another town were reported to exist; and lastly, General Prejevalski discovered traces of a third, and very large city, near the south shore of the lake. This place was known locally by the name of Kunah-Shahr, or "old town," and was thought, by Sir H. Yule, to be the remains of the *Lob* of Marco Polo and Mirza Haidar. Marco Polo, whose narrative dates from more than two hundred years before that of the Mirza, speaks of the town as still in existence in his day—he makes no mention of ruins—and there is nothing on record to point to its having been buried by the sand, like *Katak*. The latter place is not mentioned by Marco Polo, nor does General Prejevalski seem to have heard of it, by that name at least, though it may possibly be represented by the ruins he was told of, called Gás-Shahr, which seem to lie more in the direction of the shifting sands than the other two, that he tells us of.

Mirza Haidar's account of the overwhelming of *Katak* by the sand, is interesting and graphic, though, no doubt, overdrawn. The process has been well described by Dr. Bellew, who with Sir D. Forsyth saw it in operation at a place called Urdum Padshah, some forty miles to the north-east of Yangi Hisar. The sand waves were found to advance very gradually, but no estimate could be formed of the yearly rate. When the hillocks of sand become piled against walls or buildings, they grow in height, till at length they fall over and engulf the object that obstructs them. This last phase of the process would be assisted by a violent wind or storm, and it appears to have been a storm that brought about the catastrophe narrated by our author. The sand in no case falls from the sky like snow, as described by Shaikh Jamál-ud-Din in the text, though, no doubt, the air would be full of sand during a storm of wind; indeed, the Shaikh himself says enough to show that the disaster at Katak was known to be impending long before it occurred, and that the storm was only the final incident. The subsequent action of the sand in laying bare, but little injured, villages or buildings and their contents, in the course of its advance, was found by Dr. Bellew to take place much as Mirza Haidar relates. It may be remarked here, that the air in Eastern Turkistan is at all times, except just after a fall of rain (which seldom occurs) filled with a thick haze, and the sky is dark from the mist of impalpable dust or sand held in suspension. Rain clears the mist away, but immediately the fall has ceased, the sand begins to rise once more, in whirling columns, and forms small clouds, which at length grow and coalesce till, in a few hours, the dry haze has formed again in every direction.

As regards the name of *Katak*, the texts in the British Museum all have it spelled in this way, and Sir D. Forsyth specially mentions that in his copy of the *Tarikh-i-Rashidi* the spelling was the same. In some copies, however, it appears to read *Kanak*—a question only of a dot—and some discussion was at one time raised as to the real name. This need not now be followed up. Dr. Bretschneider gives, as Chinese names for Lake Lob, *Yen-tse* (salt marsh), *Po-si-hai*, and *Pu-chang-hai*, the last meaning "reedy sea, or lake." *Shên-Shên* was also a Chinese name for the Lob region. (Bellew in *Yarkand Report*, pp. 27-9; Forsyth in *J. R. G. S.*, 1877, pp. 1 *seq.*; Prejevalski, *Kulja to Lob Nor*, pp. 76–7; Bretschneider, *Med. Researches*, ii., pp. 191 and 344.)

[1] Perhaps *Oikul*, as marked on modern maps in the neighbourhood of Aksu.

some persons were seated in a retired spot. The Khán sent to fetch these people, and they were seized, bound and brought before him, inasmuch as they had transgressed the commands of the Khán, and had not presented themselves at the hunt. The Khán asked them: "Why have you disobeyed my commands?" The Shaikh replied: "We are strangers, who have fled from the ruined town of Katak. We know nothing about the hunt nor the ordinances of the hunt, and therefore we have not transgressed your orders." So the Khán ordered his men to set the Tájik free. He was, at that time, feeding some dogs with swine's flesh, and he asked the Shaikh angrily: "Are you better than this dog, or is the dog better than you?" The Shaikh replied: "If I have faith I am better than this dog; but if I have no faith, this dog is better than I am." On hearing these words, the Khán retired and sent one of his men, saying: "Go and place that Tájik upon your own horse, with all due respect, and bring him here to me."

The Moghul went and led his horse before the Shaikh. The Shaikh noticing that the saddle was stained with blood (of pig) said: "I will go on foot." But the Moghul insisted that the order was that he should mount the horse. The Shaikh then spread a clean handkerchief over the saddle and mounted. When he arrived before the Khán, he noticed that this latter was standing alone in a retired spot, and there were traces of sorrow on his countenance. The Khán asked the Shaikh: "What is this thing that renders man, if he possess it, better than a dog?" The Shaikh replied: "Faith," and he explained to him what Faith was, and the duties of a Musulmán. The Khán wept thereat, and said: "If I ever become Khán, and obtain absolute authority, you must, without fail, come to me, and I promise you I will become a Musulmán." He then sent the Shaikh away with the utmost respect and reverence. Soon after this the Shaikh died. He left a son of the name of Arshad-ud-Din, who was exceedingly pious. His father once dreamed that he carried a lamp up to the top of a hill, and that its light illumined the whole of the east. After that, he met Tughluk Timur Khán in Aksu, and said what has been mentioned above. Having related this to his son, he charged him, saying: "Since I may die at any moment, let it be your care, when the young man becomes Khán, to remind him of his promise to become a Musulmán; thus this blessing may come about through your mediation and, through you, the world may be illumined."

Having completed his injunctions to his son, the Shaikh died. Soon afterwards Tughluk Timur became Khán. When news of this reached Mauláná Arshad-ud-Din, he left Aksu and proceeded to Moghulistán, where the Khán was ruling in great pomp and splendour. But all his efforts to obtain an interview with him, that he might execute his charge, were in vain. Every morning, however, he used to call out the prayers near to the Khán's tent. One morning the Khán said to one of his followers: "Somebody has been calling out like this for several mornings now; go and bring him here." The Mauláná was in the middle of his call to prayer when the Moghul arrived, who, seizing him by the neck, dragged him before the Khán. The latter said to him: "Who are you that thus disturb my sleep every morning at an early hour?" He replied: "I am the son of the man to whom, on a certain occasion, you made the promise to become a Musulmán." And he proceeded to recount the above related story. The Khán then said: "You are welcome, and where is your father?" He replied: "My father is dead, but he entrusted this mission to me." The Khán rejoined: "Ever since I ascended the throne I have had it on my mind that I made that promise, but the person to whom I gave the pledge never came. Now you are welcome. What must I do?" On that morn the sun of bounty rose out of the east of divine favour, and effaced the dark night of Unbelief. Khidmat Mauláná ordained ablution for the Khán, who, having declared his faith, became a Musulmán. They then decided that for the propagation of Islám, they should interview the princes one by one, and it should be well for those who accepted the faith, but those who refused should be slain as heathens and idolaters.

On the following morning, the first to come up to be examined alone was Amir Tulik, who was my great grand-uncle. When he entered the Khán's presence, he found him sitting with the Tájik, and he advanced and sat down with them also. Then the Khán began by asking, "Will you embrace Islám?" Amir Tulik burst into tears and said: "Three years ago I was converted by some holy men at Káshghar, and became a Musulmán, but, from fear of you, I did not openly declare it." Thereupon the Khán rose up and embraced him; then the three sat down again together. In this manner they examined the princes one by one. All accepted Islám, till it came to the turn of Jarás, who refused, but suggested two conditions, one of which was: "I have a man named Sataghni Buka,[1] if this Tájik can overthrow him I will become a Believer." The Khán and the Amirs cried out, "What absurd condition is this!" Khidmat Mauláná, however, said: "It is well, let it be so. If I do not throw him, I will not require you to become a Musulmán." Jarás then said to the Mauláná: "I have seen this man lift up a two year old camel. He is an Infidel, and above the ordinary stature of men." Khidmat Mauláná replied, "If it is God's wish that the Moghuls become honoured with the blessed state of Islám, He will doubtless give me sufficient power to overcome this man." The Khán and those who had become Musulmáns were not pleased with these plans. However, a large crowd assembled, the Káfir was brought in, and he and Khidmat Mauláná advanced towards one another. The Infidel, proud of his own strength, advanced with a conceited air. The Mauláná looked very small and weak beside him. When they came to blows, the Mauláná struck the Infidel full in the chest, and he fell senseless. After a little, he came to again, and having raised himself, fell again at the feet of the Mauláná, crying out and uttering words of Belief.[1] The people raised loud shouts of applause, and on that day 160,000 persons cut off the hair of their heads and became Musulmáns. The Khán was circumcised, and the lights of Islám dispelled the shades of Unbelief. Islám was disseminated all through the country of Chaghatái Khán, and (thanks be to God) has continued fixed in it to the present time.

EXTRACTS FROM THE ZAFAR-NAMA.

CHAPTER IV.

EXPEDITION OF TUGHLUK TIMUR KHÁN INTO THE KINGDOM OF MÁVARÁ-UN-NAHR.[2]

SINCE the country of Mávará-un-Nahr, owing to the events above related, was in a state of disruption and confusion, Tughluk-Timur Khan (son[3] of Davá Khán, a descendant of Chaghatái Khán), King of Jatah, to whom by right of descent this country belonged, having called together his officers and courtiers, and having made ready an army, set out, in a manner becoming a great conqueror, towards Mávará-un-Nahr. This was in the month of Rabi Assani, 761 of the Hajra, [March A.D. 1360] corresponding to the year of the Mouse [Sichkán] of the Tartar cycle. Thirty years had elapsed between the death of Tármashirin[4] and this event—and during this period there had reigned eight khans of the race of Chaghatái. When Tughluk Timur Khan arrived at Chanák Bulák, which is near the river of Khojand, in the plains of Táshkand, he consulted with his princes and generals, and they decided that the wisest plan would be for Ulugh Tuktimur, of the tribe of

[1] Bellew (who, however, is not translating but summarising from the *Tarikh-i-Rashidi*) tells this story somewhat differently, and ends by saying: "Toghluk Timur was at this time twenty years of age, and he died ten years later, in 764 A.H. (1362 A.D.)." (*Yark. Report*, p. 148.)
[2] Transoxiana.
[3] Should be grandson.
[4] He died 738 A.H., which would make twenty-three years; while all th texts of the *Zafar-Náma* in the British Museum say thirty-three years.

Karáit,[1] Háji Beg of the tribe of Arkenut,[2] and Begjik of the tribe of Kánghali,[3] to go forward and reconnoitre. The three princes hastened to carry out these orders, and when they had crossed the river of Khojand, Amir Báyázid Jaláir, together with his people, joined them, and they all proceeded together in the direction of Shahr-i-Sabz.

Amir Háji Barlás having collected troops from Kesh, Karshi, and that neighbourhood, set out to oppose these combined forces. But on reconsideration, judging the plan to be unwise, he turned with his own force towards Khorásán, before the two armies had come into conflict.

[1] The *Karai*, or *Karait* (the final *t* is only the Mongol plural), are usually described as a Mongol tribe, and Rashid-ud-Din, according to Dr. Erdmann, includes them in his list of Mongol tribes. Sir H. Howorth, however, gives reasons for believing them to be Turks, and also for regarding them as one and the same people with the Kirghiz, or the "Hakas" of the Chinese. Before the rise of Chingiz Khan, they occupied large tracts of Southern and Central Mongolia, and were, in fact, the nation ruled over by Wang Khan, or Prester John, so famous in mediæval history. They were subdued by Chingiz about the beginning of the thirteenth century, and afterwards became so much scattered, that fragments of their tribes have been found in various localities all over Mongolia, and as far west as the country now known as 'the Kirghiz Steppes.' In the latter part of the twelfth century they were perhaps the most powerful of all the nomad nations of northern Asia, and are doubtless the people who displaced that other important nation, the Uighurs, from north-western Mongolia, and drove them southward. (See Howorth, *J. R. A. S.*, 1889, pp. 361 *seq;* and Erdmann, *Ubersicht der . . . . Türkischen, etc., Völkerstämme*, Kasan, 1841.)

[2] Some of the texts may read *Azkenut* instead of *Arkenut*, but the tribe intended can scarcely be other than the *Alaknut* of Deguignes' list, or the *Olkhonod* of Howorth. The latter author speaks of six tribes—the *Kunkurat*, *Inkirass*, *Olkhonod*, *Karanut*, *Kurulat* or *Kurlut*, and *Ilkijin*—who formed a confederacy under the name of *Kunkurat*. They were of Turki origin, and inhabited the north of Mongolia. In the *Institutes of Timur* the name is written *Arkenut;* and in Rashid-ud-Din's list, *Alkunut*. The last writer classes them as *Tartars*. (See Howorth, *Hist. of Mongols*, i., p. 703; Deguignes, *Hist. des Huns*, iii., p. 3; Davey's *Inst. of Timur*, p. 19; and Erdmann as above.)

[3] The *Kángali*, or *Kánkali*, were, at the time of the rise of the Mongols, an important Turki tribe whose country lay north of Transoxiana, between that of the *Kipcháks* on the west, and Moghulistan on the east. They appear to have been much intermixed with the *Kipcháks*, and are thought by Howorth to have been the ancestors of the modern *Nogais* and some of the Turkoman tribes. Abul Gházi mentions the *Kankali* as living on the Chu and Talas rivers in times previous to the Mongol ascendency. Dr. Bretschneider tells us that they are frequently spoken of in Chinese historical works of the Mongol period, the name being generally represented as *Kang-li*, or sometimes *Hang-li*. The tribe was known to the Kin dynasty of China as early as the eleventh century, when one of their chiefs is said to have offered to become a vassal of the Chinese Emperor. They were a warlike people, and at a later period the Mongol Khans utilised their services as soldiers, and even as generals. Rashid-ud-Din also classes the *Kankali* as Turks. (Howorth, *Hist. of Mong.*, i., p. 18; Bretschneider, i., p. 301; Abul Ghízi, p. 38; Erdmann as above.)

CHAPTER V.

INTRIGUES OF TIMUR WITH AMIR HÁJI BARLÁS—HIS RETURN FROM THE BANKS OF THE JIHUN AND HIS MEETING WITH THE THREE PRINCES.

[Arabic verses]:

Judgment is preferable to the valour of heroes;
The former is the first of virtues, the latter stands second;
But when these two are united in one person,
That person can attain the highest summits of fame.

[Persian verses]:

With judgment thou canst put a whole army to rout.
One man with a sword can kill as many as a hundred men.[1]

The events about to be related, all testify to the truth of these statements. For when Amir Háji Barlás, heard of the advance of the army of Jatah, he abandoned his own country and set out for Khorásán. He crossed the desert and arrived at the River Jihun. Amir Timur[2] saw well that if he continued in this policy of self-preservation, his native country would go to ruin, and his inherited dominions would fall into confusion, for in that same year his father Amir Trágái had died.

[Verses]: His father was dead and his uncle had flown:
The people were exposed to the ravages of a stranger.
Its enemies had placed the tribe in danger:
It was become as an eagle without wings or feathers.

Under these circumstances, although he had not passed the age of twenty five, and his intelligence had not yet received the enlightenment of great experience, Amir Timur determined upon setting these affairs in order, and with this intent took counsel with Amir Háji, saying: "If the kingdom remains without a head, great evils will most surely come upon it, and the people will be entirely annihilated by the violence and perfidy of enemies."

[Verses]: A kingdom without a head is like a body without soul;
Certainly a body without a head is as good as destroyed.

"Since you wish to proceed into Khorásán, I think I had better return to Kesh, and when I have comforted and encouraged the inhabitants of that place, I will go thence to the court of the Khán. I will confer with the

[1] Here follow some rhetorical phrases and more verses, which are omitted in the translation. Their burden is the superiority of intelligence over the sword.

[2] Known as Tamerlane, Timurlang, etc. He is always spoken of in the texts of the *Zafar-Nama* as "*Sahib-i-Kirán*," or "Lord of the Conjunction"; but I propose to call him throughout "Amir Timur," which is not only correct, but is sufficient to distinguish him from other Timurs. Major C. Stewart, in the Preface to the *Mulfuzát Timuri*, translates "*Sahib-i-Kirán*" as "Lord of the Auspicious Conjunction."

princes and nobles of the State, so that this country and the people, who have been entrusted to our care by God, may come to no harm."[1]

Having thus spoken he departed. Amir Háji was fully convinced that the words of Amir Timur were divinely inspired, and therefore accepted all his decisions and approved all his plans. When Amir Timur arrived at Khuzár, he met Háji Mahmud Sháh Yasuri, who was acting as guide to the advance body of the army of Jatah. The troops were advancing with all possible haste, whetting the teeth of their lust for plunder and desire for booty, and sewing themselves purses in expectation of the treasure and wealth to be found in that country. Amir Timur succeeded in arranging an amnesty with the generals of this force, saying: "Wait here while I go and see the princes and, with them, determine upon some reasonable and advisable plan." The wise words of that prince were as heavenly utterances, and had such an effect on the soldiers, that, in spite of their eagerness to advance, they remained where they were. Amir Timur passed safely on, and when he reached Kesh he met the three Amirs of Jatah, who had themselves just arrived there. After friendly greetings had been exchanged, they expressed to him their satisfaction at hearing that he was going to submit himself to the Khán; and they appointed him governor of the district, which had formerly belonged to Amir Karáchár—that is to say, the district round about Kesh, together with its dependencies; with the result that, by his wise conduct, the torrent of distress and calamity which threatened to overwhelm this country was turned aside, and the people again enjoyed that repose which they had lost all hopes of recovering. [Verses] . . . .

In the opinion of the most ignorant people, it seemed that a great piece of good fortune had befallen Amir Timur, but Fate had still a thousand successes in store for him.

After this, Amir Timur took leave of the princes and threw the shadow of his protection and care upon the tribe. He commanded troops to be collected between Shahr-i-Sabz and the River Jihun, and in a short time, having mustered a very large army, set out, together with Amir Yasuri. At this time a dispute arose among the princes of Jatah, who having withdrawn all their troops from Mávará-un-Nahr, returned to the headquarters of Tughluk Timur Khán. After that, Báyázid Jaláir, with the whole of his following, joined the side of Amir Timur and Amir Khizar Yasuri.

CHAPTER VI.

TUGHLUK TIMUR KHÁN'S SECOND INVASION OF MÁVARÁ-UN-NAHR.

When desire for the government of Mávará-un-Nahr a second time seized the skirt of Tughluk Timur Khán's enthusiasm, he prepared an innumerable army and, in the month of Jamád-alávla of the year 762 (A.D. 1361), corresponding to the year of the Ox in the Tartar cycle, he again marched for that

[1] He probably means that he will make friends with the chiefs, and persuade them not to do the country any injury.

country. When he arrived at Khojand, Amir Báyázid Jaláir came to offer him his services. Amir Báyán Salduz also, as a sign of his obedience, went forward as far as Samarkand to meet the Khán, and Háji Barlás, although at the time of the Khán's first invasion he had opposed him, trusting to Providence, now presented himself before him. In the meanwhile the Khán had given orders to his men to capture Amir Báyázid and put him to death. Amir Háji Barlás, fearing a similar fate, fled towards Kesh. He got together some of his own tribe and led them across the Jihun, but they were attacked by the Kashmir[1] regiment of the Jatah army, who were pursuing them, and a battle took place, in which Jughám Barlás was killed, and Amir Háji retired to Khorásán. On his arrival at Khorasha, which is a village of Buluk-i-Juvin,[2] a dependency of Sebzvár, he was seized by a band of brigands and, together with his brother Idegu, was killed. After the conquest of Khorásán (which event made Amir Timur feel himself in some way avenged) and after some of them[3] had been put to death, that village became a fief of the heirs of Amir Háji, and up to the present time the inhabitants thereof are their subjects and agents.

Among the Amirs at the court of Jatah was a certain Amir Hamid, of the tribe of Kurlukut,[4] who was distinguished above his peers at the court by his wisdom and common sense. He had free access to the Khán, and whatever he proposed in the way of advice or approval, was acceptable. At this time he began to praise and extol the virtues of Amir Timur to the Khán, and he begged the Khán to restore to the prince, the territory that was his by right of inheritance. The Khán lent a favourable ear to his entreaties, and a messenger was immediately despatched to fetch Amir Timur. The prince accordingly came to the Khán, received from him the warmest welcome,

[1] All the texts have the word "Kashmir," and there can be no doubt of the reading. The question is as to the fact mentioned. It seems almost impossible to imagine that there was a regiment of Kashmiris in the service of the Moghul Khans. No doubt the Buddhists of Kashmir had intercourse with those of Eastern Turkistan, and more especially with Khotan; and a certain number may have found their way into the service of the Khans, but they must have been differently constituted to the Kashmiris of the present day, if they became soldiers. Possibly all strangers who came into the country from the side of Kashmir were called Kashmiris, and if so there may have been, among them, Hindus and others with sufficiently warlike qualities to enlist as fighting-men. But perhaps the most likely explanation is that they were slaves, or descendants of slaves, and of prisoners, carried off during the earlier Mongol invasions of countries in the direction of Kashmir. In this case, little but the name of Kashmiri would have remained to such people, a century and a half later.

[2] Probably the plain of Juvain (or Jagatai Juvain), which lies to the north and north-west of Sabzawár in Khorasan. *Buluk* means "a district." *Khorasha* most likely stands for Kudáshah, the name of a village in the Juvain plain, marked on modern maps.

[3] By the word "them," the brigands seem to be intended.

[4] Probably the *Karluk*, in the Mongol plural, is the tribe meant. The *Karluk* were certainly Turks by origin, and in Sir H. Howorth's opinion were of the Uighur race. Rashid-ud-Din enters them under the Turki tribes, pure and simple. At the time of Chingiz, they appear to have inhabited the country north of the Tian Shan, but later they probably pushed farther towards the west. From Dr. Bretschneider we learn that the *Karluk* are repeatedly noticed in the Chinese histories under such names as *Ko-erh-lu*, *Ha-la-lu*, etc. (See for Howorth, Sect. IV. of Introduction; Rashid-ud-Din in Erdmann's *Ubers. d. Türk. Völkerstämme;* Bretschneider, ii., pp. 39–41). Communities of Karluks are found at the present day in and around Badakhshán, where they are regarded as Turks and speak the Turki language.

and was appointed Governor of Kesh and Tumán,[1] together with their dependencies.

In the winter of that year, the Khán determined to make war upon Amir Husain,[2] and set out against him. Amir Husain, for his part, also raised an army and led it as far as the River Vakhsh. Here he pitched his camp. When the Khán had passed the Iron Gate[3] and arrived near to where Amir

[1] For *Tumán*, probably *Kármun* (sometimes written *Kermine*) should be read. The town stands on the Zaráfshán, to the north-east of Bokhara.

[2] Husain was grandson of the Amir Kazagán, a prince of the tribe of *Tahit* (according to Pétis de la Croix) who had revolted against Sultan Kazán, the "Grand Can"—that is, the Khákán of the Chaghatai. (*Hist. de Timur Bec.*, i., p. 2.) The word *Tahit* is probably a corruption; it should perhaps read *Tait*, a difference only of a dot under one letter.

[3] The texts, in this place, have *Darband-i-Ahanin*, or "Iron Gate," but in all other places *Kulugha*, the name by which the pass was usually known. It is often mentioned by ancient travellers, but has very rarely been visited in modern times, at any rate up to within the last few years, or before the Russians became possessors of Samarkand and Khokand. The gates, in ancient times, were a reality, for the Chinese traveller Hiuen Tsang, who passed the Darband in 630 A.D., describes the defile as "closed by folding gates clamped with iron." (See Sir H. Yule in Wood's *Oxus*, 1872, p. lxix.) At the time of Chingiz Khan, when Chinese travellers frequently went backwards and forwards between China and the conqueror's camp in various parts of Central Asia, the pass of the Iron Gates is frequently mentioned under the name of *Tie-men-Kuan* (literally, Iron Gate barrier); and one of them, the Taoist monk Cháng Chun, describes his passage through the defile in 1222, with carts and an escort of a hundred Mongol and Muhammadan soldiers: "We crossed the mountains in a south-east direction and found them very high. Masses of rock were lying scattered about. The escort themselves pulled the carts, and took two days to pass to the other side of the mountains." (*Chinese Mediæval Travellers to the West*, by Dr. E. Bretschneider, 1875, pp. 41, 42.) The gates themselves seem, thus, to have disappeared by the thirteenth century, and they had certainly done so at the beginning of the fifteenth, when Ruy Gonzalez Clavijo visited the spot, in the course of his embassy (1403–5) from Henry III. of Spain to Amir Timur. He wrote: "These mountains of the Gates of Iron are without woods, and in former times they say that there were great gates covered with iron placed across the pass, so that no one could pass without an order." (See *Embassy of Ruy G. Clavijo to Court of Timur*, by C. R. Markham, Hakluyt Series, 1859, p. 122.) From the time of Don Ruy down to 1875, when the Russian Hisar Expedition passed the Darband, no European appears to have seen (or, at any rate, to have described) the defile. Mr. N. A. Mayef, who accompanied the Russian Expedition, described the spot thus: "The famous ravine of the Iron Gate winds through a high mountain chain, about twelve versts to the west of Derbent. It is a narrow cleft, 5 to 35 paces wide and about two versts long. It is known now as Buz-ghala Khána (*i.e.*, the House of Goats). Its eastern termination is 3540 feet above the sea; its western termination 3740 feet. A torrent, Buz-ghala Khána bulák, flows through it. . . ." (*Geogr. Magazine*, Dec., 1876, p. 328.)

The term "Iron Gate," or at any rate "Kulugha," seems often to have been applied to narrow defiles in mediæval times; thus there is the gate in the "Wall of Alexander," near Darband, on the west shore of the Caspian, which is still, according to Sir H. Yule, called in Turkish *Demir-Kápi*, or Iron Gate. Another is the defile of Talki leading from the Sairam (Nor) or Sut (Kul) lake southward, to the Ili river. This was called *Kulugha* by Turki-speaking people, and *Timur-Khalaga* by the Mongols; and Dr. Bretschneider explains that the word *Khalaga*, or *Khalga*, means, in Mongol, a pass or gate, while *Timur* signifies iron. The Chinese traveller Chang-Te, in 1259, passed through the Talki defile, and described it as "very rugged, with overhanging rocks." He speaks of it by a transliterated Mongol name which stands for "iron roadway." Possibly—though I think not—it may be this Talki *Kulugha* which the historians of Timur refer to when, in recording his last expedition but one against the Jatah Moghuls, they describe the route taken by the division of the army commanded by Timur's son, Omar Shaikh Mirza, from Yulduz towards

Husain was encamped, the two armies came in sight of one another and were preparing to engage, when Kaikhosru of Khatlán, together with his men, left the side of Amir Husain and joined the army of the Khán, thus breaking the order of battle of the former.[1] When Amir Husain perceived this, he turned and fled. The victorious Khán went in pursuit of him, and crossing the Jihun, penetrated as far as Kunduz. His troops pillaged all the country round about, as far as the mountains of Hindu Kush, and spent the following spring and summer in that region.

Kashghar. At any rate the Iron Gate near Kesh, in Transoxiana, cannot have been meant, as Pétis de la Croix, in reading the *Zafar-Nama*, and Price, relying upon the *Rauzat-us-safá*, seem to have assumed. From the Yulduz valley, Omar Shaikh is made to return to Andijan by way of Kuchar, Uch-Turfán, and Kashghar, and to fight a battle with an Amir of Jatah in the pass of *Kulugha*, on the way. While it is scarcely conceivable that he should have marched first into the heart of Transoxiana, there have met with a Jatah Amir far in the rear of Timur's army, and then have returned to Andijan, it is just possible, though improbable, that he may have first made an expedition north-westward to the Talki defile and thence back to Kuchar. I suspect that in the hills between the Yulduz and Kuchar, there was yet another defile known by the name of *Kulugha*, or 'Pass,' and that it may be represented on modern maps by the pass of Kui-Kule. This view is supported by the circumstance that the victory over the Jatah Amir is mentioned, in the *Zafar-Nama*, as having been won before Omar Shaikh's arrival at Kuchar, and without any allusion to a return march northward, for after the battle, he is said to have *continued* his march by way of Kuchar, etc., to Kashghar. In this case, the translators have probably been led into calling the pass "Iron Gate," on account of the name *Kulugha* being identical with one of those used for the Darband-i-Ahanin near Kesh. In all likelihood, there were many passes in various parts of Turki and Mongol-speaking Asia, which were known simply by the name *Kulugha*, though they may have had more specific local names besides, such as *Timur*, or *Demir, Kulugha*. The error fallen into, in this case, was to apply the Persian translation of one of these specific names, to all *Kulugha*, or passes. (See for *Talki*, etc., Bretschneider's *Researches*, i., p. 127, and ii., pp. 34–5 and 230.)

[1] Amir Husain had put to death Kaikobád, the brother of Kaikhusru (*Hist. de Timur Bec.*, i., p. 191.) These Zoroastrian names, occurring in Khatlán at this period, are remarkable. As regards the state or province of Khatlán, Khutlán, or Khotl, Sir H. Yule located it (in 1872) somewhat north of the present Koláb and west of Darwáz; but Mr. Mayef, who travelled in this region three years later, believes Kurgán-Tube (*i.e.*, Kurghán Tipa) on the lower Surkháb (or Vákhsh) and a short distance west of Koláb, to have been the centre of the ancient Khatlán. He quotes Ibn Dast, an author of the tenth century, to the effect that the kingdom of Khotl, or Khatlán, included the lower valley of the Vakhsh and that of the Kafir-nahán, with the town of Kabádian, and reached also to Faizabad on the upper waters of that river. Khatlán existed at least down to the end of the fifteenth century, for in 1498 we find Khusru Shah, of Kunduz, bestowing the governorship of it on his brother Wali. Both the State and the name have since disappeared. (See Yule *J. R. A. Socy.*, vi., pt. 1, 1872, p. 97, and his map in Wood's *Oxus*, 1872; Mayef in *Geograph. Mag.*, Dec., 1876, p. 328; Erskine *Hist. of India*, i., p. 200; and *Memoirs of Baber*, pp. xxxii. *seq.*) The Chinese of the Ming period knew the country by the names *Ko-te-lang* and *Ḥa-ti-lan*. (Bretschneider, ii., pp. 277 and 315.)

CHAPTER VII.

THE RETURN OF TUGHLUK TIMUR KHÁN TO HIS OWN CAPITAL.

On the approach of autumn, the Khán set out for Samarkand, and on the journey gave orders for Amir Bayán Salduz to be killed, according to the code of the Moghuls.[1] When he reached Samarkand, he had the whole of Mávará-un-Nahr under his command and rule, and all the nobles and princes of the country were compelled to swear allegiance to him. Some, however, whom he suspected of treachery, he treated as he had treated Amir Bayán Salduz. Others, whom he found he could rely on, he bestowed favours and distinctions upon. He entrusted the government of the conquered districts to his son Ilyás Khwája Oghlán, and he assigned to him a number of the amirs and soldiers of the army of Jatah, over whom he appointed Begjik. Amir Timur was charged with the most important duties in the administration of the State, under the orders of the young prince; and when the Khan had assured himself of the sagacity of Amir Timur, he handed over the whole direction of the State to him, and returned to his own seat of government. Tughluk Timur, in short, again left the country of Mávará-un-Nahr. He had given supreme authority over all the princes and people of Jatah, to Amir Begjik, and had deputed Amir Timur to look to the welfare of the people. But Amir Begjik did not obey the instructions of the Khán, for not only did he exercise tyranny and violence, but even attempted open revolt [against the Khán]. When Amir Timur saw that the orders of the Khán were not being complied with, and that, in consequence, the State would fall into disorder, he did not think fit to stay any longer in the country, but fled, with the intention of discovering Amir Husain. Since he could learn no news of the whereabouts of Amir Husain, he turned towards the deserts.[2]

[1] The term is *Ba Yásák rasánidan.* It may be taken to mean, to try a man and punish him (in this case with death) according to the system of the *Yásák.*

The *Yázák*, or *Yássá*, *Yáza*, etc. (sometimes called the *Turah*), was the legal code of the Mongols, said to have been instituted by Chingiz Khan. Pétis de la Croix hands it down in twenty-two sections, but says that there were other sections which have not been specified by the authorities he used. Deguignes summarises from Pétis, but omits the 22nd section. Section 3 of the Yásák forbids any prince, under pain of death, to cause himself to be proclaimed Khan, without having first been elected by a general assembly, or Diet (called *Kuriltai*), formed of the chiefs of the nation. (Pétis de la Croix, *Hist. de Genghiz Can*, p. 98: Deguignes, *Hist. des Huns*, iii., pp. 72–3.) Renaudot, on the authority of Mirkhund and Khundamir, calls the *Yáza* the religion of the Mongols, but this can hardly be correct. (*Ancient Accounts of India and China*, 1733, p. 139.) Baber often alludes to the *Turah*, and expressly says that they were not "of divine appointment," though they had been held in respect by all his forefathers. Erskine translates the word "Institutions" (of Chingiz Khan), and says, "they seem to have been a collection of the old usages of the Moghul tribes . . . probably merely traditionary, and never reduced into writing." In Baber's days they were still respected among the wandering tribes, but did not form the law of his kingdom, "since they had been introduced before the Musulman religion, and were, in many respects, inconsistent with the Koran." (*Baber*, xlviii., *seq.*) Sir H. Howorth has fully discussed the Yáza or Turah in the *Indian Antiquary* for July, 1882. In Amyot's *Dict. Tatare-Mantchou-Français* (1789, i., p. xviii.) *Toura* or *Taourát* is said to be the Arabic equivalent of *Yássá*.

[2] Mirza Haidar breaks off here at an interesting part of the adventures of Timur and Husain. The *Zafar-Nama* goes on to relate how Timur wandered

In short, the substance of what we find in the Moghul traditions is, that Tughluk Timur Khán's dominions extended as far as Samarkand, and even further, but no precise facts have come down to us. Amir Buláji, who has been already mentioned as having raised Tughluk Timur Khán to the Khánate, sought nine privileges for himself from the Khán, which privileges had been granted to his ancestors by Chingiz Khán, and which my family have inherited. I have seen them myself. They were written in Kunduz, in the Moghul language, and I mention this circumstance because, by it, the Moghuls prove that the Khán's rule extended as far as Kunduz. It is stated, in the *Zafar-Náma*, that the Khán died in the year 764. The Moghul traditions say that Tughluk Timur, at the age of 16, was brought from [the] Kálmák [country] by Amir Buláji, as has been related; at the age of 18 he became Khán, at the age of 24 he became a Musulmán, and died at the age of 34. He was born in the year 730.

CHAPTER VIII.

ILYÁS KHWÁJA KHÁN.

THE Moghuls have preserved no traditions concerning this Ilyás Khwája Khán, but I have heard my father mention his name, and the *Zafar-Náma* makes occasional mention of him, in connection with other events. These passages I have transcribed in substance.

CHAPTER IX.

RETURN OF AMIR HUSAIN AND AMIR TIMUR TO TAIKHÁN AND BADAKHSHÁN, AND THE TREATIES BETWEEN THEM.

THE two princes then proceeded to Kunduz, and there collected some troops from the tribe of Boldái.[1] Thence they marched towards Badakhshán, and

on through the deserts of Khiva, till at length he found Husain near the wells of Saghej; how they went on together to Khiva, where Takil, or Jakil, the governor, tried to seize them by treachery—a design which they frustrated by again taking to the desert, where they met with a series of adventures, until at last they fell in with friends, and collected a small force willing to follow them. (*Hist. de Timur Bec.*, i., pp. 45–54.) These were the adventures of Timur which attracted the attention of Gibbon.

[1] Or Buruldai—the reading is uncertain.

when they arrived at Taikhán,[1] they concluded a peace with the Kings of Badakhshán and effaced every trace of bitterness of feeling. From there again they went to Arhang,[2] where they crossed the river onto the side of Sáli-Sarái,[3] and advanced towards Khatlán; then, having traversed the desert, they arrived at a place called Gulak,[4] where they encamped. In accordance with the words "and we have ordained the night as a time for repose," they retired to rest. After Amir Timur had taken off his clothes, with the intention of going to bed, and had withdrawn his blessed feet from the fatiguing companionship of his boots, Amir Husain sent a person to beg him to come to him, and when he arrived, he found, among those present in the assembly, Pulád Bughá and Shir Bahrám. Amir Husain began to make complaints of Shir Bahrám to Amir Timur, saying: "We are now close upon the enemy; this is not the time for him to abandon us; it is not acting in an honourable way." Amir Timur did his best to induce Shir Bahrám not to desert them, but without success, and this latter set out for Biljaván.[5]

In the meanwhile, the news was confirmed that Tughluk Salduz and Kaikhusru were advancing with the army and many of the Amirs of Jatah, and besides these there were assembled, between Jálá[6] and the "Bridge of Stone" [*Pul i Sangin*],[7] Timur son of Bubakan, Sárik, Shengum, Tughluk Khwája brother of Haji Beg, Kuj Timur son of Begjik, and other commanders of thousands [*tuman*] and regiments [*kushun*] with fifty thousand

[1] *Taikhán* is often found written for Talikán. There were several places of this name in Khorasán and Persia, but the town alluded to here is the one which lies about forty-four miles east of Kunduz. Abul-feda tells us that it was distant from the border of "Khotal"—*i.e.*, Khatlán—seven farasangs, or some twenty-eight miles. (Reinaud's transl., ii., pt. 2, p. 207.)

[2] *Arhang* (or Arheng, or Arhenk) has been shown, by Sir H. Yule, to have been a small state lying "astride upon the Oxus," to the north-west of Talikán, and near the present Hazrat Imám. Pétis de la Croix mentions its being on the south of the Oxus, near Sáli-Sarái, but his geography is not always quite accurate. In the *Institutes of Timur*, Arhang is spoken of in connection with Khatlán, and as if adjoining that province (p. 90).

[3] *Sáli-Sarái* is marked by Pétis on the north bank of the Oxus, and may perhaps be represented by the present village of Sarai, shown on some modern maps about twelve miles below the mouth of the Kokcha. Sáli-Sarái is often mentioned in the *Zafar-Nama*, and was no doubt the site of a ford across the Oxus. (*Hist. de Timur Bec.*, i.)

[4] A village called *Guli-zindan* is marked on Mayef's map, about halfway between the Bridge and Baljuán, which may perhaps represent Gulak. (*Geo. Mag.*, Dec., 1876.) It is obviously the same place as that mentioned lower down, under the name of *Kulak* or *Dasht-i-Kulak* (p. 238).

[5] Baljuán—of modern maps.

[6] Or *Sar Jála*—probably a spot lying northward of the Bridge.

[7] This bridge is often mentioned by mediæval and even ancient authors. (See Yule in Wood's *Oxus*, p. lxxxii.) It spans the Upper Vakhsh (or Surkháb), where the river is crossed by the road leading from Baljuán, north-westward to Faizabad and Kafirnahán. The first modern description of the locality was that of Mr. Mayef, after his journey of 1875. He wrote: "Where the Vakhsh approaches the boundary of the Khanate of Bukhara, it rushes through a narrow valley, hemmed in by the steep slopes of the Nur-tágh and Khoja-Yukur [ranges]. This defile, at one of its narrowest parts, where the rocks approach each other within twenty paces, is spanned by the well-known stone bridge of Pul-i-Sengi. An exceedingly difficult path leads up to this bridge from the bank of the Vakhsh . . . . At many parts of it steps are cut into the rock. . . ." (*Geographical Mag.*, Dec., 1876, p. 328.) Kostenko's Gazetteer says the length of the bridge is ten paces, and that it is supported on two projecting rocks, rising high above the level of the river, which is not more than twenty paces in width. The steps cut in the rocks are also mentioned here. (*Russian-Turkistan Gazetteer*, Calcutta, 1882, ii., p. 182.)

men, though more than six thousand had deserted the royal camp. But Amir Timur placed firm trust in the assistance of God, and comforted his men with the verse, "How many armies small in number, have overcome infinite hosts, by the permission of God," which he seemed to hear repeated in his ear by a voice from the unseen world.

[Verses]: Though the ocean of the world be full of alligators,
And desert and mountain full of tigers,
If a man have good fortune for a friend,
Not a hair of his head will be touched.

With two thousand brave men, he marched out to meet the enemy, and the opposing forces met on the Stone Bridge. A battle ensued which lasted from early morning till nightfall; and during all that day these brave and experienced warriors fought, until they had no strength left to continue. Moreover the inequality of the forces was great.

Amir Timur, considering the situation, saw that victory could not be with his side, if the sword of valour were not brightened with the polish of good counsel, and he understood that if the arrow of courage were not let fly from the thumb-stall of deliberation, its whistling would not sound to them as news of triumph. These things he pondered in his mind, until the reed of assurance and conviction, painted a picture of welfare and safety upon the tablet of his enlightened intelligence.

CHAPTER X.

TIMUR'S PASSAGE OF THE RIVER AT THE STONE BRIDGE, AND THE FLIGHT OF THE ARMY OF JATAH.

Amir Timur ordered Amir Musa, Amir Muvayid Arlát and Uchkará Bahádur, with a force of 500 picked men, to wait for the enemy near the Stone Bridge, while he himself, with 1500 men, swam the river at midnight and took up his position on the mountains. On the following day, the sentinels of the enemy saw, by their footprints, that they had crossed the river during the night; and they were very much perturbed in consequence. When night set in, Amir Timur commanded his soldiers to light a great number of fires on the summits of the highest of the mountains; and at the sight of these fires the enemy were seized with fear and terror, so that they lost heart and fled. Thus did God, without the trouble of a battle, scatter this numerous army, which was in the proportion of ten warriors to one of their opponents. "Verily God giveth the victory to whomsoever He will."

The enemy being thrown into flight and confusion, Amir Timur rushed down the mountain with his army, like a raging lion or a mighty boiling torrent, and pursued them as far as Gujarát[1]—falling upon them with his life-taking sword and his soul-biting lance, till the road was covered with

[1] This name may read *Gujaráb*. I cannot identify the place.

the heaps of their slain. In this place he halted, victorious and happy, while Amir Husain with the rest of the army continued the pursuit. This victory helped to spread the fame of Amir Timur and much encouraged his troops. Feeling the reality and importance of the advantages he had just secured, Amir Timur again set out with two thousand men; and when he arrived at Kuhlagha,[1] the people of Kesh and the districts round about, fleeing from the army of Jatah, kept coming to him in detachments, with offers to serve him if he would protect them. Out of the two thousand men Amir Timur had brought with him, he selected three hundred as his own special bodyguard. With these he advanced, commanding the rest to stay behind. He then sent on two hundred of these men, under the Amirs Sulaimán Barlás, Chakui Barlás, Bahrám Jaláir, Jaláluddin Barlás, Saifuddin and Yultimur, to Kesh, telling them to divide into four squadrons, and ordering every man to suspend from either side of his horse, a large leafy branch, in order that much dust might be raised and so cause the governor of Kesh, if he saw them, to beat a retreat.[2] They carried out his orders exactly, so that when they entered the plains of Kesh, the governor, frightened at the sight of so much dust, took to flight, and they entered the town, where they occupied themselves with the appointment of officers and the like.

Thus the boundless favour of God descended in such a manner upon this king, that by means of sparks of fire he was able to put an army to flight, and with dust to conquer a town.

[Verse]: The evil eye was distant from him, for greater successes than these it is impossible to conceive.

At that time Ilyás Khwája Khán was encamped at Tásh Arighi, which is four *farasangs* distant from Kesh; he had round him his nobles and princes and an innumerable army. About this time Tughluk Timur Khán died. Ulugh Timur and Amir Hamid came to announce the news to Ilyás Khwája Khán and to bring him back to his tribe, that he might rule in his father's stead.

Meanwhile, Amir Timur, with one hundred chosen men, having marched all the night, came to Khuzár, and when day broke, the people of that town learnt the arrival of that royal prince and hastened out to kiss the ground in obeisance to him. He then combined the troops of Khuzár and Kesh, and put Khwája Sálibari in command of the rearguard. With this mighty army he set out for Chekadálik, and on arrival there, pitched his camp. At that place too, he was joined by Muhammad, son of Salduz, with seven regiments, and he remained there seven days. In the meanwhile, Amir Husain arrived with his own forces, and with those that Amir Timur had left behind at Kuhlagha. Shir Bahrám also, who had separated from them in the desert [or plain] of Gulak, in order to visit his own people, now rejoined them, after an absence of forty-three days. They then all set forth together, under the command of Amir Timur and Amir Husain, in the direction of Khuzár, and on their arrival there, visited the tomb of Khwája Resmes,[3] in the name of whose blessed spirit they made a solemn alliance and swore eternal friendship.

[1] The Iron Gates.

[2] Lit. "and if a *darugha* [superintendent] were there he would flee."—R.

[3] There appears to be something wrong about this name. It should be, probably, the tomb of Shams-ud-Din.

CHAPTER XI.

THE DREAM OF AMIR TIMUR, WHICH HE LOOKS UPON AS A GOOD OMEN, AND WHICH INDUCES HIM TO MAKE WAR ON ILYÁS KHWÁJA KHÁN.

THE Prophet (upon whom be the peace of God) said: "True dreams are one of the forty-six gifts of prophecy," and the explanation of this tradition is that when the all-knowing, all-powerful God (may He be exalted and magnified), places upon the forehead of some great person the distinctive mark of His favour, He so enlightens him that He causes him to understand the secrets of the invisible world, reveals unto his human spirit the things that are to come to pass, and makes him aware of occurrences that have not yet taken place. Joseph was informed, by revelation, of the coming of his father and brothers several years before that event took place. And Muhammad, Prince of the Prophets, had revealed to him the conquest of Mekka.

In the same way, as Amir Timur was one day reflecting upon the straits he was in, and the smallness of his army in comparison with that of the enemy, and considering what would be the best line of action, he fell asleep, and heard a voice say to him, in eloquent language: "Be of good cheer and grieve not, for God has given you victory." When he awoke from his slumber, he asked, "Did anyone speak?" All present replied, "Indeed not!" So he was convinced that the words were spoken by a voice from heaven, and that the sweet-scented breeze of good news had blown from the rose-garden of God's graciousness and favour. His confidence in the assistance of God was absolute, and he went to Amir Husain with fresh enthusiasm and renewed vigour, telling him what had happened. The good tidings were spread about among all the troops, and they were much encouraged; their obedient hearts blossomed out, as do the rosebuds with the zephyr of the morn.

CHAPTER XII.

BATTLE OF AMIR HUSAIN AND AMIR TIMUR WITH THE ARMY OF JATAH. VICTORY OF THE AMIRS OVER THE JATAH.

AMIR HUSAIN and Amir Timur, having offered up praise and thanksgiving to the Padishah of Padishahs (may His name be exalted), mounted their horses and began to make preparations for battle. They divided the army into two parts; Amir Husain commanded the right wing, and raised the victorious standard, while Amir Timur led the left wing of his troops, who were so accustomed to victory. Having arranged all this, and having put the army into order of battle, they went forward.

The enemy meanwhile were at Tásh Arighi, and they, in the same manner, divided their forces into two parts; Ilyás Khwája Khán and Amir Hamid commanding the left wing, and Amir Tuk Timur and Amir Begjik the right. The opposing armies, having drawn themselves up in order of battle,[1] attacked one another with vigorous onslaught.

[Verses]: The world and time ranged themselves on his side,
You would have thought he was about to overcome the universe.
Nor the shining sun nor the moon looked more brilliant than did his army.
His troops on a sudden raised a loud cry
And their spear points made the clouds bright.

The fighting began at a place called Kaba Matan, and clamour and shouting filled the vault of the heavens. The first attack was made upon the soldiers of Amir Timur, by the scouts of the enemy, who were boasting of the superiority of their army in numbers, and were burning for the fray.

But Timur, keeping his foot as firmly fixed upon the spot where he was standing, as was his kingdom upon its foundations, seized his bow and arrow and made his left arm like an *Alif* and his right arm like a *Dál*.[2]
[Verses] . . . .

And his soldiers, in imitation of their king, discharged their missiles into the souls of the enemy, just as the starry army of the moon let fly their shooting stars; and the reed of the arrow—according to the words "we have ordained them as missiles against the evil spirits"—made such writing with the blood of the scouts, that not one of them remained alive. . . .[3]

Among those slain were Tuk Timur, a Beg, brother of Begjik, Daulat Shah, and two princes besides, who were both of them leaders of the other army.

[Verses]: Of all these daring men not one was left,
But all fell wretchedly, of life bereft.

The two armies then rushed upon one another, and blood flowed from the enemy as if it were tears from a thousand eyes.

[Verses]: They charged one another like great mountains;
The desert became a sea of blood;
You would have said that tulips had
Sprung up on the face of the earth.[4]

The attacks and charges of the veteran warriors grew more frequent, and the waves of the ocean of combat increased. Amir Timur, in accordance with the blessed promise (thanks be to God, who has aided and blessed us), was able to overcome and put to rout this enormous army, in comparison with which his own was but as a drop of rain. "And there is no victory but from God."

Amir Ilyás Khwája, Amir Begjik, Iskandar Oghlán, Amir Hamid and Amir Yusuf were taken prisoners. But the generosity, common to all Turks, was favourable to the Khán, for the soldiers who had captured him, when they recognised him, without saying anything to their leaders, mounted him

[1] *Yasál.* Pétis de la Croix says "formed a crescent."—R.
[2] That is, he drew his bow to the ear, straightening his left arm like the straight Arabic letter *alif*, and bending his right like the crooked *dál*.
[3] The rhetoric, which continues for some lines, is omitted.—R.
[4] This is in allusion to the blood-red tulips which cover the ground in spring, in some parts of the Central Asian steppes.

and Begjik on horseback and set them at liberty. But the other captives they kept bound. On the same night, Amir Timur continued his march until he reached the River Yám, in order to cut off the retreat of the enemy, of whom many had been killed.

[Verse]: From their blood, the water of the stream became like wine.

Amir Chagu and Amir Saifuddin, at his command, marched against Samarkand. They conquered this town in the beginning of the year 765 of the Hajra [A.D. 1363], corresponding to the year of the Crocodile [Lui] of the Tartar cycle.

Amir Timur, who was attended by success in all his endeavours and desires, hastened to hold counsel with Amir Husain and Shir Bahrám, and then set out in pursuit of the enemy. Having crossed the river at Khojand, he fixed his royal camp at Tashkand, and there, in order that his good fortune might not be quite perfect, he was afflicted with a few days' sickness. [Verses] . . . .

Both Amir Timur and Amir Husain were for a short time a prey to a malady in that place. But they were soon released from the house of sickness; and the illustrious Princess Uljái Turkán arrived in safety from Kar.[1]

[Verse]: Bilkis again returned to Sulaimán.

Amir Timur then resolved to return, and therefore recrossed the river at Khojand. Being seized with a desire to hunt, he threw out a ring of beaters round a large extent of country, and Amir Husain did the same thing in a place called Dazák Bulbul. They set out from opposite directions towards Akár Kamár. Several days were spent in pleasure and amusement, according to the words, "Seize the opportunity while you may," and then they returned in safety to Samarkand.

At the joyful advent of this augmenter of happiness and decorator of kingdoms, the people of that district were illumined by the protecting dust of the royal prince, so that the evils of the buffetings of events, which had crept in among high and low, were cured by the healing properties of his humanity and encouragement.

CHAPTER XIII.

CONFERENCE [KURILTAI] BETWEEN AMIR HUSAIN AND AMIR TIMUR; AND THE RAISING OF KÁBIL SHÁH OGHLÁN TO THE RANK OF KHÁN.

When the countries of Mávará-un-Nahr and Turkistán, together with all their dependencies, had been delivered from the domination and oppression of the people of Jatah, no one of the chief princes or more important generals

[1] There is nothing to show where the first part of this campaign took place, and I cannot trace the names. It seems that the Jatah army invaded the valley of the Zaráfshán, and if so *Yám* may stand for Jám, to the south-west of Samarkand, and *Kaba Matan* for Mitan, to the north-west of it. *Kar* may also be read *Kaz* or *Gaz*.

would submit to the orders and commands of another;[1] for all the chiefs of tribes, making boast of the large number of their subjects and followers, wished to retain independence and would suffer no control. For it has been said: A number of people without a central unity to direct them, will perish, and a kingdom without a ruler to give laws to the inhabitants, and prevent them transgressing the same, will most certainly fall into a state of disorder.

[Verses]: A world without a leader is like a body without a head.
A headless body is worth less than the dust of the road.

Under these conditions, Amir Husain and Amir Timur took counsel together, and determined that it would be advisable to set up, as Khán, one of the descendants of Chaghatai Khán, while for the execution of this plan they convoked an assembly of all the chiefs and princes, in the year 765 of the Hajra [A.D. 1363-4], to discuss the settlement of the affairs of the State. They finally determined to appoint Kábil Sháh Oghlán as Khán. He was the son of Durji, son of Ilchikádi, son of Davá Khán. In order to avoid the trials and troubles of public life, he had taken to ways of poverty and solitude, and had clothed himself like a darvish. They resolved to divest him of his poor garments, and to array his noble figure in the richly-embroidered robes of the Khánship. To this end:

[Verses]: They prepared a splendid banquet,
That what was small might become great.
They sought the whole world over
For gold and silver and gifts.

They succeeded in placing Kábil Sháh Oghlán upon the throne; and, as was customary among the Turkish Sultans, he was presented with a goblet.[2]

[Verses]:
All the mighty rulers and proud princes, at one time
Bent the knee nine times in obeisance to him.

Amir Haidar Andarkhudi[3] was given over to Zinda Hásham, who executed him on that same night. [Verses] . . . .

When the country had once again been brought under the rule of Amir Timur, he made a great display of his liberality and hospitality, and gave a great feast in honour of Amir Husain. His own stewards prepared the banquet.

Amir Timur showed much favour to his own special subjects, and bestowed suitable presents on Amir Husain.

[Verses]: He gave him the most magnificent gifts,
Such as horses, swords, helmets and belts.

Since the father of Amir Haidar was on the most friendly terms with Amir Timur, he was invited to the feast; for his intelligence had received brightness from the polish of experience of long years. With him and Amir

[1] The meaning is perhaps: they would not submit to Timur and Husain.—R.

[2] That is: They presented him with the royal goblet of the Sultans of Turkistan.—R.

[3] Of Andarkhud, or *Andkhui*.

Husain, he discussed the advisability of setting Amir Hamid and Iskandar Oghlán at liberty; and Amir Husain (in spite of the words

[Verses]: When your enemy falls into your hands
Keep him at a distance, lest he hurt you again and you will repent)

out of consideration for the noble-mindedness of Amir Timur, did not refuse his entreaty, but gave sanction for the two prisoners to be released.

As soon as Amir Husain had set out for Sáli-Sarái, his residence in his own province, Amir Timur sent Amir Dáud and Amir Saifuddin to release the two prisoners, and to bring them back with all respect and honour; but Báyázid and Aiman, who had the custody of Amir Hamid and Iskandar Oghlán, on seeing the two messengers, thought they had come to kill Amir Hamid, and therefore hastened to put him to death, one giving him a blow with a mace and the other striking him with a sword. Such was the end of Amir Hamid. When Amir Husain heard of this, he said: "The work of the servant was better than the work of the master," and at once sent a messenger in search of Iskandar Oghlán, to kill him.

[Verse]: Against the arrow of destiny there is no shield.

During the winter of that year, Amir Husain and Amir Timur devoted their attention to the internal affairs of the State, so that the country attained a condition of perfect peace and prosperity.

CHAPTER XIV.

THE BATTLE OF THE MIRE.[1]

From the garden abounding in thorns and adorned with flowers, the sweet zephyr reached to nostrils of those whose souls had been sent upon the battle-field of misfortune and grief. They heard the good tidings that God often crowns our best endeavours and most fervent wishes with calamities and hardships. [Verses] . . . .

Happiness often results from the traces left by misfortune, and a state of equanimity and success often has its origin in distress and failure.

[Verses.] . . . .

The course of events in the time of Amir Timur is a proof and example of the above truths.

For when the winter (during which he had devoted his time to the peaceful administration of the affairs of his State) had passed, and spring at length arrived; (When the warrior spring had raised the standards of the tulips and

[1] Known as the battle of *Lai*—*i.e.*, mud or mire. It appears to have been fought on the right bank of the Sihun (Jaxartes) between Chináz and (old) Tashkend. Pétis translates: "Bataille des Bourbiers."

had led out his army of green plants into the plains of gardens and meadows,

[Verses]: The morning breeze led out his army towards the fertile plains
And made ready the weapons and arms of war.
He made spears of the buds and shields of the roses,
The spearpoints he made from sharpened thorns)

[When spring set in] news came that the hosts of Jatah were again on their way towards this country [*i.e.*, Mávará-un-Nahr]. Amir Timur began at once to collect his army together, and sent to inform Amir Husain of the report. The latter ordered Pulád Bughá and Zinda Hásham, son of Muhammad Aperdi, and Malik Bahádur to collect their forces and set out with all possible speed to join Amir Timur. They met, and at once marched together against the enemy. On their arrival at Akár,[1] they inspected the cavalry and beasts of burden, and remained there several days to take advantage of the excellence of the pasturage. Departing thence, they crossed the River Sihun[2] and encamped [on the opposite side]. Amir Husain hastened on in the direction of the enemy, with a large body of men, till he came to the banks of the river, where he caught sight of some of their outposts.

Amir Timur now removed his camp to the river-side, between Chináz and Tashkend, and commanded his men to fortify their tents, which they did with great care. Meanwhile Amir Husain crossed the Sihun with his whole army, and halted in the entrenchments [*murchál*] destined for his troops. The enemy had also encamped on the same side of the river, having reached it at early morn. Amir Timur and Amir Husain once more advanced, and as soon as the scouts of the two forces came in sight, preparations were made for battle and each army was arrayed in fighting order. Amir Husain commanded the right wing, and Tirlánji Irlát led the rearguard; his vanguard was under the command of Ujá Betu Irdi,[3] Shir Bahrám, Pulád Bughá, Farhád Aberdi, Malik Bahádur, and many other valiant soldiers. Amir Timur, who was the soul of the whole army, led the left wing, and he appointed Amir Sár Bughá, with the tribe of Kipchák, to the rearguard, and Timur Khwája Oghlán to the vanguard. Close at his side he kept Amir Chágu, Amir Saifuddin, Amir Murád Barlás, Abbás Bahádur, and many other brave men of the sword.

In this order they attacked the enemy, but in pursuance with the words: "It is an evil day for you when you boast of your own strength or numbers," they were not spared from an unexpected punishment, for the army of Jatah, which, in spite of its superiority in numbers, had been defeated at Kaba Matan, now that they found their opponents exceeded them in numbers, had recourse to magic, and sought aid from the Jadah stone, which possessed supernatural properties.[4]

[1] This spot must have been near the left bank of the Sihun, not far below Khojand, and is probably the place called Akár Kamár above (p. 29).

[2] Some MSS. of the *Zafar-Nama* say they crossed the Sihun *at* Khojand.

[3] This name might read Ulja Yetu Aberdi.—R.

[4] The superstition of the *Jadah* stone is often alluded to by Baber. Erskine says the stone was called by the Arabs *Hajar-ul-Mattar*, or the rain stone, by the Turks *Yedeh-tásh*, and by the Persians *Sang-i-deh*. The author, a little lower down, speaks of Jadah as the name of a magician. The stone had the virtue of causing the rain to fall or to cease; but in the course of time the original stone, which was given by Noah to Japhet, was either lost, or the name

[Verses]: The army of Jatah had not strength for the fight,
So they sought help from the magic stone.
With the stone of Jadah, who was a magician,
They filled the world with wind and rain,
The clouds roared with thunder and the winds howled.
A thunderbolt fell upon the earth.

Although the sun was in Orion, a host of dark clouds suddenly filled the sky. The thunder resounded and the lightning flashed. The elements rushed out from the ambush of destiny into the open plain of the ether, and the thunderclaps re-echoed round the azure vault of heaven. The arrows of lightning were shot out, in all directions, from the bow of the thunder-clouds, and the rain shot down its whistling darts. It seemed as if the Fates had again become a prey to the love of rebellion and confusion. Such a quantity of water descended from the eyes of the stars, that the Deluge seemed to occur a second time. And the voice of Noah was again heard to pray for the cessation of the waters of heaven.

The beasts of the field began to swim about in the water like fishes; and the feet of the horses stuck so fast in the mire, that the skin of their bellies adhered to the crust of the earth, while the damp caused their bones to become bare. They were afflicted with *Asterkha*, and began to lose their flesh and become paralytic, their bones being loosened. The feathers of the arrows fell out: the notches came off; while clothes and accoutrements became so heavy with the damp, that neither cavalry nor infantry were able to advance. In consequence of all this, our host[1] lost their confidence and courage. But the army of the enemy, remaining where they were, covered themselves over with felt, and as far as they were able, preserved their clothes and arms from the violence of the rain. When our army came up to

---

of God, which had been engraved upon it, was worn away. "It is pretended, however, that others, with a similar virtue, and bearing the same name, are still found among the Turks; and the more superstitious affirm that they were originally produced and multiplied by some mysterious sort of generation from the original stone given by Noah to his son." Mir Izzat Ullah, who was sent into Central Asia by Moorcroft, mentions the Jadah stone as one of the wonders of Yarkand. "He says," writes Erskine, "that it is taken from the head of a horse or a cow; and that if certain ceremonies be previously used, it inevitably produces rain or snow. He who performs the ceremonies is called Yedehchi. Izzat Ullah, though, like Baber, professes his belief in the virtues of the stone, yet acknowledges that he was never an eye-witness of its effects." (Memoirs of Baber, Intr., p. xlvii.; also Klaproth's translation of Izzat Ullah in *Mag. Asiatique*, ii., p. 33.)

In the *Habib-us-Siyar* an instance is given of Tului, son of Chingiz Khán, having recourse to the Jadah stone (here *Sang-i-yadda*) to produce a fall of snow as a means of concealment, when hard pressed by the enemy during his invasion of China in 1230. (See Price's *Mah. Hist.*, ii., p. 542, who translates the word "lapis imbrifer.")

The word *Jadah*, it may be remarked here, has no connection with *Jade*. It was in reality, as Sir H. Yule tells us, a bezoar, or antidote, much used in the Middle Ages by the Arabs and others. The bezoar was usually a hard concretion found in the bodies of animals, to which antidotal virtues were ascribed. "The bezoar," he adds, "was sometimes called *snake stone*, and erroneously supposed to be found in the head of a snake." (Glossary, p. 68.)

A complete note on the Jadah stone, containing numerous extracts from Oriental authors, will be found in Quatremère's *Hist. des Mongols en Perse*, p. 428.

[1] Viz., the army of Timur and Husain.

them, they threw aside their felt coverings and offered battle with fresh horses and uninjured arms; then the combat began in good earnest.

[Verses]: The cries and shoutings of the two armies
Fill the whole world, right and left.

The spheres ring again with the cries of the heroes and the sound of the *kerranái*.[1]

Amir Timur, by the aid of God, made a charge with the left wing, and overcame the right wing of the enemy, which was led by Shenkummuyán, brother of Amir Hamid; and when Ilyás Khwája Khán saw this, he fled in confusion. But meanwhile fortune had deserted the right wing of our army, for the enemy's left, led by Sharáwal and Háji Beg, attacked and overcame our right; they drove Tilánji[2] and Zinda Hásham back to where Amir Husain was posted, and the body-guard of the latter being terrified, turned and fled. But Pulád Bughá and Shir Bahrám stood their ground and displayed the utmost courage. Háji Beg continued the attack and outflanked our right. Farhád and Orong Timur[3] were astounded at the sight of this. But Amir Shams-ud-Din, on the other hand, having withdrawn the hand of bravery from the sleeve of temerity, made, with his men, a great display of courage.

And now the fuel of the ardour of Amir Timur took fire; he seized his sword

[Verses]: And made such sparks fly from it that
The sun in comparison seemed dark.
He charged down like a roaring lion.
[He wore] his iron helmet, bearing the crest of a dragon.

He charged the enemy with seventeen regiments [*kushun*]; the wind of his onslaught threw fire and fear upon the harvest of their stability, so that Amir Shams-ud-Din, terrified at the fierceness of Timur's attack, was obliged to turn the reins of power from the field of battle, and to set the face of helplessness and defeat in the direction of flight. This success of Amir Timur gave Amir Husain an opportunity to re-assemble his troops, and having done so, he stood his ground.

[Verses]: From the victory of this host-crushing Sháh
The army received new life into its body.

Amir Timur sent his servant Tábán Bahádur to Amir Husain, saying: "It is time for the Amirs to advance. Let us, together, make such a charge that we may cause an earthquake among the proud princes of the enemy: so that they may lose all power to resist us and all strength to oppose us."

But in proportion as the power of Amir Timur rose, so did the star of felicity of Amir Husain begin to decline, and his happiness to approach the evening of distress, according to the text, "God doth not work any change in the people, until they have altered their own individual selves." During this period, his nature underwent a great change; he lost his former stability

[1] A kind of horn or trumpet. Pétis de la Croix says it was a trumpet eight feet long, used in the army. (*Hist. de Timur Bec*, i., p. 87.)
[2] May read: Petlanji.—R.
[3] Or perhaps: Erek Timur.—R.

of character, and began to adopt evil habits and practise evil deeds. [Thus] when Tábán Bahádur came before him, Amir Husain abused him much in words, and then struck him so violently that he fell to the ground.

Amir Timur then sent Malik and Hamdami, who were two of Amir Husain's adherents, to tell their master that he must most certainly come, in order that no time should be lost; but Amir Husain, having heard the message, began to abuse the messengers and let loose upon them the tongue of violence and menace; then he added: "Did I run away that you should thus press me to advance? Whether you are victorious or whether the enemy carry the day, there is not one of you shall save his soul from my avenging hand."

Thereupon Malik and Hamdami, much enraged, left his presence and hastened to Amir Timur, to whom, on their arrival, they said, "It is no use your persisting in the fight." Amir Timur was persuaded by them and did not oppose their advice, but withdrew the hand of intention. Since the ranks of both armies had been so much broken that the left wings of the opposing forces were facing one another, each soldier encamped [lay down to rest] where he happened to find himself.

[Verses]: The soldiers of both armies lay down to rest
And did not stir from their places till day had broken.

During that night Amir Husain sent several times to request that Amir Timur should come to him, but the prince would not give ear to his entreaties. [Verses.] . . . .

When, on the following morning, the two hosts again joined in battle, the army of Jatah was routed and fled. Our troops were pursuing, when they suddenly caught sight of the standard [*Tugh* or *Tuk*] of Amir Shams-ud-Din, who had separated himself with a large body of soldiers from the rest of the army. Thereupon the pursuers abandoned their object and turned to attack Shams-ud-Din, while the defeated army again rallied and made a violent onslaught upon our men. Thus our side, after it had gained a victory, was in its turn defeated, and in their haste to get away, many of our men perished in the mud and swamps. The enemy pursued them and put numbers of them to the sword, so that there remained nearly ten thousand slain of our forces on the field of battle.

This battle took place on the 1st day of Ramazán of the year 766 of the Hajra [A.D. 1365], corresponding to the year of the Serpent (Yibán) of the Moghul cycle; and astrologers have shown that this event coincided with the tenth conjunction of the triple aerial conjunctions in the Scorpion. This I only mention, that my history may be complete, but I do not wish to infer that events are caused by celestial influences, for "God alone has influence over creation."

After this defeat, the princes retired to Kesh. All the chiefs of tribes began to cross the Jihun with their people. Amir Husain said to Amir Timur: "It would be expedient for you to cross the river with your household and troops"; but Timur replied, "Others may cross if they like, but as for me, my patriotism will not permit me to leave my country to the molestation of foreigners. I will again collect an army and attack the enemy."

Amir Husain then left him and retired to Sáli-Sarái; then he made all his people cross the Jihun, and taking an out-of-the-way route, he reached a place called Shibartu, where he halted. From that place he despatched spies, intending, if these brought news of the approach of the army of Jatah, to take flight at once towards Hindustán.[1]

As soon as Amir Husain had departed from Kesh, Amir Timur turned his mind to preparations for meeting the enemy. He mustered twelve regiments and sent forward eight of them, under the command of Timur Khwája Oghlán, Charuchi,[2] and Abbás Bahádur, to reconnoitre the country round Samarkand. But on the way Charuchi took to drinking much wine, and the liquor made a strong impression on him: as has been said [Arabic]:

> Wine is like the wind: When it passes over a perfume, it becomes fragrant: but becomes tainted when it passes over a corpse.

He became intoxicated and began to talk wildly, and very much frightened Daud Khwája and Hindusháh by saying: Such a one (meaning Amir Timur) purposes to send somebody to seize you, to take you before Amir Husain, and to have you killed without delay. [His companions] consequently were much alarmed, and running away, gave themselves up to the enemy. When they reached Kukung, they met the reconnoitring party of the army of Jatah, under the command of Kapak Timur, son of Ulugh Tokatmur Sharáwal, and Angirchák, son of Háji Beg. They offered to act as guides to them and brought them to the place where Timur Khwája Oghlán, Charuchi and Abbás were stationed; these they put to flight, together with all their forces. When Amir Timur heard all this, he knew that he must be patient yet a little longer, and that impetuosity was of no avail.

He crossed the river at Amuyah[3] and went and encamped at Balkh, where he again assembled his scattered tribe. He called to his side Tumán Kapak Khán and Tumán Bughái Salduz; he also appointed a certain number of men to defend the banks of the river, and get what news they could of what was passing on the other side.

Timur Khwája Oghlán was punished for his misconduct, and from this point Fortune continued to favour Amir Timur. [Verses.] . . . .

[1] That is, Husain fled to the Hindu Kush, whence he might, if necessary, take refuge in India. *Shibartu* is no doubt the pass often mentioned by Baber, which seems to have been much used in those days. It is usually called *Shibr* or *Shabar* nowadays, and will be found on modern maps a little to the east of Bámián. For a refugee crossing the Oxus at Sáli-Sarái, the Shibr Pass would be one of the most convenient, if not the nearest route, to take towards India. (See *Baber's Memoirs*, p. 139, and other places.)

[2] Or Cha-urchi.

[3] *Amuyah*, or *Amol*, was a ford over the Amu or Oxus, in frequent use during the Middle Ages, and in the time of Timur. There was also a town of the same name, which stood near the bank of the river, in a direction about south-west from Bokhara, and either on, or very near, the site of the present Charjui. (See note, p. 170.)

CHAPTER XV.

SIEGE OF SAMARKAND BY THE ARMY OF JATAH.

In the meanwhile, the army of Jatah reached Samarkand. Now at that time, this town had no citadel, but Mauláná-Zada Samarkandi, Mauláná Khardak Bukhári and Abu Nasr Kului Naddáf influenced the people of Samarkand to defend and fortify the town; and, despite their want of a princely leader, they offered stout resistance to the besiegers. They were bent on saving their city from the domination and tyranny of the people of Jatah. But when the inhabitants were beginning to tire of their efforts and to lose perseverance, God came to their aid and caused a pestilence to appear among the horses of the cavalry of Jatah, so that three-fourths of them died. Consequently, the besiegers were obliged to retire, and the great majority of them returned on foot, with their quivers strapped to their backs. Since the people of Samarkand had so well defended their State, and had offered such determined opposition to their enemies, those among them who had most power became inflated with pride, and tried to obtain precedence over their equals by stirring up sedition and rebellion in the town.

At the time of the retreat of the Jatah army, Amir Timur had sent Abbás Bahádur to Kuhlagha[1] to spy out the land of Jatah, and when he was informed of the events above related—of the state of the people of Jatah and of the retreat of their army—he sent to Amir Husain to inform him also of the state of affairs, and to advise him to proceed in the direction of that country. When Amir Husain heard the news which the messenger brought, he was beyond measure pleased, and immediately set out from Shibartu towards Sáli-Sarái. Amir Timur, having caused his household and people to cross the river, had sent them to their native land, and had started himself on horseback to meet Amir Husain. They met in the plain of Baklán,[2] and having embraced one another in the most respectful manner, they held a long discussion about what had already happened, as well as about the future. It was finally decided that they should proceed together towards Samarkand early in the following spring. Then Amir Timur returned, crossed the Jihun, and encamped at Karshi. Karshi is so-called because Kapak Khán built a palace at [that spot which is] 2½ *farasangs* distance from Nakhsheb, and in the Moghul language a palace is called *Karshi*.

There Amir Timur remained during that winter; and he caused to be erected on the spot a citadel [Hisár], which was completed by the end of the winter.

[1] The Iron Gate.

[2] Or Baghlán, which would be on the direct road from the Shibr Pass to Sáli-Sarái.

CHAPTER XVI.

THE LAST DAYS OF ILYÁS KHWÁJA KHÁN, AND EVENTS THAT TOOK PLACE AFTER HIS DEATH.—THE DOMINATION OF KAMARUDDIN.

There are no traditions or stories extant among the Moghuls relating to Ilyás Khwája Khán. We learn, however, from the *Zafar-Náma*, that it was upon him that the Khánship devolved after the death of Tughluk Timur Khán. During his reign, there took place his victory of the battle of the Mire, the siege of Samarkand and the abandonment thereof, on account of the epidemic which fell among his horses. He only survived these events a very short time. But an account of the events immediately following the death of Tughluk Timur Khán, as recorded in Moghul tradition, will be given below. For, although knowledge of what happened after the death of Ilyás Khwája Khán is with God only, we know, from Moghul traditions, what occurred after the death of Tughluk Timur Khán. From these sources we learn that there were five brothers: (1) Amir Tulik, who has been mentioned in connection with the conversion of the Khán to Islám; (2) Amir Buláji; (3) Amir Shams-ud-Din, who is mentioned in the *Zafar-Náma* as having taken part in the battle of the Mire (which passage I have copied into this book); (4) Amir Kamaruddin, of whom I shall speak later; (5) Amir Shaikh-i-Daulat, of whom no traces remain.

After Amir Tulik's death, the office of *Ulusbegi* was given to Amir Buláji, and when this latter followed his brother to the dwellings of eternity, the office of *Ulusbegi* devolved upon his son Amir Khudáidád. But Amir Kamaruddin, going down on his knees before the Khán, said to him: "The office of my brother should first come to me, for his son is only seven years of age and is not fit for the duties attached to the position." Tughluk Timur Khán would not pay any attention to him, but appointed the then seven-year-old Amir Khudáidád to the office. Kamaruddin was a violent man, and was angry at being superseded by a child of seven; but he could do nothing. When, subsequently, the Khán died he revolted. The *Zafar-Náma*, on the other hand, says that he raised a rebellion after the death of Ilyás Khwája Khán. However this may be, it appears that on the death of the Khán, Kamaruddin gave vent to that rancour which he had so long cherished in his breast, and (according to Moghul traditions) put to death in one day, eighteen sons of the Khán, and assumed the style of Khán for himself. The country of Moghulistán fell into a state of disorder.

One of Tughluk Timur Khán's sons, who was still at the breast, being concealed by Amir Khudáidád, and his mother, Mir Aghá, was spared. Kamaruddin sent everywhere in search of him, but they were successful in hiding the child from his spies.

Kamaruddin devoted his attention to the affairs of the State, but in consequence of the hostility of the Amirs, there was disorder and strife in the country. Moreover, the invasion of Moghulistán, which Amir Timur and his army undertook at that time, was a serious obstacle to internal progress. Meanwhile Amir Khudáidád sent Khizir Khwája Khán from Káshghar to the hills that are between Káshghar and Badakhshán, that he might be safe from the machinations of Kamaruddin; which matter shall be presently related, but first of all it will be well to give an account of Kamaruddin and his times.

CHAPTER XVII.

HISTORY OF KAMARUDDIN.

It has already been said that Kamaruddin tried to assume supreme authority, but that he met with determined opposition from the Amirs. Thus it was that Kumzah, together with Uzbeg Timur (who was of the tribe of Karáit), went over to the side of Amir Timur. Then Amir Timur raised an army, and himself remaining within his own dominions, sent Amir Bahrám Jaláir, Khitái Bahádur, and Shaikh Ali Bahádur to the territory of Almátu.[1] On reaching the banks of the river Áishah Khátun they attacked the men of the Karáit.[2] After this battle, having concluded a peace, they returned. But Amir Timur not approving the peace, invaded the country in person. This expedition is related in the *Zafar-Náma* as follows:—

The successful Amir Timur, who when he had once undertaken any business was never content till he had carried it through to the end, was dissatisfied with the gentle way in which his generals had treated the enemy, in watering the plains of enmity and warfare with peace. For this reason he sent royal mandates in all directions for troops to be collected [verses] . . . . A victorious and veteran army assembled before the palace of the Sháh—an

[1] The modern *Vierny*. (See note, p. 182.)

[2] Properly *Karai*, or *Kirai*, is the name of the tribe, though it is sometimes written *Girai*. The final *t* is merely the Mongol plural. (See note, p. 16, above; also, for some remarks on this passage and the word "Karait," Howorth ii., pp. 13, 14.)

army countless as the sand of the desert. When he had passed Sairám and Yangi[1] in safety, with his victorious standard, the enemy fled before him, and he reached a place called Sangarigháj,[2] when many prisoners and much booty fell into the hands of his conquering host.

At Adun Kuri,[3] Amir Musá and Zinda Háshám, in spite of all the former benefits they had received from Amir Timur, again began to devise plans of treason and deceit, and with treacherous designs conspired together, [taking into their confidence] the son of Khizir Yasuri, named Abu Ishák. They took a solemn oath that when they reached Kará Samán they would by some stratagem seize the 'Lord of the Conjunction' while hunting, and they laughed over the thought of their foolish plan. The Khánzáda Abu Maáli Turmadi and Shaikh Abu Lais of Samarkand, who were already sworn enemies of Amir Timur, now joined in this conspiracy.

But some one happening to get knowledge of the affair, informed Amir Timur thereof. Thereupon his majesty summoned the offenders to appear before him. They were brought in [and thrust] upon their knees, and on being interrogated, were found guilty of high treason and rebellion.

But as the Queen Sarái Mulk Khánim[4] was the niece of Amir Musá, and because the chaste Princess Akka Begi had been promised in marriage to him, Amir Timur said to him: "Although the crime you have committed is a grave one, nevertheless as we are relations, I will forgive you and take no vengeance upon you. [Verses] . . . . Your connection with me and your white beard have given you hope of life. Were it not for these, I should give the command for your evil-intentioned head to be severed from your body." And to the Khánzáda he said: "As your family is connected with the household of the Prophet (upon all of whose descendants be peace) I shall not consent to your receiving any ill-treatment; you must however quit this country." He commanded Abu Lais to make the pilgrimage to the Hijáz. The son of Khizir Yasuri, being the brother of the wife of Amir Saifuddin, appealed to the clemency of the 'Lord of the Conjunction,' and so escaped from the abyss; thus the tablet of his soul was cleansed of its sins with the pure water of royal beneficence and mercy. A royal mandate was issued, ordering Zinda Háshám to be conveyed, bound, to Samarkand, and there closely confined. When Amir Timur returned to his seat of government [Samarkand] he gave the governorship of Shibarghán, and the position which had been held by Zinda Háshám, to Bayán Timur, son of Ak Bughá.

[1] May be read Tanki or Panki, but no doubt *Yangi* is intended, *i.e.*, Táráz. (See notes, pp. 63 and 79-81.)

[2] Or Sangarnifáj.—R.

[3] This may be read as Pétis has read it: Adun Kunzi. I cannot identify the spot.

[4] Sarái Mulk Khánim was, according to Pétis de la Croix, Timur's chief wife, and mother of Shah Rukh Mirza. (*Timur Bec.* i., p. 225.)

CHAPTER XVIII.

THE THIRD INVASION OF JATAH (THAT IS TO SAY MOGHULISTÁN) BY AMIR TIMUR.

ON Thursday, the first day of the month of Shabán of the year 776 of the Hajra [A.D. 1375], Amir Timur, having collected an army, marched out towards Jatah—which is equivalent to Moghulistán. On the route he encamped at the Rabát-i-Kataán, when the coldness of the weather caused the sun suddenly to withdraw behind the veil of the clouds, and much rain and snow began to fall.

[Verses]: No one ever yet saw so much snow.
The world looked like a morsel in the snow's mouth.

The violence of the storm deprived the soldiers of their strength, and they were soon no longer able to look after their horses, because of the risk they ran of losing their own lives; in this way many of the men died and a quantity of horses perished. Amir Timur, being moved to pity at this sad state of affairs, commanded them to break up the camp and return to Samarkand, where they remained about two months, until the rigour of the season had in some measure abated. On Monday, the 1st of the month Shawál, at the beginning of the year of the Hare (Tushkán), he again led out his army against the country of Jatah—which is equivalent to Moghulistán.

He sent Amir Záda Jahángir forward to reconnoitre; and to accompany him he sent Shaikh Muhammad Bayán Salduz and Adilsháh, to whom he had entrusted the tribe of Jaláir, on the death of the latter's father, Bahrám Jaláir. Having passed Sairám, they came to a place called Jarun, where they seized one of the soldiers of the army of Jatah and sent him on to Amir Timur. When he was asked for news of Kamaruddin, who was of the tribe [*Umák*] of Dughlát, he related that Kamaruddin had collected an army and was then stationed at Keuk Tubeh,[1] waiting for Háji Beg, but that no news of the advance of Amir Timur had reached Kamaruddin. Timur then ordered the reconnoitring party to hasten forward, while he himself soon after followed them.

When Kamaruddin heard of these doings, he withdrew his army to an inaccessible spot called Birkah-i-Ghuriáu[2] [the Pond of the Ghuris]. In that place there are three very deep ravines, through which flow three great rivers. Kamaruddin having crossed two of these valleys with his army, pitched his camp in the third, protecting the approaches thereto with barricades and entrenchments.

But Prince Jahángir marched forward at the head of his experienced soldiers, to the sound of the drums and war-trumpets. After they had

[1] Or Kuk Tipa: the "blue hillock."

[2] The Turki MSS. says *Arshál Atár*. I cannot find either name on any map; but, taking the probable position of the Jatah army into consideration, it is possible that *Otár*, some forty miles west-north-west of Kastek, may represent *Arshál Atár*.

wounded and killed many of the enemy with their arrows, they came to close quarters with them, and when night fell, all the enemy took to flight; so that on the morrow not a single man of the army of Jatah—that is to say, Moghulistán—was found in the camp. But our victorious soldiers followed in their pursuit, and put to death many of those heretics. When the sun had risen, Amir Timur arrived on the spot with the rest of the army. He thereupon sent Amir Sayyid Dáud, Husain and Uch Kará Bahádur in pursuit of the enemy. In accordance with his orders, they followed the course of the river, and Husain was drowned in the river. On reaching the enemy's country they began to ravage and pillage, and seized many of their horses. But they spared those Hazáras who submitted, and having disarmed them sent them on to Samarkand. Amir Timur advanced as far as Báiták[1] with the purpose of meeting the enemy, while he sent Amir Záda Jahángir with one regiment to look for Kamaruddin, that he might defeat him and take him prisoner. The prince accordingly set out with a body of men, and laid waste the country of Uch and Firmán.[2] He came upon Kamaruddin in the mountains, and pursued him beyond the limits of his own country; he also captured much booty and took many prisoners. Among the latter were Tumán Aghá, the wife of Kamaruddin and her daughter, Dilshád Aghá. The prince sent news of his success to Amir Timur, who during fifty-three days had not moved from Báiták. When, however, this joyful intelligence reached his ears he immediately set out for Kara Kasmak, which hill he ascended and awaited the happy return of his son Jahángir. On his arrival, the latter, having respectfully kissed Amir Timur's feet, presented him with a quantity of booty, horses and sheep, after which he obtained for Dilshád Aghá the honour of saluting the Emperor. [Verses.] . . .

Amir Timur, on leaving this encampment, descended to Atbáshi and thence proceeded to Arpa Yázi,[3] where he spent a few days in festivity and rejoicing. There, too, Mubárakshah Makrit, who was a commander of 9000, and one of Timur's oldest friends, showed his respect for the Amir by causing a grand festival (*tái*) to be organised in his honour. And he so gained Amir Timur's good graces that he obtained for his son, Khudáidád, the succession to the honours and titles of Salár Oghlán and of Husain, who had both perished in the late war.

[1] Mr. V. P. Nalivkine mentions "Baitok" as a village in the Andiján district of Farghána, and says that its ancient name was "Paitoug." (*Hist. du Khanat de Khokand*, p. 14.)

[2] Possibly the first of these two places may stand for *Ush*, near the eastern borders of Farghána, but I know of no place with a name like *Firmán* in this direction. Dr. Bellew has "Uch Burhán or Uch Turfan;" the latter place, however, would seem to lie too far east to suit the narrative, while the former was to all intents and purposes Káshghar. Dr. Bellew himself tells us (*Kashmir and Kashgar*, p. 309) that the *Uch Burhan* ridge is on the left bank of the Tumán River, while the modern Káshghar stands on the right bank, having been built there after the destruction, early in the sixteenth century, of the old town, which was on the left bank. Had *Firmán* been so near Káshghar as to form almost a part of the town, the name of Káshghar would certainly have appeared in connection with that of *Firmán*. Like *Kara Kasmak*, which occurs immediately below, it was probably the name of an uninhabited spot, or camping ground, and should be looked for in the hills to the north-west of Káshghar. Severtsoff's map, though loaded with detail, does not contain these names. (See also p. 304, for *Uch Barkhán*, which Mirza Haidar puts at three *farsákhs*, or twelve miles, from Káshghar.)

[3] Arpa and Yázi: two rivers springing from the same range of hills near the eastern confines of Farghána. (See map for the position of the pass.)

CHAPTER XIX.

MARRIAGE OF AMIR TIMUR WITH THE PRINCESS DILSHÁD AGHÁ.

AMIR TIMUR, in accordance with the text of the Korán : "Thou shalt marry whatever woman thou pleasest, even unto the number of four women," set the eye of his favour upon Dilshád Aghá, and resolved to marry her. The officers of the Court made preparations for grand festivities. Wine and song and instrumental music were not wanting, and the whole ceremony was conducted with the greatest pomp and magnificence. The revels having been brought to a close, Amir Timur broke up his camp, and crossing the Yázi Dabán,[1] went and pitched his royal tents at Uzkand. Here he received his eldest sister Kutlugh Turkán Aghá, who, accompanied by several princes and nobles, had arrived from Samarkand; she had the honour of kissing the Emperor's feet, and took part in the festivities which were now again renewed at the Court. From Uzkand they proceeded to Khojand, when Adilsháh, being obliged to show his submission, organised feasts and merry-making in honour of Amir Timur, and made him presents of horses in order that his homage might gain the Amir's approval. His heart, however, was of another colour, for he had really the design of taking him by surprise in the midst of the rejoicings. But Amir Timur (whom God used to watch over continually) by his happy intuition, observed signs of this hidden treason, and detected the evil intentions of the conspirators by their movements. He thereupon rose from the banquet, mounted his horse and returned to his camp.

At the time when he was advancing to attack Kamaruddin, Shaikh Muhammad Bayán Salduz, Adilsháh Jaláir and Turkán Arlát had resolved to seize Amir Timur whenever an occasion should present itself. But their schemings were of no avail against one who was so carefully watched over by the Eternal: and thus he reached his capital without accident. He then disbanded his soldiers, while he himself went to take up his winter quarters at Zanjir Sarái, which is two marches to the west of Karshi. During the winter Adilsháh arrived, and having paid his respects at the palace, confessed to the Amir the evil designs he and the other conspirators had had against him. When Timur heard this, he was wise enough to pretend not to have heard, and showed Adilsháh great favour. When the winter had passed, he issued an order for his soldiers to muster, with the object of making another war upon Khwárizm. All the generals, princes, and soldiers having assembled round his palace, he ordered them to seize Shaikh Muhammad Bayán Salduz and to put him on trial. After his case had been heard, his guilt being clear, he was handed over to the brother of Harimulk Salduz, a relation of his own, whom he had unjustly killed with his sword. The brother avenged Harimulk by killing Shaikh Muhammad in a like manner. Ali Darvish, son of Báyázid Jaláir, was also put to death after being found guilty; while the government of the Tumán of Salduz, together with the administration of justice and police [*Sabt*], was entrusted to the brave Ak Timur Bahádur.

[1] Evidently the pass (Dábán) between the Yázi and Arpa rivers, alluded to in the last note.

CHAPTER XX.

THIRD EXPEDITION OF AMIR TIMUR INTO KHWÁRIZM, AND HIS RETURN ON ACCOUNT OF THE REVOLT OF SÁR BUGHÁ, ADILSHÁH AND BAHRÁM JALÁIR.

IN the beginning of the spring of the year of the Hajra 777 [A.D. 1375], or the year of the Crocodile (Lui) of the Tartar cycle, Amir Timur, being encouraged by his former good fortune, determined to make an expedition into Khwárizm, preferring war to feasting. [Verses] . . . .

Having, therefore, appointed Amir Ak Bughá Governor of Samarkand, and having sent Amir Sár Bughá, Adilsháh Jaláir, Khitái Bahádur, Ilchi Bughá and other commanders of thousands, with 30,000 horsemen, to Jatah (which is equivalent to Moghulistán), he gave them express orders to seek diligently for Kamaruddin, and to kill him wherever they might find him; he then raised his own victorious standard and set out for Khwárizm with a numerous army. On reaching a place on the banks of the Jihun, called Sihpáyah, he saw Turkan' Arlát approaching on the other side of the river. The latter, however, feeling that the end of his life had come, did not deem it advisable to advance, but fled back with his men to Kuzruán.[1] Amir Timur thereupon sent Pulád after him with a few men. They marched day and night, and having passed Andkhud they came up to the fugitives at Fáryáb,[2] which is on a river, where Turkan, with his brother Turmish and their men, taking up their position on the bank of the river, offered them fight. The enemy stood like lions at first, but they were at length defeated and compelled to take to flight, the victorious army following close upon their heels. Pulád alone came up to Turkan. His horse being fatigued, Turkan dismounted and ran forward on foot; he then struck Pulád's horse with the shaft of an arrow, and before the latter could rise from the ground, aimed at him another arrow, which only passed through Pulád's helmet. Then Pulád, becoming more

[1] A corruption, probably, of *Khorásán*, a province which extended, at the end of the fifteenth century, eastward to Balkh and north-eastward to the Amu.

[2] These movements are not intelligible. *Faráb*, or *Fáryáb*, was an ancient name of Otrar on the Sir or Jaxartes, but there is also a Faráb near the right bank of the Amu or Oxus, to the south-west of Bokhara, and though Pétis de la Croix (*Hist. de Timur Bec*, vol. i., pp. 260–1) specially explains that the *Fáryáb* of the text means Otrar, this is obviously impossible. It seems, however, that there was a third *Fáryáb*, for Abul-feda, on the authority of the *Loláb*, speaks of a "small locality" of that name in the environs of Balkh. He also quotes Azizi to the effect that *Fáryáb* was situated twenty-two parasangs, or about eighty-eight miles, from Balkh, but in which direction he does not mention. Again, he tells us Ibn Haukal states that the water of this *Fáryáb* comes from Tálkán—a place not far from Marv-al-Rud—this latter being some forty parasangs, or four days' journey, east of Marv-i-Shah-Jahán, and situated probably not far east of the Murghab. It is this last *Fáryáb* (now no more) that seems to be indicated in the text. But, in any case, the movements of Pulád's pursuing force are inexplicable, as it could not have passed Andkhui (or Andkhud) to reach a spot near the Murghláb, or 160 miles east of Marv-i-Shah-Jahán. (See Abul-feda, ii. (2), pp. 195–6 and 198.) The only map I know of that shows this *Faryáb* is that of James Fraser, who marks the place about halfway between Balkh and Marv-al-Rud. (See *Hist. of Nadir Shah*, 1742.)

furious,[1] made a bold rush at him, and they wrestled together for some time, till at last Pulád got the upper hand, and crying out, "Long live Amir Timur!" struck Turkan to the ground. He then cut off his head and returned in triumph.

Amán Sarbadál, who had gone in pursuit of Turkan's brother, Turmish, came up with him, overcame him, and severed his head from his body. His corpse became meat for the wild beasts, while the heads of the two were taken before Amir Timur.

Of those Amirs whom Timur had sent into Jatah (that is to say, Moghulistán),[2] Sár Bughá and Adilsháh, when they found the country empty,[3] prepared another plan of revolt; they seized Khitái Bahádur, and Ilchi Bughá, while Hamadi, whom Amir Timur had made Governor of Andakan [Andiján], allied himself with them. Having collected their tribes, namely, the Jaláir and the Kipchák, they set out against Samarkand, and began to lay siege to it. But the inhabitants defended themselves so successfully with arrows and darts, that they could not surround the town. Amir Ak Bughá, who was governor of the town, wrote of this matter to Timur, who having passed Kát[4] had just attained Khás, when this news reached him. He immediately made preparations to return, and, having sent forward his son Jahángir, in command of the vanguard, he himself followed with a large army. When he reached Bokhárá he put his men into fighting order, and went and encamped at Rabát-i-Malik.

Prince Jahángir came up with the enemy at a place called Karmina, where a battle took place. The air was filled with the sound of cymbals, and much blood was shed. But the Prince Jahángir, relying on the aid of the eternal God, at length overcame the enemy, who fled into the deserts of Kipchák, where they put themselves under the protection of Urus Khán.[5] Timur Beg, finding himself victorious, returned in peace to his capital. He then divided the tribe of Jaláir between his Amirs, and appointed his son Omar Shaikh Governor of Andakán [Andiján].

Adilsháh and Sár Bughá remained in the service of Urus Khán. But at length their thirst for rebellion again got the better of them, and once, while Urus Khán was absent at his summer quarters, they ran away, and drawing the sword of treachery from the sheath of infidelity, made war on Uchibi, a lieutenant of the Khán, and killed him. They then fled to the court of Kamaruddin in Jatah (that is, Moghulistán) and tried to stir up in him a spirit of revolt.

[1] *Puláditar*: more steely; a play on the word *Pulád*, which means *steel*.—R.

[2] It may be observed here that it is Mirza Haidar, and not the author of the *Zafar-Náma*, who interpolates on each occasion the remark: "*Jatah ki 'ibárat i Moghulistan ast*"—that *Jatah* is equivalent to *Moghulistan*.

[3] *I.e.*, offered no resistance.—R.

[4] Marked on Pétis de la Croix's map (vol. i.) near the bank of the Oxus, a little above Khiva. Erskine mentions Kát as the ancient capital of Khwarizm, and says it lay twenty-four miles from Hazarásp down the Amu. (Baber, p. xxix.; see also Sprenger's map No. 3 in *Post-und-Reiserouten des Orients*.)

[5] Ruler of the White Horde of Kipchak, and a descendant of Juji Khan.

CHAPTER XXI.

AMIR TIMUR'S FOURTH EXPEDITION INTO JATAH (THAT IS, MOGHULISTÁN).

AFTER Sár Bughá and Adilsháh had attached themselves to Kamaruddin, they used every possible means to rekindle in him the old fire of enmity which he naturally cherished against Amir Timur. Kamaruddin finally led an army into the country of Andakán, where the Hazára of Kudak, deserting Omar Shaikh, joined the side of the enemy. But Omar Shaikh, having taken up a fortified position in the mountains, sent a messenger whose name was Dáshmand, to Amir Timur to tell him that the enemy had arrived with a large army, and that they had overrun the whole of Andakán. Amir Timur was much enraged when he heard this, and immediately set out with all haste for that country. When Kamaruddin heard of the advance of Amir Timur he retired from the place where he was encamped, and having caused his household and tribe to leave Atbáshi, he hid himself, with 4000 cavalry, in a place of ambush. When Amir Timur reached that spot, being quite unaware of the trap [which Kamaruddin had] laid for him, he sent forward the whole of his force in pursuit of the enemy.

There stayed behind, however, of the army, 5000 cavalry and several brave generals, such as Amir Muayad, Khitái Bahádur, Shaikh Ali Bahádur and Ak Timur. Khitái Bahádur and Shaikh Ali Bahádur discussed how the enemy could best be destroyed. They determined to display the utmost bravery and audacity, and thereupon set out in pursuit of the foe, so that finally there did not remain more than 200 men with Amir Timur.

Kamaruddin, now seizing his opportunity, rushed out of his ambuscade with his 4000 cavalry, sword in hand, bent on avenging himself on Amir Timur. But Timur recalling to mind the words of the Korán: "How many small armies have overcome great hosts by the help of God!" was in no way disturbed or alarmed, but encouraged his men and opened his heart to them, saying: "Victory is from the Giver of all good gifts: not from the multitude of soldiers is it to be obtained. Your sole duty is to acquit yourselves like men; for should you show even the smallest sign of cowardice or hesitation we are lost."

No sooner had he said these words than he turned his charger against the enemy, and full of trust in God, entered the fray. [Verses.] . . . .

After the fight was over, Timur avowed that it was only by the aid of Heaven that such a mere handful of men could have overcome a force of four thousand cavalry, bent on vengeance. . . . [Verses and rhetoric.] . . . .

One day after this event, he fell asleep, and there appeared to him, in a dream, Shaikh Burhán-ud-Din Kilij (upon whom be the mercy of God). Amir Timur advanced towards him with great reverence, and asked him to pray to God for the recovery of his son Jahángir, whom he had left on the bed of sickness at Samarkand. The Shaikh answered, "God be with you"; but of his son he said nothing. When Timur awoke from his dream, he felt convinced that his wishes concerning his son were not fulfilled, and was so distressed about Jahángir's safety that he despatched Bu Kutlugh, his private secretary, with a letter (from Sang), that he might obtain correct news of his son. As soon as his secretary had started, he had another disturbing dream about Jahángir, and became more anxious than ever, saying to his courtiers: "I sadly fear I am for ever separated from my son; do not hide the truth from me any longer." But they, going down on their knees, took a solemn oath, saying: "Thy servants have absolutely no news of this matter, and have heard nothing of your son's condition."

Departing thence, they again met with Kamaruddin at Sang Zighaj; a fight took place, and they again put him to flight. Amir Uch Kará followed close after him, and when [the pursuers] had gone a little way, Kamaruddin, being surrounded by the Amir's soldiers, turned round with eight of his followers. His horse was killed under him by an arrow, and he himself only just managed to escape on foot, covered with wounds. In the same fight Pulád received an arrow wound in the hand; by chance, also, a fire broke out, and the efforts which Pulád made to extinguish it, so increased the inflammation of his wound that he died.

CHAPTER XXII.

THE DEATH OF PRINCE JAHÁNGIR.

Amir Timur having left Atákum, crossed the Sihun and arrived at his capital, Samarkand, where he found

[Verses]: The people wearing clothes of black and grey
And tears of sorrow streaming from their eyes.
And all had sprinkled dust upon their heads
And as a sign of mourning beat their breasts.
They came in haste to greet their lord the king,
Their heads they bared, and on their necks they hung
Black felt and sackcloth, thus they left the town
Filling the air with moans and lamentations.
"What pity that Jahángir, just and good,
Should thus be carried off in early youth,
As is a flower by the cruel wind."

When Amir Timur heard these wailings he could no longer doubt but that his forebodings had been correct. The death of his son, which he now learned, caused the whole world for him to become black; his cheeks were continually wet with tears, and life became almost unbearable to him. The kingdom, which should have been overjoyed at the return of its mighty monarch, was become, instead, a place of desolation and mourning. The whole army, clothed in black and grey, sat down in mourning. The generals put dust upon their heads, and their eyes were filled with the blood of their hearts.

Though the Emperor was greatly overcome by grief at the loss of his son, his noble intelligence fully realised that this world is but transitory, and that every being must inevitably perish at some time—that we must "Verily all return unto God." These considerations brought healing to the wounds of his sorrow. He, moreover, instituted many pious works, and ordered alms to be distributed in the form of food to the poor and indigent. His son's body was carried to Kesh, where it was buried, and over the grave a beautiful building was raised.[1] The prince was twenty years of age when he died. He left behind him two sons, one called Mirza 'Muhammad Sultán, by his wife Khánzádah, and the other, Mirza Pir Muhammad, by his wife Bakhtimulk Aghá, daughter of Ilyás Yasuri. This second son was born forty days after his father's death, which happened in the year 777 of the Hajra [A.D. 1375–6], the year of the Crocodile (Lui) of the Tartar cycle.

When Prince Saifuddin[2] heard of this sad event, he became weary of life, and begged Amir Timur to allow him to retire to the Hijáz.

CHAPTER XXIII.

AMIR TIMUR SENDS AN ARMY AGAINST KAMARUDDIN.[3]

Amir Timur was so much afflicted by the death of his son, that he neglected almost entirely the affairs of the State.

[Verses]: What value has this world compared with heaven?
Upon the other world my mind is set.
Why should I, for a meagre clod of earth,
Be forced to keep my spirit bound in chains?
Why for the sake of living our short life,
Should I be made to run the whole world o'er?

But the chief men among his nobles and princes came to him, and having done him obeisance, said: "The Almighty Creator and wise disposer of the affairs of the universe has appointed kings on the earth to protect the sons of men, and administer justice to them."

[Verses]: But if the mighty King do fall asleep,
His State will surely sink into corruption;
And if the Sultan's sword be not kept bright,
The mirror of religion will grow dim.
The Sultan is the Shadow of the Giver of All Light,
And from his Shadow should the world become both fair and bright.

* * * * * *

[1] Or mausoleum.—R.

[2] Uncle of Amir Timur.

[3] This incursion appears not to have been counted as a fifth expedition into Moghulistan, as will be observed from the heading of the next chapter. Also, from Mirza Haidar's statement in the ensuing one, it appears that he regarded Timur's expeditions against the Moghuls to have numbered five in all, while Pétis de la Croix reckons six.

If the desire of their noble sovereign was to please God, nothing could be more acceptable in the eyes of the Preserver of Mankind, than the administration of justice and care for his subjects, for the most perfect and wisest of all men (upon whom be the most excellent prayers) said that he preferred one hour of his life, which should be spent in the administration of justice, to sixty or seventy years spent in worship.

Amir Timur accepted favourably the counsels of his servants, feeling that it was purely out of affection for himself, that they had addressed these words to him, and he thereupon began again to turn his attention to the affairs of the State. He also reassembled his troops and prepared them for an expedition.

At this time, news arrived that Adilsháh Jaláir was wandering about the hills of Karájik, with a few other persons; whereupon Amir Timur despatched Barát Khwája Kukildásh and Ilchi Bughá, together with fifteen horsemen, in search of Adilsháh and his party. They set out from Samarkand in the night, and when they reached Otrár a few chosen men were despatched to the mountains to look for Adilsháh. They eventually found him in a place called Aksumá, when they seized him and put him to death, in accordance with the Yásák. Aksumá is a column [*mil*], built on the summit of the mountains of Karájik, to serve as a watchtower (*didah báni*) whence one may look out over the plains of Kipchák.[1]

Sár Bughá also, who having deviated from the high road of reason, had become rebellious and fled, now, after two years' absence, being led by the true guide of the intelligence, returned again to court. He was pardoned by the merciful monarch, and received the government of his own tribe and country.

Soon after this, Amir Timur saw fit to send his son Omar Shaikh against Kamaruddin, and with him he also sent Amir Ak Bughá, Khitái Bahádur and other Amirs, commanding them to do their utmost to sweep the enemy from the face of the earth. Thus intent on making a great effort, they set out with all possible speed. In the desert of Kurátu they came upon Kamaruddin, and by the aid of the Almighty, their swords of emerald hue became ruby-coloured like pomegranates, with fighting, and the faces of their opponents grew amber-coloured with fear. Their charges were so fierce that at length the enemy had to fly, scattered in all directions. When Kamaruddin had fled, the victorious army pillaged all his country and returned home laden with booty.

[1] This tower, it seems likely, may have stood at the spot marked on some maps of Turkistan, "Ak sumbe ruins." The site appears to be on a spur of the range now called Kára-tágh, and would overlook the plains of Kipchák from a distance. Dr. Bellew calls the tower "a red-brick pillar built on the Kara Cháe hill.' (*Yarkand Mission Report*, p. 152.)

CHAPTER XXIV.

AMIR TIMUR'S FIFTH EXPEDITION INTO JATAH (THAT IS, MOGHULISTÁN).

No sooner had these victorious troops returned from their attack on Jatah (or Moghulistán), than Amir Timur resolved to make yet another expedition into that country, that same year. He sent forward, as an advance party, Muhammad Beg, son of Musá (who, on account of his connection by marriage with Amir Timur, had a high opinion of himself), Amir Abbás and Ak Timur Bahádur. Marching, in obedience to orders, day and night, they came up with Kamaruddin at Bughám Issigh-Kul, and after a fierce fight, put him to flight. They then ravaged his country, and took his men prisoners. Amir Timur himself pursued Kamaruddin as far as Kuchkár.[1]

At this place news reached the Emperor's ears that Toktámish Oghlán,[2] having lost his faith in Urus Khán, had come in hopes [of good treatment] to pay his respects at court. The Emperor at once commanded the Amir Tumán, Timur Uzbeg, to go and meet Toktámish with all possible honour and ceremony, and accompany him back. Amir Timur returned from the direction of Inaghu and alighted at Uzkand.[3] Thence he reached Samarkand in safety.

On his arrival at the capital, Toktámish Oghlán was brought before him by Timur Uzbeg and others of the nobles. Amir Timur received him with affection, and with all the honour due to a prince, none of the prescribed ceremonies being neglected; for after he had given a great feast in Toktámish Oghlán's honour, he loaded him and his retinue with magnificent presents, such as gold and jewels, robes of honour and girdles; arms, armour, horses, camels, tents, cymbals (*kus*), chargers, slaves, standards, and such like things; and as a proof of the extent of the love he bore him, the Emperor paid him the honour of calling him his son.

END OF EXTRACTS FROM THE ZAFAR-NAMA.

CHAPTER XXV.

THE LAST DAYS OF AMIR KAMARUDDIN.

I HAVE heard from certain Moghuls that, towards the end of his life, Kamaruddin was afflicted with dropsy.[4] While he was in this state news came, one day, that Amir Timur was approaching with

[1] Kuchkár, or Koshkar, is one of the head streams of the Chu, to the south-west of Issigh Kul. (See the map.)

[2] Toktámish was nephew of Urus, and subsequently became Khan of the White Horde. (See note 5, p. 45).

[3] This sentence may also be read—"turned aside from the road to Inaghu." Instead of the form *Inaghu*, Dr. Bellew has read *Jumghál*, and this is likely to be correct, or nearly so; for another of the head streams of the Chu, in the immediate neighbourhood of Kuchkar, is called *Jumgán* or *Jumgál*. I can find nothing to answer to *Inaghu*.

[4] Some details, descriptive of the foul symptoms of the disease, are omitted.

his army; but Kamaruddin was too weak to mount his horse or to hold the bridle. So his people carried him into the depths of the jungle, and left him there with two of his concubines, and provisions for a few days. The rest then fled. After the invading army had withdrawn, and the scattered inhabitants had returned, they sought for Kamaruddin in the jungle, but not a trace of him or of his attendants, either dead or alive, could be found. Thus were the people released from his oppression.[1] After his disappearance Amir Timur's mind was set at rest with regard to Moghulistán, and he made no sixth invasion of that country. In fine, the Moghuls enjoyed peace and rest.

CHAPTER XXVI.

THE COMMENCEMENT OF THE REIGN OF KHIZIR KHWÁJA KHÁN, SON OF TUGHLUK TIMUR KHÁN.

It has been mentioned above, that Tughluk Timur Khán's youngest son was Khizir Khwája Khán, and that while he was yet at his mother's breast, he had been saved from the cruelty and enmity of Kamaruddin by Mir Ághá, the mother of Amir Khudáidád. When Khizir Khwája Khán attained the age of twelve years, [his friends] still fearing Amir Kamaruddin, removed him from Káshghar. Amir Khudáidád wished him to be accompanied by a few trustworthy men, but Mir Ághá opposed this plan, saying: "Do not send any of your own servants, for when the boy becomes Khán, base born people [such as they] will become influential, and then they will prove enemies to yourself and your children. They will imagine that the people do not pay them sufficient respect, but say among themselves, 'These are only servants.' For this reason rather send others than your own retainers—send strangers." So twelve men were sent with him, of whom every one eventually became an Amir, and many of their descendants are alive now. Among their number was Arjirák, from whom are descended the Amirs of Itárji; Tájri of Khwárizm, from whom are sprung the Amirs of Kunji; while another was of the tribe of Chálish Siádi [or Sayyádi]; and

[1] Amir Kamaruddin was one of five brothers who were governors of districts in Moghulistan, and were heirs of former Dughlat Amirs (*i.e.*, provincial governors), originally appointed by Chághatai Khán. The brothers were Tulik at Kashghar, Bulaji at Aksu, Kamaruddin at Atbáshi, Shamsuddin, who is mentioned as having taken part in the battle of Lai (or the mire), and Shaikh Daulat, of whom nothing but the name can be traced. Tulik, the eldest, was succeeded as Ulusbegi by Bulaji, and he by his son Khudáidád, who was seven years old when his father died. (See Bellew, *Yark. Report*, p. 151.)

his sons also became Amirs, with the style [*lakab*] of Kushji, but they are also called Kukildásh.[1] These persons all attained the rank of Amir, as did also the remainder of the twelve.

In short, they conducted Khizir Khwája Khán up to the hills, which lie between Badakhshán and Káshghar. But as the spies of Kamaruddin got news of his hiding-place, he was obliged to abandon it and take flight to the hills of Khotan. Then again fearing discovery, he passed on from this place to Sárigh Uighur,[2] Jurján,[3] and Lob Katak,[4] in which regions he remained twelve years. On the death of Kamaruddin, search was made for Khizir Khwája Khán, and Amir Khudáidád sent some people to fetch him from where he was in hiding. As soon as he was brought in, Khudáidád called the people together and raised him to the Khánship. Thus did the splendour of the Khán come to illumine the sovereignty of the Moghuls, so that the affairs of Moghulistán prospered.

The Khán then concluded a peace with Amir Timur, who formed an alliance with him by marrying Tavakkul Khánim,[5] a maiden from the royal haram. During his reign the Khán undertook a holy war [*ghazát*] against Khitái. He, in person, attacked and conquered Karákhoja and Turfán, two very important towns, situated at the border of Khitái, and forced their inhabitants to become Musulmáns, so that at the present time it is called "Dár al Islám"[6] As a seat of the Moghul Khákáns this country stands next in importance to Káshghar. It is moreover related that, in that campaign, this country was divided up in the manner ordained by the Holy Shariat. And there fell to the lot of the Khán, one piece of satin and one grey cow.[7] The Khán's object in doing this, was the glorification of the realm of Islám.

[1] The Turki MS. has *Bukuldásh*; the Persian ones have *Kukildásh* (or *Gukildash*), meaning sworn friend or foster brother, which is no doubt the right reading.

[2] The country of the Sárigh or Yellow Uighurs lay to the east of Khotan and Chárchan. (See notes, pp. 9 and 349.)

[3] *Chárchán*, or *Chárchand*, between Khotan and the Lob Nor country.

[4] Or *Lob Kanak*, the district about Lake Lob. (For *Katak* or *Kanak*, see note, p. 12).

[5] She was the Khan's daughter.

[6] Which of the two towns—Turfán or Karákhoja—was called *Dár al Islám*, or 'the Seat of Islám,' Mirza Haidar leaves his readers to conjecture. They are in reality some twenty-six or twenty-seven miles apart. In our author's time Turfán was the more important, and was usually the residence of the Khan of the State. But in earlier times Karákhoja was a place of consequence, so that it is very uncertain which may have been regarded as the capital, and the Seat of Islam, at the date he is speaking of. It is possible also, that he may mean to indicate the whole state, or province, of *Uighuristan*, as he afterwards calls the Khanate which lay east of the modern Kuchar, and had for its capital Turfán. He is much given, as will be seen, to using copulate, or dual, names for countries or districts, and sometimes speaks of this same province of Uighuristan as "Chálish-Turfán." (For the identity of Karákhoja (the Chinese Ho-Chou) with the ancient Kao-Chang, etc., see Sec. v. of the Introduction.)

[7] The 'piece of satin' and the 'grey cow' may have been some emblems of

It is related in the *Zafar-Náma*, that as soon as Amir Timur had satisfied his lust for conquest in the north, south and west, he prepared an expedition against the countries lying to the east, especially against Khitái, which is the most important of them; and a long description is given of the [projected] expedition, the substance of which is that he mustered an army of eight hundred thousand men, supplying them with provender sufficient for seven years—as was the custom in the armies of Irák and Rum.[1] As the country lying between Khitái and Mávará-un-Nahr was but little cultivated and thinly populated, he ordered each man to take, in addition to other supplies, two milch-kine and ten milch goats, telling them that when their supplies should be exhausted, they were to milk these animals; and when, in turn, the milk should come to an end, they were to convert the animals themselves into provisions.

Having completed these preparations, Amir Timur set out from Samarkand, and for that winter took up his quarters [*kishlák*] in Turkistán. While there, he sent to ask Khizir Khwája Khán if it would be possible to cultivate the ground [in Moghulistán], in order to furnish supplies for the army.

I have frequently heard my father (upon whom rest the mercy of God) relate that in the beginning of the spring the new kimiz[2] had come in, and on that day, according to an ancient Moghul custom, a great feast had been prepared. As Amir Khudáidád was on the point of offering a cup of kimiz to the Khán, one of the chief nobles announced the arrival of an ambassador from Amir Timur, and stated the purport of his mission. [The noble] added: "It is much to be regretted that we have not power to resist him, and that we should be compelled to pay him tribute." At these reflections, the cup of kimiz fell from the hands of the Khán, whereupon Amir Khudáidád said: "You must now drink of the cup of tranquillity (*ráhat*), in conformity with this couplet:

> To grieve over what has not yet come to pass is taking sorrow in anticipation.
> 'Tis better that I should defer to the morrow the things of to-morrow."

Then he added: "It has been said that if an apple be thrown up to the sky, God has had time to bestow a hundred blessings before it descends again. Ere another year be passed, how many thousand favours may He not confer! This consideration ought to bring you comfort."

---

power, or both may be corruptions of place-names, due to bad copying. There is, however, no doubt as to the reading of the texts; the words are *Yak Atlás wa Yak Gáw Kabud*—words in which I can trace no names of provinces or districts.

[1] Persia and Turkey.

[2] Kumiz or Kimiz is a bitter beverage made from fermented mare's milk.—R.

Scarcely had he done speaking, when they saw advancing rapidly from the shore of Lake Kariás, a man mounted on a black horse, and clothed in white robes. He rode on as far as the executioner's tent, where it is customary to dismount. This man, however, rode on without stopping, right past the station of the guards who were sitting in a line. The chamberlains [*yasávul*][1] ran up from every side to try and stop him in his course, but he did not slacken his speed till he came up to where the Khán was standing. Then he called out in a loud voice: "Amir Timur is no more, he has died at Otrár!" Having uttered these words he again rode off at full speed. Many horsemen were sent after him, but none could overtake him; and no other intimation of the news was received. However, after an interval of forty-five days, information came that Amir Timur had died at Otrár; so there no longer remained any doubt about the matter, and the Khán was relieved of all anxiety and distress.

The Khán was born before the year 770 of the Hajra, and the above recorded events took place in 807[2] of the Hajra. But it is not known how long the Khán survived Amir Timur—God knows best.

When the Khán ascended the throne of the Khánate, the foundations of the State, which, under the usurpation of Kamaruddin and the ascendency of Amir Timur, had been much shaken, were once more strengthened and consolidated. Old customs and rights, which had fallen into disuse or oblivion, were revived, while the affairs of the kingdom and the business of the nobles were restored to order. Among other matters that received attention was the restoration to his rights of Amir Khudáidád.

For in the reign of Chingiz Khán there had been granted to the ancestors of Amir Khudáidád the following seven privileges [*mansab*][3]: 1. *Tabl* (or the drum). 2. *Alam* (or the Standard), the former being called in Turki "*nakára,*" the latter "*tumán tugh.*" 3. Two of his servants might wear the "*Kushun-tugh.*" *Kushun-tugh* is synonymous with "*chápár tugh.*" 4. He might wear the *Kur*[4] in the councils of the Khán, though it is a custom among

[1] *Yasávul* may be translated chamberlain, or sometimes mace-bearer.

[2] Timur's death took place in February, 1405, or about the middle of the Hajra year 807, which began on 10th July, 1404, and ended 28th June, 1405.

[3] In the text used by Mr. Erskine, twelve *mansab*—privileges or prerogatives—appear to be mentioned. (See *Hist. of India*, i., p. 43, where, however, no detail is given.) From his abridged MS. translation at the British Museum, it is evident that Mr. Erskine found only *eleven* detailed, as is the case in the three texts used by Mr. Ross. Dr. Bellew (*Yarkand Report*, p. 153) has ten, and his list differs in many respects from the one given above. The word *mansab* means, properly, *office* or *dignity*, but here *prerogative* or *privilege* best answers the meaning. A good account of these prerogatives is given by Professor Blochmann in his *Ain-i-Akbari* (pp. 364–5), as derived from the *Akbarnamah* of Abul Fazl.

[4] Perhaps *girdle* or *garter*, though the text would appear to imply the meaning *quiver*. Dr. Bellew translates: *qur*, "armour" (p. 153), and Mr. Blochmann,

the Moghuls that no one but the Khán may carry his quiver in his hand. 5. Certain privileges in connection with the Khán's hunt.[1] 6. He was to be an Amir over all the Moghuls, and in the *firmáns*[2] his name was to be entered as "Sirdár of the Ulus of Moghuls." 7. In the presence of the Khán, the other Amirs were to sit a bow's length further than he from the Khán.

Such were the seven privileges bestowed upon Urtubu by Chingiz Khán. When Amir Buláji had brought Tughluk Timur Khán from the land of Kipchák, and had set him on the throne of the Khánate, he, in return for his services, received in addition to the seven privileges above enumerated, two others, so that he enjoyed nine in all. The first of the new privileges was, that he should have the power of dismissing or appointing Amirs of *Kushuns* (that is, Amirs who had one thousand followers) without applying to, or consulting with, the Khán; and the second was as follows: Buláji and his descendants should be permitted to commit nine crimes without being tried. On committing the tenth offence, trial should be conducted under the following conditions:—The accused should be set upon a white two-year-old horse; under the hoofs of the horse, nine folds of white felt should be placed—as a token of respect—and he should in that position address the Khán, while the Khán should speak to him from an elevation. When the interrogatory and investigation had been conducted in this fashion, if the offence should be a mortal one, and the other nine crimes should also be proved against him, two Amirs should stand by and watch him while his veins were opened and all his blood drawn from his body. Thus he should perish. Then the two Amirs, wailing and lamenting, should carry his body out.[3]

These nine privileges were contained in a *firmán* issued under

"a collection of flags, arms, or other insignia, which follow the king wherever he goes" (p. 50).

[1] These are given in the texts, but are unintelligible to some of the best translators to whom Mr. Ross has shown the passage. Erskine also failed to translate it in his abridged MS. at the British Museum. Dr. Bellew has "*jirga*—hunting circle—with power to punish, according to rule, those who infringed its regulations." Mr. Blochmann writes: "He could enclose (*qurq*) a forest as his private hunting-ground, and if any one entered the enclosure, he forfeited his personal liberty" (p. 364).

[2] Written orders.—R.

[3] The nine original prerogatives carried with them the title of *Tarkhán*—a very ancient rank, or order of nobility, among the Mongols. (See Yule, *Cathay and the Way Thither*, pp. 287 and 436). The *Tarkháns* are constantly spoken of by Asiatic authors as a tribe, but this need not imply that they were of any particular racial descent. Distinctions between tribes and orders, or families, are not always accurately drawn. Thus Amir Timur, in his *Institutes*, enumerates twelve of the forty tribes (*Aimáks*) which had submitted to his government: Barlás, Tarkhán, Arghun, Jalair, Tulkchi, Duldi, Moghul, Sulduzi [Salduzi], Tughai, Kipchák, Arlat, and Tatar. Some of these names imply race distinctions: others only orders or families. (Davy's *Institutes of Timur*, p. 91.) The word Barlás means "hero," and some of the others may have special meanings also. Mr. R. B. Shaw translated *Tarkhán* by "Franklin."

the seal of Tughluk Timur Khán, which I once saw myself. For it was handed down in our family, and ultimately came into the hands of my father (upon whom be the peace of God). It was however destroyed or lost, in the disturbed times of Sháhi Beg Khán.[1] It was written in the Moghul language and character, and bore the date and place of the year of the Hog, at Kunduz; which goes to prove that Tughluk Timur Khán's rule extended as far as Kunduz. No one alive now knows anything about the reign of that Khán, but I have copied into this history the account of it given in the *Zafar-Náma*.

Since Khizir Khwája Khán had been saved from the yawning abyss of Kamaruddin's violence, and had been placed upon the throne of the Kháns, by the aid of Amir Buláji's son, Amir Khudáidád, he rewarded the latter Amir by superadding three privileges to the nine existing ones; making the prerogatives of Amir Khudáidád twelve in number. Thus:

10. That on the occasion of festivals, when the Khán's chamberlains [*yasávul*] arranged the ranks, one of the chamberlains of Amir Khudáidád, taking part in the proceedings, should stand on the right hand side, holding the Khán's cup: another on the left side, should hold the cup of Amir Khudáidád, and those two cups were to be exclusively reserved for the Khán and Amir Khudáidád.

11. That he should set his seal on all *firmáns* that might be issued, but that the Khán's seal should be set above his.

12. [No 12th *mansab* is mentioned in any of the texts].

Such were the twelve prerogatives [*mansab*] for which a *firmán* was granted to Amir Khudáidád, after whose death they descended to his son Amir Muhammad Sháh Kurkán. When this latter died, they devolved on Amir Sayyid Ali Kurkán, the son of Muhammad Sháh's brother, and after Sayyid Ali to Muhammad Haidar Mirzá Kurkán his son, and after him to his son Muhammad Husain Mirzá Kurkán, father of the present writer Muhammad Haidar, known familiarly as Mirzá Haidar.

After the martyrdom of my father, my uncle, Sayyid Muhammad Mirzá, attached himself to Sultán Ash-Shahid-Sultán Said Khán; the Khán Said Shahid confirmed all these privileges to my uncle. The particulars of the matter are recorded in the Second Part of this *Tarikh-i-Rashidi*. These privileges (that is to say, the first [seven] of them) were in force from before the year 625 of the Hajra, which is the date of Chingiz Khán,[2] down to the death of the Khán and the murder of my uncle, the date of which was the

[1] Shaibáni Khan, the Uzbeg leader.

[2] This date is intended, evidently, for that of Chingiz Khan's death, which is usually taken to be 1227. The Hajra year 625 began 12th December, 1227, so that nearly the whole of it fell within 1228. But the date of the death of Chingiz is very variously stated in different chronicles.

1st of Moharram, 940 of the Hajra.[1] When this calamity took place and the Khánship came to Sultán Rashid, the customs of our forefathers were exchanged for other, and very different, practices.

Praise be to the gracious Creator, in that when my turn arrived to be created, he made me a free man and independent of the Kháns, for the great "*mansab*" He has granted me, is but an atom of those boundless favours which are the salvation of this world and the next. In the same way that thou hast made me materially free, make me also spiritually independent and prosperous!

[Verses]: Oh! God, make all the world my ill-wishers,
And keep me apart from them all.
Keep my heart from worldly matters,
And cause me to have but one purpose and aim in life.

CHAPTER XXVII.

MUHAMMAD KHÁN, SON OF KHIZIR KHWÁJA KHÁN.

THIS Muhammad Khán was the son of Khizir Khwája Khán, who had, besides Muhammad Khán, other sons; among these were Sham-i-Jahán Khán and Nakhsh-i-Jahán Khán.[2] After Isán Bughá Khán, excepting Tughluk Timur Khán, there was no one left in the country of the Moghuls who was of the first rank of Khákáns. This fact I have already mentioned. After the death of Tughluk Timur Khán, Amir Kamaruddin murdered all Tughluk's sons, so that there was no one left but Khizir Khwája Khán. (This I have also already stated.) This last Khán left many sons and grandsons; the details of the lives of all of them have not, however, been preserved in the Moghul traditions. In fine, I have recounted what I considered worthy of belief regarding the history of the ancestors of the Khákáns. But I have not been able to learn any details concerning their uncles and cousins. Consequently I have only mentioned the sons of Khizir Khwája Khán, as for example, Muhammad Khán: for in him the race of Moghul Khákáns came to an end.

Muhammad Khán was a wealthy prince and a good Musulmán. He persisted in following the road of justice and equity, and was

[1] Said Khan died on this date. The author's uncle, Sayyid Muhammad Mirza, was murdered by the Khan's son and successor, Rashid, a week or two afterwards. The 1st Moharram, 940, fell on 23rd July, 1533.

[2] The discrepancies of various authors regarding the sons and successors of Khizir Khwája have been remarked upon in the Introduction. See Sec. ii., pp. 40 *seq.*

so unremitting in his exertions, that during his blessed reign most of the tribes of the Moghuls became Musulmáns.

It is well known what severe measures he had recourse to, in bringing the Moghuls to be believers in Islám. If, for instance, a Moghul did not wear a turban [*Dastár*], a horseshoe nail was driven into his head: and treatment of this kind was common. (May God recompense him with good.)

In the Moghul records it is stated that Amir Khudáidád himself raised six Kháns to the Khánate, and this Muhammad Khán was one of the number.

Muhammad Khán built a *Rabát* on the northern side of the defile of Chádir Kul. In the construction of this building he employed stones of great size, the like of which are only to be seen in the temples [*Imárát*] of Kashmir. The *Rabát* contains an entrance hall 20 *gaz*[1] in height. When you enter by the main door, you turn to the right hand along a passage which measures 30 *gaz*. You then come to a dome which is about 20 *gaz*, and beautifully proportioned. There is a passage round the dome, and in the sides of it; and in the passage itself are beautiful cells. On the western side there is also a mosque 15 *gaz* in height, which has more than twenty doors. The whole building is of stone, and over the doors there are huge solid blocks of stone, which I thought very wonderful, before I had seen the temples in Kashmir.[2]

[1] Whether the diameter or the height of the dome is not stated. A great variety of *gaz* are in use in India, Bokhara, and other places. Baber made his *gaz* about thirty inches, but it was popularly taken at a little less, perhaps about twenty-seven inches. Mirza Haidar's *gaz* may be assumed as about equal to Baber's. (See *Memoirs*, p. 4; also note, p. 256.)

[2] The ancient temples in Kashmir are noticed again towards the end of the history. The *Rabát*, or traveller's rest-house (caravan-sarai) here recorded to have been built by Muhammad Khan at a short distance north of the Chadir Kul, would seem to be in existence still. Its ruins stand on the main road from Almati (*i.e.*, Vierny) to Kashghar, by way of the Nárin fort, and they have been seen, of late, by several European travellers. One of these is Dr. N. Seeland, whose account of the building is quoted, in English, by Dr. Lansdell, in his recently-published book of travels in Chinese Turkistan, and is so confirmatory of Mirza Haidar's description, that it may usefully be transcribed: "The traveller," says Dr. Seeland, "is not a little astonished to see a stone construction, hoary with age, about 48 paces long by 36 wide, with a flat roof, from the middle of which rises a rough, half-ruined cupola about 25 feet high. The entrance, fairly lofty and vaulted, conducts to an interior without windows. Under the cupola is a sort of chamber or hall, with vaulted wings, 9 feet high, of rooms or cells running off in four directions in the form of a Latin cross. The entrance wing has lateral corridors on one side only, and in these, as in those of the other wings, openings from 30 to 36 inches are contrived in the wall. They lead to separate cells, which are square at bottom, circular at top, and perfectly dark, except where the ceiling has, in some cases, fallen in. The entrances are so low as sometimes to necessitate crawling, and the interiors have no trace of chimneys, niches, or places to sit or sleep. No trace exists of refectory, kitchen, or even fire-place, throughout the building, which is constructed with mortar of fragments of local blueish and reddish schist. In the central hall are a few remains of plaster, but none of ornamentation." On the whole, Dr. Seeland considers that the building has no resemblance to other rest-houses or caravan-sarais in Central Asia, but I am not aware that he connects it with any ruin dating from the time

In the time of Muhammad Khán, the learned Mirzá Ulugh Beg was reigning in Mávará-un-Nahr by the appointment of his father, Mirzá Sháh Rukh; he was the founder of the famous observatory and the author of the astronomical tables called *Zij Kurkán*. Mirzá Sháh Rukh was king of Khorásán and Irák. The dates of his birth and death are not known, but if we refer to other dates, we find that he must have died before 860 of the Hajra. (But God knows best.)[1]

---

of the Nestorians. Dr. Lansdell does so, conjecturally. He infers that the Rabát, being on the "direct route between the Christian see of Káshghar and the Christian settlements on the Chu, it seems not improbable that the ruin may represent the monastery indicated on the Catalan map." A reference to this ancient map—it was constructed in 1375—will, however, scarcely aid us in falling in with Dr. Lansdell's conjecture. In the first place, the "monastery of Armenian Friars and Body of St. Matthew" is marked on the reduced fac-simile published in Yule's *Cathay*, as standing on the margin of Lake Issigh-Kul, that is, just at a spot where we know, from the narratives of modern travellers, many remarkable remains are to be seen—some on the shore, but mostly at the bottom of the lake, near the shore. The site of Muhammad Khan's Rabát would be some 180 miles to the south of the lake, by the Nárin road, or 120 miles in direct distance. In the second place, Dr. Lansdell cites, from Dr. Bellew, a passage purporting to be from the *Tarikh-i-Rashidi*, to the effect that Muhammad Khan "converted the ancient Hindu temple (resembling, in the massive blocks of its stone, the temples of Kashmir) called Tásh-Rabát, on the pass to the Chadir Kul, into a fortified post to protect his capital (Kashghar) from the incursions of the Kirghiz." The strange circumstances about this quotation are: (1) that I have been unable to find the passage in either of Dr. Bellew's works (*The Yarkand Mission Report* or his *Kashmir and Kashghar*); and (2) that no one of the texts of the *Tarikh-i-Rashidi* in the British Museum, contains anything about the origin of the stones used in building the Rabát. These texts state, simply and clearly, that which has been translated above, and nothing more. Thus, all that can be said is: (1) almost contemporary evidence proves that Muhammad Khan built a Rabát of huge stones; (2) that this building stood in a region where Nestorian Christianity flourished in the Middle Ages; and (3) in a land where many ruins, whose origin is not yet determined, are known to exist. I have not been able to obtain Dr. Seeland's full description, but may remark that no mere conjectures to the effect that the Tásh-Rabát is unlike ordinary rabáts, or that it is like a monastery or what not, would shake the very clear evidence of Mirza Haidar. What he states, when coupled with Dr. Seeland's discovery, is interesting enough. The descriptions of the building and its geographical position agree, in a remarkable manner, in identifying Dr. Seeland's ruin with Muhammad Khan's Rabát.

[1] Strange as it may appear in the case of so eminent a personage as Ulugh Beg, Mirza Haidar's statement that the date of his birth is not known, is correct. It is known, however, that he began to reign at Samarkand in A.H. 812 (or A.D. 1409), some thirty-eight years before the death of his father Shah Rukh, who was the fourth son of Amir Timur. At Shah Rukh's death in A.H. 850 (= 1446–47 A.D.) he was succeeded by Ulugh Beg, who, however, only continued to reign for a further period of two-and-a-half years. In the dissensions and wars which took place after Shah Rukh's death, Ulugh Beg was taken prisoner and put to death by his own son, Abdul Latif (Ramzán, 853, or 27th October, 1449). Thus Mirza Haidar's calculation of the approximate date of Ulugh Beg's death is not greatly in error, though the circumstance that he should be able to give only an estimate, shows that the chronology of his history is not always to be relied on. As the author of the astronomical tables, Ulugh Beg has a world-wide reputation. It is said that not only was the design his, but that he assisted in the computation of tables. The chief computers were, according to Erskine, first, Maulana Saláh-ud-Din Musa, better known by the name of Kázi-Zádah Rumi; then (after the Kázi-Zádah's death) Maulana

CHAPTER XXVIII.

SHIR MUHAMMAD KHÁN, SON OF MUHAMMAD KHÁN.

MUHAMMAD KHÁN, also, had several sons, two of whom were Shir Muhammad Khán and Shir Ali Oghlán. Shir Muhammad Khán succeeded his father, and as long as he governed, the people were peaceful and prosperous. During his reign, his brother Shir Ali Oghlán died at the age of eighteen, and thus never attained to the rank of Khán. He, however, left one son, Vais Khán by name, between whom and Shir Muhammad Khán there arose great disputes, as will be related below. Shir Muhammad Khán, who was also a contemporary of Mirzá Sháh Rukh, enjoyed a longer reign than Muhammad Khán.

CHAPTER XXIX.

EARLY LIFE OF VAIS KHÁN.

SULTÁN VAIS KHÁN was the son of Shir Ali Khán;[1] after the death of his father, he was in the service of his uncle, Shir Muhammad Khán. After a time he began to find this condition irksome, and therefore fled from the court, and took to the life of a robber [*Kazáki*]. Many distinguished Moghul youths volunteered to follow him. Among this number was my grandfather Mir Sayyid Ali. I am the grandson of Vais Khán, on my mother's side. Amir

---

Ghiás-ud-Din Jamshidi; and, lastly, Ibn Ali Muhammad Koshji. The geographical tables were first published in England by Graves in 1711, and the tables of fixed stars, by Hyde, of Oxford, in 1768. In France, Lalande published the astronomical tables in 1792. Baber, in his description of Samarkand, notices the college, observatory, and other buildings erected by Ulugh Beg. The observatory, he says, stood on the skirts of the hill of Kohik, and was three stories in height:—"By means of this observatory, and its astronomical apparatus, Ulugh Beg Mirza composed the Zich-Kurkáni, which are followed at the present time, scarcely any other being used." Mr. Schuyler was shown a hill called Chupán Atá, near the city of Samarkand, on which the observatory is said to have stood. There is now, however, no trace of it. (See Stanley Lane Poole's *Muhammadan Dynasties*, p. 268; Erskine's *Hist. of India*, i., p. 105; *Ib.*, *Mem. of Baber*, p. 51; E. Schuyler's *Turkistan*, i., p. 233; also Beale's *Oriental Biograph. Dict.*, 1881, p. 276; and d'Herbelot's *Bibliothèque Orientale*).

[1] Properly, Shir Ali *Oghlan*, not *Khán*. He is called by Erskine and some other writers *Shir Kuli*. But *Ali* and *Kuli* may easily be taken one for the other by Persian copyists. (See the Genealogical Table attached to this volume.)

Sayyid Ali is my paternal grandfather,[1] and this Amir Sayyid Ali was the son of Sayyid Ahmad Mirzá, son of Amir Khudáidád. I think it is fitting in this place to give the history of Amir Sayyid Ali.

CHAPTER XXX.

AMIR SAYYID ALI AND STORIES RELATING TO HIM.

As has been already mentioned, Amir Khudáidád lived in Moghulistán in the service of the Kháns. His native country was Káshghar, which had been given as a fief [*akta'a*] to his ancestors, by Chingiz Khán. This matter however will be referred to in the Second Part, when I speak of the country of Káshghar.

Amir Sayyid Ahmad[2] had an impediment in his speech, and only those who were accustomed to hear him speak, could understand him. He was also hard of hearing, so that it was necessary to speak very loudly to him in order to make him understand. His father sent him to Káshghar as governor, which position he retained for a considerable time, till at length Khwája Sharif, one of the nobles of Káshghar, became very powerful and all looked to him for help and advice. Khwája Sharif was a noble-minded man, but he was displeased with Sayyid Ahmad Mirzá, so he handed over the government to Mirzá Ulugh Beg, while Amir Sayyid Ahmad fled from Káshghar to his father, and soon afterwards died.

Amir Ali, the son of Sayyid Ahmad Mirzá, lived with his grandfather, Amir Khudáidád, who loved him better than all his other children; for he was without rival in stature and strength as well as in courage, talent and understanding. He used to be called Sayyid Ali *Alif.*[3]

When Amir Sayyid Ali took the daughter of Isán Bughá Khán for his son Muhammad Haidar Mirzá (as will be related below), he marked his joy by striking a nail into a wall, which I have myself seen. If one man stand upright, and a second, placing his feet on the first, also stand upright and stretch out his hand, he will not reach the nail by about an ell [*gaz*].

On this account[4] Amir Khudáidád loved Amir Sayyid Ali better than all his children.

[1] Sayyid Ali was the author's great-grandfather, as he shows elsewhere. (See Genealogical Table of the Dughláts in Sec. ii. of Introduction.)

[2] It is curious that this Khan's name should be written sometimes *Amir Sayyid Ahmad*, and at others *Sayyid Ahmad Mirza*, within a few lines. The texts, however, have been followed as they stand.

[3] In allusion to his upright figure—like the letter *alif.*

[4] On account of his stature, etc.

At this time a certain Ahmad Mirzá, one of the Timuri Mirzás of the line of Mirzá Sháh Rukh, having fled [from his own country] had come [to Moghulistán]. He had [with him] a sister, for whom Amir Sayyid Ali conceived a great affection; so much so that Amir Khudáidád and others begged her to become Amir Sayyid Ali's wife. She, however, refused, saying: "I cannot stay in Moghulistán, but if he will accompany me to my own country, it can be arranged." She then immediately set out for her own country, accompanied by Amir Sayyid Ali. When she arrived at Andiján, Mirzá Ulugh Beg despatched a man to kill Ahmad Mirzá, and himself married his sister, at the same time throwing Amir Sayyid Ali into prison at Samarkand, where he remained one year. Here he fell sick of dysentery, and when on the point of dying, Amir Ulugh Beg sent for the doctors, whose remedies, however, were all without effect. One day somebody brought some kumiz. The Mirzá implored the doctors, saying: "As the medicines have done me no good, I should much like to try a little kumiz, for which I have a great craving." They at last agreed [to grant his request] as a desperate experiment, saying: "It will very likely give him strength." They then gave him as much kumiz as he wanted, and from that moment he began to show signs of recovery. On the following day they gave him some more, and he became perfectly well.

About this time, Mirzá Ulugh Beg was going to wait on his noble father Mirzá Sháh Rukh. Amir Sayyid Ali being quite recovered, Mirzá Ulugh Beg ordered a horse and arms to be given him, that he might accompany him to Khorásán. His object was to show off Amir Sayyid Ali to the people of Khorásán, as if he would say: "This is the sort of booty we take in Moghulistán." One night when the Mirzá was in his tent, the torch-bearers were passing by, and he saw Amir Sayyid Ali with his bow, which was fourteen spans long—longer than that of anybody else. The Mirzá thought to himself: "If this man wishes to aim his arrow at me, who will be able to prevent him?" He became very nervous, and immediately sent for Amir Sayyid Ali and said to him: "This journey into Khorásán must be very irksome and unpleasant to you. You can return to Samarkand: when I get back I will give you leave to go to Moghulistán; and you shall be the intermediary between myself and Shir Muhammad Khán, so that matters may be settled in a peaceable way."

So he gave him leave to return, and sent a man to accompany him. He also wrote to the Governor of Samarkand, telling him to treat him with every mark of respect. But he sent a secret message to the governor telling him to keep Amir Sayyid Ali in prison.

When Amir Sayyid Ali arrived at Samarkand with his companion, he gathered from the behaviour of the latter that he was not going to be well treated. When they had entered the town, his companion placed him in a house, and himself went before the governor. No sooner was he gone than the Amir left the house, on foot, and proceeded to Táshkand. When the man returned to the house from visiting the governor, he found the Amir's horse, and arms, and servants, but the Amir himself had disappeared. They inquired after him from his servants, who replied that he had just departed on foot. They then searched carefully for the Amir, but could not find him.

Meanwhile the Amir had fallen in with some Kalandars on the road, and having dressed himself as one of them, arrived in safety at Táshkand. The Kalandars gave the Amir the name of Ashtar Abdál, and bestowed on him some of the provisions out of their wallets. Thus, in the guise of a Kalandar, he reached Taráz, which is another name for Yángi,[1] where he was recognised by the Shaikh of the "Shrine of the Companions of the Cave," which is called in Moghulistán "Mamlakat Atá."[2] The Shaikh sent his son Shádika with the Amir, and caused him to be conducted into Moghulistán and brought before Amir Khudáidád. This Shaikh Shádika became one of the Amir's intimates, and gained the title [*lakab*] of Vafádár [the Faithful]. There are descendants of his still alive, but they have not attained to any celebrity.

At the time when the Amir re-entered the service of his distinguished relation, Amir Khudáidád, Vais Khán had separated from his uncle Shir Muhammad Khán, and had taken to highway robbery. Amir Khudáidád said to Amir Sayyid Ali: "I think you had better go and join Vais Khán, for if you stay here you may come to some harm." He then selected sixty young men and despatched them with Amir Sayyid Ali, to Vais Khán. The Amir

[1] This name is written in the Persian texts in such a way that it may read *Yngi*, *Yinki*, *Niki*, or even *Maski*. In all probability *Yángi* is intended, though the word is spelled without an *alif*. Further on, the author tells us that *Yángi* is another name for *Taráz*, and as other writers state the same thing (see note, pp. 79–80) I think it is fair to assume that the name here written *Yngi* is merely an oversight—that an *alif* has been omitted by mistake. The position of ancient Táráz or Tálás has given rise to some discussion, while several writers have been led to the opinion that Táráz stood on the Sir, and was merely another name for the town of Turkistan, or for Otrar. Modern investigation, however, has shown these views to be untenable. That Táráz was situated on, or close to, the banks of the Tálás river, there can no longer be any reasonable doubt. The names of town and river are practically one; and there seems to be no reason to question the conclusion arrived at by Mr. Schuyler, that the ancient Táráz stood, probably, very near the site of the modern town of Aulia-Ata. He speaks of some ruins on the Tálás, ten miles below Aulia-Ata, which were called by the natives Tiume-Kent (Tumi Kand ?), and thinks that, on investigation, they may perhaps prove to be the remains of Táráz. Sir H. Howorth, Dr. Bretschneider, and Captain Valikhanof are of the same opinion as Mr. Schuyler. (See Howorth, ii., p. 286; Schuyler, ii., pp. 120–1; Bretschneider, i., pp. 18–19 and 228; Valikhanof in *Russians in C. Asia*, p. 104.)

[2] Or, perhaps, *Malikát Atá*.—R.

served the Khán well, and obtained in return the Khán's sister, Uzun Sultán Khánim, in marriage.

Countless were the laudable actions which Amir Sayyid Ali performed whilst in the service of the Khán. They would, however, take too long to relate. I have mentioned a few of them in my account of Vais Khán.

CHAPTER XXXI.

EPITOMISED ACCOUNT OF WHAT PASSED BETWEEN SHIR MUHAMMAD KHÁN AND VAIS KHÁN.

WHEN Vais Khán, as has been related above, fled from his uncle Shir Muhammad Khán, a number of people attached themselves to him, and they took to plundering in, and on the confines of, the territory of Shir Muhammad Khán; especially in the neighbourhood of Lob Katak and Sárigh Uighur.

It is related that when Uzun Sultán Khánim was given in marriage to Amir Sayyid Ali, this latter, in order to procure food for the feast, went out hunting, and returned, having killed two stags [*Gavazan*], which were eaten at the banquet. From this, one can form some idea of the splendour of the marriage festivities.

But [Vais Khán] finding little scope for activity in that country, [left it and] went to Turkistán. At that Amir Shaikh Nuruddin, son of Sár Bughá Kipchák, one of Amir Tìmur's greatest generals, was Governor of Turkistán. With him [the Khán] had some intercourse, and since he was at enmity with Shir Muhammad Khán, he gave his daughter Daulat Sultán Sakanj,[1] in marriage to Vais Khán. He also gave the Khán much assistance in his attacks on Shir Muhammad Khán, and for a long time there was continual conflict between Vais Khán and his uncle, the latter being as a rule, victorious. One of these encounters took place at a spot in Moghulistán called Karang Káingligh. Vais Khán, after a long and rapid march, surprised Shir Muhammad Khán in his camp at midnight. [The assailants] were four hundred strong. When the alarm was raised, Shir Muhammad Khán threw himself into a ditch, while Vais Khán, surrounding the camp, searched till dawn for Shir Muhammad Khán, slaying all whom he met. Yet, notwithstanding their search and the violence they used towards the people in the camp, no trace of Shir Muhammad Khán was to be found. When day broke they fled. Then Shir Muhammad

[1] The Turki MS. has Daulat Sultan Begum.—R.

Khán came out of the ditch, and his men having again collected round him, he set out in pursuit of Vais Khán, who only saved himself after a hundred narrow escapes. In fine, this hostility continued between them until the natural death of Shir Muhammad Khán, whereupon Vais Khán succeeded to the Khánate.

CHAPTER XXXII.

THE KHÁNSHIP OF VAIS KHÁN.

WHEN his turn came, Vais Khán showed himself to be religiously inclined; he was moreover distinguished among his race for his bravery. Since he had forbidden the Moghuls to attack Musulmáns, he made war against the infidel Kálmáks; and though he was frequently defeated by them, he persisted in hostilities against them, not wishing to relinquish the holy war [*jahád*]. He was twice taken prisoner by them. The first occasion was in a battle at a place called Ming Lák, where the Khán, having been seized, was led before Isán Táishi. This latter thought to himself: "If he is really a descendant of Chingiz Khán, he will not do me obeisance, but will look upon me as an inferior." When the Khán was brought in, he dismounted (for he was on horseback) and [Isán Táishi] advanced towards him with great respect [*Sar-Zadah*].[1] But the Khán turned away his face and did not raise his hands. Isán Táishi was then convinced, and treating the Khán with much honour, set him at liberty. The Khán, on being asked afterwards why he had not done obeisance [to Isán Táishi] replied: "If Isán Táishi had treated me in a lordly manner, I should, out of fear for my life, have approached him with reverence. But since he came towards me with bowed head, it occurred to me that the hour of my martyrdom had arrived; and it is not fitting for a Musulmán to do homage to an infidel, or to countenance his actions, therefore I did not salute him." It was the Khán's faithful observance of his religion that saved him from the abyss.

On another occasion, he fought a battle with this same Isán Táishi at a spot called Kabáka, on the confines of Moghulistán. Here, too, he suffered defeat. His horse being shot under him by an arrow, the Khán was obliged to continue on foot. He was on the point of being captured, when Amir Sayyid Ali, dismounting

[1] *Sar-Zadah* usually means "ill-mannered," but here it is obviously intended, literally, "with bowed head."—R.

from his horse, gave it to the Khán, while he threw himself on his face on the ground. The infidels, thinking him dead, shot an arrow at his head. When they came near enough, the Amir contrived to lay hold of one of them (who happened to be a man of some distinction), and lifting him up by his coat, turned him from side to side as a shield against the arrows, running all the while by the side of the Khán's bridle, so that it was impossible to shoot an arrow at the Amir. In this way he continued fighting and carrying the man by his clothes for a whole *farsákh*, till they came to the River Ailah. He then threw the Kálmák into the water, and seizing the bridle of the Khán's horse, entered the stream, which came up to his chest. Several men were drowned. The Khán's horse began to swim, while the Amir held up its head, and thus safely conducted the Khán, mounted and armed, across the river. Many men were drowned on that day.

It is related that the Khán had with him, on that occasion, two cousins, Hasan Sultán, who wore red armour, and Lukmán Sultán, who wore blue [*kabud*]. They were both drowned on entering the stream. Amir Sayyid Ali, keeping hold of the Khán's bridle with one hand, did his best to save these two men with the other, but could not reach them. The Khán declared he could distinguish their red and blue jackets deep down in the water. Vais Khán gave Amir Sayyid Ali five presents [1]— one for each [of the following] acts. (I.) He had given his horse to the Khán and had himself remained on foot. (II.) He had seized the Kálmák. (III.) He had used him as a shield for a whole *farsákh*.[2] (IV.) He had brought the Khán fully armed and mounted across the River Ailah.[3] (V.) Although he had hold of the Khán, he twice stretched out his hand to save the drowning men. The Khán then added: "I know that the Amir has such strength that if one of my cousins had been able to seize him by the hand, the Amir would have saved him too, and brought him across the water." In consideration of these five actions, he gave the Amir five

[1] The word is *juldu*, which signifies in Turki "royal gift," a "prize," or a "trophy," for valour.

[2] The *farsákh*, or *farasang*, is usually reckoned at four statute miles.

[3] There is nothing to show in what locality this fight took place. There were Kalmáks on both the northern and eastern "confines" of Moghulistan, and I can find no trace of Kabáka. In all probability, however, it was on the upper *Ailah*, which may also be read *Ilah*, and is the river nowadays called the "Ili," which passes by Kulja and flows into the Balkásh lake. "Ili" is the Chinese pronunciation, while the Turki-speaking people of the present day call it "Ila." As regards its being on the "confines of Moghulistan," as the author has it, Bretschneider quotes Quatremère's translation of the *Masalek-Alabsár* to the effect that the Ili river, in the first half of the fourteenth century, formed the eastern boundary of Mávará-un-Nahr. (*Med. Researches*, i., p. 18.) But the limit was soon afterwards pushed much farther westward, and at the time of Vais Khan could hardly have been formed by the river. The extreme upper and lower waters of the Ili, however, were near two of "the confines."

Aimáks as a reward. 1. Turkát. 2. Hibat Shirá Sut. 3. Uzbeg, a tribe of Khotan. 4. Darugha, also a tribe of Khotan. 5. Kukanit, also a tribe of Khotan.[1]

Sultán Vais Khán had another combat with Isán Táishi, in the vicinity of Turfán, and was again defeated and taken prisoner. Isán Táishi said [to Vais Khán, on his being brought before him]: "This time I will only set you free, on your giving me your sister Makhtum Khánim, as a ransom." There being no help for it, Makhtum Khánim was given to him, and the Khán was set at liberty. It is commonly reported that the Khán had sixty-one engagements with the Kálmáks: once only was he victorious; on every other occasion he was put to rout. (But God alone knows the truth.) I have frequently heard from Mauláná Khwája Ahmad that the Khán was a very powerful man, and that he used, every year, to go hunting wild camels in the country round Turfán, Tárim, Lob and Katak, which places I have spoken of in the Second Part. When he killed a camel he would skin it with his own hands, and take the wool to his mother Sultán Khátun; the Khátun would spin it and make it into shirts and breeches for him, which he wore with sumptuous robes outside. In Turfán water is very scarce, and it was the Khán himself who irrigated the land. He did not get his water from any stream, but having dug a deep well, drew from it a supply of water for irrigation. Khidmat Mauláná told me the following story of his uncles, who used to say: "We have often seen the Khán, during the hot season, with the help of his slaves, drawing water from the well in pitchers [*kuzah*], and pouring it himself over the land." His agriculture was carried out on such a small scale, that the produce of it never attained the value of an ass's load; but this served him for a yearly supply of food.

He was a disciple of Mauláná Muhammad Káshání, who was a disciple of Hazrat Khwája Hasan (may God perfume his tomb), and Khwája Hasan was a disciple of Hazrat Kutb-i-Masnad Arshád Khwája Baháuddin Nakhshband[2] (may God bless his spirit). Being a king did not prevent Vais Khán from passing his time in such studies [as theology]. During the reign of this prosperous Khán, Amir Khudáidád went on a pilgrimage to Mekka. Moghul records state that Amir Khudáidád raised six

[1] All five Aimáks are probably only small local clans. No. 2 may also read *Habit-shará-nut*.

[2] This Khwája Baháuddin (sometimes, though probably wrongly, called *Shaikh* Baháuddin) was the founder of a sect, or an order, of Sufis known as the "Nakhshbandi." He is said by Mr. Beale (*Oriental Biogr. Dicty.*) to have died in Persia in the year 857 A.H. (1453), and to have been the author of a work on Sufi-ism called the "*Dalil-ul-Ashikin.*" As late as 1886 there lived at Bokhara a noted Pir, or religious leader, called Ir Nazar Khwája, Samarkandi. Ir Nazar claimed to be a descendant of Khwája Baháuddin, and was (perhaps is still) regarded as the chief of the Nakhshbandi Order in Central Asia.

Kháns to the Khánship, "with his own hand." They were as follows:—Khizir Khwája Khán (whom we have mentioned), Sham-i-Jahán Khán, Nakhsh-i-Jahán Khán, Muhammad Khán, Shir Muhammad Khán, and lastly Vais Khán.

CHAPTER XXXIII.

AMIR KHUDÁIDÁD AND HIS JOURNEY TO MEKKA.

I HAVE already told the history of Amir Khudáidád in part; but in this chapter I have to relate the rest of his deeds and his death. All the Moghul traditions are agreed as to the country over which he was Amir. I remember hearing from my father (upon whom be the grace of God) and from my uncles (may the pardon of God be on them) that their father had 24,000 families under him. He was Amir before the year 765 of the Hajra [A.D. 1363–4] and he made his journey to Mekka before the year 850 of the Hajra [A.D. 1446-7]. He was Amir for ninety years.[1] He exercised absolute power over the whole of Káshghar, Yárkand, Khotan, Aksu, Bái, and Kuchár. In spite, however, of all this, he was never a wealthy man, and during most of his life had not even a horse to ride. When travelling from place to place, the people of the country used to furnish him with a horse. And in the army it was just the same. He spent much of the revenue of his State in releasing and ransoming Musulmán prisoners. In those days the Moghuls were constantly attacking Turkistán, Shásh and Andiján, and carrying off Musulmáns as prisoners. The Amir would buy these prisoners from the Moghuls, and supply them with provisions and transport to enable them to return home. He used also to provide them with tents, in which they had room to kneel down and say their prayers. In the performance of good actions such as these, and pious works, did the Amir pass his life.

[1] A little lower down, the author tells us that Mir Khudáidád was ninety-seven years of age when he went on pilgrimage to Mekka. Both ninety years for the length of Khudáidád's reign and ninety-seven years for his age, are probably mere figures of speech, intended to indicate a great number. A man of ninety-seven could not accomplish a pilgrimage from Kashghar to Mekka and Medina, as Khudáidád is said to have done, and in all probability his reign was much less than ninety years. The chronology throughout this part of Mirza Haidar's history is very loose and cannot be relied on. He probably had only rough estimates—little more than guesses on the part of his informants—to go upon, and if in the case of so prominent a person as Ulugh Beg, he could be several years in error, there is no reason why he should be more accurate in that of the Beg's contemporaries. As Mirza Haidar's is the only book (so far as we know at present) that gives the history of this branch of the Moghuls, as a whole, there is no other chronology by which his dates can be tested.

There are also many miracles attributed to him. One of them, that was related to me by Khidmat Mauláná Khwája Ahmad, I will quote here. Khwája Záhid of Káshghar was a great and pious man.[1] Amir Khudáidád sent a person from Moghulistán to beg for one of Khwája Záhid's handkerchiefs. The Khwája's wife, however, thought that it was not fitting to send the Khwája's handkerchief to a Moghul in Moghulistán, and that it would be a sin to do so. Therefore she sent one that was not the Khwája's. When it was brought to the Amir, he, with much praise-giving, wiped his face therewith. But the next moment he returned it to the messenger, saying: "If this is, in truth, the handkerchief of the Khwája, I have no need of it." So the messenger returned and gave it back to the wife of the Khwája. At this she was much astounded and told the Khwája what had passed. Khwája Záhid reproved his wife, saying: "The Amir is one of 'this sect;'[2] why did you act thus?" Thereupon the Khwája sent his own handkerchief. When the messenger delivered it over to the Amir, he, having wiped his face with it, said: "Verily this is the kerchief of the Khwája—and I have faith in the Khwája." Many miracles, such as this, are recorded of the Amir.

At last when the Amir reached the age of ninety-seven, he was possessed of a very strong desire to make the pilgrimage to Mekka. But in spite of much entreaty, Vais Khán refused his consent to this step. The Amir secretly sent to Mirzá Ulugh Beg, saying: "If you will come, I will disable the Moghuls and deliver them into your hands." Now, as Mirzá Ulugh Beg had suffered much annoyance from the Moghuls, and was continually engaged in repressing them, he immediately mounted his horse and set out [for Moghulistán]. When he reached a famous town in Moghulistán called Chu,[3] the Amir having deserted his own troops, joined Mirzá Ulugh Beg; and, in consequence, the Moghuls were scattered in every direction. When the Amir met Mirzá Ulugh Beg, he said to him: "I committed this act because I could not obtain leave to go to Mekka: this was my excuse for coming over to you, but now I don't see fit to go." They then left that place, the Mirzá treating the Amir with all possible honour and respect. When they reached Samarkand, Mirzá Ulugh Beg said to Amir

[1] The Turki MS. says "zealot."—R.

[2] Probably the "sect of sorcerers," or something equivalent, is meant. Secret sects or bodies, as the Bábis in Persia for instance, are, in fact, spoken of as "that sect," "this tribe," etc.

[3] In some MSS. this name may be read *Ju*, but three dots instead of one under the first letter would convert it into the name of the river *Chu*, which flows through the western part of Moghulistan, and it is possible that there may have been at this period a town, or *aul*, of the same name on the banks of the river. There is every reason to believe that about the time here spoken of, there were large *auls* and ruins of ancient towns on and near the banks of the *Chu*, though perhaps not actual towns, in the proper sense of the word. The word for "town" or "city," however, is one that is much misused by Oriental writers.

Khudáidád: "There is no one who knows so much about the *Turah*[1] of Chingiz Khán as you do; I beg you to tell me all its regulations, as I have a great desire to know all about it." The Amir replied: "We have completely discarded the infamous *Turah* of Chingiz Khán, and have adopted the *Shariat* [or Muhammadan Law]. If, however, Mirzá Ulugh Beg, in spite of his common sense and good judgment, approves the *Turah* of Chingiz Khán, I will teach it him, that he may adopt it and forsake the *Shariat.*" The Mirzá was much perturbed at these words, and did not learn the *Turah.*

In short, the Amir went to Mekka. When my father (God have mercy on him) went to Khorásán, as I have mentioned in the Second Part, he found there one of the generals of Sultán Husain Mirzá, named Sultan Ali Barlás, who was a very old man, being nearly one hundred years of age. He had been held in great honour by the Mirzá. My father questioned him concerning his ancestors and their times. He replied: "My father's name was Sháh Husain Barlás. He was one of the Moghul Barlás, and a distinguished Mir. Amir Khudáidád travelled with him from Moghulistán." When my father heard this story, he became greatly interested and begged [the Barlás] to narrate the whole history. The latter began: "I was quite a boy when Mir Khudáidád undertook his pilgrimage to Mekka, and my father accompanied him, for he was in the service of the Amir. We fled from Moghulistán and wandered from town to town, till we set out upon the journey to visit the holy town of Mekka; when we had been a few days on our return journey, the Amir asked where Medina was; they told him that Medina lay in a different direction. At this the Amir was much distressed, and said: 'I have come a great distance and suffered many privations; yet I have not made the *tawáf* [circuit] of the garden of the Prophet (may the peace and prayers of God be upon him); and it is a long journey home again.'

"He then gave all his servants and porters leave to return home with the caravan, sending with them many letters and messages for his children in Moghulistán. One of these letters has passed down from father to son into my possession, for it had always been carefully preserved in our family. In short, the Amir and his wife started for Medina, unencumbered, making an Arab go in front to guide them. My father sent me with him too, so I was of the Amir's party. After a long journey we arrived at Medina. The Amir made the *tawáf* of the garden of the Prophet (upon whom be the most excellent of prayers), and we passed the night in the house of a darvish. As night came on a

[1] *Turah*, as we have seen, was another name for the *Yásák* or *Yázá* of Chingiz Khan.

great change manifested itself in the Amir. He called my father (*i.e.*, Sháh Husain Barlás) and said to him: 'Read me the chapter called *Ya-sin;*' when my father came to the verse '*Mislahum Balá,*' the Amir expired. We were all astounded at this occurrence. With the break of day, many of the nobles and people of Medina came to the house, asking: 'Did not some one die here last night?' and when we told them, they began to condole with us, and said: 'We have this night seen the Prophet in our sleep, and he said to us: a guest has come to me to-night; he had made a very long journey to visit me, and he has died here during the night: bury him at the foot of the tomb of the Commander of the Faithful, Osmán.' Then the Prophet drew a line with the end of his stick. As soon as we awoke, we went and found that a line had been drawn there. Happy the man who has been honoured with such a favour! The nobles of Medina buried the Amir at the feet of Osmán, with great honour. On the following night the wife of the Amir died also, and she was buried near where her husband had been laid."

When Sultán Ali Barlás reached this point in his narrative, my father showed signs of great happiness; whereupon they questioned him as to the cause of his delight. My father replied: "This Amir Khudáidád was my grandfather." Sultan Ali Barlás immediately got up and having embraced my father, said: "What I have told you is true. But no news of the death of the Amir ever reached Moghulistán, for on our return journey we settled down for some time in Irák, and then in Khorásán, and no one brought the news into Moghulistán. Thanks be to God that I have been able to give this news to you, and tell you what a noble death Amir Khudáidád died."

Moghul tradition says that when Amir Khudáidád went to Mekka, his rank and titles were given, by Vais Khán, to the Amir's eldest son Mir Muhammad Sháh.

CHAPTER XXXIV.

THE MARTYRDOM OF VAIS KHÁN.

A SHORT time after the departure of Amir Khudáidád for Mekka, and the accession of Mir Muhammed Sháh to his father's rank and titles, Vais Khán's destiny was achieved. It came about in the following way. Sátuk Khán—one of those men upon whom Amir Timur had conferred the title of Khán—had been placed within four strong walls in the centre of the town. The place is called nowadays, in Samarkand, *Hiyát-i-Khán* [the walls of the Khán].[1] It is a large place and each division of it has a separate name. One of them is the *Hauz-i-Bostan-i-Khán* [the reservoir of the Khán's garden], which is one of the loveliest spots in Samarkand. In the days of Amir Timur, Yusurghátmish Khán[2] occupied this place; he, however, went away to Irák, and Sultán Mahmud Khán was appointed to the Hiyát-i-Khán in his stead. All the mandates [*manshur*] of Amir Timur bear the name of these two Kháns. So also the mandates of Mirzá Ulugh Beg bear the name of Sátuk Khán. Mirzá Ulugh Beg removed this Sátuk Khán from the Hiyát-i-Khán, and put some one else in his place, whom he also made Khán. He then sent Sátuk Khán into Moghulistán.

Vais Khán was in Issigh Kul, at Bakábulung.[3] I have heard Mauláná Khwája Ahmad say: "Khwája Abdul-Karim, my cousin, who was on very intimate terms with Vais Khán, used to relate that one Friday, just before the service, Vais Khán, who had performed his ablutions and had been shaved, came to me and asked: 'Of what is my head, in its present state of cleanliness, worthy?' I replied: 'A jewelled crown.' He said: 'No, it is worthy of martyrdom.' He had scarce uttered those words when a messenger came running up, to say that Sátuk Khán had arrived. Vais Khán immediately ordered them to sound the drums, while he himself began to put on his armour. The men who were near at hand quickly gathered round him, and they set out to meet the enemy. There was a stream running between them. When the two forces came in contact, the Khán himself charged forward, and wished to make his horse jump the stream, but the horse sank up to his head [in the mud] on the bank of the river. One of the servants of Mir Muhammad Sháh (Jákir by name) was such a good archer that he had not a single rival in the whole tribe, and for this reason the Khán had begged him of Mir Muhammad Sháh, for his own service. At the moment when the Khán fell from his horse, Jákir arrived on the spot, and mistaking the Khán for one of the enemy, aimed an arrow at the waist of the Khán, who on being struck rolled over on his back. Then Jákir recognised the Khán, and threw himself upon him.[4] When the news reached

[1] Perhaps, better, the *Enclosure*, or *Garden of the Khán*.

[2] This name usually stands *Suyurghátmish*. His nominal reign dates from 1369 to 1388, and that of Mahmud from 1388 to 1398. (See S. L. Poole's *Muham. Dynast.*, p. 268.) They were both puppets set up by Timur, and what Mirza Haidar briefly relates of them here, shows how they were treated by the great Amir.

[3] Or *Yakábulung*; but the Turki MS. does not mention the place. There are two rivers called *Bakbulan* in Moghulistan, on Ritter and Oetzel's map, but neither is near Issigh Kul. One is some distance to the north-west of the lake, and the other a tributary of the lower Chu. The name of *Karabulun* occurs on the east shore of the lake, and though less like the word in the text than is *Bakbulan*, it may represent the spot mentioned by the author.

[4] Probably "ran to his aid" is intended

Sátuk Khán, he set out for the spot and, on his arrival, lay the Khán's head upon his breast, but the last breath of life had fled."

The Moghul tribe were in the greatest disorder and, moreover, refused to obey Sátuk Khán; so that this latter could no longer remain in Moghulistán, but retired to Káshghar. Here he was overpowered by Karákul Ahmad Mirzá, who was a grandson of Amir Khudáidád. Soon after this, Mirzá Ulugh Beg sent an army to Káshghar. They seized Karákul Ahmad Mirzá and carried him off to Samarkand, where they cut him in half.

CHAPTER XXXV.

RUIN OF [THE PARTY OF] IRÁZÁN AFTER THE DEATH OF VAIS KHÁN.[1]

AFTER the death of Vais Khán, the tribe of the Moghuls fell into great disorder. But they became more tranquil when they learnt the news of the death of Sátuk Khán. Vais Khán left two sons, Yunus Khán and Isán Bughá Khán. Yunus Khán was the elder, and [at his father's death] was thirteen years of age. There arose a dispute among the princes [as to who should succeed]. There were two men named Irázán Bárin and Mirák Turkomán, who had first of all been in the service of Amir Khudáidád, and afterwards in that of his son Mir Muhammad Sháh; but at the death of Vais Khán, these two men had separated themselves from Mir Muhammad Khán [Sháh ?], by force of arms, and having attached themselves to Yunus Khán, began to stir up rebellion in his favour; while the rest of the people were on the side of Isán Bughá. But as most of the generals were on the side of Isán Bughá Khán, it became impossible for the party of Yunus to remain in Moghulistán. So Irázán and Mirák Turkomán, together with thirty thousand households and Yunus Khán, set out for Samarkand, while Isán Bughá Khán and the rest of the Moghuls remained in Moghulistán.

[1] The *Virání* of Irázán seems to have been a long-remembered event among the Moghuls. The word may mean *ruin*, *devastation*, or *calamity*, also *expulsion*, *dispersion*, etc. In reality it was the party of Irázán Bárin that was ruined and expelled, though the calamity fell on the Moghul tribe generally, and more especially, perhaps, on their chiefs, a number of whom were massacred. Baber mentions the matter in his *Memoirs*. He says three or four thousand families accompanied Irázán and Mirák, when these two carried the young Khan off to Samarkand. Ulugh Beg gave them a bad reception, imprisoning some and dispersing the rest in all directions: "so that 'the Dispersion of the Irázan' has become an era among the Moghuls." (*Memoirs*, p. 11.)

CHAPTER XXXVI.

RECEPTION OF YUNUS KHÁN AND IRÁZÁN, IN SAMARKAND, BY MIRZÁ ULUGH BEG.

WHEN Mirzá Ulugh Beg heard of the approach of Irázán Bárin and Mirák Turkomán, he set out from Samarkand to meet them. On their arrival, he promised to supply them with provisions, and said: "Every household must come into the fort separately, where the members will have their names written down; each Moghul will receive an ass's load of provisions and then pass on." Thus, hopeful of supplies, the people entered, but when they arrived at another door they were obliged to wait. Then their chiefs were killed and the rest of them were taken prisoners. Of all that entered the fort no one came out again to tell his story. Mirzá Ulugh Beg finished this business in a few days, and then despatched Yunus Khán, with a fifth of the spoil, to his father Mirzá Sháh Rukh. The Khán was kindly treated—more like a son than a prisoner. He was sent to Mauláná Sharaf-ud-Din Yazdi, that under him he might continue his studies. Many of the Mauláná's verses and *Kassidas* are dedicated to the Khán.

He spent altogether twelve years with the Mauláná, in the acquirement of science and letters. In fact, as long as the Mauláná lived he remained with him, but on the death of the latter, he quitted Yazd and made a journey through Irák, Arabia and Fárs. He was twenty-four when the Mauláná died, and he returned to Moghulistán, as *pádisháh*, at the age of forty-one, as will be mentioned below (if God will).

CHAPTER XXXVII.

KHÁNSHIP OF ISÁN BUGHÁ KHÁN, SON OF VAIS KHÁN, AFTER THE RUIN OF IRÁZÁN.

AFTER Mirák Turkomán and Irázán had carried off Yunus Khán to Samarkand, the whole of Moghulistán became subject to Isán Bughá Khán: all the Amirs offered to serve him, and thus the affairs of the Khán made great progress. Amir Sayyid Ali was untiring in his efforts to help the Khán, and as soon as the latter was firmly established on the throne, Amir Sayyid Ali begged him for permission to go to Káshghar. For, as I have already related, Khwája Sharif of Káshghar had given that place to Ulugh Beg Mirzá, and had expelled Mir Sayyid Ahmad, the father of Amir Sayyid Ali. Mirzá Ulugh Beg had, in the first place, appointed Amir Sultán Malik Duládái to be Governor of Káshghar, and after him Háji Muhammad Sháyistah, and after him Pir Muhammad Barlás.

Amir Sayyid Ali pointed out that it was a very fitting opportunity for him to go to Káshghar, and added: "I will see if I cannot restore to our family its old possession, of which for forty years it has been deprived. If I fail I shall merit your scorn." The Khán thereupon gave his consent.

CHAPTER XXXVIII.

AMIR SAYYID ALI'S EXPEDITION TO, AND REDUCTION OF, KÁSHGHAR.

AT this time, the greater part of Mangálái Suyah was under the administration of the Dughláts. But Andiján and Káshghar had fallen to the government of Samarkand; while Issigh Kul, from the numerous vicissitudes to which it had been exposed, was sinking into disruption; the rest of the country, however, was still in the hands of the Dughlát Amirs. Just at this period the brothers and cousins of Amir Sayyid Ali were [governing] in Aksu, Kus and Bái. Amir Sayyid Ali came to Aksu, and leaving his family there, proceeded to Káshghar. When the Amir arrived in Aksu, a great conflict arose between himself and his two brothers, Mumin Mirzá and Sayyid Mahmud Mirzá. The Amir came off victor, in the end, after having killed many of his relations. About this matter there are many conflicting traditions. It appears, at all events, that he first got the upper hand of his relatives and then set out for Káshghar. He had 7000 men in his following. When he arrived within the territory of Káshghar, Háji Muhammad Sháyistah repaired to a place called Uch Barkhán, which is about three *farsákhs* distant from Káshghar, to oppose him, with 30,000 cavalry and infantry. But at the first attack of the Amir, Háji Muhammad Sháyistah took flight. The Moghuls started, in hot haste, after the Chaghatái, who in order to gain greater freedom in their flight, threw aside their armour before the enemy were able to overtake them, and uttered cries of distress. For this reason the battle was called "Salái Begum," that is to say, "*Mir-i-man biandázam*," or "I throw down my Mir." This was one of the most famous battles ever fought in that country, and formed an epoch in its history. The people of Káshghar enabled the fugitives to creep into the citadel, while the Amir laid waste and pillaged all without, and then departed with the spoil.

The following year, when the corn was ripe, the Amir returned, and no one dared to leave the city. Háji Muhammad Sháyistah fortified himself in the citadel, while the Amir ravaged the whole country round. He laid siege to, and captured, one of the neighbouring fortresses, called Aláku, and again retired.

Then Khwája Sharif went to Samarkand to implore the assistance of Mirzá Ulugh Beg. While he was there, the Mirzá one day asked him: "Are there any donkeys in Káshghar?" Khwája Sharif replied: "Since the Chaghatái have come, there are a great number of donkeys." Khwája Sharif took Pir Muhammad Barlás with him to Káshghar, while Mirzá Ulugh Beg withdrew Háji Muhammad Sháyistah to Samarkand. When Pir Muhammad Barlás arrived in Káshghar, the people gave him the surname [*lakab*] of Bangi, but they derived no benefits from him,[1] and Khwája Sharif began to despair of the Chaghatái.

When the Amir advanced against Káshghar for the third year in succession, the people of that country addressed a complaint to Khwája Sharif, saying: "We have lost the crops of two successive years; if we lose this year's crop too, there will be a famine in our country."

On the Amir's arrival in Káshghar, the people of that town, having bound Pir Muhammad Barlás, gave him up to the Amir.[2] The Amir thereupon divested Pir Muhammad Barlás of his mantle of life, and entered the town of Káshghar, where he administered justice to the people. He governed the country during twenty-four years; and under him the State was so prosperous and happy, that he is talked of to this day. During all this time, the Amir paid so much attention to agriculture and the breeding of cattle and sheep, that when he died, leaving three sons and two daughters, one of his sons, Muhammad Haidar Mirzá, my grandfather, received as his share 180,000 sheep.

I once heard from Khwája Fakhruddin, a merchant of noble birth and pleasant of speech, that the Amir occupied himself with hunting during three months every winter. No one but soldiers were allowed to take part in the royal hunt. But as many soldiers as the Amir was able to provide for, used to join in the party, and during those three months, each one was supplied with meat and flour, which was distributed to them at the different halting-places [*manzil*]. On some days as many as 5000 sheep were given out,

[1] That is: this change of governor did not improve the state of affairs.

[2] Lit., as an *istikbál*—*i.e.*, the present offered to a person of consequence, by those who go out to meet and welcome him on his arrival.—R.

together with a proportionate amount of flour and barley and hay. Some years, 3000 persons were in attendance on the Amir, and each one was given his provisions. The inhabitants of the different villages were always anxious for the Amir to come to stay in their village, and the hunting party, on its arrival, would make them participate in their own store of good things. Fakhruddin used to relate that on one occasion, when they had alighted in our village, which is Artuch,[1] the Amir's master of the hunt [*Mir-shikár*] having brought some flour, gave it to a poor woman to bake, promising her, as a wage for her work, one of the six loaves, which were to be made from the flour he had supplied her with; but when the woman brought the loaves, he refused to give her one of them, saying: "I supplied the flour and the wood and the salt; what have you deserved of me?" At that moment the Amir happened to be passing by on horseback. He stopped and asked the woman what her trouble was: the woman laid her complaint before the Amir, who then questioned the master of the hunt. As this latter acknowledged the truth of the poor woman's story, the Amir said to him: "Why did you not bake your own bread, instead of troubling this woman?" The Amir then sent to a blacksmith's-shop for some pincers, and caused all the wretched man's teeth to be drawn from his head. I have repeated this tale as a proof of the Amir's justice. There are still existing in Káshghar, many sacred edifices and charitable institutions, which were founded by the Amir. During the twenty-four years of his government, many important events occurred, which shall hereafter be related in detail.

CHAPTER XXXIX.

THE QUARRELS OF ISÁN BUGHÁ KHÁN WITH HIS AMIRS.

When Yunus Khán left the country, the whole tribe submitted to Isán Bughá Khán, and for a few years the country enjoyed repose. The Khán, however, by reason of his youth, was but lightly esteemed by his Amirs. One of the Amirs, a certain Timur of the Uighur tribe of Turfán, had enjoyed the special favour of the young Khán; the other Amirs being annoyed at his elevation, and at the small degree of attention they themselves received, could no longer contain their wrath, and one day, in the

[1] No doubt *Artush*, or *Altun Artush*, on the spurs of the hills, one short march north of Kashghar—a favourite summer resort of the townspeople.

presence of the Khán, seized the unfortunate man and cut him in pieces. After this there was a division among the Amirs, and the Khán, much alarmed at what had taken place, fled.

When this news reached Amir Sayyid Ali in Káshghar, he at once set out for Moghulistán. He found the Khán at Ak Kabás, and, accompanied by a few men, carried him off to Aksu, of which town he made him governor.

Meanwhile the Moghul Amirs were acting each in his own way. Mir Muhammad Sháh had taken up his abode in Atbáshi, but after some correspondence and promises of friendship, between himself and his nephew Amir Sayyid Ali, he joined the Khán in Aksu; he was beloved and esteemed to the end of his life.

Another was Mir Karim Bardi, who was also a Dughlát. He built a fort on the frontier of Moghulistán, on the side of Andiján and Farghána. It stood on the summit of a hillock at a place called Alábughá, and its ruins are still to be seen. He spent his time in ravaging and plundering Andiján and the Musulmáns.

Mir Hakk Bardi Begjik went to dwell in a place called Kui Sui, which is in Issigh Kul. Here he built a fort, and put his wives and family on the island in Issigh Kul,[1] that they might be

[1] This appears to mean that *Kui Sui* was the name of the island. There are now no islands in Issigh Kul, but the name of *Koi-Su* is found, on some maps, among those of some small rivers discharging into the eastern end of the lake. Kostenko tells us that although no islands exist, there are numerous shoals in its waters, and since there is every reason to believe that the level of the lake has altered within historic times, it is possible that some of these shoals may have been above the surface four hundred years ago. He points to some evidences of the lake having fallen rather than risen, but he is speaking of geological periods in one instance, and of a statement of the local Kirghiz, that the water has subsided "during the last ten years," in another. Mr. Schuyler gives a good account of the lake and comes to a different conclusion. He writes: "Lake Issik-Kul, which is a large body of water, 120 miles long by 33 wide, has at present no outlet. Its shores, however, afford indubitable evidence of *numerous* elevations and depressions." He admits that "at one time" the water may have reached the bases of the mountains 100 feet above its present level, but adds (in another place): "the fact that ruins are visible under the water would seem to show either a subsidence of the soil, or that the lake is higher than it once was." He relates that "diamond-shaped tiles, some plain red, others covered with a blue glaze, have been obtained partly from the lake and partly from ruins, ploughed up by the peasants. At a place on the northern side of the lake called Koroi-Saroi, and in two places at the eastern end, remains of submerged cities are still to be seen a few feet under water. Many objects have been found here, some thrown up by the waves and others fished out of the water, chiefly broken pottery and pieces of metallic vessels." He mentions the discovery of two ornamented copper kettles, a lamp bearing an inscription in an unknown alphabet, etc., and continues: "These ruins have never been carefully investigated, but in 1869 General Kolpakofsky examined some of them, and says that between the mouths of the streams 2nd and 3rd *Koi-Su*, at seven feet from the shore and at a depth of three feet, there are visible traces of brick walls which go parallel to each other at a distance of a few feet until the depth of the lake prevents their being seen. He also saw a large stone, on which was carved the representation of a human face, and which he succeeded in getting out of the water. Subsequent observers, who had succeeded in rigging out a boat, assured me that especially near the river Tub, on a clear day, they could see the remains of buildings."

safe from the attacks of the Kálmáks. Having done this, he went forth to lay waste Turkistán and Sairám. The Amirs of Jarás and of the tribe of Bárin went to join Amásánji Táishi, son of Isán Táishi, who was [chief] in the land of the Kálmáks,[1] while Káluji and Balgháji and several families joined Abulkhair Khán[2] in Turkistán. The Amirs of Kunji and several others wandered, in confusion and disorder, over the desert plains of Moghulistán.

But when Isán Bughá Khán had become firmly established in Aksu, first of all Mir Muhammad Sháh came to him [and submitted], and after that, others returned to him in numbers. The Khán, too, repenting of his former deeds, began to treat his people with great kindness. As soon as he had regained complete authority, he made a simultaneous attack upon Sairám, Turkistán and Táshkand, and having devastated these countries, returned home. This expedition took place before the year 855 of the Hajra [1451]. A second time also, he made a similar foray into this country. At that time Sultán Abu Sáid Mirzá was *pádisháh* of Mávará-un-Nahr. He pursued the Khán and overtook him in Yángi,[3] which in books of history is called Taráz. The Moghuls

---

Issigh-Kul means warm lake, and is the equivalent of the Chinese *Jhe-hai.* Other Chinese names are *Yen-hai,* salt lake (for the water is brackish), and *Tsing-hai,* or clear lake, By the Kirghiz it is sometimes called *Tuz-Kul,* meaning 'salt lake,' and by the Kálmáks *Timurtu Nor,* or 'iron lake,' on account of the ferruginous sand found on its shores. Schuyler remarks that old Chinese maps place the city of *Chi-gu* on the shores of Issigh-Kul, while the Catalan map of 1375 (as noted already) marks on the southern shore, a Nestorian monastery containing the bones of St. Matthew. Bretschneider mentions a curious statement found in the work of Arab Shah, who reports that Amir Timur, in 1403, banished a Tartar tribe (the Kara Tatar) from Asia Minor "to the fortress *Dowaira,* which was situated in the middle of the lake called *Issicoul.* This lake, he says, was at the boundary between the dominions of Timur and Moghulistan." The passage is apparently taken from Pétis' translation of the *Zafar-Náma,* or *Hist. de Timur Bec.* Thus two native authors, writing in the fifteenth and sixteenth centuries respectively, mention islands in Lake Issigh-Kul. (See Kostenko, *Turkistan, English tr.,* i., pp. 155–6; Schuyler, i., p. 54; ii., pp. 129–31; Bretschneider, ii., pp. 244–5.)

[1] *Taishi* was the title by which Kálmák chiefs were designated, and from the combination *Khán-Taishi,* the word *Contaish,* used by early European writers for a Kálmák king, is said to be derived. The statement made by the author that "Amasanji Taishi was in the land of the Kálmáks," contains, probably, an omission of the word *chief* or some equivalent of it. It should probably read: "Amasanji Taishi was chief in the land. . . ."

[2] Abulkhair was the chief of the Uzbegs in and about the plains of Kipchak, Mávará-un-Nahr, and Turkistan, and grandfather of the famous Shaibáni, or Shahi Beg, Khán. He died 1469.

[3] This is the second time that Mirza Haidar gives an equivalent for *Táráz,* which may be read in several different ways, as for instance *Yangi, Maniki, Masiki, Baiki,* etc. It is more than probable that *Yangi* is intended, but Erskine, when preparing his *Hist. of India,* seems to have read, in this place, *Masiki.* He notes that Baber refers to the event mentioned in the text, thus: "Baber says that Abu Said advanced beyond *Yangi,* and gave Isanbugha a severe defeat at a town in Moghulistan called Aspera. (*Mem.,* pp. 11, 12.) Mirza Haidar makes him overtake the Khán at *Masiki,* in books called *Táráz.* . . . Otrar is known by the names of *Taraz, Yangi* (or *Yangi Kent*), and, it would appear, of *Masiki.*" Baber does say, on the first page of his *Memoirs,* that "in

fled without offering battle, and Sultán Abu Said Mirzá returned to his own country [Mávará-un-Nahr]; but when he had taken

former times" there was a city called *Yangi*, "known in books of history by the name of *Otrár*," but he adds that in his own time it was in ruins and depopulated. Quatremère also took *Táráz* to be another name for *Otrár*, because the latter had at one time borne the name of *Yangi*. But there are, and have been at all times, many towns of the name of *Yangi*, or *New*, either used alone or combined with *Kand*, *Hisar*, *Shahr*, etc., just as we have everywhere in England, Newton, Newport, Newcastle, etc. Indeed, in most countries the adjective "new" is one of the commonest parts of place-names.

Táráz, as we have seen in note 1, p. 63, was without doubt situated on the *Tálás* river, probably at or near the modern Aulia-Ata, and would therefore have stood about one hundred and sixty miles, in direct distance, to the eastward of *Otrár*. Thus the only inference is, that two places of the same name are spoken of by some of the Oriental writers. There was indeed a third in this particular region, for Mr. Lerch, in 1867, explored and made us acquainted with the ruins of an ancient *Yángi*, or *Yángi-Kand* on the Sihun, some distance below Otrár.

As regards Baber's *Yangi*, mentioned in reference to the pursuit of the Moghuls by Abu Said, it is obvious that neither of those on the Sihun can be indicated, for we are clearly told (1) that the Moghuls were flying towards their own country, and (2) that they were defeated at *Asparáh*. If they had passed by *Otrár*, they would not have been going in the direction of Moghulistan, and there is no *Asparáh* in that direction. In order to retreat to Moghulistan, on the other hand, they must necessarily have passed by, or near, Táráz, while beyond that place they would have come to *Asparáh*. Thus there is, I think, sufficient evidence to identify the *Yángi*, or *Yangi-Kand*, of Mirza Haidar with *Táráz*, and to regard the *Masiki* of Erskine as a mere misreading of the text he used. Moreover, it seems possible that he may have been misled into this reading through the frequent mentions by Baber, in his *Memoirs*, of a place which he writes *Masikha*. Athough, as Erskine himself has shown in his map, it is an entirely different place, and should never be confused with his *Masiki* or *Yangi*, still the writing in the original text may have misled him.

But if Erskine read *Masiki* as an equivalent for *Táráz* he is not singular, for Quatremère thought that the original of Haidar Rázi might possibly be read in the same, or nearly the same, way. Thus he translates the "meadows of Talas and Kentchek which are vulgarly called *Meski* and *Taraz*"; though he notes that perhaps the word *Meski* may stand for *Yangi*. This, however, is only a question of reading the texts—not of the identification of the places—and an inspection of the text of Haidar Rázi, would probably show that the word was written in the same way as Mirza Haidar has written it.

Farther on, in this history, we shall see that Mirza Haidar again refers to *Táráz* as a city mentioned in books, where "it is written that the Moghuls call *Táráz, Yangi*." Here there is no question of any other reading of the text. He adds that traces of several other ancient towns are found in the same neighbourhood, but that "it is not known which of these old cities was Yangi, or what were the names of the others." This point may be cleared up by a reference to Quatremère's translation of the *Masálak Al Absár* (a work of the first half of the fourteenth century), where we are told that from Samarkand to Yangi twenty days' journey was reckoned, and that the latter city consisted of four towns, separated one from the other by a distance of one "parasang." Each town had its own particular name, one being called Yengi, the second Yengi-bálik, the third Kenchak, and the fourth Tálás (or Táráz). Again, in the *Haft Iklim* (Quatremère) it is said that "Táráz . . . bore also the name of Yangi"; while in the geography of Sádik Ispaháni (Ouseley) we find the two names coupled together thus: "Yangi-Tiráz, a city of Turkistan." The Arab writer, Mukadasi (according to Sprenger) included *Táráz* in a list of towns belonging to the province of *Isfiján*, which is the ancient name for Sairám, near Chimkent. Istákhri and Idrisi (according to the same authority) make the distance from Samarkand to *Táráz* twenty-two and twenty-three days respectively. Ibn Khordádbah reckons it about five days (twenty-six farsákhs) from *Isfiján*; while Arab Shah (on Bretschneider's authority) places it about four days from Sairám (which

Khorásán, he repaired to that country.[1] Isán Bughá Khán went to Andiján, where Mirzá Ali Kuchuk, having been put in command by Mirzá Sultán Abu Said, had fortified the citadel. The Khán had troops enough to enable him to surround the citadel with a triple line of men. He ran mines in every direction. The outer fort was taken. . . .[2] Finally peace was concluded, and many complimentary presents given [*pishkash*]. The Khán having taken possession of the whole district of Andiján, departed. There are to this day in Káshghar, descendants of the men who were made prisoners in this war, and they are Moghuls.[3]

When Sultán Abu Said Mirzá heard this news, he was at a loss to know how he could put a check on Isán Bughá Khán. For if he advanced into Moghulistán, the Khán would withdraw to the farthest extremities of the country, whither it would be impossible for the army of Samarkand to follow him, and when the army should retreat the Khán would follow after it.[4] Again it was out of the question to be always sending people to oppose him; for Isán Bughá's strength and numbers generally proved obstacles to the Amirs who were sent.

All this time Mirzá Sultán Abu Said was intent upon an expedition against Irák, but on account of the trouble and annoyance caused him by Isán Bughá Khán, he was not able to carry out his plan of marching into Irák. So he sent to summon Yunus Khán, the elder brother of Isán Bughá Khán, from Irák,

---

agrees fairly with Khordádbah), though he makes it fifteen only from Samarkand. These distances, except perhaps the last mentioned, would suit well for a position on the *Tálás* river.

On the whole, no further evidence is, I think, needed to demonstrate (1) that *Maski*, or *Masiki*, is only a misreading of *Yángi*; and (2) that *Yangi* and *Táráz* were one and the same place and stood on, or about, the same site as the modern Aulia-Ata—though there were several other *Yangis* in Central Asia. It may be added here that D'Avezac gives some curious variants of the name Yangi Kand or Yangi-Kent, culled from old authors—*viz.*, *Iankine, Ianekin, Iakynt, Sakine, Sarguit*, etc.

(See Baber, pp. 1, 11, 12, 101, 102; Erskine's *Hist.*, i., p. 47; Yule's *Cathay*, p. ccxiii; Schuyler, i., pp. 404, and ii., pp. 120-1; Bretschneider, ii., p. 252; Sprenger, pp. 19, 22, 23; Quatremère, *Not. et Extr.*, xiii., pp. 224–26; D'Avezac, *Receuil de Voyages*, iv., pp. 505 and 513; Sadik Ispaháni, p. 56; Howorth, ii., pp. 286 *seq.; Thonnelier, Dic. Géogr.*, pp. 45 *seq.*)

[1] Sultan Abu Said Mirza was great-grandson of Amir Timur, and grandfather of Baber. He was ruler of Mávará-un-Nahr from 1451 to 1468, and at the time spoken of in the text (863 H., or 1459) had also conquered Khorasán and Balkh. He was perhaps the most powerful chief then ruling in Central Asia, and his capital, Herat, was famed for its institutions, its architecture and its men of learning.

[2] An unintelligible passage of six words occurs here.—R.

[3] This is the literal translation of the sentence. The meaning probably is, as Erskine has inserted it in the Introduction to his *Hist.* (p. 48)—"and they are become perfect Moghuls."

[4] This is exactly the difficulty that Timur experienced in dealing with the Moghuls under the leadership of Kamaruddin. Their traditional tactics, as described here, seem alone to have rendered them formidable to their western neighbours.

where, as has been already mentioned, Yunus was living at that time; he then despatched Yunus Khán against Isán Bughá Khán, in order that while the two brothers were engaged in fighting one another, his own country might enjoy a little peace. The Moghul Amirs who had separated from [Isán Bughá] Khán and all those who, having built castles, would not yield obedience to him, the Khán did not oppose in their proceedings, in the hope that they would again return to [their allegiance to] him.

At that time Abulkhair Khán exercised full power in the Dasht-i-Kipchák. He had been at war with the Sultáns of the race of Juji; while Jáni Beg Khán and Karái Khán fled before him into Moghulistán. Isán Bughá Khán received them with great honour, and delivered over to them Kuzi Báshi,[1] which is near Chu, on the western limit of Moghulistán, where they dwelt in peace and content. On the death of Abulkhair Khán the *Ulus* of the Uzbegs fell into confusion, and constant strife arose among them. Most of them joined the party of Karái Khán and Jáni Beg Khán. They numbered about 200,000 persons, and received the name of Uzbeg-Kazák.[2] The Kazák Sultáns began to reign in the year 870 [1465–66] (but God knows best), and they continued to enjoy absolute power in the greater part of Uzbegistán, till the year 940 [1533–34 A.D.]. Karái Khán was succeeded by Baranduk Khán, who was in turn succeeded by Kásim Khán, the son of Jáni Beg Khán. Kásim Khán subdued the whole of the Dasht-i-Kipchák. His army numbered more than a million [a thousand thousand] men. Excepting Juji Khán, there had never reigned a greater Khán than he in that country. He was succeeded by his son Mimásh Khán, who was succeeded by his brother Táhir Khán. During the rule of this Táhir Khán, the Kazáks began to diminish; after him his brother Birilásh reigned. During his rule there were only 20,000 Kazáks left. In 940 he died, and the Kazáks disappeared entirely. From the days of Isán Bughá Khán to the time of Rashid Khán,[3] friendly relations generally existed between the Moghuls and the Kazáks. But Rashid Sultán upset this state of affairs, as will be related (God willing) in the account I shall give of Rashid Khán.

[1] Another reading of this name is *Jud Kuzi Báshi*. It is not traceable on modern maps.

[2] This brief statement is valuable, as showing not only how this particular tribe came into existence, but, generally, how a new tribe with a new name may arise from mere local circumstances and passing events. For some remarks on this particular event and on the passages which follow, see note 1, p. 272, and Howorth, ii., p. 6.

[3] Isan Bugha reigned from 832 to 866 H. (or 1429–62 A.D.). Rashid's reign dates from the end of 939 H., or 1533, and lasted till 973 H., or 1565–6; but the alienation of the Kazáks took place in the early years of his rule. Thus the alliance continued for about a hundred years. Regarding the author's statement that the Kazáks "disappeared entirely" from about the year 940 H. (1533), see note 1, p. 272, and Sec. vi. of the Introduction.

CHAPTER XL.

THE COMMENCEMENT OF THE KHÁNSHIP OF YUNUS KHÁN.

SULTÁN ABU SAID MIRZÁ, son of Sultán Muhammad Mirzá, son of Míránsháh Mirzá, son of Amir Timur, got the upper hand of his cousins and took Samarkand from Abdullah Mirzá of Shiráz. After the death of Mirzá Bábar Kalandar,[1] son of Mirzá Báisanghar, son of Mirzá Sháh Rukh, son of Amir Timur, there was no *pádishàh* in Khorásán. So [Sultán Abu Said Mirzá] took possession of Khorásán; his heart was set upon appropriating for himself Irák also, but, as has been mentioned, the opposition of Isán Bughá Khán prevented him from absenting himself upon so long an expedition. He therefore sent to fetch Yunus Khán, the elder brother of Isán Bughá Khán, from Irák (the reason of whose going to Irák has been explained above), and having established his court at Kushk-i-Bágh-i-Zághán,[2] he instituted princely feasts in honour of the Khán. They made many compacts and agreements, and among other things, Sultán Abu Said Mirzá said to the Khán: "In Amir Timur's first expedition, his generals would not obey him as they should have done. Now, if he had ordered them all to be put to death, he would but have weakened his own power. The generals said to him: 'You should appoint a Khán, whom we must obey.' So Amir Timur appointed Suyurghátmish Khán over them, and the generals submitted to the Khán. All *firmáns* were issued in this Khán's name, but Amir Timur kept careful watch over him. After his death, his son Sultán Mahmud Khán was appointed in his stead. But from the reign of Amir Timur down to the time of Mirzá Ulugh Beg, the power of these Kháns was only nominal; and in my own time the Kháns have generally been prisoners in Samarkand. Since I have ascended the throne, my power is so absolute that I have no need of a Khán; so now I have divested you of the garments of poverty and, having clothed you in princely robes, am sending you back to your native country on the following conditions:—For the future you must not follow the example of your ancestors and say, 'Amir Timur and the race of Amir Timur are our vassals, and have been for generations.' For although it was formerly so, things have changed now, and I am

[1] His real name was Abdul Kásim Baber. (See Genealogical Table of Timuri, attached.)

[2] The *Bágh-i-Zághán* is a celebrated garden situated outside the north-western angle of the walls of Herat. Its foundation is attributed to Shah Rukh and his wife Gauhar Shád Aghá, and thus dates from the first half of the fifteenth century. (See Khánikoff in *Journ. Asiat.*, 5 série I., xv., June, 1860, pp. 537–43, and plan.)

pádisháh in my own right; thus, now if you are going to be my vassal, you must bear the name of 'servitor' [*Khádim-i-Makhdum*] and do away with the name of 'friend.' You need not, however, write to me in the way the Kháns used to write to the Timuri Mirzás, but in a friendly way;[1] and these conditions are to apply to your sons and your sons' sons." Yunus Khán agreed to all these conditions, and swore a solemn oath to abide by them. He was then allowed to depart, accompanied by all the Moghuls who were in that district.

CHAPTER XLI.

DETAILED ACCOUNT OF THE PROCEEDINGS OF YUNUS KHÁN.

I HAVE only given a summarised account of Yunus Khán in the above Chapter; I will now enter more into detail.

Yunus Khán was the son of Vais Khán, son of Shir Ali Oghlán, son of Muhammad Khán, son of Khizir Khwája Khán, son of Tughluk Timur Khán. I have never heard the date of his birth, but from the date of his death and the length of his days, it may be inferred that he was born in the year 819 of the Hajra [1416], but God alone knows. He succeeded to the Khánate upon the death of his father, Vais Khán. There was much dissension between himself and his brother Isán Bughá Khán, and the Amirs; Irazán and Mirák Turkomán had seized the Khán and several of the chiefs of families, and had taken them to Ulugh Beg in Samarkand. This was when the Khán was sixteen years of age. This disaster [*viráni*], which took place in the year 832 of the Hajra, forms, down to the present day, an epoch among the Moghuls.[2]

Mirzá Ulugh Beg sent the Khán to his father, in the manner related, and the Khán was received with all honour and respect by Mirzá Sháh Rukh, who put him under the guidance and care of Mauláná Sharaf-ud-Din Yazdi. The Mauláná was a man of profound learning, and had not an equal in all Samarkand, Khorásán or Irák. In former times enigmas [*muammá*] were of a different sort to what one commonly meets with nowadays. This new kind was introduced by the Mauláná, and he has written a book concerning the solution of these enigmas. He is the author, too, of the *Zafar-*

[1] The meaning probably is—"Before the world, and officially, you are only my vassal or subordinate, but you may write to me privately as a friend, and not with the humility that the Khans had to use to the Timuri Mirzas."

[2] Or, more literally, one of the principal dates in Moghul history.—R.

Náma. He also wrote some mystical commentaries on poetry,[1] and he has never been excelled, at any time, in this style of commentary. Many other works were written by him, which it would take too long to enumerate here. I only wish to demonstrate how very talented he was. The Khán studied twelve years under him, with the result that there never was, either before or after, so wise a Khán as he, among the Moghuls.

When Khidmat Mauláná died, the Khán left Yazd and made a journey in Fárs and Azarbáiján. He profited much by his travelling, and gained great experience of life. He finally selected Shiráz as a residence; there he mixed with the learned men of the place, and acquired many useful sciences and crafts, so that he became known as Ustád Yunus.

In the meanwhile, Mirzá Sultán Abu Said had seized Khorásán, and was meditating the conquest of Irák, but was prevented from carrying out this project, by the frequent incursions of Isán Bughá Khán into Farghána, Shásh and Turkistán, which caused all ideas of an expedition into Irák to be temporarily abandoned. In the year 860 of the Hajra, Mirzá Sultán Abu Said sent people to summon the Khán from Shiráz, under the conditions above mentioned, and to conduct him to Moghulistán. The Khán was then forty-one years of age.[2]

[1] Or commentaries *in* verse; the text is uncertain.—R.

[2] Among the works of Sharaf-ud-Din, the best known to Europeans is the *Zafar-Náma* (called sometimes the *Tárikh-i-Sáhib Kiráni*), so copiously cited by Mirza Haidar at the beginning of this history. Besides being an author, Sharaf-ud-Din is said to have been an astronomer, and to have assisted Ulugh Beg in the observations used for the astronomical tables. The *Zafar-Náma* may be described as a panegyric, as well as a history, of Amir Timur, and was dedicated to Shah Rukh Mirza in 1425. A French translation by M. Pétis de la Croix was published in 1722 and 1723, though it had been completed some years before the translator's death, which occurred in 1695. Sharaf-ud-Din died in the year 858 H. (1454 A.D.) according to Dr. Rieu, so that we ought here to have a date for fixing the life and reign of Yunus Khán. If Yunus was twenty-four years old in 858 (as Mirza Haidar says at p. 74), and returned to Moghulistan as Khán when he was forty-one, he must have remained in exile for seventeen years after the Mauláná's death, and thus began to reign only in 875 H., or 1470–1. If, however, his capture took place in 832, and he was then sixteen years of age, he must have been forty-two when the Mauláná died in 858, and forty-four at his restoration, if that event occurred, as the author states, in 860. There is thus an irreconcilable difference of fifteen years in the date of the beginning of his reign. Baber gives an account of these transactions, but, unfortunately, mentions no dates. He says that five or six months after the arrival of Yunus at Shiráz, Sultan Ibrahim (second son of Shah Rukh and Governor of Fars) died, and was succeeded by his son Abdulla Mirza, under whom Yunus took service, and remained seventeen or eighteen years—until he was summoned to Herat, and made Khan of Moghulistan by Sultan Abu Said Mirza. Farther on it will be seen that our author says Yunus was born in 818, and died, at the age of seventy-four, in 892. If this is correct, and if his capture should date from 832, he would at that time have been fourteen years old. This leaves only a difference of two years in his age to be reconciled, but it does not clear up the discrepancy in the date of the commencement of his reign. (See Rieu's *Brit. Mus. Catalogue*, i., p. 173; Beale's *Orient. Biogr. Dict.*; Erskine's *Baber*, p. 11; Erskine's *Hist.*, i., pp. 45 and 49.)

CHAPTER XLII.

ARRIVAL OF YUNUS KHÁN IN MOGHULISTÁN.

I HAVE already shown that in Moghulistán, each Amir had fortified himself where he happened to be. After this demonstration of contumacy, and the murder of Timur Uighur, Isán Bughá had withdrawn to Aksu. When Yunus Khán arrived in Moghulistán, the first of the Amirs to join him was Mir Karim Bardi; and after him, Kunji, together with several of the dispersed Moghuls, entered the Khán's service. The Khán then married the daughter of Mir Pir Haji Kunji, who was at that time an Amir Tumán of the Kunji [clan] and enjoyed absolute authority. Her name was Isán Daulat Begum. By her the Khán had three sons, each of whom will be spoken of in his proper place. Of the Begjik Amirs in Issigh Kul, Mir Pir Hakk Bardi had died, and had been succeeded by his nephew Mir Ibráhim, who also came and attached himself to the Khán.

All these Amirs offered their services to the Khán, but as they had for so long a time been acting independently, and each one for himself, they did not fulfil their duties, or offer the Khán fitting allegiance. Nevertheless, he humoured them in every way possible.

When some years had passed in this manner, the Khán set out against Káshghar. Amir Sayyid Ali was now grown very old, so that he could no longer sit on horseback. He sent a messenger [to ask help] of Isán Bughá Khán, and meanwhile fortified himself in the citadel of Káshghar. Isán Bughá Khán happened, at the time, to be in Yulduz of Moghulistán, which is on the eastern side of his dominions. When the message reached him, he immediately collected a large army, which numbered 60,000 men; with this force he marched from Yulduz, and arrived at Káshghar eleven days later. Only 6,000 men were with him, the others were still on the road [so great had been the rapidity of his march]. He was then joined by the Amir with 30,000 men. A battle was fought at Khwán-i-Sálár, which is about three *farsákhs* from Káshghar in the direction of Aksu. The fight was fiercely maintained, but finally Isán Bughá Khán and Amir Sayyid Ali were victorious. [Yunus] Khán was compelled to take flight, while his wives and family fell into the hands of Amir Sayyid Ali. At that time Mihr-i-Nigár Khánim, the eldest child of Yunus Khán, by Isán Daulat Begum, was still at the breast. They were supplied with necessaries and sent after the Khán.

When Yunus Khán reached Moghulistán, he was deserted by his followers, and finding it was impossible to remain in that country, he left it and proceeded to Khorásán, where he presented himself before Mirzá Sultán Abu Said. But the Khán was in such a state of destitution, that he could find nothing to offer as a present [*pishkash*] to the Mirzá. So the Khán said to Buyán Kuli, who was one of his most devoted servants: "I am going to give you as a slave to the Mirzá, by way of a 'pishkash.'" And as the man offered no objection, the Khán presented him to the Mirzá, and entreated the Mirzá, saying: "You must give me some country [*viláyat*] as a possession, so that I may inspire the Moghuls with confidence." The Mirzá gave him Yatikand,[1] which is on the confines of Andiján. When the hour of the Khán's departure arrived, Buyán Kuli began to weep. The Mirzá questioned him as to the cause of his tears. Having told his story, the Mirzá took pity on him, and supplying him with a horse and provisions, sent him along with the Khán.

On re-entering Moghulistán, the Khán was once more joined by his scattered adherents. At this time Amir Sayyid Ali died in Káshghar. On the dome of the mausoleum of Amir Sayyid Ali, which is in Káshghar, is written the date 862. Yunus Khán was relieved of much anxiety by the death of the Amir.

CHAPTER XLIII.

RULE OF MIRZÁ SÁNIZ IN KÁSHGHAR AFTER THE DEATH OF HIS FATHER, MIR SAYYID ALI.

THE Amir died leaving two sons. The elder was Mirzá Sániz, whose mother was of the family [*kabilah*] of the Amirs of the Jarás; and the younger was Muhammad Haidar Mirzá, whose

[1] This name is subject to many different readings, not only in the *Tarikh-i Rashidi*, but in other Asiatic histories, and has been frequently transliterated *Banikand*, *Yanikand*, *Batikand*, *Itikand*, etc. Mirza Haidar, however, gives, lower down (p. 180), the Persian equivalent for it as *Haft Deh*; and this settles the question, for *Haft Deh*, or *Seven villages*, translated into Turki, would become *Yati-kand*. This last form has been adopted, therefore, whenever the name occurs. He tells us that the district was situated on the confines of *Andiján*, but in this instance, it is possible that he may be using the word *Andiján* to denote the whole province of *Farghána*—in fact, as an equivalent for *Farghána*. In some modern maps a district called *Itikand* or *Itikent* is marked to the north of the Sir, and between the modern town of Khokand and Tashkand; but it seems hardly possible that this district can represent the *Yatikand* of the fifteenth century. It must have stood on the north-western confines of Farghána, and would have constituted the extreme western limit of Moghulistan. (See note 1, pp. 180–1.)

mother was Urun Sultán Khánim, the aunt of Yunus Khán. According to Moghul custom, Sániz, being the elder, succeeded to the government. He was a violent, but generous man. Out of respect and reverence for his mother, and his love and affection for his brother, he gave Káshghar and Yángi Hisár to the Khánim, and Muhammad Haidar Mirzá [respectively], while he chose Yárkand for his seat of government.

Although Muhammad Haidar Mirzá was cousin to both Yunus Khán and Isán Bughá Khán, yet he naturally sided with the latter, because Amir Sayyid Ali had chosen Daulat Nigár Khánim, the daughter of Isán Bughá Khán, as a wife for Muhammad Haidar Mirzá.

Soon after the death of Mir Sayyid Ali, Isán Bughá Khán died also; this was in the year 866. His son Dust Muhammad Khán succeeded to the Khánate. Muhammad Haidar Mirzá allied himself with Dust Muhammad Khán, while Sániz Mirzá, on the other hand, became a partisan of Yunus Khán. Under these circumstances it became impossible for Muhammad Haidar Mirzá to remain in Káshghar, so he left, and joined Dust Muhammad Khán in Aksu.

After this, Sániz Mirzá governed Káshghar so well, and administered justice so evenly, that his time was looked back on with envy by those who came after him. He ruled during seven years, and died in the year 869 [1464–5]. He fell from his horse while out hunting, and ran five arrow-heads into his loins, causing wounds which proved fatal. After his death, the inhabitants of Káshghar brought Muhammad Haidar Mirzá to their town, while Dust Muhammad Khán advanced on Yarkand, where he married the widow of Sániz Mirzá, Jamál Aghá by name, who had given Sániz Mirzá two sons, viz.: Mirzá Abá Bakr and Omar Mirzá, and one daughter, called Khán Sultán Khánim, all of whom the Khán took back with him to Aksu. (I will speak about them below.)

CHAPTER XLIV.

KHÁNSHIP OF DUST MUHAMMAD KHÁN.

When Isán Bughá Khán died (a natural death) he was succeeded by his son Dust Muhammad Khán, who was then seventeen years of age. He was an eccentric youth, and his actions were unreasonable. He was never for a moment in his senses. He much affected the ways of Kalandars, and gave himself and all his Amirs such names as are usually borne by Kalandars. His own name was Shams Abdál, and in the same way, all his courtiers and public officers were called Abdál this and Abdál that, and had to transact their business under these names. He was, moreover, excessively generous.

He reigned seven years. During this time he made expeditions against Yárkand and Káshghar. First of all he attacked Yárkand, where, after the death of Sániz Mirzá, the Amirs had shut themselves up in the citadel. The Khán asked them to surrender the widow of Sániz Mirzá: when she had been given up to him, he asked for the children, of whom they sent the eldest son Mirzá Abá Bakr. He then ceased hostilities, and went on to Káshghar. At the time when he had set out against Yárkand, Muhammad Haidar Mirzá, upon the entreaty of the people of Káshghar, proceeded to their town. When the Khán neared Káshghar, Muhammad Haidar Mirzá set out to meet him; the Khán sent him to Yángi Hisár, while he himself entered Káshghar, and when he had plundered it, he returned to Aksu. In consequence of this, Muhammad Haidar Mirzá was much enraged, and went over to the side of Yunus Khán (as will be mentioned below). Soon after Dust Muhammad Khán's return to Aksu, he gave his sister, Husn Nigár Khánim, to Mirzá Abá Bakr in marriage. But Mirzá Abá Bakr was much alarmed at the unbalanced state of the Khán's mind, and finally fled to his noble uncle Muhammad Haidar Mirzá, in Káshghar, whither his wife was, soon after, permitted to follow him.

Not long after this, the Khán fell in love with one of his father's wives, and in consequence tried to obtain permission from the Ulamá for an alliance with her. He put to death seven of the Ulamá in succession, who decided against the union. At length the Khán came to Mauláná Muhammad Attár, reeling with drunkenness and with a sword in his hand, and said to him: "I want to marry my own mother; is it lawful or not?" The Mauláná, who was one of the most learned of the darvishes and a most pious man, said to the Khán: "For such a one as you it is lawful." So the Khán immediately ordered preparations for the marriage to be made. But on the night of the nuptials he saw his father, in a dream, mounted on a black horse, who, coming up to him, said: "Oh! wretched one, in that after we have for one hundred years been Musulmáns, thou shouldst apostasise and become an infidel." [His father] shot him below the ribs with an arrow, then dismounting, he rubbed his hand on the bottom of a kettle, and blackened the Khán's face, who thereupon awoke, in alarm. Breathless and penitent, he rushed out of the house of his mother and washed himself. He was seized with an acute pain in the side, which, in the morning, developed into fever.

The people sent for Mauláná Muhammad Attár, and said to him: "It was you who granted the *fatvá* [decree legalising this marriage].” The Khán said: “Do not blame the Mauláná; for I had already killed seven persons when I asked his opinion, so what could the poor Mullá do?” But the Mauláná said: “I gave you no *fatva*, I simply said that [the marriage] was lawful for an infidel such as you are.” Dust Muhammad Khán was next seized with pleurisy [*Zatuljamb*] and died after six days' illness at the age of forty, in the year 873 [1468–9]. Khwája Sharif of Káshghar devised the following chronogram on his death: “*U Khuk murd*”: that pig died. He had reigned seven years. On his death great disorder ensued. He left one son, Kabak Sultán Oghlán, who was seized by some of the people and carried away to Turfán and Chálish,[1] while Yunus Khán came down and captured Aksu.

CHAPTER XLV.

SECOND RETURN OF YUNUS KHÁN FROM [THE COURT OF] SULTÁN ABU SAID.

When Yunus Khán was sent back by Sultán Abu Said into Moghulistán, he was, on his arrival in that country, again joined by all the Amirs; he remained there some time, his headquarters being generally Yatikand. He was not, however, able to enter the territory of Isán Bughá Khán. When the latter and Amir Sayyid Ali died, Dust Muhammad Khán became *pádishúh*, and was joined in Aksu by Muhammad Haidar Mirzá, while Sániz Mirzá, who had been at enmity with Muhammad Haidar Mirzá, attached himself to Yunus Khán, to whom he was of great service. Yunus Khán entered Káshghar several times, but the Amirs of Moghulistán refused to stay there, so the Khán was always compelled to withdraw. This happened several times, but I will not give any details, as it would take too long, and the accounts I have heard differ considerably. The substance of the whole matter is that the Khán was very fond of cities and houses, but the Amirs and soldiers of Moghulistán always avoided the towns, and for this reason the Khán spent most of his time in Moghulistán. When Sániz Mirzá died, the Khán was joined by Muhammad Haidar Mirzá. A short time after this, Dust Muhammad Khán also died, whereupon Yunus Khán entered Aksu and subdued the subjects of Dust Muhammad Khán, while the son of this latter, Kabak Sultán Oghlán, was seized by some of his well-wishers, who fled with him to Turfán.

[1] Jálish or Chálish—the modern Kará-shahr.

Yunus Khán wished to dwell in Aksu. In comparison with Moghulistán, Aksu is like a town;[1] but he concluded, from the manner of the Moghuls, that if he stayed there much longer, they would all go over to the side of Kabak Sultán Oghlán, so he was compelled to call together all his tribesmen and return with them to Moghulistán. At this time Amásánji Táishi, son of Isán Táishi (whom I have mentioned in connection with Vais Khán) came to Moghulistán. For Isán Táishi had given him [in marriage] Makhtum Khánim, sister of Vais Khán, as a ransom for the Khán's life, and by her he [Amásánji Táishi] had two sons and one daughter. When Vais Khán had bestowed his sister, he had obliged his brother-in-law to become a Musulmán, and they were married with Muhammadan rites. The Khánim caused all her following to become Musulmáns, and named her two sons Ibráhim and Ilyás, and her daughter Kádir Bardi Mirzá, after Mir Karim Bardi. This conversion to Islám was the cause of a conflict between Ibráhim Ung and Ilyás Ung, on the one hand, and Amásánji Táishi on the other. (In the language of the Kálmáks the son of a Khán is called "Ung.") Amásánji fled before them into Moghulistán with thirty times 100,000 men, while it is stated, that eighteen times 100,000 stayed behind with Ibráhim Ung and Ilyás Ung. These two, however, quarrelled with the Khán of the Kálmáks, and therefore fled from that country into Khitái with 10,000 men. The rupture [*viráni*] between the brothers [and Amásánji] took place before the death of Dust Muhammad Khán, which occurred in 873. The flight of Ibráhim Ung and Ilyás Ung into Khitái took place, probably, in 910 [1504–5].[2] These two both died in Khitái. Ibráhim left one son, Bábulái by name, whose descendants are still to be met with in that country, and who still bear the same name of Bábulái. Mansur Khán made a holy war [*ghazát*] against Khitái and came in contact with that very tribe (as will be mentioned shortly).

But Amásánji Táishi, having separated himself from Ibráhim Ung and Ilyás Ung, came to Moghulistán. Near the River Ailah he came upon and defeated Yunus Khán. In that fight many Moghul Amirs were killed . . . .[3] and all the Moghul *Ulus* moved

[1] Meaning that although Aksu is only a small place, life there would be town life, while in Moghulistan it would be the life of the steppes.

[2] This passage is somewhat obscure. The word *viráni* should mean *ruin, devastation*, or *expulsion*, rather than *rupture*, and it appears to refer to the flight of the brothers into Khitai, or Chinese territory. But the dates which the author mentions show, I think, that the conflict between them and Amásánji, and the latter's flight into Moghulistan, are the events he speaks of when using the word *viráni*. If this is correct, a period of thirty-six years, or more, elapsed between those events and the retreat of the brothers into Chinese territory, *i.e.*, from some date prior to 873 (1468–9) to the year 910 (1504–5). These occurrences are not traceable in the translations from the Chinese history of the Ming dynasty, published by Dr. Bretschneider in his *Mediæval Researches*.

[3] A passage of five words here is unintelligible.—R.

towards Turkistán, spending the winter at a place in Turkistán, on the banks of the Sihun, called Kará Tukái.[1] Buruj Oghlán made a raid upon them, as will be hereafter related.

CHAPTER XLVI.

EVENTS WHICH FOLLOWED ON THE DEATH OF DUST MUHAMMAD KHÁN; THE SUPREMACY OF YUNUS KHÁN, AND THE MURDER OF BURUJ OGHLÁN, SON OF ABULKHAIR KHÁN UZBEG.

IN the year 855 Abulkhair, a descendant of Juji, was *pádisháh* in the kingdom [*yurt*] of Juji Khán, son of Chingiz Khán—that is in the Dasht-i-Kipchák; and he was the greatest king [*pádisháh*] of his time. After his death[2] his people became very demoralised, and a number of them joined the Kazáks, Karái Khán and Jáni Beg Khán (whom I have had occasion to mention). There was a standing quarrel between these two Kazáks, and the sons of Abulkhair Khán. For this reason the sons of Abulkhair were also at enmity with the Moghul Kh… For these last had always been the supporters of Karái Khán and Jáni Beg Khán. At the death of Abulkhair Khán, his subjects gathered round his eldest son Buruj Oghlán.[3] Seeing that Karái Khán and Jáni Beg Khán had become very powerful, Buruj Khán thought he had better keep at a distance from them, and so retired to Turkistán.

When [the inhabitants of] Turkistán learnt the news of the advance of the Moghuls on their territory, and having ascertained that Yunus Khán was at Kará Tukái, [they sent] Buruj out with all speed [to attack him]. On that day the Khán happened to be out hunting with all his men near the banks of the Sihun. Buruj, crossing the river on the ice at mid-day, found the camp of the Khán undefended; he had 20,000 soldiers with him, and there were at that time 60,000 families of Moghuls. They entered the camp

[1] Possibly the *Kara Sengir Tukai* of modern maps. (See map attached.)

[2] Abulkhair died in 874 A.H., or 1469–70 A.D. (See Howorth, ii., p. 690, where, however, the A.D. year is, by an oversight, printed 1489).

[3] The name of Buruj Oghlán does not appear, as Sir H. Howorth has pointed out, in the list of Abulkhair's sons. His eldest son was Shah Badágh Sultan, the father of the renowned Shahi Beg, or Shaibáni, Khan; and Sir H. Howorth is disposed to think that Buruj was only another name for Sháh Badágh. This is probable, for several of the Abulkhairi Uzbeg chiefs had second names, or nicknames. Dr. Bellew calls Buruj Oghlán the son of Jáni Beg, who was a grandson of Abulkhair; but apart from the fact that the name does not occur among Jáni Beg's sons, as they are known to us, a man of that generation would have been too young to take the part ascribed to him, at the time mentioned by Mirza Haidar. (Howorth, ii., p. 691; Bellew, *Yarkand Report*, p. 159.)

and each soldier made himself master of an untenanted house. They settled down in the Khán's camp, occupying themselves with the appropriation of all the wealth and spoil they found there.

When news of this matter reached the Khán he immediately abandoned the hunt, and set out in the direction of his camp without waiting to collect his men; when he reached the river he found it was frozen over. Now the Khán's camp was pitched on the [opposite] bank of the river. The Khán could blow the horn [*nafir*] better than any one of his day, and all his men knew the sound of his blast. He now gave a loud blast on the horn, and then rushed across the ice, accompanied by six men, one of whom was bearer of the great standard [*Shash Tughji*]. The women [hearing the approach of the Khán] seized all the Uzbegs who were in their houses. When Buruj Oghlán heard the sound of the horn and saw the six men and the standard, he rose up with the intent of mounting his horse, but the female servants had seized both his groom [*akhtaji*] and his horse. Some women [at that moment] came out of their houses and seized Buruj Oghlán, when the Khán, arriving upon the scene, ordered them to behead him; this order was carried out immediately, and of the 20,000 Uzbegs a few only escaped. The Khán then again settled down, victorious, in his camp. On the morrow, when the army had reassembled, the pursuit of the enemy was continued, and all the Sultáns of Abulkhair Khán who survived, were scattered in different directions. They will be mentioned, separately and individually, in different parts [of this book].

CHAPTER XLVII.

SHAIKH JAMÁL-UD-DIN AND HIS CAPTURE OF THE KHÁN.

HAVING passed the winter at Kará Tukái, the Khán proceeded in the spring to Táshkand. At that time there was, in Táshkand, one of the Amirs of Mirzá Sultán Abu Said, Shaikh Jamál-ud-Din Khar by name. Sultán Abu Said Mirzá had just died in Irák,[1] and had been succeeded in the rule of Khorásán by Sultán Husain Mirzá; while his son, Sultán Ahmad Mirzá, succeeded him in Samarkand. The government of Hisár, Kunduz and Badakhshán had devolved upon his son, Mirzá Sultán Mahmud, and Mirzá Omar Shaikh became *pádisháh* of Andiján, and *vali* of Farghána. Yunus Khán made all three of these Mirzás his sons-in-law. (I will mention

[1] Abu Said died 873 A.H.=1468-9 A.D. Beale (*Orient. Biogr. Dict.*) gives the exact date as 25 Rajab, 873, or 8th February, 1469.

each of them in his proper place.) In short, this Shaikh Jamál Khar was one of Sultán Abu Sáid's Amirs, and had been appointed Governor of Táshkand, subject to Mirzá Sultán Ahmad of Samarkand; but his allegiance to the Mirzá was very imperfect. The Khán, on account of the scarcity of barley in Moghulistán, came to Táshkand, where he mixed freely and unsuspectingly with the above-mentioned Mirzás. For the Khán had come without any apprehensions; but his Moghul followers had sent secretly to Shaikh Jamál Khar, inviting him to come and oppose the Khán, to which the Shaikh, after much persuasion, agreed. He approached the Khán as if to do him homage, but when he drew near, all the men who were with the latter, went forward to meet the Shaikh, leaving the Khán alone. The Khán asked where his men were going, to which they answered that they were going to meet Mir Shaikh Jamál. When Shaikh Jamál Khar came up to the standard and drum of the Khán, he remained on horseback; there was no one with the Khán, so the Shaikh sent one of the Khán's own servants to seize him, which was easily managed. The Khán was bound and kept in prison one year. The whole Moghul *Ulus* submitted to Shaikh Jamál.

Isán Daulat Begum, the wife of Yunus Khán and mother of his children, has been mentioned above as the mother of Mihr-i-Nigár Khánim, who was given in marriage to Sultán Ahmad Mirzá, and of Kutluk Nigár Khánim, who was wedded to Mirzá Omar Shaikh. This same Isán Daulat Begum was given, as a present, by Shaikh Jamál Khar, to one of his most distinguished officers. When the Begum heard of this, she made no objections, but appeared pleased. They then informed Khwája Kalán (as this officer was named) of the Begum's pleasure: he too was much pleased, and in the evening went to her house. He found her servants standing outside. He himself entered her room. Now, before his arrival, the Begum had arranged with her female attendants [*dáhán*] that on a given sign from herself, they should make fast all the doors of the house. So when Khwája Kalán had entered the room, having fastened the doors, the female attendants laid hold of him and put him to death, by stabbing him with knives [*kizlik*]. When day broke they threw his body outside. Some persons seeing the Khwája's dead body, went and reported the matter to Shaikh Jamál, who sent to ask the Begum the meaning of it all. The Begum replied: "I am the wife of Sultán Yunus Khán; Shaikh Jamál gave me to some one else; this is not allowed by Muhammadan law, so I killed the man, and Shaikh Jamál Khar may kill me also if he likes." Shaikh Jamál commended her words, and, taking pity on her, sent her back with all honour to the Khán [her husband].

When the Khán had been one year in prison, Amir Abdul Kudus, the nephew of Amir Karim Bardi Dughlát, with the assistance of a body of men, fell on the Shaikh and slew him. He then brought the head of the Shaikh to the Khán, and set him at liberty. The Amirs, who had gone over to the Shaikh, now returned to their allegiance under the Khán. They explained that the reason for the hostility they had shown him was, that he had always tried to make them settle in towns and cultivated countries, but that these places were hateful to them. So the Khán repented and said: "Henceforward I will give up all idea of living in towns and cultivated countries" [*shahr u viláyat*]. To record this event they invented the chronogram: *sar-i-khar giriftah Abdul Kudus*, which is enigmatical; for "sar-i-khar" is equivalent to the letter "*khá*" and has to be added to [the numerical value of] Abdul Kudus in order to produce the date 877 [1472–3].

At this time [in the same year] the Kálmáks returned to their own homes [*yurt*], and Moghulistán being left unoccupied, the Khán led his Moghuls back to their country.

CHAPTER XLVIII.

CONCERNING WHAT PASSED BETWEEN YUNUS KHÁN AND THE KINGS OF MÁVARÁ-UN-NAHR, AFTER THE MURDER OF SHAIKH JAMÁL KHAR.

As soon as the Khán had again established himself on the throne of the Khánate, the Moghuls and the Amirs made him promise never, for the future, to attempt to make them dwell in cities or cultivated countries [*shahr u viláyat*], which had been the cause of all their sedition and revolts. The Khán was obliged to comply, and they then re-entered Moghulistán, which had been vacated by the Kálmáks. During several years the Khán never even made mention [*hawá*] of towns or houses, so that at length the Moghuls became much attached to him.

Muhammad Haidar Mirzá, who was in Káshghar, yielded fitting obedience to the Khán, from whom he, in return, received demonstrations of paternal affection; and complete tranquillity prevailed in Moghulistán and Káshghar.

Soon after the Khán's return, the followers of Kabak Sultán Oghlán (son of Dust Muhammad Khán), who had fled in the direction of Turfán, having killed their master, brought his head to the Khán. But the Khán, in spite of Kabak having been his enemy, was (for Kabak's brother's sake) very angry, and ordered the murderers [to be put to death] by way of retaliation.

The Khán had now no enemies remaining on any side. After

he had killed Buruj Oghlán, he sent his eldest daughter, Mihr Nigár Khánim, to Sultán Ahmad Mirzá, son of Sultán Abu Said Mirzá, saying: "Sultán Abu Said Mirzá turned the enmity that existed between Moghul and Chaghatái into friendship. I wish now to cement this friendship with a family alliance, and therefore offer my daughter, as a wife, to the son of Sultán Abu Said Mirzá." Mihr Nigár Khánim remained in the haram of Mirzá Sultán Ahmad as long as he lived. (I shall have more to say of the Khánim in the second part of this work.)

After the Khán's return to Moghulistán, when Shaikh Jamál Khar had been put to death, he gave his daughter, Kutluk Nigár Khánim, who was younger than Mihr Nigár Khánim, in marriage to Omar Shaikh Mirzá, son of Sultán Abu Said Mirzá. This was in the year 880. There existed between the Khán and Omar Shaikh such an affection as is seldom even found between father and son. Omar Shaikh used to go and spend a month, or two months, at a time in Moghulistán, and sometimes he would bring back his father with him to Andiján, and the Khán would be his guest for a month or more. About this time Omar Shaikh tried to induce the Khán to march on Samarkand, and after depriving his brother Mirzá Sultán Ahmad (the eldest son-in-law of Yunus Khán) of the throne, to set him (Omar Shaikh) upon it, in his brother's stead. But the Khán would not hear of such a measure. When Sultán Ahmad heard of his brother's scheme, he set out to oppose him with an army. But Omar Shaikh Mirzá appealed to the Khán for succour, giving him, at the same time, some of his own territories. Thus Sultán Ahmad was hindered from making an invasion. This state of affairs was constantly recurring. It was, however, at length agreed that the Khán should come every winter to Andiján, attended only by his own personal servants; leaving the *Ulus* of the Moghul in Moghulistán. Omar Shaikh Mirzá was to give to the Khán whichever of his territories the latter might select. In the spring, the Khán was to return to Moghulistán, and the Mirzá again take possession of his own territories.

On one occasion, Omar Shaikh Mirzá, being in great fear of his brother, sent to Yunus Khán for support, while he gave over to him Akhsi. The Khán took up his winter quarters in Akhsi, hearing of which, Sultán Ahmad Mirzá abandoned his hostile intentions. Omar Shaikh Mirzá, though his mind was set at rest with regard to his brother, nevertheless did not like the Khán's residing in Akhsi. For Akhsi was the largest town in Farghána, and its capital. On this account he rose in arms against the Khán, and fought a battle against him at the Bridge of Tiká Sagrutku.[1]

[1] This name has been transliterated accurately, as it stands in the Persian text—the Turki texts are wanting here. The meaning would be "the camel's

The Khán at first remonstrated with the Mirzá, but in vain; and a battle ensued in which the Mirzá was defeated and taken prisoner. He was brought bound before the Khán, who rose up to meet him and ordered his hands to be set free. He then made him presents and sent him away, saying: "Return home at once, that your men be thrown into confusion. I too will follow you to your house." When Omar Shaikh Mirzá returned to Andiján, the Khán allowed his ***Ulus*** to go back to Moghulistán, while he himself proceeded to Andiján with his family [*kuj*] and a few followers. He remained in the house of the Mirzá for two months, and nothing disturbed their friendship.[1]

On another occasion when the Mirzá called on the Khán for assistance, he gave him Marghilán. While the Khán was in Marghilán, his Holiness, the Axis of pious works, the Cynosure of the pious, the Beloved of God, Khwája Násiruddin Ubaidullah (may God sanctify his spirit) came there in order to bring about a reconciliation between the Khán and Omar Shaikh Mirzá, on the one hand, and Sultán Ahmad Mirzá on the other. I have often heard from trustworthy narrators, that when his Holiness arrived near Marghilán, all the Moghuls and the inhabitants of the town came out to meet him [in *istikbál*], but none of the Moghuls had the presumption to approach him [to salute him], such was their great regard [for this holy man]. Men and women halted at a distance and, dismounting, fastened their horses to the ground, while they themselves kept their eyes fixed on the dust of the road. His Holiness then approached them. There was one among his retinue who recognised the Khán, and he said to his Holiness, "This is Yunus Khán." His Holiness immediately dismounted, and having raised the Khán's head from the ground, embraced him.

I once heard from his Holiness, the Refuge of Piety, Mauláná Muhammad Kázi (upon whom be mercy), who on a certain occasion went to Marghilán, the following: "I had heard that Yunus Khán was a Moghul, and I concluded that he was a beardless man, with the ways and manners of any other Turk of the desert. But when I saw him, I found he was a person of elegant deportment, with a full beard and a Tájik face,[2] and such refined

leap." Most likely, however, the name should read *Tekka Sagrutku* instead of *Tiká*, and should mean "the goat's leap." Baber records this battle as having taken place "to the north of Andiján, on the banks of the Sihun, at a place called *Tika-Sakaratku*, which derives its name from this circumstance, that the river, in flowing past the skirt of a hill, becomes so much contracted in breadth, that it is said that on one occasion a mountain goat leaped from the one bank to the other." (*Memoirs*, p. 9.)

[1] Lit.: No vexation came between them.—R.

[2] Or Tajik "features." That is, the Mauláná found Yunus to be of an Aryan, and not of a Mongoloid cast of countenance, a circumstance that shows how little of the Moghul was left, even in the fifteenth century, in a Khan of Moghulistan.

speech and manner, as is seldom to be found even in a Tájik." In short, when his Holiness had seen the Khán, he addressed letters to all the Sultáns round about, saying: "I have seen Yunus Khán and the Moghuls. The subjects of such a *pádisháh* are not to be carried off captives. They are people of Islám." From this time forth, no more Moghuls were bought or sold as slaves in Mávará-un-Nahr and Khorásán—for before this, the Moghuls had been purchased as other Káfirs are purchased.

CHAPTER XLIX.

RULE OF MUHAMMAD HAIDAR MIRZÁ IN KÁSHGHAR.

After the death of Sániz Mirzá, son of Amir Sayyid Ali, the government of Káshghar was given to Muhammad Haidar Mirzá, son of Amir Sayyid Ali (as was related above). When he had become firmly established in that place, Dust Muhammad Khán died.

Yunus Khan, in order to satisfy the Moghul *Ulus*, gave up all intention of inhabiting cities and cultivated lands. Muhammad Haidar Mirzá, in Káshghar, acknowledged the supremacy of the Khán, who in return treated him in a fatherly way. Muhammad Haidar Mirzá reigned in peace and prosperity for twenty-four years in all: that is from the year 869 to 885 (or sixteen years) he had absolute authority; and for the remainder, partial authority only.[1]

The family of Yunus, as we have seen, had for some generations past, intermarried in several directions. His origin, therefore, combined with his Persian training, would account for his appearance being unlike that of ordinary Moghuls.

The word *Turk*, in this passage, taken in connection with *Moghul*, is obviously used in a general, sociological, sense, and is intended more as a distinction to *Tájik* than as a race-name. But this subject has been treated of already in Sec. iv. of the Introduction, and need not be further discussed here. It may be remarked, however, that the word *Tájik*, though in this instance employed in its racial sense—for the speaker is pointing to the Khan's Aryan features—meant also, in many cases, merely a "foreigner," and more especially a "western foreigner." It was in this sense that the word was used at p. 14, above, in the story of the wrestling match between the priest and the Moghul. Some remarks on this subject also, will be found in Sec. iv. of the Introduction.

[1] Thus the remainder would be the eight years from 861 to 869. Erskine makes these periods "six years with imperfect, and eighteen years with full, authority." But the MSS. used for this translation read as in the text above. (Erskine's *Hist.* i., p. 539).

CHAPTER L.

BEGINNING OF THE REIGN OF ABÁ BAKR MIRZÁ.

ON the death of Sániz Mirzá, Dust Muhammad Khán went to Yárkand, and took the widow of Sániz Mirzá to wife. He then proceeded to Aksu, taking with him Abá Bakr Mirzá, the eldest son of Sániz Mirzá. Not long after this, he gave his sister Husn Nigár Khánim, in marriage to the young Mirzá. But Abá Bakr, fearing the unsoundness of Dust Muhammad Khan's mind, fled to his uncle Muhammad Haidar Mirzá; and Dust Muhammad Khán sent Husn Nigár Khánim after him to Káshghar (all of which I have already related).

Dust Muhammad was a very brave and generous man, and of so great a height, that if he stood on foot in the midst of a hundred people, any one seeing him would have said he was on horseback. But Muhammad Haidar Mirzá having inherited his power, did not know the value and importance of an army. The distinguished generals and captains which Amir Sayyid Ali had collected round his person during a life of eighty years, were in the time of Muhammad Haidar Mirzá, for the most part dead, and those who yet remained alive, were worn with age; while their sons and grandsons had no relations with Muhammad Haidar Mirzá. All the young men and the princes [*mirzázádah*] were in favour of Mirzá Abá Bakr. It would be a long story, to recount all the details concerning those who were parties to these intrigues; moreover, though it is only twenty years ago,[1] not one of them is alive now, and the various and conflicting reports which were at that time spread about, are now entirely forgotten. It is, however, certain that Mirzá Abá Bakr fled from Muhammad Haidar Mirzá, and presented himself before the Governor of Yárkand. Showing him a forged order, he, by cunning and deceit, made himself master of Yárkand. He then sent certain persons to his uncle Muhammad Haidar Mirzá, offering complete submission to him, which the Khán accepted, and sent him, for his own service, 3000 young princes from Káshghar. His brother, Omar Mirzá, who was in Káshghar at the time, now came to join him in the government of Yárkand. They united their efforts in an attempt to subdue Khotan. Having mentioned this town here, I think it necessary to say something about Khotan and its governors.

[1] It was, in fact, much more than 20 years—rather about 60 or 70 years.

CHAPTER LI.

ACCOUNT OF THE MIRZÁS OF KHOTAN.

KHOTAN is one of the most famous towns in the East. In the Second Part, I have given all that I have been able to learn from histories, and other books, concerning Khotan. When the Amirship [*Imárat*] of the Dughláts descended to Amir Khudáidád (upon whom be mercy), he divided all the dependencies of the Dughláts among his children and his brothers. Thus to his youngest son, Sayyid Ahmad Mirzá, he entrusted Káshghar and Yárkand. Amir Khudáidád had two maternal brothers [*umm-valad*], Ilyás Sháh and Khizir Sháh by name. To the former he gave Aksu, and to the latter Khotan, making them both subordinate to Sayyid Ahmad Mirzá, to whom he granted the power of their dismissal or appointment. These two, like all his other officers, used to come and wait on the Mirzá yearly, and then, when they were granted leave, they returned to their respective provinces. This practice was observed until the time of Amir Sayyid Ali.

When Amir Sayyid Ali gave Aksu to Isán Bughá Khán, there was, in the service of the latter, one of the grandsons of Ilyás Sháh Mirzá, who was also named Ilyás Sháh, and who, till the time of Dust Muhammad Khán, had the command of the fortress of Aksu. But after Amir Sayyid Ali, there were in Khotan two brothers, descendants of Khizir Sháh Mirzá; the name of one was Khán Nazar Mirzá, and of the other Kul Nazar Mirzá. The former reckoned himself equal in strength and power of the arm, to Mirzá Abá Bakr, nay even to Amir Sayyid Ali. He showed a spirit of independence, and threw off the old allegiance to Káshghar. Mirzá Abá Bakr begged permission of Muhammad Haidar Mirzá to go and conquer Khotan, on the ground that Khán Nazar and Kul Nazar had sought to deviate from that high-road of obedience, which was one of the conditions of their inheritance. Muhammad Haidar Mirzá, being himself displeased with these two [governors] granted the demand, and encouraged him [in the undertaking]. Thus Mirzá Abá Bakr acted freely in the matter of Khotan.

Khán Nazar Mirzá had made himself an iron club, which no one but he could lift with two hands; he, however, could wield it with one hand, and whatever he struck with it, were it a horse or a cow, inevitably fell. But his younger brother, Kul Nazar Mirzá, was a young man of great modesty. These two brothers aimed at becoming kings.

CHAPTER LII.

CAPTURE OF KHOTAN BY MIRZÁ ABÁ BAKR AND THE EXTIRPATION OF THE MIRZÁS OF KHOTAN.

In those days, when Mirzá Abá Bakr was intent on the conquest of Khotan, he had with him Omar Mirzá. His elder brother did not approve of his proceedings, and wished to join issue with him. Upon Mirzá Abá Bakr ascertaining this, he contrived to lay hands on him, and having blinded him, sent him to Muhammad Haidar Mirzá. After the destruction [*virání*] of Káshghar, Omar Mirzá went to Samarkand, where he was treated with kindness, till, in the year 921, he returned to Káshghar. Here he died, and was buried in the mausoleum of Amír Sayyid Ali.

In short, Abá Bakr being released from the molestations of his brother, continued his march upon Khotan. On the first occasion he made peace; on the second, matters were again concluded with a treaty. The two governors mounted, and having met and conferred together, they arranged the conditions of the peace, and took a solemn oath upon the Word of God, in confirmation of the agreement. Mirzá Abá Bakr, having given the bond to his own servants, handed the Korán [the *Kalám Ullah*][1] to one of his nobles, telling him to take it to Khán Nazar Mirzá. When Khán Nazar Mirzá stretched out his hand to take the "Kalám Ullah," the noble seized his hand with both his own, while others attacked him from every side with swords: for the followers of Mirzá Abá Bakr, having previously agreed upon this, had been standing ready. He was taken quite by surprise. None of the retainers of Khán Nazar Mirzá being able to use their arms [to help him], they fled, while some others who had been appointed for the business, seized Kul Nazar Mirzá. The two brothers were put to death with the sword, and by this ruse their seed was eradicated from Khotan; thus did Abá Bakr conquer Khotan and gain absolute power. Having finished this affair, Abá Bakr started on an expedition against his uncle, Muhammad Haidar Mirzá.

[1] That is, he handed the copy of the Korán containing the treaty: for treaties and solemn engagements are usually written and sealed, by Musulmáns, in copies of the Korán.

CHAPTER LIII.

THE STRATAGEM OF ABÁ BAKR, BY WHICH HE CAUSED MUHAMMAD HAIDAR MIRZÁ TO EXPEL HIS OWN AMIRS.

After the death of Sániz Mirzá, Dust Muhammad Khán (as has been mentioned) took to wife the widow of Sániz Mirzá, whose name was Jamák Ághá. He, moreover, gave Káshghar to Muhammad Haidar Mirzá. These events took place in the year 869.

On the death of Dust Muhammad Khán, Muhammad Haidar Mirzá married Jamák Ághá, who was the mother of Mirzá Abá Bakr and of Omar Mirzá. By her, Muhammad Haidar Mirzá had two sons: my father Muhammad Husain Kurkán, and my uncle Sayyid Muhammad Mirzá. After the conquest of Khotan, Mirzá Abá Bakr became still more powerful. In vain were the reflections and protestations of his Amirs, who represented that his whole career, from beginning to end, had been one of tyranny: that he spared no one: that he had seized Yárkand by stealth and by the employment of unheard-of perfidy: that after he had put out the eyes of Omar Mirzá, he had put to death Khán Nazar and Kul Nazar. How could the world look with the eye of trust upon such a man? He still longed for Káshghar, and his sole object in life was to make his kingdom into a sausage [*kulmah*].[1] In spite of their laying these matters before Muhammad Haidar Mirzá, the latter, on account of his affection for his nephew, made light of it all; and his wife, who was the mother of his children, and the mother of Mirzá Abá Bakr, said to him, in opposing the remonstrances of the Amirs: "He is your son: Yárkand belonged to one of your Amirs. Since Yárkand was the capital of his father, it is his by right, but you did not give it him. If he has been presumptuous, he at least counted on your forgiveness. What matter if they make him out a bad man to you? Khotan, too, was in the possession of another. What harm was there in his superseding [the usurper]?"

In this manner she excused all the actions of Mirzá Abá Bakr; so that Muhammad Haidar Mirzá was appeased and comforted; but when she touched on the hostility which Abá Bakr had displayed towards Muhammad Haidar Mirzá, she declared that it was all owing to the Amirs who had spoken badly of the Mirzá. She then secretly wrote to Mirzá Abá Bakr, asking him how she was to excuse his hostility [to her husband], and stating the reason she had already given. Then Mirzá Abá Bakr, in conformity with

[1] Meaning, apparently, to stuff it fuller and fuller.

this, replied: "As long as the Amirs are in power, I cannot offer fitting service, for they seek to do me harm by vilifying my character to you: if you will dismiss these Amirs, I will be not only a son to you, but a slave also." Muhammad Haidar Mirzá, in the simplicity of his heart, credited these lies and discharged his Amirs. Since the most influential of the generals were thus removed, the power of his kingdom was broken; and Mirzá Abá Bakr began to ravage all the country round about Káshghar and Yángi Hisár; but as all the greatest generals had been dismissed, there was no one to watch over and protect the country.

CHAPTER LIV.

YUNUS KHAN GOES TO HELP MUHAMMAD HAIDAR MIRZÁ AGAINST MIRZÁ ABÁ BAKR, WHO DEFEATS THEM BOTH.

Amir Abdul Kudus, who was mentioned above as having slain Shaikh Jamál Khar and released the Khán from prison, was treated with great kindness by the Khán, and had been given the title of Kurkáni; all the privileges [*mansab*] of the clan [*Tumán*] of Dughlát had been bestowed upon him. In consequence of this he grew proud and presumptuous, and treated the Khán in such a way as to make him frightened at his own acts; but it would take too long to explain all this. Abdul Kudus, however, finally fled to Káshghar, to Muhammad Haidar Mirzá, who had just dismissed his generals, on which account his affairs had fallen into confusion, and he was repenting his deed. When Abdul Kudus arrived, he treated him with every respect, gave him his own daughter Ághá Sultán Sultánim in marriage, showed him marked favour, and having raised an army, sent him against Mirzá Abá Bakr. He fell upon the Mirzá, who was on a plundering foray in Yángi Hisár. Mir Abdul Kudus was, however, defeated, in spite of his force being greater than that of his enemy. He was so ashamed of himself that he did not go back to Muhammad Haidar Mirzá, but moved first to Sháhnáz, and then set out on the road to Badakhshán. He went with 300 men to Mirzá Sultán Mahmud, who showed him every kindness and attention, and bestowed on him the government of Khust, which is one of the most important districts in Badakhshán and Kunduz. He was [afterwards] slain in that country by some infidels of Katur.[1]

[1] Khust, or Khost, is a district on the northern slopes of the Hindu Kush, between south and south-east of Kunduz, and lies very near the hill tracts known in our times as Káfiristán, or the country of the Siáposh and other Káfirs. Sir

In short, after the departure of Mir Abdul Kudus, the power of Mirzá Abá Bakr increased. With his deceit and cunning, he had caused Muhammad Haidar Mirzá to send away his greatest generals and commanders, and he had defeated Mir Abdul Kudus; so that dark days had come upon the transactions of Muhammad Haidar Mirzá. Jamák Ághá repented of what she had done, but it was of no avail. Finally Muhammad Haidar Mirzá made ready an army of nearly 30,000 cavalry and infantry, and took the field against Mirzá Abá Bakr, who opposed him with 3000 men. A fierce battle was fought, and Muhammad Haidar Mirzá suffered defeat. Having come to Káshghar, he told his noble uncle Yunus Khán all that had happened, and begged his assistance. The Khán selected 50,000 men from his own army, and out of the affection he bore his nephew, marched in person against Abá Bakr. Muhammad Haidar Mirza having again collected an army, joined the Khán, and they all proceeded together against Yárkand. Mirzá Abá Bakr fortified the citadel of Yárkand. The Khán halted on the eastern side of the citadel. On the next day Mirzá Abá Bakr drew out his cavalry and infantry from the citadel into the suburbs: they were 3000 in number, all the sons of the generals and chiefs [*mirzádah* and *behádurzádah*] of Mir Sayyid Ali, whom Muhammad Haidar Mirzá had slighted. But Mirzá Abá Bakr had collected them in a body. The Khán arrived from one side with a large army and Muhammad Haidar Mirzá from another. Mirzá Abá Bakr did not direct his force to any extent against Muhammad Haidar Mirzá, but brought all his strength to bear upon the Khán, and after many attacks and retreats, finally put him to flight. When the Khán fled, Muhammad Haidar Mirzá also took flight, and thus this great army was defeated.

When the Khán and Muhammad Haidar Mirzá arrived at Káshghar, the Khán said to the latter: "Thinking it would be an easy matter, I only brought a small force. Stop in your own country this year; next year I will come with a complete army

---

H. Yule quotes several authorities who show that among the Kafir tribes which inhabited this region, between the thirteenth and the present centuries, was one called *Katur*, or *Kitaur*. Baber, in his Memoirs, also speaks of a division of Kafiristan, to the north-east of Kabul, called *Kattor;* while Col. J. Biddulph tells us that the family name of the rulers of Chitral is *Kature*, and he adds that "the name of *Kator* seems to have been applied to the country in early times, before the present *Kature* family was founded." The name *Shah Katur* occurs more than once in the line of Chitral rulers. Thus the *Katur* of the text would point to Kafiristan and probably also to Chitral, for it is quite possible that, though divided now, the two states may have been one in the fifteenth century. According to Ritter, the Kafirs were a people much feared by the Musulmáns of Badakhshán at the beginning of the fifteenth century, and used to exact tribute from them. There is nothing improbable, therefore, in the story of the Kafirs raiding into the neighbouring district of Khust and killing the Musulmán governor. (See Yule, *Cathay*, p. 554; Biddulph, *Tribes of the Hindu Kush*, p. 148; Baber, p. 140; Ritter, *Erdkunde*, vii., pp. 206–7).

and will settle [Abá Bakr's] affairs." The Khán then returned to Moghulistán, while Muhammad Haidar Mirzá remained in Káshghar.

CHAPTER LV.

YUNUS KHÁN'S SECOND EXPEDITION AGAINST YÁRKAND, AND HIS DEFEAT AT THE HANDS OF MIRZÁ ABÁ BAKR.

In the following year, 885, the Khán came to Káshghar with the whole of the Moghul troops, who numbered 60,000 men. Here he was joined by Muhammad Haidar Mirzá, who had a better ordered army than he had had the year before, and they advanced together on Yárkand. The two forces together amounted to 90,000 men, cavalry and infantry. Mirzá Abá Bakr again fortified himself in the citadel, as he had done the year before. He had mustered an army of cavalry and infantry to the number of about 5000. The cavalry consisted of 3000 of those princes of whom I have spoken—chosen young men, whom Muhammad Haidar Mirzá, in his ignorance, had let slip out of his power. The 2000 infantry were chosen archers, all of whom the Mirzá had brought together by promises and hopes [of gain]. The Khán's army encamped in a circle round [the town].[1] The Khán himself took up his quarters in Kálu Aj Bári, a well-known place to the north-east of Yárkand.

After the afternoon prayer, distinguished men from the battalions and divisions [*kushun u tábin*] of the Khán's army advanced, of their own accord, before the citadel and opened the battle. Mirzá Abá Bakr's force issued from the citadel in the following order: between every two horsemen there was an archer on foot, and in front of each archer there was another foot-soldier bearing a shield. A hard fight took place; but the Khán remained in his own quarters. Some persons came and gave him such a vivid description of the battle that he longed to go and see it himself. So, without putting on his armour, he started for the scene of action with a small number of followers. On reaching the edge of a ravine they saw that the infantry of both sides were engaged in close fight. From this position they could not see very distinctly, so the Khán descended into the ravine, and came on to the road in order to get a better view—for the ravine was a road-way. When the Khán came down, the infantry became more daring, and fought most fiercely. At that moment Alim Shaikh Bahádur, who was one of

[1] Lit.: the army formed a ring and encamped.

the Khán's most distinguished warriors, was in his tent; he heard that the Khán had gone to watch [the battle], and it occurred to him that he would go and display his valour, that he might become distinguished above his equals. Having fastened on his armour, he passed before the Khán, and then went in among the infantry who were engaged in the battle.

There was some ground between the infantry of the two armies, and on either side was an enclosure for herding cattle [*gávbandi*]; between these two enclosures was a level passage. Alim Shaikh Bahádur rode up this passage and charged the infantry of Mirzá Abá Bakr, until he came upon a foot-soldier with a shield, who, seeing him come on unchecked, did not attempt to withstand him, but having thrown down his shield in front of the horse of Alim Shaikh Bahádur, ran away. The horse, being terrified at the fall of the shield, reared so badly that Alim Shaikh Bahádur, not able to keep his seat, was thrown. The infantry who were on the other side of the enclosure, now jumped over it and seized Alim Shaikh Bahádur. Meantime, the cavalry of Mirzá Abá Bakr charged the Khán's infantry, but these, not deeming it advisable to stand their ground, turned and fled, being followed by those who had come to watch the battle.

The Khán had descended from the [edge of the] ravine, but those who were with him now counselled him to re-ascend. The Khán set out in all haste along the road in the ravine, but when his men, who were on the top, saw him approaching in haste, they fled [in a panic]. So that when the Khán emerged from the ravine, he found all his men had taken flight, and that his army was in confusion. He thereupon returned to his camp in order to reassure his men; he tried beating and striking them, but not one of them would move from his place. In the meanwhile Mirzá Abá Bakr engaged the infantry, who had come down by way of the ravine; he attacked with his cavalry those who had been watching the battle, charging up the ravine unresisted, then pursuing [the fugitives] until his cavalry threw them into confusion. When the Khán's army—already disordered—saw this state of affairs, they suddenly turned and fled: all the Khan's efforts to rally them were ineffectual. When the cavalry of Mirzá Abá Bakr came on, the Khán himself took to flight. Thus was this enormous army defeated in the space of one hour.

The Khán retreated to Káshghar, while most of the army deserted him and escaped to Moghulistán. [The Khán] advised Muhammad Haidar Mirzá not to remain in Káshghar, so the Mirzá accompanied the Khán to Aksu, taking with him 5000 families. Many of the Káshghari went to Andiján, so that Káshghar was left clear for Mirzá Abá Bakr. These events occurred in the year 885. At that time my father, Muhammad Husain Mirzá Kurkán, was twelve years of age. When Muhammad Haidar Mirzá went to Aksu with Yunus Khán, the son of the latter, Sultán Mahmud Khán, took my father with him into Moghulistán, where they became great friends; and to the end of his life he called my father "*Dásh*," which in the Moghul language means "friend."

CHAPTER LVI.

EARLY DAYS OF SULTÁN MAHMUD KHÁN, SON OF YUNUS KHÁN.

As an account will be given of Sultán Mahmud Khán, it is necessary to say a few words about his early life.

When Sultán Yunus Khán returned a second time from Khorásán, Amir Sayyid Ali had died, and Sániz Mirzá had sought the assistance of Yunus Khán, as has been mentioned. Yunus Khán, in those days, often went backwards and forwards to Káshghar. At that time, the Khán sent Amir Ziá-ud-Din (who was one of the most eminent Sayyids of Káshghar) to Sháh Sultán Muhammad Badakhshi, in Badakhshán, to ask one of his most immaculate daughters in marriage. Sháh Sultán Badakhshi was of the race of Sikandar Zulkarnain, Filikus Rumi.[1] Sikandar, after he had conquered the regions of the world, consulted with his wise men, saying: "Find me a place which shall be out of the reach of the princes of the earth [Sultáns of the time], in which I may place my descendants." The councillors chose Badakhshán, and they wrote a Book of Regulations [*Dastur ul amal*]; so that as long as the regulations were observed, no one prince could prevail in this country.

From the time of Sikandar down to the time of Sháh Sultán Muhammad, nobody had attacked Badakhshán. Thus they had ruled from generation to generation. When the kingdom passed into the hands of Sháh Sultán Muhammad Badakhshi, he discarded the "*Dastur ul amal*" of Sikandar.[2] He was a prince of great natural gifts and refined taste, and he left a "*Diván*," which is exceedingly beautiful. His "*takhallus*," or poetical name, was Láli. His elegance and clearness of style were so great that he altered [the wording of] the "*Dastur ul amal*" to suit his own taste.

[1] Alexander the Great and Philip of Macedon. *Filikus* appears to be the usual Oriental corruption of Philip.

[2] The fanciful nature of this account of Badakhshán need hardly be pointed out. It is based, probably, on the claim made by the princes of Badakhshán to be descended from Alexander the Great, rather than on any history of the country known to Mirza Haidar.

He had six daughters. He gave one of them to Sultán Masud Kábuli, who was a descendant of Amir Timur. Another he gave to Sultán Abu Said Mirzá, who had, by her, a son named Mirzá Abá Bakr. The Mirzá, after the death of his father, engaged in war with Sultán Husain Mirzá, and caused much disturbance in his kingdom (all of which is related in the Histories of Mir Khwánd and of Khwánd Mir, of Herat). A third daughter he gave to Ibráhim Barlás, who, by her, had Jahángir Barlás, who at the end of the Chaghatái rule [*daulat*] became chief minister. His fourth daughter, whose name was Sháh Begum, he sent to Yunus Khán, at the request of Sayyid Ziá-ud-Din Káshghari. He gave his fifth daughter to Sayyid Sháh Buzurg Arhangi (who will be mentioned below); and the sixth to Shaikh Abdullah Barlás, who, by her, had Sultán Vais Barlás, Mizrab Barlás, and Sultán Sanjar (all of whom will be spoken of in their proper places); they are moreover mentioned in the Histories of Mir Khwánd and Khwánd Mir, of Herat.[1]

In short, Sayyid Ziá-ud-Din brought Sháh Begum back with him to Káshghar, and delivered her over to the Khán. Yunus Khán had two sons and two daughters by Sháh Begum. The eldest of all was Sultán Mahmud Khán. He was born in 868. Next to him came Sultán Ahmad Khán (whom I shall mention separately). The two daughters were Sultán Nigár Khánim and Daulat Sultán Khánim (of these also I shall have occasion to speak hereinafter). Before Sultán Mahmud Khán arrived at years of discretion, the Amirs of Moghulistán (as I have recorded) had behaved rudely and disrespectfully to Yunus Khán. By the time Sultán Mahmud Khán was grown up, most of these Moghul Amirs were dead. Yunus Khán, with the help of his son Sultán Mahmud Khán, obtained complete ascendency and control over the Moghuls, and over those of their Amirs who were still alive.

On the occasion of Yunus Khán being defeated before Yárkand and retiring to Káshghar, he was not acccompanied by Sultán Mahmud Khán; for Mahmud remained behind in Moghulistán, to keep the people in order.

Yunus Khán, both to quiet the apprehensions of Muhammad Haidar Mirzá, and for his own pleasure, spent that winter in Aksu. They sent the son of Muhammad Haidar Mirzá, Muhammad Husain Mirzá, who was then twelve years of age, to Sultán Mahmud Khán, with whom he became very friendly; the two remained on good terms, and used to call each other "*Dásh*" [friend]. Muhammad Husain Mirzá stayed in Moghulistán with Sultán Mahmud Khán, and was treated with great honour and respect.

[1] Most of the names mentioned in this paragraph will be found in the table of the house of Timur appended to Sect. ii. of the Introduction.

CHAPTER LVII.

THE WAR THAT AROSE OUT OF A DIFFERENCE BETWEEN YUNUS KHÁN AND MUHAMMAD HAIDAR MIRZÁ IN AKSU.

THAT winter the Khán went to Aksu. Aksu is situated on the edge of a ravine. It has two forts, one of which the Khán gave to Muhammad Haidar Mirzá, while he established himself in the other. That winter passed peacefully. On the setting in of spring, Yunus Khán wished to move into Moghulistán. He therefore said to Muhammad Haidar Mirzá: "Now that the first spring has come I am going into Moghulistán. You stay here and make your men cultivate the land. I bestow the country of Aksu on you. When harvest-time comes round, it will also be the end of the season for summer quarters in Moghulistán. The horses will be in good condition, and we will then go to Káshghar and settle scores with Mirzá Abá Bakr. I shall march from Moghulistán and you from here. We will meet in Káshghar, and there make all final arrangements."

Having agreed upon this plan of action, the Khán appointed people to go to Moghulistán with the flocks. He [also] sent to collect the flocks destined for Moghulistán. But some rebellious men tried to instil into the mind of Muhammad Haidar Mirzá, that when the Khán arrived in Moghulistán he would plunder the Mirza's people; and many like impossibilities did they suggest, such as could only proceed from Satan; but the Mirzá, in his simplicity, gave ear to all they said, and began to consider how he might avert these evils. Those devils [*Shiátin*] said to him: "When the flocks reach the Khán, and he is able to make a start, we will influence his younger son, Ahmad Khán, who is accompanying his father, to separate himself from him. We will then fortify ourselves in this citadel and defy the Khán. When the hour of the Khan's departure comes he will suspect nothing, and will march into Moghulistán, while we shall remain established in Aksu."

This base and senseless plan was acceptable in the sight of Muhammad Haidar Mirzá. Just as the Khán was about to start, they suddenly closed the gates of Aksu. Sultán Ahmad Khán fled to Muhammad Haidar Mirzá; and they all rose in rebellion. Yunus Khán sent a messenger to the Mirzá, to treat with him, but to no purpose. So the Khán finally abandoned his march, and entering the other fort, put it into a state of defence. He then despatched a messenger to Sultán Mahmud Khán, who after seventeen days arrived with a force of 30,000 men. Conflicts took place daily, till at the end of forty days a famine broke out in the fort of the Mirzá. The promoters of the rebellion began to desert nightly. Sultán Ahmad Khán, alarmed at his own want of filial piety, came to his parents with apologies and prayers for forgiveness, but the Mirzá stood out. Suddenly the fort was taken by a general assault. The Khán immediately sent some Amirs to prevent it from being plundered. The Amirs went, but their efforts were of no avail, for the men who had made the assault were not of the sort that could be withheld. After a hundred struggles they seized the Mirzá and brought him before the Khán. As they approached, they were beginning to bind the Mirzá's hands, but Yunus Khán cried out to prevent them. So they brought the Mirzá forward just as he was. The Khán called him to him, and having upbraided and rebuked him severely, said: "Why did you do this? Abandon your rebellious intentions, so that I may depart. Remain here. [But if] again you rebel [think] what will happen."[1]

Muhammad Haidar Mirzá was ashamed, and stood with bowed head, at the thought of his ill-advised actions. The Khán then said: "All is well now, I have given you Aksu, and you should stay there." The Mirzá replied: "How can I remain now in Aksu, since so many of my men have gone away?" The Khán, thereupon, gave the Mirzá 3000 horses, and said: "Accompany me into Moghulistán; I think, too, the wisest plan will be for me to go to Káshghar, as soon as the corn is high, and try and take that town for you . . . ."[2]

In short, Muhammad Haidar Mirzá accompanied Yunus Khán into Moghulistán. When the spring came to an end, the Khán turned his thoughts to Káshghar. At the same time Sultán Ahmad Mirzá was planning an expedition from Samarkand, against Farghána, from which country he wished to expel his brother Omar Shaikh Mirzá. As soon as Omar Shaikh Mirzá heard of his brother's intention, he sent in great haste to Yunus Khán, begging assistance; for by this means he had frequently (as has been mentioned above) been delivered from the cruelty and violence of his brother Sultán Ahmad Mirzá. On the arrival of the news, the Khán set out for Andiján. Now the Khán did not wish that there should be any strife between his two sons-in-law, and had always tried to keep them at peace with each other. On the Khán's entry into Andiján, he was received by Omar Shaikh Mirzá; he was shown great honour, and the province of Ush was given to him. The Khán spent that winter in Ush. Entrusting the rest of the Moghuls to the care of Sultán Mahmud Khán, he

[1] This passage is most obscure. It reads: "*An gáh yághi-gari bekun. In chi-tur mibáshad?*"—R.

[2] Some high-flown passages treating of the mercy of kings are omitted here. —R.

sent them back to Moghulistán, while he himself made his winter quarters in Ush, and appointed Muhammad Haidar Mirzá as administrator [*váli*]. When Sultán Ahmad Mirzá heard of the arrival of the Khán, he abandoned his project. And thus Omar Shaikh was rendered safe from his brother. When winter had passed, the Khán came again to Moghulistán. [On the eve of his departure] the Khán said to the Mirzá: "You have always suffered great annoyance in Moghulistán. I have now given you this country of Ush. Stay here till next winter, when I will return. [In the meanwhile] govern the country, as my deputy."

He then left for Moghulistán, while Muhammad Haidar Mirzá remained in Ush. The Mirzá begged his own son, Muhammad Husain Mirzá, of the Khán, and kept him at his side.

CHAPTER LVIII.

MUHAMMAD HAIDAR MIRZÁ ATTACKS MIRZÁ ABÁ BAKR IN KÁSHGHAR, AND IS TAKEN PRISONER BY HIM.

WHEN Sultán Yunus Khán reached Moghulistán, Omar Shaikh Mirzá sent an official [*dárugha*] to Ush to replace Muhammad Haidar. The [last-named] Mirzá and his men were not capable of marching into Moghulistán, and it was also impossible for them to remain in Ush. He placed his two sons, Muhammad Husain Mirzá and Sayyid Muhammad Mirzá, under the care of Omar Shaikh Mirzá, and himself set out for Káshghar, thinking that as Mirzá Abá Bakr was his brother's son and his own wife's son, he would go to him and would offer him terms of peace. Under such illusions he approached Mirzá Abá Bakr, who immediately seized him and threw him into prison, where he remained one year. At the end of a year he was sent to Badakhshán, which was at that time ruled by Mirzá Sultán Mahmud, son of Mirzá Sultán Abu Said. Abdul Kudus, who was the son-in-law of Muhammad Haidar Mirzá (and who has been spoken of already), was at this time with Mirzá Sultán Mahmud. He [Muhammad Haidar Mirzá] was entertained for a short time as the guest of the Sultán; he then came to Samarkand and paid his respects to his Holiness Násiruddin Ubaidullah (may God bless his spirit) and waited on Mirzá Sultán Ahmad, who received him in a friendly way, and arranged to come to the Mirzá yearly, on the occasion of two festivals [*aid*].

Mirzá Sultán Ahmad had three brothers: Osmán Mirzá, Sultán Valad Mirzá, and Talak Muhammad . . . .

In the meanwhile a person came from Yunus Khán to fetch Muhammad Haidar Mirzá. Not feeling in the least fettered by the kindness Sultán Ahmad Mirzá had shown him, he went to the Khán. This matter will be mentioned in connection with the life of the Khán and his entrance into Táshkand.

CHAPTER LIX.

YUNUS AND THE MOGHUL ULUS ENTER TÁSHKAND; PEACE IS ESTABLISHED BETWEEN SULTÁN AHMAD MIRZÁ AND OMAR SHAIKH MIRZÁ AND SULTÁN MAHMUD KHÁN.

THE story of the quarrels and contests that arose between the two brothers, Omar Shaikh Mirzá and Sultán Ahmad Mirzá, is a long one, and has no place in this history; it has however been given in detail in the history of Mir Khwánd. But it is, nevertheless, necessary to mention in this book, that on the death of Shaikh Jamál Khar, Táshkand passed into the [power and] jurisdiction of Omar Shaikh Mirzá, as did also Sháhrukhia, which has a fortified castle [*kalah*]. Mirzá Sultán Ahmad became an enemy to Omar Shaikh Mirzá on the subject of these two places, and a fierce dispute arose between them. When the hostility of Mirzá Sultán Ahmad was directed against Táshkand, Omar Shaikh Mirzá desired the Khán [to come and help him] in Táshkand.

The same year that the Khán had left Ush and had given it over to Muhammad Haidar Mirzá, Omar Shaikh Mirzá, after the arrival of the Khán, dismissed Muhammad Haidar Mirzá, who went to Káshghar, where he was thrown into prison. The Khán was then in Moghulistán. When autumn [*tirmáh*] [2] set in and the hostility of Mirzá Sultán Ahmad was directed against Táshkand, Omar Shaikh Mirzá invited the Khán to [come and help him in] Táshkand. He gave Sairám to the Khán. In the same way that he had given him Ush out of Andiján, so he gave him Sairám out of Táshkand. When the Khán turned towards Sairám, the Moghuls, who could not on any terms put up with

[1] Here follows an obscure passage regarding the precedence of the three brothers, which baffles translation.—R.

[2] The word *Tirmah* is usually, if not always, found in dictionaries to signify "the first month of summer." Throughout Central Asia, however, it means *autumn*, and seeing that in some passages of this history, the context shows that Mirza Haidar uses it for *autumn*, I have applied it everywhere for that season.

towns and cultivated lands, having led astray the Khán's younger son, Sultán Ahmad Khán, fled back to Moghulistán. The Khán did not follow them, for in the family of the Moghul Khákáns there remained no rivals [of the Khán] who were worth considering. So he let the people go back to Moghulistán, while he himself went on to Sairám and there passed the winter.

The Khán also sent his elder son, Sultán Mahmud Khán, against Sultán Ahmad Mirzá, with 30,000 men. From the side of Farghána came Omar Shaikh Mirzá, with an army 15,000 strong. These three armies neared each other, and a desperate conflict was about to ensue, when the news of what was passing reached his Holiness Násiruddin Ubaidullah (may God bless his hidden soul). He at once set out, sending a person in advance to announce that he was coming. When the tidings reached the three Sultáns, they all halted where they were. When his Holiness arrived, he alighted in the camp of Sultán Ahmad Mirzá, and sent messengers to the Khán and to Omar Shaikh Mirzá, begging them to make peace. No one could resist the entreaties of the blessed mind of his Holiness. Such was his spiritual and moral influence, that he calmed these three Pádisháhs, who had each come for some object of his own, with an army in fighting order, and caused them to sit together on one carpet [*zalicha*],[1] while he sat in their midst and dictated to them conditions of peace, to which they assented. Táshkand was to be made over to Yunus Khán. The two brothers who disputed with each other the possession of Táshkand, were to give up their dispute and concede the place to the Khán.

His Holiness Mauláná and Sayyid Ná Mahdumi Mauláná Muhammad Kázi (upon whom be mercy and forgiveness) has written in the appendix [*zail*] to his "*Salsalat ul Arifin*," that this occurrence is among the miracles of his Holiness [*i.e.* of Násiruddin Ubaidullah]. It is related there: "the meeting was so solemn that, in the intensity of my emotion [*dahasht*] I overturned the table-cloth [*dastár khwán*]; when the meeting was terminated his Holiness said: 'It is well, I must now retire, for I am an old man and can only bear a certain amount of fatigue.'

"The three kings returned, each one, to his own army. His Holiness departed in the direction of the river of Khojand and performed his ablutions [*vazu*] at the waterside. Turning to me he said: 'Mauláná Muhammad can write an account of my deed.' His Holiness the Mauláná says that this was his reason for undertaking the composition of his book—the *Salsalat ul Arifin*.

"In short, Sultán Ahmad Mirzá repaired to Samarkand, Omar Shaikh Mirzá to Farghána, and Sultán Mahmud Khán to

[1] This is probably a corruption of the Turki word *zilcha* or *zilucha*, a long pile carpet made of wool.—R.

Táshkand. Yunus Khán also went to Táshkand, and his Holiness, following him, met him again there. I [Muhammad Kázi] have heard from my uncle, that one day in the assembly of his Holiness [Násiruddin Ubaidullah] the conversation turned upon Sultán Mahmud Khán, and one of those present said: 'It is strange how proud this prince is of his own grandeur.' His Holiness replied: 'Proud as the Pádisháh may be, I will make him fill his skirt with earth [*khák*]; glory and grandeur belong to God alone. Hence how can even Sultán Mahmud Khán be proud.' It chanced that at that very moment the Khán came to pay his respects to his Holiness. It was prayer time, and his Holiness had risen for prayer. When prayers were about to begin, a censer was noticed in which were some embers. His Holiness said: 'Embers and censers, while prayer is proceeding, are abhorrent. Therefore the fire must be extinguished with some earth.' In spite of the number of people present, the Khán sprang up and, going outside, filled his skirt with earth, which having brought in, he sprinkled on the fire; this he repeated several times, until the fire was extinguished. And he begged of those present that they would allow him to perform, quite alone, this service of fetching the earth. After the Khán's departure all the companions of his Holiness expressed great wonder."

This peace and meeting of the Kháns in Táshkand took place in 890. His Holiness remained for a while in Táshkand and then returned to Samarkand. It was the practice of all the princes of that time, to employ one of the disciples of his Holiness as a medium of communication with him. Sultán Mahmud Khán employed for this purpose Mauláná Kázi. About this matter I have heard many anecdotes, which, please God, I will give in their proper place.

CHAPTER LX.

END OF YUNUS KHÁN'S LIFE.

The Khán, being firmly established in Táshkand, begged the daughter of Sultán Ahmad Mirzá—Karáguz Begum—in marriage for his son Sultán Mahmud Khán. The arrival of Karáguz Begum will be mentioned hereafter. But in the interim Sultán Yunus Khán was seized with paralysis, was bedridden for nearly two years, and died, suffering, at the age of seventy-four. No other Chaghatái Khákán ever reached such an advanced age: most of them, indeed, died before they reached the age of forty. The Khán was born in

818 and died in 892. He was buried near the tomb of Puránvár Shaikh, Kháwand-i-Tuhur [Master of Purification], in Táshkand; and a large mausoleum was built over the spot, which stands to this day and is very renowned.

During his illness, the Khán heard that Muhammad Haidar Mirzá had gone from Badakhshán to Samarkand, so he sent to summon the Mirzá to him. Muhammad Haidar Mirzá left Samarkand, came to the Khán, and waited on him throughout his illness. He was a skilled surgeon and physician. The Khán, during this period, would not allow Muhammad Haidar Mirzá out of his presence for one hour; and he treated the Mirzá's children with hospitality. The Mirzá's son, Muhammad Husain Mirzá, who had remained with Omar Shaikh Mirzá, had gone to Sultán Mahmud Khán in Andiján, before Muhammad Haidar Mirzá had come [to attend on the Khán]. He lived always in the same house and room as the Khán, as shall be related below.

CHAPTER LXI.

WAR BETWEEN SULTÁN AHMAD MIRZÁ AND SULTÁN MAHMUD KHÁN.

Sultán Yunus Khán died in the year 892, and in the course of the same year, Sultán Mahmud Khán was raised to the Khánate with Moghul rites. When the news of the death of Yunus Khan got abroad, Mirzá Omar Shaikh and Mirzá Sultán Ahmad became intent on renewing hostilities with one another. Omar Shaikh Mirzá sent a large number of his staunchest and most trustworthy followers to occupy the fort of Ushtur in Táshkand, which was an impregnable stronghold. Sultán Mahmud Khán led his forces, in person, against that fort. A fierce battle took place; so fierce, indeed, that it is still talked of among the Moghuls. The castle was taken by assault, and all the faithful adherents of Mirzá Omar Shaikh were put to death; no one escaped: they all died fighting. From this victory great strength accrued to the Khán, while the Mirzá lost all power of opposition.

The year following, Sultán Ahmad Mirzá's Amirs impressed upon him that he had given up Táshkand to the Khán without proper cause, and that the longer the Khán's people remained there, the more annoying it was to them. His Holiness sent word to say that he was mistaken, and that he ought to make peace with the Khán, who would do him no injury: why should he annoy him? Finally, however, the Mirzá collected an army 150,000 strong, and led it against Táshkand. The Khán passed through the suburbs of Táshkand and stood facing [the advancing enemy]. Between them flowed a stream which it was impossible to cross. The armies remained there during three days. In the army of the Sultán was a certain Sháhi Beg Khán, the son of Sháh Badágh Oghlán, the son of Abulkhair Khán. After the death of Buruj Oghlán (which has been described above)[1] Sháhi Beg Khán underwent many hardships (as we are told in histories). Finally, as he was not able to hold his own in the steppes, he betook himself to Mávará-un-Nahr, and became a follower of Sultán Ahmad Mirzá, or rather he became a retainer of one of the Sultán's Amirs. He was in this army, and had 3000 followers. When Mirzá Sultán Ahmad had remained three days [on the bank of the river], Sháhi Beg Khán sent to Sultán Mahmud Khán to ask if he would meet and confer with him. That same night they met: he from the one side and the Khán from the other; and they agreed that on the morrow the Khán should attack Mir Abdul Ali, the master of Sháhi Beg Khán, who, on his part, undertook to throw the army into disorder, and then to take flight.

On the next day the Moghul army was drawn up in battle array, and the infantry passed the Chir; the cavalry also entered the stream, when the infantry of the other side began the battle. The Moghul army directed its force against Mir Abdul Ali. At this moment Sháhi Beg Khán turned and fled with his 3000 men, and throwing himself on the baggage [*partal*] of the army, began to plunder the Moghuls. In fact, wherever this disordered rabble found themselves, their device was to fall upon the baggage, so that the army of Mirzá Sultán Ahmad was put to flight. But the river Chir, which the people of Táshkand call Parak, was in front of them, and most of his soldiers were drowned in it. The troops of the Mirzá suffered a severe defeat, while he, discomfited and beaten, fled to Samarkand. He proffered many excuses and apologies to his Holiness, who again arranged a peace between the Khán and Sultán Ahmad Mirzá. The discussion about Karáguz Begum was resumed, and after various formalities had been gone through, they brought Karáguz Begum to the Khán. This victory did much to raise the Khán in the estimation of the surrounding Sultáns, who henceforward stood in great fear of him, and thus his position became secure.

[1] See note, p. 92. The mention of Buruj here appears scarcely to bear out Sir H. Howorth's supposition, though it does not disprove it.

CHAPTER LXII.

ARRANGEMENT FOR THE MARRIAGE OF MY FATHER INTO THE KHÁN'S FAMILY.

MY father Muhammad Husain Kurkán, (may God illumine his proof) from the time of his quitting Káshghar to this date, had always been in the service of Sultán Mahmud Khán, except for the two years that he spent with Omar Shaikh Mirzá (all of which has been related above). The Khán was on such close and friendly terms with my father, that they always lived in the same room; their houses adjoined, and they confided household matters to each other.

When anything was brought for the Khán, something like it was also brought for my father. When the Khán went out riding, two horses would be brought, one of which my father would mount and the Khán the other. Whenever the Khán put on a new robe, another like it used to be found for my father. Thus, in no matter was any distinction made between them. Till the time when the Khán married Karáguz Begum, he spent most of the day in the common apartment [*hajra-i-máhud*], and in the evening would go into his haram, whilst my father remained in the outer chamber. When the Khán was seated on his throne, they used to place a carpet in front of it, so that my father might sit down and lean against the throne; thus the two used always to arrange [the affairs of the State] together. Sometimes the Khán used to say to my father, apologising the while: "I am obliged by family affairs to retire to the haram, while you remain in the outer apartment; this makes you appear like a palace guard [*yátish*], and is inconsistent with terms of friendship and concord."

A year passed in this way, when the Khán contracted an alliance with the Kurkáni, in the person of Khub Nigár Khánim, who was his senior by one year. She was the third daughter of Yunus Khán, by Isán Daulat Begum; and her eldest daughter was Mihr Nigár Khánim, who had been given in marriage to Sultán Ahmad Mirzá (of whom I have spoken at greater length in the Second Part). The second daughter was Kutluk Nigár Khánim, whom Omar Shaikh Mirzá took to wife; and their children were Zahir-ud-Din Muhammad Bábar Pádisháh, and Khánzáda Begum, of whom I shall speak below. The third daughter was this Khub Nigár Khánim, who was given in marriage to my father, and is my mother. I will give a record of them in their proper place, in Part II. Sultán Yunus Khán had two other daughters by Sháh Begum Badakhshi: the elder, Sultán Nigár Khánim, was sent to

Sultán Mahmud Mirzá in Hisár, who had children by her, as is mentioned in the Second Part. The younger was Daulat Sultán Khánim, also mentioned in the Second Part.

In short, the Khán apologised, saying: "It is not reasonable that I should always go into the haram at nights, and leave you here in the palace, as if on guard. It is not worthy of our friendship." On this account he gave orders for the preparation of festivities, and showed [his friend] every mark of sympathy and regard. During two years the preparations continued. Then he gave Khub Nigár Khánim in marriage to my father. In the meanwhile Mirzá Sultán Ahmad, Omar Shaikh Mirzá, and Sultán Mahmud Mirzá died, as shall be presently related.

Urátupa [1] was included in the administration of the Khán, who granted that country to my father; he established himself there, and extended its limits over some of the bordering districts, all of which is related in Part II.

CHAPTER LXIII.

EVENTS IN TÁSHKAND DURING THE RULE OF SULTÁN MAHMUD KHÁN. THE LAST YEARS AND DEATH OF THE KHÁN.

Before the Khán made peace with Sultán Ahmad Mirzá and married Karáguz Begum, he captured Táshkand. He seized and threw into prison Muhammad Mazid Tarkhán, who had been appointed Governor of Turkistán by Mirzá Sultán Ahmad; and this Muhammad Mazid Tarkhán was one of the principal causes of the peace, for he was a relation, on the mother's side [*tághá*], of Mirzá Sultán Ahmad. When the Khán conquered Turkistán, he had in his service Sháhi Beg Khán. As a reward for the services he rendered in the battle of the Chir (which has been described above), the Khán made over Turkistán to him; and on this account disagreement arose between the sons of Karái Khán and Jáni Beg Khán (of the Kazák) and Sultán Mahmud Khán, who had previously been on terms of friendship. [They complained, saying:] "Sháhi Beg Khán is our enemy; why did you send him to oppress us in Turkistán?" In a word, in consequence of this quarrel, between

[1] *Uratippa* or *Uratupa* is the Persian form; *Uratubé*, the Turki—generally corrupted by the Russians into *Uratiube*—and meaning "high mound." Old names for this place are *Oshrusene*, *Usrushna*, *Satrushna*, etc., while Mirza Haidar, farther on (p. 154) writes it *Ushtur Ushna*. (See Schuyler, i., p. 312; Sprenger, p. 19, and Erskine in *Baber*, p. xli.)

Sultán Mahmud Khán and the Uzbeg Kazák,[1] two battles took place, the Khán suffering defeat on both occasions. The cause of these defeats was that the most distinguished of his generals had left Yunus Khán. For the Khán had, in common with all who succeed to power, the defect of not knowing the value of men of worth, and [of imagining] that whomsoever they favour becomes, for that reason, a valuable man, which is, of course, impossible.

However, in conformity with these pernicious principles, the Khán patronised some of the lowest of his people, who were continually engaged in trying to decry the old and influential Amirs. This they carried so far as to induce the Khán to put to death five of the great Amirs, each of whom was the head of a department [*sar daftar*], and to extirpate their families; while in their places, five of those base-born men were set up. At the time when the difference arose between Sultán Mahmud Khán and the Uzbeg Kazák, on account of Sháhi Beg Khán, and a war ensued, these five base-born men were generals: hence the defeat. That dread and esteem of the Khán, which by the successful efforts of the five Amirs, had taken possession of the hearts of the neighbouring Sultáns, had now disappeared. In the meantime Omar Shaikh Mirzá was killed by a house falling on him: this was in the year 899. When this news reached Sultán Ahmad Mirzá, he set out with an army against Andiján, to prevent it falling into the hands of the Moghuls. The Amirs of Omar Shaikh Mirzá behaved bravely, and raised his son, Zahir-ud-Din Muhammad Bábar Pádisháh, who was then twelve years of age, to the throne: they also applied to Sultán Mahmud Khán for assistance. When Sultán Ahmad Mirzá reached Marghilán he fell ill, and so made terms of peace and turned back; but he died on the road, just forty days after the death of Omar Shaikh Mirzá. Sultán Mahmud Mirzá came from Hisár, and set himself up on the throne of Samarkand in his brother's stead. He reigned six months; he then died a natural death, and was succeeded by his son Mirzá Baisanghar.

Sultán Mahmud Khán coveted the throne of Samarkand. He marched towards that town and met Baisanghar in battle, at a place called Kámyái. As the generals were the [above mentioned] base-born persons, the enterprise failed and the Khán was defeated. This was a very famous battle, and its date is as celebrated with the Moghuls as among the people of Samarkand. The Khán then returned to Táshkand, when these same low-born men persuaded him that it was fitting for them to support Sháhi Beg Khán, in order that he might take Samarkand and Bokhárá, and bear all the duties of the State, while they themselves remained at their ease in Táshkand. This appeared reasonable to the Khán. Much

[1] One MS. reads: " . . . . between Sultan Mahmud Khan and the Uzbeg Khan and the Kazák Amirs."—R.

as my father condemned this advice and used his influence over the Khán, he was in no way able to prevent the latter helping and supporting Sháhi Beg Khán, till he had taken Samarkand and Bokhárá. This needs a detailed account, which will be given in Part II. along with incidents in the life of Bábar Pádisháh.

In a word, with this assistance, Sháhi Beg Khán took Samarkand, and obtained complete control over it. His army increased to 50,000 men ; and Uzbegs from on all sides flocked round him. His first attack was directed against the Khán, who began to despair; but much as he and his ignoble advisers might gnaw the hand of vexation with the teeth of regret, they could not help themselves. In the meanwhile Sultán Ahmad Khán, who (as I have mentioned) had remained in Moghulistán, hearing of the Khán's distress, came to his brother's aid, and these two Kháns together, gave battle to Sháhi Beg Khán, but they were defeated. Sháhi Beg Khán, having treated them both with courtesy and respect, sent the Khán into Moghulistán ; he, however, kept the Moghul soldiers with him, as will be related in Part II.

The two brothers, Sultán Mahmud Khán and Sultán Ahmad Khán, went to Moghulistán, where Sultán Ahmad Khán died, as shall be presently related. Sultán Mahmud Khán reached Moghulistán and for some time underwent many hardships there. Finally he presented himself before Sháhi Beg Khán, counting on the favour he had once shown him. But Sháhi Beg Khán said to Sultán Mahmud Khán : "Once I was kind to you, but a second act of mercy would be the cause of the ruin of my kingdom." He then put to death the Khán and his children, both great and small, on the banks of the river of Khojand. The chronogram "*Lab-i-daryá-i-Khojand*" gives the date of the event—914 [1508–9]. The particulars will be given in Part II. of this History. The matter is mentioned briefly here to save repetition.

CHAPTER LXIV.

SULTÁN AHMAD KHÁN.

SULTÁN AHMAD KHÁN was the son of Yunus Khán, who has been mentioned above. When his father used to go and take up quarters in Táshkand, Ahmad, with a number of Moghuls who objected to towns and settlements, parted from his father, and stayed behind in Moghulistán. It would take too long to relate all that he did and [to describe] his administration in Moghulistán; but the substance of the matter is that it required ten years of residence in the country, before he could bring the people fully under his control. He was obliged to suppress some of the Amirs: among others the Irlát, who were powerful chiefs, and had offered him much opposition. A battle ensued in which he overthrew their race; he also put to death Amir Sultán Ali Jarás, who, since the time when the Amirs rose in opposition to Isán Bughá Khán, had never become reconciled to any of the Kháns.

The Káluji were the most numerous of all the tribes in Moghulistán. At this time, a number of their chiefs joined together, and one night attacked the Khán's camp, killed all whom they found there, and poured a shower of arrows upon the tent of the Khán, who sustained several wounds. At last one of the attacking party entered the tent intending to kill him, but he rose up with drawn sword to meet the man; they dealt each other severe blows, and the intruder fled wounded. After this, several persons, having dismounted, tried, together, to force an entry. Sut Im Bahádur, who was one of the most important men in the Khán's court, at this moment arrived on the scene, and when the assailants saw that somebody was coming, they remounted and attacked him. He was quite alone, but nevertheless, offered them fight, and a considerable time elapsed before they were able to kill Sut Im Bahádur. They then again turned to attack the Khán. Hearing the noise, men came riding up from all directions to the tent of the Khán. At last the Káluji, having no longer power to resist, turned and fled. All these were the intimates of the Khán, and no one suspected them of such [treacherous] intentions. They fled to the Kálmák. As soon as the Khán had recovered from his wounds, he pursued them whither they had gone, but it took him two years to root them out.

After this, the affairs of the Khán became more prosperous, and no one in Moghulistán dared to oppose him. He made several successful inroads on the Kálmák, and put a number of them to death. He fought two battles with Táishi Isán, and was victorious in both. The Kálmák stood in great awe of him, and used to call him Álácha Khán; *Álácha*, in Moghul, means *kushánda* [the slayer], that is to say, "the slaying Khán." This title adhered to him. His own people used to call him Álácha Khán. He is now spoken of by the Moghuls as Sultán Ahmad Khán, but all the neighbouring peoples call him 'Álácha.' Also one finds 'Álácha' written in the Histories of Mir Khwánd and of Khwánd Mir, of Herat, and others.[1]

[1] *Ilácha* is the Persian corruption of *Alácha*, and in the Persian texts of the *Tárikh-i-Rashidi*; it is found written in this way; but *Alájá*, Mr. Ross informs me, would be preferable to either. In Mr. Shaw's dictionary of the language of Eastern Turkistan (p. 12) the word *Alách* is shown as a proper name, but the author adds that it is also "a comprehensive name given to the tribes of Kuzzáks and Kirghiz, from some eponymous ancestor." Can this ancestor be Sultan Ahmad Khan—a Moghul?

After these events, he carried on hostilities with the Uzbeg Kazák, for the reason already stated in the story of Sultán Mahmud Khán. For Sultán Mahmud Khan had, on two occasions, gone to war with the Uzbeg Kazák, and had been defeated on both occasions; on which account Sultán Ahmad Khán attacked the Uzbeg Kazák and utterly routed them three times.

Whatever they had done to his elder brother, Sultán Mahmud Khán, he, in turn, did to them. He, moreover, kept Moghulistán under such strict supervision, that during seven or eight months the Kálmák and Uzbeg were unable to approach the country. When he had satisfactorily disposed of the affairs of Moghulistán, he turned his attention to the question of Abá Bakr and Káshghar. In the year 905 (which is also the year of my birth), when he came to Káshghar, he found that Abá Bakr had gone to Yárkand, leaving Káshghar and Yángi Hisár fortified, garrisoned and stored. The officers of Mirzá Abá Bakr attacked the Khán several times, both in the citadel of Káshghar and at Yángi Hisár, all of which would take too long to relate. At length, Sultán Ahmad Mirzá [1] took the citadel of Yángi Hisár by storm, and after that, Káshghar being deserted by its garrison, who fled, he captured that place also.

He spent that winter in Káshghar, and removed his family thither from Moghulistán. At the end of the winter he marched against Mirzá Abá Bakr, in Yárkand. Mirzá Abá Bakr would not come out of the citadel, and when they [the attacking force] saw that an entry was impracticable, they went up into the hills near Yárkand, to carry off the flocks and plunder [the country]. Then, having taken quantities of cattle and booty, they returned towards Káshghar. But Mirzá Abá Bakr, leading a powerful army out of Yárkand, went and blocked the Khán's road in the mountains. A fierce battle was fought, in which, at length, the Khán's army was put to flight. The defeated Khán then descended to Káshghar, but being unable to remain there, he fled into Moghulistán.

One year after this event, news of the victory gained by Sháhi Beg Khán over Sultán Mahmud Khán reached him. Prompted by brotherly love, he set out to offer his services to his distinguished brother. Leaving his eldest son, Mansur Khán, in his own place, and giving him the style of *Khán*, he took his two other sons, Sultán Said Khán and Bábáják Khán, with him to Táshkand. The two Kháns met in Táshkand, and exchanged the salutations and formalities usual on such occasions. (An account of this matter is to be found in Part II.) In short, they discussed how they might frustrate the plans of Sháhi Beg Khán, and finally a battle took place between the latter and the two Kháns, at Akhsi, in which the two Kháns were defeated, and both of them made

[1] Should be Sultan Ahmad *Khan*.

prisoners. Sháhi Beg Khán, observing the duties of the situation, permitted them both to return to Moghulistán; but the greater part of the Moghul *Ulus* he would not allow to depart. These two Kháns went to Moghulistán, passing that winter in Aksu. [There] Sultán Ahmad Khán was attacked with so violent a paralytic seizure, that the doctors were unable to relieve him, and he died in the winter of the year 909 [1503–4]. (May Paradise be his dwelling.)

Sultán Ahmad Khán was a very religious prince and a devoted Musulmán. He was versed in the Holy Law [*Shar'*][1] and most of his affairs were governed by it. He was a high-minded, though violent, man and was distinguished for his daring. He was intelligent, of sound judgment and modest. He was especially affable towards darvishes, and towards learned and pious men. During most of his life he granted pensions to the poor, and gave away one-fifth of his income in charity. In his beneficence and virtuous habits he had, in his time, no rival. He died at the age of thirty-nine.

More will be said of him in the Second Part.

CHAPTER LXV.

MANSUR KHÁN (MAY HIS SINS BE PARDONED!)

He was the eldest son of Sultán Ahmad Khán, who, when he went to join his brother Sultán Mahmud Khán in Táshkand, set up Mansur, as Khán, in his own stead. This was in the year 909, when Mansur Khán was nineteen years of age. At his father's death, his uncle, Sultán Mahmud Khán, left Aksu and came into Moghulistán. Mansur Khán then established his court in Aksu, where a dispute arose between himself and Mir Jabár Birdi, such as is wont to arise between rival heirs; and Mir Jabár Birdi's life became imperilled. The only means he could devise for saving himself, was to send off a messenger to Mirzá Abá Bakr [to ask him to come to his aid]. This was exactly what the Mirzá would have prayed God for; so he set out for Aksu with an army of 30,000 men. Mir Jabár Birdi hastened out to receive Mirzá Abá Bakr. The advance-guard and scouts of the Mirzá's army were in readiness.

When news of this reached Mansur Khán, he fortified Aksu,

[1] Lit.: from the Shar' he derived no vexation.

and, leaving a garrison in its fort, repaired to Bái and Kusan.[1] Mir Jabár Birdi, as a mark of confidence, delivered over to Mirzá Abá Bakr the fort of Uch, which was his own residence and domain. They entered Aksu together, took the fort by storm, and laid hands on all the treasure and hidden wealth which Sultán Ahmad and his people had amassed during twenty-five years. This, together with the people of Aksu, both Moghul and peasant [*ráyat*],[2] they despatched to Káshghar, Mir Jabár Birdi sending his own family in front of all the rest, to prove his entire trust in Mírzá Abá Bakr: for he looked upon a show of confidence as his source of safety. Mirzá Abá Bakr asked him if that were his family. He replied: "There might be difficulties in the way of taking them in the rear of the party, so they can go now. I will stay here a few days to pillage and plunder the surrounding neighbourhood; then I will load your army with booty, and will bring back both the booty and the army to you, in Káshghar.'

The Mirzá was pleased with this boast of Mir Jabár Birdi, whose family he took, with the rest of the people of Aksu, to Káshghar; while he left, with the Mir, an army of 10,000 men, who were to bring on whatever had been left behind.

Mir Jabár Birdi led the Mirzá's army against Bái and Kusan, making several raids into those territories, and carrying off the horses. When he calculated that the Mirzá had arrived in Káshghar, he abandoned the army of the Mirzá, which, frustrated and disappointed, returned to Káshghar, while Mir Jabár Birdi remained in the province of Aksu.

These events were disastrous to Mansur Khán, and his position became very weak. He repented of having persecuted [attempted to take the life of] Mir Jabár Birdi, who was his maternal uncle,

[1] One MS. reads *Kus* and others *Kusan*. Both names were used for the same place, as also *Kos*, *Kucha*, *Kujar*, etc., and all appear to stand for the modern *Kuchar* of the Turki-speaking inhabitants, and *Kuchê* of the Chinese. An earlier Chinese name, however, was *Ku-sien*.

The neighbourhood of Kuchar shows traces of very ancient civilisation; it must have been one of the chief seats of Buddhism in Eastern Turkistan, and it abounds still in remains of Buddhistic buildings, sculptures, cave dwellings, etc. It was in this district that Capt. H. Bower obtained, in 1888, the famous birch-bark Sanscrit MS. described by Dr. Hoernle in *J. A. S. B.*, vol. lx., pt. i., no. 3. The book was dug out of the foot of what appears to be an ancient "chorten," of which several are to be found in the Kuchar district. Capt. Bower also notices that one of these "chortens" is to be seen on the north bank of the river at Kashghar. The one out of which the MS. was obtained, stood just outside the subterranean ruins of a city called *Mangai*, which are situated about 16 miles from Kuchar, on the banks of the Shah-yar river. "The town," writes Capt. Bower, "must have been of considerable extent, but has been greatly reduced owing to the action of the river. On the cliffs on the left bank, high up in mid air, may be seen the remains of houses, still hanging on to the face of the cliffs. . . . . I was told that other similar towns may be seen in the district." (See Proceedings R. A. S. B., Nov. 1890). The book was found by Dr. Hoernle to be written in the Gupta alphabet, and to date from the sixth century A.D.

[2] *Ráyat*, in this sentence, appears to mean the natives of the soil, as distinguished from the foreign Moghuls.

the brother of his mother Sáhib Daulat Begum. In the meantime, news of Mir Jabár Birdi reached him. He thereupon sent messengers to him, offering apologies. Having made a covenant with him, he brought him back and bestowed upon him even greater favours than his father, Sultán Ahmad Khán, had done before him.

After the return of Mir Jabár Birdi to the court of Mansur Khán, the affairs of the latter assumed a more favourable aspect. At that time the people of the different tribes were engaged in hostilities with one another, and these, as far as was possible, he pacified. This is a long story, and I do not recall further details. In short, while these things were passing, news arrived of the discord, in Moghulistán, between Sultán Mahmud Khán and Sultán Said Khán and Sultán Khalil Sultán. Thereupon Mansur Khán entered Moghulistán, and again met his paternal uncle Sultán Mahmud Khán. At this audience he also met Sultán Said Khán and Sultán Khalil Sultán, who were his younger brothers.

After this division had occurred, Sultán Mahmud Khán was no longer able to remain in Moghulistán, being incapable of directing his affairs there: so he repaired to Mávará-un-Nahr (as has been told) and was there slain.

When Mansur Khán heard of Sultán Mahmud Khán's expedition into the [*viláyat*] country [of Mávárá-un-Nahr], he marched against his brothers, who were in Moghulistán with the Kirghiz and the rest of the Moghuls, who had stayed behind. On his arrival, a battle took place in Chárun Chálák. The fight was a fierce one, and ultimately Mansur Khán came off victor. The two brothers fled to "*the viláyat.*"[1] On reaching Andiján, the governor of that place put Sultán Khalil Sultán to death: but his brother, Sultán Said Khán, escaped to Kábul; all of which is related in Part II.

Mansur Khán carried off to Chálish[2] and Turfán, all those of the Kirghiz, and other Moghul tribes, whom he found in Moghulistán. As the Kirghiz were the originators of all the revolts in Moghulistán, he put most of them to death by stratagem. A few of them, however, fled to Moghulistán. After this he made inroads on the Kálmák and was, as a rule, victorious. Thus the affairs of the Khán prospered; though from time to time, he met with opposition from the side of his brothers. One of them, Aiman Khwája Sultán, twice rose against him and was twice subdued, without more being said; however, on the occasion of his revolting a third time, he was seized and handed over to Yáráka Atáka, who received orders to put him to death. But instead of obeying, he hid Aiman Khwája Sultán, telling the Khán that

[1] Into which *viláyat*—*i.e.* country or province—is not mentioned, either here or where it occurs just above. In both instances it is probably Mávará-un-Nahr that is intended, though the word appears to be used, in this and other Persian books, to denote any foreign country—as is the case in modern Hindustani.

[2] The modern Kara-shahr.

he had carried out his commission. A year after this, Bábáják Sultán, another brother of the Khán, fled from him, and betook himself to Bái and Kusan.

These two places, since their destruction [*virán*] by Mirzá Abá Bakr and Jabár Birdi, had fallen into desolation and ruin. But Bábáják came and cultivated the ground, and restored the fort which had been destroyed. Then Mansur Khán came against Bábáják Sultán, and in the first place, tried to bring him to terms of peace, but Bábáják said: "How can I put any trust in you? Aiman Khwája Sultán was also your brother, and you slew him like an enemy: I have no longer any faith in you." Then Mansur Khán repented of having killed Aiman Khwája Sultán, and could make no reply. But Yáráka Atáka interposed: "I had the presumption to act in opposition to your orders, and kept your brother alive." Mansur Khán was very grateful, and on account of this action, raised Yáráka Atáka to a very high rank. He then sent Aiman Khwája Sultán to Bábáják Sultán, who thereupon came and offered submission to the Khán, and made terms of peace.

In the meanwhile, news arrived of the victory Sultán Said Khán had obtained over Mirzá Abá Bakr, and of his conquest of Káshghar. Bábáják Sultán sent Aiman Khwája Sultán to Said Khán, who was rejoiced at his coming. (Bábáják Sultán and Mansur Khán were born of the same mother; as were also Sultán Said Khán and Aiman Khwája Khán.) This is related more fully in Part II.

Mansur Khán stood in great fear of Sultán Said Khán, because he had been the cause of the death of Sultán Said Khán's own brother, Sultán Khalil, and many violent disputes arose between them. Mansur Khán was convinced that this would cause an eternal enmity between them, but contrary to his expectations, Sultán Said Khán sent an ambassador, with an escort, to his elder brother Mansur Khán, and begged for an interview. The meeting took place between Aksu and Kusan in the year 912,[1] in which Sultán Said Khán declared his submission and obedience to Mansur Khán, and ordered the *Khutba* to be read in the latter's name; thus a complete reconciliation was brought about between the two brothers, as a result of which their countries, during a period of twenty years, enjoyed the most perfect peace and security. Any one, for example, could travel alone from Kámul,[2] in Khitái,

[1] The date 912 is wrongly transcribed in all the texts. It should be 922, as is shown in the next chapter but one, where a chronogram for the event in question is given, which works out 922—obviously the correct date—1516.

[2] Nowadays usually called *Kumul*—sometimes *Kámil*. The modern Chinese name is *Hámi*, as it was also at the time of the Mings, who were coeval with the events here related. More ancient names were *I-gu* and *I-chou*. Sir H. Yule mentions a Bishop of *Kumul*, about the middle of the thirteenth century, and believes the place to have been a Nestorian Sec. (Klaproth's *Tableaux Historiques*, map; Yule's *Marco Polo*, i., p. 213).

to Andiján, without having any duties levied upon him; and would be taken every night, as a guest, into some house [on the road]. May God place these two just and righteous brothers in the Garden of Paradise!

During these twenty years, Mansur Khán made several holy wars against Khitái, and always returned *mansur* [victorious].[1] In one of these holy wars, Mir Jabár Birdi met his death, as did also Bandagi Khwája Tájuddin Muhammad. This latter was one of the Khwájas of Kuṣan, and was descended from Mauláná Arshad-ud-Din, who converted the Moghuls to Islám, as has been already related. He made his studies under Mauláná Ali Gharrán of Tus (upon whom be mercy), and also spent much time in the company of that Axis of Axes, Khwája Nasiruddin Ubaidullah, and participated in the benevolent glance of his Holiness

I once heard from the lips of Khwája Tájuddin the following: "I was one day visiting his Holiness, and was seated near him, when he remarked that it was necessary to abstain from 'doubtful morsels.' I looked round the company, and saw they were all men of piety; I was the only one present who was not an abstainer [an ascetic], and I took an oath that, from that time forward, I would eat no food that was not pronounced absolutely lawful by him. So have me excused if I touch not any food at your table." I have mentioned this to show what a pious and abstinent man Khwája Tájuddin was. He was in attendance on Sultán Ahmad Khán and Mansur Khán for fifty years, or rather these Kháns were his disciples. And he accepted, during all this period, neither offering nor gift, whether it were from the Kháns or the Sultáns or the generals of the army, or from peasants or merchants. The Khwája occupied himself, also, with commerce and agriculture. And from these occupations there accrued to him, by the blessing of the Most High God, great wealth. And what urbanity did he not show, every year, towards the Kháns and the Amirs! The poor and indigent—nay, more, the peasant, the villager, the artisan, and the merchant, all profited [by his wealth]. For this reason no one denied him anything, and all the affairs of the kingdom were laid before him in detail. He was, in very truth, a great and loving—a generous and zealous man.

In one of the holy wars against Khitái, he was slain before Mansur Khán's eyes. (May God's mercy be upon him.) When Mansur Khán had disposed of these holy wars in Khitái, he fought a pitched battle with the Uzbeg Kazák at a place in Moghulistán called Arish,[2] where he was defeated; and Sufi Mirzá, who was a

[1] For some remarks on these wars, see Introduction, Sec. V.

[2] This *Arish* in Moghulistan can hardly be traced for certain, though names such as *Arys*, *Arystyn*, etc., often occur on the detailed Russian maps of the region which represents Moghulistan. In all probability it was situated towards the eastern confines of the Moghul territory, and can scarcely be the same as the

Begjik and the chief minister of the Khán, was killed. After this event [Mansur] made fewer expeditions from Chálish and Turfán.

Subsequent to the death of Sultán Said Khán, he marched against Aksu. Twice he failed and was obliged to retire, and in the year 950 he died (may God illumine his proof!) at the age of about sixty years. Except Yunus Khán, no other Khán of the Chaghatái line attained such an age. He ascended the throne,[1] in the year 907, at the age of sixteen, and reigned forty-three years. No other Chaghatái Khán ever reigned as long as this. Nor did any of the Moghul Kháns enjoy so long a life and reign. He adorned his days from the first to the last with blessings and charitable gifts. He passed the whole of his time in the study of the holy law, or the reading of the Korán. I have heard from his intimates that he used to spend about one-fifth of his time in directing the affairs of the State, and all the rest in perusal of the Korán [*tilavat*],[2] prayer [*davat*], the prescribed prayers [*namáz*], and in reciting the names of God [*Izkár*]. It would be hard to find any one among the Pádisháhs, or even among the most pious men [*ahl-i-suluk*], who disposed of their time better than he did. And in consequence of this he was blessed with a long life and earthly happiness, such as no one but he, of his line, has ever enjoyed. May God bless his heavenly life as he did his days upon earth! Amen. Oh God of both worlds!

He excelled in the conduct of life, in intelligence and prudence, and was skilled in state management and the control and organisation of armies. By his nature he was not at all addicted to the customs and ceremonies of kings, or to the grandeur and magnificence of Kháns, but rather tried to do without ceremony, and to live as simply as possible. In no way whatever did he make any distinction between himself and the rest of his people. He knew the Korán by heart, and had a very accurate *Reader*, who was better versed in the Korán than any one else in the country. His name was "Háfiz Magas-i-sag."[3] But in his innermost nature, this man was so unbalanced and his acts were so revolting, that to mention them would be a reason for withdrawing behind a curtain! It was under this man that Mansur Khan learnt by heart the *Kalám-Ullah*. Some of his officers one day suggested, in private, to the Khán that Háfiz Magas was not worthy to be his teacher, seeing that his mind

Arish mentioned in Part II. (p. 378) in connection with Ak-kum, as that place appears to have lain beyond the north-western limits of Moghulistan. (See note 4, p. 378.)

[1] That is to say, the throne of Aksu and Turfan.

[2] *Tilávat*—reading and meditating on the Korán. The *Namáz* means the five prescribed prayers or litanies of the day—the Arabic *salát*. *Dávat* literally means "supplication," and is used for private, or spontaneous, prayer.—R.

[3] The name would mean "the Háfiz of the fly of the dog." A Háfiz is one who has committed to memory the whole of the Korán.

was totally unsound. . . .[1] Thus it is evident that Mansur Khán was a religiously inclined monarch. He spent the whole of his life in the practice of Islám.

He left behind him two sons, Sháh Khán and Muhammad Sultán, and one daughter, whom Sultán Said Khán took for his son Rashid Sultán, as is mentioned in Part II.

CHAPTER LXVI.

SHÁH KHÁN, SON OF MANSUR KHÁN.

At the end of his life, Mansur Khán had raised his eldest son Sháh Khán to the throne, while he himself withdrew to the cell of retirement. His son succeeded to all his authority, and is at this day—952 [1545]—the reigning Khán in Turfán and Chálish. But in his treatment of his father's adherents, in his direction of the Khánate, and in his regal proceedings, he has adopted displeasing ways, and has become notorious for his bad manners, of which it is unnecessary for me to speak. Even while his father was yet alive, he had stained the garments of good reputation with the pollution of disobedience, and he does not now regard the memory of his distinguished father in the way that is becoming and fit; nor has he shown such signs of piety and prosperity as would be worthy of his good father.

It is the practice of historians to recount everything as they find it, whether worthy or unworthy of mention. For it is not their object to write down the good qualities of princes, and to omit all their bad actions, but rather to reproduce all facts without discrimination, in order that they may leave behind them a record of the people of this world. Thus all men in power, as well as others, reading their histories, may profit by their advice, and may see what have been the various fruits and results of praiseworthy habits, on the one hand, or blameable actions on the other: also that they may accept the lesson to be learnt from observing the way in which the memory of different princes has been preserved, and may, in short, incline to good deeds and avoid evil ways.

[1] The remainder of this passage is unfit for translation. In Persian it stands as follows: "In Háfiz Magas láík ustádí níst chi dar ghráyat bí i'tidálí ast. Az jumla ánki úrá darín rúzhá ba máda gáví girifta-and. Shágirdiyi Khán úrá chi munásib báshad." Khán guft: "Man azú Kalám-Ullah yád míkardam, máda-gáv ú vaz'-i-badan yád nakhwáham girift."

CHAPTER LXVII.

SULTÁN SAID KHÁN, SON OF SULTÁN AHMAD KHÁN.

SULTÁN AHMAD KHÁN had eighteen sons. The eldest was Mansur Khán, of whom I have just spoken. Next to him came Iskandar Sultán, who died a natural death, after his father. Then came Sultán Said Khan, who was fourteen years of age when Sultán Ahmad Khán went to [the assistance of] his elder brother, Sultán Mahmud Khán. He had taken with him, on this occasion, two of his sons: namely Sultán Said Khán and Bábáják Sultán.

While the two Kháns were together, Sultán Said Khán passed his days in the cell of instruction of my father, and under the kindly protection of my uncle. [This lasted] up to the time of the battle at Akhsi, between the two Kháns and Sháhi Beg Khán (which has been mentioned). In the flight which ensued, Sultán Said Khán was struck by an arrow in the thigh, and the bone was broken: so he threw himself onto a side path.[1] After the flight and rout had subsided, some of the people of that district found him, but as his leg was broken, they did not remove him from where he lay. After a few days had passed, and he was almost recovered, they took him before Shaikh Báyazid, Governor of Akhsi. An account of Shaikh Báyazid and of his brother, Sultán Ahmad Tambal, will be found in Part II. Shaikh Báyazid kept Sultán Said Khán in prison.

In the year following, when the corn was high, Sháhi Beg Khan again came against Farghána and Sultán Ahmad Tambal. Sultán Ahmad Tambal and Shaikh Báyazid, together with all their brothers, were put to death by Sháhi Beg Khán, who then possessed himself of Farghána. Sultán Said Khán, who was in prison, by the order of Shaikh Báyazid, was now released and conducted before Sháhi Beg Khán, who treated him as his own son, and being moved to pity at his sad condition, took him to Samarkand. From there he took him on his campaign against Hisár and Kunduz, at the time when Khusrau Sháh had just subjugated the provinces of Hisár, Kunduz, and Badakhshán. When he had brought this enterprise to a close, he again returned to Samarkand. He next invaded Khwárizm. But on the occasion of this expedition, the Khán fled from him and came into Moghulistán. He journeyed by way of Uzun Ahmad as far as Yatikand.[2] His uncle, Sultán Mahmud Khán, was at that time in Yatikand; with him he passed a few

[1] *Paighula*—side path or sheltered nook.—R.

[2] See for this name note, p. 180.

days, but finally, being wearied with the careless way in which his uncle conducted the affairs of the State, he departed and went into Moghulistán to visit his brother, Sultán Khalil Sultán, who was governor of the Kirghiz.

He remained four years with his brother, among the Kirghiz in Moghulistán. During this period many transactions took place between Sultán Mahmud Khan, Mansur Khán, and these two brothers. The result of these proceedings was that Sultán Mahmud Khán found, on account [of the opposition] of his nephews, that he could no longer remain in Moghulistán. So he went to seek Sháhi Beg Khán, in hopes of kind treatment. But Sháhi Beg Khán, as has been related, put him to death on the river of Khojand. When Sultán Mahmud Khán went abroad [to *viláyat*] to visit Sháhi Beg Khán, these two brothers remained in Moghulistán and the Kirghiz country. In the meanwhile, news of the approach of Mansur Khán's army reached them. For Mansur Khán had led out an army from Chálish and Turfán against his brothers, in order to seize the land of the Khirghiz and Moghulistán. So Sultán Said Khán and Sultán Khalil, having collected all the [fighting] men of the Kirghiz and the Moghuls, took up a strong position at a place called Charun Chák,[1] ready to receive the enemy. On the arrival of Mansur with his army, the signal for battle was given, and finally Sultán Said Khán and Sultán Khalil Sultán were defeated. Mansur Khán made the Kirghiz march into Chálish, as has been mentioned in the account of Mansur Khán. Sultán Khalil Sultán escaped from the fight with a considerable number of men, and came to Farghána, [hoping] to fall in with his uncle Sultán Mahmud Khán, and to be kindly treated by Sháhi Beg Khán. But when he reached Akhsi he was put to death by Jáni Beg Khán, a cousin of Sháhi Beg Khán, and governor of the country of Farghána.

Sultán Said Khán, for some time after the battle, took to robbery, but events soon came about which rendered impossible for him further sojourn in Moghulistán. (These events are described in Part II. To avoid repetition they have only been given in epitome here.) In this state of hopelessness Sultán Said Khán went to Andiján, and thence to Kábul, to visit his (paternal) cousin Bábar Pádisháh, the son of Omar Shaikh Mirzá, who received him with honour and kindness, and with whom he stayed for three years at Kábul.

When Sháh Ismáil [defeated and] slew Sháhi Beg Khán in Marv, Bábar Pádisháh moved from Kábul to Kunduz, taking Sultán Said Khán with him. At this same time Sayyid Muhammad Mirzá, son of Muhammad Haidar Mirzá, and uncle of the author

[1] Or *Járun Ják*—probably the same name that at page 125 was written *Chárun Chálák*.

of this history, invaded Andiján and, driving Jáni Beg Sultán out, became himself master of the country. He then sent messengers to inform Bábar Pádisháh of what he had achieved. Bábar Pádisháh thereupon sent Sultán Said Khán and what Moghul Amirs he had in his service, to Andiján. On his arrival there, Sultán Said Khán was received with ceremony by his uncle Sayyid Muhammad Mirzá, who also delivered over to him the whole of the territory which he had just subjugated. The Khán showed my uncle every mark of honour, and according to the ancient Moghul custom, conferred upon him the title of *Ulusbegi*,[1] which became his hereditary office.

Meanwhile Mirzá Abá Bakr, having set his heart upon the kingdom of Farghána, had collected an army in Káshghar, and was on the road to Andiján. The Khán marched out to meet him with an army of 1500 men. The two forces came into contact at a place called Tut-lugh,[2] about two *farsákhs* from Andiján. By the help of God [that small body] of 1500 men overcame an army 20,000 strong, after a very fierce struggle, and in consequence of this victory the fame of Sultán Said Khán was established among the surrounding Sultáns. The Uzbeg Sultáns from Farghána then began to assemble on the borders of Samarkand and Táshkand. Afterwards, Bábar Pádisháh engaged these Sultáns in a battle at Hisár Shádmán, and was victorious. By this victory he was enabled to rid Mávará-un-Nahr of all the Uzbeg, and he himself mounted the throne of Samarkand. In the month of Rajab of the year 917,[3] the Khán was again firmly established in Andiján. In the early spring [*avval bahár*] of the same year, the Uzbeg again entered Táshkand. Ubaid Ullah Khán advanced in the direction of Bokhárá, in the neighbourhood of which place he fought a battle with Bábar Pádisháh, who had come out to oppose him. Ubaid Ullah Khán was victorious, and Bábar Pádisháh retired defeated to Samarkand, whence, withdrawing his family and all his belongings, he fled to Hisár. Thus the Uzbeg recovered their ascendency. The Khán remained in Andiján.

Bábar Pádisháh, meanwhile, appealed to Sháh Ismáil for assistance. The latter sent Mir Najm, one of his Amirs, with 60,000 men, to the Pádisháh, who having joined his own troops to these, marched on Samarkand. The Khán, in the meantime, having

[1] That is, "chief of the tribe." This title seems to have been a very old one among the Moghuls, though strangely enough the words *ulus begi* are both Turkish. At the time in question here—within the sixteenth century—it could have carried with it little more than a nominal office, though at an earlier period the *Ulusbegi* appears really to have been ruler of his tribe, and the title then was perhaps equivalent to "King."

[2] Previously written *Tut-Luk*.

[3] June or July, 1511.

harassed the Uzbeg in the neighbourhood of Andiján, also marched towards Samarkand, and encountered Suyunj Khwája Khán near Táshkand. All the other Kháns and Sultáns had assembled in Samarkand and Bokhárá to oppose Bábar Pádisháh. But in the battle near Táshkand, between the Khán and Suyunj Khwája Khán, the former had 5000 men and the latter 7000; after a hard fight, the Khán was defeated and fled to Andiján.[1]

Your servant, the author of the present history, having taken leave of Bábar Pádisháh, at the time when he went to join Mir Najm, entered the service of the Khán, who was in Andiján, and had just sustained a defeat at the hands of Suyunj Khwája Khán. In the spring, the Khán went to the court of Kásim Khán, who was ruler of the Dasht-i-Kipchák. At that time his army numbered 300,000 men. Kásim Khán received him with so much respect and honour that the Khán remembered it for years after. On his return from that visit, he distinguished me from among my equals with the connection [*musaharat*] of Kurkáni. All this is related in Part II.

In the early spring of the year 920 all the great Uzbeg Sultáns, with a very numerous army of warriors, advanced against Andiján. The Khán, not deeming it wise to offer fight, retired into Moghulistán before the foreign army reached Farghána. When he arrived at Yatikand they held a council of war, and acting on the timely advice and persuasion of my uncle Sayyid Muhammad Mirzá (who was brother to Mirzá Abá Bakr), they marched towards Káshghar, where a terrible battle was fought, in which the army of that place was routed and obliged to retire within the fort of Káshghar. The Khán then marched on Yángi Hisár, which he besieged for three months. At length the inhabitants entered into a capitulation with my uncle, and delivered up the fort.

On this news reaching Káshghar, the army that was in that town abandoned it. When the fugitives joined Mirzá Abá Bakr in Yárkand, he too resolved on flight, and took the road to Khotan. The Khán pursued him to Yárkand, and then sent on troops after him, as far as the mountains of Tibet. Much booty in the shape of cloths, goods, cattle and horses fell into the hands of the Moghul army (as is described in the Second Part).

The accession of the Khán to the kingdom of Káshghar was in Rajab of the year 920.[2] At the end of that winter Aiman Khwája Sultán, who was brother to the Khán, by the same father and mother, came from Turfán, as has been stated above. He instigated and encourged his Amirs in the matter of the extermination of Mansur Khán, explaining to them the decline of the

[1] One MS. has "fled to Hissar," but Andiján is obviously right. Dr. Bellew's MS. appears to have had Andiján.

[2] May and June, 1514.

Khán's power, and dwelling on the enmity that had existed in Moghulistán, in times past, towards the Khán. But the Khán said: "He is the elder brother; in former times I did not pay him due respect, and consequently he punished me. I ought on this account to bear him no enmity. The most fitting thing for me to do, is to apologise to him for my shortcomings, and offer him reparation for the past." He then sent ambassadors bearing words of peace and submission. At this message, Mansur Khán, whose soul had come to his lips, from fear and foreboding, now received new life and joy without bounds. He came in fear and trembling to the conference [*mulákát*], which was held between Aksu and Kusan. The Khán showed him great honour, and agreed to read the *Khutba* and strike coins in his name. And all the ill-feeling that he had formerly borne Mansur Khán, he now changed to brotherly affection and obedience. From this peace and reconciliation between the two brothers, resulted such security and prosperity for the people, that any one might travel alone between Kámul or Khitái and the country of Farghána, without provision for the journey and without fear of molestation. Some ingenious person, to commemorate this peace, invented the following chronogram, "*Du lashkar ba nishát*"—that is, 922. ["Two armies in happiness."]

The next year, when Muhammad Kirghiz had made raids into Turkistán and Farghána, and had plundered the Musulmáns, the Khán, in his desire to protect Islám, looked upon this action as an insult. He therefore set forth to attack Muhammad Kirghiz, whom he seized and threw into prison, where he remained for fifteen years.

In 928 [1522] the Khán took his son Rashid Sultán into Moghulistán. He subdued the whole of Moghulistán and the Kirghiz, and a number of the people of Moghulistán supported Rashid Sultán. Finally, on account of the superiority of the Mangit,[1] the Uzbeg

[1] The name here rendered *Mangit* is subject to several different readings, such as *Manfakit*, *Man'akit*, etc.; but there can be little doubt that the author is pointing to the tribe of *Mangit* or *Mangut*. The word occurs again in connection with the same events lower down, though it is there spelled differently, (see p. 374). Still it would seem permissible, on historical grounds, to assume that the tribal name of *Mangit* is intended. There is little to be found on the subject of these people. Abul Gházi tells us, quite shortly, that they descended from Chingiz's grandfather Bartan Khan, while Rashid-ud-Din, according to Erdmann, includes them in his list of 'Black Tatars,' or tribes who were originally Mongols; but beyond these brief references to them, in the later Middle Ages, they do not appear to have attracted much attention. They are said to have been a people akin to the *Nogai*, and at about the period alluded to in the text (1522) were inhabitants of the Kipchák steppes. They are known also to have become adherents of Sháhi Beg Khan shortly before this date, and it seems quite possible that they may have had sufficient power to expel the Uzbeg Kazák from the Kipchák steppes, if these were their enemies. At a long subsequent date—in the eighteenth century—the descendants of these Mangit rose in influence, till their chiefs became a ruling dynasty in Bokhara. (See Abul Gházi, p. 76; Erdmann's *Temudschin*, pp. 168 and 219; and S. L. Poole's *Muham. Dynast*, p. 277.)

Kazák, being no longer able to remain in the Dasht-i-Kipchák, came over into Moghulistán, to the number of 200,000 persons. It was impossible to resist them, so Rashid Sultán retired with his men to Káshghar.

Meanwhile the Khán invaded Badakhshán, and conquered half of it, which is, to this day, subject to the government of Káshghar. This is a long story. The disputes that arose out of the claims to its inheritance made by Sháh Begum (who has been mentioned) are related in Part. II. of this History.

The Khán twice invaded Badakhshán, once in the year 925 and again in 936 [1519 and 1529–30]. In the year 934 the Khán sent me, with Rashid Sultán, to Balur, which is a country of infidels [*Káfiristán*], between Badakhshán and Kashmir,[1] where we conducted successfully a holy war [*ghazát*], and returned victorious, loaded with booty and covered with glory.

A short time after this, it came about that some malicious and impure devils set up Aiman Khwája Sultán in Aksu. This town, which from the date of the conquest of Mirzá Abá Bakr (909), to the year 913, had been in a state of ruin, was now rebuilt by Aiman Khwája Sultán.

The Khán sent me, together with Rashid Sultán, to Aksu, whence we drove out Aiman Khwája Sultán, and sent him to Káshghar. Then, having set in order his military and civil affairs, I left Rashid Sultán in Aksu and re-entered the service of the Khán. Aiman Sultán was despatched to Hindustán, where he died a natural death. At the end of the year 938 [1532] the Khán made a holy war on the infidel country [*Káfiristán*] of Tibet,[2] sending me forward in advance of himself. I had taken several of the forts and subdued most of the country of Tibet, by the time the Khán

[1] *Balur* or *Bolor* included Hunza, Nagar, Gilgit, Yasin, Chitral, &c., as will be seen further on, note, p. 385.

[2] It may be noted here, that the only name for the province of *Ladak* ever used by Mirza Haidar is *Tibet*. In this he is at one with all the Turki-speaking inhabitants of Central Asia, down to the present day. The word *Ladak*, or more properly *La-tags*, is a purely local one. The inconvenient circumstance, however, is that throughout the *Tarikh-i-Rashidi* the name of *Tibet* is applied not only to *Ladak*, but to the whole of the provinces under the rule of the priestly government of Lassa—that is, to the region generally known in Europe as *Tibet*. In reading the *Tarikh-i-Rashidi*, therefore, it is necessary to discriminate between *Ladak* and *Tibet* proper, on every occasion that the word occurs. In the present instance the author is speaking of *Ladak* only. The province of Baltistan (called always by our author *Balti*), which is situated to the north of Kashmir and west of *Ladak*, is known as *Little Tibet* in all the neighbouring regions, and to most Oriental writers; while *Ladak* is sometimes termed *Great Tibet* by way of distinction. The Jesuit missionary Desideri, in the MS. narrative of his travels during the early part of the last century (in possession of the Hakluyt Society) nearly always refers to *Baltistan* as "the first Tibet," to *Ladak* as "the second Tibet," and to *Tibet* proper, or Lassa territory, as "the third Tibet." The word *Tibet*, it may be added, though seldom or never used by the natives of any of the Tibetan provinces, is of purely Tibetan origin, as explained by Mr. W. W. Rockhill in the *Journ. Rl. As. Socy.* for Jan. 1891, p. 5. It has come to Europe, however, through Central Asia.

came up with me. The two armies together formed a body of 5000 men, which was a larger number of people than all Tibet could support in winter time. So the Khán saw fit to send me, in company with Iskandar Sultán, to Kashmir, with 4000 men, while he himself proceeded to Balti, which is a province between Tibet and Balur. He spent the winter there, engaged in a holy war, and in the spring returned to Tibet.

I entered Kashmir that winter, and at the end of the season[1] fought a pitched battle with the kings [*malik*] of the country. Thanks to the Most High God, I came off victorious, and exterminated the whole army of Kashmir and the kings. I might also have subdued the whole of the country, had it not been for some of those malignant persons who, by their words and actions, throw things into disorder, and who rendered the further reduction of the country impossible.[2] Peace was made with the kings of Kashmir, and the daughter of Muhammad Sháh, the Pádisháh of Kashmir, was given in marriage to Iskandar Sultán, while the *Khutba* was read and the coins struck in the Khán's name. All the wealth of Kashmir, that it was possible to collect, was brought, in the spring following that winter, to the Khán in Tibet. The Khán, on my return, honoured me with every mark of royal benevolence and favour, and sent me to Ursáng, which is the *Kibla* of Khitái and Tibet,[3] while he himself set out for Káshghar.

[1] The winter of 1532–3.

[2] The author is referring to "malignant persons" in his own camp—*i.e.* to one Ali Taghái and others of the Moghuls, as will be seen in Chap. cii. of the Second Part.

[3] *Ursang* can be no other than Lassa, under a corruption of the Chinese names of the two chief or central provinces of Tibet—viz., *Wu* and *Tsang*. These two names are nearly always coupled, and used together to denote Tibet proper as a whole, so that Mirza Haidar, hearing them paired in this way—*Wu-Tsang*—applied them to the capital city instead of to the country. Nothing is more common among Asiatics than to give the name of the country to its chief town, or to employ the name of the capital for the country at large. In this case, Mirza Haidar is only using what may be termed the official Chinese designation for the country, at the time he wrote, for during the Ming period, as well as during that of the Mongols (which preceded it), *Wu-Tsang* or *Wu-sz'-tsang* was the name for Tibet which had been adopted in the official histories and geographies. Later, the name became changed into *Si-Tsang*, or Western *Tsang*, and Tibet is known to the Chinese of the present day by this combination. The two outer provinces of Lassa-governed Tibet are *Kám*, lying to the east of *Wu*, and Ngari to the north-west of *Tsang*. All the country to the north of *Wu-Tsang* and *Ngari* is usually known as *Cháng-tán*, or the Northern Plain—an elevated desolate region with which the Lassa government seems scarcely to concern itself.

When Mirza Haidar speaks of *Ursang*, as the "Kibla"—the cynosure, the point of adoration—of the Chinese and Tibetans, he could not have indicated Lassa more distinctly, although further on, in the Second Part, he gives some additional particulars concerning *Ursang*, which could apply to no other place than Lassa. His spelling of the name has arisen from the difficulty, which every Persian or Turki speaking Asiatic finds, in pronouncing the combination *ts*—a difficulty just as formidable as the pronunciation of the *st*. The insertion of the letter *r*, too, in foreign names, is not an uncommon practice with Persian writers, as *Amur* for Amu, *Manchur* for Manchu, etc. (Comp. Bretschneider, ii., pp. 23–4, 221, etc.)

At the time of his arrival [in Tibet] he had become very weak and much reduced, from *dam-giri*,[1] and during the whole period of his sojourn in Tibet he never quite recovered. Nevertheless, he was obliged, under any circumstances, to make the [return] journey. When he reached a spot where *dam-giri* was prevalent, his pious soul took flight to the regions of the blessed. This was at the close of the year 939.[2] All this is fully related in Part II. of this History.

CHAPTER LXVIII.

CONCERNING THE LAUDABLE VIRTUES AND RARE ATTAINMENTS OF SULTÁN SAID KHÁN.

SULTÁN SAID KHÁN was a noble, happy, and prosperous prince, and was adorned with acquirements and good qualities. He was nearly forty-eight years of age when he went to take up his abode in the dwellings of God's mercy. His conduct of life was irreproachable. His conversation was both graceful and eloquent, whether in Turki or in Persian, and when he showed favour to any one, he used to blush before speaking. He was always gay, open-hearted, generous and affectionate. For example, a certain Maksud Ali had struck the Khán in the left shoulder with an arrow, in some battle; [so severe was the wound] that the Khán suffered from it for two years and nearly died of it. During the time of his suffering, some men captured Maksud Ali, so that the Khán might wreak his vengeance upon him. But when he was brought before the Khán, he treated him kindly, and though he had only one garment by him, gave it him. He also took him into his own society, and made him his companion, saying: "I was vexed, but thou art welcome [*nik ámadi*]," and they continued good friends the rest of their lives. He performed many similar acts of generosity, several of which will be found recorded in Part II. His liberality reached a high degree of perfection. I was twenty-four years in his service. Such was his munificence that his household supplies were sometimes quite exhausted, and the royal larder was some days so empty, that he would go and take his meals in the haram. For the same reason his expenditure exceeded the revenue of the State.

[1] The word here is *damgir*—lit. breath-seizing or choking; but the malady the writer points to is that of shortness of breath, and other distressing symptoms, produced by the rarefied air at great altitudes. (See note, p. 413).
[2] The year 939 ended 23 July, 1533.

He was also greatly distinguished for his bravery. I was present at an attack which was led by him in person, and have described it in Part II. Moreover, I never saw his equal as an archer, among all the Moghul, Uzbeg, or Chaghatái *Ulus*, either before or since. I have myself seen him shoot seven or eight arrows in succession, without missing his mark. When hunting deer, hares, or game birds, he would never fail to hit them with his arrow. And in the battles he fought against the Kirghiz and others in Moghulistán, he became celebrated for the way he discharged his shafts into their midst. Generosity such as his I have seldom seen. On one occasion, an assassin came and sought to take his life, but not finding an opportunity, stole a horse from the Khán's stable and rode off. He was captured on the road, with the horse, and brought back. The prisoner said to the Khán: "I came on a mission [*davá*], but could find no opportunity of carrying it out, so I said: I will take a horse from the Khán's stables, then I shall at any rate have done something." The Khán's men all wished to kill him, but the Khán said to me: "Hand him over to your servants that they may take care of him, and do with him whatever you tell them." When the people had dispersed the Khán said to me: "As a thankoffering to God for having preserved me from that man, give him the horse he stole from me. Then tell your men to let him secretly out of the camp, so that when he returns to his fellows they may not look upon him with contempt. Thus the poor man will, in a measure, have executed his mission."

Further, I never saw a more accurate reader than the Khán. However faulty the orthography might be, he would read off verse or prose without hesitating, in such a way that listeners might suppose he knew it by heart. He wrote *Naskh Tálik* excellently, and his spelling in Turki and Persian was faultless. He also composed letters [*inshá*] well in Turki: other people could only have composed them with great difficulty and application. I have rarely met with such power and capability in writing verse [*shir*]. He never said poems by heart, but in assemblies and social gatherings, if any collection of odes [*diván*] that was at hand was opened, and he was given any metre and rhyme, he would extemporise a poem. If he repeated a poem once or twice, everybody could remember it; but he was not pleased if any one made a copy of it.

I have remembered, and here reproduce, some of the extempore poems which the Khán recited in the assemblies. [Turki verses . . . .]

I only once knew him make verses in Persian.[1]

[1] The author cites one "Bait" of the Khan's Persian verses, which, however, is omitted in the translation.

He performed on the *'ud*, and the *sihtara*, and the *chártára*, and the *ghachak*, but best of all on the *chártára*.[1] He had a sound knowledge of bone-cutting, and was skilled in making arrows.

CHAPTER LXIX.

ABDUR RÁSHID KHÁN, SON OF SULTÁN SAID KHÁN.

AT this date of 953,[2] Abdur Rashid, the most excellent son of Sultán Said Khán, is on the throne of the Kháns, and I (your most despicable slave), Muhammad Haidar, have inscribed and adorned my history with his glorious name. This book, beginning with an account of Tughluk Timur Khán (who was the first among the Moghul Khákáns to be converted to Islám), down to Sultán Yunus Khan, is compiled from oral tradition and contemporary accounts, when they have not been found contradictory. Conflicting traditions have been omitted, on account of their probable inaccuracy. The history, from Yunus Khán down to the end of the reign of Sultán Said Khán, has been fully treated of in Part II. But in Part I. I have only given this portion of the history in epitome, as it is long, and much repetition would not embellish my work.

As, however, there is no account of Abdur Rashid Khán in Part II., it is fitting to give it in this place.

At the time when the Khán [Sultán Said] was in Moghulistán with his brother Sultán Khalil Sultán, Mansur Khán also entered that country, and a battle was fought between them at Chárun Chálák, in which the two brothers were put to flight. After being routed, they found that they could no longer remain in Moghulistán, so they retired in distress to Andiján, where the Khán was put into confinement. But he managed to escape, and went to Kábul, where his cousin Bábar Pádisháh was. (All of this is related in

[1] *El 'Ud*, the Arabic name, whence our word *Lute*. Either the *Sih-tára*, a three-stringed instrument, or the *Chártára*, one of four strings (the tetracord), may be the original of the European *guitar* or cithar; but it is not clear from which name the word guitar has descended. Either one could be the parent. Badger's dictionary gives the word *kitárah* for *guitar*, but it is possible that the Arabs adopted the guitar (as they are known to have adopted the lute) from Persia, and with the instrument, probably, the name. The *Ghachak*, according to the dictionaries, should be a kind of violin—or, at any rate, a stringed instrument.

[2] That is, 1546 A.D., when the author was composing his history.

Part II.) The mother of Abdur Rashid Khán was one of those tribes-people whom his father had married, while they were in his service. She was with the Khán when he was thrown into prison in Andiján, but the malignant Uzbeg had separated her from the Khán, by whom she was seven months with child, of this same Abdur Rashid Khán. When the Khán joined Bábar Pádisháh at Kábul, news reached him that his servant was delivered of a son. The Khán told this news to the Pádisháh, who said to him: "Call this boy Abdur Rashid, because it rhymes with Sultán Said Khán." And this is the origin of the name of Abdur Rashid, who was his father's successor.

When my uncle, Sayyid Muhammad Mirzá, went to Farghána and attacked the Uzbeg under Jáni Beg Sultán, he cleared the country entirely of Uzbeg impurities, and sent a messenger to the Pádisháh in Kunduz, who brought him back Sultán Said Khán. Abdur Rashid Khán had fallen into the unclean hands of the Uzbeg, but in consequence of these successes, he recovered his liberty and joined his noble father. When my sister, Habiba Sultán Khánish, came from Samarkand, the Khán married her, and entrusted Abdur Rashid Sultán to her care. She reared him with motherly attention and love, and Amir Ghuri Barlás was appointed his governor [Atábeg]. He was at that time three years of age. Two years later Amir Ghuri Barlás died, and according to the Moghul usage, his office was given to his uncle, Ali Mirák Barlás Khán. Thus Ali Mirák Barlás was appointed Atábeg to Abdur Rashid Sultán, and the charge of his education was given to Mauláná Muhammad Shirázi, a learned and noble-minded man, who passed all his valuable life in the service of the Moghul Khákáns. He was chief judge [*Sadr-i-Sudur*] at the court of Sultán Said Khán, where he exercised great influence.

This Mauláná was in truth the Atábeg of Rashid Sultán, while Ali Mirák Barlás held the office only nominally.

Rashid Sultán was born in the year 915 [1509-10]. In 928, when he was thirteen years of age, the Khán brought him into Moghulistán.

When Khalil Sultán was killed by Jáni Beg Sultán at Akhsi, his son Bábá Sultán was still at the breast, and like Rashid Sultán, was kept a prisoner by Jáni Beg Sultán. At the time when Farghána was subdued, he was brought to the Khán, who came to love this nephew more dearly than he loved his own children. He gave the child in charge to Khwája Ali Bahádur, who had formerly rendered great services to Sultán Said Khán, and appointed the Khwája, Atábeg to Bábá Sultán. The Khwája was a Moghul, and had spent most of his life in Moghulistán; he was very devoted to that country, and was always longing to be there. For this reason he begged the Khán to give Moghulistán and the Kirghiz country to Bábá Sultán, saying that he himself would take [the boy] to Moghulistán, and would arrange the affairs of the Kirghiz and of Moghulistán. The Khán consented to this, and wished to send [them] off. My uncle, since he was father-in-law to Bábá Sultán, did not overstep the bounds of loyalty, but as he disapproved of the plan, he represented [to the Khán] that the Moghuls had an unbounded love for Moghulistán. If Bábá Sultán were once established in that country, all the Moghuls would want to live in Moghulistán; if the Khán forbade the undertaking, Bábá Sultán would be offended; while if he did not forbid it, the departure of the people for Moghulistán would be a source of injury to the Khán; much anxiety would be caused, and the situation would give rise to many difficulties. "But if, [he went on to say] Rashid Sultán takes him there, he is your son, and it can do you no harm for the people to follow him. Even if evil should result, you have only to control him—a course which cannot injure him. Although Rashid Sultán is very young, it is advisable that he should go into Moghulistán."

No one supported my uncle's opinion. Mirzá Ali Tagháí in particular supported the side of Bábá Sultán.

In the meanwhile, Khwája Ali Bahádur died (a natural death), so that the proposal was entirely abandoned, and the Khán's attention was turned to Rashid Sultán, but heated discussions constantly arose concerning that matter. My uncle did his utmost to settle the affairs of Rashid Sultán quietly, and represented [to the Khán] that the right course to take was to release Muhammad Kirghiz from prison, where he had now been for a long time. He should [my uncle said] be brought out; a selection should be made from among the Moghuls who had flocks and herds and were desirous of returning to Moghulistán, and these, accompanied by some of the great Amirs, should all be sent off [to Moghulistán] together.

Finally the Khán approved my uncle's plan, and carried it out as had been suggested.

Having created Mirzá Ali Tagháí commander-in-chief, and appointed Muhammad Kirghiz, Amir of the Kirghiz, he sent them away. Just at this time Ali Mirák Barlás died, and was succeeded in the service of Rashid Sultán, by his son Muhammadi bin Ali Mirák Barlás; he also accompanied the expedition.

Finally, at the insistence of my uncle, the Khán gave to Rashid Sultán one-third of all his regal possessions, whether in men, soldiers, money, tents, or felt dwellings [*khargáh*], and despatched him into Moghulistán. On the day of the departure of Rashid Sultán, [the Khán] sent to the haram for all his accoutrements, and said to me: "Fasten on his sword and quiver for him, and help him to mount his horse; it may be a good omen, and in the art of war he shall be your pupil." I performed this service, and the Khán himself, having stood up, repeated several times the *Fátiha*,[1] and then said: "Do not forget that it was Mirzá Haidar who first fastened on your sword for you, and that you are his pupil; should any one ask you, whose pupil are you in the art of war, what answer will you make?" Rashid Sultán replied: "[I shall say] that I am the pupil of such a one." The Khán said: "He is my pupil." Having repeated this several times, and having once more recited the *Fátiha*, the Khán sent the party off.

On the arrival of Rashid Sultán in Moghulistán, Muhammad Kirghiz brought together all the Kirghiz and entirely subdued Moghulistán, where at that time there was a large army. It would take too long to recount the details. However, in consequence of the opposition which Rashid Sultán and his followers and allies met with from the Uzbeg Kazák, and also because of the hostility of the Kirghiz, he was obliged to return to Káshghar. Then followed those incidents in connection with Bábá Sultán and Sháh Muhammad Sultán which I have given in Part II. Muhammadi Barlás was also concerned in these matters, for it was to him they entreated the Khán to give the heritage of Sháh Muhammad Sultán, by way of retaliation. My uncle and I, however, opposed this plan.

In short, in the winter of that year, 934 [1528], the Khán sent me with Rashid Sultán to Balur, and in Balur I managed all the affairs of the army. Rashid Sultán was then eighteen years of age. He had no cultured men in his service, and had never had practice in conversation [*kasb-i-muhávara*]. Those about him were all a sect of Muhammadans, who, though men in form, were but brutes in their manners, and what could he learn from the brutal ways of those people? In spite of my own want of power and capacity [*istitáat*], I was superior to these people, and I passed my time with Rashid Sultán. So that when we returned, some little time after, the Khán found his son quite another person, and he said several times, both before me and in my absence, to Rashid Sultán, that he was delighted [*mastwar*] with me. I had made Rashid Sultán a son to him, in that he had won many victories with this army; and [he added] "thanks be to God, my son has come so near to being what my heart would desire him to be."

Meanwhile news came of the revolt of Aiman Khwája Sultán who was at Aksu, and in spite of my own and my uncle's efforts, we were unable to quell it. The account of this, and of the execrable proceedings of Mirzá Ali Taghái, will be found in Part II.

Finally, I was sent, together with Rashid Sultán, to Aksu. When

[1] *Fátiha*—the "opener" or "beginner," *i.e.* the opening chapter of the Korán. —R.

we reached that town the whole population came out to receive us. Aiman Khwája Sultán presented himself before the Khán. I remained six months in Aksu, where I conducted satisfactorily all military and civil affairs. Before this, one day in Moghulistán, the Khán was eating almonds; he broke one with his (blessed) teeth, and found that it had two kernels. He thereupon sent for Rashid Sultán and myself, and gave one kernel to each of us, saying: "It is an excellent and significant custom that when two men wish to become friends, each should eat one of the kernels from a double almond, and then become friends to one another. Thus, like the two kernels in one shell, nothing will separate them, and though two in appearance, they will really be one. I have told you to do this that you may be friends." Both of us then respectfully kissed the ground, and drew our horses close together. The outcome of which was that, while we were in Aksu, we lived in great concord. Our affection, our unity, our mutual regard and confidence were beyond description, and our friendship was confirmed by sworn covenants. If I were to write down a description of our friendship and concord, the reader would certainly doubt whether such a state of things really existed, and would attribute it to mere rhetoric. In a word, after six months we parted with a hundred regrets at separation, but in hope of meeting again, and I returned to wait on the Khán. At the hour of bidding farewell I extemporised an ode [*ghazal*], of which I here give four verses. [Verses] . . . .

The year after my returning to his service, the Khán entered on a holy war in Tibet, sending me on in advance, so that before the Khán joined me, I had achieved a great deal in that country. An army of 5000 men was now in Tibet—a number that the country was unable to support. So I was obliged to retire to Kashmir, with Iskandar Sultán, younger brother of Rashid Sultán. Having passed the winter in Kashmir, I returned to the Khán the following spring. This I have related [elsewhere], so there is no object in stating [details] here. While with the Khán in Tibet, he sent me to destroy the Idol-Temple of Ursáng, while he himself returned to Yárkand. I made a journey of four months; but the Khán died on his way home. The Amirs who were with him at the time, sent express messengers to Rashid Sultán to acquaint him with the event. They also sent the news to my uncle, who came to be present at the Khán's funeral, and to take part in the lamentations [*azá*]. On the 10th of Moharram, 940 [2nd August, 1533], Rashid Sultán arrived, when my uncle, having raised lamentations [by way of condolence], entered the presence of Rashid Sultán and was immediately put to death, together with Ali Sayyid, who was the sworn friend of my uncle. To commemorate the date of the martyrdom of these two men, the chronogram

"*Kutilá fi(á)l-moharram*" [940] was invented [meaning: the two men were killed in the month of Moharram.]

It is the practice of the humane and the usage of the generous (and of these two qualities kings make boast) that when a person at any time renders them some particular service, they reward that person with various presents and favours. My uncle was the son of the daughter of Yunus Khán, and for generations [his family] had been at the head of the affairs of the Moghul Sultáns and Khákáns. I have explained the prerogatives of the office of *Ulusbegi*, in Part II. My uncle was one of the most distinguished men in the service of Rashid Sultán's father, so much so that no one was more valued or prized than he; for he had rendered some most important services to Sultán Said Khán. The first was the conquest of Andiján, which became the keystone of the Khán's dominions.

His second service was on the expedition against Káshghar, where he made such exertions, that had he not been of the party, all hope of taking Káshghar would have been relinquished. The Khán was in consequence grateful for his services, and rewarded him with favours in proportion. If my uncle had never been of service to Rashid Khán—nay, had he even committed offences against him, his faults ought to have been overlooked. But in addition to this, his invasion of Andiján delivered Rashid Khán out of the hands of the Uzbeg. It was, moreover, owing to the efforts of my uncle that Rashid Khán subdued Moghulistán—an event which was the cause of enhancing his dignity, and the commencement of his prosperity. For had the advice of Mirzá Ali Taghái and Khwája Ali Bahádur been followed, Bábá Sultán would have been sent to Moghulistán instead of Rashid Khán. He had always endeavoured to represent Rashid Sultán in a good light to the Khán. Aiman Khwája Sultán had married his daughter, and by her had five sons, who were my uncle's grandsons; yet, notwithstanding this, when it was suggested that Rashid Sultán should be set up in the place of Aiman Khwája Sultán, and that this latter should be driven away, he made no objection, but rather exerted himself to the utmost to further the plan. It is not worth while here to detail his services.

It was most astounding that all this should have been ignored, and that he should, though innocent, have been put to death. It is therefore all the more fitting that his story should not be told more fully; what God willed came to pass. Moreover, the retribution for this act is in His power; and we should read and remember the verse, "Verily we belong to God, and unto God we return." It is the more strange that those very mischief-makers who had caused a rupture in the affairs of Rashid Sultán, were those whom he raised to high dignities. In short, Mirzá Ali

Tagháí was appointed successor to my uncle, and was sent to Káshghar, where, on his arrival, he omitted no act of cruelty, such as putting to death my uncle's children and relatives. . . . .[1]

In a word, the accession of Rashid Khán was characterised by the shedding of innocent blood, and by an absence of humanity. [Verses. . . .] In the sight of the wise and pious, it is not right to shed blood, even for the kingdom of the whole world. After the murder of these faithful men, Rashid Khán established himself upon the throne of the Khánate. When the news of the death of the Khán reached Mansur Khán, he marched against Aksu, and Rashid Khán went out to meet him. Mansur Khán returned without achieving his object, and Rashid Sultán likewise returned to his seat of government. The attempt was afterwards repeated by Mansur Khán; Rashid Khán also marched out again, and returned with success and spoil. The Amirs in the service of the Khán became apprehensive, on account of my uncle having been put to death without cause. On this account they lost all confidence, and Mirzá Ali Tagháí fled towards Karatigin. [Verses. . .]

When Mirzá Ali Tagháí fled from that execrable devil,[2] he was joined by the rest of the Amirs; and having seized some of the Khán's children, they all made off to Khotan and rose in open rebellion. Rashid Khán then went after them; all the people [of Khotan] came out to receive him, except a few of the Amirs who remained in the fort. These [Amirs] were all bound and brought before Rashid Khán, who spared their lives, but ordered them all to be banished. Thus he did not kill these men who had committed a crime and were deserving of death, and whose neglect of duty had been proved, though, on the other hand, he had publicly murdered my uncle, in spite of his near relationship, his countless services, his innocence of all offence, and his strong protestations of loyalty.

[Verses.] No one can comprehend the ways of this lower world,
The Godhead seems always to be upside-down,
All faithful men come to a bad end, and the wicked triumph over them.

After he had finished this affair of the Amirs, he banished all his

[1] Here follows a tradition concerning Muhammad and his son-in-law Abul As, which, having no bearing on our history, is omitted in the translation. The story is taken, says Mirza Haidar, from the work of Shaikh Sáid Kázaruni, entitled *Siyar-unnabi*—"The Virtues of the Prophet." (See Rieu's *Catalogue Brit. Mus.* ii., p. 621 a.)

[2] It appears, at first sight, that the author is here alluding to the Khan, Abdur Rashid; but my impression is that Muhammadi Barlás is meant. In spite of the bitterness of feeling which Mirza Haidar evinces against Abdur Rashid, he is careful not to abuse him; but with the Barlás it is otherwise, and seeing that a little lower down we are told that the Khan was led and ruled by Muhammadi Barlás, who is called by various abusive names, it seems likely that he is the person here referred to as an "execrable devil."

paternal aunts and sisters and mothers; among the rest Zainab Sultán Khánim, who had been the favourite wife of Sultán Said Khán. He next contracted an intimacy and friendship with the Uzbeg-Shaibán, who had been old enemies (as has been already related), and did his best to exterminate the Uzbeg-Kazák, who were old friends; and to the Uzbeg of both sides [tribes] Rashid Khán gave his own sisters in marriage. As the Uzbeg-Shaibán were old enemies, Rashid Khán put an end to this [enmity] by giving his sister [in marriage], which was a base action. In short, having allied himself with the Shaibán, he entirely crushed the Uzbeg-Kazák. Still if we leave aside all consideration of the ancient covenant, the overthrowing of the Uzbeg-Kazák was, in truth, a mighty achievement. Since the time when Sultán Yunus Khán defeated Buruj Oghlán at Kará Tukái (in the year 877) up to this date, there have been many battles between the Uzbeg and the Moghuls, and the Uzbeg have always been victorious; for during all this time the Moghuls had never gained a single success over the Uzbeg. But Rashid Khán did gain a victory over them, and this exploit of his was a really great one. For although his grandfather, Sultán Ahmad Khán, overcame the Uzbeg (as has been related), yet it was only in plundering forays; he never won a victory over them in a real pitched battle. Rashid Sultán defeated their troops in order of battle.

Up to this point I have heard the story of Rashid Sultán from reliable sources in Hindustán and Kashmir, and have committed it to writing. After his victory over the Uzbeg he marched on Andiján and Turfán. But the sources from which I derived the details of this matter not being trustworthy, I have not thought fit to enter them, and have therefore drawn in the reins of my pen from [writing] of these things.

All those unworthy acts with which people have reproached Rashid Khán, were committed either for the sake, or through the efforts, of Muhammadi Barlás. The origin of this man's influence is not evident, for neither had he rendered such service as to merit elevation in rank, nor had he ever displayed such great bravery or good qualities, as to gain for himself distinction.

Rashid Khán was led, mounted, [*murtakib*] by him in all his affairs. If I were to relate all, the reader, who has not himself witnessed these things, would regard them as incredible. The epithet of "Himár" [Ass] which is applied to the tribe of Barlás, was, indeed, fully applicable to that particular Barlás. It would be quite out of place for me to relate how he urged Rashid Khán on to kill, or banish, his uncles and mothers and Amirs, and to change his haram; therefore I have thought it better to avoid this matter altogether.

At the present time the Most High God has delivered Abdur

Rashid Khán from that calamity, and has carried off the ass [*himár*] with the drunkenness [*khimár*] of death. It is to be hoped that, this time, the reins of power may become united in the hands of intelligence, and that trouble may be kept at a distance. Also that the Khán may follow in the approved ways of his honoured father and distinguished ancestors; that his mind may be enlightened, and that he may not, for the sake of an ass, engage in the extirpation of meritorious persons.

May the Most High God, of His gracious favour, cause justice to issue from the throne of the Khánate for many years to come! May the Khán avoid all that is displeasing in the sight of God and His Prophet, and may he repent him of his former deeds! Amen! Oh Lord of the worlds!

Though Abdur Rashid Khán's powers of discrimination were faulty, he was strong of body, sound of limb, and without an equal in the art of conversation. Excepting his father, I have rarely seen an archer like him. He was brave even to rashness. In elegant conversation he was as a peerless pearl; and he had also written several letters to a great personage. He played several instruments to perfection, and had great aptitude for all arts and crafts. Once, for example, he cut a tree out of paper, and painted all the branches, the leaves, and the trunk in their proper colours; he did it so skilfully that even the masters of that craft were astounded. Since the time of my absence has been protracted, I cannot answer for all his acquirements. But in those arts which I was myself cognisant of, I know him to have excelled. Not being a musician, I cannot praise his performance on instruments with justice,[1] nor can I say anything of what he acquired during my absence. He was, besides, a good Musulmán and inclined to justice and equity. But, by allowing himself to be influenced by the violent Muhammadi, he performed many unjust acts. Please God that he may now persist in the path of justice!

CHAPTER LXX.

END OF PART I. OF THE TÁRIKH-I-RASHIDI.

What right have I, with my poor learning and my want of capacity, to attempt to make my styleless reed flow upon the white [sheet] of literature?

[1] This must have been written about the time when, according to Abul Fazl (the historian of Akbar), Mirza Haidar was giving so much attention to music that he neglected the affairs of the Kashmir State, of which he was regent. (See Erskine, *Hist.*, ii. p. 368, and Sec. i. of the Introduction to this volume.)

My justification lies in the fact that I have, during my life, collected many authentic facts concerning those Moghul Khákáns who were Musulmáns, and have also myself played a part in their history. At the present time there is no one but myself who knows these traditions. Thus, if I did not make the attempt, it is probable that the memory of the Moghuls and their Khákáns would be altogether lost.

The history of the Moghuls and their Kháns can be of little interest to any but the Moghuls themselves, for they have now become the most remote and insignificant of tribes, whereas formerly they were, through the power and resolution of Chingiz Khán, the lords of the world. Chingiz Khán had four sons to whom he left the world, dividing the cultivated countries and deserts into four parts, and giving one quarter of the earth to each of these sons. Every mention in histories of the *Ulus Arbaa*, or "the four hordes," refers to these four divisions. The learned Mirzá Ulugh Beg has written a history which he has called *Ulus Arbaa*. One of the "four hordes" is that of the Moghul, who are divided into two branches, the Moghul and the Chaghatái. But these two branches, on account of their mutual enmity, used to call each other by a special name, by way of depreciation. Thus the Chaghatái called the Moghul *Jatah*, while the Moghul called the Chaghatái *Karáwánás*.[1] At the present date there are no Chaghatái left excepting the kings, who are the sons of Báber Pádisháh; and the place of the Chaghatái is now occupied by some [other] civilised people. But of the Moghuls there are still about 30,000 in the neighbourhood of Turfán and Káshghar. Moghulistán has been seized by the Uzbeg and the Kirghiz. Although the Kirghiz belong to the tribe of Moghul[2] they have, on account of their repeated rebellions against the Khákáns, become separated from them. All the Moghuls have become Musulmáns, but the Kirghiz are still infidels, and hence their hostility to the Moghuls. The Moghuls have become a most isolated and paltry people. No one but a Moghul could be interested in this history; but though fully recognising my lack of literary capacity, I have not shrunk from doing the best in my power.

[1] Some remarks on these interesting points will be found in the Introduction, Sec. iv.

[2] This is a somewhat embarrassing statement. It would seem, at first sight, that the author means to class the Kirghiz and Moghuls as one people, or race; but the word *Kaum* in the text, meaning "tribe" or "nation," is not, I think, used in a racial sense. The sentence runs, *Agarchi Kirghiz ham Kaumi az Moghul ast* . . . , and my impression is that the author means the connection between the two people to be regarded as a political, rather than a racial one: that is, that the Kirghiz were understood to belong to the Moghul kingdom, or were one of the tribes subject to the Moghul Khans, while the Uzbegs had no connection with the Moghuls. The word *Kaum* is often used in a very broad sense in Persian. It is unfortunate that neither of the Turki MSS. used for this translation contains this part of the history.

It is the practice of authors to excuse themselves, and beg for pardon if they have made any mistakes or blunders in their work. But I will not make such apology as those who say:—"If there be any mistakes or blunders"—for I know that my book is full of mistakes from beginning to end. My object is not to extol my own merit, but simply to write a memoir, that the history of the Moghuls may not be entirely forgotten; and that if, by chance, any of the Moghul Khákáns should wish to know his genealogy, he shall be able to find it in this book.

Of those Moghuls who were not Musulmáns, I have not mentioned more than the names; for an infidel, though he attain to the splendour of Jamshid and Zohhák, is not worthy of having his life commemorated. This *Tárikh-i-Rashidi* was completed at the end of the month Zulhijja of the year 953,[1] in the town of Kashmir (may God defend her from ruin and destruction) five years after I, Haidar Mirzá son of Muhammad Kurkán, had ascended the throne.

[1] February, 1547.

END OF PART I.

TARIKH-I-RASHIDI.

PART II.

PROLOGUE.

I WOULD lay before the wise and critical that I, the least of God's servants, Muhammad Haidar, known among my intimates as Mirzá Haidar, son of Muhammad Husain Kurkán, have been continually possessed of the thought that the rank and dignity which historians attain to, is not so high that one should have a craving for it. Still, there can be little doubt that this poor history (which has been driven by the whirlwind of pride and the waves of ignorance and intoxication, from the sea of incapacity upon the shores of small literary attainment) may be regarded as of some value by the divers in the ocean of excellence, who have concealed in the shells of perfection, the pearls of poetry and the precious stones of prose. According to the saying: "Necessity makes lawful that which is forbidden," and because certain important events in the annals of the Moghul Khákáns have been entirely forgotten, I was induced, as far as time should permit, to narrate some of the most trustworthy facts in their history.

When the Moghul power was high, many eminent men flourished, and some wrote their people's history. Now, for more than a hundred years nothing of the sort has been done—no trace of these men remains, nor of their writings. Nor does any sign remain of their prosperity and civilisation, except here and there a ruined tower or fortification; and in some towns the relics of a monastery, a college, a mosque, a portico, or a minaret, still exist, because their foundations being of stone, or for some other reason, God willed that they should endure. No vestige of these men survives and no one knows anything concerning them. For during this long lapse of time, all have become strangers to the old customs and ways of learning. Since the conversion of the Moghuls to Islám, more especially, no history of them has been written. But the learned men of Mávará-un-Nahr and Khorásán and Irák, who have written the annals for their own kings, have made mention of the Moghuls, just where it has suited the context, while they have paid no attention to them when not connected with their own country. Among these histories may be mentioned the *Mujma ut Tavárikh*[1] of Khwája Rashid-ud-Din; the *Tárikh-i-Guzida*[2] of Khwája Hamid Ulláh Mustaufi; the *Zafar-Náma*[3] of Mauláná Sharaf-ud-Din Ali Yazdi; the *Tárikh-i-Manzum*[4] of Mauláná Abdur Razzák; and the *Ulus Arbaa*[5] of Mirzá Ulugh Beg. Among these I have sought carefully for any mention of the Moghul Khákáns, but have found nothing very connected [*ba tartib*]. In my early years, I was much drawn to the study of the history of my forefathers, and in those days there were still alive some of the Moghul Amirs and nobles (some over one hundred years of age, some under). But it never occurred to my father or my uncles to commit to writing what they had heard concerning the Khákáns, from their parents, and other trustworthy sources. And now they have all been dead for some time. [On this account] I intend, God willing, to write an account of the Moghuls after their conversion to Islám, basing my facts upon histories and reliable traditions, in addition to what I have myself witnessed in my own times. But not finding that I had capacity or talent sufficient to justify my setting out on this bold venture, I have resolved to begin by making a trial on those events of which I have been an eye-witness, and then, should I by the grace of God succeed, I will proceed with my original plan of writing the history of the Moghul Khákáns.

[1] The correct title of this work is *Jámi 'uttavárikh.* It is a general history of the world from the earliest times to A.H. 700, and gives a special account of the Moghuls. (See Dr. Rieu's *Catalogue*, i., p. 74.)

[2] A general history from the earliest times to A.H. 730, by Hamid Ullah Mustaufi, Kazvini. (Rieu, i., p. 80.)

[3] A history of Timur.

[4] The proper title is *Matla'i Sa'adain va Majmu-i-Bahrain*, by 'Abdur Razzák bin Ishák us Samarkandi—("Manzum" here, may mean "well arranged.") (Rieu, i., p. 181 b.)

[5] A history of Chingiz Khan, his ancestors and descendants, down to the time of Timur. (Rieu, i., p. 164.)

CHAPTER I.

BEGINNING OF PART II. OF THE TÁRIKH-I-RASHIDI, WHICH CONTAINS, IN DIFFERENT PARTS, WHAT TOOK PLACE AMONG THE MOGHUL ULUS AND THE UZBEG AND THE CHAGHATÁI.

AT the time of my birth, which was in 905, and for which the chronogram *Nur Chashm Sháh* has been found, the power of the Moghul Khákáns was, compared with former times, on the increase; but at this period, the towns of Moghulistán (which is another name for Kará Khitái)[1] fell into ruin, till in the beginning of the

[1] This mention of Kara-Khitai is curious, and the geographical indication accords with what we know, from other sources, to have been the centre of the Kara-Khitai dominion about the beginning of the thirteenth century, when the power of that dynasty was at its best. What Mirza Haidar means to explain, in this passage, probably is that Moghulistan stands on the ground which the Kara-Khitai country occupied before the time of Chingiz, when all previous sub-divisions were swept away. In other words, he seems to have found it more convenient to go back to ancient times for a single name to denote the region, than to explain its whereabouts geographically, or to describe its limits according to the ever-shifting divisions of the period subsequent to Chingiz's conquests. But there is no reason to suppose him to mean that Moghulistan was, at his time, known as *Kara-Khitai*, or that it was a land inhabited by a race of that name. The Kara-Khitai must have disappeared, as a nation, some two centuries before Mirza Haidar's day. Indeed, they could hardly at any time have been regarded as a nation in the western parts of Central Asia, but only as a ruling dynasty, supported by a fighting force, composed of their own and other foreign races, sufficient to subdue certain weaker nations, and to rule them for a time, until some stronger power should arise and displace them. In this way they resembled most other Asiatic dynasties that have appeared in history, and their period of power was perhaps even shorter than most others, for it lasted for less than a century.

In race the Kara-Khitai (or Kara-Kitan) appear to have been Manchu, though perhaps a good deal mixed with Mongol tribes, for their home was in southern Manchuria—the Liao-tung of modern times—and bordered on south-eastern Mongolia. To the Chinese they were known as Kitan or Liao. In the tenth century, they conquered the small section of northern China which was then known to western nations as *Khitai* or Cathay, where they set up the dynasty called by the Chinese "the Liao." As a Chinese dynasty, their kings ruled for about two centuries, and it was only just before their overthrow, in the early part of the twelfth century, that they first appear in Central Asia as a conquering horde. At this time a certain Liao prince, one Yelui Taishi, escaped westward from "Cathay," gathered an army (composed of what races is not clear), and overran, firstly Eastern and Western Turkistan, and subsequently Khwarizm. In these regions, and at about this period, he and his people seem to have acquired the name of *Kara-Khitai*, or "Black Cathayans," while the Chinese spoke of them as *Si Liao* or *Western Liao*. In a short time, the whole country between Hami (or Kumul) in the east, and the Aral in the west, became subject to them, while their capital seems, as far as can be ascertained, to have been situated near the banks of the river Chu—in the heart of the *Moghulistan* of our author's time. The identity, as well as the position, of the Kara-Khitai capital has been made a subject of much discussion, for it is mentioned by several

year 889, when Yunus Khán, [who affected] towns and cultivation, came into power. Most of the Moghuls had never possessed or even lived in a village—nay, had never even seen cultivation. They were as wild as the beasts of the mountains. The explanation of this is that the country of Shásh, together with its dependencies, was under the rule of the Moghuls, as were also all the deserts of Moghulistán. It would be tedious to relate this here, but, God willing, it will be mentioned in the First Part of this history.

My father was Muhammad Husain Kurkán, son of Muhammad Haidar Kurkán, son of the Amir, Lord of the Sword and the Throne, Sayyid Ali Kurkán, son of Amir Sayyid Ahmad, son of Amir Khudáidád, son of Amir Buláji. It was this Amir Buláji that introduced Islám, and changed the darkness of unbelief into the light of faith.

After my father entered the service of Sultán Mahmud Khán, son of Sultán Yunus Khán, sun of Vais Khán, son of Shir Ali Oghlán, son of Muhammad Khán, son of Khizir Khwája Khán, son of Tughluk Timur Khán (who also lightened the dark night of heathendom with the rising sun of the dawn of Islám), he was treated by the Khán with the utmost favour and honour (as is mentioned at greater length in the First Part of this history [*Tárikh-i-Asl*]) and had the title of Kurkán conferred upon him, as well as the honour of marriage with Khub Nigár Khánim. This

---

different names in the records of different nations. Thus the Chinese knew it by the name of *Hu-sze-wa-erh-du*, *Gu-sze-o-lu-du*, etc., the Turki writers by that of *Balasakun*, while the Mongols (as is stated in the *Tarikh-i-Jahán-Kushai*) converted Balasakun into *Ghar-bálik*. No doubt the Chinese forms "wa-erh-du," "o-lu-du," etc., stand for the Turki word "Urdu"—city or capital; while "bálik" in Mongol means the same thing. Dr. Bretschneider is therefore probably right in identifying the "Gu" (it should be Ghar) of the Chinese and Mongols with the Balasakun, which, according to all probability, stood in the valley of the Upper Chu, and in deeming it the site of the Kara-Khitai capital. It was, at any rate, in and about the region of the Chu valley, that they seem to have flourished most, during their short period of power; and it was in this region, after being partially subjected by the Naiman, that Chingiz Khan finally broke them up.

As regards the name of *Kara-Khitai*, it appears to me that these people were regarded by the Turki-speaking nations of the west as northern Chinese, or Cathayans, though differing from them to some extent. The word "Kara," though meaning "black," is constantly used in Central Asia to denote a difference, a variety, and especially a lower variety. It is difficult to find an English equivalent; but the Urdu word "Kacha" (raw), as used in India, would perhaps more nearly translate "Kara" than any English term. In this way "Kara" is sometimes applied, at the present day, in Mongolia and Turkistan, to Chinese from certain parts of China, though they may be Chinese of the lightest complexion; also to some tribes of Kirghiz who differ, in colour, in no way from other Kirghiz, and so on. In naming wild animals too, the word is made use of in this manner—to denote a variety. Thus the Kara-Khitai were, to the western foreigner, not the real, the true-bred (the "pakká") Khatai, but a variety, or offshoot, of them, and therefore denominated by an adjective.

(See Bretschneider, i., pp. 208, *seqq.*; Howorth, ii., pp. 16–20.)

alliance was contracted in Shásh in the year 899. After this he received the country of Ushtur Ushna (which is known now as Urátippa), together with as much of the surrounding country as he could bring within his power. He then had leave to depart, and spent nine years in the administration of the government of that district. During this time many important events occurred. I was born after my father had governed for six years.[1]

I think it proper here to mention who were the princes who at this time ruled in the surrounding countries.

In the country of Farghána, whose capital is Andiján, after the death of Mirzá Omar Shaikh Kurkán, son of Sultán Abu Said Kurkán, serious quarrels and disputes arose between his two sons, Zahir-ud-Din Muhammad Bábar Pádisháh Gházi and Mirzá Jahángir,[2] in spite of their youth; and these quarrels were chiefly owing to the enmity of their respective Amirs. There ensued many victories and defeats, some of which shall be mentioned in this Epitome.

In the country of Samarkand and Bokhárá, endless wars and contests arose between the three princes, Báisanghar Mirzá and Sultán Ali Mirzá (the sons of Mahmud Kurkán, son of Sultán Abu Said Kurkán) and Sháhi Beg Khán, son of Sháh Badágh Sultán, son of Abulkhair Khán, than whom, in his lifetime, there was no more exalted chief on the throne of the Juji.[3] Of these wars and disputes I will speak hereafter.

In Khorásán, Sultán Husain Mirzá[4] was at the height of his power and magnificence. From time to time the dust of dissension rose up between the father and his sons, but this the Mirzá, with his wisdom and sagacity, soon caused to subside.

In Irák, after the death of Sultán Yakub, son of Uzun Hasan,[5] the Sultáns (his sons) by reason of their youth, were unable to direct the affairs of the State, and Sháh Ismáil (who had made his violence felt in the world) taking advantage of the situation, invaded the country, entirely exterminated the rest of those Sultáns, and upset all the affairs of the state and of religion.

In the Dasht-i-Kipchák and the *Ulus* of Juji Khán, Baranduk Khán[6] was in power, and all the Juji Sultáns were subservient to him. They have sought to rival the rain-drops in their numbers.

[1] That is in 905 H. = 1499–1500 A.D.

[2] See, for these names, the Genealogical Table of the house of Timur attached to this volume.

[3] Compare the genealogical table of Uzbeg Khans in Stokvis, i., p. 158.

[4] Otherwise known as Abul Gházi Hussain, or Sultan Hussain Baikará. He was great-grandson of Timur's son, Umar Shaikh. (S. L. Poole, p. 268; or Stokvis, i., p. 156.)

[5] Of the line of Ak-Koinlu, or White Sheep Turkomans. (See S. L. Poole, pp. 254–5; or Stokvis, i., p. 119.)

[6] Son of Karai Khan, son of Barák, etc., of the White Horde. (Comp. Howorth, ii., p. 685; and Stokvis, i., pp. 158 and 163.)

What took place between them and the Moghuls will be hereinafter related.

In Shásh, which is better known as Táshkand, Sultán Mahmud Khán held sway.

I must now turn to the story of Yunus Khán, without which the thread of my history would not be connected.

CHAPTER II.

REIGN OF YUNUS KHÁN; ACCOUNT OF HIS LIFE AND LIST OF HIS OFFSPRING.

Yunus Khán was the greatest of all the Chaghatái Kháns, and before him there was, in many respects, no one like him in his family. None of the Chaghatái Kháns who preceded him had passed the age of forty; nay, most of them never reached that age. But this prosperous Khán attained to the age of seventy-four. Towards the end of his life, growing repentant and devout, he became a disciple of that Refuge of the Pious, Nasiruddin Khwája Ubaidullah (in this history, wherever the term "His Holiness" is used, it refers to the Khwája), and him the Khán followed with piety. He was also acquainted with many other Shaikhs, and used to associate with them. His nature was adorned with many high qualities and virtues; he possessed also many acquirements, among which may be mentioned the reading of the Korán. He was of an even temper, his conversation was charming, and he had a quick perception. He excelled in penmanship, painting, and other accomplishments conformable with a healthy nature, and was well-trained in singing and instrumental music. He studied under Sharaf-ud-Din Ali Yazdi, with whom he spent twelve years, and travelled much in foreign countries. Of all these acquirements and travels, a more full account will (God willing) be given in the First Part of this history. He was graced with good qualities and perfect manners, was unequalled in bravery and heroism, and excelled especially in archery. In a word, no one of all his family can be compared to him. The Khán had seven children.

1. Mihr Nigár Khánim, whom he gave to Sultán Ahmad Mirzá. She died childless.

2. Kutluk Nigár Khánim, whom he gave to Omar Shaikh Mirzá. She had two children: Khánzáda Begum, who still honours the throne of chastity, and Bábar Pádisháh, who has illumined the

world with the radiance of his power and his exploits, as I have recounted in the First Part, and will relate again in this Epitome whenever it suits the context.

3. Khub Nigár Khánim, who was given to my father, as has been mentioned above.

4. Sultán Mahmud Khán, a short notice of whose history will be given.

5. Sultán Ahmad Khán, known as Álácha Khán, of whom, also, I shall speak briefly.

6. Sultán Nigár Khánim, who was given to Mirzá Sultán Mahmud, son of Sultán Abu Said. She had one son, who is known as Mirzá Khán; and his son Sulaimán is, at the present time, king of Badakhshán.

7. Daulat Sultán Khánim, who fell into the hands of Timur Sultán, son of Sháhi Beg Khán, at the sacking of Táshkand. She too will be mentioned farther on.

CHAPTER III.

END OF THE REIGN OF YUNUS KHÁN. LIST OF HIS SONS. THE REIGN OF SULTÁN MAHMUD KHÁN AND THE REASON OF HIS RUIN.

At the beginning of the reign of Yunus Khán, all the Moghuls dwelt, according to their old custom, in Moghulistán; they avoided all towns and cultivated countries [and regarded them] with great repugnance. They were Musulmáns in nothing but the name; in fact, not even in name, for they were carried off into the countries round about, and sold as slaves like other infidels. After the Khán had had the happiness to kiss the feet of his Holiness, the latter wrote letters to all the surrounding Musulmán rulers, saying: "We have seen Sultán Yunus Khán, and it is not lawful to molest a tribe whose chief is so good a Musulmán."

From that date, no more Moghuls who had been carried off, were ever bought or sold as slaves, in a Muhammadan country. The Moghuls had always been this kind of [nomadic] people. The Khán felt that until they settled down in cultivated countries and towns, they could never become true Musulmáns. He therefore exerted himself to the utmost to bring their settlement about. When the Khán was leading away the Moghuls to Táshkand, a number of them who were loth to go, having seized the Khán's younger son, Sultán Ahmad Khán, abandoned the party and stayed behind in Moghulistán. The Khán meanwhile arrived in

Táshkand with his elder son, Sultán Mahmud Khán, and the rest of the Moghuls. It would be tedious to relate their proceedings in this Epitome, but they will (God willing) be given in the First Part. When Yunus Khán went to the palace of eternity, he left the kingdom to Sultán Mahmud Khán, and the Moghuls, according to their custom, placed him on his father's throne. It is a common occurrence that those who inherit what their father has left them, do not appreciate its worth; thus the new Khán, undervaluing the great Amirs who had served his father, expelled them and set up, in their stead, weak-minded and base men: while his old friends being defeated, old enemies, who styled themselves new friends, now gained the supremacy. But in this new order of things, the Khán found it difficult to withstand these [new advisers]; nay, was incapable of keeping together his kingdom. When Alácha Khán heard of this, although he was occupied with rebellions and seditions on the confines of Moghulistán (which was under his rule), he did his best to punish those [who opposed him], and then, setting up his eldest son, Mansur Khán, in his own place, hastened to the court of his brother. This was in the year 907 [1501–2].

A year and a half previous to this meeting of the two Kháns, my mother journeyed from this transitory abode to the dwellings of eternity. She had six sons: two of them had died at the breast, four survived her, and of each of these I will speak hereafter.

One of the most curious facts in my own history is the following. While I was yet at my mother's breast, I was subject to such severe hæmorrhoids that the doctors gave up all hope of my recovery. My mother, before bearing me, had been four times disappointed in child-birth [*ájiza*]. She had prayed very earnestly to God to grant her a son, and after much prayer and supplication on her part, I came into existence; hence the unbounded love which my mother had for me. When my malady became alarming, she turned in every direction in search of help, till at length she went to Mauláná Muhammad Kázi, who was one of the most distinguished of the companions of his Holiness: so much so that even at this time his family have many disciples. When he had looked on me with his Christ-like glance,[1] he became very thoughtful, and after he had gone out said: "If I had known that the Mirzá's son was in such a grave condition, I should not have come." He ordered no remedy, except frugality, and then went on his way.

One morning he sent one of his servants to my parents, to tell them that the Most High God had sent to their child the wine of recovery and the meat of life, from His heavenly abode. When

[1] Christ is always connected with healing in the Muhammadan mind.—R.

my parents heard this good news, they set out that same morning to the place of worship of this holy man, and laid their prayers before him. From that same day, marked signs of improvement showed themselves in me; and up to the present time I have never had a return of the hæmorrhoids. I would point out that in this matter two miracles were performed—one being my recovery without the aid of medicine, the other the fact that the malady never returned. And this is the more wonderful miracle of the two, for hæmorrhoids generally last all one's life. From that date to the end of his life, the Mauláná helped and instructed me, both publicly and privately.

The story of each [of the children] will be told in the proper place.

After these events my mother departed this life.

Shortly afterwards Sháhi Beg Khán, with the inopportune aid of Sultán Mahmud Khán, conquered Samarkand and Bokhárá, and defeated the Timuri Sultáns: in particular Bábar Pádisháh, who was Sultán Mahmud's nephew, and almost like a son to him. After [these successes] having changed his assurances of obedience and friendship, into boasts of pride and insubordination, he began to sound the drum of revolt.

In the meanwhile Sultán Ahmad Tambal, who had been in the service of Omar Shaikh Mirzá, although he belonged to the race of the Moghul Amirs, revolted in Andiján, on account of the improvidence of the Khán, and having got possession of that place, began to shoot the arrows of insurrection at the target of sovereignty. The two Kháns consequently went to crush him—Sultán Mahmud Khán, leaving his son Sultán Muhammad Sultán in Táshkand with a strong army, wherewith to oppose his perfidious enemies. My father, too, had been left in Urátippa to oppose Sháhi Beg Khán. And they imagined that the latter could not pass between these two armies. But in reality he looked upon it as an opportunity to be seized, thinking that he would never again find the two Kháns with so small a force. Therefore he hastened from Samarkand to Fargháná, passing by Urátippa on his road. [My father] thinking he had come to lay siege to the town, began to busy himself with its defence. At the hour of afternoon prayer, [Sháhi Beg] came and encamped close to the town. After the sun had deprived the world of its light, and had thrown the shadows of night upon the eyes of all creation, he broke up his camp and marched away with all possible speed, so that before the men in the fort had begun to inquire in which direction he had gone, he was many *farsákhs* away. When it was discovered that he had marched towards Fargháná, several messengers in succession were despatched, to give notice to the Kháns of his approach. The messengers and the enemy arrived at the same moment. Neither the army of Táshkand nor that of

Urátippa, had time to come to the aid of the Kháns. The two Kháns had with them 15,000 men, because in the beginning of the year they had [collected a large force] to attack Tambal, whom they had severely handled, and whose power they had entirely subdued. For this reason, they felt sure that he would now resolve on flight as a last resource. They had taken Bábar Pádisháh with them, in order that after things were settled, they might set him up on his father's throne and then return home.

The Kháns had not yet reached Andiján. Akhsi, which is one of the strongest forts in that country, was occupied by Shaikh Báyazid, brother of Tambal; he was treating about submission, and for that reason they had tarried near the fort. At this juncture, Sháhi Beg Khán came up with 30,000 men, and all his Sultáns, such as Kuchum Sultán, Suyunjuk Sultán, Jáni Beg Sultán and others. They had hardly time to draw up in line, when, after a short conflict, the Kháns were put to rout by the overpowering numbers of the enemy. Their horses being rendered useless with fatigue, the two Kháns were taken prisoners. Bábar Pádisháh fled to the hills on the south of Fargháua. Sháhi Beg Khán behaved with magnanimity, and having taken possession of Táshkand, dismissed the Kháns with every mark of favour, saying: "With your help and assistance I have won my power: I took you captive, but do not kill you: I let you go."

In this place, I call to mind the story of the tax-gatherer [*amaldár*]. A certain governor had imposed a fine upon a tax-gatherer, and went so far as to torture him [in order to make him pay it]. But a generous Khwája took pity on him, and bought him out of the hands of his creditors [by paying] the price of the fine, and taking him home with him, showed him every kindness and attention. One day the tax-collector was sitting with his son, and they were talking confidentially, while the Khwája was listening on the other side of the wall. The son said to his father: "How can we ever worthily repay the Khwája for his kindness?" The tax-collector answered: "As soon as I am again in office, the matter will be simple." The son then asked: "How will it be easy to repay his generosity?" His father replied: "When they have again entrusted me with an office, I will press the Khwája very hard, and will give him over to the creditors, who will fine him heavily, and when it has come to a matter of life and death for him, I will take all his money, and with a part of it will buy him off again."

When the news of the capture of the Kháns reached Táshkand, Sultán Muhammad Sultán carried off into Moghulistán, all that he was able of his people and family, and of the Moghul *Ulus*, causing my father and my uncle to follow him with all the money they could collect.

When the Kháns were captured, Sháhi Beg Khán said: "I have always wished to arrange a marriage, but it has never been granted me; to make up for this [disappointment] I must now form three marriage alliances." The youngest sister of the Khán, Daulat Sultán Khánim, who has been mentioned above in the list of the children of Yunus Khán, was married to [Sháhi Beg's] son Timur Sultán.[1] He took for himself Aisha Sultán Khánim, better known as Moghul Khánim, and gave to Jáni Beg Khán, Kutuk Khánim; both of these princesses were, in their chastity, bright as the sun and pure as the moon. Some of their children are living now, and are ruling in Mávará-un-Nahr.

On the return of the Kháns to their old residence, in Moghulistán, the younger fell ill, and at the end of the year 909, wandered from the garden of earthly dominion to the fields of Paradise.

From Khwája Tájuddin Muhammad, who inherited from his ancestors the office of Shaikh-ul-Islám of that country (and who was, in truth, a most admirable, austere man, and endowed with many good qualities) I have heard the following: "When the Khán was extremely ill, I said to him, 'It is commonly reported that Sháhi Beg Khán has caused poison to be put in your food; if your Highness is also of this opinion, I will bring some of that powerful antidote, which comes from Khitái, and administer it.' The Khán replied, 'Yes, indeed, Sháhi Beg Khán has poisoned me, and the poison is this: having risen from the most degraded station to the highest elevation, he has taken us two brothers prisoners and then set us at liberty. This disgrace is the cause of my succumbing to illness. If yours is an antidote against this kind of poison, it may prove efficient.'"

Sultán Ahmad Khán had eighteen sons.

(1.) The eldest, Mansur Khán, from 909 to the present date of 948,[2] has ruled over his father's dominions with absolute power. An account of him will be given in this Epitome.

(2.) Iskandar Sultán, who died a natural death, soon after his father's demise.

(3.) Sultán Said Khán, whose history will be related. Wherever "*the Khán*" is spoken of in an absolute way, in this Epitome, it is this Khán that is meant.

(4.) Bábáják Sultán, who is still in the service of Mansur Khán.

(5.) Sháh Shaikh Muhammad Sultán, who, together with his haram and some of his children, was killed by the fall of his palace during an earthquake.

[1] In Stokvis' table of the line of Juji, the son of Shahi Beg is shown as 'Yár Muhammad.' I do not know the authority for this name. (*Manuel d'Hist.*, p. 158.)

[2] A.H. 948 (1541 A.D.) will then be the date of compiling Part ii. of the *Táríkh-i-Rashidi*—or the Epitome.

(6.) Sultán Khalil Sultán, of whom I shall have occasion to speak in connection with Sultán Said Khán.

(7.) Aiman Khwája Sultán, who will also be mentioned in the same connection.

(8.) Chin Timur Sultán, who for some time was in the service of Mansur Khán, whom he afterwards abandoned, and entered the service of "the Khán." Mansur Khán had him brought back, but he again fled; this time going to the court of Bábar Pádisháh in Hindustán. Here he rendered good service, and was in return treated with the utmost honour and respect by the Emperor. He died of a violent dysentery at Agra, where he was buried.

(9.) Yusun Timur Sultán, who like his brother, being tired of always going backwards and forwards between the two Kháns, fled to the Kazák and thence to Turán; thence again to the court of Ubaid Ullah Khán in Bokhárá. From there he went to the court of Bábar Pádisháh; him also the Emperor treated most kindly, and he is now in Hindustán.

(10.) Tukhta Bughá Sultán, who also went to Hindustán, where he died a natural death.

The other sons died natural deaths, at different times.

Sultán Ahmad Khán had four daughters.

(1.) Lál Shád Khánim, whose mother was a slave whom the Khán had married [*umm-valad*]. Although she was outside the circle of distinction, she was finally married to Muhammad Amir Mirzá, son of Amir Jabar Birdi, who was a Dughlát, and to their family alone belonged the office of *Ulusbegi* in the time of Álácha Khán.

(2.) Máhim Khánim, who was given to Builásh Khán, son of Uyuk Sultán.

(3.) The third was married to me, as will be related below.

(4.) Khadija Sultán Khánim. After the death of Sultán Ahmad Khán, Mirzá Abá Bakr, whose story will be told in connection with the Khán, took possession of Aksu, the capital of Álácha Khán's dominions. In those days Khadija Sultán Khánim fell into the hands of Mirzá Abá Bakr. He, however, treated her kindly and gave her to his son Jahángir Mirzá. When the latter was slain, she was given to Sháh Muhammad Sultán, son of Sultán Muhammad Sultán, son of Sultán Mahmud Khán, as will be related.

CHAPTER IV.

EPITOMISED ACCOUNT OF THE MARTYRDOM OF SULTÁN MAHMUD KHÁN AND HIS CHILDREN.

On the death of Sultán Ahmad Khán, Sultán Mahmud Khán resigned to his brother's children all the country and people that had belonged to their father, from the frontier of Khitái to the confines of Káshghar, viz.: Turfán, Chálish, Kucháh [Kuchar], Aksu and Uch [Ush-Turfán], while he himself withdrew, with those few of his own people who yet remained, to the deserts of Moghulistán. There he spent five years, during which time nothing of importance happened to him. At length those same base men who had caused the night shadows of ruin to overcloud the dawn of the Khán's reign, filled his mind with evil suggestions, saying: "Sháhi Beg Khán will treat you kindly, but even if he does not, he will at least allow us to return to this corner of corners." My uncle used to relate that one day after the death of Álácha Khán, he was at the court of Sultán Mahmud Khán in Aksu, where the Khán, being friendly and talkative, asked him: "Is the position of scullion[1] in Táshkand better than that of king in Aksu?" My uncle replied: "Verily it is, if the scullion is allowed to perform his office." At these words the Khán was very wroth.

In short, these base men succeeded in bringing the Khán to Farghána. When news of this reached Sháhi Beg Khán, he was in Uláng-zádagán. He at once despatched a party of men to find him. These men were coming in exactly the opposite direction to the Khán, whom they met and slew, together with his five young sons, at Khojand. To commemorate the date of their martyrdom the chronogram "*Lab-i-daryá-i-Khojand*" = 914, was devised. (This matter I will also speak of elsewhere.)

Sultán Mahmud Khán had six sons, five of whom suffered death with their father. His eldest son was Sultán Muhammad Sultán. When the Khán was setting out from Moghulistán, in the hope of being well treated by Sháhi Beg Khán, Sultán Muhammad Sultán had done his utmost to dissuade his father from going, but his words being of no avail, he separated from his father and stayed behind in Moghulistán. From circumstances which, God willing, will be related in the First Part [*Tárikh-i-Asl*], he was not able to remain in Moghulistán, but went in dire distress to Baranduk

[1] The word in the original is *Dastmál-shui*, meaning, literally, "towel-washer."

Khán and Kásim Khán [1] in the Dasht-i-Kipchák. His followers, hoping that Sháhi Beg Khán had received Sultán Mahmud Khán well, led him by a wrong road and brought him to Táshkand, where the Uzbeg sent him to join his father. He left one son, whose name was Sháh Muhammad Sultán. His history will be given in my notice of the Khán.

CHAPTER V.

THE REST OF THE HISTORY OF MY FATHER, MIRZÁ MUHAMMAD HUSAIN KURKÁN.

When the Kháns fell into the hands of Sháhi Beg Khán at Aksu, my father was at Urátippa. When Sháhi Beg Khán passed between [the two armies] it was not possible for my father to form a junction with the Kháns, and he found it necessary to go to Karátigin. At that time Khusrau Sháh, one of the Amirs of Mirzá Sultán Mahmud, son of Sultán Abu Said, was in possession of Hisár, Kunduz and Badakhshán. After the death of Mirzá Sultán Mahmud, he had blinded his son Sultán Masud Mirzá, and when Báisanghar Mirzá, son of Sultán Mahmud Mirzá, fled from Samarkand, Khusrau Sháh sent messengers to him to express his repentance, saying: "What I did, was from fear for my life, for Sultán Masud Mirzá had the intention of killing me; but now, in compensation for that act, I will serve you so faithfully that, however much my infamous act may have brought down upon me the execrations and curses of mankind, my conduct for the future will procure for me their favour and applause." In this manner did he make abundant promises and protest so much, that he deceived Báisanghar Mirzá also, and sent that worthy prince into the next world, as if he were an arrow from a bow.

Thus he brought the whole of the dominion of Sultán Mahmud Mirzá under his own power. But these successes filled his mind with pride and vainglory. When he was thus at the height of his power, my father arrived in Karátigin, and Khusrau Sháh desired an interview with him. My father accordingly went to Hisár; and Khusrau Sháh, having received him in the Bágh-i-chinár, with the utmost distinction and friendliness, said to him: "I look upon your gracious visit as a blessing from God; for it is the season of Sháhi Beg Khán's supremacy. My fear is that though this year his mind is set upon the conquest of other territories, he

[1] The Turki MS. only has Kásim Khan's name here; but it is probably correct. (See Erskine, *Hist.*, i., p. 192.)

may next year turn towards this quarter. I have never been to war with the Uzbeg, and do not know their mode of warfare. For every tribe has its own special methods, whether in war or in negotiation. The arrangement of these matters differs with each people according to time and place, and until their methods are known, it is difficult to contend with them. Now, as you have many times had to do with the Uzbeg, both in peace and in war, and have experienced, when at war with them, both victory and defeat, make known to me all that you have learned, that I may be guided by what you tell me. As my reliance is on you, and my hope, I beg you to accept, in confirmation of my confidence, Sultánim Begum, daughter of Sultán Ahmad Mirzá, and one of the princesses, [of my family] that she may be a bond of union between us."

Such idle words and many more did he utter, and set on foot grand preparations for the marriage.

The destruction [*viráni*] of Táshkand and Urátippa was in the season of Cancer,[1] and this affair took place in the end of the season of the Balance.[2]

Meanwhile, news arrived of the invasion of Sháhi Beg Khán, and all the adherents of Khusrau Sháh fled in different directions. Those who possessed castles, fortified themselves in them, and those who had none, fled to the hills and the remote valleys and glens. No one troubled himself about his neighbour. As all Khusrau Sháh's people were scattered in confusion, my father also took refuge in Karátigin, which is a country of mountain fastnesses. Among these mountains they encountered a very severe winter. It began to snow as soon as they arrived, and for one whole month the weather did not clear, so that the snow reached to a depth of twelve spans, and for those who had settled in the valleys, or lived in houses, there was no possibility of changing their abode.

Now Sháhi Beg's purpose in coming [to Hisár] was not to seize Khusrau Sháh, but just to try whether Khusrau Sháh had power to withstand him or not. In that inroad he did not commit much violence. Whatever plunder did fall into his hands, he seized upon. He then returned, with the conviction that when he came a second time he would frighten away [Khusrau Sháh] as a fly from a dish, with a mere wave of his hand. That winter he also wished to test the people of Khorásán. Using the same means, he marched on Balkh, where the governor at that time was Sultán Kulunják, acting under Badi-uz-Zamán Mirzá, son of Sultán Husain Mirzá. He commanded his men to invest the town, and spent the whole of that winter in besieging it. The Khorásáni were, in

[1] About June—1503. [2] The end of autumn.

spite of their numerous attacks on the enemy, unable to relieve Balkh. Thus, during that winter, he weighed Khusrau Sháh and the Khorásáni in the scales of experiment, and found that neither of them equalled himself in weight.

But while Sháhi Beg Khán was engaged in besieging Balkh, Khusrau Sháh was left free from molestation, and his men again assembled. In short, his affairs began to prosper, and he sent messengers without intermission to Sháhi Beg Khán, with suitable expressions of friendship, which Sháhi Beg Khán returned in kind. That winter, when Khusrau Sháh was recovering his peace of mind, news arrived from Karátigin that there had been a great fall of snow, so that no one was able to get away. Khusrau Sháh immediately despatched 20,000 men, under his brother Mir Vali.[1]

Those in Karátigin were under no apprehensions from anything on his side, but remained where they were, far and near. When they learned the approach of the army, they immediately mustered all the men they could, to the number of about 500, and occupied the pass. The snow was so deep that no one dared leave the road. Both sides dismounted and the fight commenced. It lasted from morning till night. Finally our people had no arrows left, for on both sides every arrow that was shot was lost in the snow. The enemy were very numerous, and advanced to the fight in detachments; while as soon as the arrows of one detachment were expended, another came up to take its place and continued the fight. But we had on our side only one body, and towards evening, our arrows being entirely expended, our people turned and fled. Among the Amirs of my father, who died of arrow-wounds in that fight, were Bāgh Yasár Oghlán, Khush Rái Kukildásh, and several more. My father escaped, with six others, towards the hills of the country of Farghána, which lie on the eastern side of that country, between Káshghar and Andiján. In those mountains are people whom they call Jagirák, and who, at that time, were great cattle-stealers. Not long after this, however, they were exterminated by Mirzá Abá Bakr.[2] But Khusrau Sháh had carried away all our

[1] Only one text gives the name of Mir Vali. He was also brother of Báki Chaghaniáni, so often mentioned by Baber. He played a considerable part, but eventually fell into the hands of Shahi Beg, who beheaded him at Samarkand in 1504. (Erskine, *Hist.*, i., pp. 95 and 212.)

[2] The country of the Jagirák must have been in the mountains which bound the upper part of the Alai valley on the north, and separate it from the lower country of Farghána. Seeing that the tribe is said to have been exterminated about the beginning of the sixteenth century, it is scarcely surprising that no trace of them, or of the name of their country, should remain. Baber mentions the tribe, calls it a very numerous one, and says that they inhabited "the mountains that lie between Farghána and Káshghar." Secure in these mountains, they refused to pay tribute, and accumulated great numbers of sheep, horses, and yaks. Baber describes how, in A.H. 900, he sent a force to plunder them, taking 20,000 sheep and 1500 horses, which he divided among the soldiers of his army, then in a state of destitution. (*Memoirs*, p. 35.)

servants and retinue to Kunduz, where they spent one year as best they could.

Having reached this point in my narrative, if I omitted to give a short account of Sháhi Beg Khán, the chain of my history would not be continuous.

CHAPTER VI.

HISTORY OF SHÁHI BEG KHÁN.

When the great judge and disposer of all things determines to exalt some mortal with the crown of sovereignty and make him illustrious, he so arranges that great warriors and intelligent councillors assemble round his person, who may defend him from his enemies and ill-wishers, and make all far-sighted men blind and all attentive men deaf, so that father and son, brother and brother, are at enmity with one another. These words may serve as a preface to the story of Sháhi Beg Khán.

He was the son of Sháh Badágh Sultán, the son of Abulkhair Khán. After the death of Abulkhair Khán, disputes arose among those whom he had left behind. To such a length were these quarrels carried, that each one went in a different direction, and thus all the men of noble lineage—the Sultáns and the Mirzádas—who were held in esteem by the people, were scattered. In this confusion, Sháhi Beg Khán, after much suffering and wandering, being driven to extremity by want, went to Mávará-un-Nahr, where Sultán Ahmad Mirzá, son of Sultán Abu Said Mirzá, was reigning. Sultán Ahmad Mirzá was a powerful king, and had round him Amirs of such dignity and pretensions that they aimed at having kings in their service. One of these Amirs was Amir Abdul-Ali Tarkhán, Governor of Bokhárá. Sháhi Beg Khán became his vassal, and was entered as one of his retainers. In like manner several other Sultáns entered his service. From this circumstance, an estimate may be formed of the splendour and dignity of Sultán Ahmad Mirzá. As long as Sultán Ahmad Mirzá remained in the bonds of this life, Sháhi Beg Khán stayed in the service of Abdul-Ali Tarkhán. The Mirzá and Abdul-Ali Tarkhán died at about the same time, after which Sháhi Beg Khán went to Turkistán and sought the protection and favour of Sultán Mahmud Khán, who did not deny him what support and assistance lay in his power to give, till finally, by means of the aid afforded him by the Khán, Sháhi Beg Khán took possession of Samarkand and Bokhárá. Then the number of his troops rose from two or three hundred to 50,000;

or rather to 60,000. From the time of his going to Turkistán, by the help of Sultán Mahmud Khán, his power had increased daily. All the Sultáns and Amirs, and other adherents of Abulkhair Khán, who had been wandering aimlessly in the wastes of the Dasht-i-Kipchák, now joined him; and thus he arrived at power.

After the reduction of Samarkand and Bokhárá, he turned against his own benefactor. Thus was the protector undone by the dependant. When news of this reached the ears of Álácha Khán, he set out from Moghulistán to his brother's aid. The result, as has been briefly related above, was that he captured and set at liberty the Khán [Mahmud], and took from him as many of the Moghuls as was possible. Thus to his Uzbeg army there were added 30,000 Moghuls. [Verses] . . . .

Leaving Táshkand, he did not tarry long in Samarkand, but proceeded to ravage Hisár and to besiege Balkh (as has been mentioned). Having passed the winter of 909 [1503–4] in the siege of Balkh, he went, in the beginning of spring, to Samarkand, and remained a month or two in the open country [*Sahári*] round that town. He then turned his victorious arms against Andiján. The first year, when he captured the Khán, he did not trouble himself with Tambal or Andiján, being fully occupied in settling the affairs of Táshkand. Moreover, before the conquest of that place, Shaikh Báyazid had hastened fearlessly out to receive him, and had shown him signs of loyalty. Tambal also had proffered him timely assurances of devotion, with all of which he showed himself contented, and returned that same year. Having thus set his mind at rest with regard to the Moghuls and Táshkand, and having had an opportunity of forming an estimate of the Hisári and the Khorásáni, he wished first of all to settle the question of Andiján and Tambal, that he might, with a calm mind, proceed with the reduction of Hisár and the extermination of Khusrau Sháh, which was the first step towards the conquest of Khorásán.

When he reached Marghinán, which is one of the chief towns of Farghána, Tambal abandoned all the forts in Farghána, and collected a force within the fort of Andiján. On this news being brought to Sháhi Beg Khán, he and all his wisest advisers were agreed that this bringing together, into one place, of the troops [of Tambal] only made the conquest easier for them. With all speed, therefore, they hastened to Andiján, and being sure that they should find him, prepared for a siege; it was resolved that Sháhi Beg Khán should conduct the siege in person, while the rest of the Sultáns should ravage and spoil the country round, seizing the forts and men, and laying waste the whole region. The next year they would return to complete the work of devastation. But the hand of fate seized Tambal by the collar and hastened him to his end. He came out of the fort saying: "Let us meet them in the open field"; and he led 10,000 men out of the walls. When Sháhi Beg Khán arrived, Tambal, judging of their numbers from the dust they raised, retired. But before he could reach the fort, many of his men had fallen by the edge of the sword, and Tambal and his brothers, broken and terrified, crept into the citadel. It had been decided that that year they should lay waste his territories[1] and then return home, so that the enterprise should be easy the next year. He himself, however, went to meet his fate: and thus the undertaking which was to have been accomplished the year following, was achieved in forty days. When Sháhi Beg Khán saw that the fugitives, in terror of their lives, had taken refuge in the fort, he resolved to shut them up and to push the siege vigorously forward.

After the defeat in Karátigin, my father crossed to the country of the Jagirák.

The most surprising thing of all was that, although news had reached [Tambal] of the movements of Sháhi Beg Khán, instead of making preparations to withstand the advance of Sháhi Beg Khán, he went to attack my father, in Jagirák. The Jagirák, allying themselves with my father, took up a strong position in the valley of Turuk Sháran.[2] On the arrival of Tambal, fighting began and lasted continuously for three days. I have heard my father say: "On the third day we had used every means in our power to hold our ground. When night fell we became very thoughtful and distressed, wondering what would become of us if the enemy renewed the attack, for most of our active men had been killed or wounded, and there was no one left. How will it be with us to-morrow? But when day broke we were filled with astonishment and wonder, for on going up to the top of the hill, we saw the army hurrying away with all possible speed, in divisions and detachments. Our joy and gratification knew no bounds, and we immediately sent off some of those who were not wounded, or whose wounds were not mortal, to obtain information. One man was brought in. He said that at midnight some one had brought news [to Tambal] that Sháhi Beg Khán had reached Kand Bádám, and on learning this, he had set out without delay. This news caused fresh life and immeasurable joy to spring up in us. We forthwith sent a messenger to Sháhi Beg Khán, to say that we had come to that country in great distress, owing to the confusion of times; that when news of the arrival of the Khán reached us it was as if life [*ján*] had come to us; whatever the royal mandate should lay upon us we were ready to perform. Our messenger

[1] That is, the Uzbegs should lay waste Tambal's territories.

[2] See note 2, p. 165. From the position of Jagirák and from what follows, it would appear that *Turuk Sháran* was in one of the valleys of the north slope of the Alai mountains. It could not have been far to the south and east of *Kand-Badám.*

reached Andiján on the second day of the siege. He was immediately sent back to tell us that we were desired to hasten on without delay, and that everything we could hope for or desire would be done for us. We were very apprehensive, but having no other place to go to, and deeming it the most advantageous plan for ourselves, we set out with light hearts.

"When I came into the Khán's presence, he showed me all honour and respect, and received me in the most friendly way, saying to all his Sultáns and Amirs: 'Muhammad Husain Kurkán is our guest; I expect you all to entertain him as a guest.' And every day, while the siege was in progress, all the Sultáns and Amirs entertained us with feasts and banquets and showed us marked attention.

"On the morning of the forty-first day, Tambal mounted to the top of one of the towers and called out with a loud voice: 'I am a Mirzá, remember my services and the time of our infancy. Tell me what I should do—[and I will do it].'" (Now Tambal was my father's foster brother.) My father continued: "Although I had been very badly treated by him, it made my heart sad to see him in this evil plight, and I asked: 'Why do you not strengthen the fortress?' Tambal replied: 'I cannot continue hostilities; what is to be done?' I answered: 'The only hope for the helpless is surrender.' Timur Sultán was present. Tambal at once came out of the fort with his brothers. He came in confusion and alarm, and threw his arms round my neck. They [the Uzbeg] granted him no respite, but that same hour put them all to the sword. They then closed the gates of the fort, and would not allow any kind of plunder or rapine to be carried on."

That country was then given to Jáni Beg Sultán, and Sháhi Beg, accompanied by my father, retraced his steps and arrived in Samarkand. [There] they spent a few days in military preparations, after which they set out to attack Khusrau Sháh. On reaching Hisár, they found the fort defended by Shiram Chahra, a dependant of Khusrau Sháh. Sháhi Beg Khán conducted the siege in person, but after a few days Shiram Chahra begged for quarter, and coming out, surrendered the fort. The Khán, observing his promise,[1] let Shiram go. Shiram stayed for a time among the followers of the Khán, and many who had formerly been attached to him, now rejoined him.

It is not known how it came about, but the same day that the Khán began, personally, to lay siege to Hisár, he also sent a mandate to Mahmud Sultán, ordering him to take as many men from the army as he wanted, and to advance on Kunduz.

Khusrau Sháh for a long time past had been filling Kunduz with stores, provisions and treasure, and had proclaimed that he

[1] A promise to give quarter seems to be implied.

had supplies enough to last him for twenty years. If all else should fail [he said] we shall, at least, be able to remain inside the fort for twenty years, dead or alive.

While he was busy with this vain boasting, news came that Sháhi Beg Khán was laying siege to Hisár, and that Mahmud Sultán was crossing the River Amuya.[1] That same hour, abandoning all his stores, he packed up whatever he could, and in the utmost confusion and disorder, set out for the hills, hoping there to find a refuge. A few days later, Mahmud Sultán entered Kunduz, where I myself happened to be, with my sisters and my younger brother. It has been stated already, that a marriage connection had been formed between my father and Sultánim Begum, and after the above related circumstances, we were carried off to Kunduz. During our sojourn there, Sultánim Begum gave birth to a son, named Abdullah, whose history will be told in various connections. My father had accompanied Mahmud Sultán, for the greatest intimacy existed between them. The reason for this was as follows. In his earlier days, Sháhi Beg Khán had made every possible effort to obtain supreme power, and was bound by no promises or agreements. Whenever an occasion offered he pushed his ambitious projects: if he was successful he would say: "It was God's will"; if he failed he was always ready with a thousand excuses and pretexts. In this way, frequent misunderstandings arose between him and Sultán Mahmud Khán. The wonder is that in every instance, his pretext, such as it was, should have been accepted. It would be tedious to enter here into the details of this matter, which will be given in the First Part [*Tárikh-i-Asl*]. I will, however, give one instance in this place. Sháhi Beg was then in Turkistán at the height of favour and prosperity, when Sultán Mahmud Khán led an army against Tambal. After three days' march, in consequence of some untoward events (mentioned in the *Tárikh-i-Asl*) his projects were frustrated and he marched back again. All the Amirs who had come from [beyond] the frontiers to join the army, now returned and settled down again within their own territories.

[1] The ancient town of *Amuya* or *Amol* stood some three or four miles from the left bank of the Oxus, on the road from Merv to Bokhara. According to the Arab geographers followed by Sprenger, the distance from Merv was calculated at 36 *farsakhs*, and from Bokhara at 19 f. by one authority and 22 f. by another. The ferry crossed to *Ferebr* (Farab) on the right bank, a name still extant on modern maps, near Charjui, which latter place, indeed, represents the ancient *Amuya*. The name of the river—*Amu*—is said by some of the Arab writers to have been derived from that of the town, but possibly this statement should be reversed. The Chinese travellers of the Mongol period called the river, *Amu* and *An-bu*. In the Turki MSS. used for this translation, by Mr. Ross, *Amur* is written where *Amuya* stands in the Persian. The addition of the letter *r* is not, however, unfrequent in Turki renderings of foreign names, as remarked in note 3, p. 136 above, on *Ursang*. (See Sprenger, pp. 16 and 17, and map I. Bretschneider ii., p. 62.)

When news of the Khán's expedition reached Sháhi Beg Khán in Turkistán, he at once placed the foot of ambition in the stirrup of enterprise, and marched to attack Táshkand. He sent Mahmud Sultán against Sairám, which in old books is called Isbijáb,[1] but while on his road he learnt that the Khán had returned. He instantly sent a messenger to say that his Highness had set out to punish his rebellious vassal Tambal, while he had come to protect Táshkand, and [the Khán's] family and household. (Though except himself there was no one to hurt them.) Hearing of his Highness's return to his capital, he had also returned, and, in effect, he did go back to Turkistán. He moreover despatched swift messengers to Mahmud Sultán, enjoining him, likewise, to molest no place, but to return. But before the messengers could arrive, Mahmud Sultán, supposing Sairám to be unprotected, had begun to plunder. The Governor of Sairám was Amir Ahmad, one of the Itáráji Amirs, and uncle of Tambal, but unlike his nephew, he was a worthy man and a devoted servant to Sultán Mahmud Khán. He went out to check Mahmud Sultán, and the two forces met, when Mahmud Sultán was seized and brought bound before the Khán. The Khán sent for my father, who, on his arrival, begged that the prisoner's life might be spared; therefore he [Mahmud] was treated with great kindness and then allowed to depart. On this account a very close intimacy and warm friendship sprang up between my father and Mahmud Sultán. He accompanied Mahmud Sultán to Kunduz, and there caused us to rejoin his own party; thus our families and households arrived at Shahr-i-Sabz, a town which Sháhi Beg Khán had given to my father as a fief. From the time of the return from Balkh to that now mentioned, only one spring had elapsed. At the beginning of the winter, Sháhi Beg Khán set out against Khwárizm, while my father fled into Khorásán.

In this place, for the proper understanding of what followed, it

[1] *Isbijab*, or *Asbijab*, is a name frequently employed by the early Arabian geographers. It has been thought by some modern writers to be the old name for *Chimkend*, but here is a distinct statement that *Sairám* is its modern representative. The present *Sairám* lies only some seven or eight miles distant from *Chimkend*; but Sir H. Yule gives reasons for believing that the town of that name mentioned by authors in the fifteenth century, stood some distance farther east. He notices that Hulagu, on his march to Persia in the thirteenth century, reached *Sairám* the second day after passing *Talas—i.e. Táráz;* also that Rashid-ud-Din speaks of an ancient city of vast size called *Kari-Sairam*, near *Talas*. Sir H. Yule does not mention the date to which Rashid-ud-Din refers, and the book he quotes is, I regret, not accessible to me. If, however, the city was ancient in Rashid-ud-Din's time (end of thirteenth century), it is just possible that the modern Sairam may have been in existence at the time of Mirza Haidar's history. The distance between the modern Sairam and Aulia-Ata (which, as we have seen, was about on the site of Táráz) is as nearly as possible 110 miles, or about five ordinary marches in that country. Thus, if the older Sairam lay two marches westward of Táráz, the distance between it and the modern town would not be great. (See Yule's *Cathay*, p. cc. Kostenko's *Turkistan*, ii., p. 23).

will be necessary to give some account of Bábar Pádisháh and Sultán Said Khán. Some further details will, God willing, be given in the First Part.

CHAPTER VII.

BIRTH AND PARENTAGE OF BÁBAR PÁDISHÁH: HIS CONNECTION WITH THE MOGHULS; AND HIS EARLY HISTORY.

THERE existed anciently, between the Chaghatái and the Moghuls, a bitter enmity. Moreover, from the time of Amir Timur till that of Sultán Abu Said Mirzá, some one of the race of Chaghatái Khán, son of Chingiz Khán, had always been placed on the royal throne, and was honoured with the title of King, in spite of the fact that he was [in reality] a prisoner, as one may gather from the royal mandates. When it came to the turn of Sultán Abu Said Mirzá to reign, this king discarded the old custom; Yunus Khán was summoned from Shiráz, and was sent into Moghulistán to oppose his brother Isán Bughá Khán. But in this Epitome there is no space for an account of the removal of the Khán to Shiráz, of the Khánship of Isán Bughá Khán, or of the reign of Sultán Abu Said Mirzá.[1]

To be brief, Sultán Abu Said Mirzá said to Yunus Khán: "The old order of things has been changed; you must now lay aside all your [former] pretensions: that is to say, the royal mandates will be issued in the name of this dynasty [*tabaka*], and henceforth there must be friendship between us, and a bond of union."

When Yunus Khán came to Moghulistán, he, after thirty years of hardship and suffering, got the upper hand of Isán Bughá Khán, as will be briefly related in connection with the history of Sultán Said Khán and Mirza Abá Bakr.

The noble mind of Yunus Khán was thus set at rest; Sultán Abu Said Mirzá changed an old enemy into a new friend. Yunus Khán was desirous of making a return for his kindness, and [said to himself]: "Perhaps in the same way that he has changed an old enemy into a new friend, I will change a friend into a relation." To this end, he gave to the three sons of Mirzá Sultán Abu Said (namely, Sultán Ahmad Mirzá, Sultán Mahmud Mirzá, and Omar Shaikh Mirzá) three of his daughters in marriage; the names of

[1] The main facts regarding Yunus' exile in Persia have been noticed at pp. 74 and 84–5; while some remarks concerning the Khanship of Isán Bugha II. will be found in the Introduction, Sec. ii.

these three daughters being Mihr Nigár Khánim, Sultán Nigár Khánim, and Kutluk Nigár Khánim. (These have all been already mentioned.)

As Farghána, the country of Omar Shaikh, was situated on the borders of Moghulistán, [Yunus Khán] became more intimate and friendly with him than with either of his brothers: indeed, the Khán made no distinction between him and his own children, and whenever they pleased they used to come and go between each other's countries and residences, demanding no ceremony, but being satisfied with whatever was at hand.

On the occasion of the birth of Bábar Pádisháh, a messenger was sent to bear the good tidings to Yunus Khán, who came from Moghulistán and spent some time with [Omar Shaikh]. When the child's head was shaved, everyone gave feasts and entertainments. Never were two kings known to be on such terms of intimacy as were Yunus Khán and Omar Shaikh Mirzá. In short, the Pádisháh was born on the 6th of Moharram of the year 888. Maulána Munir Marghináni, one of the Ulamás of Ulugh Beg Mirzá, discovered the date in the [numerical value of the letters] of *Shash Moharram*. They begged his Holiness to choose a name for the child, and he blessed him with the name of Zahir-ud-Din Muhammad.

At that time the Chaghatái were very rude and uncultured [*buzurg*], and not refined [*bázári*] as they are now; thus they found Zahir-ud-Din Muhammad difficult to pronounce, and for this reason gave him the name of Bábar. In the public prayers [*khutba*] and in royal mandates he is always styled 'Zahir-ud-Din Bábar Muhammad,' but he is best known by the name of Bábar Pádisháh. His genealogy [is as follows]. Omar Shaikh Kurkán, son of Sultán Abu Said Kurkán, son of Sultán Muhammad Mirzá, son of Mirán Sháh Mirzá, son of Amir Timur Kurkán. And on the mother's side: Kutluk Nigár Khánim, daughter of Yunus Khán, son of Vais Khán, son of Shir Ali Khán, son of Muhammad Khán, son of Khizir Khwája Khán, son of Tughluk Timur Khán. This prince was adorned with various virtues, and clad with numberless good qualities, above all of which bravery and humanity had the ascendant. In the composition of Turki poetry he was second only to Amir Ali Shir. He has written a *Diván*, in the purest and most lucid Turki. He invented a style of verse called "Mubaiyan," and was the author of a most useful treatise on Jurisprudence, which has been adopted generally. He also wrote a tract on Turki Prosody, superior in elegance to any other, and put into verse the *Rasala-i-Válidiyyah* of his Holiness. Then there is his *Vakái*[1] or Turki History, which is written in a simple,

[1] The "Memoirs" of Baber. It is interesting to notice that about ten years after Baber's death, his Memoirs were in the hands of Mirza Haidar. Baber died

unaffected, and yet very pure style. (Some of the stories from that work will be reproduced here.) He excelled in music and other arts. In fact, no one in his family before him ever possessed such talents as his. Nor did any of his race ever perform such wonderful exploits, or experience such strange adventures, as did he. He was twelve years of age when his father, Omar Shaikh Mirzá, died. In his *Vakái,* which, though in Turki, is written in very elegant and florid style, he says: "On Monday, the 4th of Ramazán, Omar Shaikh Mirzá having flown from the top of the precipice with his pigeon and his pigeon-house, became a falcon, at the age of thirty-nine."[1] This occurred in the year 899, and after his father's death Bábar Pádisháh was raised to the throne, being, at that time, twelve years of age. There was so much dissension between Báisanghar Mirzá and Sultán Ali Mirzá (the sons of Sultán Mahmud, son of Sultán Abu Said),[2] that neither of them had strength enough to protect Samarkand. When information of this [state of affairs] reached Andiján, the Emperor set out to attack Samarkand. Although the Mirzás had become very weak, they offered him stout resistance; but finally, Báisanghar having no power left, abandoned the town and fled towards Hisár, where he was put to death by Khusrau Sháh (as already mentioned). The Emperor took Samarkand, and quartered in it as many of the troops of Andiján as was possible, while the rest returned to Andiján, some with his permission, some without.

On the arrival of Tambal, of whom we have spoken, he, in conjunction with some other Amirs, set Jahángir Mirzá, younger brother of the Emperor, upon the throne.

The Chief Judge [*Kázi*] of Andiján, a very pious and religious man, who had done everything in his power to forward the

---

in 937 A.H. (26 Dec. 1530), and Mirza Haidar was in India from about 943 to 947. It was probably at this time, therefore, that he acquired a copy of his cousin's Memoirs. The pity is that he says nothing to enlighten us regarding the gaps, or lost chapters, in the Memoirs.

[1] Baber, in his Memoirs, describes his father's death. After mentioning that Akhsi, where Omar Shaikh lived, "is situated on a steep precipice, on the very edge of which some of its buildings are raised," he continues, according to Erskine's translation (p. 7): "Omar Shaikh Mirza was precipitated from the top of the steep, with his pigeons and pigeon-house, and took his flight to the other world." In Pavet de Courteille's translation from the Turki, the passage stands: "Se changea en faucon" (i. p. 11). The allusion to a "falcon" in this connection, I cannot explain.

[2] In the very detailed table of the descendants of Timur, given by Prof. Blochmann, in Vol. I. of the *Ain-i-Akbari,* the name of Sultan Ali does not appear among the sons of Sultan Mahmud Mirza. Only three sons are entered there—viz., Baisanghar Mirza, Masud Mirza, and Khan Mirza; but we know that the last of these had also another name—that of Sultan Vais Mirza, which does not appear in Prof. Blochmann's table. It is possible, therefore, that Ali may have been a second name of one of the two other brothers, but as this is merely a conjecture, I have added the name of Ali to the abbreviated table of Timuri attached to this volume. (See note, p. 203).

Emperor's interests, was wantonly put to death. A short time before the murder of the Kázi, the adherents of the Emperor had strengthened and defended the fort of Andiján, and had sent letters of entreaty [to the Emperor], representing that if he did not come quickly, Andiján would fall, and that after it Samarkand would also succumb. On receiving these letters, the Emperor left Samarkand, and set out for Andiján. On reaching Khojand, however, news was brought him that the enemy had won the day. The Emperor, having left one place, and lost the other, was greatly perplexed, and betook himself to his uncle, Sultán Mahmud Khán.

The Emperor's mother, and her mother, Isán Daulat Begum, went to their son and sister. This sister was my mother. On this account the Emperor, also, stayed in our country. His hosts exerted themselves to the utmost on his behalf, and after many severe hardships, after many victories and defeats, the Emperor once more became ruler of Samarkand. He fought many battles with rival claimants for Samarkand, and experienced both victory and defeat. At length he was besieged, and when all his power of resistance had gone, he gave his sister, Khánzáda Begum, to Sháhi Beg Khán, and making some kind of treaty, left Samarkand, which thus fell again into the hands of Sháhi Beg Khán. It would be very tedious were I to relate all the details; however, to be brief, the Emperor [again] repaired to his uncle. Having given up all idea of [regaining] Samarkand, he determined to secure Andiján. The Kháns also, having bound the girdle of endeavour round the waist of fatherly love, exerted themselves to the utmost to take Andiján, that they might give it to the Emperor, with the result which has been mentioned above. After the last battle, in which the Kháns fell into the hands of Sháhi Beg Khán, the Emperor fled to the hills on the south of the country of Farghána, where he underwent many hardships and innumerable misfortunes. Moreover, his mother was with him, as were also most of his servants, together with the family and children. In that journey (and verily, as the Prophet himself said, "Travelling is a foretaste of Hell") they all suffered great hardships, and with difficulty reached, at length, the territory of Hisár, which is the capital of Khusrau Sháh, hoping that they might participate in the humanity for which he was renowned. But he, like the heavens, changed, and averting the face of compassion, turned the back of unkindness towards that master of benevolence. But beyond this he did not do them any injury. And thus, in the same state of dejection, affliction, apprehension, and evasion, they passed on towards Ghuri and Baklán. When they reached this quarter, the back of their strength being broken, and the foot of vigour being bound, they tarried for a few days.

How often in misfortune is there a hidden blessing! Although waiting in that place was a cause of great affliction to them, it turned out most providentially, and in a way which the most far-sighted person could not have foreseen. For at this very crisis, the advance of the standards of Sháhi Beg Khán on Hisár, and the approach towards Kunduz of the drums of Mahmud Sultán, caused the boasting Khusrau Sháh to desert his kingdom, as has been related above. He, too, fled to the hills of Ghuri; and on his arrival there, learnt that the Emperor was still among the mountains. That same night his servants and retinue, both great and small, from the Mir to the groom, all flocked to the court of the Emperor. Khusrau Sháh saw nothing left for it but to hasten also to offer his services. Yet this man had put out the eyes of one of the Emperor's cousins, Sultán Masud Mirzá, and had brought Masud's brother, Báisanghar Mirzá, to the bier, after having raised him to the throne; also, at the time when the Emperor had arrived on his frontier, he had, with extreme harshness, ordered him to quit the country.

Moreover, Mirza Khán, a younger brother of the cruelly-treated Mirzás, whose father and mother were both closely connected with the Emperor's father and mother, had shared in all the Emperor's sufferings and trials in the mountains, and was at this time with him. When Khusrau Sháh arrived in the Emperor's presence, Mirzá Khán petitioned that he might be put to death, by way of retaliation for his treatment of his [Mirzá Khan's] two brothers. The Emperor, whose natural disposition was a humane one, said to Mirzá Khán: "It would be a pity, a thousand pities, to compare two good angels with this devil of a king, and to such purpose did he pierce the pearls of love with the diamond of mercy, that at last he caused Mirzá Khán to desist from his demand and be satisfied. When Khusrau Sháh looked upon the Emperor and Mirzá Khán, the forehead of his folly became moist with the perspiration of shame, but the Emperor wiped it clean with the sleeve of forgiveness and the skirt of pardon. When the audience was terminated, the Emperor commanded the treasurers to take back all the property, treasure, horses, etc., which they had brought to him, just as they were, although he had only one horse suitable to his rank, and that was used also by his mother. From this an idea may be formed of what necessaries [he had at his command]. He ordered that none of [Khusrau's] effects should be confiscated. Although the Emperor was very needy, he would not take any of the presents, but gave him back all his arms and treasures untouched, and declined all that was offered. This is one trait out of a thousand, in the Emperor's character. Khusrau Sháh, having obtained permission to go to Khorásán, separated from the Emperor, and proceeded to his destination. It is astonishing that, with such a force as he had, he did not attempt to defend his own State. Having got some help from Khorásán, he went and attacked Kunduz, where he was put to death without much ado. Verily the murder of a master, or a master's son, is a portentous deed!

The Emperor, in one night, became master of 20,000 men, together with great Amirs, such as Báki Chaghániáni,[1] Sultán Ahmad Karául, Báki Nila Furush and others, who took office under him.

[Having made the necessary preparations] they set out against Kábul. After the death of the Emperor's uncle, Ulugh Beg Mirzá of Kábul, Mukim, son of Zunnun[2] Arghun, one of the Mirzás of Sultán Husain, had taken possession of Kábul. Immediately on the arrival of the Emperor, he went out to oppose him, but seeing the enemy's superior numbers, he fled back and prepared to defend himself in the fort of Kábul. At length, being unable to hold out, he begged for quarter and surrendered the fort. Faithful to his agreement, the Emperor allowed him to proceed to Kandahár, with all his effects and followers. From that date, 909, to the present date, 948, Kábul has remained in the hands of the Emperor and his descendants.

Having brought down my history to this point, it is time to turn to the proceedings of Sultán Said Khán; also to those of my father, of his journey to Khorásán, and of his relations with the Emperor. The first part will be given briefly, and the latter part in detail.

CHAPTER VIII.

BEGINNING OF THE STORY OF SULTÁN SAID KHÁN, SON OF SULTÁN AHMAD KHÁN, SON OF SULTÁN YUNUS KHÁN, AND THE SUFFERINGS AND HARDSHIPS HE ENDURED AT THE OUTSET OF HIS CAREER.

[Here follows a somewhat lengthy dissertation on the advantages of misfortune, into which is introduced an anecdote in verse concerning Moses, taken from the "*Salsalat-uz-Zahab*" or "Golden

[1] The texts differ here. The Turki MS. has *Kálghán Chághátai* in the place of Báki Chaghániáni. The latter name, however, is certainly correct, as is evident from a reference to Baber's memoirs (pp. 128, *seqq.*), where these transactions are set forth. Báki of Chaghánián was a younger brother of Khusrau Shah, and is described by Baber as "a man of much weight." The country of *Chaghánián*, it may be remarked, was situated on the middle and upper courses of the Surkhan and Káfirnahán rivers. The name is now obsolete.

[2] Usually written *Zulnun*. For an account of his life and lineage, see Erskine's *History*, i., pp. 262 *seqq.*

Chain" of Abd-urrahman Jami, and also an account, in prose, of the Education of Nushiriván the Just.] Wherever in this Epitome *the Khán*, in an absolute sense, is mentioned, Sultán Said Khán is meant.[2] This Khán had many wonderful adventures. As one of the chief objects of this Epitome is to set forth the virtue and ability of the Khán, I shall enter into detail.

His most noble lineage has already been given. From the time of his birth to the age of fourteen, he spent his days under the fond care and kind protection of his father. When he reached the age of fourteen, his father, Sultán Ahmad Khán, better known as Álácha, wished to go to the assistance of his elder brother, Sultán Mahmud Khán. He therefore appointed his eldest son, Mansur Khán, to fill his place on the throne, and took with him to Táshkand, two sons who were younger than Mansur Khán, namely, Sultán Said Khán and Bábáják Sultán. The Khán was with his father at the battle of Akhsi, in which the Kháns were captured, as has been mentioned. When the army was thrown into disorder and every man was trying to save his own life, the Khán also took flight, but at that moment he was struck in the thigh by an arrow, which, piercing his armour, struck the bone. As his father's army was routed he had no means of escape. Some men of the district captured him, and as he was, at the time, unable to walk, they refrained from carrying him as a present to anybody, but took care of him for a few days.

Sháhi Beg Khán returned in haste to settle his affairs in Táshkand. By the time the Khán had recovered his strength, Shaikh Báyazid had taken upon himself the government of Akhsi. The Khán, as soon as he was sufficiently recovered to be moved, was brought before him, and by his orders was thrown into prison, where he remained a whole year.

When Sháhi Beg Khán arrived [in Táshkand] he seized and put to death Tambal, and gave the government of Andiján to Jáni Beg Sultán. When this latter came to Akhsi, the Khán was brought before him. Jáni Beg Sultán recommended him to the favour of Sháhi Beg Khán, who received him with compassion, kept him in his fatherly care, and denied him nothing. He, moreover, took the Khán with him on the expedition in which he conquered Hisár and Kunduz.

I have heard the Khán relate, in terms of wonder and admiration, that when Sháhi Beg Khán had conquered Hisár, news was brought of the taking of Kunduz by Mahmud Sultán. Sháhi Beg Khan, having entrusted Hisár to Hamza Sultán and Chaghánián to

[1] It is to be regretted that the author does not carry out his intention in this matter. In many places he forgets himself, and calls other Khans "*the Khan*," thereby causing some confusion. To make matters clear, I have usually had to insert the full name on these occasions.

Mahdi Sultán,[1] set out quietly on his return. "As the pass of Darband-i-Ahanin [The Iron Gate] was very difficult [continued the Khán], and as the army was much burdened with booty, they made the journey, *farsákh* after *farsákh*, by way of Buya and Tirmiz. While the victorious army was encamped at Buya, I was sitting once, at midday, in the royal tent [*majlis*]. The hour for the assembly had not yet arrived, and only a few of the king's intimates were present, when somebody with a terrified countenance and wild appearance came in great haste, and laid a letter at the foot of the royal throne. As [Sháhi Beg] perused the contents of this letter a great change came over him, and before he had finished reading it, he rose up and went in to his haram, giving orders for his horse to be brought. He remained for some time in the haram; but after midday prayers came out again and mounted his horse. He was attended by a great number of people. Then it was made known that Mahmud Sultán had died a natural death in Kunduz, and that his body was on the way [to the camp]. When Sháhi Beg Khán had got some distance away, we saw a great crowd in pitch-black clothes, such as captives wear. Having placed the bier upon the ground, they drew up in two lines behind it. When [Sháhi Beg Khán] saw this, he made a sign for all the Sultáns and others to dismount and follow in his train. These, having obeyed, began to raise cries of grief and lamentation, and we, in the camp, also commenced to utter moans and wailings. When those attending the bier approached, he ordered all who were with him to draw up in a line, while he himself rode forward until his horse's head was just above the bier; he then gave a sign for everyone to keep silence, and thereupon those who were with him ceased from rending their garments and tearing their beards. He then called one of the Amirs of Mahmud Sultán, and said to him such things as are usual on occasions of condolence. After this he remained silent for a while, never showing the slightest change in his countenance, nor shedding a tear. At the end of an hour he raised his head and said: 'The death of Mahmud is a good thing: men have been wont to say that the power of Sháhi Beg Khán was upheld by Mahmud: let it now be known that Sháhi Beg Khán was in no way whatever dependent upon Mahmud. Carry him away now, and bury him.' Having said this, he turned away, and all present were astounded at his boldness and composure."

The death of Mahmud Sultán was a great loss to the Moghuls, for he was, in every respect, a thorough Moghul [and they recalled all he had done for them].

[1] These two Uzbeg chiefs had formerly been in Baber's service, but had deserted him to join his enemy Sháhi Beg. Afterwards, at the battle of the Iron Gate (916 A.H.=1510 A.D.—after Sháhi Beg's death) they fell into Baber's hands and were put to death. (Erskine, *Hist.*, i., pp. 145, 309 and 315).

When Sháhi Beg Khán reached Samarkand, Sháh Begum arrived from Moghulistán. The details are briefly these: Sháh Begum was the mother of the Kháns, was daughter of Sháh Sultán Mahmud, King of Badakhshán, and of the race of Iskandar Zulkarnain. She had accompanied her son, Sultán Mahmud Khán, into Moghulistán. But those base advisers, of whom I have already spoken, provoked a quarrel between the mother and her son—a son who had been so obedient to her, that he had never even mounted for a ride without her permission. Between these two, they contrived to raise the dust of vexation and wrath. For they—cunning advisers that they were—decided to send Sháh Begum to Sháhi Beg Khán to solicit a country for herself, because she found living in Moghulistán distasteful. Such was the impracticable mission upon which they sent Sháh Begum. Now, as the Begum was a very sensible woman, she went under this pretext, and thus left her son, before those base advisers could bring about an open rupture, which would cause endless scandal and reproach to herself. The rumour was that she had gone to entreat [Sháhi Beg Khán], while she was [in reality] in Samarkand enjoying the company of her children.

At this same time [Sháhi Beg Khán] led an army into Khwárizm, and my father fled to Khorásán, as shall be presently related.

The Khán told me: "After the Mirzá's flight we were so overcome with apprehension, that sixteen of us having banded together, we fled from Samarkand, and journeyed by way of Khutuk and Kará Tukái to Sairám. Thence we went on to Moghulistán by way of Uzun Ahmad, and arrived at Haft Deh, which is better known as Yatikand,[1] where Sultán Mahmud Khán was living at

[1] This name has occurred several times already (see pp. 87 and note, 130, etc.), but has been subject, in the texts, to many different readings, such as *Batikand*, *Banikand*, *Yanikand*, etc., etc. Here, at last, we have in the Persian translation of it, which the author himself gives as *Haft-Deh*, a distinct guide to *Yatikand*, the Turki (as Haft Deh is the Persian) equivalent for "seven villages," or "seven towns." But though he has thus fixed the name for his readers, he still leaves them in the dark as to the situation of *Yatikand*. In the passage under note, he appears to regard it as lying within Moghulistan—and probably at some distance within it—for *Sairam* (either old or new, see note, p. 171) must have been near the frontier, and he mentions *Uzun Ahmad* (a place I cannot trace though, see below) as situated on the road between the two. As the party had come from Samarkand—*i.e.* from the south-west—they were journeying probably towards no point south of *Sairam*. We have, therefore, to look for *Yatikand*, according to the indication in this passage, somewhere to the east or north-east of *Sairam*. But at p. 87 the author says *Yatikand* was on the confines, or in the territory, or even suburbs, of *Andiján* (az náhiyat i Andiján); and he appears always to mean the *town or district of Andiján* alone, when he uses that name, and not the *province* to which the town belonged. The latter he always speaks of as *Farghána*. Thus, according to this indication, *Yatikand* would have to be sought to the south or south-east of *Sairam*. In modern times the province of *Farghána* came to be called *Andiján*, and the only solution of the discrepancy which I can suggest is that perhaps Mirza Haidar, in one instance, has also used

the time." It has been already related that after the death of Sultán Ahmad Khán, Sultán Mahmud Khán came into Moghulistán. The latter was a weakly prince and very lax and careless in the affairs of State.

Now Moghulistán is a country which does not admit of any such negligence and callousness in its administration, and for this reason Sultán Mahmud Khán was not able to remain there long, but came, with a desire to live a civilised life, to Yatikand, where there is [indeed] some cultivation. When he had been there a short time, the Khán went and attached himself to his uncle, Sultán Mahmud Khán. The Khán passed some time in the service of his uncle; but he was an energetic and enterprising man, and being unable to endure the negligence and indolence of his uncle, he fled from his court. Sultán Mahmud Khán sent a party after him to bring him back. After three days' march he was overtaken, when a fight ensued. In the heat of the action, a certain Maksud Ali, one of the courtiers of Sultán Mahmud Khán (and a man skilled in instrumental music and singing), displayed great valour, and the Khán seeing that the brunt of the battle was supported by him, rode up to attack him. Thereupon Maksud Ali turned and fled, but while retreating faced round and shot an

---

Andiján to denote the entire province. For this reason I have made the translation of "az náhiyat" read "on the confines"—a reading which, at any rate, points to a position within Moghulistan. If this suggestion be accepted, *Yatikand*, or *Haft-Deh*, would have stood probably in the south-western extremity of Moghulistan, and on the northern slopes of the range which forms the limit of the valley of the Sir; or possibly near the more westerly of the head streams of the Talas river, and thus not very far distant from Taráz. When (on p. 131) the author speaks of the Khan passing on from *Yatikand* to Moghulistan to visit his brother Khalil, it should be remembered that Khalil was at that time chief of the Kirghiz only, and that the Kirghiz tribe did not occupy the whole of Moghulistan. In all probability, therefore, that passage may read: "went farther on into Moghulistan."

It is somewhat strange that we should have no better cue for fixing the position of *Yatikand*, for it was evidently, about the period in question, a place of some importance. It may be worth while to remark that its identification has been somewhat embarrassed by the application, on Arrowsmith's map of 1878, of the word *Itikent* to a district of Kuráma, in the angle formed by the Sir near *Khojand*. I do not know on what authority the name, so located, rests. The district in question is practically that of the modern *Kuráma* itself—between the river and the hills, and almost exactly opposite *Khojand*. In this locality, however, the *Yatikand* of our history cannot be sought: it is, in the first place, a quarter which lay altogether outside of Moghulistan, while secondly, no traveller making for it from Samarkand could have taken Sairam on his road. *Itikent*, as placed by Arrowsmith, must have belonged either to the province of *Shásh* (*i.e. Tashkand*) or to *Farghána*; and was in one of the most thickly-populated and highly-cultivated parts of Central Asia, while this could not have been the case with *Yatikand*, as is evident from the narrative. As regards *Uzun Ahmad*, Kostenko in his itineraries, mentions a stream of that name in the mountains between the *Bish-Tásh* pass and *Katmán-tipa*, more than 100 miles in a direct line to the south-east of Aulia-Ata (Táráz), and consequently too far in the same direction to suit the narrative, or to point in any way towards Sairam, old or new. (See *Turkistan*, ii., pp. 58–9.)

Kara Tugai is very possibly to be identified with the Kara Sengir Tugai of the accompanying map—one of the numerous "Tugai" on the Sir.

arrow, which struck the Khán in the left shoulder. The collar-bone was broken, and passing under his left shoulder blade the arrow reached his right shoulder blade. [In this state the Khán tried to overtake Maksud Ali], but in spite of his efforts, his hand would not wield the sword, and his enemy got away in safety. The Khán then turned back [from the pursuit]. His wound proved very serious, and during two years he was deprived of the use of his right eye and his right arm.

Later in the day Maksud Ali fell into the hands of one of the Khán's men, who thought to himself: if I bring him alive to the Khán, that he may put him to death with his own hands, he will be more grateful to me [than if I bring him dead]. So he took him alive before the Khán. But the Khán, assuming a cheerful air, called to him and said: "I am glad you have fallen into my hands. I was sorry [for what had happened]." And although he had only one garment by him, he gave it him, together with a present of some horses, and kept him in Moghulistán to the end of his days, always looking on him with the eye of favour.

The Khán's generosity was quite unbounded. Other examples will be given in their proper places. In short, after being wounded and enduring great hardships, he joined his brother Sultán Khalil Sultán. This latter, after the death of his father, had fled from Mansur Khán into Moghulistán, and had joined the Kirghiz, who are the "wild lions" of that country. They made him their chief. He remained some time with his brother, but finally war broke out between them on the one hand, and Sultán Mahmud Khán, in alliance with Mansur Khán, on the other, which led to victories and defeats, struggles and conflicts, and great and wonderful battles. In those fights such wounds were inflicted, that no reasonable person would consider them capable of being cured. But the details are not worth describing. These hostilities continued from 910 to 914, when Sultán Mahmud Khán, being hard pressed by his nephews and the people of Moghulistán, went over to Sháhi Beg Khán (as has been related). Mansur Khán then attacked his two brothers, Sultán Said Khán and Sultán Khalil Sultán, who had remained in Moghulistán. They, for their part, met him in the open field at Almátu,[1] one of the most celebrated places in Moghulistán, when after a hard fought battle the Sultáns were worsted.

Sultán Khalil Sultán, all his prospects of success in Moghulistán being shattered, followed his uncle [Mahmud], in the hope that

[1] This place stood on a southern tributary of the river Ili. The name, though usually written *Almaty*, is still in use for the modern Russian fort and town of *Vierny*, which was built in 1854, on the banks of a small river, called by the Kirghiz *Almatu*. The name is derived, Mr. Schuyler says, from the abundance of apples (in Turki, *alma*) which grow in the neighbourhood. (Bretschneider, ii., p. 33; Schuyler, ii., p. 145.)

Sháhi Beg Khán had received the latter kindly; and when he reached Akhsi, Jáni Beg Khán having seized [him] delivered him to my uncle Sayyid Muhammad Mirzá, Sultán Ali Mirzá Begjik and Tubra Tiághuth, [with the order] that he should be drowned in the river. They, being obliged to obey this order, drowned the unfortunate Sultán in the river of Akhsi. It will be mentioned later, how the Khán, a short time after this event, heaped favours and patronage upon those men whose brother he had murdered.

When the Khán escaped from the field of battle, he was accompanied by about fifty men with their cattle and followers, all in great want. Broken and discomfited, they came from Almátu to Dulán (about fifteen days' march at a medium pace). On arriving there, they began to grow less afraid of the enemy. That same day, they came across a man whom they seized and interrogated. He informed them that at Uruk, which was distant about three days' march, at an even pace, there was encamped a body of the tribe of Bahrin, who intended to go to Káshghar and seek the protection of Mirzá Abá Bakr. "And I," he added, "have fled, and am on my way to join the Kirghiz." They then all sat down [and held a consultation]. Some suggested that the Khán should himself go and mix with that tribe: haply by that means he would obtain a little help from them. And Khwája Ali Bahádur, in particular, urged this plan (for he was himself of the tribe of Bahrin), and he was, moreover, a bold and daring man, and an unrivalled archer. When the Khán fled from Samarkand and entered the service of his noble uncle Sultán Mahmud Khán, Khwája Ali Bahádur was in Yatikand, in the service of one of the officers of Sultán Mahmud Khán. When the Khán arrived, he entered [his uncle's] service with the greatest eagerness. On the occasion of the Khán's flight, when he received the arrow-wound from Maksud Ali, the musician, Khwája Ali Bahádur, had displayed great valour in the contest, and had shown proofs of singular daring, which did not escape the notice of the Khán, who, from that day forward, bestowed on him his special protection and favour. In the battles that took place in Moghulistán, he usually distinguished himself by his heroic acts. But besides his bravery and prowess, he was also noted for his sagacity, intelligence, and perception; wherefore at that time most [of the Khán's] affairs were submitted to him for decision.

Now as he was strongly in favour of the proposed plan, [while all the rest objected to it], Khwája Ali represented that if the Khán went with a body of men, [the Bahrin] would be frightened, and think he had come to attack them. It was impossible to drive these ridiculous ideas out of their minds, which had become a prey to the whispering of devils; and it seemed that a new cause of dissension and violence would arise. [The Khwája] thought the wisest plan was that he, in preference to any of the other followers, should be selected to accompany the Khán. He suggested that they should remain where they were for five days, to see if they would approve of his going. If, thus, their minds could be pacified and their vain fears and foolish ideas be changed to good faith and confidence—well and good. "If not," said he, "let us all go, as quickly as possible, and make common cause with [the Bahrín]."[1]

This suggestion was approved, and the Khán and Khwája Ali set out together. They made a three days' journey, passing only one night on the road, and arrived at their destination at breakfast time.

When these dastardly men heard of their arrival, they came with unbounded impudence before him, not observing any of those marks of respect which are customary among the Moghuls. Then Khwája Ali addressing them said: "All adventurous persons who have obtained their desires, have watched for a favourable opportunity to seize with both hands the skirts of men of power." While his words were yet unfinished, they cried out: "Down with this babbler of idle words! What use has a Khán for a hundred households? We have nothing to offer him!" So saying they drove the Khán back to his friends, and seized Khwája Ali; they took away the led horse of the Khán, which he was holding, and threw its bridle towards the Khán. On seizing Khwája Ali, they carried him off to their tents.

The Khán, in alarm for his life, fled back with all speed, fearing lest they might take him and deliver him into the hands of Abá Bakr. Being terrified at this idea, he hastened to rejoin his men, looking round him on all sides as he went [to see whether he was being pursued].

Once, when the Khán was relating this story, I asked him: "Did you not dread [the thought of] solitude and desolation?" He replied: "Not so very much, for I had once before been left alone in Moghulistán, and had spent some days in solitude, in the same way, but afterwards joined my people again."

When he had gone a short way, he perceived something black in the distance; whereupon he withdrew to a secluded spot and, fastening his led horse there, stood waiting in ambush. He soon discovered that it was a man, and waited till he came near; then, placing an arrow [in readiness] in his bow, he leapt out of his ambush upon the new-comer, who had no time to get away, but threw himself in terror from his horse. The Khán then recognised that this man was the slave who had fled to the Kirghiz from his own party, who had been captured at Dulán, and had given in-

[1] The texts here are very confused, and the meaning of the whole paragraph (beginning with the words: "Now as he was strongly . . .") is in some degree uncertain. Some passages of it are not contained in the Turki MS.—R.

formation of [the presence of] those dastardly people [the Bahrin]. He, on his part, recognised the Khán, and kissed his stirrup.

The Khán asked him for news of his men, and where they were now encamped. The man replied: "When you went away with Khwája Ali Bahádur, a dispute arose among your men. It came about in this way. Somebody said: 'Last night I happened to be near the Khán's tent, when I heard Khwája Ali Bahádur say to the Khán: Our people are in a very broken condition [and there is nothing to be done with them]; they have hardly anything left; but our opponents have cattle and property in abundance, because every one of [the Khán's] dependants is either a Mir or a Mirzáda, and wishes to have power and precedence over others, which they cannot possibly obtain. Moreover, we cannot attain any object or carry out any scheme by means of such people. It will be best for us, therefore, for the reasons I have given, to separate from these men and to go and join the other side. Let these people go wherever they choose, while we avail ourselves in every possible way of the services of our opponents. And with this plan the Khán will be greatly pleased. [I tell you] the Khán does not intend to return.'

"At these words the people became very despondent and grieved; and each one, forming whatever plan seemed best to himself, they split up into factions. One party under the leadership of Uchku Muhammad Mirzá, Sháh Mirák and Zikul Bahádur, set out for Turfán, the capital of Mansur Khán. Another division under Kará Kulák, took the road to Andiján, in the hope that the Kháns who had preceeded them had been well received by Sháhi Beg Khán. And a third division, under the direction of Khush Gildi Kukildásh and Aziz Birdi Aghá, resolved to go to the court of Mirzá Abá Bakr in Káshghar. Thus did they form themselves into different parties."

The Khán used always to say: "When I learnt these facts, I was filled with amazement and alarm. Dismay took possession of my mind. I asked him how many days ago this had happened; he replied that on the particular day he had left them, the discussion had taken place, and they had separated.

"I then dismounted, and for a while remained buried in thought. At length I resolved to leave my horse in the impenetrable jungles of Nárin, and myself to lie in ambush for antelopes; and when I had killed them, to eat their flesh and to clothe myself with their skins; thus I would spend several years, until I should see how events might fall out.

"With this intention, having withdrawn my led horse to one side, I set out on my road."

[It must be understood that] it is a custom among the Moghuls, for the bravest of their youth to spend a long time alone, either in the deserts, the mountains or the forests, at a distance of one or two months' journey from any of their fellow creatures, and to feed and clothe themselves with the flesh and skins of antelopes. Such persons they esteem as brave and manly; and it is, in fact, a very difficult and dangerous mode of life.

[The Khán] having resolved upon this strange and perilous adventure, gave the slave his liberty, and set out on his own design. He spent the night in what he considered a suitable spot, and on the morrow again started on his road. But first of all he surveyed the country, in accordance with the Moghul practice of circumspection and caution. For it is their custom, in the morning, to examine carefully the road by which they have just come, and also to reconnoitre that by which they intend to travel the same day; the travellers having ascended a piece of rising ground, and having carefully inspected both the roads, then give some fodder to their horses, which have been tethered all night. The purpose of this vigilance which they practise is, that if anybody should happen to be following them, and should have come on during the night, he would be seen, and could be guarded against. When the horses have grazed long enough, and no one is visible in either direction, the road is again taken at midday, and the journey continued till midnight, so that no one may discover the traveller or his nightly resting-place. Such is the cautious practice of the Moghuls.

The Khán, looking round carefully on all sides, after a short time descried something black on the road by which he had come the day before, and began to fear lest those tribesmen, regretting that they had let him go, were come in pursuit of him. But he presently saw that it was only one person, and that there was no one behind him, as far as he could see. Then, as was his practice, he placed himself in ambush. He noticed that this man was ever and again uttering cries, as if calling for somebody. And as he came nearer [the Khán] recognised his voice as that of Khwájá Ali Bahádur. He rushed out to meet him, and the Khwája, also recognising the Khán, dismounted, and they both began to weep as they met in affectionate embrace.

One can imagine the extent of the Khán's joy at this meeting. Having made an end of weeping, [the Khán] asked the Khwája where he had been and what had befallen him. The Khwája replied: "They carried me off and kept my horse, and placed me in the house of one of my acquaintances. After a while a decrepit and frail old woman, who claimed a blood relationship with me, came to me secretly and began to heap reproaches on my head, saying: 'Some have been known to serve a Khán yet unborn, or an Amir still in his cradle, and to have reaped their reward; yet you, with your lack of zeal, have deserted a great

Khán, who is worthy of a throne and a crown, and in your sluggishness have debased yourself. Rise up: if you have not a horse, I have left mine tied up in such and such a place: take it and go!' Then my old enthusiasm, which seemed to have died within me, revived: I hastened out and went to the spot she had indicated, found the horse, and here I am."

The Khán, having bestowed thanks and praises on him, said: "When I found myself alone, I resolved upon the following plan" (and the Khán proceeded to relate to him, from beginning to end, what has been told above). Khwája Ali Bahádur replied: "Peace on you! It was a most excellent resolve for a brave man like yourself, under existing circumstances. And it is all the better that it should have been so. But now it is possible to proceed with greater comfort and ease. However, even if we do spend a few years in this way, we must get news of the world whenever we can; for the wheel of the spheres does not always turn in the same groove, and we must be on the look out for any opportunity that may arise to again obtain the control of affairs. We must also be bold."

The two then set out with strong hearts and cheerful spirits, riding bridle to bridle. On the following day they noticed in front of them some black objects: and the same care and precautions were observed as on the other occasion. As the objects approached, they recognised the two brothers of Khwája Ali Bahádur, Tika and Ali Mirák, and two of his sons-in-law, Asil Pulád and Buzana [each one accompanied by his servant].

After this meeting, the Khán's position was as sovereignty compared with that of the day before. The new-comers were then asked their story. They related what has been mentioned above, and added: "Khush Gildi and Aziz Birdi, who had determined to go to Káshghar, separated from us yesterday." With these two came Sukár and some of the Káluchi (who were relatives of a certain woman of the name of Makhtum, with whom, during the time of the great disturbances in Moghulistán, the Khán had contracted a marriage), and they brought with them several horses from the royal stables.

Having announced this news, the whole party set out in pursuit without delay, and came upon the fugitives towards the end of the night; when these heard the sound of the hoofs of the approaching horses, they were filled with dismay and alarm. The Khán and his companions called out to each one by name, and they, recognising his voice and that of the others, were filled with joy. They came, running, to the stirrup of his Excellency the Khan and, kissing his feet, gave vent to expressions of thankfulness.

The Khán, being rejoined by Khwája Ali, was relieved of the distress of solitude, but now, on falling in with Tika and his party, he had become a veritable king, compared with his former position. When, under the guidance of these men, they had rejoined the party who had separated from them, the Khán was overjoyed at the prospect of a meeting with a slave, who was his wife. All were delighted at coming together again, and hoped that that night they would enjoy a refreshing sleep. The Khán, in the same hope, had already taken off his boots and coat, when Aziz Birdi Aghá came and persuaded him to put them on again. Although it was apparently a trouble to do so, it was at least a fitting precaution, so he consented, in order to quiet Aziz Birdi, and with one boot off [and one boot on] he slumbered peacefully on the breast of his wife. For he had taken no rest for several nights and days, and was exceedingly fatigued from rough travelling and watchful nights. The full enjoyment of sleep had not yet come to him, when he heard a war cry [*suran*] and the sound of giving and taking of blows. Before the Khán could jump out of bed, he saw by the light of the burning camp that the enemy were upon them, and were dealing out blows to right and left. He had just time to gird on his quiver, when Khwája Ali arrived. They rushed together, from the blazing camp into the darkness, and began to shower down arrows upon the enemy who were doing their work in the light, and in the same way, the men from the camp came out on all sides into the darkness, and began to discharge their arrows. The enemy, who were all mounted, then withdrew from the light, and the Khán's men, who were on foot, shot at them from different ambuscades. On account of the darkness it was not possible to judge of the great numbers of the one side or the small numbers of the other. Some of the men, in imitation of the Khán, were engaged in discharging arrows, while the rest had gone back to secure the horses.

As a fact, this hostile band was part of an army which Mirzá Abá Bakr had sent to Moghulistán, with orders to seize and treat, in the worst possible way, any one who might be found in the deserts of Moghulistán. The continual raids of these followers of Mirzá Abá Bakr caused great distress in Moghulistán, and threw the Moghuls and Kirghiz into disorder. [The assailants] who were a division of the force spoken of, had come on at the time of afternoon prayer, and when they had seen the Khán's party arrive and halt, they had crept into concealment till late in the night. They then seized all the horses, which had been turned out to graze, and when darkness was nearly over they made their night attack. There were no horses left in the camp[1] except a few fat animals, which had been retained for purposes of war. These were saddled, and mounted by the men, and some of the

1 The Turki text has, in place of "in the camp"—"among the Khan's suite." —R.

women of the Khán's haram; while two or three other women were sent off by their husbands, who found horses for them. The Khán's horse was saddled and brought to him. When day dawned all were in the greatest straits. Moreover, except for the two or three women already mentioned, all the wives and children of our party had fallen into the enemy's hands, and there was no time to take leave or bid farewell. The scar of disappointment was marked upon their foreheads, and they never saw each other more. But those who fled, drove their wives and men and horses before them. The Khán and all those who had any courage and strength, followed after them. The cursed enemy came close on their heels, and pursued them with the greatest ardour, being, moreover, supplied with changes of horses.

Whenever the enemy approached, the Khán with a few men, turned round and plied them with arrows, and kept them at bay until his own party had got well on, when he again let loose the reins of flight till he overtook them. Thus did they fly fighting; and shot their arrows with their faces towards their friends and their backs to their enemies. This state of affairs continued till the hour of the "prayer of sleep." The night attack took place in the desert plains [*chulgái*] of Utluk, which are called Ankghun Archa, and by the time of the "prayer of sleep" they had reached Kumala Káchur,[1] which represents a distance of five days' journey at a medium pace. The feeble ones, both women and men, at the time of flight and distress, were concealed in the glens and forests, while the rest hid themselves wherever they thought most safe.

With the exception of the Khán's wife and two or three other women, and a few men who had remained, most of these people were captured; only a few escaped. When evening-prayer time came, fear of the enemy left them but little peace of mind. They were all scattered, every one hiding in the jungle of Kumala Káchur; and from the excess of their terror, some of those whose horses were tired out, left them and crept into the forest on foot.

When day dawned, they all came out onto an elevation, and still concealing themselves, looked carefully round. They could see no trace of the enemy. They waited patiently till midday, when wherever they happened to be, they called out, and by means of their cries were able to find one another; [they also found] those whom they had sent into the glens, and of whose fate they

[1] The spelling of these names is very uncertain; but in whatever form, I can find no trace of them, even on Severtsoff's detailed map of Zungaria, &c. They were probably mere local names of uninhabited and unimportant spots; though it is possible that "*Ankghun Archa*" may have some connection with the "*On Archa* marked on modern maps, seeing that this place stands on a river (a right tributary of the upper Narin—just east of the Son Kul) called the *Ottuk*—of which perhaps *Utluk* may be a mis-rendering. The author, however, gives no indication of the quarter of Moghulistan where these adventures took place.

were till then ignorant, not knowing whether they had been captured or not.

Returning, they looked to see what had become of these people. They found that, excepting the Khán's wife [haram] and one or two other persons, all had been discovered and carried off captive. They remained where they were during that day, for they had not sufficient strength left to proceed. Moreover, they did not know whither they could go. They discussed the matter in all its aspects: every one made suggestions, and held his own views upon the matter; but all their plans were quite impracticable. One proposition was that they should live in the forests, and banish from their thoughts all desire for civilisation. This, however, was not considered to be feasible, as it was impossible to exist in the forests without the [necessary] weapons, etc. After seeking everywhere, they found that all their quivers were empty. At last they found one arrow in the Khán's quiver: in the rest there were none left but *tir-i-gaz*.[1] [And with only one arrow there was certainly nothing to be achieved, so perforce this idea must be banished from their minds. Another proposal was that] they should enter the Dasht-i-Kipchák, which at that time was an asylum and refuge of the Moghul Kháns. But this again was impossible, on account of their want of arrows [and other weapons. A third suggestion was that they should go to Káshghar. But they came to the conclusion that] to go to Káshghar was as good as to walk, living, into a grave.

With Mansur Khán it was but yesterday that they had fought a battle, and all their sufferings and calamities were due to him. At length they decided upon going to Andiján; for it was possible that Sháhi Beg Khán had given Sultán Mahmud Khán a favourable reception.

The Khán repeatedly related these details to me, and he used to add: "Those who advised our going to the country of Sháhi Beg Khán, did so out of their ignorance of his true character. However strongly those who knew him protested, and pointed out the absurdity and danger of the scheme, which the others had made appear so plausible, they would not be dissuaded. I, for my part, showed my objections and disapproval in a hundred ways; for had I not been a whole year with Sháhi Beg Khán? I well knew and understood his temperament, the ways of his Sultáns, and the intentions of his Amirs. I knew very well that he would ill-treat us, which he did, but when I said this to these ignorant men, they replied: 'Then what is to be done? All our proposals are considered impracticable or impossible! [But in going to Sháhi Beg Khán] there is some hope of safety. If anything else suggests itself to your enlightened mind, tell us of it: for in every matter

[1] Probably arrows of one *gaz* in length.

we are willing to follow and obey you, mind and body.' Much as I thought the matter over, I was unable to find a solution of the difficulty, or offer any other suggestion; and finally I, with my eyes open, and in spite of what I knew, became myself a promoter of that very plan for which I had so severely reproved my men. For, in truth, there was no choice left. Knowingly and deliberately I rushed upon calamity!

"On the morrow, having prepared myself for death and my heart for martyrdom, I set out to pay homage to Jáni Beg Sultán, which was the first step to entering the service of Sháhi Beg Khán. And there was no great difference between that stage[1] and the bottom of the tomb."

These events took place in the year 914,[2] just two months after the murder of Sultán Mahmud Khán, and one month before Sultán Khalil Sultán was drowned in the ocean of mercy, all of which has been mentioned above. Sultán Khalil Sultán was the full brother of the Khán.

At this date Bábar Pádisháh was established on the throne of Kábul, and his power was nearly absolute.

Having reached this point in the Khán's story, it is necessary for the better understanding of the history, that I should now revert to the stories of my father and Bábar Pádisháh.

CHAPTER IX.

FLIGHT OF MY FATHER MUHAMMAD HUSAIN KURKÁN FROM BEFORE SHÁHI BEG KHÁN INTO KHORÁSÁN; WITH SOME INCIDENTAL BIOGRAPHICAL NOTICES.

It has been related above, how Kunduz submitted without resistance, on the advent of the victorious army of Mahmud Sultán; also how I, after being confined in prison by Khusrau Sháh for a year, obtained my release, went and joined my father, and together with all the members of my family, proceeded to Shahr-i-Sabz, which Sháhi Beg Khán had given to my father [together with its dependencies].

In the beginning of Sagittarius, Sháhi Beg Khán marched on Khwárizm.

All the heads of the Moghuls, whether Sultáns or Amirs,

[1] Instead of the words "that stage," the Turki MS. has:—"the service of Jani Beg Sultán."—R.

[2] 1508-9 A.D.

together with their train, were dwelling among the Uzbegs, and fear and apprehension continually occupied their hearts.

In the meanwhile, Mahmud Sultán, who had always been a defender of the Moghuls, died in Kunduz, whereat all the Moghuls, and especially my father, were much afflicted and saddened. For Mahmud Sultán had borne him such love, and had bestowed so much kindness on him, that if ever one of Sháhi Beg Khán's nobles wrote a letter of cruelty or violence upon the tablet of the imagination concerning my father, he would draw a line through it with the pen of his protection; or else would erase this writing from the tablet of the rancorous heart of the evil-minded man, with the penknife of punishment. In fact, he recognised it as his duty to side with my father in all things. His death was a source of great uneasiness to the Moghuls in general, and to my father in particular. But Sháhi Beg Khán said privately to Amir Ján Vafá, who was an intimate friend of my father, that he would on no account whatever leave Khwárizm until he had reduced it, and it was clear that the siege[1] would be a very protracted one:—"There are, at the present moment, about 30,000 Moghuls among our Uzbegs. So long as any of the Moghul chiefs remain, these men will continue to serve them, and never enter our service. If a favourable occasion presents itself, they will do to us that which we did to them. The first among them is Muhammad Husain Kurkán; I think of him all day, but feel that to kill him would be like killing one of the Kháns—an act that would obliterate all the kindnesses I have ever shown the Kháns. Hence, it will be best for you to announce to him my intention, so that he may rise up with all speed and escape while he has yet a foot [to walk upon], and no longer tempt his fate. For after his departure, I must make all the other Moghul Amirs feel the blood-drinking scimitar."

Amir Ján Vafá immediately sent a messenger, who reached my father at the hour of midday prayer, and by the time of afternoon prayer my father, having chosen me from among his children to accompany him, together with sixteen of his servants, fled towards Khorásán. This event remains fixed in my mind like a dream or a fantasy.

In those days Sultán Said Khán was also in Samarkand. Three days after [our flight] he fled to Moghulistán; but this story has been told above.

Of those children whom my father left behind him in Shahr-i-Sabz, the eldest was Habiba Sultán Khánish; Sháhi Beg Khán kept her in his haram at Táshkand, where he also kept Aisha Sultán Khánim, the daughter of Sultán Mahmud Khán, and who

[1] The author appears to mean the siege of Khwarizm, or Khiva; but Erskine mentions that Shahi Beg was besieging Kelat (I presume Kelat-i-Ghilzai) at the time. (See *Hist.* i., p. 257.)

is nowadays better known as Moghul Khánim. After a while he married her, with various ceremonies, to Abdullah Khán, son of Mahmud Sultán.

[2.] Next in age was Ganhar Shah Begum, whom Amir Ján Vafá obtained, in marriage, for his own son Amir Yár, in return for having carried the message to my father.

[3.] I come next. I accompanied my father.

[4.] Another was Muhammad Sháh, whom one of my father's relations had taken after my father into Khorásán.

[5.] The youngest of all was Abdulláh Mirza, who has been mentioned above, as having accompanied his mother, Sultánim Begum. I shall tell his life in these pages.

In short, we left Shahr-i-Sabz, and, passing one night on the road, reached, at the close of [the second] day, the banks of the River Amuya; the cold was very severe and we only succeeded in crossing with great difficulty; without entering Balkh, we went on to Khorásán.

Those were the last days of the life and reign of Mirzá Sultán Husain, who was a grandson of Mirzá Jahángir,[1] son of Amir Timur. None of his ancestors, as far back as Amir Timur, had attained to sovereignty. Mirzá Sultán Husain, however, had, after many years of struggles and hardships, won Khorásán at the point of the sword, and during forty-eight years, while firmly established on the throne of Herat, he governed the four quarters of Khorásán. He encouraged all the arts and crafts of the world to such a degree that in every separate profession he produced an unsurpassed master.

Having reached this point, I meditated and felt that I ought to write something concerning these lords of revelation and masters of manifestation, who lived at this time. And though I did not, with my lack of capacity, seem fit for the task, yet strange to say, I could not see my way to omit recording one or two circumstances in relation to these men. In any case I will make a beginning, in the hope that, with the aid of existing memoirs [*tazkira*], which

[1] Our author should have said that Sultan Husain Mirza (Baikara) was great-grandson of Omar Shaikh, son of Amir Timur—not the grandson of Jahangir. Sultan Husain's father was Mansur Mirza, his grandfather Baikara Mirza, son of Omar Shaikh. He succeeded Sultan Abu Said on the throne of Khorásán in A.H. 878, and reigned till his death in 912 (1474 to 1507); but previous to 878 he had been ruler in Mázandarán and Gurgán. He is said, by Erskine, to have been a man of great power and reputation, and beyond comparison the most distinguished of the Princes of the house of Timur, at that time living. The capital of Khorásán was then at Heri, or Herat, which, for about half a century, was celebrated, "not merely for the splendour and dignity of its Court, the architectural beauty of its mosques, tombs, colleges, and palaces, but as being the resort of the greatest divines, philosophers, poets, and historians of the age." Sultan Husain, besides being eminent as a ruler, was also well known as a poet and a writer of fiction—under the name of Husaini. (See S. Lane Poole, *Muhamd. Dynasties*, table facing p. 268. Erskine, *Baber*, pp. lvi. and 125; *History* i., p. 77; Beale, *Orient. Biographies*.)

shall supplement the deficiencies of my humble reed, it may prove worthy of the perusal of the clear-sighted.

* * * * * * *

As it does not lie in my power to write a separate book in memory of these men, I have in this Epitome only devoted a few lines to some of them, in order to satisfy my mind and to calm my inner man. [Quatrain]. . . .[1]

Shaikh Ul Islám, the Light of Religion, Mauláná Abdur Rahmán Jámi.

He was far the greatest and most excellent and learned of all the saints and spiritual guides of the time of Mirzá Sultán Husain.

He is much too great to stand in need of any mention from my humble pen; so I will simply trace his discipleship. He was a disciple of Mauláná Sad-ud-Din Káshghari, disciple of Mauláná Nizam-ud-Din Khámushi, disciple of Khwájá Alá-ud-Din Attár, disciple of His Holiness the Kibla of the Pious, Khwájá Bahá 'ul Hakk va ud-Din, generally known as Khwájá Nakshband.

Mauláná Sad-ud-Din Káshghari.

He belonged to one of the most noble families in the country of Káshghar, and his race had produced Ulamás, and many pious and devout men and saints. Among whom was Shaikh Habib, the disciple of Shaikh Sayyid Kárdgar, disciple of Shaikh Mohibb Mujarrad.[2]

Amir Sayyid Ahmad, my great-great-grandfather, placed his son Mir Sayyid Ali in the service of Shaikh Habib, when he was very young.

* * * * * * *

Mauláná Nizám-ud-Din Khámush.

I have heard from a certain distinguished person that [even] before Mauláná Nizám-ud-Din became a disciple of Khwájá Alá-ud-Din he was an exceedingly pious and chaste man. He used to sit in the mosque of the Lawyers, and was an admirer of the spirituality of the Shaikh.

* * * * * * *

[1] Here follow some notices of saints, learned men, poets, singers and others, the bulk of which are omitted, as the persons they treat of have no connection with the history. They are all, Dr. Rieu informs me, to be found in other books; indeed, the author acknowledges that he has taken them chiefly from "existing memoirs," and has written them for his own satisfaction. As, however, three of the saints mentioned are persons of importance, and appear to have played some part in the history of the times, the brief notices of their lives have been translated, though the anecdotes regarding them have been left out; these last are not only irrelevant, but childish.

[2] The name *Kárdgar* stands in the Turki MS. *Kázargar;* while for *Mujarrad* may perhaps be read *Mujtabi*—R.

He performed many miracles, as is related in the *Nafahát ul 'uns.*

* * * * * * *

Return from the Digression.

My father arrived in Khorásán at the time when its pomp and splendour and learning were at their highest, and the fame of Herat and its people was spread over the world.

At that time the sons of Mirzá Sultán Husain, who had revolted against their illustrious father, had repented and had been allowed to kiss his feet, and they now surrounded the Mirzá's throne with honour and respect.

When my father arrived in Herat, the people came out to receive him, and attended his passage with honour. They then conducted him to a magnificent residence—worthy of his rank—which they had made ready for him.

[When my father went to pay his respects to Mirzá Sultán Husain], Mir Muhammad Baranduk Barlás, who had been one of the Amirs of Sháh Rukh and who, at that time, in respect of age, rank, understanding, intelligence, and knowledge of the laws and customs, had not his equal among the whole of the Chaghatái *Ulus*, came and spoke to my father about kneeling at the audience. My father agreed to his proposals. The Mirzá also showed my father great honour, and placed him above all his children, even above his son Bádi-uz-Zamán, who was the eldest and most respected of the Mirzá's sons. In this city, which might have been compared to Paradise, my father commanded the utmost respect and distinction, and enjoyed every possible luxury.

The Mirzá, for his personal satisfaction, had determined on an alliance between one of his granddaughters and my father. The latter did not approve of this connection, because the Mirzá was very old and afflicted with paralysis and gout, and the power of his children would not be such that, when they succeeded their father, they would be able to cope with Sháhi Beg Khán. Nevertheless, as it had been arranged, he contracted the marriage.

In the meanwhile, Sháh Begum, as has been mentioned above, went from Moghulistán to Samarkand with a petition for Sháhi Beg Khán. The latter was intent on the conquest of Khwárizm, which was a dependency of Mirzá Sultán Husain. It was on Sháhi Beg Khán's warning that my father had fled to Khorásán, and Sultán Said Khán had taken refuge in Moghulistán. Most of the Moghul chiefs had gone to the kingdom of the next world, while some had been thrown into confinement. Sháh Begum was banished and sent to Khorásán. The rest of the Moghuls accompanied the expedition into Khwárizm.

In enumerating the names of the children of Yunus Khán, I

mentioned that the eldest was Mihr Nigár Khánim, who married Sultán Ahmad Mirzá, king of Samarkand. When Sháhi Beg Khán seized and put to death Sultán Ali Mirzá and subdued Samarkand, he married Mihr Nigár Khánim. When he besieged Bábar Pádisháh in that city, for the last time, and compelled him to capitulate, he demanded Khánzáda Begum. Bábar Pádisháh gave up Khánzáda Begum in exchange for his own life, and escaped, as has been mentioned. Now as Mihr Nigár Khánim was maternal aunt to Khánzáda Begum, and as it was unlawful for both to be wedded to the same man, he divorced Mihr Nigár Khánim, and married Khánzáda Begum. The Khánim had dwelt in Samarkand. When Sháh Begum was sent to Khorásán, the Khánim accompanied her mother-in-law. My father had a maternal aunt, who had remained in Shahr-i-Sabz, whither many of her connections had fled: she, having taken my brother Muhammad Sháh with her, came with the Begum and the Khánim to Khorásán.

Before the arrival of this party, my father resolved to make the Pilgrimage of the Hijáz, but when they joined him he gave up this intention, thinking that they would be in danger if left alone in a strange land. He then decided to remove them to Kábul, where Bábar Pádisháh was, as has been related. Sháh Begum was the stepmother of the Emperor's mother; Mihr Nigár Khánim was his maternal aunt.

In short, having, with this intention, obtained leave to depart from Mirzá Sultán Husain, they set out for Kábul. A few days before they reached Kábul the mother of Bábar Pádisháh, Kutluk Nigár Khánim, died, and her death was a great misfortune to all. In spite of his mourning, Bábar Pádisháh came out to receive them, and gave the party a warm welcome, accompanied by every honour that he was able to show them. Here they spent some time in the greatest ease and comfort.

Soon after this, came news of the death of Mirzá Sultán Husain. In the natural order of things, and in conformity with recognised custom and practice, Mirzá Bádi-uz-Zamán should have succeeded his father on the throne. But Khadija Begum, one of the late Sultán's wives, who was at the head of a factious party, succeeded in getting Muzaffar Husain Mirzá, who was her own son, to share the government with Mirzá Bádi-uz-Zamán. This she did, in spite of the objections of the wise men of the time [who were at last compelled to consent to the unstable arrangement] which was in consequence carried out.

In the meantime, Jahángir Mirzá, who was in Ghazni, being discontented with the narrow limits of his territories, marched for Khorásán. [At the same time] he sent a petition to the Emperor, saying: "Sultán Husain Mirzá has lately departed this life. It has occurred to me that, at this crisis, I should go and offer my help and alliance to his sons. Probably I may be able to help them in some way." When this petition reached Bábar Pádisháh, he at once set out, with the intention that if he fell in with Jahángir Mirzá on the road, he would turn him back, or if not, would pursue his brother into Khorásán. [In either case] he would not be long in ascertaining what schemes Mirzá Jahángir had in his mind. As soon as the Emperor had resolved on this plan, he came to my father's house, and asked him to undertake the management of Kábul and its dependencies. My father would not accept the invitation, but said, in excuse: "When in Khorásán, I resolved to undertake the Pilgrimage; if I were to bind myself to the measure you propose, my resolution would be to no purpose. Let this business be entrusted to one of your great Amirs, and I will render him assistance to the utmost extent of my ability." The Emperor then sent for Nizám-ud-Din Ali Khalifa Mauláná Bábá Bishághari, Amir Ahmad Kásim Kuhbur,[1] and one or two other of his [trustworthy] chiefs, and after complimenting [my father], said to him: "I am about to start for Khorásán, having the most perfect reliance on you. These Amirs will conduct the different affairs of the State under your general supervision." Having thus spoken, and after further compliments, he set out for Khorásán.

CHAPTER X.

BÁBAR PÁDISHÁH'S EXPEDITION INTO KHORÁSÁN. TROUBLES AND CONTENTIONS IN KÁBUL.

After the Emperor's departure for Khorásán, up till the middle of the winter, all was order and quiet in Kábul. He, however, stayed away a long while, and various reports began to circulate; the main roads were also blocked by the Hazára highwaymen.

In the list, given above, of the children of Yunus Khán, it was stated that he had five daughters and two sons.

By his wife, Isán Daulat Begum, he had three daughters: [1.] Mihr Nigár Khánim, who has been already mentioned as being at this time in Kábul; having accompanied Sháh Begum from Samarkand. [2.] Kutluk Nigár Khánim, the mother of the Emperor, who died just before the arrival of Sháh Begum, the Khánim and my father, in Kábul. [3.] My mother, who died during the interval of peace [*amáni*] in Táshkand, which has been mentioned.

[1] The Turki MS. has *Kuhi* in place of *Kuhbur*—R.

By Sháh Begum he had four children: [1] Sultán Mahmud Khán; [2] Sultán Ahmad Khán; [3] Sultán Nigár Khánim, who was the wife of Mirzá Sultán Mahmud (son of Mirzá Sultán Abu Said) and the mother of Mirzá Khán; and [4] Daulat Sultán Khánim, who was wife of Timur Sultán, son of Sháhi Beg Khán. All of these have been mentioned before. From this it will be seen that Sháh Begum was step-grandmother [1] to both the Emperor and myself; and [actual] grandmother to Mirzá Khán. After the defeat of the Kháns, when the Emperor went to the hill country of Hisár, he was there joined by Mirzá Khán, who accompanied him wherever he went. And the Emperor looked upon him as his own son; for, as has been explained, Mirzá Khán's father and mother were of the same family as the Emperor's father and mother.

On account of straitened circumstances [Mirzá Khán] did not accompany the Emperor on that expedition, but stayed behind in the service of his grandmother Sháh Begum. As various reports came in concerning the Emperor and the Mirzás of Khorásán, the motherly love of Sháh Begum began to burn in her heart, and she persuaded herself that the Emperor had fallen into the hands of the Mirzás of Khorásán. Also, on account of the enmity that existed between Sultán Husain Mirzá and Abu Said Mirzá, and the bloodshed which had resulted therefrom, [she thought] that the Emperor would never escape from their power. Moreover, reports which seemed to confirm this view were constantly arriving; and it was considered time to put Mirzá Khán upon the throne in the Emperor's place.

When this plan was suggested to my father, he would not hear of it. An altercation followed which led to much sorrow; and the distress of Sháh Begum gave offence to the Kháns. All this brought much trouble upon my father, who at last, being exasperated, said: "As you will not be warned by me, I will no longer be your adviser." Nevertheless, the Emperor's Amirs, who used to come daily out of the castle to wait on my father, continued to come, as was their wont. After one month's bickering and quarrelling, Sháh Begum had quite resolved to set Mirzá Khán up in the Emperor's place.[2] My father [then] said privately to the Amirs, that it was not necessary for them to come to him any more. When the Amirs re-entered the castle, my father went away to a place called Áb-Báran, which is a day's march from Kábul, and withdrew himself from public affairs. Sháh Begum and some Moghuls [then] read the *Khutba* in the name of Mirzá Khán, and did their utmost to seize the fort of Kábul; whereupon numerous

[1] The term used is *Mádar-i-Kalán-i-Sababi*—R.

[2] The whole of this paragraph is more or less obscure, and very badly arranged; but the sense is, I think, preserved in the translation. Erskine has made it nearly the same. (See *History* i., pp. 249–50.)

fights ensued. Sháh Begum sent a letter of entreaty to my father to return, and as entreaties and remonstrances were unlimited, my father could not choose but come. During twenty-four days they laid siege to the castle of Kábul; and in the course of these operations the Emperor himself arrived.[1]

CHAPTER XI.

BÁBAR PÁDISHÁH'S JOURNEY INTO KHORÁSÁN, AND HIS RETURN FROM KHORÁSÁN TO KÁBUL.

WHEN Bábar Pádisháh went in pursuit of Jahángir, he came upon him in the mountains of Hazára. After holding a consultation, it was determined that the wisest plan would be to proceed into Khorásán, as with some aid, the sons of Sultán Husain Mirzá might be enabled to withstand Sháhi Beg Khán. So with this object in view, they turned towards Khorásán, and, on their arrival, these two brothers were warmly welcomed by the people of Khorásán, while the two Mirzás, for their part, were overjoyed at their advent. But there existed no accord between these two Mirzás. In the first place, Bábar Pádisháh knew that they were not at one; he also knew that without unity they could effect nothing. Moreover, Jahángir Mirzá, from having indulged too freely in wine drinking, was suffering so severely from dysentery, [from a disease called] *mui*, and a burning fever, that it was generally reported that Khadija

[1] This episode has no doubt been slurred over by the author, in order to exculpate his father as far as possible, but there can be no question that the latter was guilty of a serious act of treachery towards Baber, and that he gave his countenance to the schemes of Shah Begum. Baber himself seems to have regarded Muhammad Husain Mirza as one of the chief movers in the plot, and evidently felt his ingratitude acutely, though, with characteristic generosity, he spared the Mirza's life, when the latter fell into his hands. In recording the event in his "Memoirs," Baber concludes the account of it thus: "Muhammad Husain Mirza had conducted himself in such a criminal and guilty way, and had been actively engaged in such mutinous and rebellious proceedings that, had he been cut in pieces or put to a painful death, he would only have met with his deserts. As we were in some degree of relationship to each other, he having sons and daughters by my mother's sister Khub Nigar Khánim, I took that circumstance into consideration and gave him his liberty, allowing him to set out for Khorásán. Yet this ungrateful thankless man, this coward, who had been treated by me with such lenity and whose life I had spared, entirely forgetful of this benefit, abused and scandalised my conduct to Shaibák Khan [Sháhi Beg Khan]. It was but a short time, however, before Shaibák Khan put him to death and thus sufficiently avenged me:—

[*Verses*]: "Deliver over him who injures you to Fate,
For Fate is a servant that will avenge your quarrel."

Begum (after her old fashion) had put poison in his wine. For these and other reasons, he took his leave and returned to Kábul.

On reaching the Hazára mountains, he learnt that Mirzá Khán and Muhammad Husain Mirzá were besieging Kábul. Leaving the heavy baggage with Mirzá Jahángir (who, being sick, was travelling in a litter) he advanced with all possible speed towards the passes of Hindu Kush, accompanied by a small body of men. [The passes] were covered with snow. They, however, crossed them with much difficulty, and advanced, by forced marches, upon Kábul. At dawn one day they made a rapid descent upon the town. Those who were outside the fort of Kábul, and had been attacking those within, crept into concealment on every side, while those who were within, rushed out and carried off, as plunder, all that fell in their way, both within and without [the walls]. The Emperor, in conformity with his affectionate nature, without ceremony, and without a sign of bitterness—nay, with the utmost cheerfulness and good-humour—came into the presence of his step-grandmother, who had withdrawn her affection from him, and set up her grandson as king in his stead. Sháh Begum was confounded and abashed [at his generous behaviour] and knew not what to say.

The Emperor, going down on his knees, embraced her with great affection, and said: "What right has one child to be vexed because the motherly bounty descends upon another? The mother's authority over her children is in all respects absolute." He added: "I have not slept all night, and have made a long journey." So saying, he laid his head on Sháh Begum's breast and tried to sleep; he acted thus in order to reassure the Begum. He had scarcely fallen asleep, when his maternal aunt, Mihr Nigár Khánim, entered. The Emperor leapt up and embraced his beloved aunt with every manifestation of affection. The Khánim said to him: "Your children, wives and household are longing to see you. I give thanks that I have been permitted to behold you once again. Rise up and go to your family in the castle. I too am going thither."

So he went to the castle, and on his arrival all the Amirs and people began to thank God for His mercy. They made the dust of the feet of that loving king, powder [*kohl*] for their eyes. Then the Khánim conducted Mirzá Khán and my father before the Emperor. As they approached, the Emperor came out to receive them. The Khánim then said: "Oh, soul of your mother! I have also brought my guilty grandson and your unfortunate brother to you. What have you to say to them?" and she pointed to my father. When the Emperor saw my father, he instantly came forward, with his wonted courtesy, and smiling, openly embraced him, made many kind inquiries and showed him marked affection. He then embraced Mirzá Khán in like manner, and displayed a hundred proofs of love and good feeling. He conducted the whole ceremony with the utmost gentleness of manner, bearing himself, in all his actions and words, in such a way that not a trace of constraint or artifice was to be seen in them. But however much the Emperor might try to wear away the rust of shame with the polish of mildness and humanity, he was unable to wipe out the dimness of ignominy which had covered the mirror of their hopes.

My father and Mirzá Khán obtained permission to go to Kandahár. The Emperor, by entreaty and unremitting attentions, detained Sháh Begum and the Khánim. When they reached Kandahár, Mirza Khán remained there, while my father proceeded in the direction of Faráh and Sistán, with the intention of carrying out that holy resolve which he had made while in Khorásán. On his arrival in the territory of Faráh, he heard of the conquest of Khorásán, by Sháhi Beg Khán, and the overthrow of the Chaghatái. The high roads and passes were in a dangerous state, being obstructed and even closed. Thus my father was prevented from executing his purpose. This happened in the year 912.[1]

CHAPTER XII.

BRIEF ACCOUNT OF BÁBAR PÁDISHÁH'S SOJOURN IN KÁBUL, AND A FEW STORIES CONNECTED THEREWITH.

It has been already related that the Emperor, in the year 909, conquered Kábul from Mukim, son of Zunnun Arghun. [On this expedition] he was accompanied by nearly 20,000 men of the army of Khusrau Sháh. Now as Kábul was unable to support so great a host, the Emperor resolved to invade Hindustán. But on that expedition, from ignorance of the roads, they frequently came to places where provisions were scarce, and most of their cattle perished. Although there was not a single battle in that campaign, yet the army suffered a severe reverse. On their return to Kábul, many of Khusrau Sháh's men deserted him. At this crisis Sháh Begum and my father arrived in Kábul, and the Emperor proceeded to Khorásán (as has been related above).

After we went to Kandahár, in consequence of all that had passed, the people were reduced to the most afflicting want and distress. In addition to this, Jahángir Mirzá, who was at that time the stay and support of the Emperor's government, died. After the occurrence of these events, he [the Emperor] wished to strengthen his power by whatever means were available, in order that he might be firmly and securely established in Kábul. To this end, he sent an envoy to Sháh Beg in Kandahár. Sháh Beg was the son of Zunnun Arghun, who was one of the greatest Amirs of Mirzá Sultán Husain, under whom he had, during thirty years, conducted the affairs of Kandahár and Zamindáwar. Although he was a brave and intelligent man, yet by denying himself everything, he amassed great wealth. He had gone in person to Khorásán to assist the Mirzás. When Sháhi Beg Khán attacked Herat, he alone went out to oppose the advance of the Uzbeg army, and in the engagement which ensued, he was slain. He was succeeded, in Kandahár, by his son Sháh Beg. [As has been stated] the Emperor sent an envoy to Sháh Beg, saying: "Since the children of Mirzá Sultán Husain have been extirpated, it is fitting that the gates of obedience and service should be opened, and at this time there is no one in the palace of our sovereignty, who is more worthy than yourself of occupying the highest post." But in spite of all the Emperor's assurances and promises, Sháh Beg refused; for he had higher views of dignity than that of entering into a state of dependence. To be brief, this refusal led to an outbreak of hostilities. The Emperor marched to Kandahár, in the neighbourhood of which town a battle was fought, and that a very bloody one. Finally victory declared for the Emperor; the dust of flight filled the eyes of Sháh Beg's men, and they were thrown into such confusion that they were unable to enter the fort of Kandahár. Thus, without baggage, they crept on towards Sui,[1] and his good fortune was changed to desolation. So much treasure fell into the Emperor's hands, that [the gold and jewels] and Sháhrukhi [2] were divided among the army by the shieldful.

Mirzá Khán, who had stayed in Kandahár, now joined the Emperor, who returned to Kábul laden with much spoil and treasure, having left Sultán Násir Mirzá, younger brother of Jahángir Mirzá, in charge of Kandahár.

On his return to Kábul [important] news came from Badakhshán.

[1] From the abridged MS. translation at the British Museum, Erskine appears to have read this name *Sivi*, in the text used by him. If that is the correct reading, probably *Sibi* is the place indicated. In our texts, it may read *Subi* as well as *Sui*. For Baber's account of these transactions, see *Memoirs*, pp. 224 *seq.*

[2] The *Sháhrukhi* was a coin reckoned by Erskine to be of the probable value of $9\frac{1}{2}$ or $9\frac{3}{4}$ pence, when the rupee was worth two shillings. (*History*, i. Append. E.) I infer that it derived its name from Shah-Rukh Mirza, fourth son of Timur, who reigned in Khorasan, etc., from 1405–1447, and that it was a silver coin, though Col. Malleson, in his *Life of Akbar*, calls it "a gold coin of Khorasan" (p. 53). The *Sháhrukhi* does not appear in Mr. S. Lane Poole's tables.

When the country of Khusrau Sháh [1] was annexed by the Uzbeg, some of the people of Badakhshán refused to submit, and on several occasions put the Uzbeg army to flight, wherefore every commander of 1000 men [*mir hazári*] attained the rank of Sardar, and placed the heads of the Uzbeg on their pikes.[2] Their leader was Zobir Rághi.[3]

Sháh Begum laid claim to Badakhshán, saying: "It has been our hereditary kingdom for 3000 years.[4] Though I, being a woman, cannot myself attain to the sovereignty, yet my grandson Mirzá Khán can hold it. Males descended from me and my children will certainly not be rejected." The Emperor assented, and Sháh Begum and Mirzá Khán departed for Badakhshán.[5] My brother Muhammad Sháh, who was in the service of the Begum, accompanied them. As they approached Badakhshán, Mirza Khán was sent forward to announce to Zobir Rághi the arrival of the Begum, and to explain her intentions.

No sooner had Mirzá Khán left them, than the army of Abá Bakr marching from Káshghar came upon them. All the men and the Begum, and all who were of the party, were seized and carried off [to Káshghar]. An account of Abá Bakr [6] will shortly follow.

Mirzá Khán [hearing of this event] hastened to Zobir Rághi. At first Zobir treated him with respect and honour, but afterwards paid so little attention to him, that he allowed only one or two servants to wait on him. When things had gone on a short time in this way, Yusuf Ali Kukildásh Divána, one of Mirzá Khán's old retainers, conspired with eighteen other persons, and one night fell on Zobir, slew him, and set Mirzá Khán upon the throne. From that date, 913, till the end of his life, Mirzá Khán reigned over Badakhshán.

[1] Khusrau's country was the province of *Kunduz*, or more properly the territory of *Kattaghán*, of which *Kunduz* was the capital.

[2] The words are *Sir-dári*, but the passage makes no sense when translated literally. Erskine (in a note to his MS. in the British Museum) suggests a pun on the words *Sardár* and *Sir-dári*, by adopting which, the translation may stand as given here.

[3] That is, a native of *Rágh*—a hill district in north-western Badakhshán, on the left bank of the Panjah, and opposite Kuláb.

[4] Shah Begum (Khan Mirza's grandmother) was, as we have been told above, the daughter of Shah Sultan Muhammad, King of Badakhshán, and the widow of Yunus Khan, Baber's maternal grandfather. (See also Baber, p. 231.)

[5] This *Mirza Khan* (or properly, perhaps, *Khan Mirza*) was the son of Sultan Mahmud Mirza, who was third son of Sultan Abu Said and an uncle of Baber. Mirza Khan was ruler of Hisar, Khatlán and Badakhshán. His mother was Nigar Khanim, a sister of Baber's mother. Consequently he was Baber's cousin, both by the father's and the mother's side. His proper name was *Sultan Vais Mirza*, and it is not clear how he acquired that of *Khan Mirza* or *Mirza Khan*. One of his brothers, Baisanghar Mirza, had been murdered, and another, called Sultan Másud Mirza, had been blinded by Khusrau Shah. (See Baber, pp. 128 and 237).

[6] Abá Bakr was a Dughlát, and brother of the author's uncle, Sayyid Muhammad Mirza.

After the conquest of Kandahár, Bábar remained in Kábul. Those Moghuls of Khusrau Sháh's army who had stayed behind, to the number of about 3000, now raised Abdur Razzák [1] to the throne, and declared against the Emperor, who had only 500 men left with him. However, with these 500 men, he met them in a pitched battle. This was one of the Emperor's greatest battles. After much giving and taking of blows and countless hand-to-hand fights, the Emperor broke and routed the foe. In that action he personally, and alone, engaged five different champions of the enemy: Ali Sayyid Gur, Ali Sinár, and three others, and with brave strokes and sword cuts, put them all to flight.

In this same battle, Abdur Razzák Mirzá fell into the Emperor's hands, but was treated with generosity and set at liberty.

After these events, the affairs of the Emperor began to march favourably in Kábul, where he remained until the year 916 [1510], when Sháhi Beg Khán was slain, as will be mentioned below.

CHAPTER XIII.

EXPEDITION OF SHÁHI BEG KHÁN INTO KHWÁRIZM. HIS CONQUEST OF THAT COUNTRY. HIS RETURN TO MÁVARÁ-UN-NAHR, AND HIS MARCH INTO KHORÁSÁN.

WHEN Sháhi Beg Khán had disposed of the Moghuls, Sultán Said Khán fled to Moghulistán, and my father to Khorásán. Some [of the Moghuls] were put to death and others imprisoned. Sháh Begum was sent into Khorásán, while the rest of the Moghuls, [Sháhi Beg] carried with him into Khwárizm. He besieged [Khwárizm] for eleven months. Chin Sufi was then acting as governor for Mirzá Sultán Husain. During all that time no one came in answer to his appeal for help; and he fought some marvellous battles, which even now are celebrated among the Uzbeg. At length, in consequence of the dearth of provisions, most of his men died of hunger, and resistance became no longer possible; then Sháhi Beg Khán took the citadel, put Chin Sufi to death, and returned to Samarkand.

As, before the conquest of Khwárizm, he had laid siege to Balkh for six months, and had left that enterprise only half completed

[1] Abdur Razzák was another of Baber's numerous cousins. He was a son of Sultan Ulugh Beg Mirza of Kabul (son of Abu Said), and had reigned in Kabul until expelled by Mukim, son of Zunnun Arghun, late in 1503 or early in 1504. (Erskine, *Hist.*, i., pp. 211, 215, 216, 277, etc.)

(as has been related above), he now went and conquered Balkh, and then returned to Samarkand, where he passed the winter. In the spring he set out against Khorásán. Mirzá Sultán Husain had died the year before, and his sons, in their indolence and indifference, could not come to any mutual agreement. When the news arrived of Sháhi Beg Khán's approach, everything was thrown into dire confusion and disorder. Every one had some suggestion to offer, but no conclusion could be arrived at, [and while they were still engaged in these arguments] news came that Sháhi Beg Khán had reached Herat. Mirzá Zunnun led out an army [to oppose him], but [saw] that it was too late to dam the torrent with earth, or to smother the blazing fire with dust, and he was himself slain at the first onset of the Uzbeg, who forthwith entered and plundered Herat. The Mirzás all fled in different directions, and the greater part of the army did not even know how Herat had been taken. Thus easily fell that important city with its vast population.

Mir Muhammad Sálih, one of the Amirs of Sultán Abu Said, whose name is to be found in the "Lives of the Poets" [*tazkira*] discovered the date of this event, namely, 912, in the words *Fath-i-Khorásán*—"Conquest of Khorásán."

CHAPTER XIV.

THE REASON WHY MY FATHER, MUHAMMAD HUSAIN KURKÁN, SURRENDERED HIMSELF TO SHÁHI BEG KHÁN. MARTYRDOM OF MY NOBLE UNCLE, SULTÁN MAHMUD KHÁN, AND OF MY FATHER.

My father and Mirzá Khán left Kábul and went to Kandahár, whence the former proceeded, with the intention of making the Holy Pilgrimage, while Mirzá Khán remained at Kandahár. [My father] had resolved to go to Sistán, and taking the road by Neh and Bandán, to reach Kirmán; since if he travelled by way of Khorásán, he would be hindered by the importunities of the Mirzás.[1] On nearing Faráh he was met by a body of fugitives, in the most pitiable state imaginable, who told him that Sháhi Beg Khán had seized Khorásán in the manner above related.[2]

When they reached Faráh they found that the roads on every side were unsafe, and there was nothing left for my father but to remain where he was. Thus he stayed three months in Faráh. On Sháhi Beg Khán hearing of his whereabouts, he sent him a

[1] The Turki MS. has: "the Mirzas would press him to stop."—R.

[2] The Turki adds: "And we have fled from him; having said this they gave him an account of the victory, as we have given it above."—R.

most courteous invitation [which he accepted], and, accompanied by the magnates of Faráh, he went to visit Sháhi Beg Khán, who was then encamped at Uláng Káhdastan,[1] in great magnificence; but the limits of this Epitome prevent me from giving full particulars. No one would ever have imagined that change and destruction were coming over his affairs within a few years; it is wonderful how, in a short space of time, all went to ruin, in a way that will be briefly described.

In short, he received my father with every mark of attention and honour, and showered down innumerable presents upon him.

After this [Sháhi Beg Khán] went against Kandahár, where Sultán Násir Mirzá [2] was [ruling], as has been mentioned above. He laid siege to the town for forty days, and then, having made peace, he returned, carrying away much booty. During the same year there were battles between the sons of Mirzá Sultán Husain and Sháhi Beg Khán's Sultáns at Mashhad, Nishápur, Astarábád, and Turshiz. In all these encounters the Uzbeg were victorious, and the Chaghatái defeated. A great number of the Chaghatái were slain, and those who escaped became so scattered that they were never again united.

At this time, Ubaid Ullah Khan,[3] who was Sultán (and many

[1] Kahdastán appears to have been a spot in the near vicinity of Herat. It lay probably to the north or north-east of the city, but is not marked on maps now in use. (See Barbier de Meynard in *Journ. Asiat.*, 5 Série, xvii., p. 509.)

[2] Násir Mirza was Baber's youngest brother, and had been appointed Governor of Kandahar, when Baber took that place in 1507. (Erskine, *Hist.*, i., pp. 89 and 279.)

[3] Ubaid Ullah Khan (or Ubaid Ullah Sultan) was son of Mahmud Sultan (Shahi Beg's brother), and afterwards (in 1533) became Khákán, or over-lord, of the Uzbegs. It may be remarked here, that the Uzbeg government was not an absolute sovereignty, but was committed, by an electorate of chiefs, into the hands of one of their number. Sir H. Howorth likens it to that of Russia in mediæval times, and says: "It was broken up into a number of appanages, each under its own Khan, and all subservient to an over-chief who was styled Khákán, and answered to the Grand Prince in Russia, who had a similar feudal authority over the appanaged princes. On the death of a Khákán the appanaged princes met together to choose a successor; and their choice, as is usual in the East, generally fell upon the senior representative of the house, not necessarily the heir by right of primogeniture, but the oldest living representative of the senior line. It has followed, in consequence, that in many notices of Bokhara there has not been a sufficient discrimination between the line of Khákáns, or chief Khans, and those of the appanaged princes, and the two lists have been confused together." (Vol. II., p. 713.) Ubaid Ullah's private appanage was Bokhara, as mentioned in the text; but he was practically Sultan of the Uzbegs at the time in question, though Kuch-Kunji (otherwise Kuchum Khan) was nominally in that position. It appears that Ubaid Ullah ruled the whole of Transoxiana, including Bokhara, during two reigns before he was himself proclaimed Khákán in 940 H., or 1533 A.D. These reigns were Kuch-Kunji, 1510–30,
Abu-Said, 1530–33, and they were followed by
Ubaid Ullah as Khákán, 1533–39.

Mr. Stanley Lane Poole points out the "dual character of Shaibani's dynasty," and remarks that, though Samarkand was the capital. "there was generally a powerful and sometimes an independent government at Bokhara." (See S. L. Poole's *Cat. Orient. Coins in Brit. Mus.*, VII., p. xiv; also Stokvis, *Manuel d'Hist., etc.*, p. 157.)

victories were in his name), was going to Bokhárá, which was his hereditary seat of government. He begged my father to allow me to accompany him. The reason for this was that Habiba Sultán Khánish (who has been mentioned, in the detailed list of my father's children, given above) had been married by Sháhi Beg Khán to Ubaid Ullah Sultán, after [my father's] flight from Shahr-i-Sabz. So, with my father's permission, I was taken to my sister in Bokhárá.

In the winter of the same year, Sháhi Beg Khán went to attack the Kazák in Mávará-un-Nahr, that is to say, the Dasht-i-Kipchák.[1] Sháhi Beg Khán [first] took my father to Bokhárá, but when he went to attack the Kazák, he left him in Samarkand. He returned in the spring, and then set out for Khorásán, entrusting my father to the care of Timur Sultán, his son, to whom he had given Samarkand. So my father spent that spring in Samarkand, while I was living with my sister in Bokhárá.

At this time news came that Sultán Mahmud Khán had left Moghulistán and was advancing on Andiján, with complaints and demands. Sháhi Beg Khán sent to beg my father to come into Khorásán. My father accepted the invitation and went. He felt his end was drawing near, and on the tablet of his fate he recognised the hue of martyrdom. His hope of safety being more slender than a spider's web, he devoted all his attention and energy to providing for my safety, so that should his precious soul be drowned in the whirlpool of martyrdom, I at least, on the shores of safety, should be protected from risks and dangers.

On his first visit to Herat, my father had sought out a pious and talented man to be my teacher, whose name was Háfiz Miram. He was, indeed, a pious and ascetic man [*fakir*], possessed of numerous talents. He could recite the Korán [with special attention to the] modulations of the voice, and wrote the *Naskh Táalik* hand and others beautifully. My father was much pleased with him; and during [his stay in Herat] this man was his constant companion, whether in the time of contentment and pleasure, or in the days of trial and sorrow. He instructed me in the Korán and in calligraphy.

When the time came for starting for Khorásán, my father showed me, in private, much kindness, and did his utmost to console and comfort me, saying: "Your uncle Sultán Mahmud Khán has arrived [from Moghulistán] in spite of my having warned him both by word and in writing. I said to him, 'After the conquests of Amir Timur, and the devastation [*takhrib*] of Moghulistán, your forefathers, though dispersed, remained in that

[1] This is the literal translation of the passage, but it seems to imply the fallacy of regarding the Dasht-i-Kipchák and Mávará-un-Nahr as one and the same region. The meaning most likely is that Shahi Beg returned to Mávará-un-Nahr to attack, or check, the Kazáks of, or from, the Dasht-i-Kipchák.

country, and were awaiting their opportunity. Contenting themselves with scanty clothing and simple food, they took care of their people and their army. Thus passed 150 years, until the sun of your noble nature rose in Moghulistán, which is an eastern clime and the quarter where rise the lights of the Khákáns. At the middle season of your youth, in the manner of your noble ancestors, you restored the fallen Moghulistán to its former glory, and together with Yunus Khán, you seized that opportunity, which had been long sought by your forefathers, and brought under your control those states which they so earnestly coveted. Thus you spent nineteen years in complete success. It is now clearer than the day, that the power of your victorious forces cannot be compared with the numbers of Sháhi Beg Khán's army. Hence it is your obvious duty to remain in Moghulistán, both for your own personal safety and for the welfare of your people. For though you may there be exposed to many hardships, that is better than extinction. It is, moreover, quite evident to me that should you ever fall into the hands of Sháhi Beg Khán, he will subject you to the most painful of tortures, and will deem your death his own life: on no account whatever will he spare you.'

"Thus did I use all the arguments in my power to dissuade the Khán, but as often as my remonstrances reached him, certain base advisers, in their short-sighted ignorance, represented to him that 'Muhammad Husain Mirzá does not wish you to go, because lately Sháhi Beg Khán has shown him great favour, and he knows that your going would put an end to this.' To absurd representations of this kind they would add: 'It is our firm conviction that if [Sháhi Beg Khán has treated Muhammad Husain Mirzá well, in return for his services, he will treat a hundred, nay, a thousand, times better, you who have done so much more for him'].[1] After the expression of all these impossible and absurd ideas, the following answer was sent back: 'Oh! *Dásh*' (that is, oh! Friend, for these two had become 'friends' according to the Moghul custom, in their youth, and called each other by this name up to the end of their days): 'how strange it is that you should be leading such a happy life in Khorásán and Samarkand, in spite of your knowledge of the pitiable state of affairs in Moghulistán! How can you allow me to be exposed to so much suffering?' But taking my words and advice as mixed with evil intentions, he failed to recognise their truth, and came. This instance is not the same as the former one.[2] Certainly Sháhi Beg Khán will fill the cup of the Khán's hopes with the fatal wine of martyrdom, and whatever dregs remain he will cause me to drink. I now commit you to

[1] Thus in the Turki; in the Persian texts the sense appears to be the same, but is obscure.—R.

[2] That is, the times have changed now.

the care of God. Though your company would be dearer to me than my own life, I fear Sháhi Beg Khán would not allow it, and I prefer the idea of your life being prolonged, even though it involve the bitterness of separation; you must therefore bear my absence patiently. Patience is bitter, but it has a sweet fruit. Remember that when the father dies, the children are his heirs. You also have become an heir. If the bird of my life escape from the net of Sháhi Beg Khán's intentions against me, we shall have the joy of meeting again.

"Now as your teacher, Háfiz Miram, is a devout man, and is not on friendly terms with any of our people, if anything happens to me, he will, with the advice of my partisans, be able to look to your interests. Moreover, his family is also in Khorásán. It is just a year since he left them to follow me; therefore he is going along with me.

"I entrust you to the care of Mauláná Muhammad. Be careful to pay attention to all he may say to you, for he is my vicar [*khalifa*].[1] His father was my instructor and guide. From the day of his birth up to the present time, he has been my confidant and companion. I trust that he will always be your support in times of trouble, and that he will protect you through thick and thin."

Having thus threaded many pearls of good counsel upon the string of wisdom, and hung them on the attentive ear of my understanding, my father departed to go and wait on Sháhi Beg Khán, who was at that time besieging Kalát.[2] To all outward appearance he received my father with friendship, and then allowed him to proceed to Herat. When he reached Herat, a person was sent after him [to put him to death]. Sultán Mahmud Khán and his children were killed on the river of Khojand.[3] My father was buried in the mausoleum of Amir Sayyid Husaini, while Sultán Mahmud was placed in the mausoleum of Shaikh Muslih-ud-Din, Khojandi.

This happened in the year 914. For the Khán, the chronogram *Lab-i-daryá-i-Khojand* [the banks of the river of Khojand] was discovered. [Here follow some blessings upon the martyrs . . . .]

[1] Or successor. That is—he is to take my place as your father.
[2] Kelat-i-Nádiri—as the modern name is—in Khorasán.
[3] The texts are very corrupt here. I have followed the Turki.—R.

CHAPTER XV.

SOME OF THE AUTHOR'S OWN ADVENTURES.

After Sháhi Beg Khán had put my father to death, he despatched an emissary to Bokhárá with instructions to throw me into the river, and thus send me to join those who had been drowned in the river of Khojand. Although the order was an obnoxious one to Ubaid Sultán, who received it (for he was married to my sister), still it was impossible for him to refuse.

But how excellent a thing it is that the Almighty has power to check the violent and, if He so wills it, to restrain the hand of the cruel: so that, without His consent, the tyrant cannot touch a single hair of any man's head. And this is confirmed by the events of this disturbed time.[1] For, in his glory, vanity and magnificence, see how many royal families Sháhi Beg Khán destroyed, and the number of princely houses he annihilated! For example, Sultán Husaini[2] and his followers, to the number of nearly 200,000 persons; Sultán Mahmud and the Mirzás with nearly 50,000 men—these all suffered at the hands of Sháhi Beg Khán. Again the royal houses of Samarkand and of Mirzá Sultán Ahmad: to what extremities were they not all driven by this tyrant? In a short space of time, he scattered to the winds of annihilation many governors and officials, so that the dust of their existence formed towers on the plains of non-existence, which reached up to the heavens, and from the mists of their sighs a frightful whirlwind arose in the deserts.

This king, who could commit such atrocities and practise such violence, was resolved on my death, at a time when I had only just passed the half of my childhood, and did not know my right hand from my left, nor good from evil; nor had I the ability to use my strength—nay, I had not enough intelligence to execute my own wishes. I had become an orphan, without father or mother, my paternal uncles were scattered and my maternal uncles slain. I had not [even] an elder brother who could share in my grief; no friend or relation to comfort me.

That year, 914,[3] proved one of disaster for the Sultáns of the day in general, and of massacre for the Moghul Khákáns in particular. When God willed that all my uncles, aunts, and cousins should be carried off in different directions and murdered,

[1] The Turki MS. says: This is explained by what happened to myself.—R.

[2] That is: Sultan Husain Mirza, Baikara, whose poetical name was Husaini, as we have seen.

[3] 1508-9 A.D.

I was the weakest and youngest of the family. The strangest part of it all is that they were, everyone, at a great distance [from Sháhi Beg Khán], as has been mentioned above, but being helpless, nay, having no alternative, they came and threw themselves into calamity and were murdered; while I escaped, though in the town of Bokhárá, in the middle of the ocean of Sháhi Beg Khán's dominions. Since the decree of the will of the Almighty had not been issued for my destruction, but for my preservation, Sháhi Beg Khán, with all his boasting and power, was not able to touch one hair of the head of that helpless little child whom he wished to kill. (Thanks be to God, the Lord of Heaven and Earth, the Possessor of Might, Majesty, and Power.)

The details [of my escape] are briefly as follows: at the above date, my father went to Khorásán and was put to death by Sháhi Beg Khán, who also sent an emissary to Bokhárá to kill me. And although this was an act that would have been distasteful to Ubaid Ullah Khán, it was quite impossible for him to disobey the orders of Sháhi Beg Khán. He handed me over to the emissary, with instructions to throw me into the river Amu, that I might join those others who had been drowned in the ocean of divine mercy. He was engaged in investigating some of the property which my father had left [in Bokhárá], alleging that the Mirzá had said to him: "Bring my property along with my son." This occasioned a delay of a few days. During this interval Mauláná Muhammad, who was my master and my father's Khalifa, went to see Hazrat Mauláná Muhammad Kázi, who asked him: "When are you starting for Khorásán?" Mauláná Muhammad replied: "We have decided to depart in a few days." Hazrat Mauláná then said: "Come back in a little while, I have something I wish to say to you." After a time, when the assembly of faithful men had dispersed, Mauláná Muhammad came in again, and Hazrat Mauláná asked him: "How could I consent to Muhammad Husain Mirzá going to Khorásán, and now to the Mirzá's son going there too?" Mauláná Muhammad replied: "Verily, we are taking him, fully trusting in God's protection." Then, said Hazrat Mauláná: "The Holy Prophet, when his life was threatened by the infidels of Mekka, did not put his trust in standing still and being captured, but took to flight. Therefore, what you should now do is, trusting in God, to take the Mirzá and flee; and if danger or cause of fear presents itself, I am your security. You ought certainly to set out without delay."

Mauláná Muhammad used to say: "I never had any such thought in my mind, but those words of Hazrat Mauláná had a wonderful effect on me, and the determination to go and seize you and carry you away, took so strong a hold of me that as soon as I had left him, I turned my whole attention to our flight."

Having reached this point in my narrative, I think fit to give some details of the life of Hazrat Mauláná, who has been mentioned above, in connection with my illness.

CHAPTER XVI.

HAZRAT MAULÁNÁ MUHAMMAD KÁZI.

HIS name was Muhammad bin Burhán-ud-Din. His father was one of the intimate friends of Kázi Imád-ud-Din Maskin, Samarkandi, and for this reason Hazrat Mauláná was known as Mauláná Muhammad Kázi. After he had acquired a certain proficiency in the sciences, he devoted himself to the study of theology—walking in the way of God—and to this end he repaired to Khorásán. On leaving Samarkand, he went to pay his respects to that much beloved and respected example of piety, Khwája Násir-ud-Din Ubaidullah, who lived there. He asked Hazrat Mauláná where he was going. The latter replied that he was going to Khorásán. Again he asked: "Are you going for the sake of study, or for some other object?" A certain student, who was in the company of Hazrat Mauláná, said: "His greatest desire is to become a darvish." His Holiness [the Khwája] telling them to wait a little, went into his garden, and after a prolonged absence returned, bringing two letters for Hazrat Mauláná: one was a letter of recommendation to Khwája Kilán, the son of Mauláná Sád-ud-Din Káshghari; the other contained an account of the rules and practices of devotees, which he had written, and which he now gave to Hazrat Mauláná.

* * * * *

[Here follows an epitome or summary of the contents of the "Tract," which contained commendations to the study of divine truths, through following Muhammad, and warnings against associating with dancing and singing (or howling) darvishes, and against listening to heretical doctrines.]

In the *Salsalat ul Arifin*, one of Hazrat Mauláná's works, it is written: "It was most strange that in spite of the Khwája's admonition, my desire to visit Khorásán was in no way lessened; I at length obtained Khwája Nasir-ud-Din's sanction to depart, and set out for Khorásán. But as, on the road, incidents occurred which prevented me from proceeding further, I returned and entered the Khwája's service." The writer remained some time with him, and managed his private kitchen; and so great was his devotion that he used himself to come, on foot, and lay the meals before Hazrat Ishán. He, by degrees, won his entire confidence, and Hazrat Ishán used to address Hazrat Mauláná in the presence of all his most distinguished guests.[1]

In all matters, the most perfect intimacy and trust existed between them—so much so, that Mauláná Muhammad became an object of jealousy to the other companions of Hazrat Ishán and his children. And as this gave rise to much unpleasantness, Hazrat Mauláná set out for Khorásán in company with Mauláná Muhammad Amin, who was also a disciple of Hazrat Ishán. . . .

* * * * *

And there they spent six months in the enjoyment of the society of Mauláná Abdur Rahman Támi. Hazrat Mauláná then entered the service of Hazrat Ishán in Táshkand, who encouraged him and honoured him with the respectful style of "Ishán." . . . .

* * * * * [2]

It was the fashion, at that time, for every Sultán to have one of Hazrat Mauláná's disciples for a spiritual guide. Thus Sultán Abu Said Mirzá entertained Mauláná Kásim; Sultán Ahmad Mirzá, Mauláná Khwája Ali; and all the Sultáns observed this practice. Sultán Mahmud Khán was guided by Hazrat Mauláná. I have heard this last say: "I was once praising Sultán Mahmud Khán to Hazrat Ishán, when he remarked that Sultán Mahmud Khán was indeed a very capable young man, but he had one fault, which was a hinderance to his advancement. A pupil, with such an instructor, ought to do all that his instructor told him, and not rely on his own judgment; but, like a hawk, he should pounce down upon whatever prey he is sent against, whether or no he has strength sufficient, and should not hesitate and doubt, as the Khán did. It was this that prevented him rising to that elevation which his people had expected of him."

In a word, after the death of Hazrat Ishán, Hazrat Mauláná went to Táshkand, where he was welcomed with honour and devotion, and where he remained until the destruction of Táshkand, when he migrated to Bokhárá. At that time Mahmud Sultán, brother of Sháhi Beg Khán, and father of Ubaid Ullah Khán, was ruler of Bokhárá, as representative of Sháhi Beg Khán. He cultivated the society of Hazrat Mauláná and was his disciple for one winter, which greatly pleased Hazrat Mauláná, who for this reason stayed on in Bokhárá from that date to the year 916, when my father went to Khorásán[3] and was martyred. It has been

[1] This paragraph is very obscure.—R.

[2] The omissions here consist of some irrelevant anecdotes concerning these holy men. They are obscure in style, Mr. Ross informs me, and not worth translating.

[3] The Turki text adds here:—"I, also, was at Bokhára." The date should be 914.

mentioned in my own story, and will be related again, how kind Hazrat Mauláná was to me.

When the Kizilbásh [1] overran the land (as will be described), Hazrat Mauláná left Bokhárá and went to Andiján and Akhsi, where he resolved to stay.[2] There, many people became Nakhshbandi under his guidance, thus attaining high rank, and are, to this day, a blessing in the land, where they propagate the doctrines of their sect. An account of these men will be given below, in connection with the biographical notice of Hazrat Makhdumi. Wherever in this history Hazrat Mauláná, absolutely, is mentioned, Hazrat Mauláná Muhammad Kázi is indicated. Further details of his life will be given in their proper place.

[1] It frequently happens at the present time, in Central Asia, that the word *Kizil-básh* is used to denote almost any Shiah, but more especially a Persian, or Khorasani, Shiah, or the descendant of one. In the sixteenth century, it is evident from many passages in Erskine's *History*, that the native authors utilised by him meant the Persians in general, when they spoke of the *Kizil-básh;* and it appears to be in this sense that Mirza Haidar makes use of the name. The Turki words mean literally *Red Head*, but more properly *Red Cap*. The people who originally bore the name of *Kizil-básh* were, according to Sir J. Malcolm, the seven Turki tribes who had been the chief supporters of Shah Ismail during his early, successful, campaigns in the west of Persia, and whom he distinguished by a particular dress, which included a red cap. The names of these tribes are given by the historian as:—(1) the Ustájlu, (2) the Shámlu, (3) the Nikállu, (4) the Bahárlu, (5) the Zulkadar, (6) the Kajar, and (7) the Afshár. He adds:—"The swords of these tribes were consecrated . . . . to the defence of the Shiah religion; and a sense of that obligation has survived the existence of the family by whom it was first created"—*i.e.*, the Sufavi. The *Kizil-básh* would thus date from the first decade of the sixteenth century; but James Fraser, writing in the first half of the eighteenth century, attributes their institution to Shaikh Haidar, the father of Shah Ismail, which would make the date a little earlier. Sir H. Yule defines the name as that "applied to certain tribes of Turks who have become naturalised, as it were, in Persia, and have adopted the Persian language; they are in fact Persianised Turks, like the present royal race and dominant class in Persia." The name is now chiefly heard in Afghanistan and the adjoining regions of India, Persia and Turkistan. In the two first of these localities they appear, from what Mr. Denzil Ibbetson tells us, to be regarded as the residue of the army with which Nádir Shah invaded India. However this may be, it appears that they are fairly numerous in Afghanistan, and that there are some 1200 families of them in the city of Kabul alone, where they form not only an important military colony, but also a political party, in possession of much influence. (Malcolm, *Hist. of Persia*, i., pp. 502–3; Yule, *Glossary*, p. 814; Ibbetson, *Punjab Census*, 1881, i., p. 278; Fraser, *Hist. of Nadir Shah*, 1742, p. 135.)

[2] This is a loosely expressed sentence, but has been translated as it stands in the original. It does not determine whether the Mauláná stayed at Andiján or at Akhsi.

CHAPTER XVII.

RETURN TO THE HISTORY.

Before entering upon the life of Hazrat Mauláná, I had reached that point in my narrative where Hazrat Mauláná Muhammad, who was my tutor [*ustád*], had resolved that he would escape with me. Though he had previously had no intentions of this sort, the idea gained complete ascendency over his Christ-like mind. With this intent he came to me, in private, and asked me: "Do you propose to go to Khorásán now?" I replied: "Yes, I must go, for I have been sent for." He then said: "It is quite certain that Sháhi Beg Khán will put you in chains, but what he will do with you after that I cannot say." Then he added: "I have something to tell you, but will only do so on the condition that you will reveal the secret to no one." I then took a very solemn oath and swore I would not repeat what he told me, after which he said: "They have murdered the Mirzá in Khorásán, and have now sent for you. They have given orders that you are to be sunk to the bottom of the River Amu, and thus to be despatched to the next world. If you know of any one who will carry you off, then fly at once.

For death attacks alike both old and young,
And fills with fear the minds of all it strikes:"

Fear and dismay overcame me, and I began to weep: I longed to flee, in the hope of saving my life.

The Mauláná said: "You must keep this secret well hid; be on the watch: for the moment I give the sign you must hasten away."

He had a friend who lived outside the town of Bokhárá, and arranged that I should pass a few days in perfect concealment in this man's house. He informed certain of my father's servants of this plan, and arranged that on the night of our flight, these servants should take some saddle horses and start in a certain direction, in order to make the spies think that we had fled on horseback, and [thus cause them] to scour distant roads, searching only the outside of the town while not suspecting the inside.

Accordingly, the same night that we took refuge in the house of this friend, the servants took the horses and carried out the orders which had been given them. All turned out as we had expected. The spies imagined that we had escaped on horseback, and no one made search for us in the town. We remained fourteen days in the house of that excellent man. After this lapse of time, we joined a party of donkey-drivers and accompanied them to the town of Hisár Shádmán. In the bázár of that town one of my father's servants recognised Mauláná Muhammad. Fearing lest he might trace us out, we at once fled from Hisár. On the road I fell from my donkey, and dislocated my left elbow. We dared not re-enter the town, or the bázár, and in the villages we could not find a bone-setter; thus I endured the greatest agony for two months.

At Pushang, one of the villages in Khatlán, we spent some days in the house of one of its holy men, who was known as Khwája Habib Ullah. He was a benevolent person, and after diligent search found a bone-setter, whom he brought. The bone-setter broke the joint again, and set it. I had not been able to use my arm for two months, and from the intensity of the pain, had, during all that time, never slept at night. That night, however, I fell asleep.

One day, while we were there, a soldier came in and, placing his quiver in a corner, sat down. Having scrutinised the company, he came quickly forward, and said with great respect and courtesy: "Does not Khwája Mauláná Muhammad know me again? I was Mirzá Muhammad Husain's cook at such and such a time; in those days I rendered you good service." And as he gave such clear proofs of recognition, it was vain to disclaim his acquaintance. Moreover, Mauláná Muhammad seemed much pleased, gave expression to his joy, and began to enumerate the good qualities [of that man]. That day and night they spent in friendly intercourse. When day broke and he was about to depart, he stood in the doorway of the house, in a respectful attitude, and said: "Oh, Khwája Mauláná Muhammad, blessings be upon your zeal and fidelity. It was a noble and a suitable act of yours to take Mirzá Husain's son and escape with him. If I had had any power or means, I would have given my assistance; but I have not. However, if I can, in any way, further your plans, I will hasten to bear my part." So saying he departed.

A little while after, there came an intimate friend of Khwája Habib Ullah, who whispered something in the Khwája's ear; whereat the Khwája's colour fled from his face. He immediately took the man apart, and said: "Now repeat what Shaikham[1] said." The man replied: "Shaikham told me to go and tell Khwája Habib Ullah that 'this man' has fled with the son of Mirzá Muhammad Husain; the child is the cousin of Mirza Khán

[1] The only word in the texts is *Shaikham*, but no doubt reference is made to *Shaikham Mirza*, who, our author informs us lower down, was an uncle of Ubaid Ullah Khan. He was governor of Karshi, and was killed, in 1512, at the taking of that place by the Persians, under Mir Najm.

and of Bábar Pádisháh. Perhaps the Khwája is keeping him in his house, and in this case he will incur the enmity of Hamza Sultán.[1] Behold, I am going to inform the Naváb Matlab Sultán [of the matter], so that the house and home of Khwája Habib Ullah may be swept away with the broom of plunder, its dust mount to the skies, and its vapour be diffused over the earth." With these words he went away.

This Matlab Sultán was the son of Hamza Sultán, a one-eyed wretch, whose inward vision was rendered blinder than his outward sight by the darkness of tyranny. All the oppressed of those countries united, at his court, in a common protest against his tyranny. The leaves of the trees of these people's lives were constantly trembling from the violence of his blasts.

Khwája Habib Ullah remained for a while buried in thought, then raising his head, he said: "No one has delivered you over to me as hostages. I will not, from fear of being held responsible[2] for a charge I have not taken upon myself, deliver this little child into the hands of death. To do so, would be conformable neither with the teachings of Islám nor the dictates of humanity. Rise up and flee whithersoever you may be safe. And whatever chastisement may fall upon me, on your account, I will consider as treasure laid up for me in the next world." We then, having returned him thanks, bade him farewell, and set out at once.

At this time Sháh Razi-ud-Din, who was a Chirágh Kush, appeared in Badakhshán. His followers used to put to death every one they met, deeming it a means of salvation, and reward in the next world. He had caused all the roads to be stopped, so that it was impossible for us to journey into Badakhshán. Sháh Razi-ud-Din was one of the cursed Muláhida of Kohistán, whose story is to be found in all histories. Most of the people of Badakhshán are adherents of that sect. They hold the world to be without beginning or end [*kadim*], and do not believe in resurrection or a future state. They say that during the lifetime of the Prophet, it was incumbent on all to abide by the statutes of the Holy Law; but at the present time, the sole duty of man is to speak fitting words and to be faithful to their meaning. All other ordinances are futile. Sexual intercourse [*vati*] with their own kindred is lawful, and the enjoyment of it is, in no respect, dependent on marriage; thus, should one have a passion for somebody with whom its indulgence is practicable, it is lawful to gratify it—be it with daughter or son or mother.

[1] An Uzbeg chief who had at one time been in Baber's service, and afterwards, joining Shahi Beg, turned against him. Finally, in 1511, he fell into Baber's hands and was executed as a traitor, together with two other Uzbeg leaders. At the time in question here, Hamza was master of Hisár. (Erskine, *Hist.*, i., pp. 145, 315, etc.)

[2] The Turki has :—no one has made me responsible for you.—R.

It is also lawful for them to take one another's lives or property. [In fact] the sect of Mulâhida is the worst form of heathenism in the world.[1] At the time of the conquests of Sháhi Beg Khán,

[1] It is noticeable that Mirza Haidar uses the word *Chirágh-Kush* or "lamp extinguishers," as a synonym of *Muláhida*, or "the impious," for the sect he is alluding to. Properly, the designation of this sect of Shiahs is *Ismaili*, and they take their name from Ismail, the eldest son and nominated successor of Imám Jáfar Sádik. They consider Ismail as the true heir to the Imámat, and do not acknowledge, as lawful, the succession of his brother Musa, and of the five last Imáms. One branch of the sect flourished in Africa under the Egyptian dynasty of the Khalifs, while another became established in Northern Persia, where it was known by the name of *Ali-Iláhi*, as well as by that of *Ismaili*. It is not clear, however, that all the eastern, or Asiatic, *Ismaili* hold the doctrines of the *Ali-Iláhi*. Mr. Colebrooke quotes the book called *Dáhistán*, by Mullah Mohsin Fani, from which I transcribe the following extract, as it brings to light the meaning and origin of the name. "The Ali-Iláhiyah hold that celestial spirits which cannot otherwise be known to mankind, have frequently appeared in palpable shapes. God himself has been manifested in human form, but especially in the person of Ali Murteza, whose image being that of Ali-Ullah, or Ali-God, these sectaries deem it lawful to worship. . . . They imagine that Ali Murteza when he quitted this earth, returned to the sun, which is the same with himself; and hence they call the sun *Ali Ullah*. This sect does not admit the authority of the Koran as it is now extant . . . . they believe in the transmigration of God into the persons of the Imams. Some of them affirm that the manifestation of the divine being in this age of the world was *Ali-Ullah*, and after him his glorious posterity; and they consider Muhammad as a prophet sent by *Ali-Ullah*. When God, say they, perceived Muhammad's insufficiency, He himself assumed the human form for the purpose of assisting the prophet." The names of *Muláhida* and *Chirágh-Kush* are of course terms of reproach only, while that of *Assassins*, by which the Ismaili were known to Europeans in the Middle Ages, was derived from their practice of drugging their victims with *Háshish*, a preparation of hemp, and thus acquiring the designation of *Háshishin*. *Fidáwi*, another name under which they are found mentioned, means "the devoted," and was applied to them as devotees, or instruments, of the Chief of the *Assassins*—the *Shaikh ul Jabal*—or, as the literal translation ran in the Middle Ages, the *Old Man of the Mountain*. Full and interesting accounts of the *Ismaili*, the *Ali-Iláhi*, and of the dynasty of the Háshishin or *Assassins*, who ruled for about 170 years from their strongholds in the Kuhistan of Northern Persia, will be found in the works mentioned below. There is no space here to go further into the general subject; but it must be remarked that when Mirza Haidar speaks of the "cursed *Muláhida* of Kuhistan," it is to the *Assassins* of the Kuhistan of North-Western Persia that he alludes. The chief stronghold of the "Old Man of the Mountain" was at *Alámat* (the "Eagle's Nest"), about thirty-two miles N.E. of Kazvin, until the power of the dynasty was broken, by the Mongol army under Hulaku, in 1256, when the sect, as a political body, came to an end. In Mirza Haidar's time (as indeed down to the present day) they seem to have flourished in the remote hill districts of Badakhshán and the region of the Upper Oxus; and from time to time, no doubt, some of their chiefs, like Shah Razi-ud-Din of the text, obtained a certain degree of power in those localities. Here, in our times, they are known as *Ismaili* and also as *Agha-Kháni*, from the name of one of their "Pirs," or religious leaders, who took up his residence in Bombay in 1840, and whose successors still live there. The inhabitants of Shighnán, Roshán, etc., still carry tribute to him at Bombay, and reverence him as the chief of their religion.

As regards the name of *Chirágh-Kush*, it may be added that it is a term which has been applied to many religious sects, besides those of the Shiahs: indeed, it was applied to the early Christians, and is meant to stigmatise their proceedings as immoral or obscene, by conveying the charge that, after their gatherings for worship, the lamps are extinguished and obscene orgies indulged in. Thus it is merely an abusive term, invented by intolerant religious opponents. In our times, at any rate, (as far as the European traveller among them has opportunities of judging) their morality is no worse than that of their neighbours.

The best notices of these sects and their history, will be found in Yule's *Marco*

the people of Badakhshán (as has been mentioned) were acting independently; still, they had never neglected to pay tribute to Razi-ud-Din, who was a Pir-záda, or to his ancestors. At that time Sháh Razi-ud-Din was brought from Sistán into Badakhshán. But before his arrival Mirzá Khán, as already stated, had come, and having killed Zobir, set himself up as king. As the people of Rágh, as well as most of the Hazára of Badakhshán, attached themselves to him, his supremacy was absolute. All the inhabitants of Badakhshán, both far and near, openly and privately, adhered to him.

When we reached Dili Bázár, one of the chief villages of Khatlán, we heard of these events. Whereupon we debated together as to what should be done; some of the people of that place counselled us, saying: "Nik Pai Sháh, although he professes obedience to Hamza Sultán, is nevertheless a well-wisher of Mirzá Khán, and has also pretty constant intercourse with Sháh Razi-ud-Din. If you throw yourselves upon him for support and protection, he will be able to convey you to Mirzá Khán." The Mauláná, having left me in the house of some person, went to see Nik Pai Khán, to whom he explained that he was the preceptor of Mirzá Khán,[1] and that, having escaped the tyranny of the Uzbeg, he was desirous of repairing to the foot of the throne of Mirzá Khán. "If," he continued, "you will help me in this matter, your reward shall be great;[2] I shall, moreover, be able to represent your loyalty in the most favourable light to Mirzá Khán." Nik Pai Sháh received the Mauláná with great respect and honour, and instructed five of his most trusted men to escort him across the river to Rusták, which, though in ruins, was at least a place of security from the violence of the Chirágh Kush. At about the hour of midday prayer, those five men came and conveyed us across the river Amu, whence we advanced towards Rusták. When the blazing torch of the sun descended into the oven of the West, and the sparks of the stars were scattered over the smoke-streaked vault of heaven, fire fell upon the souls of those five men, and they began to brawl and wrangle. Three other poor men, who carried a little merchandise, were of our party, being bound for Kala-i-Zafar, where they hoped to realise a small profit. These [five men] said to us: "You must pay duty [*báj*]"; and what was demanded was accordingly handed over. Again they said: "To each of us, separate payment is due"; and this also they took. Finally they said: "[You have

---

Polo, i., pp. 146–8, 152–5; *Cathay*, i., pp. 153–4; Colebrooke in *Asiatic Researches*, vii., p. 339; Sir H. Rawlinson, *J. R. G. S.*, vol. ix. (1839), pp. 36–7; Bretschneider, i., pp. 112 *seqq.*; and D'Herbelot, *Bibl. Orient.* under *Ismailoun*, *Molledoun*, &c.

[1] The Turki MS. says: one of Mirza Khan's oldest attendants.—R.

[2] Literally: [Yours] shall be the reward of Gabriel.—R.

no need of money]," and they threatened to plunder us. How could five poor artless men withstand five stalwart ruffians [*ghalcha*].[1] Besides, they gave us no time, but began to bind us all, as a first step towards putting us to death. When they laid hold of Mauláná Muhammad, he called out in an authoritative and severe tone of voice: "You dare not do us any injury. Do you know who this is?" (pointing to me). "This is the brother of Mirzá Khan, who, flying from Bokhárá, is on his way to visit his brother. A great number of his servants are following after him, as fast as they can, while others have stayed behind with Nik Pai Sháh. If we do not reach Kala-i-Zafar in safety, you can imagine what will be done to you." When Mauláná Muhammad had said this, the ruffians [*ghalcha*] became mild [*sust*], and replied in their own dialect: "Take back your possessions, oh! Khwája." So saying they restored what we had given them, and turned to depart. In spite of our insistance, they would not help us any further, but returned. We, however, had no intention of returning; but putting our whole trust in God's protection, continued our road until dawn. During the day we crept into hiding, and on the following night again set out. At daybreak we reached Rusták, where we were safe from the hostility of the accursed Muláhida.

On the following day we arrived at Kala-i-Zafar. During the time of the Uzbeg domination, of which I have spoken, when the people of Badakhshán raised their heads in every corner, and the Uzbeg made several unsuccessful invasions, one of the chiefs of Badakhshán was Mubárak Sháh. He had chosen out a strong place for himself, but before he was able to complete the fortifications, the Uzbeg came upon him. He gave them battle in that place, and defeated them, and for that reason he called the fort Kala-i-Zafar [the Fort of Victory], which name is the more appropriate seeing that Mubárak Sháh was of a tribe called "Muzaffari." It is the capital of Badakhshán.[2] This Mubárak Sháh was put to

[1] The dictionary meanings of the word *ghalcha* are—villager, vagabond, rustic. The late Mr. R. B. Shaw defined it as the name applied to the Tajik or Aryan inhabitants of the mountain districts of Badakhshán, Shignán, Wákhán, Sarikol, Kuláb, Karátigin, etc. In Eastern Turkistan he found it used generally for a slave bought with money. Vambery translates it: "Der knirps, der kleine Wuchs"; and Pavet de Courteille: "Court, bas, petit homme." In any case it was a reproachful name, applied by neighbouring tribes, and not used by the people themselves. In most parts of Badakhshán, in Shignán, Roshán, and I think I may say Wákhán, the name is unknown to the inhabitants. They not only do not call themselves by it, but appear unconscious of its being applied to them by others. It is one among the many instances, in Central Asia, of one people being known to another by a contemptuous appellation, instead of by their own name. (For a full account of the so-called *Ghalchah*, see Shaw's *Ghalchah Languages*, Calcutta, 1876.)

[2] The ruins of Kala Zafar are still to be found. They stand on the left bank of the Kokcha, a little below the mouth of the Argu river and above that of the Teshkán stream. The Kokcha valley contains several traces of mediæval times; for instance, the ruins of a fort called Ai-Khánim (on an isolated hill near the mouth of the river, and on its right bank), which is said to have been destroyed by

death by Zobir Rághi, who had defeated him, but who was, in turn, killed by Mirzá Khán, as already mentioned. [Mirzá Khán then ruled Badakhshán] and resided in Kala-i-Zafar.

Mirzá Abá Bakr had taken many of the upper [*báládast*][1] Hazára of Badakhshán, and the lower [*páyán*] side, which is flat country, he had joined on to the Uzbeg states, which lie on the borders of this territory. But the best of the country that was left between these [two territories] was under the sway of Sháh Razi-ud-Din, the Chirágh Kush, and his Muláhida. Mirzá Khán encountered many difficulties and hardships in Badakhshán. When I came to him, he gave me a warm and affectionate welcome. Eighteen days before my arrival, Sultán Said Khán had come to visit him, [had stayed a short time] and then left [for Kábul], as will be presently related. I remained one year in the service of Mirzá Khán. The rest of my adventures will be told after the account of the Khán's journey to Kábul.

CHAPTER XVIII.

ADVENT OF SULTÁN SAID KHÁN IN ANDIJÁN. HIS CAPTURE AND ESCAPE TO BÁBAR PÁDISHÁH IN KÁBUL.

It has already been stated that Sultán Said Khán had passed some time in the service of Sháhi Beg Khán, and was consequently well acquainted with his disposition and that of his nobles. He felt assured that Sháhi Beg would not spare the Moghul Sultáns, merely in recognition of having once been released by them, after

Chingiz Khan. Above Kala Zafar also, and nearer to the present capital, Faizabad, there are the remains of a stone bridge, among the scattered blocks of which, one of my party in 1885, found an Arabic inscription to the effect that the bridge had been built by Shah Sultan Muhammad, in the year 884 H. How long Kala Zafar remained the capital of Badakhshán I am not aware, but it appears from the narrative of Mirza Haidar that it could only have been founded towards the end of the fifteenth century. It was still the capital of Badakhshán in 1516 when Humayun took refuge there, but beyond that date I have met with no mention of it.

[1] The word *báládast* seems to be used throughout the *Tárikh-i-Rashidi*, with the meaning of a "hill," or "highland, district"; while the word *Hazára* denotes the inhabitants of such districts, and becomes therefore the equivalent of "highlander," without reference to any racial consideration or to the meaning of the word. I have never heard it used in this way, but to judge from the report of Munshi Faiz Bakhsh (1870) it must still be commonly met with, for he speaks of the inhabitants of Wákhán, Hunza, etc., as *Hazára*, and the former of these places must have been one of the "báládast Hazára of Badakhshán" mentioned in the text. (See Faiz Bakhsh in *J. R. G. S.*, 1872, p. 472.)

having fallen into their hands.[1] So, whenever he had heard praises bestowed on Sháhi Beg Khán, he had protested. Ultimately, things came to such a pass in Moghulistán, that he had no resource left but to surrender himself to the Uzbeg.

Under these conditions, he entered Andiján. The government of the province of Farghána was, at that time, in the hands of Jáni Beg Sultán. He had given Andiján to Khwája Ali Bahádur, who was one of Sháhi Beg Khán's most trusty men, and whom he now promoted to the rank of *Atálik*[2] [guardian]. He was partially mad, but, in military and state affairs, exceedingly capable.

The Khán reached Sulát-Kand,[3] which is one of the dependencies of Andiján, but, before he told his name and descent, asked the inhabitants what had happened to Sultán Mahmud Khán, and whither Sultán Khalil Sultán had been sent. They answered him: "Sultán Mahmud Khán and all the Khákáns of the Moghuls, who have come here, have been sent to the City of Non-Existence, by the Gate of Martyrdom."

At this announcement, the thread of the Khán's hope, which was slender as a spider's web, snapped in two. But he did not regret that he had come, for he had done so as a last resource, with his eyes open and knowing the risk he was running. Khwája Ali Bahádur sent people to seize whatever they had brought with them, and imprisoned the Khán in an apartment which was above the gateway of the citadel of Andiján.

On the morrow, when the glorious sword-bearer of the East drew his sword from the sheath of the horizon, and caused its dazzling brightness to illumine the earth, the resplendent world was utter darkness in the eyes of the Khán, who was sent, with his hands tied to his neck, to Jáni Beg Khán in Akhsi. But Khwája Ali Bahádur was depressed and sorrowful; he felt deeply for the Khán, but as he did not dare to disobey Sháhi Beg Khán's orders, he could not so much as think of releasing the Khán.

[1] This passage is obscure and the translation somewhat uncertain.

[2] The proper meaning of *Atálik* is "guardian" or "tutor." In speaking of Bokhara and the Kipchák country, Sir H. Howorth (on the authority of Senkofski) tells us that: "Originally the duties of the *Atálik* consisted in superintending the education of the heir to the throne and looking after his household. Afterwards the *Atálik* became one of the chief dignities of the Court, almost equal to those of Divan-begi and Grand Vizier, and eventually, having become hereditary and fallen into vigorous hands, the holders of the post became the virtual rulers of the country, like the Merovingian mayors of the palace, and succeeded like them . . . . in usurping the chief authority of the state." (Vol. II., p. 869). A modern instance of what Sir H. Howorth states here, was the career of the late Amir Yakub Beg, who, when he first began to exercise power in Eastern Turkistan, and while nominally in the service of Buzurg Khoja of Khokand, assumed the title of *Atálik Ghàzi*, but soon afterwards abolished his chief, styled himself *Amir-ul-Mumnin*, and reigned independently.

[3] On Ritter and Oetzel's map of 1841, a small place near Ush, to the south-east of Andijan, is marked as *Lát Kend*, which may possibly represent *Sulat-Kand* of the text. Neither name appears on modern maps.

Before sending him off he had despatched a special messenger [to announce the Khán's approach]. At about that time, Jáni Beg Sultán had fallen from his horse onto his head, and his brain had become severely deranged, so that now, most of his actions and words were inconsistent with a healthy understanding, and the reins of memory fell from the hands of his intellect. On the day that this news was brought to him, it chanced that his brain was influenced by the spirit of Islám and the Holy Law (the Most High God had ordained this, for the purpose of delivering the Khán), and he said: "I am not an executioner that I should endeavour to take any man's blood." He then ordered a letter [*nishán*] to be written to Khwája Ali Bahádur, saying: "The Moghul Sultán who has come [to you] has not been delivered into our custody. It would not be acting in conformity with the statutes of the Holy Law were I to take his life. [It behoves me] to open to him the meadows of mercy and safety, that he may wander whither he will." [Such was the purport of his letter.]

When the Khán related these incidents to me, as he frequently did, he used to say: "I had, for a long time, felt quite assured that the Uzbeg would spare none of the Moghul Sultáns, and had become so convinced of this, at the time of my first visit to Andiján, that when I arrived there [on this occasion], and [1] certain pious men had written to me and sent prayers [for me to repeat], I said in reply to them: 'One of the conditions [of prayer] is that nothing impossible should be prayed for; now my deliverance must be reckoned among impossibilities, and therefore these prayers for my safety would be ill-advised.' To which they answered: 'Though these prayers may not have the power to bring about deliverance from the imminent peril in which you stand, yet on account of them, God will give you a greater reward in the next world.' On this assurance I repeated the prayers which they had sent me. I began also to turn over in my mind my chances of safety, and how my escape might be achieved, but not one of the ideas that occurred to me seemed feasible. If, for example, Sháhi Beg Khán were now to die, how could his dying in Khorásán, at the time when they were going to put me to death in Akhsi, in any way further my escape? If, again, Jáni Beg Sultán were to die, his death would not throw the affairs of the Uzbeg into such confusion that, during the disturbance, my escape could be effected. In short, I could not conceive any possibility or probability of deliverance. As we drew near to Akhsi, we saw a horseman riding towards us; I was persuaded that he was coming to put me to death, and wondered how he would do it. But when he approached, we found that it was Maulána Haidar Kharsuz, one of the notables of Andiján. Throw-

[1] The Turki MS. interpolates here: I was quite prepared for martyrdom.

ing himself from the saddle, he came and kissed my stirrup, with joy and delight that knew no bounds, and said: 'Good news for you! Jáni Beg Sultán has issued an order for your release. The joyful mandate is now being brought by Dust Ali Chulák.' It then occurred to me that he was saying this just to set my fears at rest, so I said: 'May God reward you with good things! As for me, I have withdrawn my mind from life, and therefore do not stand in need of such comfort." But Mauláná Haidar reiterated his assertions, and was confirming them with the strongest asseverations and the most solemn oaths, when Dust Ali Chulák arrived, and commanded my guard [*muvakkal*] to return, to escort me back to Khwája Ali Bahádur and perform all the details of the mandate concerning me. Thus, from within one *farsákh* of Akhsi I was conveyed back to Andiján.

"When the mandate was delivered to Khwája Ali Bahádur, he [having read it] handed it to me. On perusing it, I found it to contain exactly what Mauláná Haidar had told me. Khwája Ali Bahádur then said: 'Though he should not abide by this decision but, changing his humour, should issue a second mandate reversing this one, still this is sufficient pretext for me; you must be cheerful, and enjoy now the soul-stirring wine-cups of the spirit of youth. Be at your ease.' However much I insisted that it was but base deceit and a mean device to pollute the cup of martyrdom with [earthly] wine, [my protestations] were of no avail.[1] Moreover, in conformity with the rules of good breeding [*ilm-i-maásh*], I was obliged to give in to his mode of thinking [and with an unwilling heart I accepted his invitation]. As the wine-cup was passed round, the rose-coloured liquor diffused itself over our cheeks, which had become yellow as saffron, from the jaundice-tainted order of the livid-souled Sháhi Beg Khán, but now opened out like the red rose or the new-blown tulip. All that day was spent in wine drinking, [and when night came on] the feast adorning torches made the banquet hall bright as the day. [The festivities had scarce recommenced] when one of Jáni Beg Sultán's chamberlains named Alláh Birdi came in and placed a sorrow-bearing mandate in the hands of Khwája Ali Bahádur, who passed it on to me, saying: 'Read thy letter.' In it was written: 'The question of the release of Sultán Said Khán has been reconsidered, and found to be contrary to the orders of the Khán. He must be sent to join those who have gone before him and who will never return: or, otherwise, according to the old Moghul custom, he must be sent to the capital, where he should, by means of the gallows, be sent to his lasting home.' On reading this ill-favoured mandate, the rosy tints of joy were exchanged for the saffron hues

[1] The Turki puts it: Now that I have mixed the wine of martyrdom, to defile my mouth with the pure wine [of enjoyment] were of no avail.

of apprehension. Khwájá Ali Bahádur grasped the situation, and asked: "What is the cause of your dejection? Read out the mandate.' So I read it aloud. Then Khwája Ali Bahádur became enraged, and said: 'His brain is disordered with mischief: whatever emanates from such a mind, if it be originally a good thought, becomes a sin, and if it be a premeditated sin—then God preserves us! When a man has escaped from the edge of the sword, or from the foot of the gallows, he is as difficult to lay hold of as quicksilver—he disappears like camphor unmixed with pepper. Where can I find him?' The chamberlain, kissing the ground of respect, said: 'It is not reasonable that you, Bahádur, should deviate from the straight-road of loyalty and adopt that of falsehood, which is the worst of qualities. You say that the Sultán, like quicksilver, is not to be caught; but he is now at your side, and of this I am a witness.' [At these words] Khwája Ali Bahádur blazed up, like a fire, with rage, and cried: 'Have all the worthy services and deeds of valour I have performed in the employment of Jáni Beg Sultán, resulted in so little, that a Chaghatái like yourself (whose skirt of service is still so defiled with the pollution of hostility that no water of forgiveness could cleanse it) should come and give me the lie direct, and point out to me the straight road of loyalty to this family? I will report your answer in full to the Sultán.' He then ordered a hole to be cut out of a beam, and that the beam should be placed upon the man's neck [and he be made to sit before the gate]."

After the Khán [Sultán Said] had been invested with the robe of sovereignty of Andiján, this same Alláh Bardi was taken before him, and he was thus reminded of the man's former base conduct. But he said: "Khwája Ali Bahádur avenged me that same night, and the rancour I bore him was washed from my heart. Let him now be restored to his former post of chamberlain;" and he gave him the middle rank of chamberlain, which was a high office for him.[1]

"That night was spent in companionship, until day dawned; on the morrow, attended by a few men, we set out for Karátigin. After travelling for one day, the men sent to accompany us, having lost the right road, turned back. When Khwájá Ali Bahádur was informed of this, he vented his wrath upon these men and punished them severely." He kept the Khán with him some days, while he selected for him some distinguished and trusty persons. The first among them was Mauláná Khaliki, a talented, good, and studious man; he wrote the *Naskh-Táalik* perfectly, and composed good poetry; he was also a proficient musician. Another of them was Khwája Sálih, who was the leading merchant in the province of Andiján, and was known by every one he met on the road, while

[1] Here follows a prayer, which is omitted.

people often appealed to him for advice in their affairs. A third was Mauláná Yusuf Káshghari, who was an accountant [*muhtasib*], much esteemed in Andiján for his judgment. Another was Gadái Piri, a professional courtier [*nadim*] and a skilled musician. Another was Mir Ahmad, one of the Andiján Turks; he had travelled much and knew all the best routes. Another was Jalál, a very serviceable man. Having given him these few men as an escort, he started the Khán off a second time.

Khwája Sálih and Mauláná Yusuf were dressed like merchants, Mauláná Khaliki, Darvish Piri and the Khán were in the guise of students, and looked very like kalandars. Mir Ahmad and Jalál passed as servants of the merchants. Thus attired, they set forth and reached Kala-i-Zafar in perfect peace and safety. Here they found Mirzá Khán, who received and entertained them as well as his straitened circumstances would allow. They remained there eighteen days. Now, since Mirzá Khán was a very feeble man, some of his retainers, on account of his weakness, thought fit to offer the Khán the government of Kala-i-Zafar (which was not worth half a loaf of bread). But the Khán declined, saying: "Mirzá Khán, who is my cousin, has been exposed to a thousand hardships, by crooked fortune. It would be contrary to all rules of good feeling and justice to oppose him, or to deprive him of this [possession]." The Khán accordingly hastened to depart, and went on to Kábul. Eighteen days after his departure, I arrived at Mirzá Khán's [capital], as has been mentioned above.

On reaching Kábul, the Khán was welcomed with the utmost respect and honour by the Emperor. The Khán used to say [when telling his story]: "Those days that I spent in Kábul were the freest from care or sorrow of any I have ever experienced, or ever shall experience. I spent two years and a half at the court of this excellent Prince, in a continual succession of enjoyments, and in the most complete abandonment to pleasure and absence of preoccupation. I was on friendly terms with all, and made welcome by all. I never suffered even a headache, unless from the effects of wine; and never felt distressed or sad, except on account of the ringlets of some beloved one."

In short, the Khán remained in Kábul as the companion and confidant of the Emperor. There existed between these two great princes perfect accord and love and trust. The Khán's visit lasted from Shabán 914 to Ramazán 916,[1] at which latter date Sháhi Beg Khán fell into the hands of Sháh Ismail, and was killed by him, as will be related.

[1] From Nov., 1508, to Dec., 1510.

CHAPTER XIX.

MIRZÁ KHÁN'S LIFE IN BADAKHSHÁN. THE AUTHOR GOES FROM BADAKHSHÁN TO KÁBUL.

I HAVE mentioned that I arrived at Kala-i-Zafar just eighteen days after the Khán's departure for Kábul. Mirzá Khán was living there in exceedingly straitened circumstances, being without provisions and surrounded by the scheming natives of Badakhshán. The Tangi Bálá,[1] in which are situated the strongest places of the Hazára, had been annexed to Káshghar, as will be mentioned below. The flat country of Badakhshán, the most fertile and prosperous part of that state, was under the control of the Uzbeg; while the rest [of the land] from fear of the Uzbeg had [been abandoned and had] become a waste. What yet remained over from the panther of the mountains of enmity, on the one hand, and from the crocodile of the river of tyranny, on the other, (that is to say, the Uzbeg and the Káshghari) had passed to Sháh Razi-ud-Din, the Chirágh Kush, who, having been brought from Sistán to Badakhshán, had been appointed king [of this portion]. He had introduced the religion of the Muláhidas, and outdid the oppression of his two tyrannical predecessors. Mirzá Khán, as a Musulmán, was much harassed [by these infidels] and had scarcely the necessaries of life. That winter was passed in suffering.

In the early spring, a dissension arose among the supporters of Sháh Razi-ud-Din, which ended in their cutting off his head and laying it at the feet of Mirzá Khán. By this defeat of the Mulá-hida [Mirzá Khán] gained a little power. Thus passed the spring; and at the end of autumn [*tirmáh*] a compulsory order came from the Emperor of the following purport: "The son of Muhammad Husain Mirzá has been with you; your country is always exposed to the forays of the Uzbeg, and my mind can never be at rest as long as he remains there; you must send him to me."

When Mirzá Khán gave me leave to go to Kábul, he tried his best to procure a coloured garment for me, but was unable to find one [and was obliged to excuse himself]. On that day a most curious incident occurred. I have already mentioned that I fell from my horse and dislocated my elbow at Langar Mir Amád (which is a dependency of Hisár), and that it had been broken again and set at Pushang. Although the pain had subsided, I was not able to bend and straighten my arm. I could not bend it

[1] The *Tangi Bálá* may be translated—"the higher defiles" or "the upper ravines."

enough to touch my face with my hand, nor straighten it sufficiently to draw a bow. During the spring I spent with Mirzá Khán, a man of Badakhshán, having stolen a two year old horse from the Uzbeg, had brought it as a present [*pishkash*] to Mirzá Khán who, in turn, gave it to me. One day the Mirzá was taking a ride for pleasure, and I accompanied him on that particular horse. While we were riding along, a thorn ran into [the *khárish-gáh*[1] of] my horse. He gave two or three bounds into the air, and as I had not strength enough to keep hold of the bridle, it fell from my hand, and I was thrown on to the ground upon my injured arm. As I struck the ground, I heard a sound in my bad elbow. The shock was so violent that I fainted. After a time I came to, and found that Mirzá Khán was holding my head upon his knees. He asked me how I felt. When I had quite recovered my senses, having bound up my arm, they conveyed me to Kala-i-Zafar. There they sent for the bone-setters [*kamángar*].[2] On examination, they found that my arm had gone back to its proper place, so that after a short time I recovered the entire use of it, and no injury was traceable. This was certainly a very strange occurrence.

In a word, at the beginning of the month Rajab I left Kala-i-Zafar and the service of Mirzá Khán, and turned towards Kábul, accompanied by a party of sixteen. We only had two horses with us, and so limited was our baggage that I had nothing to lie on at night. Mauláná Muhammad, who was a sort of father to the party, had nothing but one meagre shawl, such as is worn by the poorest men in Badakhshán. What the condition of the others was, may be surmised.

When we reached Kábul, we were received by Shirun[3] Tagháí, who was maternal uncle to the Emperor and myself, and one of the pillars of state. With a hundred marks of respect, he invited me to his own house, where I was entertained with distinction and kindness. Later, the Emperor sent a messenger to say that, after three days, the happy hour would arrive when he would send for me. After that, the moon of my ascendency and [the star of my good-luck] emerged from their eclipse, and my misfortune changed to prosperity. An order came that I should have the honour of waiting [upon the Emperor]. When I came into his presence, the joy-diffusing glance of the Emperor fell upon me, and from the excess of his love and the intensity of his kindness, strung pearls and set rubies began to rain down upon me from his

[1] I can find no meaning for *khárish-gáh*. The dictionaries only give "part of a horse."—R.

[2] The word only means "bow-maker" in Persian, but is, I believe, used in India for "bone-setter."—R.

[3] In Baber's *Memoirs* this man's name is written *Shirin*, but in the *Tárikh-i-Rashidi*, everywhere *Shirun*.

benign, jewel-scattering eye. He extended towards me the hand of favour and bade me welcome. Having first knelt down, I [raised myself and] advanced towards him. He then clasped me to the bosom of affection—drew me to the breast of fatherly love, and held me thus for a while. When he let me go, he would no longer allow me to observe the formalities of respect, but made me sit down at his side. While we were thus seated, he said to me with great benevolence: "Your father and brother and all your relations have been made to drink the wine of martyrdom; but thank God, you have come back to me again in safety. Do not grieve too much at their loss. For I will take their place, and whatever favour of affection you could have expected from them, that, and more, will I show you." With such promises and tenderness did he comfort me, so that the bitterness of orphanage and the poison of banishment were driven from my mind. He then asked me: "Who was it that carried you off in flight?" I replied: "My master, Mauláná Muhammad Sadr." He then sent for the Mauláná. When he arrived [the Emperor] honoured him with many kind speeches, and kept asking him the particulars of his story, while the Mauláná several times recounted the details of our escape. [The Emperor] praised him highly and rejoiced his soul with promises of favour. [When the Mauláná had taken his leave] the Emperor said to me: "You have not yet paid your respects to Sultán Said Khán," and thereupon he ordered one of his private officers to take me to the Sultán. I accompanied this officer, and at once waiting on the Khán, benefited likewise by his joy-scattering glances. I then returned to the presence of the Emperor. After sitting with him for a short time, I took my leave, amid assurances of royal favour.

When I came out, a man advanced to meet me with great respect, and said: "I am the steward [*kalávuz*] of the abode which the Emperor has appointed for you." So saying, he led the way to an elegant mansion; its rooms were spread with many-coloured carpets and beautiful thrones [*masnad*]. Everything in the way of furniture, food, clothing, servants, and slaves, had been so fully prepared as to leave nothing to be desired in the whole building. It may be imagined how I enjoyed so sudden a transition to comfort, ease, and abundance from a state of poverty, misfortune, suffering, and hardship, which had rendered the soul weary of its confinement within the cage of the body. How can I ever show sufficient thankfulness? May God reward him with good things!

Thus I passed a long time in the service of the Emperor, in perfect happiness and freedom from care; and he was for ever, either by promises of kindness or by threats of severity, encouraging me to study. If he ever noticed any little virtue or new acquisition, he would praise it in the highest terms, commend it to everybody, and invite their approbation. All that time, the Emperor showed me such affection and kindness as a fond father shows his son and heir. It was a hard day for me when I lost my father, but the bitterness of my desolation became scarcely perceptible, owing to the blessed favours of the Emperor.

From this time, to the year 918 [1512 A.D.] I remained in his service. Whenever he rode out, I had the honour of riding at his side, and when he received friends, I was sure to be among the invited. In fact, he never let me be separated from him. When I was studying, for example, directly my lesson was over he would send someone to fetch me. And in this fatherly manner did he continue to treat me till the end of my stay [*tá akhar-i-hál*].

CHAPTER XX.

EXPEDITION OF SHAHI BEG KHÁN AGAINST THE KAZÁK, AND THE BEGINNING OF HIS DECLINE.

As Sháhi Beg Khán had filled the cups of the Kháns and my father with the wine of martyrdom, and had made them drink it to the last dreg, so also was his own cup of life full, and his fortune departed; for has it not been said: "The wine which thou hast made others drink, that must thou also drink of in the end"? The goblet of his prosperity was upset, and that which he had caused others to taste, he was himself, in turn, obliged to drink to the dregs. To be brief, as soon as he had set his mind at rest concerning the Kháns and my father, Sháhi Beg Khán carried devastation in all directions. In the year 915 [1509 A.D.] he proceeded against the Kazáks. At that time, although Baranduk was Khán, yet all the business of government was conducted by Kásim Khán. In spite of his great power, Sháhi Beg Khán had not force enough to withstand Kásim Beg. At that period, the numbers of his army exceeded 20,000. In winter time every one stayed in some place [1] where there was fodder for the cattle. In the middle of the winter, Sháhi Beg Khán was engaged in plundering on every side, but he soon returned, his object being not to remain too far from his own country.[2] About the time above mentioned, he made his last expedition, but the strength of his horses and soldiers was quite exhausted; he himself remained in

[1] In the Turki MS.: Were scattered in all directions.—R.

[2] This passage is obscure. It may mean that he never stayed away long at one time.—R.

the district of Kuk Káshána, and having detached a force, whose horses had some strength left, sent them forward. This party fell in with a few men, whom they despoiled and made prisoners.

One day they had halted for the sake of feeding their horses, when news came that Kásim Khán was close at hand. This news alarmed them. Buyun Pir Hasan, one of Kásim Khán's Amirs, having heard of the invasion of the Shaibáu, advanced against them with his own followers; he spread the report that Kásim Khán was approaching, and had let himself be seen in the distance. Sháhi Beg Khán's men, being fully persuaded that Kásim Khán was really upon them, abandoned all they had seized—nay, even all they had brought with them—and retreated, in the utmost disorder and confusion, to Sháhi Beg Khán, bearing the news of Kásim Khán's approach. Sháhi Beg Khán at once ordered them to sound the drum of departure, without paying attention to anything [but getting away]. Those who liked stayed, those who wished to go went. Broken and in disorder, they reached Samarkand at the end of the winter. [Sháhi Beg Khán] himself went on to Khorásán, where he spent the spring.

In the beginning of autumn [*tirmáh*] he led an army against the Hazára; but search as he might, he could not find a trace of them in the Hazára mountains. For they had crept into hiding, so that it was impossible to find them. He returned by way of the passes, and along the bottom of a ravine where flows the River Halman [Helmand]. There were but few roads by which it was possible to descend the ravine, and these were extremely difficult. It was well nigh impossible for an army of that magnitude to pass by one or two paths, or to carry away [sufficient] water [or to water the horses and beasts of burden]. They marched as they could for several days, but from want of water they lost their courage. Numbers of the cattle perished; and this army, too, having received the decree of defeat, returned to Khorásán. As it was winter, and as two armies in succession had fared thus badly, he gave his soldiers a general leave of absence [allowing every man] to return to his own home and country, whether he came from the confines of Turkistán or the farthest extremity of Irák and Kirmán. At this juncture, news came that Sháh Ismail was advancing on Khorásán. Now, as the army was dispersed, Sháhi Beg Khán did not think it advisable to remain in Herat. He sent messengers to the surrounding districts, to summon the Sultáns and Amirs to assemble in Merv, whilst he himself proceeded thither; and when he reached Merv he found Sháh Ismail was already close upon him, as shall be presently related.

CHAPTER XXI.

THE BEGINNING OF HOSTILITIES BETWEEN SHÁHI BEG KHÁN AND SHÁH ISMAIL. DEATH OF THE FORMER AT THE HANDS OF THE LATTER.

It is written at the beginning of this Part, and is mentioned in the list of the kings who were reigning in the different countries in the year 905, that Sháh Ismail had gained complete dominion over Irák. His dynasty had driven the Perfect Law [*Shariat*] out of that country, and had brought about general massacres. However, there is no room in this Epitome for an exposition of his misdeeds. When the frontiers of Sháhi Beg Khán's states came to border on Irák, the Uzbeg used to make forays into those parts of Irák which immediately adjoined Khorásán. On this account Sháh Ismail sent an envoy to Sháhi Beg Khán, bearing suitable gifts, together with a letter, which ran as follows: "Hitherto the dust of dissension has never settled upon the skirts of our thoughts to such an extent as to raise a cloud of enmity. Let the path of fatherly conduct be observed on your side, and on this side the bonds of filial relationship shall be established. [Verses]

Plant the tree of friendship: for its fruit will be the desire of your heart;
Root up the sapling of enmity, which produces countless griefs."

When the bearer of this missive arrived[1] at the court of the Khán, the [following] answer was returned: "It is fitting that every man follow the profession of his father. If he follows his mother he is going backwards. For Uzun Hasan withdrew himself from the circle of kings, on the day that he gave his daughter in marriage to your father, as did also Sultán Yakub, son of Hasan, in giving him his sister. You had a right to make claims on your mother's side, so long as there was no son in the world like me—Sultán, son of a Sultán. As the proverb says: 'Let the son do the father's work, and the daughter the mother's.' [Verses]

Kings know the secrets of the business of the realm.
Oh! Háfiz, thou beggar, sitting in the corner, do not complain."

Having exhausted his eloquence, Sháhi Beg Khán sent back by the envoy a staff [*ásá*] and a beggar's bowl [*kachkul*], adding:

[1] The Turki MS. is fuller here; it says: Having performed the requisite observances, they laid the presents before the Khan and submitted the letter for his perusal. When Shahi Beg Khan had acquainted himself with the contents of this excellent epistle, he made answer . . . .—R.

"In case you have forgotten your father's trade, I remind you of it. [Verses.]

> Oh! my friend, if you value your life give ear to good counsel;
> Ye happy youths, listen to the wisdom of the sage old man.

If you place your foot on the step of sovereignty think of your own danger. [Verses.]

> He may clasp the bride of sovereignty firmly to his breast,
> Who dares to kiss her amid the clashing of keen swords."

So saying, he dismissed the envoy from Irák, while he himself led an army against the Hazára. The envoy, on his return, delivered the reply to Sháh Ismail, who, on hearing it, said: "If it is incumbent on every son to follow his father's trade, we, being sons of Adam, ought all of us to practise prophecy! If sovereignty had been confined to the hereditary descendants of kings, there would have been more Pishdádi, and never any Kaiani. How would Chingis himself have become king? and where did *you* come from?

> [Verses.] Oh! youth, do not boast of your dead father;
> Do not, like a dog, take delight in bones!"

Then, in return for his presents, he sent Sháhi Beg Khán a spinning-wheel and spindle, saying: "You wrote in your letter to me, 'Whosoever would clasp the bride of sovereignty close to his breast . . . .' I, too, say the same thing, and behold, I have bound on the girdle to offer you fight, and have placed the foot of contest in the stirrup of fierce warfare. If you come out to meet me face to face in battle, our claims shall be thereby decided. And if you will not fight, go and sit in a corner and busy yourself with the little present I am sending you. [Verses.]

> We have had many experiences in this monastery of Recompenses.
> Whosoever quarrelled with the Family of the Prophet was defeated."

Sháhi Beg Khán had disbanded his army, and was in Merv when this letter arrived. He despatched expresses to every quarter to collect his forces, but before even the troops of the neighbouring districts could assemble, Sháh Ismail arrived and pitched his camp in the vicinity of Merv. During three days there were continual skirmishes, and the army of Sháhi Beg Khán began to muster from all directions. Sháh Ismail then came out from the broken ground [where he was camped], and when the pickets of the Uzbeg army saw this movement they reported it. The Uzbeg [at once] imagined that the enemy had repented having come, and were about to turn back. At the hour of afternoon prayers, on the *ruz-i-shak* of Ramazán in the year 916 [1510 A.D.], they marched out, with a force of about 20,000 men. Some of his advisers, such as Amir Kambar and Amir Rái, represented that: "To-day we had better suspend hostilities [and not pursue Sháh Ismail]; for Ubaid Ullah Sultán and Timur Sultán are encamped with 20,000 men at a distance of one *farsákh;* [to-morrow they will come and join their force to ours]. Moreover, it has been positively ascertained that the enemy, in thus returning, either means to retreat or [to draw us on to] battle. If they wish to fight, we had better [wait until more of our troops have assembled from the surrounding districts] and engage them with as large a force as possible. And if they are really in flight, there is no necessity for the chief to pursue them in person. Ubaid Ullah Sultán, Timur Sultán, and a few other Amirs can follow them, while His Majesty the Khán can travel quietly and leisurely, stage by stage, right into Irák. It is evident that in the case of his retreating from this place, our men can drive him forward and rout him, so that he will not have strength to establish himself even in Irák." To this the Khán replied: "[You have said well] nevertheless, to make war on Sháh Ismail is a holy war, and one of importance: moreover there will be much plunder, and it would be a sacrifice of gain in this world and advantage in the next, were I to share [this undertaking] with the Sultáns. We must be bold." So saying, he [mounted his horse and that same hour] set out [in pursuit of Sháh Ismail]. When they had crossed the broken ground and entered the open plain, they saw that the enemy had halted, and they calculated them to be 40,000 strong. Before the Uzbeg army had time to get properly into fighting order, the Turkomán contingent charged them. When Sháhi Beg Khán's men saw themselves outflanked by the enemy, they lost their steadiness and turned in flight. But the leaders of the army stood their ground, till at length Sháhi Beg Khán and all his officers were killed. No history has recorded, nor has any one read or heard of [another] battle in which all the commanders of the army were slain.

When the fugitives reached the fort of Merv, every man of them who was able to do so, took his family and fled, while such as were unable, repeated the verse [from the Korán] about separation from wife and children, and then departed.

Now, most of the Moghuls had been sent to Khorásán by Sháhi Beg Khán, so that they might be further from the Kháns and from Moghulistán. When the Uzbeg reached the River Amu, they fell into the hands of these Moghuls, who did not fail to plunder them. 20,000 Moghuls then separated themselves and went to Kunduz. Ubaid Ullah Sultán and Timur Sultán were still encamped near Merv, when news of the defeat reached them.

They immediately repaired to the fort of Merv, when they seized the haram of Sháhi Beg Khán, and of several of the Sultans and nobles, together with anything that caught their eye, and went off again the same night. Of those who stayed behind, all the men were compelled, by the flashing swords of the Turkománs, to taste the wine of martyrdom, while the women were carried off into bondage. There followed, also, a general massacre of the people of Merv.

Meanwhile Sháh Ismail returned to Herat, where he commanded all the chief men [*akábir*] of the town to assemble in the Mulkán mosque, and read the *Khutba*; also, while the *Khutba* was being read, to pour out curses upon the Companions of the Prophet and the faithful Aisha. When the chief men were met together in the mosque of Mulkán, they carried out that unseemly order, and then remained silent, until Háfiz-ud-Din, who was the preacher [*khatib*], was conducted to the pulpit. Háfiz ascended the pulpit and gave out praise and thanksgiving to the Bestower of all good gifts, and praises to the Lord of all living things [the Prophet]. When the turn came for the blessed names of the Companions of the Prophet, the hand of honour and piety seized the collar of [faithfulness to] Islám and gave him the courage of Háfiz, so that he, preferring the good things of the next world, and eternal felicity, to this transitory life, said: "For many years I have read the *Khutba* in accordance with the *Sunna*. To-day, the sun of my life has reached the west of old age. If it were the dawn of my days, I might not have hesitated to perform this act of infidelity to preserve my young life; but now that my days are just drawing to a close, what benefit could I derive from such an act of blasphemy [*kufr*]?" So saying, he proceeded to read out the names of the Companions, with the customary honour and respect. The accursed Kizilbásh (may God curse them) rose up to a man, and pulled the hoary-headed Háfiz down from the pulpit, by his collar, trampled him under their feet, and then cut him in pieces; while the great men of the city all fled.

On the following day, the Shaikh-ul-Islám (who has been mentioned among the great men of Khorásán) was sent for by Sháh Ismail. When the Shaikh came into the king's presence, the king turned to him and said: "Oh, Shaikh! you are a learned man. It is a pity you should commit an error. Come and curse the Companions and adopt the Shia faith." The Shaikh then opened his lips and said: "Oh, my son! what do you know of religion, that you should point out the way thereof to me? Bring before me those cowardly men who are nothing more or less than infidels and worthy of death, and who have brought you to this sad plight. If their words convince me, I will renounce my own faith and enter their sect. But if the superiority of my religion is proved against them, then you will renounce your corrupt belief and adopt my pure faith."

Then Sháh Ismail turned to his Ulama and asked them what they had to say to this. They replied: "With people such as these words are of no avail."

That hundred times a wretch twice turned towards the Shaikh ul-Islám and said: "Come, Shaikh, renounce your sect." But the Shaikh retorted insultingly: "Oh, cursed infidel, may your mouth be filled with the earth of malediction, and your head struck with the stones of execration! You, who are deceived by false and wicked guides, and cannot distinguish between the path of life and the road to perdition: what do you know of religion, or of sects? How do you know Satan from God the all-merciful? By what science, learning, intelligence, or perception can you distinguish the true from the false, that you should lecture me on the True Faith?" On hearing these scornful remarks, the king laid hold of his bow and let fly an arrow at the Shaikh, which struck him. The Shaikh pulled the arrow out, rubbed some of the blood that issued from the wound, over his blessed face and white beard, saying: "Thanks be to God, that after a life of eighty years spent in the confirmation of the True Faith, and the refutation of false doctrine, I have seen my white beard stained with the blood of martyrdom." That black-faced heretic [*bad-kish*] then drew another arrow from his quiver [*kish*], and shot it at the Shaikh. He then gave orders for him to be carried out and hanged on a tree, and for the tree to be afterwards cut down from the root. The Shaikh fell with the tree, and they carried him away and burned him in the Malik bazaar. Try as they might, they could not make the blessed breast of the Shaikh to burn, and he lay for some time in the bazaar exposed to the kicks of infidels. . . .[1] In short, the persecution was continued as long as Sháh Ismail remained in Khorásán.

A summarised account of the rest of his reign will follow.

[1] Here follows a rhetorical passage, explaining why God allows His faithful servants to be exposed to calamity, in the defence of the truth.—R.

CHAPTER XXII.

ARRIVAL OF THE NEWS OF THE DEFEAT OF SHÁHI BEG KHÁN BY SHÁH ISMAIL. MARCH OF THE EMPEROR FROM KÁBUL TO KUNDUZ.

IN the early part of Ramazán of the year 916 [1510 A.D.] a person came to Kábul with a letter from Mirzá Khán to the Emperor. The passes were blocked with snow, for it was the season of the beginning of Capricorn. The letter contained the news that Sháh Ismail, having come from Irák, had engaged and defeated Sháhi Beg Khán at Merv. It had not been fully ascertained whether Sháhi Beg Khán had been killed or not.[1] All the Uzbeg had recrossed the river Amu, and fled to Kunduz, where Amir Urus Durman then was.[2]

Nearly 20,000 Moghuls, having separated from the Uzbeg, had also gone to Kunduz from Merv. "I, myself," he added, "have gone over to Kunduz. If you will quickly turn the reins of your power in the direction of Kunduz, I will attach myself to you, and I have the firmest hope that you may soon recover your hereditary kingdom."

[As soon as the Emperor had read the contents of this letter] he set out with all possible speed [although it was] in the depth of winter. [He took the route] of Ab Dara[3] [since by that route] there were no high passes to cross. He kept the Feast of Ramazán[4] in the Bamián district, and at the beginning of

[1] It is somewhat singular that Mirza Haidar nowhere records the death of Sháhi Beg Khan, or gives any account of how it took place. It is fully recorded, however, by other authors. His army was completely routed by Shah Ismail at Muhammadabad, near Merv, in 1510, when Shahi Beg, attended by about 500 men, chiefly heads of tribes and persons of distinction, had to fly for his life. They were pursued and took refuge in a walled enclosure, erected for herding cattle. This enclosure had but one entrance, and as the pursuers pressed towards it, those inside attempted to escape, by jumping their horses over the wall on the far side, at the foot of which ran a river. They fell in heaps, one upon another, and Shahi Beg was crushed and smothered by those who followed him. Afterwards, his body was disentangled from the heap of men and horses, and his head was cut off and presented to Ismail, who ordered a number of barbarities to be committed with the Khan's remains. (See Erskine's *Hist.*, i., p. 303; Howorth ii., p. 708, etc.)

[2] This Amir Urus I cannot trace. He appears to have belonged to the Durman sub-tribe of Uzbegs, who nowadays occupy, according to Mayef, the valley of the lower Vakhsh or Surkháb. (*Geogr. Mag.*, Dec., 1876, p. 329).

[3] The *Ab-dara* pass, or defile, is frequently mentioned by Baber, though we never hear of it nowadays. It appears to be the name not of an actual pass (or *kotal*) across the main range, but rather that of a defile leading up to the *Shibr*, or *Shibertu*, pass from the northern side, and was used only in winter when the water was low. The name does not occur in our most recent maps. (See note p. 36.)

[4] The 2nd January, 1511.

Shawál reached Kunduz, where he was received by Mirzá Khán, and by the Moghuls who had been with the Uzbeg. Having reposed for a few days in Kunduz, after the fatigues of the journey, it was proposed that they should proceed against Hisár, where Hamza Sultán and Mahdi Sultán, two of the most eminent of the Uzbeg Sultáns, were ruling. The winter was nearly over when they passed the River Amu, at the ford of Tukuz Táram. When Hamza Sultán heard of their approach, he rode out of Hisár and repaired to Vakhsh, while the Emperor advanced to the plain [*dasht*] of Kulak,[1] which is one of the most noted localities in Khatlán. There he learnt that Hamza Sultán was in Vakhsh. That same night he set out by the higher road to surprise Sultán Hamza, and at sunrise reached his camp. Nobody was there. They searched on every side, and found a few peasants, who gave them the following information concerning Hamza Sultán: "Yesterday, at the hour of midday prayers, news came that the Emperor had pitched his camp in the plain of Kulak, whereupon [Hamza Sultán] immediately set out for that place, by the lower road." The Emperor at once started in pursuit, along the road which Hamza Sultán had taken, and at noontide prayers again found himself at his quarters of the night before. Hamza Sultán, for his part, had reached the camp at dawn, and found a precisely similar state of affairs; he, too, set out in the track of our army, and at midday prayer time re-entered his own camp.

The Emperor and his men believed that Hamza Sultán would not be able to resist them; while Hamza Sultán, on the other hand, thought that [the Emperor] had only brought a few men with him from Kábul, and that the Moghul army, having only just arrived, would not yet have made sufficient preparations to be able to fight. As both sides entertained such ideas as these, they became afraid of one another.[2] That same night the Emperor pressed on to Kunduz, while Hamza Sultán fled to Hisár. After a few days, they each received the news of the other's flight, and both of them repeated, in thankfulness for their escape, the verse "Praise be to God who has averted from us an affliction." The Emperor, on reaching Kunduz, found that an ambassador had arrived from Sháh Ismail, bearing tenders of friendship. In the

[1] *Tukuz Tarám* means, in Turki, the nine "branchings" or "forks" of a river. The ford is not marked on any map that I am acquainted with, nor can any particular town or village of *Vakhsh* be located, nor the *Dasht-i-Kulak*. But the route taken from Kunduz to Hisar is made evident by a reference to the map in this volume. In all probability, whatever town or fort may have been known as *Vakhsh*, at the period in question, would have been situated not far from the modern *Kurghán Tipa*, or the *Kurgan Tube* of Russian maps. (See pp. 21 and 24.)

[2] The author seems to have fallen into an inconsistency here. As all the texts, both Persian and Turki, read alike, the translation is allowed to stand. If each side thought the other weak, it is not clear why they should have dreaded one another and avoided a battle.

meantime Khánzáda Begum, the Emperor's sister, had come from Khorásán [having been sent by Sháh Ismail]. It has been already related how the Emperor, at the siege of Samarkand, had given his sister, Khánzáda Begum, to Sháhi Beg Khán, as a ransom for his own life, and had thus escaped. The Begum was taken into Sháhi Beg Khán's haram, and by him, had a son named Khurram Sháh Sultán. After this, the Khán [Sháhi Beg] began to fear that she might, in concert with her brother, plot against his life; he therefore divorced her, and gave her to Sayyid Hádi, one of the most eminent Sayyids of the *Sayyidátái*[1]—a man who was held in the greatest respect and honour by himself and the Sultáns and all the Uzbeg. Sayyid Hádi had been killed in the battle of Merv, and the Begum and her son had fallen into the hands of the Turkománs. When Sháh Ismail discovered that she was Babar Pádisháh's sister, he treated her with great attention, and sent her back, with an ambassador bearing costly gifts, to the Emperor. When Khánzáda Begum arrived [the Emperor was overjoyed] and despatched Mirzá Khán to Sháh Ismail laden with presents, and charged with protestations of submission, good faith, and entreaties for support and assistance. Sháh Ismail received him well, and having acceded to his requests, speedily gave him leave to return.

During this interval, a messenger came from my uncle to announce that he had entirely cleared Farghána of the Uzbeg, and that he had brought that country under his complete control, so that the extermination of the Uzbeg and the conquest of Mavará-un-Nahr would now become an easy matter. This brings me to the next chapter.

CHAPTER XXIII.

BRIEF ACCOUNT OF THE PROCEEDINGS OF MY UNCLE SAYYID MUHAMMAD MIRZÁ, AND DETAILS OF THE CONQUEST OF THE COUNTRY OF FARGHÁNA.

At the time of the devastation of Táshkand, my father's brother, Sayyid Muhammad Mirzá (who is everywhere spoken of in this book as "my uncle" in an absolute sense), was in Táshkand, in

[1] In order to explain who were the Sayyids and the Sayyidátá, I cannot do better than cite Sir H. Howorth. He informs us (on the authority of M. Schefer) that the former "were all who claimed descent from the Khalifs Osman and Ali, through the daughters of the Prophet. The Khojas claimed descent from the Khalifs Abu-bakr and Omar, by other women than daughters of the Prophet. The Sayyids had precedence of the Khojas. The latter were divided into two categories, the Khojas Sayyid-ata, who possessed deeds proving their descent, and the Khojas Juibari, whose title-deeds were lost, and who could only appeal to tradition and repute." (Vol. ii., p. 870.)

the service of Sultán Mahmud Khán. When the Kháns went to attack Andiján, they first of all easily subdued Kásán, and gave it to my uncle; they next proceeded to Akhsi, whither Sháhi Beg Khán had also gone, and there a fight ensued, which has been already mentioned. On the news of Sháhi Beg Khán's victory reaching my uncle, he left Kásán [immediately], and though he himself had not been defeated, he joined those who were flying into Moghulistán. When Sultán Mahmud Khán went into Moghulistán (as has been mentioned) my uncle remained with him until the death of Sultán Ahmad Khán. After this event (as has also been related) the Khán said to my uncle, in disparagement of Aksu and Moghulistán: "The position of towel-washer in Táshkand is better than that of king in Moghulistán." To which my uncle responded: "Verily, it is better if one is allowed to wash towels." The Khán was offended at these words, and some of those base men [*arázil*], whose manner it always is to slander good people behind their backs, strove to aggravate the Khán's anger to such a degree as to cause him to put my uncle to death, and succeeded in preventing any reconciliation ever being effected between the two. However, the Khán said: "He is too near a relation for me to take extreme measures with. As he has no evil intentions against me, let him take himself off; let him go to Mansur Khán at Turfán." My uncle, therefore, was sent to Turfán, while the Khán himself went to Moghulistán. In journeying towards Turfán, my uncle allied himself, at Aksu, with the survivors of Sultán Ahmad Khán's people, who had remained in that province.

When Sultán Mahmud Khán came to his brother in Aksu, his son, Sultán Muhammad Sultán, and Amir Ahmad Itárji were left in Moghulistán, with some other persons, and on the whole ruled with success. They sent out some men who brought my uncle; and he and Sultán Muhammad Sultán lived on the most friendly and intimate terms, until one night some assassins [*fidái*], disguised as servants, came and murdered Amir Ahmad. It was never discovered by whose order this deed had been done.

After this, the entire government of Moghulistán, and the authority of Sultán Muhammad Sultán, devolved upon my uncle. But for want of the old army and of able councillors [*sahib-i-rái*] my uncle's affairs did not prosper. All the old stock and the chief councillors were with my father, and had accompanied him to Hisár, so that nothing could be accomplished with the hundred men or so, that my uncle had with him.

During that time, Sultán Said Khán and Sultán Khalil Sultán, together with the Kirghiz, made repeated forays into Moghulistán, so that my uncle [at length] fled from that country to Yatikand, which was the residence of Sultán Mahmud Khán. Those same base men [*arázil*] again commenced their intrigues, and caused my uncle to be seized and sent to the Uzbeg. Jáni Beg Sultán was at the time in Andiján, and to him my uncle was taken. Jáni Beg Sultán did nothing [to injure him], but rather treated him with his wonted kindness and consideration. With him my uncle remained until the time of Sháh Ismail's conquest, and the Emperor's expedition from Kábul.[1]

In the spring following the winter when Sháhi Beg Khán was killed, all the Sultáns of the Uzbeg assembled in Samarkand; Jáni Beg Sultán also went thither, taking my uncle with him. At that meeting, the Sultáns came to the conclusion that not one of the Moghuls who yet remained in Mávará-un-Nahr, should be left alive. But to this Jáni Beg Sultán would not consent. He dismissed my uncle, and all the Moghuls who were in attendance upon him, [permitting them] to go to Andiján and join their families. My uncle, however, placed no trust in the permanence of Jáni Beg Sultán's decision, and fearing a change in his humour, got away with all speed. Soon after this, Jáni Beg Sultán regretted the action he had taken, and sent some men in pursuit of these Moghuls, with orders to put to death any they should find of them. My uncle had only just escaped in time. On his arrival at Andiján he joined the remainder of the Moghuls and the people of Andiján; with these he raised a revolt, and drove all the Uzbeg out of the country of Farghána. He then sent a messenger to the Emperor, by way of Karátigin,[2] to inform him of these events, and to beg him for help, as has been mentioned above. The news filled the Emperor with joy.

CHAPTER XXIV.

BÁBAR PADISHÁH LEARNS THE SUCCESS OF MY UNCLE SAYYID MUHAMMAD MIRZÁ, AND SENDS SULTÁN SAID KHÁN TO HIS AID IN ANDIJÁN.

Before this news reached Kunduz, a deputation of the leading men [*sahib-i-rái*] of the Moghuls, such as Mir Sharim, Mir Mazid, Kul Nazar Mirzá, Amir Ayub, Mir Muhammad, Mir Ibráhim, Yadgár Mirzá, Kará Sultán Ali Mirzá, Mir Ghuri Barlás, Amir Dáim Ali, Mirzá Muhammad, Mir Beg Muhammad, Mir Kambar, Sháh Nazar Mirzá, Kutluk Mirák Mirzá, and others, came and represented to the Khán, at a private interview, that if he desired it they would

[1] Viz., in 917 A.H., or 1511 A.D.

[2] The word often reads *Kair Tagin*, and in the present instance all the texts spell it in that way. I have, however, adhered to *Karátigin* throughout, as that is known to be the real name of the country.

make away with the Emperor, and set him [Sultán Said Khán] in his place. [For at that time there were 20,000 Moghuls armed and fully prepared, while there were not more than 5,000 Chaghatáis.] But the Khán replied: "During the period of the hurricane of Sháhi Beg Khán's conquests, when the buffetings of the waves of calamity and contention dashed in pieces the ships of the life and prosperity of the Moghul Khákáns, [and they had all been drowned in the ocean of annihilation] I saved myself upon the plank of concealment, and arrived at length at the island of Kábul, which Bábar Pádisháh had contrived to save from the violent shocks of the billows of events, and where he then was. On this island, the Emperor protected me with the utmost benevolence. Now that I have attained the shore of prosperity, how malicious, how ungrateful it would be for me to perform so ignoble an act. [The Holy Law and the dictates of humanity prevent my entertaining any such base thoughts.]" By the hand of Amir Kásim Kuchin, who stood in the place of guardian to the Emperor, he sent the following message: "Praise be to God, the affairs of [your] State are to-day prosperous, and the various peoples are turning their faces towards the palace of that Refuge of the Nations [your Majesty]. The Moghuls, more especially, who are distinguished above all other tribes by their numbers and their strength, and whose Amirs have been the most eminent of Amirs, have always devoted their energies to the advancement of the work of their colleagues [*ibná-i-jins*]; they now turn to your Majesty. It is no longer expedient for me to remain near you; it is fitting that our ancient union should be changed to separation. If your Majesty send me to some quarter, where it will be possible for the bonds of our old affection to remain fastened, it will contribute to the welfare of both."

Just at this time news came from Andiján, together with my uncle's petition for help. The Khán was immediately sent off to Andiján, together with every one that thought fit to go. These events will be presently related, if it please God.

CHAPTER XXV.

ACCESSION OF BÁBAR PÁDISHÁH TO THE THRONE OF MÁVARÁ-UN-NAHR.

After the Khán had been despatched to Andiján, Mirzá Khán arrived with the auxiliary force which had been sent by Sháh Ismail, and thus the power of the Emperor became complete. Then, without delay, his Majesty marched for the country of Hisár; on learning which the Uzbeg, on their part, collected their forces, and under the leadership of Hamza Sultán, Mahdi Sultán, Timur Sultán, and several others of their great Sultáns, set out to oppose the Emperor. Kuchum Khán—who had been set up in the place of Sháhi Beg Khán—Suyunjuk Sultán, Jáni Beg Sultán, Ubaid Ullah Sultán, and all the other [Uzbeg] Sultáns, had assembled and encamped at Karshi, which was originally called Nakhshab. When the Emperor approached the Pul-i-Sangin, Hamza Sultán advanced and occupied it. Both sides remained encamped for nearly one month. Finally it became apparent that the Uzbeg force was numerous, their Sultáns renowned, and that it would be a difficult matter to resist them. The Uzbeg, on their part, came to the conclusion that the Emperor was unable to withstand them, and crossed the river by swimming it below the Pul-i-Sangin. Intelligence of this reached [Bábar] at about afternoon prayer-time, and he immediately broke up his camp and advanced towards Abdara, a locality where there are mountain fastnesses. They continued to march at their best speed all through that night, until the midday prayers of the following day, when they reached a spot which the most experienced leaders considered strongly enough protected to justify a halt. At midnight news came that the Uzbeg were advancing in full force; the commanders announced this simultaneously to the whole army, and up to daybreak every man was busy getting his arms ready [for action]. About sunrise . . . .[1] our pickets came in and reported that the Uzbeg army was approaching. Thereupon the Emperor mounted his horse and rode to the top of some rising ground. He saw that there was only one road by which the enemy could advance; on the left hand of the elevation [on which he stood] there was another hill, and between the two there was a deep ravine, through which, also, only one road led. When the enemy had deployed on the level plain, they saw that it would be no easy task to ascend [the first mentioned] hill. Timur Sultán

[1] A rhetorical interpolation of three lines, descriptive of the victory of the day over the night, is omitted here.—R.

and some of the other Sultáns, with about 10,000 men, detached themselves from the rest of the army and began to mount the other hill. Against these the Emperor sent Mirzá Khán with a detachment of brave warriors. At this moment his eye fell upon a body of men, and he asked who they were.[1] When [my father] had left Kábul, there were nearly 3000 of his hereditary retainers, [who had come from Khorásán to Kunduz with the Moghuls]. The chiefs and leaders of these men, the Emperor had taken into his own service, and some of the remainder became attached to myself. It was upon this latter body that the Emperor's eye now fell. They replied: "We are Mirzá Haidar's followers." The Emperor then [addressing me] said: "You are still too young to take part in such serious affairs as these. Stay by me; [keep by you] Mauláná Muhammad and a few others, and send the rest to the aid of Mirzá Khán."

When my retainers came up with Mirzá Khán, the Uzbeg made a charge, bearing down [*bar dashtand*] every one who was in front of Mirzá Khán, till they came close upon the Mirzá himself. At that crisis my retainers arrived on the scene. Their leader was Ataka Fakir, whose name was Ján Ahmad Ataka;[2] hereafter, wherever his name occurs, he will be called by the latter style. He attacked the Uzbeg with the men under him, and put them to flight. Then those who had fled from before Mirzá Khán rallied, and returning to the fight, drove the enemy back. In the midst of this confusion and scuffle, one of my men took one of the enemy prisoner, and led him before the Emperor, who viewed it as a good omen [*fál*], and said: "Inscribe the name of Mirzá Haidar upon the first trophy [*juldu*]." Thus, fighting continued on the left of the army till evening. But on the Emperor's side [of the army] there were no engagements, for the road was very narrow, and his position was not easy of approach from either side. At the hour of afternoon prayers the brave warriors, having left the Emperor's presence, dismounted and encamped. At nightfall [*bigáh*] the enemy found it impossible to encamp where they were, on account of the absence of water—for none was to be had except at a distance of one *farsákh*—so, with the object of being near water when night came on, they retreated. The infantry, who had descended [the hill], ran after them, shouting Hai! Hai! [and making a great noise]. That portion of the enemy's army which was opposite to Mirzá Khán, also became anxious to retire, as soon as they saw that Hamza Sultán, who was in their centre [*ghul*],[3] was in retreat. As long as the two armies remained facing each other, neither side

[1] For this passage the Turki MS. substitutes: The Emperor asked them who they were. They replied, "We are Mirza Haidar's followers."—R.

[2] The Turki MS. says: Their leader was a poor man [fakir] named Jan Ahmad.—R.

[3] Ghul is a Mongolian word, also written *Kul*.—R.

prevailed over the other. But when the enemy turned to retire, those of Mirzá Khán's men who had been facing them, [suddenly] made a charge, and the enemy at once fled. When the centre saw this division put to rout, they too let the reins of self-possession fall from the hand of stability, and likewise turned and fled. It was at the hour of evening prayers that Hamza Sultán, Mahdi Sultán, and Mamák Sultán, who had been captured, were led before the Emperor, who did to them that which Shaibáni had done to the Moghul Khákáns and the Chaghatái Sultáns.[1]

From night to morning and from morning to the next night, did our men pursue the Uzbeg—as far as the frontier [of the State] of Darband-i-Ahanin. The whole of the victorious army now assembled in Hisár, when further help arrived from Sháh Ismail, besides bodies of men from all the surrounding tribes, so that the entire force amounted to 60,000 men. They next marched out of Hisár and proceeded to Karshi. Most of the Uzbeg Sultáns were in Samarkand, while Ubaid Ullah Khán had fortified himself in the castle of Karshi. All [the Emperor's] councillors (and they were those who solved the difficult questions of State) were against laying siege to Karshi. "It would," they argued, "be far wiser to push on to Bokhárá. For if Ubaid Ullah keeps himself strongly fortified and garrisoned in the castle of Karshi, Bokhárá, which is devoid of troops and full of fools, will fall easily enough into our power. He has nothing to gain by staying in Karshi. [God forbid that, fearing to remain there,] he should abandon the fort and come out."[2] The Emperor agreed with these opinions, and passing Karshi, went and encamped [at a distance of one stage beyond it]. Scouts came, in rapid succession, to report that Ubaid Ullah had come out of the fort of Karshi and was on the road to Bokhárá. At that same hour the Emperor mounted his horse, and set out with all speed in pursuit of the Uzbeg. He marched night and day until he reached the city. The pursuers drove the Uzbeg out of Bokhárá into the deserts [*chul*] of Turkistán, plundering as they went.

When the Uzbeg Sultáns who were assembled in Samarkand heard this news, they were suddenly filled with terror and fled, scattered and dismayed, to different parts of Turkistán.

Now when the Emperor arrived in Bokhárá, he sent back the

[1] Baber's account of these transactions is wanting in his Memoirs. The battle here described took place early in 1511, while the period 1508 to the beginning of 1519 is one where a break occurs in his Memoirs. It is known, however, that he put the two first-named Sultans to death as traitors, for they had, at one time, been in his service, and had deserted him to join the cause of Shaibáni. (See Erskine, *Hist.*, i., p. 145.) The antecedents of Mamák do not appear to be recorded anywhere.

[2] The meaning of these obscure passages appears to be, that Ubaid Ullah alone was formidable; that he was too strong to admit of an attack on Karshi, and might also prove dangerous if he came out to attack Baber.

auxiliaries of Sháh Ismail,[1] after praising them for their services and bestowing upon them adequate rewards, while he himself, victorious and covered with glory, proceeded to Samarkand. All the inhabitants of the towns of Mávará-un-Nahr, high and low, nobles and poor men, grandees and artizans, princes and peasants —alike testified their joy at the advent of the Emperor. He was received by the nobles, while the other classes were busy with the decoration of the town. The streets and the bazaars were draped with cloth and gold brocades, and drawings and pictures were hung up on every side. The Emperor entered the city in the middle of the month of Rajab in the year 917, in the midst of such pomp and splendour as no one has ever seen or heard of, before or since. The angels cried aloud: "Enter with peace," and the people exclaimed: "Praise be to God, Lord of the Universe." The people of Mávará-un-Nahr, especially the inhabitants of Samarkand, had for years been longing for him to come, that the shadow of his protection might be cast upon them. Although, in the hour of necessity, the Emperor had clothed himself in the garments of the Kizilbásh (which was pure heresy, nay almost unbelief), they sincerely hoped, when he mounted the throne of Samarkand, (the throne of the Law of the Prophet) and placed on his head the diadem of the holy Sunna of Muhammad, that he would remove from it the crown of royalty [*Sháhi*], whose nature was heresy and whose form was as the tail of an ass.

But the hopes of the people of Samarkand were not realised. For, as yet, the Emperor did not feel able to dispense with the aid and support of Sháh Ismail; nor did he consider himself sufficiently strong to cope single-handed with the Uzbeg; hence he appeared to overlook [*mudára*] the gross errors of the Kizilbásh. On this account, the people of Mávará-un-Nahr ceased to feel that intense longing for the Emperor which they had entertained while he was absent—their regard for him was at an end. It was thus that the Emperor began [already] to flatter the Turkománs, and associate himself with them.[2]

[1] Erskine, in his *History of India*, notes that the historian Kháfi Khan (following the Tarikh-i-Alam Arai Abási of Mirza Sikandar) makes Baber dismiss the Persian auxiliaries after the march to Samarkand; while Mirza Haidar states here that they were sent away from Bokhárá. Erskine prefers the statement of Kháfi Khan, and thinks that dismissal from Bokárá would have been premature under the circumstances and, therefore, improbable. (Vol. i., p. 316, footnote.)

[2] It appears, from what Erskine remarks, that much difference of opinion exists among Asiatic historians as to some of the events of this period—viz., 916 to about 921 A.H.—an interval which falls just within one of those gaps which unfortunately occur, in several places, in the course of Baber's Memoirs. In this instance, the gap extends from the beginning of 914 to the beginning of 925 (May, 1508, to January, 1519), so that his own explanation of his transactions with Shah Ismail is wanting, and difficulty has been found in fixing their exact dates. It would appear that Indian historians, such as Firishta, Kháfi Khan, and Abul Fazl, differ entirely in their views from the Persian writers, Iskandar Beg and Khundamir. The former group state that the coin was struck and the

CHAPTER XXVI.

THE KHÁN'S JOURNEY TO ANDIJÁN AND EVENTS THAT OCCURRED THERE.

It has been recounted above, that the Emperor sent the Khán to Andiján. Along with him he sent, of the Moghul Amirs, Mir Ghuri Barlás, Mir Dáim Ali and his brother Ahmad Ali, Mahmud Kuli, Mirzá Muhammad Begjik and his brother Beg Muhammad; of the tribe of Dughlát, Sháh Nazar, Mirzá Ali, Kutluk Mirák; of

---

Khutba (prayer for the sovereign) was read in Baber's name, while the Persian authors affirm that Ismail's name was employed as that of sovereign in 917 (1511). Again, when referring to the subsequent battle with the Uzbeg under Ubaid Ullah at Kul Malik, the Indian writers make Baber's army very small and that of Ubaid Ullah very numerous, while one of them (Abul Fazl) goes so far as to give Baber the victory, though he acknowledges that the Emperor had to beat a retreat. Mr. R. S. Poole, who has gone thoroughly into the subject (taking the coinage of the period as his principal guide), cites Khundamir to show that there was an agreement between Baber and Ismail, to the effect that if Transoxiana were to be conquered by the Allies, the prayer and coinage should be in the name of the Shah. He then, in support of Khundamir, points to a recently-discovered coin of Baber's reign in Transoxiana, which bears the Shia formula and the names of the twelve Imáms; and concludes from this, and some other numismatic evidence, that "Baber caused the Khutba to be said and the coinage to be struck in the names of Shah Ismail, as over-lord and himself as vassal." This indeed is evidence that cannot easily be gainsaid, and it derives something very like confirmation, when the religious bias of the various authors who have commented on these transactions is considered. Their historical opinions appear to be governed, to a great extent, by their sectarian feelings, and in no case is this more evident than in that of Mirza Haidar. There can be no question that, whatever may be the true facts regarding the Khutba and the coinage, Baber gave great offence to the Sunnis by acting in subordinate alliance with the fanatical Shia, Ismail, and by adopting the national costume of the Kizil-básh, for himself and his men. This was an outward and visible sign of subordination to Shia interests, which all would feel and understand. Shah Ismail had lost no opportunity of insulting the Sunni religion, and as Mirza Haidar relates, had treated some of their most revered divines with barbaric cruelty. It is scarcely surprising, therefore, that Mirza Haidar should speak with bitterness of the transactions of his cousin and protector, with the Persian Shias and their Turkoman allies at this period, or that even his historical statements should, to some degree, be underlaid with rancour. It should not be forgotten, however, that in accordance with one of the curious anomalies of the times, Mirza Haidar had a family connection with Baber's opponent, and the enemy of his own race. Ubaid Ullah was his brother-in-law, and it is remarkable, throughout the *Tárikh-i-Rashidi*, that the tie of relationship often counted for a great deal. On the other hand, Baber owed Shah Ismail a debt of gratitude for rescuing his sister, Khánzáda Begum, as related at p. 239.

With regard to the missing pages in Baber's Memoirs, Mr. R. S. Poole believes that their absence may be accounted for by a desire, on the part of the autobiographer, to hide the traces of proceedings which he could only look back upon with shame. This view, I cannot help thinking, requires some substantiation. In the first place, the objectionable connection with the Shias extended only over the period 916 to 921—some five years—while the gap in the Memoirs embraces the eleven years, from 914 to 925. If the object of the writer had been to hide the traces of events of the shorter period, there would seem to be no reason for also destroying the record of an additional period of six years. Secondly, this gap in the Memoirs is not the only one; there is another, which extends from late in the year

the Kunji Amirs, Kul Nazar Mirzá, Khanánki[1] Mirzá, Amir Kambar, son of Haidar Kukildásh Barki, and others. All these departed in the train of the Khán. This party, on their arrival at Andiján, were received by my uncle and the Amirs who had assisted him in the conquest [*istikhlás*] of Farghána, such as Sultán Ali Mirzá Begjik, Pishka Mirzá Itárji, Tubra Nuyághut and others, who all came and kissed the Khán's stirrup.

After the Khán had come to Andiján, the Uzbeg Sultáns in Samarkand heard of his arrival and of the support he brought the Moghuls of Andiján. [Moreover] as was mentioned above, Hamza Sultán, Mahdi Sultán and Timur Sultán, together with a few other Sultáns, had assembled in Hisár with the intent of opposing the Emperor. Although Ubaid Ullah Sultán knew that Sháh Ismail had given over [the kingdom of] Mávará-un-Nahr to the Emperor, and was not going there in person, he [Ubaid Ullah Sultán] nevertheless, by way of precaution, stayed and occupied Karshi. What happened to him has just been mentioned. Jáni Beg Sultán, Kuchum Khán and Suyunjuk Sultán advanced towards Akhsi and Andiján, in order to check the downfall of Farghána. The Khán had made no preparations in Andiján, when news of their approach arrived, but he then despatched Sultán Ali Mirzá and Tubra Nuyághut Mirzá to Kásán. As the castle of Kásán was not well fortified, these men went and made it strong. It was the first place which the Uzbeg Sultáns attacked, and they reduced it to straits. On learning this news, the Khán sent all the captains of his army to the hills of Kásán, [hoping that] although they were not strong enough to cause the Uzbeg to fear them,[2] yet they might, at least, be able to harass their flanks, and inflict some discomfort and annoyance on them; also that the force in Kásán would thereby be somewhat encouraged.

When this body was sent to [help] the Kásáni, news of the event reached the ears of Abá Bakr Mirzá, who had just come from Káshghar, with the project of seizing the kingdom of Farghána. He had taken possession of all the country above Andiján, such as

---

908 to the end of 909, and a third, where nearly six years are wanting, viz., from 926 to 932. Yet in these periods, it is nowhere suggested that Baber was concerned in proceedings of which he had reason to be ashamed, or the evidence of which he desired to obliterate. In the third place, it is noticeable that in each case where a gap occurs, the narrative breaks off suddenly in the middle of a sentence—a circumstance that points rather to the accidental loss of certain sheets of the manuscript, than to premeditated destruction, or a design to omit any particular events. The matter, however, need hardly be pursued in detail here. (See Erskine, *Hist.*, i., p. 321; R. S. Poole, *Cat. of Coins of Shahs of Persia in Brit. Mus.*, 1887, pp. xxiv., *seqq.* Also, on the general question of Baber and Ismail, Howorth, ii., pp. 712–13.)

[1] This name is very uncertain. It may be read *Jánki*, and perhaps in other ways.

[2] The Turki MS. has: to meet the Uzbeg face to face.—R.

Uzchand[1] (better known as Uzkand), Mádu[2] and Ush, which comprise the best parts of Farghána; and he now [on hearing that these troops had left Andiján] marched towards that place intending to lay siege to it. [He imagined that the fort of Andiján was a very strong and large one, and that, without the necessary siege appliances, it could not be taken by a party of two or three thousand assailants. Therefore, he first got ready some engines [*manjanik*], ladders, etc., and then set out for Andiján]. When news of this was brought to the Khán, he and all his people were filled with the utmost alarm.

In the meanwhile the Uzbeg Sultáns had delivered a simultaneous attack on the fort of Kásán, had made breaches on all sides and applied the scaling ladders. Such was the violence of their assault that those within the fort, giving up all hope of being able to defend it, made their escape by the gateway on the side removed from the river. All the Uzbeg army had dismounted and were on foot; they had not thought of the garrison taking flight, and before they had time to get back to their horses and mount, the fugitives had gone a great distance. But those who lagged behind they put to death, together with the people of the fort.[3]

The garrison that had escaped from the fort, fell in with those captains who had been sent to the hills of Kásán to succour them. They now all went straight on, until they arrived at a spot within half a *farsákh* of Andiján, where they found Abá Bakr Mirzá encamped, with all his siege appliances made ready; for he had determined to deliver an assault from all sides, early the next morning. This same night the army arrived from Kásán. [On the morrow the enemy] advanced with the intention of storming the fort, quite ignorant of the fact that the Khán's troops had arrived. At early dawn, the Khán in person issued from the castle, and drew up his troops in order of battle. Mirzá Abá Bakr, on his side, brought forward his force ready to lay siege to the castle. The opposing armies met at a place on the road called Tutluk; both sides at one drew up, and raising their battle-cries, began the struggle. It would take too long to detail all the particulars of this battle. In short, the standard of the Khán was filled by the winds of victory and success, while the faces of his enemies were covered with the dust of death and destruction. The victorious

[1] Or it may be read *Urchand.*

[2] Known nowadays as *Mádi* or *Mád.*

[3] The Turki translator reverses the order of the two paragraphs which end at this point, and which begin with the words: When this body was sent. . . . He introduces his second paragraph with the following interpolation: "When Aba Bakr Mirza heard the news of the Khan's arrival in Andiján, and the storming of Kásán by the Uzbeg Sultans, he desired to bring within his power the country of Farghána, and left Káshghar. . . ."

breezes of the Khán scattered the enemy (who in strength and numbers might be compared to mountains) like chaff before the wind. Thus the army of Mirzá Abá Bakr suffered an overwhelming defeat. All of the enemy who were taken captive by the conquering army, were brought together, and the order was issued for them to be put to death in the park [*kuruk*] of Andiján. Having, accordingly, made them sit down in lines [the victors] began to kill them. At that moment my uncle [Sayyid Muhammad Mirzá] placing the knee of intercession upon the ground of entreaty, said to the Khán: "Praise and gratitude we owe to God for this victory, for it is the key by which may be opened the whole kingdom of Káshghar. I sincerely hope that Káshghar may fall into our hands with the same ease. But these prisoners whose execution is permitted by, and is in accordance with, the laws of retaliation [*mazhab-i-intikám*], are all natives of the country [of Káshghar]. If you do not spare them here, it will be as if you had committed a general massacre in that place itself—an act that would, in the end, be a cause of repentance and regret [to yourself]. If his Highness the Khán will forgive these men, who yet remain, and hand them over to me as my share of the spoil, his reward in this world and the next will be enhanced by such an act of mercy." When the entreaty of my uncle reached the blessed ears of the Khán, he drew the line of forgiveness with the pen of pardon, upon the tablet of the existences of those prisoners. Thus about 3000 persons were rescued from death. Then, raising up their hands in prayer, they filled the air with acclamations of thanksgiving.

This important victory caused the Uzbeg to keep the foot of reflection yet longer within the skirt of hesitation. Following this event, news arrived of the defeat which Hamza Sultán had suffered from Bábar Pádisháh, and of his death, by the Emperor's order, after the battle [which has been mentioned]. A short time afterwards, intelligence was received of the Emperor's march on Samarkand and his reception by its inhabitants; also that the Uzbeg, who were in the city, had taken flight and therefore were unable to surround him. After these occurrences, the Emperor and the Khán reigned absolute in Samarkand and Andiján, respectively. Sháh Ismail returned to Irák. The Emperor gave Kábul and Ghaznin to his younger brother, Sultán Násir Mirzá. The Uzbeg all collected together in Turkistán. The rest of the events that ensued will, please God, be recounted below [1]—how, for example, the Khán and Sultán Khalil Sultán came, one after the other, to Andiján. Sultán Khalil Sultán left one son, who was still at the breast, named Bábá Sultán; and the wife of the Khán, who has

[1] The Turki MS. interpolates here: It has been mentioned above that Sultan Khalil Sultan was put to death, at Akhsi, by Jáni Beg Sultan.—R.

been mentioned above, was with child, at the time when the Khán was put to flight by Khwája Ali Bahádur the Uzbeg:[1] she fell into the hands of the Uzbeg, and after a short time was delivered of a son. The Khán arrived in Kábul at the same moment as this news.[2] The Emperor said to the Khán: "As your illustrious name is Said, it would be very suitable to call him [the child] Abdur Rashid," and the Khán decided upon that name. Both [these Khánzáda], Bábá Sultán, son of Sultán Khalil Sultán, and Abdur Rashid Khán, son of Sultán Said Khán, were taken in charge by Tutuk Khánim, daughter of Sultán Mahmud Khán, who, at the destruction of Táshkand, had been captured by Jáni Beg Sultán, as has been mentioned. When the Khán gained his victory at the battle of Tutluk, and drove the Uzbeg out of the country of Farghána, these two Sultáns were brought to him. I shall speak of them hereafter.

Having reached the story of what passed between the Khán and Mirza Abá Bakr, my history would not be complete without a brief account of the Mirzá's career.

CHAPTER XXVII.

SHORT ACCOUNT OF MIRZÁ ABÁ BAKR.

Amir Sayyid Ali, my great-grandfather [*sivum jadd*], whose history will, God willing, be told in the First Part, had two sons: Sániz Mirzá, whose mother was of the line of the Jarás Amirs, and Muhammad Haidar Mirzá, my grandfather, whose fortunate and blessed name has devolved upon me. His mother was an aunt [*amma*] of Sultán Yunus Khán. On the death of the great Amir Sayyid Ali, his elder son, Sániz Mirzá, according to the ancient Moghul custom, succeeded to his father's throne. After seven years, he went to join his father in the next world, leaving two sons, the first Abá Bakr Mirzá and the second Omar Mirzá. The mother of these children was married [afterwards] to Muhammad Haidar Mirzá, in conformity with the Moghul custom of *Yangalik.*[3] By her, Muhammad Haidar Mirzá also had two

[1] There appears to be some mistake here, as Khwája Ali Bahadur can hardly have been an Uzbeg. The Turki MS. seems to read: "At the time when Khwája Ali Bahadur was taking the Khan from the Uzbeg."

[2] The Turki version is: The Khan was in Kabul when this news reached him.—R.

[3] *Yanga* means "aunt by marriage," or "wife of an elder brother;" the custom being, apparently, that a younger brother should take to wife the widow of his elder brother.

sons: the first was my father Muhammad Husain Mirzá, and the second my uncle Sayyid Muhammad Mirzá. After the death of Sániz Mirzá, the government of all the districts of Káshghar devolved upon Muhammad Haidar Mirzá, who for a period of twenty-four years ruled with perfect justice and impartiality. He was a prosperous man, for he had inherited great riches; he always realised his desires, and examined into details; [he experienced no trials or troubles]. But those young men in whose conduct, indications of bravery and intelligence were traceable, he failed to encourage. Most of those experienced and wise men whom Amir Sayyid Ali had gathered round him, during a space of eighty years, had died by the end of Muhammad Haidar Mirzá's life, or if they were not actually dead, they were only decrepit old men [*shaikh-i-fáni*], whose hands and intellects were no longer capable of guiding or controlling. Their sons [had developed into incapable young men] quite unworthy of their parents. At this time, Mirzá Abá Bakr was about twenty years of age, and was in the service of his guardian [*abwi-mááb*] uncle [Sayyid Muhammad Mirzá]. He mixed and associated, in the most friendly way, with the princes and youths [of the court], while they, for their part, from equality of age and from fellow service, became very devoted to him. Mirzá Abá Bakr was so open handed and generous, that in a few days he distributed all his property and household possessions, as if they were plunder [*batáraj midád*]. One day, one of his followers, hearing of some spoil, came in great haste, but found everything gone, and that others had already exhausted the booty. So he came and laid hold of the skirt of Mirzá Abá Bakr, who was standing at the door of his own house, saying: "Although I have come the last [and am disappointed of booty], nevertheless I have found a good pledge [which I will not give up until a ransom is paid]." At these words Mirzá Abá Bakr laughed, and bought himself free from the man with a large sum. In a word, his liberality was so unbounded, that all men flocked to him.

At this period he went to Aksu and Moghulistán, and paid his respects to Dust Muhammad Khán, son of Isán Bughá Khán. Dust Muhammad Khán treated him with honour, and after giving him his own sister in marriage, allowed him to depart. It would take too long to tell this story, and the details would carry us too far afield. In short, he managed, by one means or another, to reduce Yarkand, which is one of the most renowned cities of the province of Káshghar, and is distant four days' journey from the town of that name. To-day Yarkand is the capital of Káshghar.

He had collected 3000 men in his following, who had to oppose 30,000. When his troops reached that district, he openly sounded the drum of ascendency, and rang the bells of independence.

Muhammad Haidar Mirzá went out to meet him with an army of 30,000 infantry and cavalry, but he was defeated and fled. He sought refuge with Yunus Khán, who was his cousin. The Khán also undervalued the strength of Mirzá Abá Bakr, and did not take his whole army. He came against him with 30,000 armed men. Muhammad Haidar Mirzá again made ready his forces, as best he could, and set out [with Yunus Khán]. This time, also, [Mirzá Abá Bakr] sallied forth from the gates of the citadel of Yarkand with 3000 chosen men, and defeated and scattered these two armies; and Yunus Khán and Muhammad Haidar Mirzá both retired, crestfallen, to Káshghar. The Khán passed into Moghulistán, and in the following year returned with the whole of his troops. On this occasion, Mirzá Abá Bakr had made fuller and better preparations. He strengthened his cavalry by embodying with it lightly-armed archers on foot, as he had done on two former occasions, and engaged in such a battle [as the tongue of the reed is incapable of describing]. His men then again became bold, and showed more steadiness [and courage] than ever, so that they easily put to rout that numerous army; and the Khán, with Muhammad Haidar Mirzá, returned once more, defeated, to Káshghar. But this time it became impossible for Muhammad Haidar Mirzá to remain in Káshghar, so taking his household with him, and accompanied by Yunus Khán, he went to Aksu. Meanwhile Mirzá Abá Bakr gained complete domination over the whole of the kingdom of Káshghar. After this, he put out the eyes of his full [*yak záda*] brother Omar Mirzá, and then banished him from his territories. Omar Mirzá went and lived in Samarkand. [Subsequently] when [Sultán Said] Khán took Yarkand and Káshghar, Omar Mirzá returned to Káshghar, where the Khán paid him unbounded honour and attention, until his death.

The affairs of Muhammad Haida Mirzá and of Yunus Khán will be related in the First Part; the object of this chapter is to give a brief account of Mirzá Abá Bakr.

For forty-eight years he remained firmly established and successful in Káshghar, exercising always absolute authority [*istilá*]. During this period [he was attacked] on one other [1] occasion, when Sultán Ahmad Khán, son of Sultán Yunus Khán (and known as Álácha Khán), in the course of the year 905, came against Káshghar. But his army likewise was put to rout, as will be mentioned in the First Part.

After the above mentioned victory over Sultán Ahmad Khán, Mirzá Abá Bakr began to extend his conquests on all sides. In the first place, he sent an army into Tibet. It gained glorious victories, subdued most of the districts of Tibet as far as the

[1] In the Turki is inserted: encouraged by their two former successes.—R.
[2] The Turki MS. has: a third time.—R.

frontiers of Kashmir, and carried such desolation [*zabun*] into those countries, that nobody was left to withstand him. He next sent armies in the direction of Balur, which gained decisive victories and carried off untold booty. After this, he sent a force into Badakhshán, where he subdued most of the Hazára of Badakhshán. At the time when Sháhi Beg Khán was making the whole world tremble, Mirzá Abá Bakr despatched an army to Andiján and reduced Jáni Beg Khán to great straits. He took Ush, Mádu and Uzkand from the Uzbeg, and reduced the whole of Moghulistán to such a condition, that not a single Moghul was able to remain in the country,[1] as already mentioned in the history of the Khán. The reason of their [the Moghuls] passing into Andiján has been explained. All the Moghuls who were in Moghulistán fled in different directions before the prowess of his army. Even the Kirghiz, who are the ravening lions[2] of Moghulistán, were no longer able to stay there, but had to join Mansur Khán in Chálish. After the death of Ahmad Khán, and the arrival of Sultán Mahmud Khán in Moghulistán, Mirzá Abá Bakr went to Aksu, which he seized, together with Uch,[3] and carried off all the people from the neighbourhood of the latter place. He also left a garrison in the fort of Uch. My object in relating the prowess and valour of Mirzá Abá Bakr, and the extent of his conquests, is to show what a great warrior Sultán Said Khán was, to have defeated such a man, as he did, at the battle of Tutluk.

CHAPTER XXVIII.

THE EVIL DEEDS AND WICKED WAYS OF MIRZÁ ABÁ BAKR.

One of the obligations I have imposed on myself in writing this Epitome [*mukhtasar*] is, that what I have heard from other people and on good authority, I would briefly rehearse, when it was of importance; but what I have not witnessed myself, I would not dwell on too long, for fear of exaggeration, which I desire to avoid. But what I have witnessed or taken part in, that I have written as personal experience. I have divided the strange life, the evil deeds, and the depraved conduct of Mirzá Abá Bakr into three sections. Firstly, what I have heard from others and from trust-

[1] The Turki adds: there was nothing left for them but to go to Andiján, prepared to die.—R.

[2] *Shir-i-bisha.* Lit.: lions of the forest.—R.

[3] The place now known as *Ush Turfán.*

worthy reports: this I have stated briefly; secondly, what I have myself seen or heard [directly], but which I could not bring myself to relate; and thirdly, what I have myself witnessed, and have written down in this Epitome. But this is only as one in a thousand incidents—a little out of many—a long story cut short.

Heaven forbid that any reader of these pages should accuse me of exaggeration or of slander. If I had deemed it permissible to depass the limits [of truth] in any way, I should not have said anything about Mirzá Abá Bakr, for he was my uncle. But if I were to omit his history, all other facts connected with him would be obscure and incomprehensible. It is my duty both to shun exaggeration and to avoid omissions. The truth is that for more than forty years Mirzá Abá Bakr ruled supreme. Towards the end of his life, the spirit of tyranny so mastered his nature, that if an offence was committed against him, though the offender might not be liable to any sentence according to the law, yet his evil heart was not satisfied with killing him once, but desired the death of the sinless sinner, a thousand times over.

If any one had, in the slightest degree, opposed him, and he only heard of it ten years after, he was sure to punish, not only the offender, but likewise his children, relations, connections, and dependants. On this account, his subjects grew so submissive to his government, that nobody dared dream of acting contrary to his orders. When he had brought his authority to the point of complete supremacy in all things, he made such a collection of wealth, in treasure, property, mules and cattle, as surpasses all reckoning.

He used to set culprits to work, involving difficulty which was proportionate to the gravity of their offence; he arranged for the separate employment of men and women, but he got some work out of everybody. [For instance] he ordered the old cities [known as] Kázik[1] to be excavated by these [prisoners], and the earth dug from them to be washed. If there were anything big, they would come upon it in digging, while anything small [such as gems] they would find when they washed [the earth]. In this way, innumerable treasures in precious stones, gold and silver, were discovered. I have heard some of his confidants say that a

[1] The word *Kázik* has proved somewhat of a puzzle, and I am not quite satisfied that the author's meaning is correctly rendered, either in this passage or in those immediately below, where the word is used. In all it occurs five times; but the texts are so obscure that, in some places, it may be read as the name of a person, rather than that of ruined towns, generally. Mr. Ross informs me that there is a verb *Kázmak*, in Turki, meaning "to make excavations, or excavating," while *Kázik* signifies, literally, "a spade." But from the context it appears rather that *Kázik* stands for *excavations*, and has been applied, in a general way, to the sites of ruined towns, or those buried in the sands, where probably the inhabitants were in the habit of digging for treasures. In that case it would be used like "the mines," "the roads," etc. Still, it is a word that does not appear in any book relating to Eastern Turkistan and the buried cities, so far as I am aware; and I am not acquainted with it from local experience.

treasure was found in the citadel of Khotan.[1] There were twenty-seven jars [*khum*] of such a size that a man, with a quiver on, could get inside them, without stooping or bending [and without touching it on any side]. Inside each of these jars was a copper ewer [*áftába-i-mis*]. One of these ewers fell into my possession. It is a sort of flask [*surahi*] with a long narrow neck, to which is fixed a rough iron handle. In the centre of the ewer is a copper spout, the nose of which is on a level with [*barábar*] the mouth of the ewer. The height of it is, at a guess, over one and a half *gaz.*[2] When filled with water, two persons had great difficulty in lifting it, and they could not carry it from one place to another. Inside each of the jars was placed one of these ewers, filled with gold dust, and outside [the ewers] the space was filled with *bálish* of silver. In historical works, such as the *Jahán-Kushái*, the *Jamiut-Tavárikh*, and others, a *bálish* is thus described: "A *bálish* is 500 *mithkál* [of silver], made into a long brick with a depression in the middle."[3] I had [at that time] only heard the name [and

[1] The Turki translator changes *Khotan* into "the old city of Yarkand," and very possibly he may have made the alteration with some reason—perhaps in accordance with local traditions, with which he may have been acquainted. Many stories, it may be remarked, are current in the country, to this day, concerning Abá Bakr and his treasures.

[2] See note, p. 58. The *gaz* as used by Baber, was estimated by Erskine, from a variety of considerations, to be a little over two English feet. He concludes his remarks on the subject as follows: "A fair allowance for the pace, or *gaz*, of Baber would thus be thirty inches, which applies to his regular *tanáb* or surveying cord. But as the regulated measures were larger than the ordinary ones, we may perhaps assume two feet, or little more, as an average popular *gaz*." A great variety of *gaz* are in use in India and Central Asia, and just as the measure varies in different localities, it has probably also changed in value at different periods. In estimating Mirza Haidar's *gaz*, it will perhaps be best always to assume that of Baber, seeing that it belonged to the same regions and the same period. Baber, however, was fairly accurate in such matters as measurements, etc., but this cannot always be said of Mirza Haidar.

[3] The author is obviously alluding to the Chinese ingots of silver, called *Yuan-pao*, which appear to have been very generally known, down to the seventeenth century, as *bálish*, *balisht*, etc., among European, as well as Asiatic, writers. Sir H. Yule has an interesting dissertation on the subject in his "*Cathay*" (i., pp. 115 *seqq.*), from which it may be gathered that the true meaning and origin of the word is uncertain. The value of the *bálish*, as a measure of money, is also very uncertain, and appears to have varied at different periods; while there were *bálish* of gold and of paper, as well as of silver. The Turki dictionary states the weight of the *bálish* at 8 *miskál* and 2 *dának*. But it is to the silver *bálish* of 500 *miskáls* weight that our author alludes. The actual weight of the *miskál*, like that of most Asiatic measures, may be variable, but Mr. R. S. Poole (*Coins of the Shahs of Persia*, 1887) states it, for numismatic purposes, at 71·18 grains. At this rate the *bálish* would have weighed 74·1 oz. troy. As a rule, the modern Chinese *Yuan-pao* is made to weigh about 50 to 55 *liang* (or *taels*), and the standard *liang* is equal to 579·84 grains. Thus, if taken at 500 *miskáls*, the *bálish* would have weighed about 61½ *liang*, which is perhaps nearly correct, for at the period in question it may have been heavier than in modern times. The *Yuan-pao* (or "shoe of sycee" as it is usually called in the ports of China) is made somewhat in the shape of a shoe, or a shallow boat, and this is what Mirza Haidar means by describing a depression in the middle. In Eastern Turkistan it is called nowadays *Kurus*—a Turki word, the derivation of which I am ignorant of—and *Yámbu*, which is, of course, only a corruption of the Chinese *Yuan-pao*. Its value, in exchange with India, is usually about 165 or 170 rupees. (See also Yule's *Glossary*, under "Shoe" and "Tael.")

had never seen one myself, but had read the description in these books]. These *bálish* had been placed outside the ewers, but inside the jars. Many of them were brought, just as they were, to the treasury, which fell into the hands of the Khán's army [when Sultán Said Khán conquered Yarkand]. I myself possessed some of them. Thus [subsequently] I saw the *bálish* [and found them correspond to the description I had seen in books].

One of the most singular things that I heard from those who had worked at the Kázik was this: In every one of the ewers was a letter written in Turki, which read: ["This treasure was prepared for the expenses of the ceremony of circumcision of the son of the Khátun called Khamár."] But no one could discover who this Khamár Khátun was, nor when she had lived, nor how. How strange that in spite of witnessing such examples, man is not restrained in his lusts, desires, and vain fancies!

After the discovery of this treasure, Mirzá Abá Bakr urged forward the men employed at the Kázik, to work with greater diligence and care than before, and several other treasures were brought to light in the old cities of Káshghar, Yarkand, and Khotan. The mode of operations at the Kázik was as follows: eighteen or twenty prisoners, more or less, were secured together by a chain running from one to the other, at their backs, through a collar fastened round the neck of each. In their hands they carried spades [*kaland*].[1] They laboured both summer and winter. [During the day they worked] and at night they were put into a prison. If the prisoner's offence was very grave, neither friends, relations, nor strangers were allowed to speak to him or give him anything. So that not even one of the same gang [chain] as himself was able to tell him a story. There was an overseer to every gang, and over every eighteen of the overseers was another person, and there was one man at the head of the whole of the Kázik. If any one of these overseers, whether superior or inferior, in the slightest degree neglected his duty with regard to the convicts, as in flogging, commanding, urging them on, or throwing them into prison, and the like, he was himself consigned to a gang of convicts. Moreover, such was the strictness of discipline, that the overseers never dared to show any leniency. In fact, they could never speak a word, except officially.

Those who were confined for lesser offences, were allowed to see a relation or friend once a week; and in like manner, there were many different gradations for individual cases, from which [favours], however, not the slightest deviation, in the way of enhancement, could be made, without authorisation. [Separate] work was found for the men and the women. The above is only one example, out

[1] *Kaland* may mean a shovel or spade or pick-axe. The Turki MS gives *Katmán* which signifies a spade. Vambéry has: pelle, bêche.—R.

of many, of Mirzá Abá Bakr's cruelties. Many more instances might be mentioned, but they would disgust the reader, and the mind shrinks from narrating them.

It has been related above, that Sháh Begum, Mihr Nigár Khánim, my brother Muhammad Sháh, and the maternal sister of my father (who was the full sister of Mirzá Abá Bakr), when they were coming from Kábul, on their way to Badakhshán, were captured by the army of Mirzá Abá Bakr. The Mirzá brought them to Káshghar. His sister, Khán Sultán Sultánim, was a very pious woman, and had spent all her life in acts of religious devotion. For a long time he allowed her no food but wine, and when she was brought to the point of death by hunger and thirst, she was made by force to drink some of that [wine], so that she died in torture and suffering, all the same.[1]

He kept my brother, Muhammad Sháh, up till the age of fifteen years among his eunuchs [*ghulám-i-akhta*]. When [my brother] reached this age [the Mirzá] ordered a roasting-spit to be thrust into his stomach, then to be driven through with a hammer, so as to come out at his back, and impale him against a wall; thus nailed to the wall, he was left [to die in agony]. From these examples, one may judge of his treatment of his nephews and nieces, and of those two noble women, the Begum and the Khánim. On consideration, I have decided to withhold my pen from further details, for I do not wish the honourable mind of the reader of this Epitome to be clouded by the darkness of that black nature; I will therefore not detain him longer on this subject.

In spite of all these [barbarities] Mirzá Abá Bakr affected great piety, and was given over to good works, charity, and almsgiving to such an extent, that he never rested from these matters; while Mullas and doctors of the law were continually in his assemblies. In all his affairs and actions he relied upon a *fatwá;* he even procured *fatwá* for the most atrocious of his deeds.[2] If the Ulama granted the *fatwá*, well and good; if they refused it, he would accuse the Mufti, find him guilty and sentence him to death, but would pretend to show him mercy, saying: "He ought, according to the law, to die, but owing to my regard for him, I will remit the sentence of death, and will give him some work to do instead." But the work he gave him was far worse than death. Among the *fatwá* he demanded were the two following.

[1] In the Turki we find: Mirza Abá Bakr practised such cruelty towards his sister, that for some time he refused her all food, and gave her nothing but wine in place of water; and that wretched woman was, at length, driven to drink one or two drops of the wine to quench her thirst.—R.

[2] In place of this passage the Turki MS. reads: Until the Ulama had granted a *fatwá*, he had no right to do anything; and in order to legalise and justify his most hideous and abominable undertakings, he would ask for a *fatwá*, and would thus show that his action was in accordance with the Holy Law.—R.

If Amr attack Zaid with the intention of killing him, Zaid does all he can against Amr in self-defence, and according to the law is justified.[1]

Again, if Khálid[2] be one who excites sedition and carries his evil intentions to another kingdom, in order to stir up rebellion in his own, the governor of his own country does all he can to prevent Khálid from going to another country, lest he may become a source of distress to his own people; and in so doing is justified by the law.

On the strength of these two *fatwá*, Mirza Abá Bakr put to death 3000 of the men of Jágirák, Uzkand, and Mádu, who had designs upon his life. And he cut off the feet of several thousands of others, with the excuse that: "if these men run away to another country, they will stir up revolt [against me]; in this manner I will keep them within my own kingdom, that they may not escape." Such were his acts of cruelty. [In this book] there is no place for a further record of them. Haply they are contained in the book of the Most Merciful of Scribes. On this account, I will now close the description of these repulsive matters.

The rest of Mirzá Abá Bakr's reign will be related presently.

CHAPTER XXIX.

UBAID ULLAH KHÁN MARCHES FROM TURKISTÁN AGAINST BOKHÁRÁ. IS MET AT KUL MALIK BY BÁBAR PÁDISHÁH. A BATTLE TAKES PLACE, IN WHICH THE LATTER IS DEFEATED. EVENTS THAT ENSUED.

WHEN the Emperor, in Rajab of the year 917,[3] mounted the throne of Samarkand, as has been stated above, the learned men and nobles of Mávará-un-Nahr were indignant at his attachment to Sháh Ismail and at his adoption of the Turkomán style of dress. When that winter had passed and spring had set in (the plentiful drops of her rain having clothed the earth in green raiment) the Uzbeg advanced out of Turkistán. Their main body marched against Táshkand, while Ubaid Ullah went to Bokhárá by way of Yati Kuduk. As the citadel of Táshkand had been fortified by Amir Ahmad Kásim Kuhbur, [the Emperor] sent him some rein-

[1] In Arabic grammars Amr and Zaid are generally taken in examples of rules of syntax, and correspond, in sort, to A. and B. in English, or Caius and Balbus in Latin.—R.

[2] Khálid is, I suppose, the typical name for a general, after the famous early Muhammadan conqueror.—R.

[3] October, 1511.

forcements, under the command of such men as Amir Dust Násir, Sultán Muhammad Duládi,[1] and others, while he himself [the Emperor] advanced on Bokhárá. When he neared the town, news of his approach reached Ubaid Ullah Khán, who [becoming alarmed] immediately drew his bridle and returned along the road by which he had just come. The Emperor pursued him, overtook him at Kul Malik, and compelled him to retreat. Ubaid Ullah Khán had 3000 men with him, while the Emperor had 40,000.[2] Ubaid Ullah Khán having repeated to the end of the verse: "And how often has not a small force defeated a large one, by the permission of God?" [faced the Emperor], and a fierce battle began to rage. God, the most high, has shown to the peoples of the earth, and especially to kings and rulers, that no boast is to be made of, no reliance to be placed in, the numbers of an army nor their equipment; for He in His might gives victory to whomsoever He will.

Thus Ubaid Ullah Khán, with 3000 shattered [*rikhta*] men, who eight months previously had retreated before this same force, now entirely defeated an army of 40,000, perfectly equipped and mounted on fine horses [*tupchák*].[3] This event occurred in Safar of the year 918.[4] The Emperor had reigned eight months in Samarkand.

When the Emperor returned to Samarkand, he was unable to get a firm footing upon the steps of the throne, and so bidding farewell to the sovereignty of Samarkand, he hastened to Hisár. He sent one ambassador after another to Sháh Ismail, to inform him of what had passed, and to beg for succour. Sháh Ismail granted his request, and sent Mir Najm, his commander-in-chief,[5] with 60,000 men, to his aid. Thus at the beginning of the winter succeeding that spring, [the allies] once more marched against the Uzbeg. On reaching Karshi, they found that Shaikham Mirzá, the uncle of Ubaid Ullah Khán, had strengthened the fort of Karshi. They, therefore, began by laying siege to the fort, which they quickly reduced. Then they put to death Shaikham Mirzá, and massacred the whole of the people of the fort, killing both high and low—the sucklings and the decrepit.

Of the Uzbeg Sultáns, each one had fortified himself in his own

[1] For *Duládi* the Turki has *Kutárlik*.—R.

[2] The Turki version of this passage is: Ubaid Ullah Khan saw that no escape was possible, and that he must perforce remain and give battle to Baber Padishah, although he had only 3,000 men to the Emperor's 40,000.—R.

[3] *Tupchák* is an Eastern Turki word meaning "a fine horse," though Dr. Bellew says it signifies "roadster," and that it is used in distinction to *árghumák* or "thorough-bred." (*Yarkand Report*, p. 70.) Baber constantly uses the word in his Memoirs, and implies a superior animal and a riding horse.

[4] April—May, 1512 A.D.

[5] Mir Najm, sometimes called Najm Sáni, or the "Second Star," was, according to Howorth, minister of finance to Shah Ismail. His real name was Yar Muhammad. (ii., p. 712.)

castle. Thus Jáni Beg Sultán had stood on the defensive in the fort of Ghajdaván. When the Turkománs had finished with Karshi, they asked the Emperor about the condition of all the fortified cities of Mávará-un-Nahr, and he described them one by one. It appeared that the easiest of all to take was that of Ghajdaván; towards it, therefore, they marched. The Uzbeg Sultáns heard of their coming, and entered the fort on the same night that the Turkománs and the Emperor, who were encamped before the place, were busy preparing their siege implements. At dawn they arranged their forces in the midst of the suburbs, and stood facing [the enemy]. On the other side, too, preparations were made for a fight.[1] Since the Uzbeg were in the midst of the suburbs, the field of battle was narrow. The Uzbeg infantry began to pour forth their arrows from every corner, so that very soon the claws of Islám twisted the hands of heresy and unbelief, and victory declared for the true faith. The victorious breezes of Islám overturned the banners of the schismatics. [The Turkománs] were so completely routed, that most of them perished on the field; all the rents that had been made by the swords at Karshi, were now sewn up with the arrow stitches of vengeance. They sent Mir Najm and all the Turkomán Amirs to hell. The Emperor retired, broken and crestfallen, to Hisár.

And now a difference arose between the Emperor and those Moghul Amirs who, when the Khán went [to Andiján], had stayed behind and entered the Emperor's service. To make a long story short, one night, Ayub Begjik, Mir Muhammad, Yádgár Mirzá and Nazar Mirzá, in company with the rest of the Moghuls, fell upon the Emperor so unexpectedly that he was with difficulty able to escape, naked, into the castle of Hisár; while [the conspirators] having plundered all they could find outside [the fort], marched away towards the mountains of Karátigin. The Emperor was powerless to oppose them: having left several of his trusted Amirs to defend the castle of Hisár, he himself proceeded to Kunduz. The whole province of Hisár, except the fort, fell into the hands of the Moghuls. The Moghuls have a proverb which runs: when a place is left unoccupied, the pigs will mount to the top of the hillock.[2] . . . They withdrew the hand of tyranny and oppression from the sleeve of violence and enmity, and seized upon the households, families, possessions and cattle of all the people. One of the most distinguished of those Moghuls, who was in my service [at one time], used to relate: "They once [by way of paying my allowance] gave me an assignment [*barát*] for obtaining provisions, which was addressed to one of the inferior officials

[1] The Turki says: The Emperor and the Turkomans advanced.—R.

[2] This saying is followed by a line containing a coarse pun, which is untranslatable.—R.

at Vakhsh. I alighted at his house and showed him my assignment. He pondered for a while; then he came out and displayed before my view about 200 horses, and a proportionate number of sheep, camels, slaves, household furniture, clothes and [various] materials, saying: 'I entreat you to let me and my children and wives go with the clothes we have on, while you take possession of all that is here, and release me from the balance of the sum that is mentioned in the order.' When I had reckoned up the value of the cattle and property, though it came to a considerable sum, it was only half of that entered in the assignment." This story shows what degree of tyranny, violence and oppression they had begun to practise. Whatever property or flocks they found among the people of Hisár, they extorted from the owners, whom they ruined with waste and extravagance. There ensued a terrible famine among the Musulmáns,[1] and in the whole town of Hisár [only] sixty persons survived. The living eat the dead, and when these had died in such a condition that no nourishment was left in their flesh, the living fell upon one another. The end of these odious and revolting scenes was, that out of those thirty or forty thousand people, only about two thousand escaped, leaving their property behind; the rest were all engulfed in the ocean of violence, or annihilated with the sword of vengeance. The women and children were led away captive by the Uzbeg, and bear the burden of the ignominy to this day.

To add to all this distress and suffering, that winter there was such a prolonged and incessant snowfall, that the plains became like hills and the hills like plains. But as for that abominable race [the Uzbeg], as their tyranny and cruelty increased, so did their prosperity decrease. They, also, began to suffer from want of grain; and as the fodder all lay buried under the snow in the plains, they had nothing to give their horses; nor could they find any corn for themselves. Thus were these cursed people likewise reduced to great distress, and became impotent.

When news of their helpless condition reached Ubaid Ullah Khán, most of whose efforts were guided [at least] by good intentions, he felt it his bounden duty, both from a desire to restore order in the country, and also from a sense of right and justice, to go and expel these evil doers. At the end of the winter, therefore, he set out for Hisár. When [the Moghuls] heard of the approach of the Uzbeg, they knew not which way to turn, for they had themselves darkened their road to the Emperor; nor did they think fit to go to the Khán in Andiján, because whenever they might enter the Khán's service, they would be obliged to do some work which they considered beneath their dignity: the hands of their

[1] By Musulmáns the Sunni appear to be meant—*i.e.*, the Uzbegs and their partisans.

tyranny would be cut off and the feet of their insubordination crushed. On this account they abhorred the idea of going to the court of the Khán. Moreover, the roads were rendered impassable by the snow. For these several reasons, they took up a strong position in the mountains of the Surkháb and of Vakhsh. On one side it was protected by the River Surkháb, on two others by the mountains, while on the remaining side was deep snow, on which they placed much reliance.

When the Uzbeg drew near, they reconnoitred on all sides and found the enemy well fortified. As the Ustád says: "Life is like snow under the summer sun." The snow on the one flank, on which they had put reliance, thawed a few days later, and left a very broad way through the defile. This wide passage caused joy to [the Uzbeg] and depression to those wicked [Moghuls]. One morning the Uzbeg charged down upon [the Moghuls], who, when they saw them coming, threw themselves into the water . . . . (Couplet). . . . Most of those wretches passed through the water to the flames of hell, some few escaped; and all those who had not reached the river, went to hell by way of the flashing scimitar. Those that survived were taken prisoners, and all the suffering that they had inflicted on the people in Hisár during a year, God Almighty now caused, by the hand of Ubaid Ullah Khán, to descend upon them in one hour . . . (Couplets) . . . . All those that escaped the Hisár river and the glittering sword, went to the Khán in Andiján, in the condition that has been described, or rather, their condition would not be possible to describe.

I have heard Mir Ayub relate: "Often, when I experienced ill-treatment from the Moghuls, and witnessed their dealings with the people [in Hisár], I have prayed to God to hasten to send down calamity upon them, that true Musulmáns might thereby be delivered." The moral to be drawn from this story is that one should shun cruelty, which embitters life and destroys happiness: one should practise justice, which strengthens prosperity and sweetens life. "Divine aid is a precious thing, and is only given to the faithful servant."[1] In short, through the villany of that tribe [the Moghuls], Hisár fell from the hands of the Emperor, and came under the domination of the Uzbeg. So long as the Emperor entertained any hopes [of recovering Hisár], he remained in Kunduz, though exposed to the greatest distress and want. Mirzá Khán possessed that country, but in spite of his entire subordination [to the Emperor], he was not able to give up his own country to oblige him. The Emperor, with his accustomed courtesy, bore the situation patiently, and made no attempt to deprive Mirzá Khán of his dominions. At last, despairing altogether of recovering Hisár, he returned to Kábul.

[1] An Arabic quotation from the Korán.—R.

When he conquered Mávará-un-Nahr, he left Sultán Násir Mirzá upon the throne of Kábul. On learning the Emperor's approach, Sultán Násir Mirzá came out to receive him, with protestations of devotion and respect, saying: "When you withdrew your foot from the throne of the glorious kingdom of Kábul, you entrusted the high honour of government to me. And I have guarded this imperial treasure for you until, through the changes of fortune and the revolving of the spheres, you have again come to place your noble foot upon the steps of the throne. I would now crave your permission to be allowed to return to my former government of Ghazna, and would be most grateful if a few Amirs, of whom I stand in need, were appointed to my service." This devotion on the part of Sultán Násir Mirzá made a deep impression on the mind of the Emperor, who showed his gratitude by many favours, and allowed him to return to Ghazna, where Sultán Násir Mirzá died soon after [*dar hamán ayyám*]. Whereupon grave disputes arose among the Amirs in Ghazna, which shall be spoken of in their proper place. The Emperor remained in Kábul until the conquest of Kandahár; after that he conquered Hindustán, which shall likewise be mentioned in its right place.

CHAPTER XXX.

ACCOUNT OF MY UNCLE, SAYYID MUHAMMAD MIRZÁ.

It has already been briefly related how the Khán, on the 14th of Safar, in the year 917,[1] separated from the Emperor, and went to Andiján; also how he defeated [Mirzá Abá Bakr] and the Káshghari [at the battle of Tutluk]. At the same time the Emperor seized Samarkand: while the Khán became absolute master of Andiján. In speaking of the children of Sultán Ahmad Khán, it was mentioned that Sultán Khalil Sultán, being in great distress, had come to Andiján, and that Jáni Beg Sultán had been affected in the brain, by falling from his horse onto his head.

At the time when Sultán Khalil Sultán came [to Andiján], Jáni Beg Sultán ordered my uncle, Sayyid Muhammad Mirzá, Sultán Ali Mirzá Begjik, and Tubra Nuyághut,[2] to kill Sultán Khalil Sultán, in order that he might be assured that they were cut off from the Moghuls, otherwise [he feared that], on the first opportunity, they would stir up a rebellion and attach themselves to the Moghul Khákáns. These three, fearing for their own lives,

[1] The 14 Safar, 917 = 13 May, 1511.
[2] The Turki MS. has: *Tubághuth.*—R.

drowned Sultán Khalil Sultán in the river of Akhsi. The Sultán was younger brother to the Khán.[1]

So long as the Uzbeg had the upper hand and were successful, these three men lived in peace; but when the Uzbeg were overthrown, they grew apprehensive lest the Khán should take vengeance upon them for that crime [and this thought was never out of their minds]. One day the Khán, in a state of intoxication, killed Tubra. It came about in this wise. Tubra was a rude, unpolished man, who had never been in personal attendance on the Khákáns, but had always lived in the deserts of Moghulistán and Uzbegistán, engaged in forays [*kazáki*] and skirmishes [*karávuli*].[2] He was ignorant of the manners of an Amir. He now looked upon himself as one of the pillars of the State, and thought that for him to speak gently or courteously to a prince was but flattery, while flattery was the vilest of qualities; that coarse speech was a sign of power, and that a rough manner and the non-observance of the rules of politeness due to a king, should be regarded as a mark of dignity in himself. The people thought he was insane, and that pride had thickened the fibres of his brain. In spite of fear and apprehension, he had certainly made roughness of speech and rude manners his second nature. One day, at a feast given by the Khán, the wine was passing freely, and Tubra's head became hot with intoxication; reason left his brain, and in its place came pride and wickedness. All those thoughts which, when sober, he kept to himself, he now let free with full force, and began to talk wildly. It was in vain that the Khán expostulated and pointed out to him that his railleries were out of place: that he should not let loose the reins of coarse speech and vulgarity. Tubra retorted in a speech reflecting on the Khan's family.[3] At this answer, the Khán quite lost control over his temper, and the harvest of his patience was consumed; he then and there gave orders for Tubra's head to be struck off and hung over the gate, as an example to all not to forget the respect due to authority.

When Sultán Ali Mirzá, who was one of the three, heard of this event, he fled to the Emperor in Samarkand, and joined his brothers, Mir Ayub, Mir Muhammad, and Mir Ibráhim. My uncle, Sayyid Muhammad Mirzá, who was their leader, was plunged into the greatest alarm. This event had occurred at Akhsi, while my uncle was in Andiján. The Khán immediately sent off Mir Kambar, in great haste, from Akhsi [to explain the matter to my uncle], saying: "Tubra was an ass; but no ass would endure him, even to buckle on his nose-bag.[4] Moreover,

[1] The expression is: *birádar-i-padar-i-mádari.*—R.
[2] The Turki says: Like a Kazák.—R.
[3] The speech, which is about one line in length, is obscure and impossible to put into English.—R.
[4] A play on the word *Tubra*, meaning a "nose-bag" for feeding horses.

he had entirely given himself up to the paths of rudeness." Mir Kambar succeeded in quieting the Khán with this message. Soon after this, the Khán himself came to Andiján. Here he treated my uncle with such friendliness and affection, as to blot out all fears from the latter's mind, and such a firm friendship was established between them, that it lasted all their lives. In later times the Khán never mentioned my uncle's name without shedding tears of affection.

[Verse] Behold the kindness and mercy of the Lord;
The servant has sinned, and the master is ashamed.[1]

After settling this matter, the Khán became firmly established upon the throne of the Khánate, until the time when the Emperor abandoned Samarkand, and the Uzbeg again obtained the ascendency in Mávará-un-Nahr. The Emperor appealed to Sháh Ismail for assistance, which came in the person of Mir Najm, with whom he again marched against Samarkand, as has been already recorded. On learning this news, the Khán set out for Andiján; and with the desire to anticipate [*pishdasti*] the Emperor and Mir Najm, before they had crossed the Darband-i-Áhanin, he attacked Suyunjuk Khán,[2] who was one of the chief Uzbeg Sultáns. With him a pitched battle was fought at a place called Bishkand.[3] But the Khán was defeated, after displaying great personal valour and receiving many wounds, and he arrived discomfited at Andiján, where he awaited news of the Emperor and Mir Najm. The Uzbeg, for their part, were unable to pursue or harass his troops to any great extent, for the Emperor and Mir Najm had turned towards Samarkand, thereby causing them great alarm. On this account, the Khán remained in Andiján, to repair the effects of his defeat and wait for news of the Emperor.

[1] From Sádi's *Gulistán*. Then follow four lines of rhetoric, which are omitted —R.

[2] He was son of Abulkhair Khan, and brother of Kuch Kunji and Shah Badágh—consequently, uncle of Shaibáni Khan.

[3] *Bish-kand* is no doubt intended for Panja-kand, a town in the Zaráfshán valley, some forty miles east of Samarkand. *Bish Kand*, or "five towns," is merely the Turki form of *Panja Kand*, which has the same signification in Persian. The case, indeed, is similar to that of Yatikand and Haft Deh, alluded to at p. 180. The movements of the three parties referred to in the text are not very clear, but they are sufficiently plain to show that *Biskand* or *Piskand*, beyond the right bank of the Sir, and south of Tashkand, cannot be the place indicated by Bish-kand.

CHAPTER XXXI.

PERSONAL ADVENTURES OF THE AUTHOR.

It has been already related that in Rajab of the year 915,[1] I left Mirzá Khán and proceeded to Kábul, to be honoured by the blessed glance of the Emperor, who welcomed and entertained me with the warmest affection. In public he ranked me with his brothers and nephews; but in private he regarded me with a truly paternal eye, as one of his own children, and I was the special object of his fatherly sympathy. So much did he comfort me, that he entirely banished from my mind the bitterness of orphanage, and grief at separation from my friends. Thus did I pass my time in perfect ease and contentment. In the meanwhile the Emperor resolved to lead an army against Kunduz, as has been already mentioned. It was the season of the polar star, and in the rigour of *Dai*,[2] when he said to me, with great affection: "The difficulty of the road and the coldness of the air are extreme. [You had better] stop in Kábul this winter. When spring comes, and the air is cleared of the bitter cold, you can come to me." But I remonstrated with him, saying: "In this country, it is the consideration and kindness of the Emperor which have enabled me to endure the bitterness of my desolation. If the Emperor leaves me behind, to whom shall I turn for comfort?" When he saw that to insist upon my remaining behind, in Kábul, would prey upon my mind and break my heart, he ordered such preparations for my journey to be made as the limited time allowed, and permitted me to accompany him to Kunduz.

As many of my father's old followers were among the Moghuls, they all hastened, at this crisis, to enter my service, bringing with them such presents and offerings as their circumstances admitted. In short, I was well equipped with arms and men. More especially [I must mention] my foster-father, Ján Ahmad Ataka, whose name will frequently occur hereafter, in its proper place; he, together with the rest of my father's old retainers, attached himself to me. This Ataka was a trustworthy man, and had distinguished himself by his personal exploits at the time of the Uzbeg ascendency. He had made a goodly collection of horses and arms, which he put at my service. It was thus that he was employed until the winter, when [the Emperor] led his army into the Dasht-i-Kulak, as has been mentioned. I personally accompanied that expedition. On

[1] Oct.—Nov., 1509.

[2] *Dai* would be the tenth month of the ancient Persian year, or December. —R.

our return from the Dasht-i-Kulak, in the spring, the Emperor sent the Khán to Andiján. The Khán was very anxious to take me with him in his service, and, I for my part, had a strong desire to go. But when I asked leave of the Emperor, his blessed heart became heavy, and he put all such ideas on one side. Thus the Khán went to Andiján, while I remained in the service of the Emperor.

Soon after this, followed the campaign of Hisár, in which the battle with Hamza Sultán and the defeat of the Uzbeg occurred. In the former engagement, the aforesaid Ján Ahmad Ataka led my men into battle, and having captured one of the Uzbeg chiefs alive, brought him to the Emperor, who promised him a reward for his bravery [*juldu*],[1] saying: "This is Mirzá Haidar's first exploit, and is a good omen." He then ordered them to record the *juldu* in the book, under Mirzá Haidar's name. This story has been already related.

I was with the Emperor when he captured Samarkand. In mentioning my father's children, I said that the eldest of all was Habiba Sultán Khánish; [she was my full sister] and had fallen to Ubaid Ullah Khán. When Ubaid Ullah fled from Karshi to Bokhárá and entered Turkistán, he was not able to look after his own family properly. Every one who could find means to make that difficult journey went; those who could not, stayed behind. Among these last was my sister, Habiba Sultán Khánish, whom I joined in Bokhárá. We then came to Samarkand, where we found my uncle, who had come, that winter, from the Khán in Andiján, on business of the State. Having settled his affairs to the best of his powers, he returned to Andiján, taking with him my sister, whom on his arrival he gave in marriage to the Khán.

In the spring of that year, when the Emperor went to encounter Ubaid Ullah Khán at the battle of Kul Malik, I was detained in Samarkand by an access of fever. When the Emperor retired to Samarkand discomfited, and then again departed [being unable to remain there], I was in a state of convalescence; nevertheless, I continued to follow him to Hisár. The Khán sent messengers several times to the Emperor to fetch me, and at last, displeased and irritated, he gave me leave to go. In my childish folly I did not (as it was my duty to do) pay attention to the Emperor's consent [but determined to go to Andiján]. Thus, on the arrival of Mir Najm, the Emperor mounted his horse and joined the expedition, while I set out for Andiján. I have already mentioned how the Emperor joined Mir Najm. I [as I say] went to Andiján; but before reaching my destination, the Khán[2] had been put to rout by Suyunjuk Khán, and returned to Andiján just as I arrived

[1] A Turki word meaning—a present made to heroes, or a reward for bravery.
[2] Sultan Said Khan.

there. This occurred in Rajab of the year 918. From that date to the day of the Khán's death, in Zulhijja 939,[1] I remained constantly in his service, and was all the while distinguished by his regard and liberality. In short, until he conferred upon me the rank of Kurkáni, I was never absent from him. At night, whereever his bed was spread, one was also spread for my convenience, at his side. At royal banquets, the right hand of my fortune was joined to the left hand of the Khán's favour. Whenever a consultation was held, my uncle was sure to be at the head of the meeting [*sar-i-daftar*], but he gave me precedence over my uncle; nay more, he did so at the request of my uncle, who used frequently to point out to the Khán that [although] I was only the son of his brother, still he recognised that my precedence over him was not only proper, but necessary. When he rode out, I always rode at his side; and when he went hunting, he used to instruct me in the sport [and initiate me into its secrets and subtleties]. He used to lead the hunt himself, for he was a keen sportsman. He never allowed me out of his sight, but used to persuade me to go hunting with him, and if ever I showed any reluctance, he would compel me to enjoy it. He used to set me various tasks to do, at the same time pointing out what benefit I should derive [from doing them], and would say: "Until young men begin to perform duties, they can never gain experience. [Otherwise] in important affairs and in large assemblies, in mosques and in the battlefield, where the leaders of the people, whether Khákáns or Sultáns or Amirs, take part, they become confused, and meet with opposition from their people. But when young men practise themselves in the business of their elders, they gain insight into the particulars of their various duties, and in all such matters as wars and the like, they acquire a certain confidence. This self-reliance gains for them the esteem of the people, which strengthens their authority. In the performance of these duties they learn to recognise their own merits and demerits, and to judge of the best modes of action.

"While in the service of my father and my uncle, I had these principles indelibly engraved upon my heart, and they used to make me perform numerous duties, that I might turn the advantages derived from them to the best possible account. What I learnt from my elders I now am teaching you, that you, in turn, may also profit by it."

Till the age of twenty-four, I was employed in every kind of service, and all that the Khán gave me to do, both great things and small, I carried out single-handed. But if, even in the councils of the Amirs, in which I had my special place, an opportunity of some service presented itself to me, the Khán would forbid my performing it, saying: "In the battlefield you must remember

[1] Rajab, 918, began 12 Sept., 1512. Zulhijja, 939, began 24 June, 1533.

your rank, so that you may not fall in the estimation of the people." When I was between twenty-four and twenty-five years of age, he bade me desist from all these services, and said: "All that I have given you to do, you have done well. Now you can return to your favourite pursuits." Thereafter, till the age of thirty, he entrusted to me the affairs of the army. But he caused me to be attended by men of judgment and experienced Amirs, and instructed me never to deviate from what they considered right, but to follow them in all matters. When several campaigns [*lashkar*] had been carried through in this way, he gave me leave to speak my mind in debates and plans of action. Up to the age of thirty I had never received this permission, nor had I ever spoken in an assembly, but had always remained silent. After sanction was accorded me, however, I spoke much, and whenever I used to speak in the assemblies, the Khán would say to me: "Explain this matter more fully, give us your proofs and your reasonings." If I explained myself well and said what was fitting, he would praise me, and desire the people to applaud; and when I did not say exactly what was right, he would add: "What he means to say is so-and-so"; and thus would improve my words and satisfy the Amirs.

When some time had passed in this way, he said to me: "I have now learnt to rely on you thoroughly;" he then entrusted to me the entire management of the army and the direction of the government, giving me, in these matters, absolute freedom of action, together with sanction to issue mandates and *firmáns*. When I returned from my expedition into Kashmir, and came to kiss the Khán's feet in Tibet,[1] he called me by no other name than "brother," both in private and in public. The details connected with [these events] will be given in the account of the Khán. I shall not record the rest of my own life until I have related the end of his.

CHAPTER XXXII.

ACCOUNT OF SULTÁN SAID KHÁN AFTER HIS DEFEAT BY SUYUNJUK KHÁN.

[Soon] after I entered the Khán's service, news arrived of the defeat of the Emperor and Mir Najm at Ghajdaván. This was at the beginning of the same winter in which the Moghuls revolted

[1] By *Tibet*, Ladak is meant here, as in nearly every case where the word *Tibet* is used.

against the Emperor, when the severe famine broke out in Hisár, [and much snow fell]. During that winter the whole of the province endured great misery and want.

At this crisis, news came of Suyunjuk Khán's march [on Andiján]. Three months previously [the Khán] had been defeated [by Suyunjuk], and his power of resistance had been broken. After much deliberation, it was resolved that my uncle should fortify himself in the citadel of Andiján; that Mir Ghuri Barlás should defend Akhsi and Mir Dáim Ali should hold the citadel of Marghinán, while the Khán should retire to the hills on the north of the province of Andiján, with his family and the rest of the army; for it would be difficult for the Uzbeg to come into the hills [to fight], and the fact that the Khán was still in the field [*birun*] would make them fear to besiege the citadels. Having decided upon these plans, they were at once put into execution. When Suyunjuk Khán learnt this, he did not see fit to advance, but abandoning his purpose, remained quietly where he was for that winter.

In the spring, news came of Kásim Khán. The incidents were as follows. When the Emperor conquered Mávará-un-Nahr, he gave Táshkand [in charge] to Mir Ahmad Kásim Kuhbur, and Sairám to the latter's brother, Kitta Beg. When the Emperor left Samarkand and went to Hisár, the Uzbeg, having regained their composure, laid siege to Táshkand, and at length reduced the defenders to great straits. One night, however, [the garrison] rushed out of the citadel, and attacking one corner of the Uzbeg army, got away. The Uzbeg looked upon their departure as a great blessing, and did not follow them, but were satisfied with the reduction of Táshkand. Afterwards, Mir Ahmad Kásim went to the Khán in Andiján, and on leaving that town, proceeded to join the Emperor in Hisár. But his brother, Kitta Beg, had put the citadel of Sairám into a state of defence, [lest the Uzbeg should come and besiege him], and could find no road for escape. All that winter he remained within his fortifications. Early in the spring he sent to Kásim Khán for help, saying: "If you will come to me, I will deliver the citadel of Sairám over to you." With such words did he entice his brother and arouse his ambition, thus bringing him against Táshkand.

But at this point, in order to understand what follows, it is necessary to say something about Kásim Khán.

CHAPTER XXXIII.

ACCOUNT OF THE KAZÁK AND THEIR SULTÁNS: THE ORIGIN OF THEIR NAME AND THEIR END.[1]

When Abulkhair had made himself master of the whole of the Dasht-i-Kipchák, he desired to remove several of the Sultáns of the race of Juji, in whom he detected symptoms of seditious designs. Karái[2] Khán and Jáni Beg Khán, perceiving the intentions of Abulkhair Khán, fled, together with a few other Juji Sultáns, to Moghulistán. This country was at the time under the Khánship of Isán Bughá Khán, who received them favourably and assigned a corner of Moghulistán for them to live in. Here they dwelt in peace.

On the death of Abulkhair, differences arose between the Uzbeg *Ulus*. As many as were able, repaired to Karái Khán and Jáni Beg Khán, for the sake of peace and security; and in this way [the two Kháns] became very powerful. Since they had first of all separated from the mass of their people, and for some time had

[1] The whole of this valuable section was translated by Erskine, and will be found in his MS. at the British Museum. As Sir H. Howorth has reproduced it in his chapter on the *White Horde and the Kirghiz Kazaks*, and has collated it with other accounts of the same events, it would be superfluous to offer any comment on the subject here. I would only remark that, when Mirza Haidar says that "in the year 944 not a vestige" of the Kazák of Moghulistan remained "on the face of the earth," he must have been unacquainted with what was going on in that country. He wrote the passage, apparently, in the year 948 H. (1541–2) in Kashmir, or about nine years after he had severed his connection with Moghulistan, and was possibly wrongly, or imperfectly, informed. Sir H. Howorth observes: "This is probably an exaggeration, but there can be no doubt that at this time the Kazák confederacy was much disintegrated." Their line of Khans continued, however, and Sir Henry traces their history, and that of their people, down to the early years of the eighteenth century.

For convenience of reference, the Khans of the Kazák of the White Horde may be detailed here, for the period of Mirza Haidar's history, as follows:—

Karai and Jáni Beg (sons of Borák)	1427–1488	A.D.	
Baranduk (son of Karái)	1488–1509	,,	
Kásim (son of Jáni Beg)	1509–1518	,,	
Mumásh (son of Kásim)	1518–1523	,,	(?)
Táhir (grandson of Karái)	1523–1530	,,	
Bulásh (*Ibid.*)	1530–15..	,,	(?)

There is some doubt about the last name. Sir H. Howorth, citing a Russian author, shows that it may have been Uziak Ahmad. The date 1523, I have taken from Stokvis, but do not know his authority for it. It is wanting in the *Tárikh-i-Rashidi*, and in Howorth. (See *Hist. of Mongols*, ii., pp. 627, *seq.*; and Stokvis, i., p. 163; but the latter's table does not agree with the above.)

[2] This is the exact transliteration of the name as it occurs in the texts, though most European authors have written it *Girai*.

been in an indigent and wandering state, they got the name of *Kazák*, which has clung to them [ever since].

On the death of Karái Khán, his son Baranduk Khán succeeded to the Khánship, while Kásim Khán, son of Jáni Beg Khán, like his father, became obedient and submissive to Baranduk Khán. In addition to Baranduk Khán, Karái Khán had many sons, and Jáni Beg Khán had others besides Kásim Khán. Among [Jáni Beg's sons] was Adik Sultán, who married Sultán Nigár Khánim, the fourth daughter of Sultán Yunus Khán, on the death of Mirzá Sultán Mahmud, son of Sultán Abu Said Mirzá. After the devastation of Táshkand, Adik Sultán abandoned Sháhi Beg Khán to join the Kazák, and was followed by Sultán Nigár Khánim. But Adik Sultán dying soon after this, Kásim Khán took Sultán Nigár Khánim to wife. At the death of Adik Sultán, Kásim Khán obtained complete ascendency, and Baranduk was Khán in name only. Finally he banished Baranduk Khán, who repaired to Samarkand and died in exile.

Kásim Khán now brought the Dasht-i-Kipchák under his absolute control, in a manner that no one, with the exception of Juji Khán, had ever done before. His army exceeded a thousand thousand. In the year 924 he died, whereupon contests ensued among the Kazák Sultáns. He was succeeded in the Khánate by his son Mumásh Khán, who, in one of the wars, died of shortness of breath,[1] and was succeeded by Táhir Khán, son of Adik Sultán. Being a harsh man, he practised much cruelty, so that his people, who numbered about 400,000 persons, suddenly deserted him and dispersed, while he was left alone among the Kirghiz, and died, at last, in misery.

Nearly 30,000 men being now collected together in Moghulistán, they appointed as their Khán, Bulásh[2] Khán, brother of Táhir Khán. But the wheel of Fate has made such strange revolutions, that for the last four years, not a trace has been visible of these people. In the year '30, the Kazák numbered a thousand thousand; in the year '44, not a vestige of all this host remains on the face of the earth. They will be frequently mentioned [in this history] in connection with the Khán. Such is the story of the Kazák.

Even previous to the time of Kásim Khán's assumption of the title of Khán, his power was so great that no one considered Baranduk Khán; nevertheless he did not wish to live side by side with Baranduk Khán, because, if near him, he would not be able

[1] The Persian texts have *dam-giri*, the Turki *tang-nafsi*. Both terms mean practically the same thing, but *dam-giri* is generally used for shortness of breath produced by the rarefied air at high altitudes, while *tang-nafsi* usually stands for ordinary asthma or other affections of the breathing organs. In the Dasht-i-Kipchák there are no high altitudes to produce *dam-giri* in its usual sense.

[2] This name may perhaps read *Tulásh*.

to pay him due respect, but would offer him opposition; and [he felt that] if he did treat him with honour, he could not reconcile passive submission with his own private convictions. He therefore kept at a distance. Baranduk Khán lived at Sarai Chuk,[1] and Kásim Khán, in order to be far away from him, went to the confines of Moghulistán. He made Karátál[2] his winter quarters, intending, early in the spring, to return to his original capital; when one of Kitta Beg's men, with some of the chief inhabitants of Sairám, arrived, bringing the keys of Sairám and beseeching him to accept the town, which he did. He then marched on Taráz, which the Moghuls call Yángi. In advance of himself, he despatched one of his own Amirs, into whose hands Kitta Beg delivered the town of Sairám. [Kitta Beg waited on Kásim Khán in person, and induced him to attack Táshkand.] Kásim Khán then set out with a countless army for Táshkand, where Suyunjuk Khán had fortified himself within the citadel. Kásim Khán arrived, spent one night outside, and then turned back again, plundering all the environs of Táshkand as he went. The rest of the events of Kásim Khán's life will be related in their proper place.

CHAPTER XXXIV.

EVENTS THAT FOLLOWED THE BATTLE WITH SUYUNJUK KHÁN; ALSO SULTÁN SAID KHÁN'S JOURNEY TO THE KAZÁK AND TO KÁSIM KHÁN.

In the spring of the year 918, the Shaibán Uzbeg (by which name is meant the followers of Sháhi Beg Khán) had become absolute masters of Mávará-un-Nahr. The fear of them had sunk into every heart. That winter had been spent in the above-mentioned plot;[3] in the spring they were busy devising further schemes, and thinking what they should next attempt, when suddenly news

[1] If this is intended for the name of a town, some possible variants are *Sarai-Juk*, *Sarai-Chik*, etc. There is a town of the last name on the Yaik or Ural river, near the northern end of the Caspian, and it is quite possible that this is the place indicated. But the text may be read "the palace of Chuk, Juk," etc., and in that case I am unable to suggest any location for it.

[2] The *Kárátál* River, which flows into Lake Bálkásh from the south, was, as Mirza Haidar states in a later chapter, on the northern confines of Moghulistan. There was a place called *Kárátál* on the upper course of the river, but it is less likely to have been the name of a town than that of a camping-ground. Both the river and the modern camping-ground, or village, are marked on the accompanying map. There are, however, other insignificant spots called *Káratál*.

[3] The Turki translator here interpolates the following explanation: The Khan in Andiján had taken counsel with the Amirs; and Suyunjuk Khan, hearing of this, had desisted from his intended march against Andiján.

of Kásim Khán's advance [on Táshkand] was brought to them. Before Kásim Khán's arrival, however, the Khán went and plundered Áhangarán, one of the most important towns in Táshkand, and I accompanied him on this foray. When, at early morn, we came upon the people of Áhangarán, they retired with their wives and children and effects into a wood, and there took up a strong position. On one side of the wood was a large river, and on the other a deep ravine, which could only be approached by one road. They would not allow the pillagers to approach, and when the Khán heard of this he put me under the care of Khwája Ali, saying: "Hold the bridle of Mirzá Haidar's horse, lest he get into some dangerous place." For I was still too young to distinguish good from evil or to keep myself out of danger. [Having entrusted me to Khwája Ali, the Khán placed himself at the head of his men and advanced on the enemy.] When he drew near them, he saw that their foot bowmen had made ambushes in every corner, and were ready to shoot. They had stretched their bows, washed their hearts of life—made straight, crooked, and the left, right. As our men advanced, the Khán stimulated and encouraged the champions of his right and the warriors of his left, warning them not to ride impetuously, but to make a charge in one body. The heroes drew their horses up in line ready to charge, and so busy were they getting into order, that they did not notice the Khán, who had made a charge all alone. It had been the Khán's intention to conceal his design from them by his words. Thus he threw himself upon the enemy before any of the others. Three men who were lying in ambush let fly their arrows simultaneously at him; but by the mediation of the Almighty, they all three missed the mark. Then the Khán made his bright sword to flash upon one of those three men who, bleeding, and in fear for his life, fell at the feet of the Khán's horse. The Khán turned against another of them; but the first had just put out his head from behind the horse, when Abdul Váhid, who was the Rustem of the Khán's warriors, having followed close behind [his master] came up and struck a blow with his sword at the wounded man's head, which sent it flying a bow's length off, while the Khán fell upon the second. Then commenced a conflict, in which all the enemy were annihilated, and where the Khán exceeded all the other warriors in valour.[1]

On his return, in safety, from this expedition, laden with booty, the Khán learnt that Kásim Khán had attacked Suyunjuk Khán in Táshkand. Whereupon he immediately set out for that town, but on reaching the pass of Kandarlik, which is situated between the provinces of Farghána and Táshkand, news came of Kásim

[1] This sentence is an abridgment of four lines full of high-flown phrases.—R.

Khán's retreat. Returning, [the Khán] proceeded to Akhsi, and having put the various forts of the province of Farghána into a state of defence, he turned towards the Kazák, his object being to make them attack Táshkand a second time. I did not accompany that expedition; being indisposed, I stayed behind.

The Khán advanced [in the direction of the Kazák] till he came to a well-known town in Moghulistán called Jud.[1] At that date Kásim Khán was nearer seventy than sixty years of age; while the Khán, being still under thirty, was in the full vigour of youth. Kásim Khán begged, on the plea of old age, to be excused from coming out [in *istikbál*] to receive the Khán. He commanded all his Sultáns to go and kneel before the Khán, and receive him. Some of these Sultáns were fifty and sixty years old; such as Jánish Khán, Sabásh Khán, Mumásh Khán, Ján Haidar Sultán, Kárish Khán, and others to the number of thirty or forty—all Sultáns of the race of Juji. When Sabásh Khán[2] and Jánish Khán (who were very old)[3] bowed, the Khán rose up, but when the others bowed he remained seated. Then Kásim Khán advanced with a courtesy which the Khán, to the end of his life, never forgot. Whenever he was spoken of, the Khán used to say that Kásim Khán was a most upright and worthy man, and would then relate the circumstances of their friendship.

On meeting, Kásim Khán approached and said: "We are men of the desert, and here there is nothing in the way of riches or formalities. Our most costly possessions are our horses, our favourite food their flesh, our most enjoyable drink their milk and the products of it. In our country are no gardens or buildings. Our chief recreation is inspecting our herds. Therefore let us go and amuse ourselves with looking at the droves of horses, and thus spend a short time together." When they came to where these were, he examined them all, and said: "I have two horses which are worth the whole herd." These two were then brought forward; (and the Khán used to say that never in his life had he seen such beautiful animals as these two). Then Kásim Khán resumed: "We men of the desert depend for our lives upon our horses; and [personally] I put my trust in no others than these two. [I could not bear to part with either of them.] But you are my esteemed guest, so I beg you to accept whichever of them appears to you the better, and to leave the other for me." Having examined the points of each, the Khán chose one which was called Ughlán Turuk; and truly such another horse was never seen. Kásim Khán then selected several others from his droves, and gave them to the Khán. He next offered the Khán a

[1] For the author's remarks on this place, see pp. 364–5.
[2] This name reads *Shásh Khan* in some texts.—R.
[3] The Turki text says: Much older than the Khan.—R.

cup of the spirit *kimiz*, saying: "This is one of our forms of hospitality, and I shall esteem it a great favour if you will drink it." Now the Khán, a short time before this, had renounced all intoxicating liquors; so he excused himself, saying: "I have foresworn such things as this: how can I break my vow?" To which Kásim Khán replied: "I have already told you that our favourite beverage is mare's milk and its products, and of these this [*kimiz*] is the pleasantest. If you do not accept what I now offer you, I am totally at a loss to know what to give you in its place, in performance of the duties of hospitality. Years must elapse before such an honourable guest as yourself again enters the house of your humble host; and now I am incapable of entertaining you. How can I make reparation for this?" So saying he hung down his head with shame, and marks of sorrow appeared upon his face. Thereupon, for his host's sake, the Khán drank the spirit to the dregs, to the great joy of Kásim Khán. Festivities [*suhbat*] then began, and during twenty days they continued to indulge together in quaffing cups of the spirit *kimiz*. The summer was just drawing to a close, and the Kazák set out, by Kázim Khán's orders, for winter quarters. Kásim Khán said: "To go and attack the Shaibáni, at this time, would involve great difficulties. Men of the desert do not think of winter at this season [without orders]. It is impossible. An expedition is not to be thought of at this time." He then dismissed his army;[1] and with the utmost courtesy and regard, he bade the Khán farewell. He himself returned to his capital, while the Khán, much pleased with Kásim Khán, returned to Andiján. It was then autumn [*tirmáh*]. A learned man, to commemorate these events, discovered the chronogram: *Ashti-i-Kazák*, or "Peace with the Kazák" [919 A.H.]

CHAPTER XXXV.

ACCOUNT OF THE MIRACLES OF MAULÁNÁ MUHAMMAD KÁZI.

At the time of Sháh Ismail's victory over Sháhi Beg Khán, and the arrival of the Emperor in Samarkand, to lend his aid to the former, Hazrat Mauláná had left Samarkand and come to Andiján, as has been mentioned above. At the period of which I am now speaking, Hazrat Mauláná was living in the province of Farghána,

[1] The Turki text says, literally: He excused his army from going against Tashkand. From the words, "The summer was then drawing. . . ." onwards to this point, the passage is obscure and involved, in all the texts.

and all the Amirs, of every degree, used to wait upon him, and profit by the blessing of his converse. I also took upon myself the duty of waiting on him frequently, and he continued to shower upon me the same kindly favours as he had done when I was a child in Uratippa (at the time of the calamities in Bokhárá); and by the blessing of which favours, I was rescued from that terrible abyss, all of which has been already explained.

Hazrat Mauláná performed miracles and wonders. Among others was the following: One of my father's retainers, Sayyidim Kukildásh, who was a disciple of Hazrat Mauláná, was one day waiting on the latter. Hazrat Mauláná, seeing that he looked sad, questioned him [as to the cause]. Sayyidim Kukildásh replied: "A certain person" (meaning me) "has come from Hisár in the hopes of obtaining the Khán's daughter in marriage, and being thus raised to the dignity of Kurkáni.[1] All the Amirs are

[1] The title here spelt *Kurkán*, is also written in a number of other ways by the Musulman authors. The difference, as it appears in translation, is in some cases only due to confusion of the *K* with the *G* in the original text, for Persian and Turki writers make no difference between these two letters. Thus the first syllable may be read *Kur* or *Gur* indifferently, and in many instances the second syllable may also be read *kán* or *gán*, according to choice. But it frequently happens that an author has written the second syllable *khán*, and in this way has implied a totally different meaning for the word. Kurkán, Gurkán, Gurgan, or Kurgan, would mean nothing in Persian or Turki, but in Mongol (transliterated *Khurghen* in Kowalowski's dictionary) it means "son-in-law," and the title is known to have been a Mongol one by origin. The matter has been much discussed, but with no very definite result; though Dr. Erdmann has come to the conclusion that there were two separate titles, and that when the word is met with under different spellings, in the best of the Persian and Turki histories, it is accounted for by the author having used two separate words, with a distinct purpose. Thus he maintains that *Kurkan* or *Gurgan*, etc., stands for 'son-in-law,' or for a prince who is allied by marriage with some "mighty monarch." In this way—its Mongol sense—it is used, he tells us, by Rashid-ud-Din, "who knows well how to draw the distinction." He also tells us that *Kurkán* or *Gurgán* represents the Chinese expression *Fu-ma*, and that the Amir Timur was called *Timur Fu-ma* by the Chinese, because he married the daughter of Chun-ti, the ninth and last emperor of the Mongol dynasty. *Fu-ma*, in fact, means 'son-in-law' in Chinese, when applied to princes, and thus is a translation of the Mongol word; but Dr. Erdmann does not mention his authority for the statement that Timur married a Chinese princess. In all probability he has found it in some of the Musulman authors, for it is a statement that several of them appear to have made, though there is good reason to believe that they were mistaken. Dr. Bretschneider says that the Ming annals use for Amir Timur the title *Fuma Tie-mu-rh*, and he goes on to remark: "Fu-ma is a Chinese term meaning 'son-in-law of the Chinese Emperor.' But the Chinese chronicler does not mean to say that the great Timur had married a daughter of the Emperor of China. Fu-ma here is a translation of the Mongol title *Gurkan* or *Kurgan*, which was bestowed only on the princes allied by marriage with the house of Chingiz Khan. In modern Mongol *Khurghen* means son-in-law." He then shows that, as a matter of fact, Timur never married a Chinese princess, notwithstanding the assertions of several writers to the contrary. "I have not been able to find," he continues, "either in the *Yuan Shi* or the *Ming Shi*, where lists of the imperial princesses, under each reign, and their respective husbands are given, any corroboration of this suggestion. The Zafar-namah, also, which notices nine wives of Timur, knows nothing about a Chinese princess among them." Timur's favourite wife was (according to the *Zafar-Náma*) one Sarai Mulk Khánim, daughter of Kázán Sultan, Khan of Turkistan and Mavara-

now opposed to this match, and it is difficult to carry through anything that the Khán's Amirs have set their faces against. This is the reason of my sorrow and dejection." Hazrat Mauláná then said: "I feel convinced that God has fore-ordained this union; therefore the efforts of the Amirs can avail nothing. This marriage will certainly take place." When Sayyidim returned, he repeated to me the words of Hazrat Mauláná, and announced the good news. It was at this time that the Khán was away among the Kazák, but a few days later he returned, and raised me to that dignity which Hazrat Mauláná had foretold. Thus, in Rajab of the year 919 I was elevated to the rank of Kurkán.

un-Nahr, who was a descendant of Chingiz. She was married to Timur in 1369, and became the mother of Shah Rukh. The next year he married another Moghul princess, named Tukal Khánim, who was a daughter of Khizir Khwája, Khan of Moghulistan, and was also a descendant of the house of Chingiz.

But the personages in Asiatic history, to whom a title in the form *Gurkhán* is most generally applied, are the kings of the Kara-Khitai or Si-liao; and more especially to that one of the line (named Ye-liu Taishi) who made himself notorious in the early part of the twelfth century. In this instance, Rashid-ud-Din, Abul Gházi, Juvaini, Mirza Haidar, and Ahmad Rázi, all agree in writing *Gur-Khán*, and three of them explain the meaning of the word to be "great" or "universal, king"—a translation which one of them (Abul Gházi, p. 50) derive from the Kara-Khitai language. There is this that is noticeable, however, in Abul Gházi: throughout his book, to whomsoever the title is applied, he (or his translator, Desmaisons) spells *Gur-Khan;* while Rashid-ud-Din (according to Erdmann) makes a distinction. Mirza Haidar also distinguishes between the two forms. He uses the word *Kurkán* as a title applied to several characters in his history, but in the passage under note here, he records that he himself, by marrying the daughter of Sultan Said, Khan of Kashghar, was raised to the dignity of a *Kurkán;* while only a few pages later (p. 287) he writes of the chief of the Kara-Khitai by the title of *Gur-Khán* or *Kur-Khán.*

It would appear, therefore, that there were two titles in use: but if this was the case, how is it that we find Shah Rukh, the son of Timur, styling himself on his coins *Gurkhan*, while those of his own son and successor, Ulugh Beg, are struck with the form *Kurkán* (S. L. Poole, as below)? These two princes were both descendants of Timur, who used *Kurkán*, and who could not possibly trace any line of descent from the *Gurkhans* of the Kara-Khitai. At first sight, this seems to be an objection to the opinion that there were two quite separate titles; but the evidence is so complete on the other side, that I do not think the coins of Shah Rukh need have much weight. In all probability the legend on them is a mere misrendering of the style *Kurkán* on the part of the designer, who was very possibly ignorant of the word *Kurkán* and its derivation, though well used to the employment of the title of *Khán* in one form or another.

If this be admitted, perhaps the most likely explanation of the matter is: that originally *Kurkán* was a Mongol title used only for sons-in-law of the Khákán (first of Mongolia, and afterwards of China), while in later times, it was assumed by all, or at any rate by many, (1) who married daughters of other reigning princes; or (2) by those who married descendants of Chingiz Khan, though not actually his daughters; or (3) that when its true signification was once forgotten, it became a mere honorific, and was perhaps made hereditary. My impression is that, as in the case of Mirza Haidar, No. 1 of the above propositions is sufficient to account for the manner in which the title was used by Timur and his descendants, and by most others who assumed it. Indeed, if applied in that way, it would suit nearly every Khan or Amir in Central Asia, for most of them must have been able to take to wife the daughter of one ruler or another, and most likely did so.

Thus Dr. Erdmann's opinion that there were two separate titles, appears to be established, although the facts he brings in support of it may not be correct. One of these titles was of Mongol origin, and meant "son-in-law"; the other,

CHAPTER XXXVI.

SOME FURTHER DETAILS IN THE SAME CONNECTION.

At the beginning of this book, in enumerating the offspring of Sultán Ahmad Khán, it was mentioned that the Khán had four daughters. The third daughter, Muhibb Sultán Khánim, on the death of [her first husband] was married to his brother, Sultán Mahmud Khán, who was martyred at Akhsi by order of Sháhi Beg Khán. Muhibb Sultán Khánim then remained with Kutuk Khánim, daughter of Sultán Mahmud Khán, and who, after the devastation of Táshkand, was given to Jáni Beg Sultán, as has been mentioned. After my uncle had risen up against Jáni Beg Sultán, and driven him out of the province of Farghána, Muhibb Sultán Khánim separated from Kutuk Khánim, who was her cousin. On the Khán's return to Andiján, she rejoined him. Of all his four sisters, the Khán loved her the best, so that when she came to him, he showed her the greatest regard and affection. The occasion of my marriage was celebrated by magnificent banquets and entertainments, which were remembered long after.

That winter the Khán took up his winter-quarters at Pishkharán, a township of Akhsi. In the middle of the same season, Mir Ghuri Barlás, Governor of Akhsi, died a natural death, whereupon the Khán moved from Pishkharán to Akhsi, where he remained the rest of the winter. Early in the spring, Mir Ayub and the Moghuls who had been in Hisár, having been defeated by Ubaid Ullah Khán, as above related, came [to Farghána].[1] The Khán gave Akhsi to Mir Ayub Begjik.

Meanwhile, news was brought that the Uzbeg were approaching. The reason for their coming was that, the year before, Kásim Khán had advanced [and had again retired], but during the whole of

---

probably of Kara-Khitaian, or perhaps Manchu origin, meant "Great Khan." Both seem to have become familiar to Western writers about the same time—the twelfth century—and they, knowing nothing of the languages in which the words originated, began, in the course of time, when writing their histories, to confuse the two.

In spelling the words, I have adopted throughout the form *Kurkán* for the Mongol title, as being the most exact and simple transliteration of it, as it is found in the *Tarikh-i-Rashidi* as well as in other texts; while the Kara-Khitai title I have written with a *G*—*Gur Khán*—in order to distinguish it as much as possible from the other. (See Erdmann, *Temudschin der Unerschütterliche*, p. 580; Bretschneider, ii., pp. 256-8; S. L. Poole, *Cat. Orient. Coins in Brit. Mus.*, VII., p. xxx.; Abul Gházi, p. 50; *Haft Iklim* in Quatremère's *Not. et Extraits*, XIV., p. 478). Klaproth, Berezin, Amyot, and many other Orientalists have discussed this subject, but there appears to be no necessity to lengthen this note by citing their views.

[1] Or perhaps to Akhsi.

the spring, the Uzbeg were afraid [that he might advance again]. When winter set in, they were fearful lest Sháh Ismail should come and avenge Mir Najm, [taking advantage of] the low state of the Amu. For these reasons they had, for a whole year, desisted from attacking the Shaibáni.[1] When Sháh Ismail returned to Irák, and Kásim Khán, likewise, went back to his original residence, and Bábar Pádisháh fled to Kábul, there was nothing left for the Shaibán Uzbeg to attend to, but an expedition against the Khán and Andiján. So that spring they set out in full force against Andiján. On hearing of this, the Khán left the province of Farghána [and went to Káshghar], as will be told.

CHAPTER XXXVII.

SHORT ACCOUNT OF SHÁH ISMAIL'S END.

FROM the time when Sháh Ismail came from Irák and killed Sháhi Beg Khán in Merv, he inspired great dread among the Sultáns on all sides. Thanks to this dread, and with a little assistance from Sháh Ismail, the Emperor was able to meet and defeat Hamza Sultán. After this, his fame spread in every direction, and following up his success, he subdued Bokhárá and Samarkand [without difficulty], as has been related. When the Emperor a second time quitted Samarkand and retired to Hisár, [he asked Sháh Ismail for help]. Sháh Ismail, thereupon, sent him 60,000 men under the command of Mir Najm. They were, however, defeated at Ghajdaván, all [the Emperor's] arms and military accoutrements being lost [while Mir Najm perished]. On this account, [the Uzbeg] feared lest Sháh Ismail should march into Mávará-un-Nahr to avenge Mir Najm. They had been expecting this event the whole year, and made no expeditions in any direction.

At that period Sháh Ismail returned to Irák, where he was attacked by the Sultán of Rum, Sultán Salim, with an army of several hundred thousand men. Sháh Ismail met him with a force of 30,000, and a bloody battle was fought, from which he escaped with only six men, all the rest of his army having been annihilated by the Rumi. Sultán Salim made no further aggressions after this, but returned to Rum, while Sháh Ismail, broken and [with his forces] dispersed, remained in Irák. A short time after this event, he went to join his colleagues Nimrud and Pharaoh, and was suc-

[1] The Turki translator uses the word *Uzbeg* here instead of *Shaibáni;* but the meaning is the *Shaibán-Uzbegs.*

ceeded by his son Sháh Tahmásp. This Sháh, likewise, was on several occasions exposed to the kicks of the Rumi army; moreover, from fear of the Rumi he was not able to maintain his accursed religion, nor uphold the evil practices of his father. He continues to sit on the throne of Irák down to the present day.

CHAPTER XXXVIII.

ACCOUNT OF THE SHAIBÁNI WHO HAVE REIGNED IN SUCCESSION IN MÁVARÁ-UN-NAHR, DOWN TO THE PRESENT DAY.

THE Uzbeg Shaibán, in the beginning of the winter of the year 918, had killed Mir Najm and defeated the Turkománs and the Emperor. In the spring of the same year they desisted from further aggressions on any side, being apprehensive both of Sháh Ismail's vengeance and Kásim Khán's invasion [*istilá*], as has been explained. But in the winter of 919 [1513], Sháh Ismail returned to Irák to oppose Sultán Salim the Rumi, while Kásim Khán in order to look to his own kingdom, went to Ubaira-Subaira.[1] The minds of the Shaibán being now set at rest with regard to these two formidable enemies, Ubaid Ullah Khán, near the end of the winter, set out for Hisár, delivered it from the tyranny of the Moghuls, and made an end of them, as mentioned before. In the spring of 920, the Shaibán marched against Andiján. On careful consideration, the Khán realised that in disputing over Andiján with the Uzbeg, there could result nothing but the dimness of trouble and ruin upon the mirror of his fortune. For those who had power to withstand them, had moved out of the Shaibán territory, and he who had offered them the stoutest resistance, namely Bábar Pádisháh, having placed the foot of despair in the stirrup of despondence, had gone back to Kábul. He thought the wisest plan for him was to retire from the country, before the enemy arrived. So the Khán set out for Káshghar, by way of Moghulistán. [Thus] the province of Farghána was joined on to Mávará-un-Nahr [under the domination of the Uzbeg].

The dignity of Khán was,[2] according to the old custom, vested

[1] This name is transliterated as written, and thoroughly pointed, in the Turki text. It is usually found in the form *Ibir-Sibir*, but other variants, such as *Abar*, *Sebur*, etc., are found among Musulman writings, while the Chinese, in the Yuan dynasty, used *I-bi-rh Shi-bi-rh*. The double name was the ordinary term for Siberia, but there was also a Tatar town of *Sibir*, in the sixteenth century, situated on the river Irtish, sixteen versts above Tobolsk. This place (as Bretschneider informs us) was the capital of the Tatar Khan, Kuchum, and was taken in 1581 by the Russians under Yermak. (See *Med. Res.*, ii., 37 and 154.)

[2] That is, after the death of Sháhi Beg Khan; see note, p. 206. The best

in the eldest Sultán, who was Kuchum Sultán, and the heir-apparent [*Kaalfa*] was Suyunjuk Sultán, who however died before Kuchum Sultán, when Jáni Beg Sultán became the heir-apparent. He followed Suyunjuk Sultán, and Kuchum soon after journeyed along the same road. The Khánship now devolved upon Abu Said, son of Kuchum Khán, and on his leaving the throne of the Khánate vacant, Ubaid Ullah Khán sat in his place. From the year 911 down to the end of the reign of the last-mentioned Khán [Abu Said], he had, in reality, conducted the entire affairs of the State; and if he had chosen to assume the title of Khán, no one could rightfully have opposed him. Nevertheless [the Uzbeg] adhered to the old rule and conferred the Khánship upon the most advanced in years. After Abu Said, there remained no one older than [Ubaid Ullah] himself, and he therefore ascended the throne of the Kháns, and continued to perfume the world with the sweet breezes of justice and the scent of right-dealing, until the year 946,[1] when he bade this transitory earth adieu, and his pure soul passed to the regions of the blessed.

I have neither seen nor heard speak of such an excellent ruler as he, during the past hundred years. In the first place, he was a true Musulmán, religiously inclined, pious and abstinent; he also regulated all the affairs of religion, of the state, of the army, and of his subjects, in conformity with the ordinances of the Holy Law; never deviating from it one hair's-breadth. He was pre-eminent for his valour and for his generosity. He wrote seven different styles of handwriting, but best of all he wrote the *Naskhi*. He made several copies of the Korán and sent them to the two holy cities [Mekka and Medina]. He also wrote *Naskh Táalik* well. He possessed the *diváns* of the various Turki, Arabic and Persian poets. He was versed in the science of music, and several of his compositions are still sung by musicians. In short, he was a king endowed with every excellence, and during his lifetime, his capital Bokhárá, became such a centre of the arts and sciences, that one was reminded of Herat in the days of Mirzá Sultán Husain. Although both the Emperor and the Khán died before Ubaid Ullah Khán, and the account of the end of his days should have been given after their deaths had been recorded, yet since the stories of the Emperor and the Khán occupy much space, and since Ubaid Ullah Khán has no further connection with my story, I have summarily completed my account of him here. I shall have no further occasion to refer to the Uzbeg in this history.

---

account of the events briefly touched upon in this section, will be found in chap. ix. of vol. ii. of Sir H. Howorth's *Hist. of the Mongols*, where all available sources of information have been laid under contribution.

[1] The year 946 began 19th May, 1539. See also Howorth, ii., p. 723, for Ubaid Ullah's death.

CHAPTER XXXIX.

REASONS FOR SULTÁN SAID KHÁN QUITTING FARGHÁNA AND REPAIRING TO KÁSHGHAR.

In the summer of the year 920, the Uzbeg Shaibán who were in Táshkand, advanced under the command of Suyunjuk Khán, against Andiján. When the Khán learnt this, he convened a meeting of all his Amirs and councillors, and they discussed what were the wisest steps to take in the matter. They tried to foresee the final issues of things, and were plunged in the ocean of meditation. [At last] my uncle said: "The neighbouring Sultáns are not inclined to sacrifice their reputation, and have gone to look after their own affairs. Our numbers are not sufficient to compete with the Shaibáni, nor are our armaments equal to theirs. If we offer their legions fight, however zealous and loyal we may be, we shall only be as men with broken weapons, and a defeat will not mean the destruction of one particular person, but will result in constant disputes and continual fighting. If, by some strange chance, matters should turn out otherwise, they will have to make reparation for what has gone before, and all their power will be destroyed. Such an advantage we should turn to account. We shall be able to make no reparation for what has passed. Nor will any amount of binding make that breakage whole.[1]

"The province of Farghána is the territory and ancient dwelling-place of the Chaghatái. The Shaibáni have deprived them of it by force and violence. We have become the guardians of the Chaghatái country. Now that all the Sultáns, in general, and the Chaghatái Sultáns in particular, have given up the contest, it would be absurd for us to engage in this dangerous affair on their account. If you wish to be on the safe side and consider the wisest plan, then block up the path of war and follow the road of flight, before the borders of this kingdom have been darkened by the dust of the enemy's army. Let our reins be drawn towards Moghulistán, which is the old home of the Moghuls; this will tend to the consolidation of the State. And yet another fact must be taken into consideration: namely, that Mirzá Abá Bakr, in the face of [the Khán's] victorious host, is like a wounded quarry, for has he not once before fought a pitched battle, at Tutluk, and been defeated? If we enter his province, and if he keeps a brave heart, he will probably again offer battle, and fighting with him will be an easy matter in comparison with fighting the Uzbeg. In fact,

[1] Down to this point, nearly the whole of this speech is obscure in meaning and the translation doubtful.

there will be little to fear and much to gain. Another point that ought to count in favour of this plan is that the Mirzá is over sixty years of age, and he has reigned close on fifty years. The Almighty has, during forty years, suffered him to exercise tyranny. The time has probably now come for his day of oppression to be changed to the night of annihilation. Moreover, he has cast aside all his own Amirs, and has neglected the leaders of his army, setting up in their places a number of mean people of low birth, who, by reason of their lack of judgment and small intelligence, stand in great fear of him. Therefore, we ought to direct all our energies, devote all our strength, to the conquest of Káshghar. Haply the opener of all gates will open to us the gate of victory. Finally, Mirzá Abá Bakr's men, who were my companions in the service of my brother, when they see me in your train, will probably return to me. And they will be a substantial assistance to us in conquering Káshghar.

"Although Mirzá Abá Bakr is my own brother, (Verse) . . . . my loyalty and devotion are to the Khán alone: and any head that will not bow to him, verily will I bring it down, though it be that of my own brother. In my devotion to the Khán, no such consideration as a tie of brotherhood shall stand in the way. In the Mirzá's downfall, I now recognise the establishment of the Khán's prosperity. If my plan is approved, let it be at once proceeded with."

When my uncle had finished his speech, the Khán, who had been listening with evident satisfaction, began to praise and commend him, saying: "My thoughts have for a long time been occupied with such considerations; but in our discussions, all the suggestions made have been either impossible or inexpedient. I find your plan most reasonable, and preferable to any other. My opinion is the opinion of Sayyid Muhammad Mirzá. If any one has anything further to say on the matter, let him speak." All the Amirs were unanimous in their agreement, and began to approve my uncle's suggestion.

Being all of one mind, the Khán, in the month of Rabi-ul-avval, of the aforesaid year,[1] left Farghána before Suyunjuk Khán had entered it, and marched towards Káshghar by way of Moghulistán. At this time Mirzá Abá Bakr executed a very surprising work, the truth of which is attested by all who were in Káshghar at the time, and I myself have seen and measured the building . . . .[2] Now, he had destroyed the ancient citadel of Káshghar a long time before, as well as its suburbs, and had carried the inhabitants off to Yarkand, while he had turned several inhabited places into cultivated fields. When he heard of the Khán's approach, he

[1] Rabi I., 920, or May, 1514.
[2] Here six lines have been much condensed, and a repetition omitted.

commanded a fort to be built on the banks of the River Tuman. I have taken the dimensions of that fort several times. It may include about fifty *jarib*, more or less, and its height in some places is twenty *matá gaz*.[1] The circumference of the towers at each angle is more than thirty *gaz*. On the ramparts, in most places, four horsemen can ride abreast. This huge fort was constructed in seven days, which is, of course, a most extraordinary feat, and confirms what has been said above, of Mirzá Abá Bakr's power and activity. It is now necessary to give some account of Káshghar.

CHAPTER XL.

DESCRIPTION OF KÁSHGHAR.

KÁSHGHAR is an old and famous town.[2] In former times the Sultáns of Káshghar were of the family of Afrásiáb the Turk, whom the Moghuls call Bughá Khán. His genealogy is as follows: Afrásiáb, son of Pish, son of Dád Nashin, son of Tur, son of Afaridun. It is thus given in the *Tárikh-i-Guzida*, which has copied from the *Mujma-ut-Tavárikh*[3] of Khwája Rashid-ud-Din Fasl Ullah. In some other histories the descent is traced yet further. But God alone knows the truth.

Among the Sultáns of Káshghar was a certain Sátuk Bughrá Khán, who was converted to Islám in his early years. During his occupation of the throne, he brought over the whole country of Káshghar to the true faith. After his death, several of his descendants ruled in Káshghar, and even in Mávará-un-Nahr, until the conquest of Chingiz Khán.

[1] The ordinary *gaz*, as we have seen (notes, pp. 58 and 256), probably measured about 26 to 28 inches. The *matá gaz*, or *gaz* for measuring goods or effects, may have differed slightly from other *gaz* in use, but probably one will suit as well as another for Mirza Haidar's loose statements. The *jarib* is a land measure, generally said to be equal to 60 square ells, or *zar*; but the value of the *zar* is very uncertain. At the present day, in Persia, it is equal to about 40 inches. Col. Jarrett shows that it is taken to mean the same as the *Tanáb* of Persia, and the *Bigah* of India, but that its value differs greatly according to locality and different historical periods. In Akbar's time it was fixed at 3600 *Iláhi gaz*; while the standard *Bigah* in the north-west provinces of Bengal, contains nowadays 3025 square yards, or $\frac{5}{8}$ of an acre. (*Ain-i-Akbari*, ii., p. 61.)

[2] The word used here is *shahr*, or town. In the following paragraph the author speaks of the "country of Káshghar," and it may be remarked that he employs the name Káshghar indiscriminately for the town, for the province, and for the whole of Eastern Turkistan as far east as Chálish, or Karashahr. In most instances his meaning is obvious, but in many others it is not so clear, and in these I have usually added either a word in parenthesis, or a brief note by way of elucidation.

[3] Usually called the *Jami-ut-Tavárikh*.

[Tái Yáng Khán fled from Chingiz Khán. Kushluk, son of Tái Yáng Khán] took Káshghar from the vassals of the Gur Khán of Kara Khitái, who had himself taken it from the vassals of the descendants of Afrásiáb. At that time Sultán Osmán, of that family, was ruling in Samarkand and in the greater part of Mávará-un-Nahr. What passed between him and Khwárizm Sháh is to be found in every history.[1]

The rebellion of Kushluk and the conquest of Káshghar by the Moghuls, I have copied from the *Jahán-Kushái*, as it stands [there].

[1] Taken separately, Mirza Haidar's facts are, in the main, correct, but his account is confusing. He derived his knowledge from books, and has stated it imperfectly. The "family of Afrasiáb the Turk" may, perhaps, be more properly called the dynasty of the *Ilak Khans*, who were, according to the best authorities, Uighurs. Some writers prefer to call them the *Kárákháni*, after the title said to have been adopted by the first Musulman chief among them. Afrasiáb himself (otherwise Bughá, or Buku, Khan) was probably a mythical personage, but the Uighur dynasty that bears his name was, no doubt, an ancient one, of purely Turki origin. It only takes a place as a practical factor in history, however, with the reign of Sátuk Bughra Khán, who was the first to become a Musulman. Sátuk Bughra is said to have ruled over all Turkistan (Eastern and Western) as far east as the borders of China, while shortly before his death, about the end of the tenth century, he is reported to have captured Bokhara. His capital was Kashghar, then called Urdukand; but not long after his death, his descendants would seem to have moved the seat of government to Balasághun. His immediate successor appears to have taken the title of *Ilak Khan*, or "Great King" or "Sovereign," which seems to have been perpetuated in that of the dynasty, though it is often wrongly written *Il-Khan*. This Ilak Khan (perhaps Nasr by name) conquered Mávará-un-Nahr about 1008, drove out the Samáni rulers, and established his authority over the country. The date of his death does not appear to be recorded, but he is said, in some accounts, to have been succeeded by his brother Toghan Khan, who is known to have been reigning at Balasághun in 1018. He, again, was succeeded by Arslan Khan I.; then followed Kadir Khan, then Arslan II., and then a second Bughra, who was in power in the year 1070; but there may have been others between those named here. Whether the second Bughra was immediately succeeded by one Mahmud Khan is not clear, but we learn, at any rate, that a Khan of that name was ruler of the Uighur-Ilak kingdom about the year 1124, when the Gur Khán of the Karakhitai invaded Eastern Turkistan and conquered it, together with Balasághun, and perhaps also Western Turkistan. At about this date, the Uighur kingdom is represented as coming to an end. But the Karakhitai do not appear to have disturbed Mávará-un-Nahr, which, as a part of the Uighur dominion, was administered by vassals or tributary Sultans. These Sultans continued to govern till 1213, when the last of them, named Usmán, was killed by Muhammad Khwárizm Shah, who took possession of the country, and held it until he was himself ousted, shortly afterwards, by Chingiz Khan, with the Uighurs as his allies.

Thus, dating only from Sátuk Bughra Khan, this Musulman Uighur dynasty flourished in Turkistan for nearly a century and a half, and in Mávará-un-Nahr for over two centuries; but their history, as we have it, is somewhat uncertain if not contradictory.

As regards the habitat of this nation, the author of the *Tabákát-i-Násiri* says that the Afrasiábi Turks under the Ilak Khans, or Afrasiábi Maliks, occupied the tracts about Káyálik and Balasághun until dispossessed by the Karakhitai.

Dr. Bretschneider may be consulted for a brief account of the Ilak Khans, which he appears to have derived from the *Kámil-ut-Tavárikh* of Ibn-ul-Athir (1160–1233 A.D.). Dr. Bellew has published a full summary of the earlier history of the same dynasty, extracted from the *Tazkira-i-Sultan Sátuk Bughra*, a work, however, which he evidently mistrusts. Mr. S. Lane Poole gives a brief sketch of their history, and a list, as far as it can be authenticated, of the Khans; and

CHAPTER XLI.

EXTRACT FROM THE JAHÁN-KUSHÁI.

WHEN Chingiz Khán carried his victorious arms into the countries of the East, Kushluk, son of Tái Yáng Khán, fled by way of Bish Báligh, to the country of the Gur Khán. He wandered about among the hills, in great want, while those tribes who had accompanied him became scattered. Some people say that he was captured by a body of the Gur Khán's soldiers, who led him before their chief; another story is that he went and presented himself of his own accord. He at any rate remained some little time at the court of the Gur Khán. Sultán Muhammad Khwárizm Sháh rose in revolt against the Gur Khán, while other Amirs in the eastern quarter, rebelled also, and put themselves under the protection of the Emperor of the world, Chingiz Khán, by whose favour they obtained immunity from the evil acts of the Gur Khán. Kushluk then said to the Gur Khán: "My tribes are very numerous, and are scattered over all the territory of Imal, Kiyák,[1] and Bish Báligh, where they meet with opposition from every one. If you will allow me, I will cause them to assemble and with their assistance [I will bring the rebels again under your authority]. Thus will I help the Gur Khán; and I will not in any way

---

lastly, Major Raverty, in his translation of the *Tabákát-i-Násiri*, furnishes a long list of Ilak Khans, together with much comment, but he does not mention his authorities. All these lists differ as to names and dates.

The word *Ilk* or *Ilak*, Dr. Terrien de Lacouperie informs us, meant *Sovereign*. It was a title first used by a Prince of the Tuküeh, and was revived by the Uighur Khans of Turkistan, who used it from the middle of the tenth century till the year 1213. Subsequently, it was revived a second time by the Mongols in Persia; Hulaku having changed his own title of *Khan*, which he had held during the reign of Mangu Kaán, for *Ilak Khan*, under the reign of Kublai Kaán. The form *Il-Khan*, often said to mean "Khan of the Ilyát"—the *Ils* or *tribes*—is therefore erroneous. (See Bretschneider, *Med. Res.*, i., pp. 252–3; Bellew, *Yar. Rept.*, pp. 121–30; S. L. Poole, *Muham. Dyn.*, pp. 132 and 134–5; Raverty, pp. 900–10; Lacouperie, *Babylonian and Orient. Record*, Dec., 1888, p. 13.)

[1] In the Persian texts this name may be read *Kabák*, *Katák*, or *Kiyák*, but the Turki reads consistently Kiyák, so I have adopted that form. If it is correct, I think there is no doubt that the *Kayálik* of some ancient writers, and the *Cailac* of Rubruk, is the place intended. It was situated, according to the most trustworthy critics, to the south-west of the Imil river, and near the modern Kopál, and in this position would accord well with what is known of the localities of Kushluk's tribes—the Naimáns, or properly the Naimán-Uighurs; *i.e.*, the *Eight-Uighurs*. (See Yule, *Cathay*, p. 576; F. M. Schmidt in *Zeitschrift der Gesellt. für Erdkunde*, Berlin, 1888, xx., Bd., Heft 3, pp. 201–5; Bretschneider, i., p. 230. Also Schuyler, i., p. 405; Valikhanoff in *Russians in C. Asia*, pp. 62 and 527; and D'Ohsson, ii., p. 516, who quotes Vásáf to the effect that in 1301 Kayálik was on the frontier, between the territories of Kaidu and the Khákán, though there is nothing to indicate where this frontier actually was.)

deviate from his commands." With such flattery and deceit did he throw the Gur Khán into the well of pride. Then having loaded him with gifts, he begged that the title of "Kushluk Khán" might be bestowed on him. The Gur Khán accepted the gifts and gave him the title he desired, whereupon, quick as an arrow shot from a bow, Kushluk left the territory of the Gur Khán and came to the country of Imal and Kiyák. When the report of the invasion of Kushluk got abroad, Tuktái, who was one of the Makrit Amirs, had fled and joined Kushluk. This was before the rumours of the conquests of the Emperor of the world, Chingiz Khán, had been spread abroad. And wherever they went, they were joined by bands of men, with whom they conducted forays—plundering and burning as they came and went.

When they heard of the successes of Muhammad Khwárizm Sháh, they sent numerous ambassadors to persuade him to attack the Gur Khán from the west. Kushluk, at the same time, was to attack him from the east, so as to bring him out of the centre [of his dominions]. [The conditions were that] if Sultán Muhammad Khwárizm Sháh should be the first to gain a victory, Almáligh, Khotan and Káshghar, which were in Kushluk's kingdom, should be ceded to him; but if, on the other hand, Kushluk should have the first success, Kará Khitái as far as Finákand should be delivered over to him. These conditions having been agreed upon, a treaty was concluded between them. (Finákand means Shahrukhia.)[1] Thus the two armies set out for Kará Khitái from opposite directions. Kushluk arrived before Sultán Muhammad Khwárizm Sháh [and defeated the Gur Khán], since the army of this Sultán was more distant. Then, having plundered his treasury, which was at Uzkand, he proceeded to Balásákun, where the Gur Khán himself was, and a pitched battle was fought at Jinuj,[2] in which Kushluk was, however, defeated, and most of his men being worn out [*kufta*]

[1] The texts throughout this extract from the *Jahán Kushai* are corrupt and obscure. In this instance the name is spelled in one text *Shahr-Khiah*, in another *Shahr-Kah*, and so on. I have no doubt, however, that *Shahrukhia* is meant; for *Shahrukhia*, as we learn from the *Zafar-Náma*, was founded by Timur, on the ruins of the ancient *Finakand*, towards the end of the fourteenth century. The author of the *Jahán Kushai*, however, died in 687 A.H., or about a hundred years before any such place as *Shahrukhia* had come into existence! The inference, therefore, is that the sentence, "*Finakand* means *Shahrukhia*," is an interpolation, either by Mirza Haidar, or by a copyist, while the bad spelling of the latter name is due to the interpolator. See Pétis, *Timur Bec*, iv., p. 207. Also Baber, p. 1.

It may be added here that the forms *Finakand*, *Finakat*, and *Binakat*, denote, without doubt, one and the same place, as Sadik Ispáhani (p. 78) expressly notes that *Binakat* was also called *Shahrukhia*.

[2] By variations in pointing, the name here written *Jinuj* may become *Jinbuj* or *Chinbuj*; it may therefore be taken to stand for the *Chinbudje* of D'Ohsson (i., p. 168), where this episode is alluded to. It was the name of a river in Turkistan, according to Bretschneider (i., p. 231), but if near Balásághun, it must have been in the extreme north-eastern quarter of that territory—near the upper left tributaries of the Chu; for it was among these streams that Balásághun (or perhaps better Balásákun) was most probably situated.

he retired and set about reorganising his army. He heard that the Gur Khán had returned from his war with Sultán Muhammad Khwárizm Sháh, and had been ill-treating the people of the province; also that the army had returned to its own country. Then, like lightning from a cloud, he rushed out to meet him, and having seized his followers, brought his kingdom and his army under his own power; he then demanded one of his daughters in marriage. Now the tribe of Náimán were mostly Christians [*Tarsá*],[1] and when he took that daughter in marriage, he made her abandon Christianity and become an idol worshipper.

After Kushluk had firmly established himself on the throne of

[1] The word *Tarsa* is rendered *Christian* here, as its most probable signification when applied to the Naimáns. It was a term, however, that was used for Buddhists, for Zoroastrians, and for idolaters. Perhaps also, among Musulmans, it may have meant any non-Musulman religion. There is much evidence to show that Nestorian Christianity was prevalent among the Naimáns in the twelfth and thirteenth centuries, as well as among other Uighurs, though it cannot perhaps be said for certain, as Juvaini is made to do in the translation at this place, that they were "mostly Christians." It is possible that his meaning may have been that they were mostly Buddhists; he, at any rate, cannot have applied the word to idolaters, as the succeeding sentence proves—the woman was made to abandon the religion called *Tarsa* and become an idolater. Thus, so much stands out clearly in this passage—that Fire-worship not being in question with the Naimáns, *Tarsa* cannot stand for any religion except Christianity or Buddhism. But Buddhism and idolatry are frequently regarded as one and the same by Musulmans, and called by the same name, so that if it could be regarded as probable that Juvaini took this view, there would remain no other translation for *Tarsa* than *Christian*. On all considerations, therefore, it is probable that the words *Christian* and *Christianity* render the author's meaning in these passages, and hence they become an important contribution to the evidence (1) that the Naimáns were, indeed, "mostly Christians," and (2) to the fact that the term *Tarsa* was used for *Christianity*.

Dr. Bretschneider remarks that the Archimandrate Palladius (in a Russian publication) states that "*Tie Sie* is the Chinese transcription of the word *Tarsa*, used by the Persians since the time of the Sassanides to designate the Christians, and sometimes also the Fire-worshippers and Magi. The name of *Tarse* is applied expressly to the kingdom of the *Yogurs* (Uighurs) by Haithon, the Armenian, in his account of the kingdoms of Asia (beginning of the fourteenth century). John of Montecorvino, in a letter written at Peking about the same time, speaks of *Tarsic* characters, meaning evidently Uighur letters." Thus the name was applied also to the Uighurs as a nation, but probably only on account of their Christianity or Buddhism—for both religions were prevalent among them.

D'Ohsson states that in the *Jahán Kushai*, Juvaini explains that the Christians (thirteenth century) were called by the Mongols *Arcaoun* [Arghun], while Buddhist monks were known as *Touines*. He also says that Rubruk speaks of the Buddhists generally as *Touiniens*, and adds that Touin is in reality the Mongol name for Buddhist ecclesiastics. He quotes, moreover, the Armenian writer Orpelian, to the effect that the Christians were known as *Arkhaioun* [Arghun]. These designations point to a well-understood difference between Christianity and Buddhism among the Mongols, but this may not have been the case among Musulmans. The term Arghun is now used in Ladak to mean a "half-breed," and it was so used also in the time of Polo in North-Western China. The real meaning of the word, in Turki, is "fair" (complexioned), and is said to have been current in Mongol as well as Turki, in the Middle Ages; but it was by no means always applied to Christians. A full discussion of the term Arghun will be found in Yule's *Marco Polo*, i., pp. 279 *seqq.* (See also D'Ohsson, ii., p. 264; Rémusat's *Nouv. Mélanges*, ii., p. 198.)

As regards the country known as *Tarse* or *Tarsia*, the reduced facsimile of the Catalan map in Yule's *Cathay* shows, in large letters, a kingdom called *Tarsia*,

Kará Khitái, he fought several battles with him [the Gur Khán ?] at Jám Bálígh,[1] and finally he surprised the Gur Khán on his hunting grounds, when having captured him, he put him to death.

The chief men of Káshghar and Khotan had also become hostile. The Gur Khán had imprisoned the son of the Khán of Káshghar. [Kushluk] now set him at liberty and sent him back to Káshghar. But the Amirs declined him, and before he had placed his foot within the city, they put him to death between the gates. At the time when the corn was ripe, Kushluk sent his army to eat or burn it. When the inhabitants had been deprived of three or four quarters of their income [*dakhl*] and corn, a famine broke out. The people of Káshghar suffered great distress, and had therefore to submit. After that, Kushluk marched away with his army. And his soldiers used to lodge in the houses of the people of Káshghar and mix with their families, so that [the Káshghari] had no homes left. [His troops] practised every form of violence and wickedness. They did everything to encourage idolatry, and no one was able to prevent them. They next went to Khotan, which they captured, and compelled all the inhabitants of the surrounding districts to abandon the religion of Muhammad, giving them the choice of becoming either Christians or idolaters. [Arabic quotation from Korán . . . .] Verily God is forgiving and merciful. Having adopted the garments of sin, the cry of the Muazzin and the confession of the Unity of the God of Believers was no longer heard. The mosques were closed and the schools abandoned. One day they conducted the Imáms of Khotan out into the plains and began to argue with them. Among their number was Imám Alá-ud-Din of Khotan. He was asked questions and gave answers, and at length they hanged him up over the door of a college. Of this matter I shall speak presently. After this, the faith of Islám having lost all its splendour, the darkness of evil spread over all the servants of God, and they raised their supplications to heaven. [Five couplets in Arabic . . . .] The arrow of their entreaties reached the target, and God heard and answered them.

When Kushluk was setting out to attack the kingdoms of

---

but the distorted geography of the times, renders any location of the region on a modern map impossible. Haithon of Gorigos, the historian (Mr. Warren tells us in his notes to *Mandeville's Travels*) expressly says that the kingdom of *Tarse* was the land of the Uighurs, and that it adjoined Tangut on the west. It can, however, hardly be said to be so placed on the Catalan map. (See *Mandeville*, p. 211, and note, p. 125.)

[1] This place stood on the north of the Tian Shan mountains, between Bishbalik (the modern Urumtsi) and the Manás river. It is frequently mentioned in this position, under the names of *Chang-ba-la* and *Jang-ba-li*, by the Chinese travellers of the thirteenth century, whose narratives have been so ably translated and elucidated by Dr. Bretschneider. It is also mentioned by King Haithon of Little Armenia in the account of his homeward journey from Mongolia. (See Bretschneider, i., pp. 67, 160, etc.; ii., p. 32.)

Chingiz Khán, the latter sent a body of Nuin[1] to check Kushluk's evil progress. He [Kushluk] was, at that time, in Káshghar. The chief men of Káshghar related that when [the Nuin] arrived, and before they had drawn up in line, Kushluk turned his back and fled, while the regiments that arrived one after the other, of the Moghuls [*az Moghulán*], demanded nothing of them but news of Kushluk. They sanctioned the "call to prayer" [*Takbir*] and the prayers [*Uzán*]; and they issued a proclamation in the town, that every one might practise his own religion. The advent of those people was held to be an act of mercy and bounty from the Almighty. When Kushluk fled, every one who lived in a Musulmán town or house, suddenly disappeared, like quicksilver; and the Moghul army went in pursuit of Kushluk. Wherever he halted, they came up behind him and drove him on, like a mad dog, until they reached the frontier of Badakhshán, which is called Darázukhán.

When he arrived at Sarigh Chupán, he missed the road, and entered a valley that had no egress. There happened to be a party of Badakhsháni hunters in those hills, and when they saw [the fugitive party] they went towards them, while the Moghuls advanced from the other side. The valley being rough, the Moghuls found walking difficult, and came to an agreement with the hunters, saying: "This band, namely Kushluk and his followers, have escaped from us; if you will capture them and give them over to us, we will do them no harm." So they went and surrounded [Kushluk] and his party, and having bound him, delivered him up to the Moghuls, who cut off his head and carried it away with them. The Badakhsháni, having found endless booty and precious stones, returned.

How clear it is that no one can ever be victorious who opposes the religion of Ahmad and the Holy Law of Muhammad; while he who promotes it becomes more successful day by day!

[1] This sentence, again, is without doubt a corruption. All the texts have "*jam' i Nuin*," and no other reading seems possible. *Nuin* would represent the well-known Mongol rank or title, *Noyan* (meaning general, or commander of 10,000); but there could not have been a body or assembly of Noyans, as the word *jam'* implies. The sentence should read, probably, that a force under one *Chabah*, or *Jabah*, *Noyan*, was sent, etc. The episode is to be found described in most of the Musulman histories, and is always given in this way: thus the *Haft Iklim* (Quatremère, *Not. et Extr.*, xiv., p. 478) says that Chingiz "envoya *Djebeh Noian*." Abul Ghazi (p. 102) has *Tchepe-Noian*. The Habib-us-Sayar (in Price's *Muhd. History*, vol. ii., p. 496) has *Hubbah Noyan*, though Price adds in a note, that the word is pointed *Jabbah*; while D'Ohsson, citing, apparently, *Rashid-ud-Din*, says that "20,000 hommes sous les ordres de *Noyan Tchebé*" were sent. This *Noyan Chabah* was a famous general of Chingiz Khan's, and his name frequently occurs in connection with the Mongol conquests. Dr. Bellew (*Yarkand Report*, p. 179) gives the meaning of *Noyan* as "a Kalmak noble." Sir H. Howorth says that among the Mongols and Kalmaks it means "a prince or any member of the Royal family;" also that, according to Quatremère, it is the title of a leader of a *tomán*, or division of 10,000 men (iii., p. 152).

CHAPTER XLII.

THE MARTYRDOM OF IMÁM ALÁ-UD-DIN MUHAMMAD OF KHOTAN, AT THE HANDS OF KUSHLUK.

WHEN Kushluk conquered Káshghar and Khotan, he changed from the religion of Jesus to the practice of idolatry, and the rest of the people he caused to abandon Hanifism and become fire worshippers. He changed the lights of the true path into the darkness of unbelief, and the service of the all merciful into the serfdom of Satan. . . .[1]

Thus far, I have copied from the *Tárikh-i-Jahán-Kushái.*

After Chingiz Khán had subjugated the whole of Káshghar, he went and set his mind at rest with regard to the affairs of Irán and Turán—nay, rather of the whole world.[2] He then returned to his capital and divided all his kingdoms among his four sons. We learn from the *Mujma-ut-Tavárikh* of Rashidi and from the *Guzida* (the former entering into detail, the latter giving it in brief), that the whole of the Dasht-i-Khizr and [Dasht-i]-Kipchák, whose boundaries are Rum, the ocean [*Muhit*] Mávará-un-Nahr, and Moghulistán, was given to his eldest son, Juji Khán. Moghulistán, Kará Khitái,[3] Turkistán and Mávará-un-Nahr to Chaghatái Khán. To Tuli he gave the whole of Khitái, while his original seat of

[1] About one folio and a half of text is omitted here, as it has no bearing on the history. It consists chiefly of Arabic phrases, etc., and is, like the rest of the extract from the *Jahán Kushai*, very corrupt and, in places, unintelligible.

It may be mentioned here that in the British Museum there is only one copy of the *Tarikh-i-Jahán-Kushai*, and that one, Mr. Ross informs me, is so corrupt that he is unable to make much use of it. It might perhaps have been advantageous, had a good copy been obtainable, to translate Mirza Haidar's extract direct from the original, as was done with the *Zafar-Náma* in Part I.; but Mr. Ross found this impossible. On the other hand, a new translation of this section of the *Jahán-Kushai* is not of great importance, seeing that the subject matter has appeared already in many other works—European as well as Asiatic—and has been well elucidated by able Orientalists. In fact, on the particular subject of the transactions of the Kara Khitai and the Naiman, etc., it is constantly used as an authority, although no translation of the whole work, into any European language, has yet been made. The author, Ala-ud-Din Ata-ul-Mulk, known as Juvaini, was born in Khorasan in 624 or 625 A.H., and died 681. He went on a mission to the Court of Mangu Khakan at Karakorum about 647 (or 1249 A.D.), and thus had, himself, travelled through the countries on which he wrote. He is probably, therefore, a good authority on all matters relating to the tribes, the geography, etc., of these regions in the twelfth and thirteenth centuries. For a full account of his life and book, see *Fundgruben des Orients* (Mines de l'Orient), i., pp. 220–234.

[2] Meaning that he conquered Iran and Turan, and the whole world.

[3] While at p. 152, the author makes Moghulistan coincide with Kara Khitai, he here distinguishes between them. The matter, however, has been explained in the Introduction; the mention, here, of two countries, may be regarded merely as one of the ordinary inconsistencies or loose expressions, in which the book abounds.

government, that is to say Karákorám and the Kálmák [country] he entrusted to Uktái. In the same manner he distributed his army and his Amirs; and in that division, the Dughlát fell to the lot of Chaghatái, who entrusted to them ***Mangalái Suyah***, which means "facing the sun" [*Aftáb rui*].[1] This country is bounded by Shásh, Chálish, Issigh Kul and Sárigh Uighur; and on the confines of these four limiting provinces are situated Káshghar and Khotan. The particular Dughlát who was established in this kingdom, was Amir Bábdághán,[2] in whose family it remained, from father to son, until the time of Mirzá Abá Bakr. The ***Jám-i-Giti Numái***[3] says that Káshghar is the most important town of the Turks, and goes on to describe several objects in it, of which now no trace remains. Among other things it says is, that people used to carry clothing of ermine [*Kakum*] and squirrel [*Sinjáb*] from Káshghar to all parts. But nowadays there are no such [animals] to be found there.

Káshghar is bounded on the north by the mountains of Moghulistán, which stretch from west to the east, and from them rivers flow towards the south. Those hills extend from Shásh, on one side, to beyond Turfán [on the other], their extremities reaching into the land of the Kálmák, which quarter none but the Kálmák themselves have seen, or know anything about. I have questioned some of those who have seen something of that country, but I can recall nothing of what they told me, which would be worthy of mention in this book. Moghulistán will [afterwards] be described shortly. From Shásh to Turfán is three months' journey. On the west side of Káshghar is another long mountain range, of which the mountains of Moghulistán are an off-shoot [*munshaib*]. This range runs from north to south. I travelled on those mountains for six months without coming to their extremity. They also shall be presently described, in the account of Tibet. From these mountains, rivers run from west to east, and to these rivers Káshghar owes its fertility [*ábádáni*]. The whole of the countries of Khotan, Yárkand and Káshghar lie at the base of these mountains.

[1] For some remarks on Mangalai Suyah, see note, p. 7.

[2] The Turki MS. reads *Bábdághán*, as did also one of the Persian texts originally, but some native reader has altered the name into *Amir Bábdá Kurkán*, in both places where it occurs. That this is a Musulman conceit, is obvious. The mention, however, of the name of a Dughlát Amir before the time of Bulaji is interesting, and is the only one I have met with in the *Tarikh-i-Rashidi*, or elsewhere, except that of Urtubu, who is spoken of by Mirza Haidar in the first chapter of Part I. as grandfather of Bulaji. He has, as he says, avoided all mention of infidels, and the Dughláts previous to Bulaji had not yet become Musulmans. Dr. Bellew makes the name of *Bábdághán* into *Amir Báyzid*, and has also misread his author, so far as to make him state that this Amir "resided in the Sarigh-Uighur region." Mirza Haidar's statement, however, refers to "Mangalai Suyah," and not to the Sárigh-Uighur country. (See *Yarkand Rep.*, p. 166.)

[3] The *Jám-i-Giti Numai* is by one Mir Giyáth-ud-Din Mansur. The British Museum does not possess a copy, but in the Catalogue of Persian MSS. in the Bodleian Library at Oxford, the work is mentioned.

To the east and south of Káshghar and Khotan are deserts, which consist of nothing but heaps of shifting sands, impenetrable jungles, waste lands and salt-deserts. In ancient times there were large towns in these [wastes], and the names of two of them have been preserved, namely Lob and Katak; but of the rest no name or trace remains: all are buried under the sand. Hunters, who go there after wild camels, relate that sometimes the foundations of cities are visible, and that they have recognised noble buildings such as castles, minarets, mosques and colleges, but that when they returned a short time afterwards, no trace of these was to be found; for the sand had again overwhelmed them. On such a scale were these cities of which, nowadays, neither name nor vestige remains! In a word, the habitable districts of Káshghar and Khotan lie along the western skirts of these mountains. On the frontier of Káshghar is the district of Artuj;[1] from there to the confines of Khotan, at Kariyá and Jariyá,[2] is one month's journey. But as for the breadth of fertility of the cultivated region (from the foot of the western range to the eastward) by travelling quickly one can leave all cultivation behind in a day or two. On the banks of every stream that comes down from that range, corn is sown and the land is cultivated.

The first of these is the River Timan,[3] which comes from a mountain standing between Káshghar and Farghána. This river flows between the ancient citadel of Káshghar, which Mirzá Abá Bakr destroyed, and the new one which he built, on the banks of this river, as has been related. Part of Káshghar is fertilised by this same river. The second river is the Kará Tázghun. In the dialect of Káshghar, Tázghun means a river.[4] It flows about three *farsákhs* to the south of the above mentioned fort. The greater part of the province of Káshghar is watered by it. At a distance of three *farsákhs* from it, is a third river called Kusán Tázghun, on the banks of which is the town of Yángi-Hisár, and its dependent districts. The town is supplied with water by this river. The distance from Káshghar to Yángi-Hisár is six statute [*shari*] *farsákhs*. At about six *farsákhs* from Yángi-Hisár is an insignifi-

[1] This place is often mentioned in the *Tarikh-i-Rashidi*. It is, nowadays, a favourite summer resort of the townspeople of Kashghar. According to the late Mr. R. B. Shaw the proper spelling is *Artush*. (*J. R. G. S.*, 1876, p. 282.)

[2] Usually *Kiria* and *Chiria*, or *Chira*. Both exist to the present day, the former as a town of some size.

[3] Nowadays called *Tumán* or *Tuman*. Mr. Shaw, in speaking of the situation of the present Kashghar—*i.e.*, the Kohna Shahr or old city—the Musulman and not the Chinese city—says the *Tuman*, or *Ara Tuman* (meaning Middle Tuman) washes the eastern side of the town. A short distance below, it joins the river Kizil; thus Kashghar is situated on the tongue of land between these two rivers. (*Loc. cit.*, p. 282–3.)

[4] Mr. Shaw says the real meaning of *Tázghun* is "a flood"; while the river in question—the *Kara Tázghun*—is also known as the *Yupurghi*. (*Ib.*, p. 283.)

cant hamlet called Kará Chanák,[1] in front of which flows another stream called Shahnáz, which waters several [other] places. The valley of the Shahnáz lies in the western range, and the [high] road from Káshghar to Badakhshán runs through this valley. On the road from Kará Chanák to Kilpin Rabát, is a resting place [*manzil*] for those coming and going [on the road]; the distance between Kilpin Rabát and Kará Chanák is five statute *farsákhs*. Further on is another halting place—a monastery [*langar*]—which is called Kush Gumbaz, an excellent stage [*manzil*] watered by the Shahnáz. It has both cultivated grounds and gardens [*bághát*] which all form a part of the foundation [*vakf*] of this "langar." Travellers enjoy the advantages which the "langar" offers. The next stage is a village called Kizil. The water there is brackish, and nobody stops there who is not obliged to. It is considered the halfway stage between Yángi-Hisár and Yárkand. It is about ten *farsákhs* from Kizil to Kuk Rabát, and from Kuk Rabát to the edge of the district of Yárkand, which is called Rabátchi, is by measurement seven statute *farsákhs*.[2] Between Rabátchi and Kará Chanák there is but little inhabited country, except for the stages that have been mentioned.

Yárkand was formerly a very important city. The old town was dug out by Mirzá Abá Bakr; it was among the excavations [*kázikha*] which we have spoken about, and much treasure was found [in it]. It is not known whether the old town was called Yárkand, or whether it had another name. In the days of my ancestors, Yárkand was a companion city to Yángi-Hisár. Mirzá Abá Bakr made Yárkand his capital. He introduced streams [into the town] and laid out gardens; and it is generally reported that these numbered 12,000, most of which were in the city and its environs. But I cannot imagine that this figure is correct. Mirzá Abá Bakr built a citadel which, in most places, is thirty statute *gaz* in height. The inside of the citadel is roughly about a hundred *chub*, and in it has been built a very high fort [*ark*]. The citadel has six gateways, which are devised for great strength. The gates themselves are placed about a hundred *gaz* within [the walls] and on either side are two towers near together, so that should any one wish to enter either of the gates, he must [first] pass between

[1] Or *Kara Khanák*. But in either form the name, according to Mr. Shaw, is nowadays unknown; it is called now *Suget Bulák*. (*Ib.*, p. 284.)

[2] Except the first two marches from Kashghar all the distances given by the author are greatly exaggerated.

For a complete analysis of Mirza Haidar's description of this road, and of his geography of all the regions bordering on Eastern Turkistan, see Mr. Shaw's paper in the *Journal of the R. G. S.* for 1876, entitled *A Prince of Kashghar on the Geography of Eastern Turkistan*. When in Yarkand and Kashghar in 1874–75, Mr. Shaw had with him, if I remember rightly, a copy of the *Tarikh-i Rashidi*, and was thus able to criticise it on the spot, with the help of native informants.

these two towers. If an enemy attack the interior, he is assailed with arrows and stones from front and rear, as well as from right and left. This system is to be met with in very few forts. In the fort [*ark*] of this citadel, magnificent buildings have been constructed; but to describe them would be tedious. In the suburbs are about ten gardens, in which are erected lofty edifices, containing about a hundred rooms each. All these rooms are fitted with shelves and recesses in the wall [*ták* and *tákcha bandi*], they have ceilings of plasterwork, and dados of glazed tiles [*káshi*] and frescoes. Along the public roads are avenues of white poplar [*safidár*], so that one may walk for a statutory [*farsákh*] and a half on every side of the city, under the shade of these trees. Streams run by most of the avenues.

The water of Yárkand is the best in the world. Every praise which doctors have bestowed upon any water is true of this.[1] It comes down from the mountains of Tibet (a month's journey distant), which are covered with snow and ice; it flows swiftly over a stony and sandy soil from south to north, and when it reaches Sárigh-Kul, which forms the extremity of the hilly country of Káshghar, it rushes on, with like rapidity, from rock to rock, leaping and tossing, for seven days [journey] in an easterly direction, until it arrives at the level ground. Here it continues its rapid course over a stony bed for two days more, and when it reaches the bed [*majari*] of the river of Yárkand, in which there are few stones, the current in some degree abates its speed. A curious fact concerning this stream is, that in the early part of the spring it becomes so small that one might almost cross it, in some places, by stepping from stone to stone. In the season of Leo, [*Asad*] it swells so much that it becomes, in places, nearly a statutory mile [*mil*] [2] in breadth, [while its depth is then nowhere less than four *gaz*], and for a distance of one *karuh* [3] it is no less than ten *gaz* in

[1] The Turki MS. interpolates here:—"The waters of Yarkand and Khotan owe their excellence to the fact that jade and gold are found in them; and they are found in no other rivers. The people of Yarkand praise the water of the Kara Tázghun very highly, and indeed it is an excellent beverage."

As a fact, the water of the city of Yarkand and its neighbouring districts should be classed among the most impure and insanitary that can be imagined. Even the natives are, nowadays, in the habit of attributing—and perhaps rightly—some of the worst diseases they suffer from, to the impurity of the drinking water. In the towns it is of course worse than in country places.

[2] All the rivers and streams of these regions are at their lowest in early spring, and rise in summer. It is strange that the author should regard so common a circumstance as "curious." What, however, is somewhat curious is that he should use the term *mil* as a measurement, for it is a word he has not previously employed. He probably derived it from some of the authors he had read, for it was often used by the Arab writers to denote a measure of one thousand paces. Whether Mirza Haidar really intends this measurement is doubtful.

[3] *Karuh* or *Kuroh*—the Kro or Kos of India—usually taken to measure about 1½ statute mile. See note, p. 424.

depth. Jade [*Yashb*][1] is found in this stream. Most of the country and districts of Yárkand are irrigated by it. At a distance of about seven *farsákhs*, flows another stream called Tiz-Ab,[2] which waters the rest of the country. For about three days' journey, at a medium pace, from Yárkand [in the direction of Khotan] are well populated towns and villages; the farthest of these is called Láhuk.[3] From this place to Khotan is ten days' slow marching, during which time, excepting at the halting places, one meets with no habitations [*ábádáni*].

In Khotan there are two rivers, called Kará Kásh and Urung Kásh,[4] in both of which jade is met with, and it is found nowhere else in the world. The waters of these two rivers are preferred [by some] to that of Yárkand, but personally, I could never find the superiority in them. Khotan is amongst the most famous towns in the world, but at the present time its jade is the only thing that remains worth writing about. One curious circumstance concerning Khotan, is that magpies[5] are never seen there; or if, at any time, one happens to appear, it is taken as a bad omen, and the people band together and drive it away.

The Imám Alá-ud-Din Muhammad of Khotan is mentioned in all histories, but no one in Khotan knows which is his tomb, nor even recalls his name. There are many other tombs there, about which nothing is known. According to tradition (the truth of which is contradicted by books on history) there lie buried there, among others, many martyrs, such as Imám Zabiha [or Zabija], Jafar Tayyár, and Imám Jafar Sádik, and several others of the Companions [of the Prophet]. But the falsehood of these traditions is evident. It is possible that some of the followers of these companions [*tabi'in*] bearing their names, came here and suffered martyrdom, for before the conversion of Káshghar to Islám, some of the followers of the companions came to Káshghar and conducted a holy war [*ghazát*] there [and at Khotan]. But the strange thing there is that the martyrs, whom they have deposited in the tombs, are sometimes exposed to view, from the sand being blown away by the wind, and no change is noticeable in them; they are recognisable, and their wounds—nay more, the very blood which has issued from the wounds, all dried up, is still visible.

[1] *Sang-i-Yashb* (or *Yashm*) is rendered in the Turki by *Kásh tásh*, in Shaw's Vocabulary, where there is also an interesting note on the subject.

[2] Now called the *Tiznáf*.

[3] The *Luk Langar* of modern maps, and the *Lakhouf* of the *Haft Iklim*. (See Quatremère, *Not. et Extr.*, xiv., p. 476.)

[4] The *Yurung Kásh* of ordinary maps, and according to modern pronunciation. On and near its upper waters, jade is still quarried. The late Mr. W. H. Johnson, who was at Karánghu-tágh on the Upper Yurung in 1865, wrote: "It is noted for the *Yashm* which is met with in the stream." (See *J. R. G. S.*, 1867, p. 7.)

[5] In the Persian *'Aka*, and in the Turki *Saghizghán*.—R.

Every one who makes the circuit [*tawáf*][1] of these graves, witnesses these things.

The tombs of Yárkand, however, belong to no one who is mentioned in histories or other books. But the people of Yárkand believe that there lie [buried there] the Seven Muhammadáns. Their story, as related by the *mujávir*,[2] is not worth recording here, but Mauláná Khwája Ahmad, who was a disciple of Házrat Ishán, and a good and industrious old man (of whom, God willing, I shall speak in the First Part), has told me that the Seven Muhammadáns were grandees [*utád*]; but I do not remember having read of them in any history. Another tomb is that of Davá Khán Pádisháh; but concerning him I could learn nothing from the *mujávir*. Suddenly Házrat Shaháb-ud-Din Khwája Khávand Mahmud passed in front of the tomb, and turning to me said: "This man possesses a wonderfully strong power of attraction [*jazaba*], and I never pass by here without being strongly drawn towards [his tomb]." The edifice is a lofty one and is covered outside with plaster, upon which are paintings and inscriptions. In spite of having examined them carefully, my efforts did not enable me to read them, for most of them were in Kufic character, but not in the Kufic which is employed nowadays. A few are in *Suls*[3] writing, but it is not inscribed in such a manner as to be easily read. Near this, is a dome, upon the archway of which is some Turki writing which is mostly destroyed. It is there written: "In the year 656 . . . . ," but the rest is obliterated and cannot be read. This date corresponds very nearly with the date of Davá Khán, better known as Davá Sahan,[4] and I am convinced that this is his tomb. I hold the proof to be conclusive for several reasons. Firstly, at that date there was no other Davá Khán reigning; and this name of Davá Khán does not indicate, in the least, that he was a Shaikh or an Imám; nor does the fact of such a magnificent tomb having been raised over him. Again the father of Davá Khán, Barák Khán, became a Musulmán in Bokhárá, received the title of Ghayyás-ud-Din, and was succeeded on the throne by his son Davá Khán.[5] From this it is quite evident that Davá Khán was a

[1] A ceremony which consists of walking round the Kaaba at Mecca, or other tombs and sacred edifices.—R.

[2] Properly the mosque sweepers, but here the guardians of the tombs.—R.

[3] *Suls* is a sort of large *Naskhi* hand.—R.

[4] As far as is known, Davá Khan died in 706 A.H. (or 1306 A.D.); the date on the dome, therefore, is just fifty years too early, and can hardly refer to the Chaghatai Khan of that name. (See S. L. Poole's *Muham. Dynasties*, p. 242; and E. E. Oliver in *J. R. A. S.*, xx., N.S., p. 104.)

The second title, given as *Sahan* in the text, is found in this form in the Turki and in one Persian MS. In another Persian MS. it reads *Chichan*.—R.

[5] Barák Khan was a great-grandson of Chaghatai. He reigned in Bokhara down to about the year 670 H. (1270 A.D.), and was succeeded, not by his son Davá, but by his great-uncle Nikpai, who reigned for two years, and was followed by a nephew called Tuka Timur for a further period of two years. It was only after

Musulmán. He is very much lauded in histories, and it is not surprising that God should have raised him to such high rank, considering his "Islám," and his noble qualities. After his death, any man who believed this to be his tomb, did it reverence, and as time went on [its identity] became an established fact; but God alone knows the truth.

If, as is indeed the case, this is the tomb of the famous Davá Khán, his story is told in histories. In the Prolegomena to the *Zafar-Náma*, Sharaf-ud-Din Ali Yazdi says: "Davá Khán was the son of Barák Khán, son of Kará Isu, son of Bámnagái, son of Chaghatái, son of Chingiz Khán. He was a powerful and worthy monarch. [Couplet. . .] Mamálikiz Nuyán, son of Amir Áihal, son of Nisun, was of the race of Karáchár Nuyán Barlás. According to the ancient charter [*Ahd-Náma*] Davá Khán was made king, and the duties and privileges of his forefathers devolved upon him. He ruled for thirty years, and through the excellent management of Altigiz Nuyán, the Chaghatái *Ulus* attained great prosperity. [Couplet. . . .] Finally having drawn a few breaths he perished." Thus far from the *Zafar-Náma*.

Within the citadel of Yárkand and near to the fort [*ark*] is a tomb called Abjáji Atá, in which is the bone of a man's thigh, in two pieces. I have always noticed this with great wonder. I once pointed it out to Khidmat Mauláná Sháh Sayyid Ashik, one of the most profoundly learned and pious Ulama in Mávará-un-Nahr, who expressed great astonishment, and said: "Let us take the measurement." He ordered to be brought the corresponding thigh-bone of a man of the present time; he broke off clods of earth of the weight of that bone and tied them up in handkerchiefs, till they were exactly the weight of the bone which was in two pieces. He afterwards counted the clods and found there were sixty. Then the Mauláná said: "The owner of this bone must have been sixty times the size of men of our time." This is indeed a most wonderful thing!

As for the tombs of Káshghar, the first is that of Sátuk Bughrá Khán, of the race of Afrásiáb, and ancestor of Yusuf Kadr Khán and Sultán Ilak Mázi. He was the first Turk to become a Musulmán, and he is related to have said: "Sátuk was the first of the Turks to become a Musulmán." [1] I have heard from darvishes that to visit his tomb is a source of great spiritual advantage. There are many other tombs, excellent accounts of which are to be found in books. Among them are those of Husain Fasl Khwája,

---

Tuka Timur that Davá attained the sovereignty—viz, in 1274. (See Chap. II. of Introduction; also S. L. Poole, *Muham. Dynasties*, p. 242; and E. E. Oliver, *J. R. A. S.*, xx., N.S., pp. 123, 127, etc.)

[1] See for some remarks on Sátuk Bughra Khan and his successors note, p. 287. The saying here attributed to Sátuk is in Arabic.

Kutb-i-Alam, Shaikh Habib, Fakih ibn Bakr and others. The strangest is the enclosure [*hazira*] of Husain Fasl Khwája, which they call the "Enclosure of the Muftis," for a hole has been made in his grave opposite to where his face is. No change has taken place: his beard is [still] perfectly straight, and he is recognisable. I have heard the Ulama of Káshghar say that whenever they had a difficult question to decide, they would write a copy of it and place it in the tomb; on the morrow, when they came, they found the answer written down. And this has been tried and tested. (The responsibility be upon their shoulders.)

All the people of Khotan and Káshghar are divided up into four classes. One is called Tumán, which means peasantry: they are dependent upon the Khán, and pay their taxes to him yearly. Another class is called Kuchin, which means soldiery, who are all dependent upon my relations.[1] A third is called Imák [or Aimak], all of whom receive a fixed revenue [*mukátáa*] of grain, cloth and the like. These people are also dependent upon my relations. The fourth class are the controllers of legal jurisdiction, and the custodians of religious houses and pious foundations; most of these are of my family. They need not, however, be specified in this place.

There are in that country one or two things quite peculiar to it. Firstly, the Jade-stone, which is found in the rivers of Yárkand and Khotan, and of which not a trace is to be found in any other part of the world.[2] Secondly, the wild camel, which if taken in such a way that it receives no injury, can be placed in a line [of camels], and will follow exactly like a domestic camel. This animal is found in the deserts to the south and east of Khotan.[3] Thirdly, in the hills of that country are wild oxen

[1] By "relations," it may be inferred that the Dughlát are meant.

[2] This statement is not quite accurate; jade is found also in Burma and Western China.

[3] The wild camel is an interesting subject, but this is scarcely the place to do more than remark that, though its existence has been mentioned by Asiatic authors for many centuries past, no one of them but Mirza Haidar, as far as I am aware, has noticed the possibility of taming it. There is, I believe, a question among naturalists as to whether the animal is really wild, or whether it is not the tame camel run wild, its form and colour having changed somewhat during the centuries it has had to shift for itself. Mirza Haidar's statement, if correct, might have some bearing on this question, though if judged by the case of the wild ass of Central Asia (the *Equus hemionus*) it would not go far. There is no question of the latter animal being otherwise than really wild, yet, if caught young, it can be readily tamed, up to the point of marching in line with tame asses or ponies, though not beyond that point—all attempts to load, saddle, or bridle it (as far as I have seen or heard in Mongolia and Ladak) being unsuccessful. The earliest mention of wild camels that I am acquainted with, is in the narrative of King Haithon of Lesser Armenia, who saw them, or heard of them, to the north of the Tian Shan, about the middle of the thirteenth century; but it is possible that the Arab authors may have mentioned them still earlier. In modern times their existence was first reported by an English explorer in 1873, and he was duly laughed to scorn by the naturalists. A few years afterwards, they were seen in the Lob region by the Russian traveller and naturalist, Prejevalski,

[*kutás*] of extreme size and nobility; they are the most ferocious of savage beasts When one of them attacks a human being, its butting with the horns, its kick, and its lick are all equally fatal. When on my journey from Tibet to Badakhshán (which journey I will speak of presently) we were a party of twenty-one persons, and on the road a *kutás* was killed. It was only with the utmost trouble and difficulty that four men were able to extract the beast's stomach. One man could not lift one of its shoulder blades. After the twenty-one persons had each carried away as much as he was able for food, two-thirds were still left.[1]

---

who obtained, from the native hunters, a skin and skeleton, which he sent to St. Petersburg. Since then they have been found, and shot, by Mr. St. G. Littledale on the skirts of the mountains to the south and east of Lake Lob, and the specimens have been brought to England. The Chinese Buddhist pilgrims of the fifth to seventh centuries do not appear to have mentioned them. It is probable that the wild camel nowhere exists, nowadays, to the north of the Tian Shan.

[1] The Kutás is the *Bos Poëphagus*, the Kháshgau, the Tibetan Yak, or Dong. Nearly everywhere in Central Asia stories are told of the ferocity of the wild yak, and of the dreadful nature, even, of the tame yak. One of the most common is the allegation that its lick is fatal. Its tongue, as a matter of fact, is peculiarly rough, and this circumstance often leads to the fable that it is made of red hot iron. The evidence of modern sportsmen and travellers by no means bears out our author, as to the ferocity of the wild yak. They are frequently shot on the eastern frontiers of Ladak, but I have never heard of an instance of even a wounded yak making a charge. Captain Hamilton Bower, in the narrative of his recent journey across Tibet, especially notices the same thing; he says, "They are extremely easy to stalk, their sight not being nearly as acute as that of most wild animals. Their powers of scent are, however, fairly good . . . I have never known one charge, even when wounded and with his assailant in view." (*Journey Across Tibet*, p. 286.) General Prejevalski also bears witness to the harmless qualities of these animals. In 1873 he wrote: "Their principal characteristics are indolence and stupidity, which render them less formidable than, at first sight, they would appear to be. If the yak were possessed of more intelligence he would be far more dangerous to the sportsman than the tiger, for one can never be sure of killing him with whatever weight of ball." As regards the dimensions of the wild yak, we have good evidence from two careful and accurate observers—General Prejevalski, in Eastern Tibet, and my friend Colonel A. E. Ward, in Western Tibet. The former, after mentioning that he had shot twenty specimens, continues: "The adult male attains to enormous dimensions. The one whose skin now figures in my collection measured 11 feet in length without the tail, which, of itself, was 3 feet: thus the total length was 2 *sazhens* [just 14 feet, English]. the height of the hump was 6 feet [*i.e.*, 18 hands], the circumference of the body in the middle 11 feet, and the weight of the animal from 35 to 40 *pouds* [11¼ to 12¾ cwt.]." Colonel Ward, who has also shot many yak, writes: "I put the measurements of a full-grown animal at 15½ to 16 hands. The bull whose horns I saw in 1869 was measured as 17½ hands, and a writer in the *Asian* [a sporting periodical published in India], in 1884, gives 18 hands as the height of a bull yak. It is not easy to measure a dead animal's height, and I think there was some error in both these. Two measurements, carefully made of big bulls, gave a record of 16 hands, and I do not think that they ever vary as much as 6 and 8 inches, which would be the case if they reach 17½ to 18 hands in height. . . . A solid bullet from a ·500 Express will be found heavy enough for yak." He also mentions that the horns, alluded to as seen in 1869, measured 31 inches in length, while another pair, in 1886, were 31½ inches long. Both these specimens were shot in the eastern part of Ladak. The circumference of the horns at the base has been found to be 15 inches. (See Prejevalski, *P. R. G. S.*, xviii., No. 1, Jan. 1874, p. 81; Ward's *Sportsmen's Guide to Kashmir and Ladak*, 3rd ed., Calcutta, 1887, pp. 76, 77.)

Again, most of the fruits of that country are very plentiful. Among others the pears are especially good, and I never saw their equal anywhere else; they are, in fact, quite incomparable. Its roses and rose-water are also excellent, and almost as good as those of Herat. Moreover, its fruits have an advantage over the fruits of other countries, in that they are less unwholesome. The cold in winter is very severe, and the heat in summer is moderate; but the climate is very healthy. The fruits, which generally are injurious when taken at breakfast or after any food, are there, on account of the excellence of the climate, followed by no evil consequences and do no harm. During the autumn [*tirmáh*] it is not the custom to sell fruit in the provinces of Káshghar and Khotan, nor is it usual to hinder any one from plucking it. Nay more, it is planted along the roadsides, so that any one who wishes to do so, may take of it.

But [Káshghar] has also many defects. For example, although the climate is very healthy, there are continual storms of dust and sand, and violent winds charged with black dust. Although Hindustán is notorious for this phenomenon [*sifat*], yet in Káshghar it is still more prevalent.[1] The cultivation of the ground is very laborious and yields but little profit. In Káshghar it is impossible to support an army upon the produce of the country. Compared with the Dasht-i-Kipchák, the Kálmák country and Moghulistán, it has the semblance of a town, but with regard to productiveness and its capacity to support an army, it cannot be compared to those steppes. The inhabitants of towns who go there regard Káshghar as a wild country [*rustá*], while the people of the steppes consider it a refined city. It is a sort of Purgatory between the Paradise of Towns and the Hell of Deserts. "Ask those from Hell of Purgatory, and they will call it Paradise."[2] In a word, it is free from the discord of men and the trampling of hoofs, and it is a safe retreat for the contented and the rich. Great blessings accrue to the pious, now, from the blessed saints who lived there in time past. From two pious persons, out of many I have seen, I have heard that when people migrate from that country to some other, they cannot find the same peace of mind, and they remember Káshghar [with regret]. This is the highest praise.

[1] The haze peculiar to Eastern Turkistan is described in nearly all modern writings on that country. It is not of the nature of the Indian dust-storm, as the author seems to imply, but is present in the calmest weather, and only disappears for a brief interval after a fall of rain or snow. The sand-storms that occur occasionally are altogether independent of the haze phenomenon. For some particulars regarding both haze and sand-storms, see note, p. 12, and Sec. III. of the Introduction to this volume.

[2] A quotation from Sadi's *Gulistán*.—R.

CHAPTER XLIII.

RETURN TO THE GENERAL NARRATIVE.

I HAD brought the Khán's history down to the point where he, having left the province of Farghána, set out for Káshghar by way of Moghulistán. As soon as Mirzá Abá Bakr heard of this, he built the citadel of Káshghar in seven days, and placed in it one thousand horse and foot, with provisions for several years, giving his own son Yusfán[1] command over them. Then, having settled whatever business he had there as best he could, he started for Yángi-Hisár, which he also supplied with provisions, arms, and siege implements, and finally went on to Yárkand.

In the meanwhile the Khán reached Atu Bum Báshi,[2] which is one of the frontiers of Moghulistán on the side of Káshghar. Leaving his family and baggage there, to follow slowly after, he marched forward with an unencumbered army. On the first night he encamped at a place called Mirzá Turki; on the second day he halted at Tushku, arriving at Artuj on the third day, and there he performed the circuit [*tawáf*] of the shrine of Shaikh Habib, an eminent Shaikh. The miracle is recorded of him that in building the monastery, one of the beams [*chub*] was found too short, and that he pulled it, and extended it [to the required length]. This beam [the Khán] saw, and having repeated verses from the Korán and uttered prayers, he begged that he might profit by the spirit of the Shaikh.

On the following day, when the troops of the east put to rout the army of the west, and in one moment seized the rays of the lights of the world [when the sun rose, etc. . . . Two couplets], they set out from Artuj and came to Uch Barkhán, a village near which the river Yutun Báshi [or Tuyun B.], which flows down from the valley of Kálik Kiyá [or Kabá], must be crossed by travellers. There is some rising ground above it, from the top of which Káshghar, which is exactly three statute [*farsákhs*] distant, is visible. On this eminence Mirzá Abá Bakr constructed a wall with battlements, reaching from the highest point of the hill down

[1] Only one MS. has "son"; the others have "his own *mir*." The name *Yusfán* is probably a corruption, though possibly it may be an abbreviation—after the Andijáni method—of *Yusuf Ján*.

[2] Perhaps the *Gulja Báshi* of modern maps, though the name of *Atu Bum Báshi* would rather point to *At Báshi*—a tributary of the Narin—a place often mentioned in this history. *At Báshi*, however, would be too far off and not quite in the right direction, while *Gulja Báshi* would be about one march above *Mirza Tirak*, as marked on maps, and that place, again, would stand about the same distance from *Tishak Tásh*, for which the *Tushku* of text would seem to be intended.

to the ravine which overhangs the river, and there he placed a gate. Implicit orders were issued that the commanders [*taváji*] should take up their stand in that narrow passage [*tangi*] and count the army. The troops passed through the defile [*tangi*] regiment by regiment, and as they passed, the *taváji* counted them and the scribes [*bakhshi*] wrote down the numbers. Besides those who stayed behind with the women and children and the baggage, and those who were strong enough to guard the roads, there were inscribed four thousand seven hundred and odd.

Though the number is small, it was composed entirely of famous generals [*sarvar*], mighty Amirs, wise councillors and brave warriors, who were ripe in experience and well tried in adversity. From the date of the devastation of Táshkand in 908, corresponding to the year of the Hog [of the Moghul cycle], to the present date 920, corresponding [again] to the year of the Hog—that is for twelve years—they had been persecuted by evil fortune, and had been continually engaged in warfare and contests and disputes. Of the four [great] tribes, three—namely the Uzbeg, the Chaghatái, and the Moghuls—had always been at variance, [Couplet . . .] as has been explained above. During those twelve years, these people had been subject to many vicissitudes and changes of fortune, and had endured innumerable reverses and trials, so that each one of them had gained great experience, and was acquainted with all the details of the art of war, such as marches and countermarches and forced marches. Nor was this knowledge peculiar to the Amirs—nay, rather, in every tribe of the Moghuls many men were to be found in whose judgment and advice every one placed reliance.

The following is a short account of some of those who passed in review that day, as well as I can call them to memory. First of all the family of Dughlát, of whom the leader—the most noble and the eldest—was my uncle, Sayyid Muhammad Mirzá. He was at that time about forty-one years of age. He was the prop and stay and overseer of the whole of that army. His wisdom and foresight were well known, and he was famed for perception and penetration. His story, and all that he did, has been already related. He was conspicuous among his contemporaries, and without an equal among the tribesmen. According to the reckoning then drawn up, he had one hundred and eighty men in his following. Next [in standing] was Kará Kulák Mirzá, who has been mentioned above, in connection with the Khán's adventures in Moghulistán. During those events, this Kará Kulák Mirzá held, at one time, the dignity of Amir, and at another, fell into the most abject poverty, until at last, leaving the Khán, he went to Andiján and there managed to live with the Uzbeg, in some way or another, exchanging the bitterness of poverty for the sweets of commerce. At the time the Khán captured Andiján, he again entered his service. In a word, this Kará Kulák Mirzá was renowned both for his courage and sound judgment, and great reliance was placed in him. In the enumeration [of the army], one hundred followers were entered in his name. [Another was] his brother, Sháh Nazar Mirzá, who had precedence over his elder brother in all matters. His retainers were entered as sixty in number. Another was Mirzá Ali Taghái; the wiles this man could devise after a moment's reflection, could not have been invented by a cunning Delilah after years of deep thought. The hump-backed old woman [who personifies] deception used to come to learn wiles and tricks from him, and to serve him in order to learn how to stir up sedition. This will be explained, in the account of the end of the Khán's days. Ninety men were entered in the list under his name. Another was his brother, Kutluk Mirák Mirzá, of whom everyone expected great achievements. Seventy persons came under his name. Another was Bahrika Mirzá, who was of the military caste [*ahl-i-kushun*], and he had forty followers.

Another was the compiler of these pages and the chronicler of this history, your humble servant. The dawn of childhood had not yet changed to the morning of youth, nor was my intelligence yet fully developed. I was but fifteen years of age. Although the Khán had honoured me with the title of Kurkán, yet on account of my youth, and immaturity, both physical and mental, I was not able to participate fully in that dignity. I however carried out as much as was possible. The retainers and followers of my father, as many as had remained behind, supported and aided me nobly in every way, so that in spite of the general scarcity of attendants upon the Moghuls, one hundred and twenty persons were entered in my name.

There were many nobles [*mirzádas*] of the Dughlát family, who were entered as single individuals, since by reason of their poverty they had no retinue. All those who were Amirs, and had a following and attendants, were mentioned [in the lists].

In this way, I propose to speak of all the families of the Moghul Amirs.

Another family [*tabaka*] was that of the Dukhtui, whose chief was Amir Dáim Ali. At that time his brothers, Ahmad Ali and Mahmud Kuli, had not yet come. This Amir Dáim Ali was one of the least worthy of the great Amirs. He will be frequently mentioned hereafter in this book. There was a serious dispute between him and [the family of] Barlás as to precedence, which was at that time still undecided. But Amir Dáim Ali took precedence whenever he could, till on the first occasion of the meeting with Mansur Khán, which shall be spoken of. The question was referred to Amir Jabár Birdi, who was a Dughlát, and of whom I have spoken above, and he decided that the Dukhtui should have precedence. After that the right of Amir Dáim Ali over the Barlás was established.

I do not recollect precisely, but I think there were more than two hundred persons recorded in the list of this family.

Another family was the Barlás, whose leader was Ali Mirák Mirzá, the maternal uncle of my paternal uncle. He had both sons and brothers. One of his sons, named Muhammad, will be mentioned later.

There were many of the Moghul Amirs and notables who were very aged, older indeed than any one else at that time in the Moghul *Ulus*; upon all matters such as the *Tura* and the *Tuzuk* they were consulted, and reliance was placed in their discretion and judgment in all important consultations and councils. Of these old men was Ali Mirák Mirzá; among others were Káká Beg, Kará Básh Mirzá, Sayyid Ali Ághá, Alláh Kuli Kukildásh, and Abdul Aziz Mirzá. Among this group of aged men too, was Ali Mirák Mirzá himself. Like the rest of the old men, he was much enfeebled by age, both physically and mentally, but his courage was still firm. In spite of his having both brothers and sons, he conducted all his own affairs, civil as well as military. In the list, the number of his retainers is nearly as great as those of Mir Dáim Ali.

Another [of them] was Háji Mirzá, who was renowned for his valour. He had more than one hundred in his train.

Another family was that of Bárki,[1] of whom the first and eldest was Mir Káká. But his extreme old age prevented him from taking part any longer in the hardships of warfare, so he entrusted his affairs to his son Mir Kambar. Many conspicuous and able men of the Bárki family accompanied the Khán from Kunduz to Andiján, and numbers of them fell in the battles that took place in Andiján. When no more of these were left, the management of the affairs [of the family] devolved upon Mir Kambar. His brothers Maksud, Háfiz, and Tuluk, were in immediate attendance upon the Khán. The following of Mir Kambar was larger than that of Háji Mirzá; I cannot, however, recall the exact number.

Another family was that of the Urdubegi; their leader was Kará Básh Mirzá, who has been mentioned in the list of old men. His sons and brothers were men of note, such as Gadái Mirzá, Sabur Mirzá, Muhammad Háji Mirzá, and Muhammad Váli Mirzá.

Another family was that of Itárji. Their chief was Bish Ka Mirzá, who had some capable sons and also some brothers. Their retinue numbered about one hundred men.

[1] *Bárki* or *Yárki*. The Turki text reads *Yárki* persistently.—R.

Another family was that of Kunji, whose chief Amir at that time was Mir Jánáka. Mir Sharun, Kul Nazar Mirzá, Mir Mazid, and Mir Jaka had not yet arrived. His retinue exceeded that of Bish Ka Mirzá in numbers.

Another family was the Jarás, at the head of whom was Munka Beg, a man distinguished among his equals for his bravery. His suite numbered more than one hundred men. He had a brother named Bábá Sárik Mirzá, who was a man of a similar nature to the above-mentioned Kará Kulák Mirzá and Mirzá Ali Tagháí. All that is said of them applies equally to him. His following was not less than that of Munka Beg. He had a brother named Shahbáz Mirzá, who, in the conduct of affairs, was not inferior to his brother.

Another family was the Begjik. The chief among them was Mir Ayub, whose history has been related in connection with Bábar Pádisháh and Ubaid Ullah Khán. He is one of the most distinguished of all the famous Moghul Amirs. During those twelve years of disturbances, wherever he was, he took the lead. Indeed, he was a man admirably qualified in every respect to bear the dignity of Amir. Nearly two hundred men were entered in his name. His brother Muhammad Beg was an extremely calm and polite man, of noble birth and breeding. His mother was a Sayyida of Tirmiz.

[Of the same family] was Sultán Ali Mirzá, whom I have mentioned above, in speaking of the Khán. Also Yádgár Mirzá, who, soon after this event, left the Khán's service, made the Holy Pilgrimage, and then rejoined the Khán, by whom he was highly honoured. After this he again made the Pilgrimage, and he is at the present time a recluse, having dealings with no man and disturbed by none. [Of these too] was Nazar Mirzá. Each of them had a following of one hundred men or less. Another was Mirzá Muhammad, who had exercised the authority of Amir among the Begjik and the Tumán of Mir Ayub, before the arrival of this latter. But when Mir Ayub came, being the elder brother, all the duties of Amir were passed over to him; he [Mirzá Muhammad] submitted to Mir Ayub, and in the administration of business was associated with him. His followers were better equipped than those of Amir Ayub. Another was Beg Muhammad, the same young man whose excellent qualities were alluded to in the account of the Khán's doings in Kábul. Among all the young men he had not his equal in courage. He had one hundred well armed retainers.

There were violent disputes between the families of Jarás and Begjik on the question of priority. On this account, the elder Amirs assembled and held an inquiry. It was at length ascertained that, in the time of each Khán, priority and inferiority had been decided by the favour [*ináyat*] of that Khán. Therefore the Khán now issued the following mandate [*yárligh*]: "I will not at present determine your precedence. You must decide it among yourselves. You must take it by turns, year by year, and whichever family shows the greatest valour, that one will take precedence." They carried out the order, but the dispute exists to the present day, and has found no settlement.

All the above-mentioned men were Amirs and commanders of regiments and detachments. There was another set of men, who, although not Mirs or sons of Amirs, had yet each his own tribe and following. They had been at the head of some of the Moghul tribes during those twelve eventful years, and having directed their affairs, had thereby gained so much experience that every one placed confidence in their advice and opinions. Among them was Khwája Ali Bahádur, of whose valuable services to the Khán in his early days in Moghulistán, I have spoken above. Another was Beg Kuli, whose name was mentioned in the history of Sháhi Beg Khán. At the time when the Emperor was defeated at Kul Malik by Ubaid Ullah Khán, and retired from Samarkand, this Beg Kuli, placing himself at the head of 3000 men, came and joined the Khán. He was a trustworthy man. Another was Ishák Bahádur, renowned for his valour and his sound judgment. Others were, Marik Bahádur, Putáji Bahádur, Kará-Uchunghál,[1] Shabán, Sultákár[2] Tufta Kuli, and Uzun Sakál Tufta Kuli. [Each of these was head of a tribe] and all were trustworthy and experienced men. Another was Tumán Bahádur, leader [*sar-khail*] of the Káluchi, and one of the most notable generals of his time. He will be mentioned in the account of the Khán's last days. Another was Malik Ali, commander [*sirdar*] of the tribe of Kárluk and a brave soldier. Another, Kulka, head [*sar khail*] of the Makrit. Another, Omar Shaikh, chief [*kalántar*] of the Shulkárchi.

All these were chiefs of tribes, and each had a retinue. There was yet another class of men, who had no following, but were quite alone; yet they had distinguished themselves above the rest, by their courage in many battles and engagements, and thus they had acquired the name of "heroes" [*bahádur*]. Some of their deeds of warlike valour will be mentioned below. A list of the names of a few of them follows: Midaka [Bahádur], Abdul Váhid [Bahádur], Khudái Kuli [Bahádur], Shakával, Yusuf Bakával, Muhammad Ali Tumán, Kishkui Divána, Kará Dána Kuli, Shaikh Nazar Yasával, Barka Yasával, Hakk Nazar Divána, Ali Kurchi, Sháh Mirák Kalandar, Bábá Kulághán, Tangri Bardi, Bái Tisha, Hakk Nazar Kughuchi, Pák [or Jabák] Mir Akhur, Pálicha Mir Akhur, Bar Mazid Mankish, Sukár Káluchi, Sukár Ukhsi, Bábarin

[1] The vowels in this name are uncertain.—R.
[2] Perhaps Naltákár.—R.

Ázuk Mirzá, and others. They were the talk of their time, and all of them heroes like Rustam, Zál, and Afrásiáb the brazen-bodied. I have mentioned a few of them, but it would be tedious to mention them all; moreover many of them have no place in this history—no connection with the main events.

CHAPTER XLIV.

BATTLES OF SULTÁN SAID KHÁN WITH THE ARMY OF MIRZÁ ABÁ BAKR AT KÁSHGHAR.

THE army having been mustered, it began to descend from the rising ground of Uch Barkhán. . . .[1] The Amirs of Mirzá Abá Bakr's troops saw the masses of soldiers from afar, and estimated their numbers at 50,000. When a nervous person counts the enemy, he mistakes a hundred for a hundred thousand. On nearing the Tomb of the Khwája, they drew their bridles to the right and turned towards a village called Sarman, two *farsákhs* from Káshghar, where there is a ford over the Timán. Crossing the Timán they passed on to a place called Sughunluk, where Mirzá Abá Bakr had laid out beautiful gardens and meadows; in these they encamped. Some of the Amirs, taking their troops, approached the citadel of Káshghar, thinking that the enemy would wish to defend the fortifications and decline to come out. They approached quite close to the citadel and were examining it and admiring how well it had been fortified, when the enemy, sallying forth, drew up in battle order and stood ready. [Couplet]. . . .

On arrival of the Amirs the battle began. Some courageous youths, to whom the day of battle was as the nuptial night, and the rumbling of the drums of war was as the murmuring of harps. . . . [three couplets] now threw themselves upon the enemy's ranks, wielding their sabres on every side. All around was disorder and confusion: victory and defeat fell sometimes to one and sometimes to the other. The enemy having turned their faces towards Báz-Shirak,[2] all the infantry and cavalry poured out of the citadel to their assistance and joined in the fray. The battle lasted till past midday. . . .[3] Then some of the Amirs sent messengers to the Khán, representing that the enemy had

[1] Three couplets, probably from Firdausi, are omitted here.—R.

[2] The passage reads: "Ru ba báz shirak shuda." Thus *báz shirak* probably stands for the name of a place; but this is not certain.—R.

[3] Some rhetoric is omitted here.

left their strong position and had descended into the plain. If the Khán wished to meet them on equal terms, now was the opportunity. Let him come before the sun should set, for then the enemy would retire to the citadel, and would not come out again. When the Khán received this message, ... [three couplets] he arranged his army in the manner above described, and went forward, but as the ground was rough and broken, the troops were not able to preserve their formation. The Amirs of the left wing were ordered to go in advance, while the centre was to follow them. The Amirs of the right wing had many of them advanced in the early morning. When the Khán drew near he said: "Let the force advance slowly, while I ride forward and see how matters are going." The Khán arrived just as the left wing had come up. The men who had been fighting [all the morning], seeing the Khán arrive, received fresh courage and were overjoyed; for they had been anxiously expecting him. They now made a combined charge . . . . [three couplets] and before the centre had time to come up, had overwhelmed the enemy.

Khwája Sáki Ali was chief minister [*mushrif-i-diván*], and was sprung from the Uighurs of Khorásán.[1] He had always distinguished himself by his extreme valour, but through his impetuosity the thread of his life was cut in two. He had been one of the first to arrive on the scene of action, and was standing with his men in the front of the army, when he saw that the Khán had come. Before all the rest, he threw himself upon the centre of the enemy, and allowed the reins of discretion to be guided by the palm of recklessness. The infantry archers had formed an ambush in a large stream called the Sarman. Khwája Sáki Ali, without hesitating, made his horse leap this stream, wishing to use his sabre against the cavalry that were standing on the opposite bank. But one of those foot bowmen who were standing in ambush in the water, shot an arrow into Khwája Sáki Ali's eye, so that it came out at the back of his head, and he immediately fell [lifeless] from his horse.

In the meanwhile the enemy had been put to rout, having been dislodged from their ground by the violence of the onslaught of the Khán's warriors. Before the whole army could come up, the advanced body pushed on, striking and killing, up to the gates [of Káshghar]. In a short space of time the King of Kings of the universe, and rightful Lord of the realm, utterly destroyed the numerous host together with its weapons and material of war. They were only just able to creep, crushed and routed, into the citadel and to close the gates. That night the Khán pitched his royal camp in the immediate vicinity [of the town], and on the

[1] Meaning Uighurs settled in Khorásán. This allusion, brief though it is, to Uighurs in Khorásán is interesting. Compare Abul Ghází, pp, 50, 51.

morrow, at break of day, again drew up his troops and approached the citadel. But as there was nobody within, except a few soldiers lightly armed, he retired to Tukuzák, where he encamped. On the following day, having crossed the river Kará Tázghun, his army went and pitched their camp at Tirák, one of the districts depending on Yángi-Hisár. Here they were joined by the families [*kuch*] who were following after them; these they left here, and marched on to the gates of the citadel of Yángi-Hisár. The men in the citadel did not come out, but there was some infantry stationed below the citadel, and upon these Midaka Bahádur (who has been spoken of already, and will be mentioned again) made a bold attack. As their position was a strong one, he retired, and they, in turn, having stood their ground for awhile, also retreated. The Khán remained several days in that neighbourhood, changing his position from place to place, in the expectation that Mirzá Abá Bakr, having collected an army, would be coming. He passed nearly two months in those parts, without hearing any news of Abá Bakr Mirzá. In the meantime Mirzá Ali Taghái and Haji Mirzá, together with a few men from every division, conducted forays round about the hills of Sárigh Kul, where they became possessed of much booty and countless sheep.

At this time Muhammad Kirghiz came to wait on the Khán and was favourably received. He begged to be allowed to go to Yárkand and bring back definite news [of Mirzá Abá Bakr]. [The Khán approving of the plan allowed him to depart], sending with him several persons of consequence. They plundered Arslán Bágh, which is two *farsákhs* from Yárkand, and found much booty, which they brought with them, together with the news that [Mirzá Abá Bakr] was doing his utmost to collect an army, and was giving out horses and arms to the peasantry and villagers. But he had no force on which he could rely. Upon hearing this the Khán set out against Yárkand.

CHAPTER XLV.

MARCH OF SULTÁN SAID KHÁN AGAINST YÁRKAND, AND SEVERAL MATTERS IN THE SAME CONNECTION.

When Muhammad Kirghiz brought the news of Mirzá Abá Bakr, all the councillors were for marching against Yárkand. If Mirzá Abá Bakr were to come forth and give them battle, well and good; if not, there was, at any rate, an abundance of corn and other necessaries round about Yárkand. They must lay siege to the citadel of Yárkand. If it should fall, Káshghar and Yángi-Hisár would naturally fall also. With such projects they moved on towards Yárkand, until they came to Sukát, a village at ten *farsákhs* distance from Yángi-Hisár.

At this place some of those who had come in flight to Mir Ayub, with neither family nor dependents, formed a plot [*daghdagha*] to desert and go off towards Karátigin and Hisár. But when their scheme was discovered, most of them were unable to get away: a certain number, however, went. While the talk about this continued, Midaka Bahádur represented that Kitta Beg had had a similar intention. This Kitta Beg is the same person who was mentioned in the beginning of this book. He was the brother of Mir Ahmad Kásim Kuhbur and when Mir Ahmad Kásim left Táshkand, he was in Sairám, which place he kept for himself for a whole year. When the Emperor retired to Kábul, and no hope was left him of relief from any quarter, he [Kitta Beg] sent a message to Kásim Khán offering to give up Sairám to him, and thus brought Kásim Khán against Táshkand. This anecdote has been already told. On leaving the service of Kásim Khán, Kitta Beg went over to the Khán in Andiján. All the Amirs approved the words of Midaka Bahádur, who said: "His flight is quite proper, because he is Bábar Pádisháh's subject, and he wished to go away. But he must not be put into chains until the matter has been more thoroughly inquired into." When the Amirs had confirmed this plan, the Khán said: "I will myself stand security for Kitta Beg, and if he gets away, I will be responsible." The Khán then sent for Kitta Beg and said to him: "They have been telling such and such stories about you. Now you are a brave man. It is not fitting that you should desert us. I have made myself security for you to the Amirs. If on this occasion you show me attachment, your desires shall be satisfied; but if you disgrace me in the sight of the Amirs by running away, that course is also open to you." To this Kitta Beg replied: "I am not such a coward as to desert just at the time of battle." He said nothing more, but remained, in silence, in close attendance upon the Khán.

In consequence of these dissensions, the proposed march on Yárkand was abandoned, and at dawn on the following day they set out in haste for Yángi-Hisár . . . [three couplets], where they arrived at midday. There was one circumstance which was most propitious for them. When the army that was occupying Káshghar heard that the Khán had marched against Yárkand, they sent a message to the Amirs in Yángi-Hisár, to the effect that the light force in occupation were uneasy on many accounts. If a few of the Káshghari were sent back to them, they would be of material aid to the garrison. The Amirs in Yángi-Hisár thinking this reasonable, sent back a large number of Káshghari to Káshghar. These men, issuing from the citadel, crossed the river of Yángi-Hisár and were proceeding [homewards], when suddenly the Moghuls[1] fell upon them, and the whole body became a prey to the Khán's army.

At this juncture, the Khán himself came up. The Yángi-Hisár men, who were all on foot, had come into the midst of ravines and streams, and rough, broken ground, but they made a brave stand. When the Khán came upon the scene, Kitta Beg pushed forward and struck Midaka Bahádur, saying: "On that day you told me that I was going to run away. Let it be seen to-day, who it is that will run away." Now Midaka was one of the most eminent warriors, and the bravest of the brave. He replied: "I have been longing for this day for years;" and therewith he pressed forward. The two charged forward upon [the enemy] [Verses] . . . . The road down which they rode was very narrow; on one side of it flowed the river of Yángi-Hisár, in which the water was surging in waves, while on the other side was a deep ravine. The road was wide enough, perhaps, for three horsemen to ride abreast. In the middle of this had been placed a gate, through which infantry could pass, and in which many soldiers in armour were posted, while outside it, others were engaged in discharging their arrows. When these two horsemen charged, the soldiers put their backs against the gate. The horse of Kitta Beg came up in advance of Midaka's, and however much the latter might use his whip, he was not able to pass in front. When Kitta Beg came near, the archers began to aim their arrows at his horse, so that it fell on the spot, and Kitta Beg was dismounted. As the passage was narrow, the horse fell into the water, while Kitta Beg advanced on foot to attack the soldiers. They, however, placed themselves so that his sword could not reach them, and Midaka, coming close after, drew his horse up and said: "Peace be on you. Let this be a sufficient display of valour; let us now return." But Kitta Beg replied: "I will not retire until you do." Now as the arrows were pouring down, like rain, from the gate, and from the top of the ravine, Midaka saw that if they advanced, both would perish; he therefore withdrew first, while Kitta Beg followed very slowly behind him. The Khán praised Kitta Beg loudly, while the people blamed Midaka, who replied: "It was not a position in which we could do the enemy any injury. Kitta Beg, in his excitement, behaved like a madman; if I, too, had made a fool of myself, the only result would have been the death of us both. I yielded to his passion." This excuse was approved by some, but not by others.

[1] Apparently those who were returning from Sukát with the Khan.

To be brief, every one took up his quarters [*muljár*] in the suburbs of Yángi-Hisár. A few days later, Mir Ayub was carried off by a form of dropsy. Towards the end of his illness the Khán went to visit him, and he said to the Khán: "I have not observed fidelity and loyalty to Bábar Pádisháh [but have broken my oath], owing to the instigation of those hogs and bears," alluding to the Moghul generals who had incited him to join in the revolt at Hisár, which has been mentioned. "That [broken] oath is now lacerating my bowels, and I am being killed by remorse. As for those hogs and bears, may God restrain His wrath from them, for causing me to break solemn vows." [Quatrain] . . . . After the death of Mir Ayub, his rank descended to his brother Muhammad Beg.

During those times there were daily engagements, and every man was eager to bring into evidence the precious stones of bravery which he had stored up in the treasure-house of his heart. Among those who distinguished themselves, were Midaka, Abdul Váhid, Khuddái Kuli Shakávul, and Muhammad Ali Tumán. Other individuals displayed their gallantry on one, or two, or three occasions, but as for these four men, there were few battles in which they did not do something remarkable, and scarcely a day passed without a battle taking place. When it was ascertained that Mirzá Abá Bakr did not intend leaving Yárkand, all were agreed that Yángi-Hisár ought to be carried by storm, and this having been determined upon, they sent off Ali Bahádur (who has been alluded to above in the list of eminent Moghuls) to Kizil, which is on the border of the desert of Yárkand, that he might reconnoitre, and watch the movements of Mirzá Abá Bakr. If, during the siege, he should make a sally, the Khwája was to return immediately with the news, so that [the Khán] might be prepared to meet him.

CHAPTER XLVI.

TAKING OF YÁNGI-HISÁR: THE KEY TO THE CONQUEST OF THE KINGDOM OF KÁSHGHAR.

In the beginning of Rajab of the year 920, the Khán disposed his troops round the citadel of Yángi-Hisár, and pitched his camp so close to it, that if *gaz*-long arrows had been aimed at his tent from the top of the citadel, they might have reached the edge of the cliff under which he had camped. The intrenchments [*murchal*] were arranged on the following plan. On the north side there was no need for intrenchments, because the fort was situated on the top of a cliff, which ended in a sheer precipice. Mines would there take no effect, while to ascend the cliff was impossible. For these reasons trenches were useless on the north side. The first tower on the west, was taken in hand by the Khán himself and the warriors of the centre, who were always in attendance upon him; these belonged to no particular regiment, but their names have been mentioned above. Another tower on the same side—west of the Khán's—was entrusted to me, and to my right were Mirzá Ali Taghái, Kutluk Mirak Mirzá, and Babrika Mirzá, who, together, were laying a mine. Beyond them, Bábá Sárik Mirzá and Shahbáz Mirzá, and a body of Báhrin, had charge of another. Farther on again, were Mirzá Muhammad Beg and Beg Muhammad Beg, who had chosen [a site for] a third. Beyond them was a tower, the gate of which looked due south. To this tower were appointed Jánka Mirzá and Bishka Mirzá; while on the south side Munka Beg had charge of another mine. At his side was yet another, under the supervision of Mir Muhammad, who had lately succeeded to the position held by Mir Ayub. Near him was Mir Kambar, then came Ali Mirák Barlás, next Mir Dáim, next Kará Kulák Mirzá, then my uncle; and beyond him was the eastern gate of the citadel, which side, like the northern, overlooks a precipice. For five days and nights all our energies were devoted to digging and advancing galleries.

The first mine that was ready to be tried was the Khán's. It went off at midnight, and that tower which had raised itself to the skies, now fell with a crash, level with the ground; but part of the original wall was left standing. On that day every one exerted himself to the utmost, and the mines were so far advanced, as to be ready to blow up the walls with very little further labour. [The strongest of all the towers was the one] given to Jánka Mirzá and Bishka Mirzá to undermine, but they made cracks along the wall for a distance of about sixty *gaz*.

While the siege was thus proceeding, one of Khwája Ali Bahádur's men brought in a certain Alika and a few generals. This Alika was the son of the commander of the citadel, who was called Amin Dárugha, and who was one of Mirzá Abá Bakr's most distinguished Amirs. To him had been committed the entire charge of the citadel of Yángi-Hisár. It came about in this way. Mirzá Abá Bakr had collected a force in Yárkand and had amassed a quantity of arms, hoping to come and relieve Yángi-Hisár. He then detached a body of picked men and sent them off to reconnoitre at Kizil, with orders to bring back any news they might learn, so that he might form his plans accordingly. This body was under the command of Pir Ali Beg, the brother of Vali Beg, who has been alluded to already. On reaching Kizil, they found that a party of Moghuls were reconnoitring in the same district. Having ascertained his exact position, they fell upon Khwája Ali Bahádur unexpectedly, the same night. The horsemen were sleeping soundly, when the din of giving and taking of blows, war cries, and trumpets startled them from their slumbers. [Verses] . . . . It was a pitch dark night—neither moon nor stars were visible—nor could friend be distinguished from enemy. [Two couplets] . . . . All who awoke were mad with confusion at the alarm, and were unable to collect their thoughts sufficiently to realise what was passing, so all fled in dismay, excepting Khwája Ali Bahádur, who did not lose his presence of mind, but stood his ground firmly, and called out to his followers by name. All who heard his voice rallied to his side, till at length a good number were gathered round him, and they too began to call their war-cry loudly. Some of those who had been stupefied by the sudden awakening, now recovered their senses, and on listening attentively, heard the voices calling the war-cry. On this their courage was renewed, and they went and rejoined Khwája Ali Bahádur. They discharged their arrows in the dark, and fought on till the brightness of dawn overcame the shadows of night, when by that light the combatants began to see [the real state of things]. The enemy became aware of their small numbers, while our men saw their own superiority.

Pir Ali Beg had but a hundred men with him, while Khwája Ali Bahádur had three hundred. Since in the darkness they had become confused and disordered, Pir Ali Beg saw that flight would be a cowardly death, while to hold his ground was to die nobly. Near to that spot was a garden; within this he tried to defend himself. Ere the sun had reached the meridian, the sun of the lives of those men had set. Out of a hundred, only two escaped to bear the news that the rest of their party had perished. The above-mentioned Alika had been wounded in the fight. To prevent his giving information, they did not send him back to his friends, but despatched him to the Khán with the heads of the slain hung round his neck—the throats running with blood. He reached the Khán at midday, and the heads of those generals were sent into the citadel as a gift. Alika was then asked for news. He replied: "Mirzá Abá Bakr has made all the necessary preparations for an expedition. All the people know that he has got horses, and arms of every kind, such as coats of mail, horse-armour, and so forth; that nothing is wanting—nay, rather there is a superabundance of all such things. But he has no generals—no renowned Amirs or brave warriors, whose strength and judgment are the very foundations of true sovereignty. For all of these, he has himself put to death. And now, in order to complete his army, he is obliged to choose men from among the peasantry, artizans and market-people, making one a Vazir, another an Amir: the first a Mir and the second a councillor. The rustic who has spent his life with his hand on the plough, and has never done any work but ploughing, how can he begin to wield a sword or hold the reins of government? Though he may try ever so hard, I am sure he cannot succeed; such foolish ideas can come to nothing." And he laid much stress upon the improbability of Mirzá Abá Bakr advancing. [Our] people, however, did not fully trust his words, but suspected that this man, drowning in the whirlpool of misfortune, was employing flattery as a means of reaching the shore of salvation.

About evening prayer time, one of Khwája Ali Bahádur's followers brought in another man who had come to him in flight. This fugitive reported that Mirzá Abá Bakr, having mustered an army, had advanced two *farsákhs* out of Yárkand, when he deserted him. Many were loth to believe this also, and imagined it to be a trick on the part of Mirza Abá Bakr, by which he hoped to retard the operations against the citadel of Yángi-Hisár; so they tortured this informant till he died, but he persisted in his story to the end, and then they believed it.

All the Amirs were for raising the siege that same night, and for marching out to meet and engage Mirzá Abá Bakr, before he should be joined by the armies of Káshghar and Yángi-Hisár. But the Khán said: "I intend to remain at the foot of this cliff until Mirzá Abá Bakr comes, and to aim my arrows at the citadel and at Mirzá Abá Bakr, until I am killed on this spot. Those who do not [wish to] follow my example, let them do what they like." When the Khán had said this, all knelt down before him, saying: "May your exalted majesty's road be [strewed] with our lives as a thousand sacrifices! Who is there among us who holds his own wretched existence more dear than the precious life of the Khán, or thinks of his own personal safety first, in this undertaking?" Then all again set to work, with contented hearts, at the mines.

At daybreak of the sixth day of the siege, the Khán rode round all the trenches and infused his own enthusiasm into the hearts of his Amirs and soldiers: praising those who had exerted themselves, and ordering to be whipped any who had been remiss. In this manner did he pass round the citadel. As he approached the trench of my uncle, some one called out from the top of the citadel. They listened. He was saying: "Let one of the followers of Sayyid Muhammad Mirzá come forward; I have something to tell him." Thereupon a man was sent forward, who [however] asked whether Kukildásh Mirzá Ali Sayyid Bahádur was there, [and if so] had they not better send him [to parley]? [So they sent him.] After a short time Ali Sayyid returned reporting that Amin Dárugha had spoken as follows: "Sayyid Muhammad Mirzá is Mirzá Abá Bakr's brother. For generations past I and my sons have been their servants. In our loyalty we have, during three months, been in peril of our lives, in spite of never having enjoyed during forty years, a moment's security from Mirzá Abá Bakr. Those whom he wished to kill he killed, and those who were left alive were all subjected to violent punishments, such as castration—that is to say, depriving of virility—cutting off the hands and feet, putting out eyes, and the like. All were sure to be exposed to some calamity. In spite of all this, I felt it still my duty to remain loyal. Now it has come to a question of life and death; the knife has reached the bone. If Sayyid Muhammad Mirzá will forget our enmity, forgive our sins, and spare our lives and our goods, we will deliver the citadel into his hands and become his vassals." When the Khán heard this message he was overjoyed, and sent Ali Sayyid back, saying that their offer was accepted.

CHAPTER XLVII.

DECLINE OF MIRZÁ ABÁ BAKR; FACTS CONNECTED THEREWITH, AND THE END OF HIS DOMINION.

One of the worst of the wicked practices of Mirzá Abá Bakr was that, having laid down the most strenuous and exacting regulations and observances, he would not be satisfied with anything less than the death of any person who should, in the least degree, infringe them. Having put that person to death for a trifling fault, he would become apprehensive of his tribe and relations, and would persuade himself that they could never be pacified. He would therefore set about their extermination, sparing neither suckling babes nor women with child; but punishing them all, from mature men to the child at the breast, so that after he had been satisfied a thousand times with their death, they died with thankfulness (as has been related before).

In short, towards the end of his life, Mirzá Abá Bakr entrusted his army and all military affairs to Mir Vali, placing the administration of the State and the people in the hands of Sháh Dána Kukildásh. These two men fulfilled their duties with the utmost possible diligence.

As has been briefly stated above, Mir Vali succeeded so thoroughly in driving the Moghuls and Kirghiz out of Aksu and Moghulistán, that for a long time none of them dared come within two or three months' journey of Káshghar.[1] All the Moghuls crept into Chálish

[1] Here, no doubt, the province of Káshghar is meant.

and Turfán, but the Kirghiz were allowed to dwell on this side of Issigh Kul. In the same manner, Mir Vali took entire possession of certain places in Farghána, such as Uzkand (which is the most important [town] of that province), Ush, Mádu, and Jágirák; all of which places lie above Andiján. He also brought under his power much of Karátigin and Badakhshán, and the districts of Balur and Tibet as far as Kashmir. All this was the achievement of Mir Vali.

Before the battle of Tutluk, my uncle endeavoured to bring about a meeting with Mir Vali, in order that they might discuss the terms of a peace. [When Mir Vali heard this] he thought my uncle must be reduced to straits and in despair; thus he might be able to seize him by deception, and send him to Mirzá Abá Bakr as a present. He felt that he could not possibly perform a more worthy or important service. These considerations induced him to assent to the interview. They met at a place agreed on, between two lines of men appointed respectively by either side, and they began to confer together in a manner suitable to the occasion. During the conference, my uncle said to the Amirs who had accompanied Mir Vali: "I have a few words to say to Mir Vali; leave us." Thereupon the Amirs rose up [and withdrew]; Mir Vali alone remained. The few words were merely a repetition of some civilities relating to Mirzá Abá Bakr, which he had already uttered in the presence of the Amirs. They then separated, and each man returned to his own army. After this, occurred the event [battle] at Tutluk, which weighed down the scale of Mir Vali in the balance of the regulations of Mirzá Abá Bakr. Mirzá Abá Bakr asked the generals who had been present at the interview what had been said; they told him all that had passed, and added: "This is what was said in our presence, but afterwards Sayyid Muhammad Mirzá spoke to Mir Vali in private, and we do not know what he said then." When, after the battle at Tutluk, Mir Vali came to Mirzá Abá Bakr's presence, the latter asked what Sayyid Muhammad Mirzá had said to him in private, and Mir Vali told him what my uncle had said. Then Mirzá Abá Bakr replied: "But that is exactly what he said before all the others; one does not demand a private interview merely to repeat such things as these." He said nothing further, but from that moment he began to suspect Mir Vali, thinking: "What Sayyid Muhammad really said to him in private he will not tell me; perhaps he is in league with him, and is planning my ruin." So he seized Mir Vali and sent him to the *Kázik*, together with his brothers. Some of them he castrated. And thus did he annihilate all these people for the simple question: "why did Sayyid Muhammad demand a private interview?" and subjected them all to hard punishments and bitter suffering. [Verses] . . . .

This is an instance of Mirzá Abá Bakr's cruelty. Another example is his treatment of Shah Dána Kukildásh, to whom were entrusted the affairs of the State and the people, and the control of the treasury. He, too, had exerted himself to the utmost in the performance of his duties. For example, the flocks of sheep he had collected at the conquest of Káshghar were beyond reckoning, and when by reason of my extreme youth I could not attend to business, and on this account did not attempt to estimate the profits of the booty [then taken], I only know that more than 15,000 sheep fell to my lot. No one on that occasion got a smaller share than myself, of Mirzá Abá Bakr's property. The soldiers who had accompanied the Khán, and the men from the armies of the Mirzá, all received an equally large share; and from this, one can form an estimate of the whole! In the same manner, his cattle and flocks, grain and treasure (which have been mentioned, and will be mentioned again), were so numerous and abundant, that the intellect is incapable of conceiving the quantity that fell to each man. All this had been amassed under the superintendence of Sháh Dána Kukildásh.

After the fall of Mir Vali, the Mirzá's suspicions extended to Sháh Dána Kukildásh, [thinking] that he might say to himself: "Mir Vali was a greater man than I am, yet the Mirzá seized him: perhaps he will seize me too." These thoughts had never entered Sháh Dána's mind, nor that of anybody else; he, however, seized Sháh Dána upon suspicion, saying [by way of pretext] that Sháh Dána had reduced the value of his property; and there, in front of the seat of judgment [*divan-khána*], he ordered people to pluck out the whole of his beard and to castrate him; while, as soon as his wounds were healed, he sent him to work [in the Kázik.]

In the places of these two [officers] he set up mean creatures [*arázil*] from among the Amirs; and, though he found himself better off than formerly as regards worldly substance, the affairs of the army ceased to flourish; for such another commander as Mir Vali was not readily to be met with. In the meanwhile, the news of the Khán's march from Andiján to Káshghar received confirmation. [The Mirzá] immediately proceeded to Káshghar, and there, in seven days, constructed a citadel, as has been explained above. By the time it was known that the Khán had reached At-Báshi, which is seven days' journey from Káshghar, the fort of Yángi-Hisár had likewise been filled with stores, arms, and all that was fitting and necessary. It was placed in the charge of a few officers in whom he reposed confidence—namely, Amin Darugha, Ján Hasan of the tribe of Kárluk, Kuli Itárji, Ajmaga Akhta and Jáni Beg Akhta, Mir Vali, Sháh Dána, and Muhammad Beg (whom he had lately castrated), together with some of their followers.

Although he had just taken many of them from the works,[1] he gave them each horses and arms, saying: "If you prove to me your devotion and loyalty, I will again take you into favour."

At this juncture, it was reported that the Khán had reached Tushgu. [Mirzá Abá Bakr] thereupon set out for Yárkand, giving his final injunctions [to the officers] in Yángi-Hisár. He promised the people that he would go and muster an army in Yárkand, and come to their relief. Upon his arrival at Yárkand he at once set about collecting forces. He filled the country with horses and arms. [There was a certain] Ustád Abdál Sháikh, who was a perfect master [*ustád*], and unrivalled in all kinds of work with hammer and anvil. After the fall of Mir Vali and Sháh Dána Kukildásh, Mirzá Abá Bakr had set up this Shaikh Abdál in the place of Sháh Dána, and I have heard [Shaikh Abdál] say that there were in the Mirzá's armoury 60,000 coats of mail [*juba*] and 12,000 sets of horse armour [*kichim*], besides other arms and accoutrements, the number of which may be judged by these figures. But the army itself was composed of peasants, artizans, gardeners, and cultivators of the soil. Upon those he judged the most capable among them, he conferred the rank of Mirzá. A hundred and twenty of them he made his own escort, and the rest all received horses and arms. [Three couplets.]

(1) It takes many a year for the natural stone to become, by the sun's power, a ruby in Badakhshán, or an amethyst in Yemen.

(2) It is many months before a seed of cotton is ready to be made into a robe for a *huri*, or a shroud for a corpse.

(3) It is many days before a handful of wool from the back of a sheep, becomes a zealot's shirt or a donkey's halter.

. . . .[2] However this may be, Mirzá Abá Bakr having mustered his army, marched with it to a point two *farsákhs* distant from Yárkand; thence he detached, and sent in advance, some picked men, who fell in with Khwája Ali Bahádur at Kizil, as has been told above. [Thus we see] that the man who was brought before the Khán at Yángi-Hisár during the siege operations, and who had been tortured to death, spoke the truth. He had deserted at the time when Mirzá Abá Bakr, having led his army two *farsákhs* out of Yárkand, sent forward the advance guard. The man had reported exactly what he had witnessed.

When Mirzá Abá Bakr had pitched his camp at this spot, he wished to pass his forces in review, but his efforts to do so were in vain. For these Amirs, who had been used all their lives to handling the yoke [*yugh*], when they now raised the standard

[1] The word is *Kár* (work), and evidently refers to the *Kázik*, or excavation works.

[2] A rhetorical passage of one folio is omitted here. It is chiefly in verse, and relates to the impossibility of a ploughman making a good soldier.

[*tugh*][1] and formed in line, thought they were thrashing corn, and got in each other's way; nor could they distinguish between right and left and centre. When their spirited steeds reared and shied, they held on anyhow to the withers, and when, in fear of their lives, they pulled at the bridle, and the horse would rear, the rider would lose his control, and slip back on the horse's haunches. If the animal started off, they would throw up the bridle and fall, like a drop of sweat, to the ground. Their bows got broken, and their arrows fell out [of the quivers]. When Mirzá Abá Bakr saw this kind of horsemanship—such soldiering and such archery—he said: "With such a troop as this, it would be dangerous to try and rob a kitchen-garden" [*páliz*]; and he returned, dispirited and anxious, to his tent, seriously meditating flight.

Following this, came news that the citadel of Yángi-Hisár had fallen; and when the people of Káshghar heard of that, they too abandoned their citadel and dispersed. On this intelligence reaching the Mirzá, he felt that further delay was useless [and that the hour for flight had come] [Couplet] . . . . Therefore, having packed up the richest of his clothes and his valuables, having divorced his kingdom, and handed Yárkand over to his eldest son, Jahángir Mirzá, he fled. [Verses] . . . .

Jahángir Mirzá, who had passed all his life in seclusion, was of a timorous disposition. Finding himself suddenly placed upon the throne of a disordered State, he did what he was able in the way of government, and then, at the end of five days (hearing that his father was at a distance, and that the enemy were near at hand), set out in flight. He collected all the treasure he could carry off, and issued a general order that every one might take what he wished. Those who were afraid of the Moghuls, accompanied him in his flight. The rest fell upon whatever treasure remained, plundering the granaries and burning, or destroying, property of all kinds.

Four days after the departure of Mirzá Jahángir, Khwája Ali Bahádur arrived with two or three thousand men, and two days later the Khán followed, all of which shall be related presently. Mirzá Jahángir retired to Sánju, which is the frontier on the high-road to Tibet, while Mirzá Abá Bakr went to Khotan. But, seeing no possibility of making a stand in the citadel there, he marched on to Karánghutágh, whither he was followed, in hot pursuit, by a party of Moghuls. As the roads were difficult, it would have been hard—nay, impossible, for him to carry off all the property he had with him; he therefore collected it all together, and set it on fire. I have heard from those who had charge of it, that there were nine hundred mule-loads of embroidered and brocaded garments. Many

[1] A play on the words *Yugh* and *Tugh*.—R.

of them were embroidered in gold in the European, Ottoman [*Rumi*], and Chinese fashions; while some of the robes were studded with jewels and all kinds of precious stones. All these were consumed in the fire; while his gold and silver vases, cups, and various kinds of ornaments set with jewels, and his saddle-bags filled with gold-dust, he threw from the bridge into the River Ak-Tásh, which flows through the middle of [the valley of] Karánghutágh. He killed his riding horses [*tupchák*] and mules; then, taking what it was possible to carry on such a road, set out for Tibet.

On reaching Tibet [Ladak], he found that all the forts which he had garrisoned had been abandoned by his men, who had fled in different directions; so that his forts and treasures had again fallen into the hands of the infidels of Tibet. Hence he could do nothing in that country. He could discern no shore of safety from amid the furious waves of hardship and trial, which tossed around him. Mirzá Abá Bakr had now for a space of forty-eight years [1] so filled the book [of life] with black records, that there was no space left to write anything more. He had devoted all his energies to accumulating earthly goods, and the pen is unable to describe his worldly magnificence. But, although he used ostentatiously to speak of the next world, and to express hopes of attaining it, yet he never performed an action that did not, as it were, open to him a door of hell or shut upon him a gate of paradise. Between himself and paradise was a long road. . . . . [2]

In short, in the fulness of time, he reaped the fruits of his past misdeeds; so that, finding it impossible to remain in Tibet, he preferred death to life. Leaving his family and children there, he departed, saying: "I am going [to give myself up to the Khán]. It is evident that I shall be killed with the poison of oppression. If this happens, bury my body in the sepulchre of my ancestors. Although I have not discharged the duties of kinship towards Sayyid Muhammad Mirzá and Mirza Haidar, I beg you to show them kindness. And if, contrary to my expectations, they should not kill me, I have still a plan [which may be executed]." With such intentions he set out, towards the middle of winter, to visit the Khán. On his way, he met with a party of his own servants, whom my uncle had sent into Tibet to fetch him, threatening them with this and that [penalty] if they did not succeed. When Mirzá Abá Bakr met them, he asked their news; they replied: "We have been sent to find you:" and then they strung together a few lies to try and reassure him. But he did not believe them, and

[1] This figure evidently has reference to Aba Bakr's reign, and not to his age. If we count from the death of Muhammad Haidar Mirza in 868, Aba Bakr's reign would be thirty-five years; but he was in power over parts, if not the whole of the country, at intervals, for some years during the Mirza's lifetime. It is not clear from what event our author dates Aba Bakr's reign of forty-eight years.

[2] Three lines of rhetoric are omitted here concerning Aba Bakr's evil deeds.

said: "All I want you to do is to take me, living, before the Khán and Sayyid Muhammad; after that, you can do what you please." They launched out into professions of readiness to comply with his wish. Then, as it was late, having said his night prayers, he went to sleep: and the saying, "Sleep is the brother of Death," was verified in his case. When he retired to rest, the men of the party consulted together, resolved to cut off his head and carry it to the Khán, [as this would appear an important service] and cause the Khán to place confidence in them.

Bad as he was, these people [should not have] betrayed their charge, and used perfidy in place of good faith. However, they cut off his head while he slept and then returned, as shall be narrated shortly. Thus were all his subjects—prince and pauper, high and low—delivered from his wickedness. [Verses, etc.] . . .

CHAPTER XLVIII.

THE CONQUEST OF KÁSHGHAR.

HAVING taken the citadel of Yangi-Hisár, in the manner above described, the Khán turned his attention to [the reduction of] Káshghar. On the third day he learnt that the garrison of Káshghar had abandoned their citadel and, taking their horses, had fled to whatever place each thought safest for himself. The Khán's noble mind being thus, in the most satisfactory manner, set at rest with regard to Káshghar, he placed the foot of success in the stirrup of victory, and drew his reins towards Yárkand, confident of success and triumph. He sent Khwája Ali Bahádur in advance [Verses] . . . The first stage from Yángi-Hisár is Sátlik, and here the Khán pitched his camp. [On the same day] news came that Mirzá Abá Bakr, having given over Yárkand to the charge of his son Jahángir Mirzá, had retired to Khotan. [On hearing this news] the Khán hastened still more, and on reaching Kizil heard that Jahángir Mirzá also had fled, and that Khwája Ali Bahádur had entered Yárkand. At the end of Rajab of the year 920, the Khán made his triumphant entry into the town of Yárkand, and with the splendour of his glittering sword, he allayed the dust of tyranny and enmity [etc.] . . . .

Before [his army] entered the town, he sent on Amir Dáim Ali and Beg Muhammad to occupy Khotan; he also despatched in pursuit of Mirzá Abá Bakr, seven brave generals—namely, Kará Kulák Mirzá, Háji Mirzá, Sultán Ali Mirzá, Nazar Mirzá, Mir Kambar, Mirzá Ali Tagháí and Beg Kuli Makrit. These seven generals started in pursuit with the greatest eagerness. This affair having been attended to, the Khán issued a general order that every one might go and plunder wherever he liked. And every man in the army who cared for pillage and booty, immediately hastened out [to take advantage of the permission]. Only a few of the Amirs, who held plundering to be derogatory, remained in attendance on the Khán. Having settled this matter also, the victorious Khán mounted the throne of the town. He then went up to the citadel [*ark*], within which were many lofty buildings, containing, each of them, rooms and upper-apartments and battlements, so numerous as to astound the beholder. And these buildings were filled with cloths, chintzes, carpets, porcelain, cuirasses, horse-trappings, saddles, bows and other things useful to man. All these things had been seized by Mirzá Abá Bakr, or procured by whatever means he chose to employ, and had been hidden away by him, so that no one might know of their existence. Of such as remained over, Mirzá Jahángir had destroyed and wasted as much as he was able; and on his departure had sanctioned a general pillage, which, until the arrival of Khwája Ali Bahádur, was carried on by the whole population—each taking what he could. When Khwája Ali Bahádur entered the town, he, likewise, devoted himself to pillage. Seven days later the Khán arrived, and he too gave his men permission to plunder right and left. Everything in the way of money, as well as the valuable cloths and stuffs, had been carried off, but the houses were still full [of other things]. Two months after the flight of Mirzá Abá Bakr, there were still great quantities of cuirasses and the like, lying about the houses and passages, that no one had cared to carry away. [Five couplets]. . . .

Thus, all that Mirzá Abá Bakr had, in the course of forty-eight years, amassed with infinite toil, and guarded with savage miserliness, he was finally obliged, with a thousand heart-rendings, to abandon; while the Khán, with one stroke of his pen, gave it all over to a general sack, and during two months the dust thereof rose to the sky. [Verses]. . . .

At the end of two months, every man returned safely—laden with plunder from different directions—and presented the Khán with tribute [*pishkash*], according to the quantity of booty he had taken. But the Khán, in order to win the hearts of his people, divided the property up into shares [*suyurghal*] in accordance with the old Moghul custom, and distributed it among his soldiers. I remember distinctly that some of the Amirs who had come from Karánghutágh, presented, besides arms [*álát*] and vases, an Andiján *man* of gold-dust. Now an Andiján *man* is sixty-four *chárik* and a *chárik* is 400 *mithkál.*[1] From this the extent of the rest of the booty may be conceived.

CHAPTER XLIX.

STORY OF THE AMIRS WHO WENT IN PURSUIT OF MIRZÁ ABÁ BAKR.

THOSE nine Amirs whom the Khán had sent off to settle affairs in Khotan and to pursue Mirzá Abá Bakr, started off with great eagerness and exerted themselves to the utmost of their powers. On reaching Khotan, the inhabitants came out to receive them, and delivered into their hands all their treasuries and granaries, their flocks and herds, and everything connected with these. Mir Dáim Ali and Mir Beg Muhammad, according to [the Khán's] orders, stayed in Khotan, and occupied themselves with the administration of the State and the government of the people. The other seven Mirs, like the seven-headed devils fighting on the top of the mountains of Káf, swept on to Karánghutágh, but when they arrived there, found that Mirzá Abá Bakr had left the mountains of Karánghutágh, and had gone on to Tibet [Ladak], in which direction it was difficult to follow him.

When they came to the bridge over which Mirzá Abá Bakr had thrown his effects, they found the roads blocked with the carcases of the *tupchák* horses [three couplets]. . . . which he had killed, and of the mules, on which had been loaded the saddle-bags [*khachir*] full of money and stuffs. I do not quite recall whether there were 900 mules or 900 strings [*kitár*][2] of mules. They next came to the spot where he had burnt his brocades, etc., and saw that these valuables were become an ash-heap from which smoke was still rising. The gold and precious stones with which these clothes had been adorned, were still remaining. These they gathered from among the ashes, and found that the jewels and rubies had not been affected [by the fire]. But the turquoises [*firuza*] had turned black, and become brittle. No trace of their

[1] No doubt Aba Bakr plundered the country and accumulated a large amount of property and some treasure, but the exaggerations of Mirza Haidar on the subject, in this chapter and the next, are too apparent to require pointing out. As regards the Andijáni *man*, if the data he gives are correct, and if the *mithkal* be reckoned at its exact numismatic value of 71·18 grains, the *chárik* should weigh 59·32 oz. troy, or, roughly speaking, 5 lbs.; so that the Andijáni *man* of gold would be nearly 320 lbs. troy and its value some £15,000!

[2] A *kitár*, or string of mules or ponies, consists, usually, of four in the hills and of five in the plains.

original colour was left. The rubies [*lál*] too, were broken into little pieces, and had changed to an ugly colour. The pearls were reduced to ashes, so that they could no longer be distinguished; also the amber—which had lost all its charm.

The Amirs and their men, having gathered what they could from the ashes, again set out upon their road, when they suddenly noticed the boxes of gold-dust shining at the bottom of the river. Indeed the jewelry [*hali*] and vessels of silver and gold, shone forth the rays of the sun, as it were, from the depths of the stream. They thereupon proceeded to attempt the recovery of these valuables, from the water. The river was rushing over the rocks in such a torrent that no one could, by any device, have entered it. So each man prepared a long pole, at the end of which a hook was attached. To reach the bottom, it was necessary to join several of these poles together. Now when Mirzá Abá Bakr had thrown these treasures into the river, he had ordered his men to cut the leather cases into pieces, so that the gold-dust might be scattered in the water. But since the cutting up of the cases took a long time, and the Mirzá was impatient to go forward, he [finally] ordered them to be thrown in just as they were, and thus they had remained from that time.

When they struck the cases, their hooks broke most of them in pieces, and [the contents] were washed away by the current. Sometimes, however, if a man took great care, it did not break, and was lifted out of the water. They were found to contain a mule's-load each. Such of the vases and vessels as had handles, or something to lay hold of, were hooked up, but nothing was recovered upon which a firm hold with the hooks could not be obtained. They only secured a very small quantity of the gold-dust; about a hundred-thousandth part of the whole. However, they were enriched by what they did secure, and got more than enough to enable them to realise all their desires. At present, as compared with those times, all this wealth and all these Moghuls are as a mere drop in the ocean.

CHAPTER L.

CONCLUSION OF THE STORY OF MIRZÁ ABÁ BAKR'S OFFSPRING.

After the victorious Khán had settled all his important affairs in Yárkand, it was discovered that Mirzá Jahángir had not followed his father into Tibet, but that he had settled down in the district of Sánju. The Khán, thereupon, sent my uncle to bring back his nephew, by some means or other. When my uncle reached Sánju, Mirzá Jahángir came out to receive him, offering rich gifts, and said to him: "It is evident to all, that during my father's reign I lived in retirement and in mortal dread of him. During all that time, I did not enjoy a single moment's security or freedom from anxiety. Fear of violence had always made me seek seclusion, and thus the eye of my nature became closed to the splendours of wealth and rank, and I have always been obliged to drink from the cup of dissatisfaction. When the evil foundations of my father's realm began to give way, and his power to crumble from the earthquakes caused by the Khán's forces, he drew me forth from my corner of seclusion, and set me upon the throne of pomp. And I, who during forty-two years, being in fear and trembling for my life, had never gained any experience of the world, how could I suddenly be expected to supervise a whole State? Besides these difficulties, it was my father's constant practice, whenever he stripped one of his children of the garments of life, to lament the unfortunate victim in my presence, saying: 'He was a full grown youth. I dreaded lest he might treat me as Shiruya treated Khusrau and Abdul Latif Mirzá treated Ulugh Beg Mirza.'[1] Hearing such things as this, I endeavoured to the utmost, for the sake of my personal safety, to appear very inefficient in my behaviour. How shall I, who have thus spent forty-two years in cultivating ineptitude and helplessness, revive, in one moment, the welfare of a State which [my father] himself has ruined? Moreover, I had no information concerning any of my father's affairs. Nor has any one ever experienced so much as an inconvenience, at my hands. Whatever the people have suffered is due to my father. They do not blame me, nor hold me responsible for his sins. Let me now go to the Khán, and spend the rest of my days in his service." Words of abject humility, such as these, and many more like them, he continued to pour forth; but my uncle comforted him, and conveyed him, together with much treasure and many horses, before the Khán.

Mirzá Jahángir was born of one of the daughters of Isán Bughá Khán, the youngest brother of Yunus Khán, who was the Khán's grandfather. At the time when Mirzá Abá Bakr captured Aksu, the residence of Alácha Khán (which event has been fully described above), the fourth daughter of Alácha Khán fell into his hands. And he took care of her and treated her with great honour. When she was of age, he gave her in marriage to his son Jahángir Mirzá. The latter, arriving now in the Khán's presence, was

[1] The allusions are (1) to a fable in the *Sháh-námah*, where Khusrau is said to have been killed by his son Shuruya; and (2) to the murder of Mirza Ulugh Beg of Mávará-un-Nahr, by his son Abdul Latif, in the year 1449.

received with respect, and this fourth daughter of Alácha Khán, whose name was Khadija Sultán Khánim, also joined the Khán, whose full-sister she was. The Khán showed favour to Jahángir Mirzá, in accordance with the verse, "I will not ascribe to thee the sins of others"; and ignoring the cruelties and hideous deeds of his father, entered him among the men of trust around his person, and promised that feasts should be celebrated in honour of Khadija out of regard for her noble birth.

One night towards the end of that winter, Jahángir Mirzá was killed in Yángi-Hisár, together with several of his followers. It was never known who committed this deed. Every one had his own suspicions, but God alone knows the truth. Mirzá Abá Bakr had many children. Several of his grown up sons he had put to death, with the most horrible tortures, for totally inadequate reasons. Of those that survived, the eldest and most honourable was Jahángir Mirzá, whose fate has been related. There were two other sons, named Turángir Mirza and Bustángir Mirza, the children of the daughter of Mirzá Sultán Mahmud, son of Mirzá Sultán Abu Said.

In the spring following the winter in which Jahángir Mirzá had been murdered, a person was sent to Tibet to bring back the family of Mirzá Abá Bakr; his wife, Khánzáda Begum, and her elder son, Turángir Mirza, were thus brought to Káshghar. In conformity with the custom of the *Yanga*, she was married to my uncle, while Turángir remained in the Khán's service, until he was drowned in the river.

Bustángir Mirza did not accompany his mother and brother. He went from Tibet to Kashmir and thence into Hindustán. (At that time Bábar Pádisháh had not conquered Hindustán.) From Hindustán he retired to Kábul, but although he was [the son of the daughter of the Emperor's uncle], his father's misdeeds made him repulsive to the Emperor, so that he could not stay in Kábul, but fled into Badakhshán, to Mirzá Khán, who was his maternal uncle. Mirzá Khán, however, instead of showing him the affection of an uncle, displayed hostility towards him on account of his father, Mirzá Abá Bakr; so that he was forced to fly from him also, and betake himself to the Uzbeg Shaibán. Suyunjuk Khán received him with the utmost courtesy and honour, saying: "He is a human being, and it is incumbent on us to treat him with kindness."

He is still about Andiján and Táshkand, where he enjoys high distinction, and is famous among the Uzbeg for his honourable conduct.

CHAPTER LI.

HISTORY OF THE KHÁN AFTER THE CONQUEST OF KÁSHGHAR.

As soon as the Khán had reduced the State to order, he bestowed liberal gifts and rewards upon his followers, especially upon those who had distinguished themselves in battle, by their courage and daring; these have been enumerated above. [Verses] . . . . He poured down favours, more plentiful than drops of rain, upon his soldiers; and by the splendour of his justice, he dispelled the darkness of tyranny which had settled on the inhabitants of the country. [Verses] . . . . The roads which had before been too dangerous to traverse, were now made so safe and tranquil as to become proverbial, that if an old woman were to travel along them, bearing a jar of gold on her head, she would not be molested. At that time there was a popular song which ran: "A solitary person may carry a jar of gold from east to west, for the respect he [the Khán] inspires, causes all corners of the earth to be safe." But what is yet more remarkable, and more creditable, is that if, for example, a woman should leave a vessel full of gold and proceed on her road, she would, on returning at any time, find it untouched. [Verses] . . . .

Into such a complete state of order did the Khán bring the kingdom, that the doors of pleasure and the gates of security were opened to high and low alike. And now all the people gave themselves up to wine and song and dancing. [Verses and rhetoric] . . .

The entire population of the country, and the Khán and his courtiers in particular, turned night into day and day into night in draining the wine cups; nor did they care to learn of events that were passing [around them]. [Verse] . . . . "I came intoxicated to thy street and I left mad: I know not how I came nor how I departed." Revelling became so much the fashion that sobriety was held as a disgrace, and drunkenness as a cardinal virtue. These illicit indulgences [*manáhi*] lasted from Rajab of the year 920, to the end of the year 928, after which time the Khán was, by the favour of Heaven, defended from exposing himself to further censure, as shall, God willing, be related in its proper place.

CHAPTER LII.

ARRIVAL OF AIMAN KHWÁJA SULTÁN FROM TURFÁN TO WAIT ON THE KHÁN.

In the middle of this winter, Aiman Khwája Sultán arrived. The explanation is as follows. In the list given of the offspring of Sultán Ahmad Khán, it was noticed that Aiman Khwája Sultán was the full brother of the Khán. After the death of Sultán Ahmad Khán, when Aksu, on account of the hostility of Amir Jabár Birdi, fell under the domination of Mirzá Abá Bakr, all Sultán Ahmad's children, together with the tribe [*Ulus*],[1] migrated to Turfán and Chálish, and Mansur Khán reigned in his father's stead.

All his brothers were in his service, as was also this Aiman Khwája Sultán, till he attained to adolescence, when, at the instigation of some seditious persons, he laid claim to the throne—an act which resulted in an insurrection [*khuruj*] and much intrigue. At first Mansur Khán acted generously in counselling him to desist and in forgiving him, but finally, since Aiman Khwája Sultán would not cease to urge his claims, Mansur Khán ordered him to be put to death. On Yáráka Atáka, the Khán's trusted servant, was imposed the duty of carrying out the order; but he took Aiman Khwája Sultán to [his own] house and hid him in an underground [chamber], spreading the report that he had put him to death. Not long after this, came news of the Khán's victory over Mirzá Abá Bakr, and the conquest of Káshghar. [Thereupon] Mansur Khán repented his deed, and showed strong marks of regret and sorrow. Yáráka Atáka represented that learned men had said: "'It is an easy matter to deprive a man of his life's breath; but life cannot be restored to a dead man.' I acted in opposition to orders, and have kept him safe." On hearing this the Khán was overjoyed, and expressed his gratitude to Yáráka Atáka, who brought forth Aiman Khwája Sultán from the house. Aiman Khwája Sultán, on being set at liberty, went to Bábáják Sultán, the full brother of Mansur Khán, who had lately settled in Kusan and Bái.

These places Mirzá Abá Bakr had destroyed, and they had remained for some time in ruins, but Bábáják Sultán restored them. He lives there to the present day. Thence, taking leave, [Aiman Khwája] proceeded to Káshghar, and when the Khán heard

[1] It is not clear what *ulus*, or tribe, is alluded to. Probably the family of Ahmad Khán, together with their relations and retainers, is all that is meant; but the word *ulus* is nowhere else used in so restricted a sense.

he was coming, his joy knew no bounds; a new delight sprang up in his heart. In accordance with his frame of mind, he began to sing: "*Har dam az in bágh bari mirasad: Táza tiráz táza tari mirasad.*" (At that time I often heard the Khán sing this song.) [Couplet] . . . . The Khán did all that was possible to make the reception of Aiman Khwája Sultán a splendid one, and in his affection, honoured him so far as to go out himself and receive him [*istikbál*]. He treated him as a brother in his domestic life [*buyutát*]. All that winter was spent in entertainments and banquets, and with the setting in of spring, princely feasts were celebrated in honour of Aiman Khwája Khán. The Khán selected men [as retainers] for him from among all the Moghul tribes. Sárik Mirzá, a Dughlát and nephew of Mir Jabár Birdi, was appointed to be his *Ulusbeg*. The greatest of his Amirs of the right wing [*báránghár*], namely, Munka Beg (who has been mentioned in the battles of Káshghar), Nazar Mirzá, brother to Mir Ayub Begjik, and others, together with a select band chosen from among the various tribes and *Ulus* of the Moghuls, were sent to Aksu [with Aiman Khwája]. The inhabitants of Aksu also, whom Mirzá Abá Bakr, after conquering the place, had led away to Káshghar, were now permitted—nay, rather urged—to return, all together. Thus, in the beginning of the year 921, Aiman Khwája Sultán repaired to Aksu.

At the time of his conquest, Mirzá Abá Bakr had laid waste Aksu and all its dependencies, and had carried its inhabitants away to Káshghar. He had also placed a lightly armed [*jarida*] garrison in Uch,[1] which is a strong place. This garrison carried on a little cultivation of the soil. When [the Khán] conquered Káshghar, he immediately sent to Uch to fortify it, in the same way that Mirzá Abá Bakr had done. Aiman Khwája Sultán, setting out at once, proceeded to Uch, and there pitched his camp. Having restored the cultivation of the town and its districts, he went on, during the second year, to Aksu, where he rebuilt the citadel. The rest of Aiman Khwája Sultán's life will be told in a fitting place.

[1] By *Uch* is meant, no doubt, Ush-Turfan.

CHAPTER LIII.

THE KHÁN (IN SPITE OF PAST ILL-TREATMENT) CRAVES AN INTERVIEW WITH MANSUR KHÁN AND SUBMITS TO HIM.

THE Almighty Creator, at the beginning of the world, so ordained that nothing but good should proceed from those beings whom He had endowed with laudable qualities and a praiseworthy character, so that even when treated badly, they should return good for evil. This truth is instanced by what follows.

It was explained at the beginning of this book, that the Khán was in Moghulistán with his brother,[1] that the Kirghiz were subject to them, and that they lived in comparative comfort and security, till Mansur Khán led an expedition against them. The opposing armies met at Chárun Chálák,[2] and a fierce battle ensued, in which these two brothers were ultimately defeated. On this account they were unable to remain longer in Moghulistán, and all other asylums in the world being closed to them, they were obliged to retreat into the province of Farghána. Sultán Khalil Sultán, the Khan's brother, was drowned by the Sultáns of Sháhi Beg Khán in the river of Akhsi, while the Khán himself was thrown into prison, whence he finally escaped to Kábul in the guise of a kalandar. The details of these events have all been given above. It was at the hands of Mansur Khán that the Khán suffered all these calamities. [Verse] . . . . The enmity of brother to brother is worse than that of other foes. But when the Khán had laid the foundations of a lasting State, had collected a countless host and gathered round him the most distinguished warriors [verses] . . . . the surrounding rulers began to be sorely afraid of his might and majesty. More especially [was he feared by] Mansur Khán, who, having fled from Mirzá Abá Bakr, had retired to Turfán and Chálish, and now had neither strength to oppose, nor place of refuge to fly to. The saying: "Alas! they have stopped my road on six sides," now became applicable to Mansur Khán. Furthermore, Aiman Khwája Sultán had attached himself to the Khán, who recounted to him all he had endured at the hands of Mansur Khán, and opened afresh his old wounds.

All the chiefs of the State, and the nobles, were unanimous in wishing to lead an army against Mansur Khán, and to attack

[1] Khalil Sultan.

[2] This place has been mentioned before under the same form. I cannot identify it, but it seems just possible that it may be the same as the *Jarun* mentioned in the account of one of Timur's invasions of Moghulistan. If this is the case, it lay probably not far to the eastward of Sairám—perhaps about the upper waters of the Talás.

Turfán. They represented that: "When he had the opportunity, Mansur Khán did what has been related; if he is given his own way, he will do such things as cannot be told. It is therefore fitting that we should fall upon him at once, and in such a way that our minds may be set finally at rest with regard to him." To this the Khán replied: "The duty of the young is obedience; that of adults is favour [*ináyat*]. If the young neglect their duty, it is incumbent upon their elders to correct them. . . . .[1] At this time, the elder brother is in the place of the father. To him reparation can be made for disobedience to the father." He then sent several ambassadors [to speak as follows]: "What I have suffered from my elder brother (that is to say, Mansur Khán) was all on account of my own shortcomings. Even if this were not the case, the elder brother is the father's successor, and although he has treated his younger brother with the reverse of kindness, how should this younger brother venture (in his position of son) to overstep the prescribed limits? [Verse] . . . . Forgiveness for past offences is now humbly solicited. May they all be swept from the recesses of your blessed memory. I would, moreover, crave for permission to kiss the carpet at your noble feet. From our [meeting] many advantages will result. One of them being that you will wash away, with the water of good-will, the stains of my offences. Another that (thanks be to God) from this victory our friends will derive strength and elation, while our enemies [will foresee] disaster and despair. If we meet in harmony, our troubles will be at an end, and the backs of all evil-wishers will be broken." Many other advantages were mentioned, which it is needless to repeat. [Verse] . . . .

When Mansur Khán saw all these ambassadors arrive, one after the other, bearing costly gifts, his soul, which had risen to his lips,[2] was refreshed with unbounded joy. After much passing backwards and forwards of envoys, and the discussion of preliminaries, an interview was arranged.

[1] Three lines of rhetoric, on the disobedience of children, are omitted here.—R.
[2] Or: "was about to take flight"; *i.e.*, from fear.—R.

CHAPTER LIV.

TRANSACTIONS OF MANSUR KHÁN.

THE context here demands some further details of the life of Mansur Khán. He was the eldest son of Sultán Ahmad Khán, son of Yunus Khán. The experiences of Sultán Ahmad Khan's elder brother, Sultán Mahmud Khán (which have been touched upon in their proper place in this book, and will be mentioned, in detail in the First Part, are briefly as follows.

[Sultán Ahmad Khán] dismissed the old Amirs of Yunus Khán, and set up in their places some mean persons [*arázil*] whose flattery suited the Khán's nature. To these men he gave up the management of all important affairs of State, and they, with their narrow-minded views and want of judgment, so worked upon the Khán, that he estranged his old friends—that is to say, the Uzbeg Kazák and the kings of the Chaghatái—and made new ones of his old enemies, thinking that they would be his true allies; but these [in the end] ruined him.

Thus Sháhi Beg Khán, after he had, with the assistance of Sultán Mahmud Khán, defeated the Chaghatái and conquered Mávará-un-Nahr, turned against Sultán Mahmud Khán and took Táshkand [from him]. [Verses] . . . . When Sultán Ahmad Khán heard of the helpless condition of Sultán Mahmud Khán, brotherly love began to glow in his heart. Seizing the skirt of fraternal affection with the hand of resolution, he, in the course of the year 907, set out towards Táshkand to the relief of his brother, leaving, in his own place, his eldest son Mansur Khán, with absolute authority and power over the whole of Chálish, Turfán, Bái, Kus, Aksu, and Moghulistán.[1] The events that now followed in Táshkand have been already related. When Ahmad Khán returned, defeated and sick, to his capital Aksu, he was met in state by his son Mansur Khán. After entering the city, he became anxious about his illness, and sent Mansur Khán away to Turfán, where the latter remained till his father's death, when he returned to Aksu. But Sultán Mahmud Khán, despising the sovereignty of Aksu, left it and went to Moghulistán. [Verses] . . . .

Mansur Khán continued to dwell in Aksu, and Amir Jabár Birdi in Uch. This Amir Jabár Birdi was a Dughlát, and filled the post of *Ulusbegi* under Sultán Ahmad Khán, by whom he had been held in the highest honour and esteem. Indeed, he was a wise

[1] The year 907 H. fell in 1501–2. At the time, it will be remembered, Abá Bakr was in possession of the rest of the Moghul dominions.

man and worthy of the rank he held; for he was without an equal as an administrator. [Verses]. . . . In those turbulent days he was of the greatest value. But Mansur Khán, for the reason explained above—namely, that heirs are not always able to estimate the value [of their inheritance]—purposed putting Amir Jabár Birdi to death, saying: "Until I have put him out of the way, I shall never feel safe on the throne." As a fact, the very reverse of this was true. When Amir Jabár Birdi [became aware of this design], though he lamented and bewailed the matter much, he exerted himself in every possible way to avert the impending danger. He continued to carry on the Khán's business and offered explanations [*sukhanán guft*]. But it was of no avail: he saw that nothing but his death would satisfy the Khán. He therefore set about planning his own safety, and sent a messenger to invite Mirzá Abá Bakr to come.

Now this had been the Mirzá's intention, independently of the invitation, so he marched at once and appeared, like a flash of lightning, at the head of 30,000 men. Amir Jabár Birdi offered him the best presents he could [command], and himself became the guide [*yazak*] of the army. He went in advance, while Mirzá Abá Bakr followed after. Mansur Khán, being informed of these movements, took away as many men as he could muster and [started for Turfán], while the rest, together with some of the Amirs, stayed to defend the citadel of Aksu. Mirzá Abá Bakr came up, and took the citadel by storm; then, forming a junction of his troops, with those of Amir Jabár Birdi, he conducted forays against Bái and Kusan. All the inhabitants of those districts were carried off to Aksu, so that the country became entirely depopulated.

Then Amir Jabár Birdi said [to Mirzá Abá Bakr]: "It must be quite evident to you, that I have now gone to too great lengths ever to expect protection at the hands of the Moghul Khákáns. For I have treated them as no one ever treated them before. I have scattered to the winds of perdition their throne, kingdom, and men: their wives and children. My loyalty now prompts me to go again, and utterly devastate Bái, Kusan and Aksu [and to carry off the inhabitants to Káshghar], while Uch must be defended by a light-armed [*jarida*] force. My household and family shall remain with you. You must give me leave to go to Chálish and the mountains around, and I will drive all the inhabitants into your hands, in order that I may make an end of the Moghul Khákáns, and have no longer any cause to fear them." Mirzá Abá Bakr highly approved of these plans, and having allowed Amir Jabár Birdi to depart, carried off his family, together with all the Moghul people. Thus did Amir Jabár Birdi make his wives and family a sacrifice for his own life; for, with the exception of two sons, he sent them all—though with many misgivings [*ihtimám*]—to Káshghar. He displayed so much energy in the whole matter, that he won the entire confidence of Mirzá Abá Bakr, who, leaving his army with him, then returned.

Amir Jabár Birdi drove the inhabitants out of all the towns, districts, open country, and uplands. The owls were left in possession of the cities and villages, while the plains were made over to the antelopes. It would be impossible to give an idea of the numbers of the flocks and herds, and the quantity of treasure that he took in those countries and cities, all of which he carried back to Káshghar. Mirzá Abá Bakr entered Káshghar in great pomp. Mir Jabár Birdi having conducted countless forays with Mirzá Abá Bakr's army, at length left it: he himself going into Moghulistán, while the army returned to Káshghar, driving the flocks before them.

Meanwhile, Mansur Khán repented of the designs he had entertained against Amir Jabár Birdi, and saw that prosperity was impossible without such men as he. So he sent a person after him, with apologies and entreaties to return. Mansur Khán was born of Mir Jabár Birdi's sister. Mir Jabár Birdi knew that Mansur Khán was sorry for what he had done; he therefore made an end of the quarrel [*az niza barkhásta*], for he saw that if he did not go quickly, the effect of separation would be the entire destruction of Mansur Khán. So having accepted apologies and strengthened matters by concluding a covenant, he set forth [to visit Mansur Khán].

There is a story current at the present time, which is very appropriate, and which I give here. Talkhak died in Tirmiz. Before dying, he expressed a wish that he might be buried at a certain cross-way, that his tomb might be high, and that on it might be inscribed in large letters: "Every one who passes by here and repeats the *Fatiha* for my soul, may he be cursed; and if he do not repeat it, may his father be cursed!" Those who were present laughed, and asked: "But how can one avoid both these curses?" [The dying man] replied: "There is one means of escape, and that is to keep away from Tirmiz."[1] This saying applies to the situation of the Moghul Khákáns and Dughlát nobles. For [they reasoned], if they imitated Mir Jabár Birdi [in his behaviour towards Mansur Khán], they would save their own lives, but would be accused of ingratitude and disloyalty; if, on the other

[1] *Tirmiz* is sometimes found written *Termedh.* The city was, in the early Middle Ages, a famous seat of learning and commerce, and stood on the north bank of the Oxus. It was destroyed during the campaigns of Chingiz, but was rebuilt in the fourteenth century, about two miles away from the river bank. During the first half of the fifteenth century, the new town was visited and described by the Moorish traveller Ibn Batuta, who speaks of it as a great city provided with fine markets, numerous gardens, and traversed by streams. It has now passed almost out of existence. (See Defrémery's *Ibn Batuta*, iii., pp. 56, 57, and Yule in Wood's *Oxus*, p. lxx.)

hand (following the example of my uncle), they remained faithful, and stood round the tomb of the late Khán, wailing and weeping, their heads would be struck off then and there: though it might be said of them that they were incapable of a cowardly action. The result of remaining in the service [of the Moghul Kháns] will in the end only be to gain the name of cowards or traitors. [Therefore, it may be said, the only way to avoid these two bad names, is not to remain in the service of the Moghul Kháns, nor to go near them.]

As my maternal uncle Mahmud Khán has said [couplet in Turki] . . . . : "No one ever met with fidelity from the world or its people. Oh, happy that man who has nothing to do with the world!"[1] [Verses.] . . .

But the pearls of these intentions found no place in the shell of the Moghul Khákán's ears. . . .[2] Thanks be to the Most High God that this servant has at length found the means of avoiding them. It were also preferable to abstain from further words on this matter.

To return to the thread of my narrative. Mansur Khán, having given him every possible assurance of safety, took Amir Jabár Birdi back into his service, and after the return [of the Amir], the Khán's affairs began again to improve.

From the year 910, which is the date of [the commencement of] Mansur Khán's disturbed and turbulent reign, to the year 922, the date[3] we have now reached in our history, Mansur Khán lived in Chálish and Turfán. During this period many important events occurred. In those times the brothers [of the Khán's family] quarrelled among themselves, and everybody in the Moghul tribes was rebellious. On this account, Mansur Khán dismissed the Arlát —an ancient order of Amirs—and, bringing the Kirghiz into his power by stratagem, put many of them to death. He once went to war with the Kálmák, and won a signal victory over them.

After these events, his government began to assume an orderly shape, which was due to the wisdom and tact of Mir Jabár Birdi. Towards the end of this period, Bábáják Sultán separated himself from Mansur Khán, and together with his following, proceeded to Kusan. Mansur Khán pursued him, in person, and besieged him. His object, however, was not to destroy Bábáják Sultán, so he sought terms of peace. The answer he received was: "Aiman Khwája Sultán was also [your] brother, and him you killed like a stranger. What reliance can I place in you, that I should make peace?" Now Aiman Khwája Sultán had devised treasonable

[1] The Persian is not clear in the above passages. I have, therefore, followed the Turki.—R.

[2] Here are omitted a passage of two lines containing an untranslatable play on words, and some verses.—R.

[3] A.H. 910 to 922 would be 1504 to 1516 A.D.

plots, and on this account Mansur Khán had ordered Yáráka Atáka to put him to death, but [instead of this] Yáráka Atáka had hidden him in an underground place, as has been already related. When Bábáják Sultán mentioned the affair of Aiman Khwája Khán, Yáráka Atáka saw the Khán was much distressed, and represented: "I had the presumption to disobey the order, [and did not put him to death]." Thereupon Mansur Khán fell to commending Yáráka Atáka, and Aiman Khwája Sultán was brought out. After this, Bábáják surrendered, and peace was made. Mansur Khán then returned, while Aiman Khwája Khán went to Káshghar, as has been mentioned already. Bábáják Sultán stayed on in Kusan, where he is to this day.

After this occurrence, negotiations for a peace ensued between the Khán and Mansur Khán. Mansur Khán came forth from Turfán, Kusan, and Bái, and sent Mir Jabár Birdi in advance. The meeting, which shall be described below, took place in the plains of Arbát.[1]

CHAPTER LV.

BIRTH OF ISKANDAR.

In the month of Jumáda II. 921, new fruit was added to the tree of the Khánate. . . . .[2] As the Khán was the grandson of Sháh Begum, who was descended from Zulkarnain, he was called Iskandar. Learned men have found chronograms for this child's birth. Among them was Mauláná Muhammad Shirázi, who was one of the great *Ulama*, being not only versed in all the sciences, but also a skilled physician. For a space of thirty years he rendered praiseworthy services to the Moghul Khákáns, and was appointed *Sadr-i-Sudur*. Some details of his life will be given below. He discovered the chronogram: "*Sháh-i-Iskandar far*" [a king equal in power to Iskandar]. Khwája Nur-ud-Din Abdul Vahid Tuhuri Kázi, who shall also be mentioned, found the date in: "*Nakhl-i-Iram*" [the tree of Iram]. Many discovered: "*Lashkará shikan*" [army breaker]. There were many more, but I have given as many as I can remember.

At that time, the Khán's health was somewhat affected by his excessive wine-drinking. He, therefore, went to Moghulistán hoping to restore his health by a change of air. On his return, he

[1] *Arbát, Arwát,* or *Aruvát,* is marked on most modern maps to the north-east of Aksu and west of Bai. There was (and perhaps is still) a place called *Arawán,* near Ush in Eastern Farghána.

[2] Five lines of rhetoric omitted.

said to me: "To you, who are like a son to me, I have given my dear sister, who is a pearl in the shell of the Khánate. My hope is that if a child should be born to you, I may be a father to him as well as you. Thus, a child with two loving fathers; two fathers with one happy child. But since you have, up to this time, no offspring, you must look upon this son of mine [Iskandar] as your child, so that what I hoped of you, you may realise in me. If eventually you should have a son, he will be a brother to this child; if you should have no children, you will have no need of another son." Favours and kind words such as these, did he express to me and his sister; we accepted them with gratitude, and feasts were instituted and presents given. The life of Iskandar shall be presently related.

CHAPTER LVI.

REBUILDING OF AKSU AND NEGOTIATIONS OF THE AMBASSADORS OF MANSUR KHÁN AND THE KHÁN.

Aiman Khwája Sultán, having been sent to Aksu, departed thither, and in the spring set about rebuilding the town, while ambassadors went backward and forward, between Mansur Khán and the Khán, to arrange a friendly settlement. In the summer the Khán's health became much impaired by excesses in wine-drinking, as was stated above, and he was finally seized with ague [*tap larza*]. Mauláná Shirázi, who was a talented man and a skilled physician, and who had spent all his life in attendance on the Kháns, pronounced a change of air to be needful. So the Khán betook himself to a place in Moghulistán, not far from Káshghar. But as he did not yet trust the people of Káshghar, he left me in Yárkand, while he himself went on his way. I did all I could to keep order in the country. At the end of the autumn the Khán returned from Moghulistán, in good health; the pure air of those plains having cured him of the malady which indulgence in wine had produced in him. He alighted in Yárkand.

CHAPTER LVII.

DEATH OF HAZRAT MAULÁNÁ MUHAMMAD KÁZI.

In different parts of this history, the life of Hazrat Mauláná has been told, down to the point where he went to Akhsi and its dependencies. Wherever he stayed the people received the blessing of his converse. In that province he gained many followers and devotees, all of whom were honoured by witnessing some miracle or wonderful act. [Verses] . . . .

When the Khán left Akhsi, Hazrat Mauláná remained there. When Suyunjuk Khán came to that town, he waited on Hazrat Mauláná and entreated him to honour Táshkand with a visit. He went to Táshkand, but a short time afterwards died . . . . . [Verses and rhetoric] . . . . His intimates and followers discovered the date of his death in "*Nakd-i-Khwája Ubaid Ullah*" [=922].[1] He was between sixty and seventy years of age, was versed in all sciences, and wrote several interesting and profitable works.

His tracts are text-books for the pious. Among his compositions is the *Salsalat ul Arifin*, written in excellent style. It is divided into three parts. The first of these treats of the manners of Shaikhs and the conditions of discipleship. The second part contains the life of Hazrat Ishán, together with the truths and sayings he uttered in various assemblies, in the language of the country; also some of his miracles and wonders. The third part comprises the sayings and miracles of various pious men. The tongue is incapable of adequately praising this book. There are about fifty parts.

Besides this work, he composed many pamphlets [*rasáil*]. Among them are answers to certain questions which, in the course of different meetings [*majlis*], I had the presumption to put to him. These, together with some rules and maxims, he put into book form, but never found an occasion of giving it to me. After his death, however, his son and successor, Mauláná Kutb-ud-Din Ahmad, sent it to me, and I have copied the whole of it, as it stood, into this work. I know well that, with my lack of literary capacity, this rough copy, written by the pen of carelessness, with the help of ignorance, will have but small merit in the eyes of critics; but I trust that the embodiment of the pamphlet will bring a blessing on my work, and that my shortcomings may be overlooked. I look to the Pardoner of all Sins to forgive me my faults and errors in this Epitome, in consideration of the truths contained in [the Hazrat's] pamphlet. [Verses] . . . .[2]

[1] The year 922 H. began 5 Feb. 1516.

[2] As the Maulana's pamphlet has no reference whatever to the history of the Moghuls, or to any historical subject, it is omitted. It is a purely religious treatise, but is not, I believe, what is usually known as the *Salsalat ul Arifin*. It occupies about four folios of the Persian texts.

CHAPTER LVIII.

MEETING OF MANSUR KHÁN AND SULTÁN SAID KHÁN, AND CONCLUSION OF PEACE BETWEEN THEM.

THE winter was passed in Yárkand, in feasting and merry-making. As Turfán was a two months' journey from Káshghar, the negotiations of the ambassadors, the settlement of the place of meeting and other preliminaries lasted a whole year. In the month of Moharram 922, the Khán started for Aksu. [Verses] . . . . He entered Káshghar in great pomp and splendour. [On the road] I had a fall from my horse and dislocated my right elbow; it was a bad accident, and I was confined for some days in Káshghar before getting well. As soon as the pain began to abate, the Khán set out again, while I remained a few days longer in Káshghar. On my arm becoming cured, I followed the Khán and came up with him at Jái Tuba, whence we proceeded stage by stage to Uch. [Verses] . . . .

At that time Aiman Khwája Sultán was living in Uch, for Aksu was not yet habitable. On the Khán's approach, he came out to meet him with gifts [verses] . . . . and invited him to come and bless his house by alighting there. He entertained the Khán with regal banquets. [Verses] . . . . [Departing again] the Khán passed Aksu and pitched his royal camp at a place called Jám, while Mansur Khán, coming from the opposite direction, reached Arbát, which is seven *farsákhs* from Jám. Mir Jabár Birdi now came and waited on the Khán, and finally settled [under what conditions the two Kháns were to meet]. The two armies were to advance and stand opposite each other in battle array; hostages were then to be exchanged; the two Kháns were to come forward, each attended by thirty men selected from his own army, and were to meet between the two lines [of troops]. As soon as these plans had been agreed upon, I was sent to Mansur Khán as a hostage. Aziz Birdi was appointed to select the men who were to accompany Mansur Khán. I was received with much affection and friendship by Mansur Khán, who poured down honours upon my head. [Verses] . . . .

When the King of the East placed his foot upon the steps of the throne of the firmament, and brought the whole world under the sway of his brightness, repulsing the powers of night, Mansur Khán set his noble foot in the stirrup, and having drawn up his troops, rode forth. On reaching the trysting-place, he sent for Bábáják Sultán and Sháh Shaikh Muhammad, who were his full brothers, and enjoined them to exercise caution and judgment. Aziz Birdi Aghá, standing at the head of the passage [between the lines], told off exactly thirty persons. From the side of Mansur Khán, Sáhib Daulat Begum, sister of Mir Jabár Birdi, and Máhim Khánim, sister [*hamshira*] of Mansur Khán, were given as hostages. The Khán advanced from the other side, accompanied also by thirty persons. At the meeting-place between the armies, awnings [*sáya-bán*] were erected. [Couplet] . . . . Mansur, advancing first, went and seated himself upon a throne under the shade of the awnings. [Couplet] . . . . Then the Khán came, and dismounted at a respectful distance. [Couplet] . . . .

When he had approached within the distance assigned by the Moghul custom, he fell on his knees [*zánu zad*]. Although Mansur Khán was the elder brother, he got up, advanced towards the Khán, and embraced him affectionately [couplet] . . . .; then taking him by the hand, he walked towards the throne. When Mansur Khán was seated on the throne, the Khán rose up and returned to the place where he had first made his obeisance. [Two couplets] . . . . He then offered him such presents as became the dignity of both; while Mir Jabár Birdi, in presenting the gifts [*pishkash*] to Mansur, made an eloquent speech, as is the custom of those who observe the *Tura*. Mansur Khán was pleased with his words, and accepted all the gifts. The Khán having knelt again, stood with his arms respectfully crossed on his breast. Mansur Khán then invited him to come and sit at his side, saying: "I know I am your elder brother, but why should you, with your high rank, be so modest before me, who am in the place of a father to you?" The Khán, having once more made obeisance, expressed his profound respect for Mansur Khán, and returned to his seat. Mansur Khan called him forward again and repeated what he had said before, but with greater emphasis. He, moreover, took the Khán by the hand and drew him towards himself, when the Khán, having knelt again, took a seat beside him. [Couplet] . . . .

Mansur Khán began by asking: "How did you fare in those disturbed times?" To which the Khán, with every token of respect, replied: "Misfortunes that end in success—separations that terminate in union—are not remembered. The sweetness of the end causes the bitterness of the beginning to be forgotten. [Two couplets] . . . . Thanks be to God, that in one moment reparation can be made for what has happened during long years." They went on, then, to discuss policy, military tactics, and justice; they also swore a solemn oath to remain at peace, and to strengthen the bonds of friendship. By the time they had finished all their business, the day was also ended. Mansur Khán next gave the Khán rich presents in the shape of horses and silver, brocades and embroidered robes. At the hour of bidding farewell, they embraced once more, and exchanged the clothes they were wearing and the horses they were riding. They finally separated in the most friendly manner, and each went back to his own army.

When Mansur Khán returned to his own ranks, he called for me and explained all the particulars of the interview, as I have given them above. Thus conversing, he accompanied me from his troops to the camp. He said: "The thirst of longing and the hunger of absence cannot be satisfied with this small quantity of the wine of union." [Verses] . . . . He continued to speak in such terms until we arrived at the camp, which we did at about the middle of the first watch of the night. At sunrise Mansur Khán sent for me, and loaded me with favours and distinctions becoming his own greatness. He then permitted me to return, and having travelled all night, I reached the Khán [on the following day]. The Khán told me what Mansur Khán had said, and showed marks of regret at separation from him. The result of this peace was that soldiers and civilians—in fact, every individual—enjoyed full repose and freedom from anxiety, and testified their thankfulness to the two Kháns.

Ingenious scholars devised many chronograms to commemorate this happy event. Among others, the date was found to be contained in "*Du lashkar ba nishát*"—Two armies in gladness—922 [1516].

CHAPTER LIX.

THE KHÁN'S RETURN AFTER THE PEACE—SUBSEQUENT EVENTS AND VISIT OF BÁBÁJÁK SULTÁN.

[After the conclusion of this affair] the Khán made for Yárkand. At Sungtásh, which is three days' journey from Uch, on the road to Káshghar, he separated from his army, and riding long stages [*ilghár*], arrived at Yárkand in six days. Here new displays of festivity and rejoicing were commenced [verses] . . . . ; and every one, according to his means, made merry and rejoiced.

At the season of the Khán's return to Yárkand, the King of Kings of the Firmament had placed the fourth throne of his sovereignty in the palace of Taurus, and the Prince of the Flowers had pitched his tent on the plains. [Verses] . . . . From the time of his accession to that day, a period of about two years, the Khán had lived in the citadel of Yárkand, both summer and winter. But this year, feeling his mind relieved of all its anxieties, when the season of flowers and foliage came round [verses] . . . . he changed his quarters from the town to the palace of Gul Bágh, [which had been] a favourite residence of Mirzá Abá Bakr. When the temperate days of spring changed to the oppressive heat of summer, the only way to keep in health was to sit under the shade of the trees. On this account the Khán retired to Gul Bágh, and there enjoyed the protection afforded by the shade of his garden. Meanwhile the army and the populace were dwelling in peace, and the nobles and pillars of the State lived in the lap of luxury and magnificence. Every brain had its scheme, and every scheme had a brain [to work it].

All the Amirs came to the palace of the Khán to sit in council; they made the following representation to him: [Most noble Khán] to-day, by the favour of God's assistance, the arm of our State is strong enough to lay low its enemies, and annihilate its opponents at one blow. If you do not take vengeance on your enemies now, when will you be able to do so? If you do not destroy them now, when will you have the power to destroy them? [Verses] . . . .

Thus were the Khán's old projects revived, and he issued a mandate [*yárligh*] for the mustering of troops and preparation for an expedition. At the close of summer [922] he marched for Andiján, to make war on Suyunjuk Khán. He gathered all his army together in Káshghar, and set out from there. On reaching Tuyun Báshi, he resolved upon a hunt, and issued stringent orders for the preparations. On the second day [the beaters] formed a ring. [Three couplets] . . . . When the hunt was at an end, they left that place and proceeded to encamp on the south side of Chádir Kul. There they learnt the approach of Bábáják Sultán. His reason for coming was, that on the occasion of Mansur Khán's interview with the Khán, Bábáják Sultán, being in the service of the former (whose full brother he was) could not go and wait on the Khán. But when autumn came round, he asked permission from Mansur Khán to do so, saying, that if he did not wait on his brother, he would be considered guilty of disrespect. Mansur Khán had given him leave, and he, having set off from his home of Bái and Kusan, was now arriving.

When he reached Káshghar, he learnt that the Khán had [just] left on his way to fight Suyunjuk Khán and to invade Andiján. He immediately moved on after him, and overtook him at Chádir Kul. The Khán, in his brotherly affection, was quite overcome with emotion, and though Bábáják was his junior in years, went out to receive him. He embraced him warmly, and bestowed upon him brotherly attentions and fatherly kindness. [Couplet] . . . . [The Khán said]: "I was then bent on avenging myself on my foes: to have summoned my brother at that juncture would have been open to misinterpretation. Thank God that we have both obtained the fulfilment of our wishes. The arrival of my brother is as the commencement of conquest and victory." So saying, the two brothers (Conquest and Victory, as it were) rode off side by side towards Andiján.

On reaching Arpa Yázi, they hunted the wild ass,[1] the deer [*gavazan*] and other animals. So much game did they kill, that the beasts of the plains and the fowls of the air were able to feast upon the flesh, without fighting for it among themselves. [Couplet] . . . . The Khán, from his ambush, brought down some quarry with every arrow he shot. When the hunt was over, a sumptuous banquet was prepared, in a delicious spot where the air was fresh as in the garden of Iram, and where [the heavens] seemed filled with birds from Paradise. Bábáják Sultán and Aiman Khwája Sultán were in attendance on their brother the Khán, surrounded by a distinguished assembly. [Two couplets] . . .

When the feast was over, Bábáják Sultán represented apologetically to my uncle: "At the beginning of the spring I was guilty of a neglect of courtesy; I had longed for years to have the happiness of waiting upon you, but my aspiration could not then be realised. After that opportunity had elapsed, I saw that it would be respectful on my part, to come to your court at Yárkand and sprinkle my eyes with the dust of your palace. On reaching Káshghar, I heard of your expedition [against Andiján], whereupon I set out in all haste after you, not waiting to collect an army or make ready the necessaries for an expedition. Thus did I come, [thinking] this time the preparations have been delayed; but next time [that I go against Andiján] my arrangements shall be perfect, and I will bring into my service all the Sultáns and soldiers, with their arms, that are to be found in my country. I will collect such a mighty host that it will be evident to friend and foe alike, that the Khán has, in his train, subjects who can rival the kings of the earth. [If this proposition is acceptable to you, well and good]; if not, it will do me no harm to change my plans. I am ready to devote myself, body and soul, to the Khán."

In reply to these words the Khán said: "For many years I have longed to see this dear brother. The most fitting form of thanksgiving is that we should return now, and spend a few days together. We will devote ourselves, until next spring, to preparations such as those described by our dear brother; we will then go forward. At the present time the occasion is not suitable; the season is too far advanced. While the enemy remains where he is,

[1] The Persian texts have *Khar-gura* as the name of this animal, and the Turki text the ordinary one of *Kulán*. It is the *Asinus hemionus*—the *Jigatai* of the Mongols and the *Kiang* of the Tibetans. The wild ass of Western India, though a somewhat different animal, is known by almost the same name as that used here by Mirza Haidar—viz., *Ghor Khar*.

we can advance whenever we choose. [Even though we do not go to Andiján at all, nothing will be lost."] So they turned back from Arpa Yázi, and travelled by a direct route towards Káshghar. Bábáják Sultán accompanied the Khán to Yárkand, and there they gave themselves over to feasting. The Khán bestowed countless presents and inestimable favours upon him; while each of the Amirs offered presents according to his rank and means. [Verses] . . . . When these hospitable entertainments had been concluded, Bábáják Sultán, having obtained leave to return to his own country, rode away in that direction. These events happened in the autumn of the aforesaid year [922 = 1516].

CHAPTER LX.

THE KHÁN'S HOLY WAR AGAINST SÁRIGH UIGHUR AND THE REASON FOR HIS TURNING BACK.

THE winter was passed in the festivities and enjoyments, above described . . . .[1] The Khán's mind had always been occupied with plans for making a holy war [*ghazát*], and after much thought he finally decided [whom he should attack]. Between Khotan and Khitái there was a race of infidels called Sárigh Uighur, and upon these people he proceeded to make a holy war. It is a twelve days' journey from Yárkand to Khotan, and most of the stages are without cultivation or inhabitants. When the Khán reached Khotan, a change in his health became evident. The holy war is one of the supports of Islám and a plenary duty. The Khán desired to discharge this obligation towards the faith; but now that his health failed him, he was obliged to appoint certain Amirs to perform the duty for him, and having thus relieved himself of this necessity, he returned [to Yárkand]. On the homeward journey, cups of wine were brought every morning, and drinking went on all through the day, so that [the Khán and his companions] were generally unable to distinguish the light from the darkness. At the end of a few days they reached Yárkand. In the autumn of that year, the expedition against the Kirghiz took place.

Those Amirs who had been sent against the Sárigh Uighur, after spending two months in the plains between Khotan and Khitái,

[1] Here are omitted ten lines of florid description, regarding the effects of spring upon nature.

returned in safety, laden with plunder, but without having seen or heard anything of the infidels.[1]

CHAPTER LXI.

THE KIRGHIZ CAMPAIGN AND THE CAPTURE OF MUHAMMAD KIRGHIZ.

In the account of the conquest of Káshghar, it was mentioned that Muhammad Kirghiz had come from Moghulistán and, in those days of strife and turmoil, had rendered good service. After the conquest he became possessed of much spoil and booty. Moreover, on his departure, the Khán had loaded him with valuable presents, such as sword-belts, vases, and drinking-cups of gold and silver. [Verses] . . . . On his return to Moghulistán all the Kirghiz had submitted to him. He conducted plundering parties into Turkistán, Táshkand, and Sairám, and created much alarm. The Shaibáni Sultáns in those districts found great difficulty in repulsing him.

On one occasion he made on inroad on Turkistán, and had started to return. At that time Abdullah Sultán, the son of Kuchum Khán, was not yet Khán,[2] but he was Governor of Turkistán. He

[1] The country of the *Sárigh Uighur*, or Yellow Uighurs (as we have seen in the note at p. 9), is probably to be sought for to the eastward of Chárchán, or perhaps nearly south of Lake Lob; though to judge from the indication of its position, derived by Dr. Bretschneider from the *Ming Shi*, it would seem to have lain somewhat farther eastward, or to the north of the Zaidam valley. It appears from Mirza Haidar's statement that the expedition occupied two months, as if the country of the Sárigh Uighurs might reasonably be looked for about one month's journey east of Khotan. The *Sárigh Uighur* are spoken of, not only in the Ming annals, but in those of the Yuans, as *Sa-li Wei-wu-erh;* while it is possible that the district of An-ting, mentioned by the Ming writers, may also be meant for the Sárigh Uighur country. Plano Carpini (the Franciscan monk who visited the court of Mangu Kaan, as the envoy of Pope Innocent IV. in 1245–47) also mentions a nation of *Sari Huiur*, among those conquered by Chingiz. Again, Abel Rémusat tells of an envoy sent from Khotan to the Chinese court in 1081, who reported that between Khotan and the Tangut country (this last would include probably the Zaidam valley) he had to cross the great desert of the "yellow-headed *Hoei-he*" (Hoeï-he à tête jaune). Rémusat raises the question whether this denomination refers to the colour of the head-dress worn by these people, like in the cases of the Kará Kalpák, the Kizil-básh, and others, or whether it points to the existence of a Turkish tribe with light hair. Judging from the numerous instances, in Central Asia, of tribes or peoples being named by their neighbours after the colour of their head-dress, it would seem likely that some yellow cap, or turban, that they may have worn, would be sufficient to account for the name. It would also seem quite likely, from the situation of their territory, that the Sárigh Uighur were a remnant of the inhabitants of the old Uighur states which lay south of the Tian Shan, and which have been mentioned in Secs. IV. and V. of the Introduction to this volume. Like the Aryan communities in Shighnán, Wakhán, etc., some sections of the Uighurs, from dwelling in remote mountain tracts, may have preserved their national characteristics and name, till a later date than the mass of the population from which they sprang. (Bretschneider, i., p. 263; Rémusat, *Hist. de la Ville de Khotan*, p. 95.)

[2] He became Khan in 1540, but reigned only six months (Howorth, ii., p. 723.)

immediately set off in pursuit of Muhammad Kirghiz, and overtook him when he was at some distance from the town. Muhammad Kirghiz turned upon him, and they closed in battle. After a [short] engagement the day was decided in favour of the Kirghiz. Most of their enemies they killed, but Abdullah Sultán was captured, kept by Muhammad Kirghiz for one day, and then sent back to Turkistán with the rest of the survivors. [Muhammad Kirghiz] sent their Khán a few horses, arms, and other suitable gifts, with the following excuse: "I made a vow that if any of the Shaibáni Sultáns should fall into my hands, I would release them. I have been true to my word, and trust that I am forgiven." When the Khán heard this he was enraged, and in the autumn of the year 923 marched upon Moghulistán with an army, to punish Muhammad Kirghiz. [Verses] . . . .

He assembled his forces in Káshghar. Khwája Ali Bahádur was appointed "Yazak" of that army. In the Turki language they called a *Karávul* [picquet or guard] "*Yazak*." On reaching Káfir Yári [they were joined by] Aiman Khwája Sultán, who had come from Aksu by way of Sárigh-at-Akhuri. In the night it was decided that the Khán should proceed by way of Báris Káun, and Aimán Khwája Sultán by way of Jauku.[1]

On the next day, Aiman Khwája Sultán marched off on the Jauku road, while the Khán proceeded in the direction of Báris Káun. As they were descending from the pass of Báris Káun, Khwája Ali sent two men of the Kirghiz, whom he had captured, with news that [Muhammad Kirghiz] and his followers were lying on the shores of Issigh Kul, at the mouth of the Báris Káun [stream], ignorant [of the approach of the enemy]. Now Issigh Kul is a month's march from Káshghar. That day they hastened their march and reached the mouth [of the pass], which is known as Hujra, at the hour of afternoon prayers. The Khán, attended by a few of his chief officers, went [to reconnoitre] and from a distance espied the tents and pasture-grounds of the enemy. After the sun's disc had sunk into darkness—when Jonas had entered the fish's mouth—the commanders gave orders that of every ten men, four were to be fully armed in the centre of the force, and six were to be equipped for rapid movements [*chápkun*]; also that every man was to make ready his arms and be prepared for an assault. By midnight all were assembled and in order. When the sun rose . . . .[2] the army was drawn up in battle array on the level ground. All stood perfectly still, and the verse of "the deaf

[1] Evidently the passes of *Barskun* and *Zauka* (as shown on our maps) which lead across the range bounding the Issigh-Kul valley on the south. *Káfir-Yári* must have been near the southern end of these passes, and *Sárigh-At* some distance to the south-east. (See Kostenko's *Turkistan*, vol. ii., pp. 66–7.)

[2] The usual metaphor on sunrise is omitted in this passage, and will hereafter usually be omitted or abridged.

and the dumb" was recited. After a short interval, when it was seen that the whole army was in perfect readiness and order, there came a sudden blast from the trumpets and horns, mingled with the sounding of drums and cymbals and snorting of horses. That portion of the army which had been told off for the attack, suddenly let loose the reins of patience [verses] . . . . and rushed down. The whole of the attacking [*chápkunchi*] party advanced, while the centre, as pre-arranged, remained in one body and supported the assaulters. When the sun had fully risen, Taka, the brother of Khwája Ali, who had distinguished himself by former services (which have been mentioned above), brought Muhammad Kirghiz bound before the Khán. The Khán said to him: "Although, by the laws of the Tura, you are guilty of death, I will nevertheless, out of benevolence, spare your blood." And he issued a mandate for his imprisonment, under the charge of my uncle. The soldiers were enriched with his droves of horses, his flocks of sheep, and his strings of camels; while all the Kirghiz whom they had made prisoners, were set at liberty. [Verses] . . . . Having remained on the spot a few days, the Khán set out at his ease for the capital, Káshghar, which, by the help of God, he reached at the beginning of the winter.

CHAPTER LXII.

DAULAT SULTÁN KHÁNIM, DAUGHTER OF YUNUS KHÁN, COMES FROM BADAKHSHÁN TO KÁSHGHAR.

I HAVE mentioned above, in enumerating the offspring of Yunus Khán, that the youngest of all was Daulat Sultán Khánim. At the devastation of Táshkand, she fell into the hands of Timur Sultán, son of Sháhi Beg Khán, and remained in his haram till Bábar Pádisháh captured Samarkand, when she joined the Pádisháh. With the departure of the latter for Kábul, she separated from her nephew and went to Mirzá Khán, who was also her nephew, and remained [with him] in Badakhshán. Mirzá Khán treated her as his own mother. On the Khán's return from Aksu, he sent for her; Daulat Sultán Khánim being his paternal aunt. The messengers bore her gifts from the Khán in the shape of horses, vessels of gold and silver and fine cloths. While the Khán was away on his expedition against the Kirghiz, she arrived at Yárkand from Badakhshán. On his return from the campaign he went to visit his aunt, and thus all her relations—all of us to whom the Khánim was either maternal or paternal aunt—had the felicity of meeting her. She remained there to the end of her precious life. An account of her end will be given at the close of the Khán's history.

CHAPTER LXIII.

CELEBRATION OF THE MARRIAGES OF AIMAN KHWÁJA SULTÁN AND SHÁH MUHAMMAD SULTÁN.

WHEN Aiman Khwája Sultán came from Turfán, he asked my uncle's daughter in marriage. My uncle willingly granted his request, and from that time forward was busy with preparations for the event. This winter the marriage festivities began.

Sháh Muhammad, son of Sultán Muhammad Sultán, son of Sultán Muhammad Khán, was still a child when his father and grandfather, together with many others, were put to death by Sháhi Beg Khán. One of the Uzbeg Amirs, taking pity on him, saved him. When the Emperor went from Kábul to Kunduz, that Uzbeg sent off Sháh Muhammad Sultán to Kunduz, where he joined the Emperor, and remained in his service until the latter returned to Kábul, when he obtained permission to join the Khán in Káshghar. [This was] one year after the conquest of Káshghar. The Khán treated him as a son and honoured him even above Bábá Sultán, his brother's son, and Rashid Sultán, his own son. While the festivities in honour of Aiman Khwája Sultán's marriage with my uncle's daughter were proceeding, it occurred to the Khán to give in marriage to Sháh Muhammad Sultán, his sister Khadija Sultán Khánim, whose story has been already related. After Jahángir Mirzá, son of Mirzá Abá Bakr, had been assassinated by some unknown hand, this Khadija Sultán Khánim, having survived him, had remained, respected and honoured, in the Khán's haram.

Thus these two important marriages were celebrated at one time. . . . . .[1]

When some time had been passed in feasting and rejoicing, an assembly of all the nobles, great men and pillars of the State, was convened, who, in the first place, fastened the marriage knot of the daughter of the Khán with Aiman Khwája Sultán, and after that, of Khadija Sultán Khánim (my maternal uncle's daughter,

[1] About sixteen lines of rhetoric, interspersed with verses descriptive of the banquets and festivities, are left out here.—R.

and the Khán's full sister) with Sháh Muhammad Sultán. . . .[1] At the same time I built myself a house, and by way of compliment, some learned men invented chronograms to commemorate the date of the event [923=1517][2]

CHAPTER LXIV.

BEGINNING OF THE QUARRELS BETWEEN THE KHÁN AND MIRZÁ KHÁN. THE KHÁN'S FIRST INVASION OF BADAKHSHÁN.

DURING the summer[3] which followed this winter, the Khán invaded Badakhshán. It came about in this way. In the story of Mirzá Abá Bakr, it was stated that after the reign of Khusrau Sháh, the Mirzá had subdued several of the upper *Hazára* [districts] of Badakhshán, such as Sárigh Chupán, Ghund, Parváz, Yarkh, Pasár and Shiva-i-Shighnán.[4] Before Khusrau Sháh was able to adopt any plan for avenging himself, he sustained a defeat at the hands of Sháhi Beg Khán. But when Sháhi Beg Khán established himself in the kingdom of Khusrau Sháh, the Mir of the Hazára refused to yield to him, and after a few engagements, the Uzbeg were repulsed. In those days, all the upper defiles [*tang-i-bálá*] of Badakhshán were held by Mirzá Abá Bakr.

After Mirzá Khán had established his power in Badakhshán, he was still trammelled [*darmánda*] by the hostility of the Uzbeg. Nor was he able to restrain the usurpations of Mirzá Abá Bakr. [The country extending] from the upper defiles [*tang-i-bálá*] as far as Sárigh Chupán, had fallen under the jurisdiction of Káshghar. "When your enemies are occupied with each other, sit down at your ease with your friends;" this saying applies to the

[1] Three lines of rhetoric omitted.—R.

[2] This is given in a verse of four lines containing the words:—*ba daulat Mirza Haidar* = 923.—R.

[3] Viz., the summer of 924, or 1518 A.D.

[4] All these names are easily recognised except *Parváz*. At first sight it would appear to stand for *Darwáz*, and I believe that to be the place intended, although the initial letter cannot be read as a *D* in any of the MSS. The Turki MS., which is usually the most perfect and trustworthy on the subject of names, specially points the letter in order to make it a *P*. Nevertheless I suspect that it is only a misrendering of a little known name. The other places named, all point to the direction of *Darwáz*, and there is every probability that, up till quite recent times, it was regarded as a Hazára (or hill district) of Badakhshán, equally with the various divisions of Wákhán, Shighnán, etc. Ghund and Shiwa are marked on all maps; Pasár is the upper division of Roshán, in which stands the village of Tásh-Kurghán, or Sonáb on the Bartang; while Yárkh, or Yárokh, is a small village and district at the lower end of Roshán, near the border of Darwáz. *Paryán*, near Jarm in Badakhshán, might possibly be a reading of *Parváz*, but it does not lie in the direction towards which the author is obviously pointing.

state of affairs [at that time]. During twelve years, the districts above the upper gorges were outside of Badakhshán, and formed a part of Káshghar. The Khán, therefore, after his conquest of Káshghar, ordered those districts to be divided into [administrative] sections as if they formed part of the province of Káshghar. Thither he sent Mir Beg Muhammad, whose story has been told above, and during [his] government, Wakhán was a *Hazára* of the *Hazáraját* of Badakhshán.

The people of Badakhshán call the frontier [between Badakhshán and Wakhán] *Darázukhán*. The Káshghari call it *Sárigh Chupán*. The people of Darázukhán took violent possession of it and appealed to Mirzá Khán for protection.[1] [They said: "Let us become the subjects of Mirzá Khán."] So Mirzá Khán took possession of the country without hesitation, his claim being that it belonged originally to Badakhshán: nay more, that Badakhshán was but another name for these *Hazárajàt*. Mirzá Abá Bakr had taken it by force. With the extinction of Mirzá Abá Bakr's power, the region should again fall within its original [kingdom of Badakhshán]. Everything returns to its prime origin. [Mirzá] Khán also contended as follows: "In consequence of Mirzá Abá Bakr's conquests, this country was cut off from its ancient attachment and was, for twelve years, under the jurisdiction of Káshghar. The Emperor, with the help of his brave troops, delivered into my power the regions usurped by Mirzá Abá Bakr. If you desire to have this kingdom it will be necessary, in the first place (on account of my relationship to the Emperor), that I should send him a salutation and beg him to despatch an army to assist me, as I am too weak [to act independently]. . . . When so requested he may answer: 'that country which I have unlocked with the key of conquest, you may take possession of without fear.'"[2] After

[1] The three last sentences are obscure, and read somewhat differently in the different texts; but I believe the true sense to be preserved in the translation. The name of *Darázukhán* is new to me: I know it neither locally, nor in any book or document, modern or ancient. It evidently originates with some Persian or Ghalcha (not Turki) speaking people. Most probably it was peculiar to the locality itself, and is now obsolete. It may be mentioned also, that the first two syllables of the name have no connection with the word *dara*, meaning a valley or gorge: that word is differently spelled. I suspect that the term intended is *Darázi-i-Wakhan*, or *Daráz-Wakhan*, and that it points to the long narrow valley of the upper Panjab, sometimes known in modern days as *Sarigh Chupán* or *Sarhad*. The word *tangi* for "a narrow" or "a strait" is often used, and even *balai* is heard occasionally for "a height" or "small table-land." It appears to me quite possible, therefore, that in the colloquial language of people who have to name briefly, and for practical purposes, the various features of a mountainous country, such a term as *darázi* may easily have grown up out of the adjective *dráz*, or *long*. Parallel instances to this kind of adjectival nomenclature are to be found in English, in such terms as the "narrows" of the Hugli, the "broads" of Norfolk, the "flats" in New South Wales, etc.

[2] This speech is so obscure and involved, that it is only possible to give a brief and freely translated abridgment of it. When fully and literally translated, it makes no sense; and even in the few sentences now standing in the text, I am

informal communications, such as these, had passed between [the two Kháns] the matter was finally concluded by the Khán marching against Badakhshán.

At the time when he determined upon this, one of Mirzá Abá Bakr's sons, whom my uncle had protected [and cared for] as a child of his own, ran away; the report got abroad that he had gone to Suyunjuk Khán to inform him of the Khán's movements, and to induce him [to attack] Káshghar. On this account I was left in Káshghar, where I busied myself with the management of all that was important in the affairs of that country. Mirzá Abá Bakr's son was overtaken on the road, and put to death by some persons who had been sent in pursuit of him.

The Khán advanced into Badakhshán and carried all before him. Mirzá Khán, helpless and in despair, took refuge in Kala-i-Zafar, and gnawed his hands with the teeth of regret, for having done what had been better left undone. When the Khán saw that absolute ruin had fallen upon [Mirzá Khán] and his country, he was moved to pity and withdrew. Mirzá Khán, moreover, realising his own [weakness] did not make any further attempt to overstep his boundaries. Down to the present day that country remains under Káshghar.

Thus was the dust of dissension raised between those two relations on account of a few acts of inhumanity. To the end of their lives they carried on official intercourse, but their protestations of friendship were usually tainted with insincerity; while [the people of] the country itself, were faithful neither to Mirzá Khán at the beginning, nor to the Khán afterwards. In short, the Khán withdrew from Badakhshán with pomp and ceremony, and on reaching Yárkand, his capital, gave himself up to all kinds of rejoicing and pleasure.

---

not sure that the author's meaning is correctly conveyed. The broad facts, however, remain: that Sultan Said Khan based his right to Sárigh Chupán on Mirza Abá Bakr's conquest and tenure of the district for twelve years, while, in the meantime, he had become the Mirza's successor, and heir to his kingdom. Mirza Khan contended that Sárigh Chupán was an integral part of Badakhshán, and had been wrongfully detached by the superior force of Abá Bakr. He confessed himself too weak to offer armed resistance, but put forward the desire of the inhabitants to live under his rule. He also reminded the Khan that it was his cousin Baber, who had put him in possession of Badakhshán (alluding to the events of 913, or 1507) and threatened to call him in again. But the Khan, feeling himself the stronger, and knowing perhaps, that Baber was too much engaged in India, at this time, to take any active interest in Badakhshán, cut all argument short by marching on Kila-Zafar.

CHAPTER LXV.

THE KHÁN'S SECOND INTERVIEW WITH MANSUR KHÁN.

In the following year, Mansur Khán purposed visiting his beloved paternal aunt, Daulat Sultán Khánim, in order that, by looking on her kind face, his grief at the loss of his father might be mitigated.[1] The Khán having agreed to this, [Mansur Khán] set out for Aksu in the summer of that year, and in the same manner, on the same spot, and with similar formalities, as on the occasion of their first interview, they met, and the bonds of affection were drawn tighter. After this, each returned to his own seat of government. From this date—926—to 928 [1520–22] the Khán and his people enjoyed perfect repose and freedom from care, nothing occurring which would be worthy of record.

CHAPTER LXVI.

CONCLUSION OF THE AFFAIRS OF BÁBAR PÁDISHÁH AFTER HIS RETURN TO KÁBUL. DEATH OF HIS BROTHER SULTÁN NÁSIR MIRZÁ. CAUSE OF THE INSUBORDINATION OF HIS AMIRS.

That point in Bábar Pádisháh's history has been reached, at which he returned from Kundáz to Kábul. He committed Kábul to the care of his brother Sultán Násir Mirzá, who [however] died from excessive indulgence in wine in the course of the year 921. [Couplet] . . . . Ghazna had belonged to Sultán Násir Mirzá, and after his death a dispute arose among the Amirs of that town, which took the form of a mutiny, in which all the Moghuls and the rest of the people in the Emperor's service joined. As for example, Mir Shiram, the uncle of the Emperor's mother, who had spent all his life in the Emperor's service; his brother, Mir Mazid, Jaka, Kul Nazar, and others; also of the Chaghatái and Tájik Amirs, Mauláná Bábá Bashághiri and his brother Bábá Shaikh. This Mauláná Bábá was one of the associates [*sharik*] of the village of Bashághir in Samarkand. He won such favour with the Emperor that, when the latter took Mávará-un-Nahr, he gave Mauláná Bábá the government of Samarkand, Uratippa, and part of Kuhistán. Others [who rebelled were] Mir Ahmad, whose

[1] The Turki MS. substitutes for this passage: "being prompted thereto by the extreme warmth of his affection for her."—R.

story has been given above, and his brother Kitta Beg (the one being Governor of Táshkand, and the other of Sairám) Maksud Karak, Sultán Kuli, Chunák, and others. These were all distinguished Amirs and great chiefs. But Satan took possession of their brains, and put there, in the place of sound reason, vainglory and wickedness, which are the outcome of cursed natures.

They rose in rebellion, putting round their necks the accursed collars left behind by Mir Ayub. In short, after a few intrigues and skirmishes, a pitched battle was fought between themselves and the Emperor. As soon as the opposing troops had been drawn up facing each other, the son of Amir Kásim Kuchin, named Amir Kambar Ali, arrived from Kunduz with a powerful force, and the rebels were defeated. [A proverb] . . . . Several of them were captured [and met with their due reward; others fled in shame to Káshghar.] Among these were Mir Shiram and his brothers, who [on the occasion of the Khán's first interview, and conclusion of peace, with Mansur Khán] had gone to wait on the Khán, and had remained for some time in his service. They were ashamed and dejected. Mir Mazid, on account of insufficient means of livelihood, went to Tibet in hopes of plunder. But at Ghazwa [1] a stone fell on his head, and he was killed.

Mir Shiram, likewise, finding it impossible to stay near the Khán, returned to the Emperor, who with his usual benevolence, received him kindly, and closing the eye of wrath on his wrongdoings, opened the eye of favour upon past services. He, however, soon afterwards, left this faithless world. The Emperor, having become firmly established in Kábul, marched upon Kandahár, which was then in the hands of Sháh Beg, son of Zulnun [2] Arghun, as mentioned above. He besieged it for five years. At length, Sháh Beg, having resolved on flight, went to Sivi, and thence to Tatta, which he took, together with Ucha and Bakar, [3] as will be mentioned in the proper place. The Emperor, having captured Kandahár, proceeded to Hindustán. He made several inroads, but retired after each one. At last, he met, in a pitched battle at Pánipat, the Ughán Sultán, Ibráhim, [4] the son of Sultán Iskandar, who was king at that time. [5] Ibráhim's army numbered more

[1] The word appears rather as *Ghazwa* in one text, but the others mention no place-name. I can find no name to answer to Ghazwa in Ladak, or on the road to it.

[2] This name, here and elsewhere, has been spelled *Zulnun* for convenience of recognition of a historical personage; but the proper spelling should be *Zu'un Nun*—as in the original texts.

[3] This would mean that he conquered Sibi and the whole of Sind from the Delta of the Indus up to near Multan; for of the many places in upper India bearing the name of *Uch*, or *Ucha*, the one indicated here is the ancient town situated on the Panjnad, 70 miles S.S.W. of Multan. See note 2, p. 431). All these names are easily recognised.

[4] The Afghan Sultan, Ibrahim Lodi. *Ughán* should read *Aoghán*.

[5] The battle of Pánipat, April 21, 1526.

than 100,000 men, but the Emperor utterly defeated him with 10,000 men. He and his army became possessed of so much treasure, that all the world, from there to Rum and to Khitái, benefited by it. The rich brocades of Rum and the embroidered satins of Khitái, which are scarce in those countries, were found in ass-loads. All this will be explained presently.

CHAPTER LXVII.

SETTLEMENT OF MOGHULISTÁN AND THE KIRGHIZ. BEGINNING OF RASHID SULTÁN'S CAREER.

In the year 928 [1522] the Khán conceived the plan of invading Moghulistán, and subduing the Kirghiz. He was prompted thereto by several considerations, the first of which was as follows: It has been mentioned that in the year 923 he had made Muhammad Kirghiz prisoner, because he, after having taken Abdullah, son of Kuchum Khán, in battle, had let him go free again, and had sent some poor excuses [for his action] to the Khán. For this he was detained in prison for five years, and the Kirghiz, who [all this time] were without a chief, carried plunder and rapine into the territories of Turkistán, Sairám, Andiján, and Akhsi; they had been guilty of many excesses, carrying off into bondage many Musulmán women and children. Although these provinces were under the government of the Shaibán, and these people were his old enemies, the Khán, being a pious and God-fearing man, was offended. He determined to avert this misfortune from the Musulmáns, and thereby to secure a high place in the next world and a good name in the present one. Besides this, Khwája Ali Bahádur, whose valiant and worthy services have been spoken of above, had, according to his natural instincts, a great longing for Moghulistán. He always complained of town life, and pined for the plains of Moghulistán. He had been appointed *Atábeg* to Bábá Sultán, son of Khalil Sultán (and a nephew of the Khán), and had had the care of his education from the age of seven till he was fifteen.

He represented to the Khán: "By the grace of God, the Moghul *Ulus*—both man and beast—have so greatly increased in numbers, that the wide grazing grounds of Káshghar have become too confined for them, and frequent quarrels arise concerning pasture. If you will issue a decree [to sanction my doing so], I will take Bábá Sultán into Moghulistán, subdue the whole of that country, and reduce the affairs of the Kirghiz to order, so that our people may have ample pasture and quiet minds." The Khán quite approved of this proposal, and held a consultation with his Amirs, who were unanimous in their concurrence, with the exception of my uncle, who said: "The first part of this plan is most reasonable, but it is not advisable to send Bábá Sultán. For the Moghuls, being originally from Moghulistán, have a natural attachment to that country, and as soon as it is conquered they will all wish to return thither. If Bábá Sultán is there, he will be offended should we forbid [the Moghuls going there]; and should we not forbid them, the whole mass of them will rush in, the inevitable result of which will be confusion and discord. Instead of [Bábá], let us send Rashid Sultán, your son; let him become ever so powerful, that cannot injure you; and if it is seen fit to hinder the people from migrating into Moghulistán, he, at any rate, will not object. If they should do so [there is nothing to be feared, for he is your son]."

In the meantime, Khwája Ali Bahádur died from excessive wine-drinking. Thus the conduct of the expedition devolved upon Rashid Sultán. Now it happened that at this time my sister (by the daughter of Sayyid-as-Sádát Khávand-záda Sultán Muhammad Arhangi) had been wedded to Bábá Sultán. Nevertheless my uncle did not allow this family tie to stand in the way, but caused Rashid Sultán to be appointed for the enterprise. Bábá Sultán was much offended, but my uncle feared nothing; he persisted in pushing forward Rashid Sultán, and proposed a plan which shall be mentioned later.

It is now necessary to give some account of the country of Moghulistán. No book contains an exact description of its localities: though incidentally, in some histories, the names of a few towns are given, and in the *Suvar-i-Akálim* and the *Taarif-i-Buldán* may be found some notices. For the most part these accounts are inaccurate; but all that can be verified in them, I will state here in abridgment.

CHAPTER LXVIII.

EXTRACTS FROM THE JAHÁN-KUSHÁI OF ALÁ-UD-DIN MUHAMMAD JUVAINI.[1]

(I HAVE copied exactly what the author has written descriptive of Moghulistán). Thus it is written in the *Jahán-Kushái*, that the dwelling, original seat, and birthplace of the Tátár was a valley devoid of cultivation;[2] the length and breadth of which was seven or eight months' journey. It is bounded on the east by the country of Khitái, on the west by the province of Uighur, on the north by Kará Kiz and Sálinkái,[3] and on the south by a side [*jánib*] of Tangut. Of these four limiting countries [*hudud*], mentioned in the *Jahán-Kushái*, Khitái is definitely known, and [can be] specified. But what [the author] calls 'Uighur' is quite unknown at the present time; it is not understood which country is meant.[4] Nor is anything now known of Kará Kiz and Salinkái, nor have any places been discovered with such names. The name of Tangut is frequently mentioned in Moghul histories. At the outset of Chingiz Káhn's conquests, he sent an army thither. Uktái Káán also, when settling his dominions, sent some persons to Tangut, among other places; and from the way it is spoken of in histories, it was evidently a very important province. At that time the king of this country bore the name of Shidarku. Most histories state that his army numbered 800,000 men. However, at the present time it is not even known where it was. Thus it is impossible to say anything about those limiting countries which are specified in books.[5]

[1] The heading is somewhat misleading, for the chapter is not an "extract" from the *Jahán-Kushai*, but rather an account of the author's own, based on that book.

[2] From the Koran S. XIV., v. 40.—R.

[3] *Kara Kiz* would be Lake Zaisan, or the place of that name on its banks; *Salinkai*, the Selenga river in northern Mongolia.

[4] The author of the *Jahán Kushai* (writing about 1259 A.D.) has perhaps better reason for making the Uighur country the western border of Moghulistan than Mirza Haidar gives him credit for. He is alluding, no doubt, to the kingdom of the Ilak Kháns in Turkistan and to Mavara-un-Nahr, which was under the rule of an Uighur dynasty down to about the year 1213, and consequently almost to within the writer's own lifetime. (See note, p. 287.)

[5] It was towards the end of the career of Chingiz, that *Shidarku* became king of Tangut; indeed the campaign which Chingiz undertook against that country, at the close of the year 1225, was his last. Tangut was, as Mirza Haidar says, a powerful kingdom at that time. It played a great part in Chinese history for about a hundred years, and Tangut rulers conquered large tracts of territory from the Chinese and the Uighurs. It may be said to have included, in its best days, all the regions lying between Turfan and the Chinese province of Shansi, together with Zaidam—the homeland of the people—and some portions of northern Tibet. The name of the king here mentioned is variously written—*Shidarku*

In the same way, some of the towns in Moghulistán are mentioned by name and described, in standard works. Among them is Balá-Sákun, which in the *Suvar-i-Akálim* is reckoned among the cities of Khitái, and called 'Khán Báligh'; while in Moghulistán and Kará Khitái they have written the same 'Balá Sákun.' They have applied the name to no other city.[1] In books of repute and

---

Shidurgho, Shidasku, etc.—while, according to the *Tabákat-i-Násiri,* he styled himself the *Tingri Khan* (or Heavenly King), and was known to the Chinese as *Li-Hien.* The country also is found mentioned under many names and corruptions of names. *Tangut, Tingit, Koshi, Kashin,* etc., are the most common among western Asiatic writers; *Hsia* and *Hosi* among the Chinese. Indeed it is this last name, meaning "west of the river" (*i.e.* the Yellow River) that has been corrupted into *Koshi,* etc. The Tibetans seem to have known it as *Minyog.* By Mirza Haidar's time Tangut had sunk to very small proportions, and it is now only a geographical expression, for there is no separate state bearing the name.

The story of Shidarku and Chingiz's last war with Tangut will be found in Sir H. Howorth's *Northern Frontagers of China* (J. R. A. S., xv., (N.S.) pp. 472 *seqq.*), the *Habib us Siyar* (Price's *Mahd. Hist.*, ii., pp. 535–6), Major Raverty's *Tabakát-i-Násiri*, pp. 1084 *seqq.*, etc.

It may be added that, according to Mr. W. Woodville Rockhill, *Tangut* is only another name for Tibet in general—the *Si Tsang* of the Chinese. "The word *Tangut,*" he writes, "is interchangeable with Hsi-Tsang, or Tibet, although since Col. Prejevalsky's travels, it has come to be used by Europeans as designating the Tibetan-speaking tribes in the Kokonor region, known to Tibetans as *Andowa* and *Panaka.*" In saying this Mr. Rockhill is, I presume, referring to the Chinese or Mongol nomenclature; as is the case also when, in another passage, he cites a Chinese work to the effect that: "The name Tangutan was originally applied to tribes of Turkish origin living in the Altai." Although the name Tangut was in use for the regions about Zaidam, Kokonor, etc., many centuries before Col. Prejevalsky's time, and although the Tangut tribes can never have been Turks (in an ethnical sense), the application of the word, as pointed out by Mr. Rockhill, is interesting and instructive. (See Mr. Rockhill's valuable papers on *Tibet* in J. R. A. S., 1891, pp. 21, 189, etc.)

[1] It is quite possible that this curiously inaccurate statement may, indeed, have some truth in it. The work the author names, may very likely call Khán-báligh —the Cambalu of Marco Polo and the Mongol name for the modern Peking—by the Turki term *Bála Sághun*—or *Bála-Sákun,* as Mirza Haidar spells it. It is known that Kárakorum was, and even is to the present day, known as *Bála Sákun,* and it seems not unlikely that the name was used, in a general way, to denote a large town, or capital of some influential ruler. Still it is evident that Mirza Haidar is not alluding here, to any capital in northern China or in Mongolia, but to the seat of the old Turkish dynasty of Western Turkistan. It is all the more strange that he should have allowed himself to fall into an apparent confusion, seeing that he cites, immediately below, an account of *Bála-Sákun* by Rashid-ud-Din, which shows that it was an altogether separate city from Khan-báligh. He had, moreover, the *Jahán-Kushai* before him, where an exactly similar description of *Bála-Sákun* is given to that in Rashid-ud-Din, who apparently copied from the *Jahán-Kushai.*

There is every reason to believe that the *Bála-Sákun* spoken of in this passage, was situated on or near the head waters of the Káragáty branch of the River Chu in Moghulistan, and that it was, up to the first quarter of the twelfth century, the capital of the Ilak Khans, or the so-called Afrásiábi Turks; while later it became, for a time, the chief town of the Kára-Khitai. (See note 1, p. 287).

As there has been some difference of opinion respecting the identity and position of *Bála-Sákun,* it may be worth while to explain, in this place, that probably the basis of our information, regarding the times when it flourished, is the brief account contributed by Ala-ud-Din Ata Mulk, Juvaini, in the *Jahán-Kushai,* a work that he completed about the year 1259. He had himself travelled through the country in question, when on a mission to the court of Mangu Kaán at

histories, Balá-Sákun is said to have been one of the cities built by Afrásiáb, and [the authors] have praised it very highly. In the *Mujmá-ut-Tavárikh* it is written: "Balá-Sákun, until the time of

---

Karakorum, and had made several other journeys in Turkistan and the neighbouring regions. He may be assumed, therefore, to have heard the rights of a story which was, in his day, not particularly ancient. His work is one of the few original ones of the period of which it treats. Unfortunately it has never been translated into any European language, but some extracts from it have been published by D'Ohsson, and these have been utilised by many subsequent writers. On the subject of the city itself, D'Ohsson's extract (i. p. 433) merely shows that the building of *Bála-Sákun* is attributed to Afrásiáb, otherwise Buku-Khan, believed (according to tradition) to have been the first of the line of so-called Afrásiábi kings of Turkistan; that it stood among fine pastures in a well-watered plain; and that after the time of the Kara-Khitai invasion, in the twelfth century, it was called by the Mongols "Gu-balik." No geographical indication of its position is given; and all that can be inferred is that it stood within the very uncertain limits of what was then called Turkistan. From another extract, however, (i., p. 167) it may—by inference again—be placed a little more precisely towards the southern part of Turkistan—*i.e.* near the northern limit of Farghána. Abul Gházi is equally unsatisfactory in his reference to the situation of *Bála-Sákun*. But some of the Arab geographers of an earlier epoch are more explicit, and they point to the city having stood at no great distance from Káshghar. Thus Abul-feda (ii., pt. 2, p. 227), quoting from a work called the *Lobáb*, says that it was on the frontier of Turkistan, near Káshghar; Mukaddasi (as cited by Sprenger, p. 19) places it within the province of Isfijáb (which was the ancient representative of the present Chimkent) and very near Merke, on one of the upper affluents of the Chu. Sprenger, also, on the authority of Ibn-Khordadba and Kodáma, gives (pp. 22–3) the distance from Isfijáb to "the capital of the Turkish Khan" as 75 farasangs, and he demonstrates (p. xxvi.) that a farasang was equal to three Arabian miles, while each of the latter he calculates at a fraction over one English geographical mile. Thus one farasang might be about 3¾ English *statute* miles, making the total distance from Isfijáb about 281 *statute* miles. Whether by "the capital of the Turkish Khan," *Bála-Sákun* is intended, is of course uncertain, but taking the nomenclature of the period into consideration, it may, I think, be concluded that this and no other town must be meant. The late Mr. E. Schuyler, who studied the subject of *Bála-Sákun* and other old sites in Turkistan, presumed this to be the case (*Geo. Mag.*, 1874, p. 389) and his opinion is worthy of attention. If 281 miles be measured off to the E.N.E. of Chimkent, so as just to clear the great range of mountains, now called the "Alexander chain," and allowing one-fifth for windings of the road, a point will be reached within the upper system of the Chu, about 50 miles west of Constantinowski, and about 33 miles east-north-eastward of Merke—or approximately in Lat. 43 and Long. 73·40 from Greenwich.

There is, however, another way of arriving, or endeavouring to arrive, at the position of *Bála-Sákun*. Mr. Schuyler (*loc. cit.*) has given, in translation, a valuable extract on the subject from the "Chronicle of the chief astrologer" at the court of the Osmanli Sultan, Muhammad IV. This author was an Arab who lived from 1630 to 1701, and is usually known as the "Munajim Báshi." Two passages from this extract run: (1) "Balasagun . . . . situated at the beginning of the 7th climate in 102° of Long., and 48° of Lat., not far from Kashghar, and considered from of old the boundary city of Turkistan." (2) "Kashghar, the capital of Turan, in the 6th climate, in 106 of Long., and 45 of Lat. . . . ." Thus the difference of longitude between the two towns would be 4° and the difference of Lat. 3°. Now the latitude and longitude of Kashghar were correctly fixed by Col. H. Trotter, R.E., in 1873–4. If we take his values (to the nearest half degree) as 39½ N. and 76 E. and apply to them the differences in the Munajim Báshi's figures, we obtain for *Bála-Sákun* Lat. 42½ N., and Long. 72 E., approximately. This would be a point altogether west of the Chu basin, on the head streams of the Tálás, about 80 miles S.E. of Táráz, (or Aulia-Ata) and about 140 miles (allowing, on this more plain section of the

the Kará Khitái, was under the rule of the offspring [and descendants] of Afrásiáb. The Gur Khán of Kará Khitái took it from one of these descendants, Ilak Khán, and made it his own capital. For

---

road, one sixth for deviations) from Chimkent. Again, it will be found that in the geographical tables of Sádik Ispáháni, *Bála-Sákun* is placed (p. 76) in Lat. 46, and Long. 107, while to Kashghar is assigned (p. 126) Lat. 44, and Long. 106. Applying the differences between these figures and Col. Trotter's value, in the same way as before, we get for *Bála-Sákun* Lat. 41½, and Long. 77, or a position just on the banks of the Nárin river, nearly fifty miles above Fort Nárin. Further, the Arab geographer Abul-feda supplies us with two more indications of the position of *Bála-Sákun*, with reference to Káshghar. One of these, on the authority of Atwál, is a perfect one, and results (when computed as before) in Lat. 43·10, and Long. 71; while the other, on the authority of Kánun, fails in the Latitude, and furnishes the Longitude only as 72½.

Thus the positions taken from the Arab writers stand:—

Munajim Báshi . .	Lat. 42·30,	and	Long. 72·00	fr. Greenwich.
Sádik Ispaháni . .	„ 41·30	„	„ 77·00	„ „
Atwál	„ 43·10	„	„ 71·00	„ „
Kánun	„ „	„	„ 72·30	„ „

The mean of these data, to the nearest half degree, would be Lat. 42½, and Long. 73; or a point near the sources of some of the heads of the Karagaty branch of the Chu, some eighty-five statute miles E.S.E. of Aulia-Ata, and about twenty-six miles S.S.W. of Merke. Other statements of the Latitude and Longitude of *Bála-Sákun* are to be found in the writings of Asiatic geographers, but as no value is given for any other scientifically fixed point in the neighbourhood, to which the figures may be referred, they cannot be utilised.

The only conclusion that can be arrived at is, that the positions assigned by the Arab authors are worthless for anything approaching an accurate determination. All that can be gathered from them is that the city most likely stood among the left head-tributaries of the Chu, and was more probably to the north than to the south of the Alexander mountains. In this way it may be said not to differ seriously with the position which Sir H. Howorth would assign to the town, after examining the narratives of the Chinese travellers, Hiuen Tsang and Hueli. He finds that the city, known in those days to the Chinese by the name of Su-Yeh, stood almost certainly on the River Chu, and not far from the northern slopes of the Alexander mountains. Also that it was the capital of the Turkish kingdom of that region, and therefore, *Bála-Sákun* under another name. This conclusion appears to be extremely likely, more especially when it is considered in connection with Hiuen Tsang's itinerary, which places Su-Yeh at 540 or 550 *li* east of Táráz, and north of a range of snowy mountains; for taking five *li* to the mile, for Hiuen Tsang's time—or about 110 miles—and allowing one-fifth for deviations along the skirts of the hills, Su-Yeh would be located about eighty-eight miles, in direct distance, eastward of Taráz (Aulia-Ata), or at a spot only just to the west of Merke. This bears out also Mr. Schuyler's contention. (See for Howorth, *Geo. Mag.*, 1875, pp. 215–17, and for Hiuen Tsang's itinerary, Beal's *Buddhist Records*, i., p. 26.)

As regards the orthography of the name, Mirzá Haidar throughout writes *Bála-Sákun*, and for this reason I have retained that form. When, however, he comes to the passage in the *Jahán-Kushai*, which includes the name said to have been given to the town by the Mongols, he writes *Ghar bálik*, while in D'Ohsson and other extracts from the *Jahán-Kushai* hitherto published, this name has always stood *Gu-bálik*, and has been translated "good city." Desiring to clear up this discrepancy, I examined, with Mr. Ross, the British Museum copy of the *Jahán-Kushai*, and am satisfied that (in that copy at any rate) the name should be read *Ghar-báligh*, or possibly *Ghur-báligh*. The passage runs ". . . . they passed on to *Bála Sákun*, which the Moghuls now call Ghar [or Ghur]-báligh. The Amir of that country claims descent from Afrasiáb." Thus in the original we find *Sákun* instead of *Sághun*, *Moghuls* instead of *Mongols*, and *Ghar* (or perhaps *Ghur*) in place of *Gu*; while there is no sentence after the word *Ghar-bálik* to indicate that the meaning of the name is "good city." (See, among other works, D'Ohsson, i., pp. 433 and 442; Bretschneider, i., p. 226.)

ninety-five years Balá-Sákun remained the capital of Kará Khitái, and all the countries on this side of the Jihun—that is, to the east of it—carried tribute to Balá-Sákun. The Moghuls call Balá-Sákun, 'Ghar-báligh.' The author of the *Suráh-ul-Lughat*, in his Supplement, says that his father was one of the traditionists [*háfiz*] of Balá-Sákun. He gives, in this Supplement, the names of eminent men [*afázil*] of every town. In Samarkand he reckons fewer than ten. But in Balá-Sákun he mentions the names of a great number of learned and notable persons, and quotes traditions concerning some of them. The mind is incapable of conceiving how there could have been, at one time and in one city, so many men of eminence, and that now neither name nor trace is to be found of Balá-Sákun. Nor have I ever heard of a place called Ghar-báligh.

Another town mentioned in books is Taráz. It is said that the Moghuls call Taráz, 'Yángi'; and this Yángi is placed in Moghulistán. There are many men of Yángi in Mávará-un-Nahr who are called 'Yangiligh.' Now in those deserts [*mafáza*], which they call Yángi, there are remains of many cities, in the form of domes, minarets, and traces of schools and monasteries; but it is not evident which of these ruined cities was Yángi, or what were the names of the others.

Another famous town was Almáligh,[1] which is known at the present day. The tomb of Tughluk Timur Khán is there, together with [other] traces of the city's prosperity. The dome of the Khán's tomb is remarkable, being lofty and decorated; while on the plaster, inscriptions are written. I recall one-half of a line, from one of the books, namely: "This court [*bárgáh*] was the work of a master-weaver [*shar-báf*]"—words which show that this master was an Iráki; for in Irák they call a weaver [*jáma-báf*] '*shar-báf*.' As far as I can recollect, the date inscribed on that dome was seven hundred and sixty and odd.[2]

There are many other cities in Moghulistán, in which traces remain of very fine buildings. In some places they still stand intact.[3] In [the district of] Jud [4] there are traces of an important town, and remains of minarets, domes, and schools. Since the

[1] Almáligh—the *Armalec* of the mediæval European travellers—was the capital of Chaghatai Khan and his immediate successors. It was situated on, or near, the Ili river, in the neighbourhood of the modern town of Kulja. During the Mongol period it was a Latin bishopric, and had previously, most likely been a Nestorian See. (See *Cathay*, pp. ccxxii., 236, etc.)

[2] The death of Tughluk Timur was about 764 H., or 1363 A.D.

[3] The Persian texts are incomplete here. The Turki MS. reads:—"In some places, where the buildings were solid they will stand, in others they have been restored, while in others again they have already fallen into ruins."

[4] This word may be read *Juv* or *Jud*, or the *J* in each case may be replaced by *Ch*. The Turki MS. has:—"a village called *Ju*." It seems possible that the region, or district, of the River *Chu* may be intended. See text, immediately below.

name of that town is not known, the Moghuls call it 'Minárá.' In the same place is also a dome made of stone, into which the following inscription has been cut, in the Naskhi writing: "This is the tomb of [titles omitted] Imám Muhammad Fakih Balá Sákuni [Arabic invocation], who died in the year 711. Written by Khwája Omar Hadávi." Jud is a district [*mauza*] of Moghulistán, of a month's journey in length. In it there are many cities like this one.

In Moghulistán there is a place [*mausa*] called Yumghál,[1] which is well known. There a dome is to be found, half fallen into ruin. The inscription on it reads: "Sháh Jalil, son of Kism, son of Abbás. . . ." The rest has broken away, so it is not clear whether this was his tomb, or whether the inscription refers to some one else. God alone knows. Such remains as these are to be found all over Moghulistán, but the names of the towns are never known. The tomb of Mauláná Sakkáki, author of "The Key" [*Miftáh*], has a lofty dome. It is situated on the banks of the River Tiká, which flows from the foot of the lake.[2] With the exception of this dome, there are no remains in that place. It was either a town of which nothing is left, or else it was there that Chaghatái Khán slew [the Mauláná], the building being afterwards raised [over the spot]. God knows best. The story of Mauláná Sakkáki is told in histories.

Beyond this, nothing is recorded of the districts [*hadud*] of Moghulistán in the histories and books of former writers, nor does any one know the [above] names nowadays. What is now known as Moghulistán has a length and breadth of seven or eight months' journey. Its eastern frontier adjoins the Kálmák country: that is to say, Báris Kul, Imál, and Irtish. It is bounded on the north by Kukcha-Tangiz, Bum Lish, and Karátál;[3] on the west by Turkistán and Táshkand; and on the south by the provinces of Farghána, Káshghar, Aksu, Chálish, and Turfán.

Of these four boundaries I have seen the southern. From Tásh-

[1] The name *Jumgál* and *Jumghál*, which occurs on modern maps in the heart of the region that was Moghulistan, may perhaps represent the *Yumghál* of the text. It is the name of one of the head tributaries of the Nárin and of a small place—encampment or village—on its banks.

[2] Which lake is not specified, but I take it to mean Issigh-Kul. The sentence may read in the Persian texts: "which flows from Bai Kul," but the Turki MS. makes the reading plain—"from the foot of the lake." Thus *Pai-i-Kul* should be read in the Persian. The *Tika* river probably stands for the Tekes, which takes its rise near the eastern *end*, or foot, of Issigh-Kul, and flows eastward.

[3] These names may be read *Bári Kul* (sometimes *Bárkul*, and in Chinese *Pa-li-Kun*), *Imil* and *Irtish*. *Kukcha Tingiz* or *Tangiz* is lake *Balkash*, and *Karátál* is the name of a river which flows into it from the south-east. *Bumlish* I cannot identify. As regards lake Balkash, Mr. J. Spörer (in *Petermann* for 1868, p. 74) says, *Tengis* is the old Kirghiz name, and that *Balkash* originated with the Zungars [who were Kalmáks]. But farther on (p. 393) he tells us that "*Balkhazi Nor*," meaning "great lake," is Kalmák, while the Kirghiz name is "*Ak Dengis*," or "white lake." The two statements are not quite consistent.

kand to Andiján is ten days' journey; from Andiján to Káshghar, twenty days; from there to Aksu, fifteen days; from Aksu to Chálish, twenty days; from Chálish to Turfán, ten days; from Turfán to Báris Kul, fifteen days;[1] and Báris Kul is the eastern boundary of Moghulistán. [The whole of the southern boundary] is about three months' march at a medium pace, for it is ninety stages. I have never visited the other three boundaries, but I have learned [something] about them from the descriptions of persons who have travelled in those quarters. The greater part of this country, which is seven or eight months' journey [in circuit], is mountain or desert,[2] and is very beautiful and pleasant—so much so, that I am incapable of describing it in words. On the mountains and in the plains, grow numberless flowers, whose names no one knows; they are not to be met with outside Moghulistán, nor can they possibly be described. The summer is, in most parts, quite temperate, so that if a single tunic [*tái kurta*] be worn, no other covering is required, though even if more be worn, the heat does not make one uncomfortable. However, in some parts of the country, the temperature inclines to be cold.

There are many large rivers in Moghulistán—as large, or nearly so, as the Jihun; for example, the Ila, the Imil, the Irtish, and the Nárin, not one of which is inferior to the Jihun or the Sihun. Most of them flow into the lake of Kukcha Tangiz, which separates Moghulistán from Uzbegistán. Its length is eight months' journey,[3] and its breadth, in some parts, thirty *farsákhs*, by estimation. In winter, when it is frozen over, the Uzbeg cross Kukcha Tangiz on the ice, and thus enter Moghulistán. By using all possible speed, they can cross in two nights and a day into Moghulistán, and can return in the same time. At the end of winter they cross with the same rapidity; but at that time of the year it is dangerous, and it often happens that the ice gives way. On one occasion a hundred and twenty families, more or less, perished under the ice. The water of this lake is sweet. The same quantity of water that flows into the lake is not discharged from it. What does flow out is about equivalent to one of the rivers which enters it. It flows down through Uzbegistán, under the name of Atal, and empties itself into the Kulzum [Caspian].

Another point of interest in Moghulistán is Issigh Kul, [a lake] into which nearly as much water flows as into Kukcha Tangiz. It

[1] These stages are about correct, according to modern itineraries.

[2] The word in the texts is *sahra*, and has been literally translated *desert;* but *sahra* is often used to designate plains, open country, or "steppes," and it is employed in this sense here.

[3] There is either some mistake in this estimate of the length of the lake, or else it is a reckless exaggeration. The estimate of 30 farsakhs (120 miles) for the breadth is also far too high, even if the broadest part be taken.

is twenty days' journey,[1] and no water issues from it on any side. It is surrounded by hills. All the water that flows into it is sweet and agreeable, but once it enters the lake it becomes so bitter and salt that one cannot even use it for washing, for if any of it enters the eyes or mouth, severe inflammation is produced; it has also a most unpleasant taste in the mouth. It is remarkably pure and clean, so that if, for example, some is poured into a china cup, no sediment appears at the bottom. The water of the rivers around is delicious. Aromatic herbs, flowers and fruit-bearing trees are plentiful, while the surrounding hills and plains abound in antelopes [*áhu*] and birds. There are few localities in Moghulistán more remarkable for their climate.

From the year 916 the Kirghiz, for the reasons mentioned above, have rendered it impossible for any Moghul to live in Moghulistán. In the year 928 the Khán resolved to subdue Moghulistán, as shall be explained.

CHAPTER LXIX.

RETURN TO THE THREAD OF THE HISTORY.

* * * * *[2]

THE flocks and herds had so greatly increased, that the plains and hills of Káshghar could no longer provide sufficient pasturage, and therefore, in order to satisfy the wants and demands of his people, the Khán formed the bold project of subduing Moghulistán. Moreover, the Kirghiz, who were for the most part devoid of faith and given over to evil deeds, had thoroughly intimidated the Musulmáns of Turkistán, Shásh and Farghána, by their constant invasions and forays. Although that province[3] was under the rule of the Uzbeg Shaibán, who were his old enemies, the Khán, on account of his devotion to the faith and out of pity for the Musulmáns, took the matter to heart, and determined that no Musulmán should be molested and no infidel should prosper; but rather that the Musulmáns should thrive and the infidels should be subdued. For these two actions he expected to gain a good reputa-

[1] If twenty days' journey in *circuit* is meant, the statement might be not far from correct. For some remarks on Issigh Kul, see note pp. 78–9.

[2] This chapter opens with five lines of rhetoric (which are omitted) showing how the Khan desired to gain fame in this world and "a high place" in the next.—R.

[3] Apparently Farghána is meant. Only the words "*án valáyat*" are used.

tion in this world and merit in the world to come. May God reward him well! [Three couplets]. . . .

Mirzá Ali Taghái, Khwája Ali Bahádur, and most of the Amirs, supporting the cause of Bábá Sultán, desired that he should be sent in command of the expedition against Moghulistán and the Kirghiz. His father, Sultán Khalil Sultán, had been leader of the Kirghiz, as has been explained; and he therefore had some right in the matter. My uncle alone supported Rashid Sultán, who was the Khán's son, and upon him the conduct of the expedition finally devolved. Active preparations were set on foot [verses]: . . . and in the course of the year 928, Rashid Sultán set out loaded with favours. Mirzá Ali Taghái was appointed *Ulus-beg*, and Muhammad Kirghiz being released from confinement, was made Amir of the Kirghiz; while brave warriors and distinguished Amirs were chosen out of all the Moghul tribes. [Couplet]. . . . Everything becoming the prince's rank and dignity was made ready; such as banners [*tugh*], trumpets, mint [*zaráb-khána*] and all kinds of furniture. Feasts were given to the Amirs and soldiers, who made merry; and favours were bestowed on all. [The Khán] gave his son much good advice. [Verses]. . . Indeed he lavished sermons and wise counsels on the young prince, who did not heed them, for is it not said: Sermons and advice are as wind to the profligates of this world? Finally, however, the army was despatched.

At the hour of his taking leave of Rashid Sultán, the Khán said to me: "You accoutre him: fasten on his quiver and sword, and mount him on his horse: it may bring good fortune. In respect of what I have told him, let him be your pupil: you shall be his master. . . .[1]

In short the Khán sent them off in the handsomest manner, and himself returned to Káshghar. [Two couplets] . . . .

With their entrance into Moghulistán, Muhammad Kirghiz marched on in advance. He brought in most of the Kirghiz, though a few fled to the farthest confines of Moghulistán. When winter set in, quarters were taken up at Kuchkár.

[1] A couplet from Sádi and five lines of rhetoric and verses are omitted.—R.

CHAPTER LXX.

THE KHÁN'S REPENTANCE.

* * * * *[1]

It has been already explained to how great an extent the Khán was addicted to wine-drinking. If, for example, he dreamt of sobriety, he interpreted it to mean that he ought to get drunk; this is [the system of] interpretation by contraries. [Turki couplet]. . . .

No one would ever have imagined that the Khán could give up this habit, but by the intervention of Providence he repented him of his intemperance . . . .[2]

In short, at the end of the winter following that spring which saw Rashid Sultán set out for Moghulistán, the Khán happened to be in Yángi-Hisár. My uncle was in attendance on him, while I was in Yárkand. I have frequently heard the Khán relate that, one night when a drinking bout was coming to an end, the following verse came into his head: "'At night he is drunk, at dawn he is drunk, and all day he is crop-sick; see how he passes his noble life! It is time that thou should'st return to thy God [and abandon these unseemly practices].' When this purpose had become fixed in my heart, I again became irresolute [and said to myself]: 'these ideas are merely the outcome of excessive inebriety. For otherwise, who could endure life without this form of enjoyment?' Thinking thus I fell asleep; when I awoke I writhed like a snake with crop-sickness, and to dispel this I called for a draught. When it was brought, the intentions of the night before again took possession of my brain, and I sent for Sayyid Muhammad Mirzá, and said to him: 'I am tired of this wine-drinking, and wish to reform.'" Now my uncle had for a long while been a disciple of the order of Yasavvi Shaikhs,[3] and practised austerity and abstinence; thus he had been greatly distressed at the Khán's shortcomings; but when the Khán now announced

[1] The five lines with which the chapter opens contain only rhetorical flights concerning "Repentance."—R.

[2] Four more lines on the virtue of Repentance are omitted here.—R.

[3] The Yasavvi Shaikhs were the followers of one Shaikh Ahmad, otherwise Hazrat Khwája Ahmad, of Yassi, who was the founder of the sect of Jahria, and died about 1120 A.D. He is said by Mr. E. Schuyler, who visited his tomb at Turkistan, to be one of the most celebrated saints of Central Asia, and the special patron of the Kirghiz. The town of Turkistan, near the right bank of the Jaxartes, is the modern representative of Yassi. There the mosque of 'Házrat' is still to be seen, which was built over the tomb of Shaikh Ahmad, by Timur, at the end of the fourteenth century, and was restored in the latter half of the sixteenth, by Abdullah Khan II., the famous Uzbeg chief. It is considered one of the holiest mosques in Central Asia. (See Schuyler, i., pp. 70-72.)

to him his desire to mend his ways, my uncle burst into tears and urged him strongly to carry out his intention. Having repented, the Khán went into the assembly; [verses] . . . . the wine-bibbers and profligates were dejected and distressed, but all the pious and the learned rejoiced, while the zealots and devotees began to thank God, and the townsfolk and peasantry stretched their hands in praise to heaven. Thus the Khán repented of his past deeds, and night and day begged the forgiveness of God for his offences. . . .[1]

CHAPTER LXXI.

HOW THE KHÁN, WISHING TO BECOME A DARVISH, INTENDED TO ABDICATE THE THRONE, AND HOW HE WAS DISSUADED.

After the Khán had been distinguished with the honour of repentance, and had entered the circle of those of whom it is said, "God loves the penitent," he passed into Moghulistán, and joined Rashid Sultán at Kuchkár.[2] Remaining himself in Kuchkár, he sent forward Rashid Sultán, with his Amirs and Muhammad Kirghiz, to the farthest limits of Moghulistán. They collected and brought back the scattered Kirghiz, thus setting [the Khán's] mind at rest with regard to this affair. In the spring the Khán went back to Káshghar. After this, he used to return every year to Moghulistán with his family, to see that the country was in order, and to confirm the authority of Rashid Sultán. In the second spring that he took his family there, most of the Moghul *Ulus*, who were able to do so, went with him of their own accord and desire. That winter the Khán and Rashid Sultán took up their quarters in Kuchkár, and at the end of the winter the Khán, leaving his family there, went back to Yárkand.

The reason for this was that, since his repentance, he had devoted himself much to the study of Sufi books; and having pondered deeply on their sayings, was greatly influenced by them. . . .[3] The Khán entered fully into the tenets of the sect, and was profoundly impressed by them. From their books and pamphlets, he learnt that the blessing [of Sufistic knowledge] was only to be attained by devoting himself to the service of a perfect

[1] Two couplets and four lines of rhetoric are omitted here. They contain much the same matter as the preceding passages.—R.

[2] The Kuchkar, Koshkur, or Guchgar river is one of the head streams of the Chu. Its valley lies to the south-west of Issigh-Kul, and appears to have been a favourite camping, and grazing, ground of the Moghuls. See the Map.

[3] An irrelevant anecdote concerning some saints is left untranslated.

[Sufi]; on this account he withdrew his mind from his earthly kingdom, while his heart became entirely detached from the world. He spent most of his time in seclusion; engaged in discussions on Sufism. Not every one was allowed to intrude on his privacy. One of his companions was my uncle, who had been a disciple of the Yasavvi Shaikh's, and who, under the guidance of that sect, practised abstinence. Most of the conferences took place in his presence. Another was Sháh Muhammad Sultán, who was a cousin of the Khán and a son-in-law of his sister, and who has been mentioned briefly above; at times I was also admitted. No one else was allowed to enter, and the people used to wonder what kind of discussions those could be, to which only these four persons were admitted. [Couplet]. . . .

It was finally decided that the Khán should go to Yárkand, and that his brother, Amin Khwája Sultán, should be brought from Aksu and set up as king in his stead. To him should be confided the whole *Ulus*, while the Khán, divesting himself of everything, should set out on his journey; haply he might thus render the Most High God perfect service. My uncle then suggested that before taking this step, preparations should be made for the journey to Mekka, and all necessaries got ready; that he would accompany [the Khán]; that wherever he was he would spend his whole life in attendance on him, and that Sháh Muhammad Sultán and myself should also be in waiting.

No sooner had these plans been determined on, than Khwája Muhammad Yusuf, son of Khwája Muhammad Abdullah, son of Khwája Násir-ud-Din Ubaid Ullah, arrived in Káshghar from Samarkand, and the news [of his arrival] reached Moghulistán. The Khwája was an exceedingly pious and austere man, and the Khán longed to wait upon him, in the hope that [in his service] his desire might be realised. So he journeyed from Kuchkár to Yárkand, where he arrived at the end of the winter and waited on the Khwája. [But] when he explained to him his resolve, the Khwája remarked: "Much has been said by wise men on this subject; such as: Remain on the throne of your kingdom, and be like an austere darvish in your ways! And again: set the crown on your head, and science on your back! Use effort in your work, and wear what you will! In reality sovereignty is one of the closest walks [with God], but kings have abused its rights. A king is able, with one word, to give a higher reward than can a darvish (however intent upon his purpose) during the whole of a long life. In this respect sovereignty is a real and practical state . . . .[1] But I will show you one line that my father,

[1] Four lines omitted, containing a quotation from Najm-ud-Din, which points out what a faithful disciple may attain to, and what an unfaithful one must forego.—R.

Khwája Muhammad Abdullah, wrote for me." And he gave the writing to the Khán. It was written: "The most important conditions, for a seeker of union with God, are: little food, few words, and few associates." This brief [sermon] sufficed to compose the Khán, and he resolved to pursue the road of justice and good deeds. He began to occupy himself, at once, with what he was able, until the words of Shaikh Najm-ud-Din should be realised. A short time after this, Khwája Nurá came, and the Khán's desire was fulfilled. In the meanwhile Khwája Táj-ud-Din arrived from Turfán.

CHAPTER LXXII.

KHWÁJA TÁJ-UD-DIN.

Khwája Táj-ud-Din was of the race of Mauláná Arshad-ud-Din, who was of the race of Khwája Shuja-ud-Din Mahmud, brother of Khwája Háfiz-ud-Din of Bokhárá, the last of the Mujtahids. During the interregnum [*fatrat*] of Chingiz Khán, this Shuja-ud-Din was brought [into this country], and of his race is Mauláná Arshad-ud-Din, who brought about the conversion of the Moghuls to Islám. All this, God willing, will be fully described in the First Part. This Khwája Táj-ud-Din is of the race of Mauláná Arshad-ud-Din. His father's name was Khwája Ubaid Ullah. He was a disciple of Mir Abdullah of Bushirábád . . . .[1] Having remained for some time in the service of Hazrat Ishan, the latter gave the Khwája leave to go to Turfán, where he was cordially received by Sultán Ahmad Khán . . . .[1]

[1] The omissions here consist of a number of names of unimportant saints, and of a brief reference to an anecdote relating to one of them.—R.

CHAPTER LXXIII.

KHWÁJA TÁJ-UD-DIN IS ALLOWED TO RETURN TO TURFÁN. THE KHÁN MAKES PEACE WITH THE KAZÁK-UZBEG. OTHER CONTEMPORARY EVENTS.

WHEN Khwája Táj-ud-Din came from Turfán, the Khán received him with due honour. He stayed one year in Yárkand, and then returned [to Turfán]. Next winter Rashid Sultán went and plundered the Kálmák, slew one of their Amirs named Báráu Tálish,[1] and acquired the honourable name of Ghází. He had his winter quarters at Kuchkár, whither the Khán went with a small attendance [*jarida*] and joined him. With the middle of the winter arrived Táhir Khán, who has been briefly mentioned above among the Kazák Kháns. After a long intercourse by means of ambassadors, it was ascertained that he had come to wait on the Khán, and to deliver over to him Sultán Nigár Khánim, the Khán's aunt.

This Sultán Nigár Khánim has been already spoken of above. She was the fourth daughter of Yunus Khán, and after the death of Sultán Mahmud Mirzá, son of Abu Said Mirzá, she was given to Adik Sultán, son of Jáni Beg Khán, the Kazák. By Mirzá Sultán Mahmud she had one child, Mirzá Khán, who became king of Badakhshán, and in the year 917[2] died a natural death. His son, Sulaimán Sháh Mirzá, is now ruling in Badakhshán. By Adik Sultán she had two daughters, the elder of whom was married to Abdullah Sultán, son of Kuchum Khán, but died soon after. The younger was given, at this time, to Rashid Sultán, as shall be mentioned. After the death of Adik Sultán, this Sultán Nigár Khánim married his brother Kásim Khán. When this last died, the Khánship devolved upon Táhir Khán, who was the son of Adik Sultán. He was very much attached to the Khánim, and even preferred her to the mother that had given him birth. She showed him her gratitude, but entreated him, saying: "Although you are my child, and I neither think of nor desire any child but

[1] *Tálish* should probably be read *Táish*, a common title among Kalmák leaders.

[2] This date is no doubt intended for 927. It is given in the texts in Arabic numerals, but in such a way that it may be easily misread (*ashr* for *ashrun*). Mirza Khan (properly Vais Mirza) was only son of Sultan Mahmud Mirza and cousin of Baber. In 913 (1507) he became ruler of Badakhshan. He is believed to have died about 926 (1520), and if the date here should read 927, as I surmise, it would be perhaps exact. Mirza Khan left one child, Sulaiman Mirza, whom Baber took care of. At the same time, Baber appointed to Badakhshan his son Humayun, who retained charge of the province till 932 (1526). (See Erskine, *Hist.* i., pp. 249, 286, 511, etc.)

you, nevertheless I am grown old, and have no longer the strength to bear this migratory life in the deserts of Uzbegistán. I wish you now to take me to my nephew, Sultán Said Khán, that I may pass my last days in a city and enjoy some quiet and repose. Moreover, in consequence of [the hostility of] the Mangit your affairs in Uzbegistán are not thriving. On account of the opposition [of the Moghuls][1] your army has decreased from 1,000,000 men to 400,000, and you have no longer strength to oppose them. I will be a mediator for you, and will bring about a reconciliation between you and the Moghul Khákáns. In this way the Mangit[2] may be kept in check."

Tahir Khán fell in with this plan and came to the borders of Moghulistán, where negotiations for peace were entered upon. He came in person to Kuchkár and waited on the Khán. The latter, from love of his aunt, rose [to receive him], saying: "Although my rising [to receive] you is contrary to the *Tura*, yet my great gratitude to you for having brought my aunt, makes it possible for me to rise." Thus saying the Khán rose, but [Táhir Khán], observing all the formalities, bowed his head to the ground, and then advanced towards the Khán, who having embraced him, showed him great honour and showered royal favours upon him. After this, his sister, the Khánim's daughter, was given in marriage to Rashid Sultán, in whose haram she is at the present time. She has children, each of whom will be mentioned in the proper place.

At the time of [Táhir Khán's] departure, Muhammad Kirghiz was captured a second time, and brought bound to Káshghar. The reason for this was that he had shown signs of insubordination, and a desire to escape to the Uzbeg. He was therefore detained in custody, but after the Khán's death he was released. The Khán now returned to Káshghar, and I was left in Moghulistán to keep the people quiet. But in spite of my efforts, I was unable to pacify the Kirghiz, who fled and again betook themselves to the remotest parts of Moghulistán, where they joined Táhir Sultán. Some of them, however, remained. In this year a son was born to the Khán.

[1] The texts do not mention whose opposition is referred to, but I presume the Moghuls are indicated (if the translation is correct), and that the speaker is alluding to the defeats which Sultan Said had recently inflicted on the Kirghiz Kazák. The next sentence bears out this presumption. But see next note.

[2] The uncertainty regarding this name was alluded to at p. 134. It occurred on that occasion once, in the form of *Manfakit* or *Man'akit*; here it is twice made use of, but is spelled differently, and in such a way that it may be read *Mankafit*, *Mikaft*, etc., etc. Dr. Rieu, however, who has done me the kindness to examine the passages in the original text, is of opinion that in both cases the incomprehensible words may stand for the tribal name of *Mangit* or *Mangut*, corruptly reproduced by the copyist. It is significant that the word, in both forms, should only occur in reference to the one subject—viz., the relations of the Kazák with the rest of the Uzbeg tribe. It is found nowhere else in the book.

CHAPTER LXXIV.

BIRTH OF SULTÁN IBRÁHIM, SON OF SULTÁN SAID KHÁN.

In the month of Shawál of the year 930 . . . .[1] [a son was born to the Khán], and he was given the name of Sultán Ibráhim. Khwája Muhammad Yusuf received him as a son, and Bábá Sárik Mirzá, whose name was mentioned in the review [of the army] of Káshghar, was appointed his *Atábeg.* Magnificent banquets were held in honour of his birth—more splendid, in fact, than any that had been held on previous occasions. The Khán loved him above all his other children . . . .[2] His life will be recounted in its proper place.[3]

CHAPTER LXXV.

THE KHÁN'S SECOND INVASION OF ANDIJÁN.

On return of the spring . . . .[4] the Khán saw fit to go again into Moghulistán to confirm Rashid Sultán's authority. He set forth from Yárkand, and on reaching Káshghar met Hazrat Khwája Nurá, who was coming from the direction of Andiján. Having had the felicity of kissing the Khwája's feet, the Khán proceeded on his journey to Moghulistán, while the Khwája went on to Yárkand. Towards the end of summer the Khán reached Issigh Kul, where he learnt that the Kálmák had approached the frontiers of Moghulistán. The Khán, putting his trust in God, hastened on with all speed to Kábikálár, which is ten marches from Issigh Kul. Here a messenger from my uncle in Káshghar brought the news that Suyunjuk Khán was dead, that the Uzbeg Sultáns were without a leader, and that a better opportunity than the present

[1] Three lines of verse, etc., omitted.

[2] Here follows a chronogram in four lines of verse, containing the word *Zill*—equal to 930—[1524].

[3] The author has not followed out his intention in this matter. He mentions Ibrahim only once hereafter, as having been taken to Kabul by his mother Zainab Sultan Khánim, on being banished from her home in Kashghar, by Abdur Rashid (see p. 467). At that time, this third son of Said Khan would have been about thirteen years of age, and even when the author wrote his history, he must have been too young to have accomplished anything worthy of record.

[4] Four lines of verse in praise of spring are left out.

one for revenge, was never likely to occur; for how long had such a day been awaited?

The reason for my uncle's remaining in Káshghar was that in the last-mentioned spring [summer], on account of the extreme heat of the weather, he had caused fresh green grass to be spread on the ground and iced water to be sprinkled over it; he had then lain down naked on it and had gone to sleep. On awaking he found that he had become paralytic [*lakwa*], and noticed an impediment in his speech. In the meanwhile, the Khán arrived at Káshghar on his way to Moghulistán, and Khwája Nurá[1] from Andiján. [Two couplets . . . .] There is a proverb which runs: "When a sick man is destined to recover, the doctor comes uncalled"—a saying which illustrates the good luck of my uncle. Khwája Nurá applied himself to his treatment, and that is why he had stayed behind in Káshghar. On learning the death of Suyunjuk Khán, he had sent off a messenger to the Khán, and when this messenger arrived in Kábilkaklá,[2] [the Khán] quickly returned. His family being in Issigh Kul, thither he went; then, taking them with him, he proceeded to Kunghár Ulang, and thence towards Andiján. [Verses . . . .]

The fort of Uzkand, which was a very strong one, was taken. [From Uzkand] he marched on to Mádu, where the fort is the strongest in all the province of Fargháma. It, too, fell an easy prey to his army. Thence they advanced on Ush. All the nobles, learned men, artisans, and peasantry in this neighbourhood were agreed that since Suyunjuk Khán was dead, it would be some time before the Uzbeg could come to any agreement. "Until they have decided upon some definite plan [of action]," said they, "let us go and strengthen and provision the fort of Andiján; then let us take up a position in the mountains. As the Khán [cannot penetrate into the Uzbeg mountains] he will not be able to touch us, nor will he succeed in laying siege to the fort." [So saying, they set out for Andiján.] But when the Uzbeg-Shaibán heard of the Khán's advance towards Andiján, without further conferring or planning, all poured into [Andiján], like locusts or ants, from every quarter. There was no time for making the necessary preparations for a siege, and the Khán was obliged to send many [of his people] back. In that expedition the Khán's army was composed of 25,000 men all told, while the Uzbeg had more than 100,000. [Couplet] . . . .

[1] Nura stands for Nur-ud-Din.—R.

[2] This is evidently the same name that occurs at the beginning of the chapter under the form *Kábilkálár*. The Turki MS. has Kápilkálár. I can trace neither this name nor that of *Kunghár Ulang*, which follows a few lines below. They were both, most likely, mere camping grounds, and consequently it may well happen that no trace of them remains. Kápilkálár must have been ten days to the eastward of Issigh-Kul, seeing that it was against the Kalmáks that the Khan was marching.

The men who had been turned away, were sent to Káshghar. The Khán himself went back to Moghulistán and joined his family, which was in Utluk—a well-known place [*mauza*] in Moghulistán. Then, leaving Rashid Sultán in Moghulistán, he returned to Káshghar, where he again waited on Khwája Nurá. These events took place in the year 931 [1524–5].

CHAPTER LXXVI.

LAST VISIT OF THE KHÁN TO MOGHULISTÁN. THE MOGHULS ARE BROUGHT TO KÁSHGHAR FROM MOGHULISTÁN; AND SOME OTHER CONTEMPORARY EVENTS.

As Rashid Sultán remained in Moghulistán, he made Kuchkár his winter quarters. Now Táhir Khán was in Uzbegistán, but some events occurred there which obliged him to retire to Moghulistán. He therefore came [and settled down] near Kuchkár, where he was joined by half the Kirghiz, to whom he gave protection in his own territories. On this account Rashid Sultán became alarmed, and in the depth of winter fled from Kuchkár to At-Báshi. On learning this, the Khán, towards the end of that same winter, repaired to At-Báshi, and joined his son at [the] Kátilish[1] of At-Báshi. [Rashid's] followers were [thus] reassured.

In the [following] spring, the Uzbeg penetrated to the eastern quarter of Moghulistán, which is called Kháss and Kunkás.[2]

All the Kirghiz who had remained with Rashid Sultán, were anxious to unite with those Kirghiz who had joined the Uzbeg. The Khán ordered me to accompany Rashid Sultán, and [we] having driven the Kirghiz out of Bumghál and Kuchkár, brought them to At-Báshi. The Khán himself went to Káshghar, in order to gather all the people together, and to see if any agreement could be brought about between them and the Uzbeg. He left me in Moghulistán to ensure law and order among the inhabitants. I accompanied Rashid Sultán, until the Khán returned from Káshghar with his family and rejoined our people; then he sent me off to the Káshghar [province] to bring Sultán Nigár Khánim into Moghulistán, that she might mediate with Táhir Khán for the

[1] *Kátilish* means the confluence of two streams: in this case probably of some stream with At-Báshi, or of the At-Báshi with the Nárin. The At-Báshi valley, situated about half way between Kashghar and Issigh-Kul, seems to have been one of the chief, and most central, camping grounds of the Moghul Khans. Most likely there was no town or village there.

[2] The rivers *Kásh* and *Kunges*, as usually written by the Russians.

settlement of a peace [with ourselves]. So I went to Yárkand, and conveyed the Khánim back to Moghulistán. The Khán was at Aksái.[1]

Before I arrived, he learnt that the Kirghiz had separated from the Uzbeg. On hearing this, he thought it advisable to go and subdue the Kirghiz, and started from Aksái [for that purpose]. When they had gone one stage, Rashid Sultán fell ill. Bandagi Hazrat Khwája [2] happened to be there, on an excursion. When he arrived, he was able in three days, by means of his Christ-like healing power, to change sickness into health.

Having delivered the Khánim into the hands of the people, I hastened on to join the army, and came up with them the same day that they left that stage.[3] I had the felicity of kissing the stirrup of Khwája Nurá, who then turned back. The Khán [at the same time] pushed forward, and in twelve days accomplished forty days' journey. The details of the matter are as follows.

When we reached Ak Kumás, the Khán sent me with 5000 men to accompany Rashid Sultán against the Kirghiz, who were then in Arish Lár.[4] On arriving at this place, we found their camp and their tents left standing. It was clear that they had fled and got away. Some of their arms and baggage [*partál*] were lying tumbled about. We concluded that they got news of [our approach]. As we proceeded, we came across some dead bodies, and several horses, wounded or killed by arrows, besides many broken arrows. After careful search, we discovered a man who was half-dead, from whom we learnt that Bábáják Sultán had come from Kusan, and attacked the Kirghiz; that three days previous to our arrival a fierce battle had been fought, resulting in the defeat of Bábáják Sultán. The Kirghiz, having despatched their families towards the Uzbeg, had then gone in pursuit of Bábáják Sultán.

Advancing yet further, we lighted upon some 100,000 sheep of

[1] No doubt a camping ground on the Aksai river, between Kashghar and At-Báshi.

[2] Otherwise Khwája Nura, or Nur-ud-Din.

[3] Meaning, apparently, one stage from the *Aksai* river.

[4] *Ak Kumás* may perhaps be identified with *Ak Kum*, between the lower *Tálás* and the *Chu;* and *Arish Lar* with Lake *Aris*, which lies to the west of the Sari river and nearly north from Ak Masjid on the *Sir Daria*. These places are a long distance from Moghulistan, and one can scarcely imagine the Moghuls following the Kirghiz so far. Still, it is evident from the text, that the chase was a long one, and it was in a north-westerly direction, for it is stated below that the Kirghiz took refuge with the Uzbegs, who occupied the steppes to the north-west. There is another, and smaller, *Ak-Kum*, on the south bank of the Ili river, a short distance above the modern fort of Ilijsk, but this would not lie in the right direction, and would not be distant enough to suit the narrative; nor is there any *Arish* in the vicinity that I am aware of. The only other possible *Arish* (or *Aris*) suggested by modern maps, would be on the river of that name which falls into the Sir, near Chimkent, but this would be a settled country to which the Kirghiz would be unlikely to fly for refuge, or the Moghuls to enter, in pursuit. The word *Lar* I can find no trace of.

the Kirghiz, which we drove along with us. As the Kirghiz had united with the Uzbeg, we were unable to offer them further opposition, so we turned back and rejoined the Khán, for the original object of this expedition was to punish the Kirghiz, and not to attack the Uzbeg. This campaign got the name of *Kui Jariki*, or the "sheep-army."

Now at that time Táhir Khán had a force of 20,000 men, but his fortune was on the decline; for his army had formerly counted a million. He began to increase his violence and severity, and on this account he was abhorred of the surrounding Sultáns and men of note. He had a brother named Abul Kásim Sultán. The people were able to judge of him by the violent treatment he meted out to this brother, whom he suddenly put to death; they therefore all at once fled from him, so that none remained but he and his son. These two hurried forward and joined the Kirghiz. This news reached the Khán when he had arrived in Káshghar.

The reason for his going there, was that the Moghuls had represented to him that the Kirghiz had united with the Uzbeg, and these latter intended to settle down in Moghulistán, while he knew that he had not strength sufficient to cope with the numbers of the Uzbeg. It would therefore be dangerous for them [the Moghuls] to remain in Moghulistán that winter. For these reasons, the Khán brought Rashid Sultán, and all the Moghuls of Moghulistán, to Káshghar.[1] Here they learned the news of the rout of the Uzbeg. At the end of the spring, it being difficult to return to Moghulistán, they remained in Káshghar. It was about the beginning of spring that Táhir Khán joined the Kirghiz. He carried off all the Kirghiz who had been left in At-Báshi, together with the droves of horses which the Moghuls had left in Moghulistán.

CHAPTER LXXVII.

REASONS FOR BÁBÁ SULTÁN'S FLIGHT, AND THE CONCLUSION OF HIS STORY.

BÁBÁ SULTÁN has been already mentioned above, as the son of the Khán's brother, Sultán Khalil Sultán. He was a mere child when his father was drowned in the river, at Akhsi, by Jáni Beg Sultán,

[1] Meaning, no doubt, to the Kashghar province, or to the hills in the neighbourhood of Kashghar. Nothing marks the decay of the Moghuls, as a nation, more strongly than this episode. They had now to abandon their own country to their enemies, and though they afterwards returned, at intervals, this was the beginning of their end.

in the year 914. After the Khán took Andiján, Bábá Sultán remained in the Khán's service, and was treated with such consideration that he became an object of envy to [the Khán's own] children. Khwája Ali Bahádur, who has been frequently mentioned, was appointed his governor [*Atáka*]. This man, as has been explained, had a plan [for seizing] Moghulistán, and taking Bábá Sultán with him. But my uncle opposed this, and arranged that Rashid Sultán should go instead. On this account, Bábá Sultán was offended. Despite the attentions the Khán showed him, his resentment increased daily, and in proportion as Rashid Sultán rose [in power], his jealousy became the more bitter. Moreover, some devils of companions (who are to be found everywhere, and who sow the seeds of hypocrisy in the soil of men's hearts) did their best to incite him to sedition and revolt; so that at length he came to the conclusion that there was nothing left but flight.

One of these men was named Mazid, a person of evil ways, whom the Khán had at first favoured, but finding that he did not perform his duties in the posts to which he was appointed, the Khán deprived him of his rank. This person found it inconvenient to remain in Káshghar, so he approached Bábá Sultán, and filled his ears with many idle tales, which Bábá Sultán, from the vanity of youth, or rather from sheer ignorance, took for truth. Among other deceitful statements, he said to him: "It is a ruler of capability such as you, that Káshghar stands in need of, and everybody is seeking for a really good king. Wherever you go, the people accept you as Bábá Sháhi. Look, for example, at Sultán Avais in Khatlán-Hisár. Failing to find a good king, he set himself up on his own account, and now bows his head to no one. If you present yourself before him, he will make you king, while he himself will advance and take the whole of Badakhshán, and accomplish much that I cannot [now] explain. The truth of the matter is, that the sovereignty of Khorásán and Mávará-un-Nahr is far more important than that of Káshghar and Moghulistán [and you may attain it]." Such idle tales as these did he string together, and by persistence, made them appear reasonable. Thus was Bábá Sultán duped by this man and one or two others of the same sort.

In the summer of the afore-mentioned year, they fled from Yárkand. The Khán did not send in pursuit of them, but said: "If they find some one better than I am, well and good; if not, they will return." Bábá Sultán fled to Sultán Avais, and thence to Badakhshán. Here he saw that he had been deceived, and that these cowardly men had misled him for their own private ends. Repentant, he returned to Káshghar. But the Khán was unwilling [that he should remain], as shall be shortly explained.

So being obliged to quit the country, he withdrew to Hindustán, where he conducted himself badly. Bábar Pádisháh gave him Ruhtak, an important town in Hisár-Firuza, where he followed his uncommendable courses, but shortly afterwards was seized with dysentery, and died in the course of the year 937, at the age of twenty-four. In his youth he had been so spoiled by the Khán, that his masters could do nothing with him, and his studies came to naught. [Two couplets]. . . . Yet he was not devoid of natural talents, for he was a skilled archer and conversed well. At an early period he was fond of me, and we were such warm friends that we always used the same tent on journeys, and the same dwelling at court. His aunt was with me and my sister with him, on which account we were always able to associate without ceremony. Then occurred the affair of my uncle; a bitterness arose between them, and he plotted against the Khán. All my warnings and reproofs were in vain, and after this our friendship began to cool. When he came back [from his flight into Badakhshán] the Khán sent me to order him away again. [On our meeting, Bábá Sultán] began to make profuse excuses and apologies and to profess regret that he had turned a deaf ear to my counsels. [Verses]. . . . Seeing him thus sad and repentant, I hoped he might persist in reforming his conduct, but on reaching India, a change for the worse came over him, and on account of his former evil associations, he never again mended his ways. [Verse]. . . . His body was carried from Ruhtak to Badakhshán, and was buried in the tomb of Sháh Sultán Muhammad Badakhshi—his grandfather on his grandmother's side.

CHAPTER LXXVIII.

SHÁH MUHAMMAD SULTÁN, AND CONCLUSION OF HIS STORY.

Sháh Muhammad Sultán was the son of Sultán Muhammad Sultán, son of Sultán Mahmud Khán, son of Yunus Khán. He was only a child when Sultán Mahmud Khán, with his [other] children, was put to death by Sháhi Beg Khán, as has been explained. One of Sháhi Beg Khán's Amirs, taking pity on this child, instead of putting him to death, kept him safe in hiding. After Sháhi Beg Khán had been killed, and Bábar Pádisháh conquered Mávará-un-Nahr, this Uzbeg Amir sent the child to the Emperor, in whose service he remained [for some time]. When the Emperor, on account of the successes of the Uzbeg, was obliged to return to

Kábul, Sháh Muhammad Sultán stayed in Badakhshán with Mirzá Khán. On hearing of the conquest of Káshghar, he went to join the Khán, who loved, and treated, him as his own son. He was brought up in the special apartments of [the Khan's] children, and when he was grown up, the Khán gave him his full sister, Khadija Sultán Khánim, as a proof of his love and a token of his perfect regard for him. [Couplet]. . . .

We spent most of our time in each other's society. During nine years Sháh Muhammad Sultán, Bábá Sultan and I had remained continually in the Khán's service. Like the three dots under the letter *Sin* in Said,[1] we were never separated, nor did we leave his service for a moment on any pretext. Our worldly goods we shared in common, and were participators in each other's praise and blame. . . .[2]

For nine years this unanimity of feeling and action continued. But at length the crooked wheel of fortune worked a change. . . .[3] In the spring following the winter in which Bábá Sultan fled, a strange circumstance happened to Sháh Muhammad Sultán. The details are as follows. There was, at this time, a certain Bábá Sayyid, son of the sister of Mirzá Muhammad Begjik, for whom Sháh Muhammad Sultán conceived a great friendship. But Bábá Sayyid was a young man who, from the first, passed the limits of decency and moderation. [Verses concerning impiety and immorality]. . . . The remonstrances, reproofs and advice of the Khán and myself were in vain; his immoral conduct could not be checked, and he went so far as to prompt the young Sultán to aspire to sovereignty. The matter was rumoured everywhere and discussed by every one, till at last the Khán saw no remedy, but to banish the young Sultán from the country. [Couplet]. . . . He therefore sent Sháh Muhammad Sultán, together with Bábá Sayyid and some attendants, to Karátigin. Two of the Amirs, Muhammadi Barlás and Amir Jánaka, attended them as an escort. But on the road Amir Jánaka showed some hostility and wished to convey the Sultán to some place [other than their destination], on which account Muhammadi Barlás seized him. Thereupon Bábá Sayyid incited Sháh Muhammad Sultán to attempt the release of Amir Jánaka, saying: "It is his fidelity to you that has exposed him to this misfortune. You must save him from the hands of Muhammadi Barlás, by main force. What can Muhammadi do to you?" Sháh Muhammad Sultán, deceived by these words, turned back and at midnight approached the party,

[1] This refers to the custom, in very careful writing, of placing three dots under the letter *Sin* to distinguish it, with certainty, from the *Shin* with three dots above.—R.

[2] This passage is slightly abridged and a quatrain omitted.—R.

[3] Six lines and some verses, on fortune reversing the order of things, are left out here.—R.

who being apprehensive [of some such danger] were standing fully armed. [As he approached] he called out: "Release Amir Jánaka!" to which they replied: "Whosoever you may be, retire! otherwise we will smother you in arrows." The Sultán heard this threat, but paid no attention to it. (Has it not been said: at night the king is unjust?) The party then let fly their arrows and, by chance, the Sultán was struck [in the breast]; he retired a short distance and then expired. Muhammadi captured Amir Jánaka.

Having acted thus violently without orders, the party were thrown into the utmost consternation and knew not what to do next. A strange discussion took place among the *Ulus*. Some who had advised the Sultán, fled. Others, the Khán reassured with promises and agreements.

In the meanwhile Bábá Sultán, who had fled the previous winter to Khatlán and Kunduz, having discovered that what Mazid and the rest of them had told him was false and groundless, returned ashamed and penitent. The Khán sent me to meet him, and I turned him back; but I supplied him with all necessaries for the journey, before bidding him farewell, as has been related. The wife of Sháh Muhammad Sultán (the Khán's sister) and Sultán Nigár Khánim and Daulat Sultán Khánim (the Khán's aunt) and also the aunt of Sháh Muhammad Sultán's father, and the Khán's wife, Zainab Sultán Khánim (Sháh Muhammad Sultán's aunt) all came and demanded of the Khán why he had ordered the death of Sháh Muhammad Sultán. Whereupon the Khán swore a solemn oath, saying: "I did not give the order." They then said: "Deliver Muhammadi over to us! that we may avenge on him the death [of the Sultán]." To this the Khán agreed.

Muhammadi appealed to me and my uncle to rescue him. He was in the service of Rashid Sultán. He begged me to use my endeavours for his security, so I took his part, and privately, but with great emphasis, represented to the Khán as follows: "The Sultáns who were brothers are all gone: this Sultán, who is your son, and still remains, will also be offended, and I too should be much afflicted [if you put Muhammadi to death], for he is a blood relation of mine." The Khán then placed the whole matter in my hands [saying: "You can act as you choose; if you wish to retaliate, do so: if you wish to let him go, the choice lies with you."] But the above-mentioned Khánims, who were all either my maternal aunts or their daughters, began with one accord to blame and reproach me, saying: "What in the world will your blood connection with the Barlás lead you to, if it make you neglect such an important duty as this? Sháh Muhammad Sultán was a closer connection by many degrees than he. If [Muhammadi] is your father's uncle, this man [Sháh Muhammad Sultán] was your own uncle, and besides this, your friend and companion. Your cousin [1] Khadija is his wife, and his wife's sister (the daughter of his paternal uncle) is of your household.[2] How can you, in consideration of all this, attach yourself to the side of Muhammadi?" [Such were the taunts and reproaches they poured down on me]; nevertheless, Fate willed that I should pay no attention to the true words of my relations; I returned falsehood for truth and would not hear of retaliation. I put Muhammadi under the care of my uncle, who carried him off into the mountainous tracts of Káshghar.

This incident led to a certain degree of ill-feeling between myself and my relations, [which was, however, dispelled a short time after]. But I was caused much trouble and exposed to great annoyance, ere I was able to deliver Muhammadi Barlás out of the hands of the Khánims; and [in doing so] I raised an executioner for my uncle and his children. I brought calamity upon myself—God forgive me! and again I say God forgive me! Since I did this unjust action, God sent this same Muhammadi [to overpower us]. Verily injustice can only bring ruin in its train. This same Muhammadi, whom I and my uncle had saved from so great a danger, neglected nothing in his endeavours to murder my uncle and his children, and to bring about the extinction of myself and my house—a house upon which four hundred years had worked no change. The Prophet said: "Whoso helpeth a tyrant, God will give the tyrant power over him." . . . .[3]

CHAPTER LXXIX.

RASHID SULTÁN AND THE AUTHOR LEAD A HOLY WAR INTO BALUR.

After the affair of Sháh Muhammad Sultán, misunderstandings arose among my relations. In the winter of the same year, the Khán commanded Rashid Sultán and myself to make a holy war on Balur. Though we had been at variance with our relations, we made it up, and set out in all haste for Balur.

Balur is an infidel country [*Káfiristán*], and most of its inhabitants are mountaineers. Not one of them has a religion or a creed. Nor is there anything which they [consider it right to] abstain from or to avoid [as impure]; but they do whatever they list, and follow their

[1] Lit.: daughter of maternal uncle.—R.

[2] By "of your household" is meant (as the Turki version explains) "your wife."—R.

[3] Some verses from the Koran and a prayer of about seven lines, are left out here.—R.

desires without check or compunction. Baluristán is bounded on the east by the provinces of Káshghar and Yárkand; on the north by Badakhshán; on the west by Kábul and Lumghán; and on the south by the dependencies of Káshmir.[1] It is four months' journey in circumference. Its whole extent consists of mountains, valleys, and defiles, insomuch that one might almost say that in the whole of Baluristán, not one *farsákh* of level ground is to be met with. The population is numerous. No village is at peace with another, but there is constant hostility, and fights are continually occurring among them.

[1] The author gives so good a definition of the region that was formerly called by Western Asiatics *Bolor*, *Balur*, *Baluristan*, *Malur*, etc., and by the Chinese *Po-lo-lo*, that further elucidation is scarcely required. In one form or another the name is found in writings dating from the seventh century down to the eighteenth. Even at the present day it may not be entirely extinct, for some twenty years ago, Mr. R. B. Shaw found that the Kirghiz of the Pamirs called Chitrál by the name of *Pálor*. To all other inhabitants of the surrounding regions, however, the word appears now to be unknown.

I would only remark that when our author gives the provinces of Kashghar and Yarkand as the eastern boundary of Balur, he appears to be somewhat at fault in his orientation. The province of Kashghar, at any rate, can hardly have formed part of the eastern boundary, if Kabul and Lughmán (the Lumghán of the text) formed the western, and Badakhshán the northern limits, as he conceives them to do. He appears to have been facing about north-west, when he imagined himself to be looking to the north, and thus to have displaced his bearings by about 45 degrees, all round the horizon. If Kashghar was the eastern neighbour of *Balur*, Badakhshán must have been the western and not the northern, and so on. Again, Sarigh-Kul and the Pamirs must have formed part of Balur, but this, from Mirza Haidar's own statements, does not appear to have been the case. His description of the country, products, and people applies obviously to the region south of the Indus water-parting range (the Eastern Hindu Kush), and not to the open Pamirs; while his return from Balur to Sárigh Chupán, also implies advent from the region south of the mountains.

Yarkand may, in a sense, have formed part of the eastern boundary, for it is possible to reckon all the uninhabited mountain masses lying between the southern plains of Yarkand, on the one hand, and Baltistán, or Little Tibet, on the other, as included in the Yarkand province. Possibly even the comparatively low-lying district of Tásh-Kurghán, though north of the watershed, may also have been included in Balur. Thus it would, perhaps, be more correct to say that the provinces of Yarkand and Baltistán formed the eastern boundary of the region in question.

The Balur country would then include Hunza, Nagar, possibly Tásh-Kurghán, Gilgit, Panyál, Yasin, Chitrál, and probably the tract now known as Kafiristan: while, also, some of the small states south of Gilgit, Yasin, etc., may have been regarded as part of Balur.

The location of Balur, or Bolor, was long a subject of uncertainty for geographers and commentators, but as the matter has now been cleared up, the old questions need not be discussed afresh. The most complete dissertation on the entire subject that I know of, is that contained in Sir H. Yule's notes in the *J. R. G. S.* for 1872 (pp. 473 *seq.*) and in his *Marco Polo*, i., pp, 187, 188, where the conclusions arrived at, are very nearly borne out by Mirza Haidar's description. The only differences are (1) that, according to our author, Baltistán cannot have been included in Balur, as he always speaks of that country, later in his work, as a separate province with the name of *Balti*, and says that it bordered on *Balur*; and (2) that *Balur* was confined almost entirely, as far as I am able to judge from his description in this passage and elsewhere, (see for example his statements pp. 405 and 417) to the southern slopes of the Eastern Hindu Kush, or Indus water-parting range; while Sir H. Yule's map makes it embrace Sárigh-Kul and the greater part of the eastern Pamirs.

Most of their battles are conducted in the following manner. Their women are employed in the management of the house and the labour of the fields; the men in war. While their wives are in their houses preparing the food [the men will be engaged in fighting]. Then the wives will come out to them and make them desist, saying it is time for a meal, and they must leave off fighting. So they separate and go back to their homes to eat their food, after which they return to the fight until afternoon prayer-time, when the women will again come on the scene and make peace, which endures till sunrise, every one having returned to his own house. Sometimes it happens that no pacification is brought about, in which case they fortify and watch their houses all through the night with the utmost vigilance. In this way do they spend the whole of their lives.

As plains and pasture grounds are scarce, the people can keep but few cattle. They own a small number of sheep and goats from whose wool they make clothes, and cows which furnish them with milk and butter; beyond these they have nothing [in the way of flocks]. The tribe of each separate valley speaks a different language [to that of its neighbours], and no one tribe knows the language of another. On account of being continually at war, few of them have seen any other village than their own. In Balur there are beautiful gardens and an abundance of fruits, especially of pomegranates, which are excellent and most plentiful. There is one kind of pomegranate which is peculiar to Baluristán. Its seeds are white and very transparent; it is also sweet, pure, and full-flavoured. Honey is also abundant.

To resume: we passed that winter in Baluristán and fought many bloody [*sab*] battles, in which victory was on our side. In the spring we returned in safety, laden with spoil, and came to Sárigh Chupán, where a fifth of the booty was set apart; and a fifth amounted to more than a thousand [loads].

In the early part of the spring of 934 we rejoined the Khán. In the summer following, Sultán Nigár Khánim, whom I have had occasion to mention so frequently in this book, died of a hæmorrhage. I discovered the date in [the word] "*khuldash.*"

CHAPTER LXXX.

SECOND EXPEDITION OF THE KHÁN INTO BADAKHSHÁN, AND THE CAUSES OF CERTAIN CONTEMPORARY EVENTS.

In the year 935 [1528–9] Bábar Pádisháh recalled Humáyun Mirzá into Hindustán. The reason for this was that Mirzá Khán (the son of Sultán Mahmud Mirzá, son of Abu Said Mirzá) had died in Badahkshán, as has been related, and left behind him a child named Sulaimán. Bábar Pádisháh took this boy and kept him near himself, placing his own distinguished son, Humáyun, on the throne of Badakhshán, where he reigned from 926 to 935.

At the time when Bábar Pádisháh had subdued Hindustán and overthrown his enemies, two of his sons had become youths—Humáyun Mirzá and Kamrán Mirzá. Leaving the latter in Kandahár, he sent for Humáyun in order that he might have one of his sons [continually] by him, so that if he were to die suddenly, there would be a successor near at hand. For these reasons he recalled Humáyun Mirzá into Hindustán. But the people of Badakhshán made the following representation to Humáyun Mirzá: "Badakhshán borders on the [territory of the] Uzbeg, who cherish in their hearts an ancient hatred for Badakhshán. [If they attack Badakhshán] our Amirs will be unable to check them." To this Humáyun Mirzá made reply: "All that you say is true, still I am unable to deviate from my father's commands. But I will do my best to send one of my brothers to you, as soon as possible." Having thus reassured the people, he started for Hindustán.

[No sooner was he gone than] the inhabitants of [Badakhshán] began to despair; and all the Amirs, with Sultán Avais at their head, despatched express messengers to the Khán, representing: "Humáyun Mirzá has gone to Hindustán, leaving this province in the hands of Fakir Ali, who is quite incapable of coping with the Uzbeg, [and therefore] of establishing tranquillity in Badakhshán. If, by such and such a date, the Khán were to come, all would be well; otherwise we must succumb to the Uzbeg. But if the Uzbeg come and attack us before the arrival of the Khán, they will not be able [by the date mentioned] to obtain a firm footing. We implore his help. Perhaps he may be the cause of our salvation. Moreover, Badakhshán belongs to the Khán by right of inheritance from his grandmother, Sháh Begum; nor is there a more rightful heir than he." So persistent were they in their appeals, that the Khán became convinced that if he did not go [to their aid] Badakhshán would fall into the hands of the Uzbeg. Therefore, at the beginning of Moharram of the year '36, he set out for Badakhshán, leaving Rashid Sultán in Yárkand.

It has been mentioned above, that Táhir Khán had been left alone, and in the winter had been deserted by the Kirghiz and all his following. On this account the Khán showed him magnanimity and did nothing. After he had been a short time among the Kirghiz, about twenty or thirty thousand Uzbeg again gathered round him; and he prepared himself in every way [for war]. [The Khán on his departure] therefore left Rashid Sultán to guard and protect the province of Káshghar. On reaching Sárigh Chupán, the Khán sent me forward with an advance guard [*manghalái*], while he followed after. I arrived in Badakhshán and learnt that Hindál Mirzá, the youngest of the Emperor's sons, had been sent from Kábul by Humáyun Mirzá; also that twelve[1] days previous [to my arrival] he had reached and entered Kala Zafar. As it was the season of Capricorn and the middle of winter, to turn back would have been difficult. So [we were obliged to] go on to Kala Zafar, where we tried to enter into some negotiations, suggesting that some of the districts of Badakhshán should be given up to us, and at the close of the winter the Khán would again retire. But they did not trust us; nay, more, they suspected us of deceit. So we finally resolved upon pillage, and, until the Khán arrived, I scoured the whole country round Kala Zafar; I brought together both man and beast, and indeed all to which the word "thing" could be applied. At the end of a few days the Khán himself arrived, and during three months laid siege to Kala Zafar, while his men carried off, from the surrounding country, the little that I had left. Near the end of winter, many of the Amirs who had sent for the Khán, came and waited on him, representing, with profuse apologies, that if Hindál Mirzá had not come, they would have hastened to meet and receive the Khán. To this the Khán replied: "It is out of the question that I should oppose Bábar Pádisháh. You sent me entreating letters, saying that you would be swallowed up by the Uzbeg, and that the presence of the Uzbeg in Badakhshán would be equally hurtful to both sides;[2] for this reason I came. As matters stand, every man ought now to return to his own home." [Thereupon] the Khán left Kala Zafar, and set out again for Káshghar.

When news of the Khán's entry into Badakhshán reached the Emperor, he was greatly displeased, and after due consideration and reflection, he despatched Sulaimán Sháh Mirzá [to Badakhshán] and recalled Hindál Mirzá [into Hindustán]. At the same time

[1] The Turki version has fifteen days.—R.

[2] Here the Turki MS. has: "equally hurtful to us and to the Emperor," which is obviously the sense intended.

he wrote to the Khán: "Considering my numerous claims [on your consideration] [and the ties that exist between us] this affair seems strange. I have recalled Hindál Mirzá, and have sent Sulaimán. If you have any regard for hereditary rights, you will be kind to Sulaimán Sháh, and leave him in possession of Badakhshán, for he is as a son to us both. This would be well. Otherwise I, having given up my responsibility, will place the inheritance in the hands of the heir. The rest you know."

When Sulaimán Sháh Mirzá reached Kábul,[1] [he found that the Khán] had retreated some time before. Hindál Mirzá, in obedience to the orders he had received, gave up Badakhshán to Sulaimán Sháh Mirzá, and proceeded to India. From that time to the present, Sulaimán has reigned in Badakhshán.

The Khán [returning from Badakhshán] reached Yárkand at the beginning of spring. On the road my uncle fell ill, and when he arrived at Káshghar, his complaint took the forms of intermittent fever, dropsy, asthma and ague, so that all the doctors who were attending him, such as Khwája Nur-ud-Din, Abdul Váhid Tuhuri, Kázi Shams-ud-Din Ali and others, were at a loss; the symptoms at last became so grave that his life was despaired of. In the meanwhile Khwája Nurá arrived from Turfán, whither he had gone on the invitation of Mansur Khán, who had said that if [the Hazrat] would honour him with a visit, he and his friends would esteem it a great blessing. [Couplet] . . . Accepting this invitation, Khwája Nurá went to Turfán, and having quenched the thirst of those parched wanderers in the desert of longing, with the wine of his presence, he returned to Káshghar. [Two couplets] . . .

My uncle's state was now such that he fainted every few minutes, and became unconscious.[2] Soon after his Holiness began to attend to my uncle, the gravity of the disease showed signs of abatement. All his remedies had a beneficial effect, yet as a fact, this was not medical treatment, but miraculous power and holy influence: for the patient had become so weak and emaciated that he could not take medicines, and in such circumstances what can a doctor do? Therefore this was a miracle.

During this time a difference arose between Khwája Nurá and his younger brother, Khwája Muhammad Yusuf, on account of the neglect of a point of etiquette. The breach widened [from day to day]. One day I went to wait upon Khwája Nurá, and found Khwája Muhammad Yusuf sitting in his presence. Khwája Nurá had worked himself into a passion, and as soon as I had taken my seat, said: "Muhammad Yusuf, why do you act thus? If you are the disciple of our father, I am the disciple of his Holiness—that is,

[1] All the texts read *Kabul*, but apparently that name is a slip for *Badakhshán*. As it stands, the sense of the passage is not evident.

[2] Some details of the symptoms of the disease are omitted.

of Khwája Ihrár Khwája Ubaidullah; and besides this I have many points of superiority over you. You are foster-brother to my eldest son. Apart from all this, I am supported by God and His Prophet; what strength have you to oppose me?" Khwája Muhammad Yusuf replied: "I also am hopeful of the help of the Prophet." Then, asked Khwája Nurá: "Are you willing that the Prophet should be mediator between us?" Khwája Muhammad Yusuf answered: "I am quite willing," and Khwája Nurá having intimated that he also was willing, not another word was said. Thus the meeting terminated.

Shortly after this, Khwája Nurá set out for Badakhshán. One day somebody came and told him that Khwája Muhammad Yusuf had fallen ill, and was asking for him. I went to visit him and found he had a fever. The Khwája said to me: "I know well that Khwája Khávand Mahmud has taken an interest in me for some time past, he is kindly disposed towards me and gives me comfort from the Prophet. But now I do not know what has become of this comfort; for not a trace of it is apparent, and I am quite convinced that I shall not recover from my present illness. Khwája Khávand, who is my brother—nay more, stands in the place of a father to me, ought not to have treated me thus; he has put aside all his brotherly love and fatherly affection." These and a thousand such lamentations did he pour into my ears. He also told me a few anecdotes, and entrusted some of his household to my care. He gave me a garment of camel's-hair and an apron, as souvenirs. In vain did I attempt to dispel his ideas [of impending death]; he only replied: "I am convinced; there is not a shadow of doubt." He died on the sixth night of his illness, on the 14th of the month Safar of the year 937. I discovered this date in "*Táir-i-Bihishti*" [a bird of paradise].

After this, the Khán sent me to Khwája Nurá to entreat him to return, which he did, and the Khán came out to receive him; he placed his head at the Khwája's feet and offered him profuse apologies. The funeral rites of Khwája Muhammad Yusuf were then performed, [including] the giving of alms, distribution of food and reading the Korán through.

But Khwája Nurá chose to dwell in Yángi-Hisár, and the Khán, in order to wait on him, left Yárkand and went thither likewise. There, they and the friends and disciples of the Khwája spent that winter. The Khwája performed wondrous things in their sight. The Khán was continually in his service.

CHAPTER LXXXI.

CAUSES OF THE RUPTURE BETWEEN THE KHÁN AND AIMAN KHWÁJA SULTÁN.

The details of this affair would be tedious and irrelevant; but it was briefly as follows. Mirzá Ali Taghái, whose name appears in the lists made at Káshghar,[1] was exceedingly jealous of my uncle, but this did not show itself outwardly. Although he tried hard [to injure him], slander and detraction could gain no hearing in the service of the Khán. As was mentioned above, the Khán gave my uncle's daughter to Aiman Khwája Sultán in marriage, and from this connection had come many fine children; thus a bond of union [which should have lasted till the day of judgment] was formed between my uncle and the Sultán.

But seditious thoughts suggested themselves to Mirzá Ali Taghái. Since the spirit of jealousy had no effect on the Khán's relations with the Mirzá, he tried to beguile Aiman Khwája Sultán, and stir up the dust of dissension between the brothers. He would thus, he thought, gain his end. For if Sayyid Muhammad Mirzá took the part of his son-in-law and the latter's children, he would have, of necessity, to break with his maternal uncle, which would suit his [Mirzá Ali Taghái's] purposes well. If, on the other hand [the Mirzá] sided with the Khán, he would be closing the eye of fatherly affection on Aiman Khwája Sultán, and his children. In this event likewise [the Mirzá] would suffer, for the cause of Aiman Khwája Sultán would be ruined, and the power of the Mirzá, in a measure, broken. Acting upon these mischievous calculations, he, by a series of misrepresentations and suggestions, made the Khán and Aiman Khwája Sultán mutually apprehensive of one another.

The details are briefly these: At the time when the Khán marched against Andiján, [Mirzá Ali Taghái] said privately to Aiman Khwája Sultán: "I perceive that the Khán has changed [in his conduct] towards you, on account of my loyalty; he wishes to set up his son Rashid Sultán in your place, and give him the province of Aksu. You must now look well to your own interests, and trusting my words, act upon them." While to the Khán, he was for ever saying: "Aiman Khwája Sultán is afraid of you without right or reason. It is very probable that he will appeal to your

[1] The author frequently refers, in these words, to the analysis or review of the Khan's army, when on the point of invading Kashghar in the spring of 920 H. (See pp. 305 *seq.*)

enemies for aid [and stir up a revolt]. But the Khán does not credit my words, and says they are the outcome of mere delusion. His evidence is that this year Aiman Khwája Sultán is committing such and such acts." [Then Mirzá Ali Taghái] sends secretly to the Sultán, saying: "The right time is now come for you to do so and so." In his artlessness and stupidity [the Sultán] does what has been suggested. Then Mirzá Ali Taghái represents to the Khán: "I told you that Aiman Khwája Sultán would do such and such a thing this year. My words have come true."

From the time of the Khán's march against Andiján until his death, a period of some six years, this sort of intrigue was continually going on. And finally the Khán became altogether estranged from Aiman Khwája Sultán. It was in vain that my uncle and I reproved Aiman Khwája Sultán; when we asked him why he acted in this way, he could give no satisfactory reply, but persisted in his course; his motives were unknown to us.

At last we discovered that it was all the work of Mirzá Ali Taghái. When Mirzá Ali Taghái remarked the great change in the Khán's feelings towards Aiman Khwája Sultán, he took advantage of the opportunity, and represented as follows to the Khán: "Since Aiman Khwája Sultán's presence in Aksu may lead to a revolt, it will be better to set up Rashid Sultán in his place, and send him to govern some district of Badakhshán. This would be greatly to your advantage. But I am fearful lest the Mirzás become angry with me. If they consent [to the arrangement] you will find it most advantageous; but it will be a difficult thing to mention to the Mirzás." (By the Mirzás, he meant my uncle and myself.)

The Khán told me of this; I replied: "In what way is Aiman Khwája Sultán preferable to your Highness' [other] servants, that this change should be necessary for the good of the State? I do not consent to it. His relationship to your Highness is [only] equal to ours. If my uncle's daughter is of his household and has children [by him], the daughter of my paternal uncle is in your haram, and these two amount to precisely the same [degree of relationship]. Rather there is the advantage [on our side] that I have been in your service for twenty-three years, and you have always singled me out for your fatherly care and brotherly love. How then shall I exchange the Khán's cause for that of the Sultán? I will forward any measure that may be for the benefit of your State, by all the means in my power."

The Khán spoke also of this matter to my uncle, who said: "[Your Highness'] opinion is always enlightened; I am ready to do your bidding on every occasion. . . .[1] Although I did not know that [the Sultán] could harm you, yet I trust your hitherto

[1] One line, containing a passage of which no sense can be made, is omitted.—R.

infallible judgment, and will do whatever is most fitting in the matter."

These discussions being terminated, the Khán explained to us his proposals. He ordered me to take Rashid Sultán [to Aksu], and after sending Aiman Khwája Sultán away from there, to place Rashid Sultán upon the throne. Aiman Khwája Sultán was to come to [the Khán's] court, and to remain there until the country should be reduced to order. All must be done to advance the affairs of Rashid Sultán. To my uncle he said: "Let all be carried out as I have ordered." I said: "With all willingness I undertake the task."

Two days later I started for Aksu. On reaching Uch I was received by Sháh Báz Mirzá, who was also mentioned in the lists at Káshghar. After leaving Uch, I was met [*istikbál*] by all the men of Aiman Khwája Sultán, who sent a message to me asking: "What has happened? How would it be for us, having set aside all considerations of relationship, to meet [in consultation]?" But I would not consent [to an interview] and said: "As there is nothing to be gained by an interview, it is not worth while to have one." I then sent a person to [the Sultán] with all the necessary provisions for a journey, and also some trusty men to accompany him. [After that I set myself] to encourage the soldiers and populace [of Aksu] and to settle their affairs in the most profitable manner; I passed the necessary orders to the old servants of Rashid Sultán, and arranged the government of the province by dividing it equally into villages and districts. Thus all the people were reassured. I stayed there six months.

Rashid Sultán was satisfied with all that was done, and there grew up between us the strongest attachment. During my sojourn, we were never apart for a moment. There was not the slightest disagreement between us. All that he did was pleasing in my sight; and all that I performed met with his approval.

Whatever I had suffered in being separated from my old friends, that is to say, Sháh Muhammad Sultán and Bábá Sultán, was atoned for in my friendship with Rashid Sultán. One day Rashid Sultán said to me: "Although formerly in Moghulistán, in accordance with the Moghul usage, and by the Khán's express command, there existed between us close friendship, and we used to give each other horses, nevertheless this fellowship was not confirmed by any vow. I am now desirous of renewing the old friendship and of ratifying it by solemn oaths." I too showed my willingness, and the conditions of our covenant were that, on my side, as long as the Khán should live, I would remain in his service; but if the Khán were to die, I would serve no one but him [Rashid Sultán]—and serve him in the Khán's place, as he had served the Khán. Rashid Sultán said: "After the Khán, I look upon you as my eldest brother. If, in public, you reverence me in the place of the Khán, I in private will honour you as you deserve, and will show you even greater kindness and favour than did the Khán. I will give such offices to your uncle and relations as you may judge best." And all this we confirmed with binding oaths. [Two couplets]. . . .

This matter being concluded, he bade me farewell, and I returned to the Khán, who was in Yángi-Hisár. He received me in a most flattering manner, and would not hear of my going back to my home in Yárkand; but instead, took me with him on a hunting expedition to Tuyun Báshi—one of the frontiers of Moghulistán. On reaching the hunting ground, we were joined by the Sultán, who came from Aksu. Soon after this the Khán had a return of his old chronic illness, which took the form of flatulence, or wind in the belly and stomach, fits of shivering, and partial paralysis. Often, after hunting, he got a chill on the stomach, and his malady returned. But on this occasion the symptoms were worse than they had ever been before. My uncle was immediately sent for from Káshghar; but by the time he arrived the doctors of the royal camp had succeeded in curing the disease, by means of effective remedies.

Still, this time the Khán was much concerned about his illness. He sent for my uncle and Rashid Sultán, and said to them: "This illness has made me very anxious. I have frequently had such attacks before; for several years they have happened annually, but this year I have been seized twice, and the second time more severely than the first. My wish now is that there should be a covenant between you (meaning my uncle) and Rashid Sultán. In Mirzá Haidar's case there is no need of renewal, for not only did I establish them on a friendly footing in Moghulistán, but they have lately again, in Aksu, concluded a satisfactory agreement." Then, addressing them both in the Turki language, the Khán continued: "Oh, Sayyid Muhammad Mirzá, if anything should happen to me, look upon Rashid Sultán as standing in my place. And you, Rashid, look upon the Mirzá as in my place also." He said many kind things besides, all of which it would be tedious to repeat here.

The Khán took up his winter quarters in Yángi-Hisár, while I went to Yárkand. Previously, when I had come from Aksu I had found the Khán busily engaged in reading with, and learning under [*irádat*], Hazrat Makhdumi Nurá.

CHAPTER LXXXII.

THE KHÁN BECOMES A DISCIPLE OF KHWÁJA KHÁVAND MAHMUD.

After the Khwája Muhammad Yusuf incident, I tried constantly to induce the Khán to place himself under the guidance of Hazrat Makhdumi Nurá. The Khán would reply: "I desire this with all my soul. Without seeking [what you suggest], I wished to resign the government in order that I might follow that most perfect guide, Khwája Nurá; but the more I examined myself, the less capable did I feel of making an open request to his Holiness. I then resolved to change my mode of living and to mend my ways, so as to render myself more fitting for his service. If I should acquire proficiency and capacity in the right path, then would Khwája Nurá show me favour, without any request on my part; but if I should fail, my petition would be fruitless. I trust that, by God's grace, I may attain my end without addressing an open request to his Holiness. If such a happy consummation should be reached I shall feel reassured." However much I insisted, the Khán always gave the same reply. A few months after my departure for Aksu, a letter arrived, directed in my name, containing certain [instructions] with regard to the affairs of Aksu; and on the margin there was some of the Khán's blessed handwriting. I have it intact before me at this moment.[1]

* * * * * * *

CHAPTER LXXXIII.

GENEALOGY AND LIFE OF HAZRAT KHWÁJA KHÁVAND MAHMUD SHAHÁB-UD-DIN.

(He is always spoken of in this book as Hazrat Makhdumi Nurá.) He received the name of Mahmud from his father, and that of Shaháb-ud-Din from his grandfather. Out of veneration they gave him the name of Khwája Khávand Mahmud . . . .[2]

I have heard Hazrat Makhdumi Nurá relate that when his father died he was twenty-seven years of age. He had heard his

[1] The omission here consists of some long high-flown passages on the subject of saints. The Khán's marginal note is not given by the author.—R.

[2] Some more irrelevant matter regarding saints and their virtues, is left out here.—R.

father say: "In Shahr-i-Sabz of Samarkand there is a garden, and in the garden a mulberry tree; and Khwája Bahá-ul-Hakk wa ud-Din Nakhshband used to sit leaning against that tree. Hazrat Ishán, on account of this blessing, bought the garden. In front of the tree is a tank. One night, on the edge of the tank, Hazrat Ishán related to Khwája Ubaid-ul-Hádi and myself as follows: "During the lifetime of Hazrat Ishán [1] I suffered from a weakness of the stomach, which the doctors of Mávará-un-Nahr were unable to cure. I then went into Khorásán,[2] where the Shaikh ul Islám, Mauláná Abdur Rahman Jámi, brought me to his own house, and in his service I remained [for some little time]. I studied some of his tracts under him." I learnt that he had received his education at the hands of Bandagi Maulavi [Jámi], and from the pamphlet which I have copied into this book,[3] it appears that Khwája Nurá read standard books under him. After the death of Jámi, he went into Irák, where he enjoyed the society of Mir Hasan Yazdi and Mir Sadr-ud-Din. He next went and studied, for a period of six years, under Mauláná Jalál-ud-Din Dáváni, and he also studied medicine under Mauláná Imád-ud-Din, who was the most eminent physician, not merely in Irák, but in the whole world. . . . .[4]

Having completed his medical studies in Shiráz, he passed into Rum, where also he devoted himself to study. Thence he journeyed into Egypt. Having performed the pilgrimage [to Mekka], he embarked at Jadda, and went to India by way of Gujrát. Thence he repaired to Kábul, where Bábar Pádisháh was at that time; and I, as already mentioned, was there also. These travels had occupied Khwája Nurá twenty-three years. When the Emperor took Samarkand, the Khwája went thither, and on the Emperor's returning to Kábul, the Khwája remained in Samarkand until the year 931, when he returned to Káshghar, as was mentioned. In those days he related: "In Samarkand I saw, in a vision, Mauláná Háji Kásim (one of Hazrat Ishán's servants) come with two horses, saying that Hazrat Ishán had ordered him to tell Khwája Nurá to take these two horses and go to Káshghar." Before the Khwája reached Káshghar my uncle was attacked by paralysis, but on his arrival the Khwája, by means of his remedies, completely restored him to health. He stayed two years in Káshghar, where his associates were enriched by his blessings.

Mansur Khán sent some persons to him, saying that no Makh-

[1] The Hazrat Ishán alluded to here, is apparently one who has not been hitherto mentioned.

[2] In the Turki stands: "In order to be cured, I was obliged to go to Khorasán."—R.

[3] Quoted *in extenso* lower down, but omitted in this translation, as having no bearing on the history.

[4] A line of rhetoric omitted.—R.

dumzáda had ever come to those corners [of the earth], Turfán and Chálish, which were the residence of the disciples of his [spiritual] fathers; these people and this country had never been blessed by a visit from the Khwája. As it would be difficult for his friends in those quarters to go to him, all their blessings would be upon him if he would come and honour them. The Khwája accepted this invitation of Mansur Khán, and set out for Turfán, where he remained nearly three years, and brought blessings to those who associated with him.

On the Khán's return from the Badakhshán campaign, Khwája Nurá left Turfán and stayed in Káshghar to attend my uncle, who, as mentioned above, had become subject to fits of vomiting [*istiská*]. Having again restored my uncle to perfect health, he proceeded to Yárkand. Here Khwája Muhammad Yusuf, as has been related above, did not come out to greet him in the prescribed manner, from which circumstance a dispute arose, which terminated as already described. After this affair he went to Yángi-Hisár, in which place the Khán also spent the winter, in order to wait upon his Holiness . . . .[1] The Khwája told me that after the death of Abdur Rahmán Jámi, he found under his pillow some rough copies, one of which he gave, written out, to me; and I have copied it here. He gave me these passages in Yángi-Hisár in the year 937 [1530–31]. . . . .[2]

At the end of the winter I went to Aksu, and there [found] the Khán and some of his adherents, high officials, nobles, and others. At their request the Khwája wrote several pamphlets. One of these is the following, which I have copied out in full. [3]

* * * * * * *

[1] About five lines left out, regarding some miracles performed by the saint, together with three verses of an ode by the author.

[2] Here follows half a folio containing Jámi's "rough copies," which need not be inserted.

[3] The pamphlet is omitted. It is entirely theological, and has no reference to the *Tarikh-i-Rashidi*, or to any historical subject.

CHAPTER LXXXIV.

JOURNEY OF HAZRAT MAKHDUMI INTO INDIA,[1] AND CERTAIN MATTERS CONNECTED THEREWITH.

THAT spring, Hazrat Makhdumi Nurá set out for India by way of Badakhshán. The Khán escorted him as far as the pass of Shahnáz,[2] [representing] seven or eight days' journey. I, being in Aksu at the time, was denied participation in this happiness. On my return from Aksu the Khán said to me: "On bidding farewell to Khwája Nurá, I begged him to recite the *Fátiha*, and just as he was about to commence I asked him, as a favour, to first of all repeat it for Mirzá Haidar and afterwards for me. He granted my request, and having first recited it for you, he then did so for me." [Two couplets]. . . . Those who were present relate that the Khán, during the few stages he made with the Khwája, was overcome with grief, and whenever the Khwája spoke, he was so overpowered with emotion, that he could not restrain his tears,—a circumstance that greatly impressed those who were present. [Verses]. . . . As this was the last time the Khán would see the Khwája, he naturally felt severely the pangs of separation.

In short, Khwája Nurá arrived in Hindustán. The frontier towns of Hindustán, namely, Kábul and Láhur, were then held by Kámrán Mirzá, who humbly begged the Khwája to stay in Láhur, but the Khwája replied: "From the first, it had been my intention to wait upon the Emperor [Bábar]; therefore I must now go and condole with Humáyun. Having performed this duty, should I return, I will accept your invitation." He then went to Agra, the capital of India, where he was received with great honour by the Emperor [Humáyun].

At that period there had arisen in Hindustán a man named Shaikh Pul. Humáyun was anxious to become his disciple, for he had a great passion for the occult sciences—for magic and conjuration. Shaikh Pul having assumed the garb of a Shaikh, came to the Emperor and taught him that incantations and sorcery were the surest means to the true attainment of an object. Since doctrines such as these suited his disposition, he became at once the Shaikh's disciple. Besides this person, there was Mauláná Muhammad Parghari who, though a Mulla, was a very [irreligious] and unprincipled man, and who always worked hard to gain his

[1] The Turki rubric reads: "Journey into Badakhshan."

[2] I do not know which of the passes reached by ascending the *Shahnáz* river, is meant by this name. It might be the *Káskásu*, or perhaps the *Kara-tásh*. The Khan appears to have returned at this time, from Aksu to one of the western towns.

ends, even when they were of an evil nature. The Shaikh asked the aid of Mulla Muhammad and, in common, by means of flattery, they wrought upon the Emperor for their own purposes, and gained his favour.

Not long after this I went to visit the Emperor, as shall be presently related, but I could never gather that he had learned anything from his *Pir*, Shaikh Pul, except magic and incantations.[1] But God knows best. The influence of Shaikh Pul being thus confirmed, Mauláná Muhammad, or rather the Emperor and all his following, neglected and slighted Khwája Nurá, who had an hereditary claim to their veneration. This naturally caused the Khwája great inward vexation. It was mentioned above that when passing through Láhur, he had been invited by Kámrán Mirzá to take up his abode in that place, and he had promised to do so on his return. In pursuance of his promise, he now set out from Agra to Láhur. Humáyun and his companions begged him [to stay], but he would not listen to their entreaties. He reached Láhur in the year 943 [1536–7]. I had arrived in Láhur just before, and I now had the honour of kissing his feet.

In those days I used frequently to hear him say: "I have seen in a vision, a great sea which overwhelmed all who remained behind us in Agra and Hindustán; while we only escaped after a hundred risks:" and thus did it come about three years later—just as he had said—as shall be presently related."[2] After the devastation of Hindustán he escaped, in safety, to Mávará-un-Nahr, by way of Káshghar.

CHAPTER LXXXV.

MIRACLES OF KHWÁJA NURÁ.

I WAS present in the assembly when Mauláná Muhammad Parghari arrived from Agra, with a letter from Humáyun Pádisháh; he also was present when the Khwája gave the answer before-mentioned. Mauláná Muhammad began to weep and begged that his sins might be forgiven him; he beseeched [the Khwája] with great earnestness to write a letter to Humáyun. The Khwája wrote: "Oh! Humá, do not throw thy noble shadow, in a land

[1] Shaikh *Pul*, *Phul* or *Buhlul*, was well-known in India as a saint and sorcerer. He was put to death at, or near, Agra by adherents of Hindál Mirza in 1537. (See Beale's *Or. Biogra. Dict.*)

[2] The author alludes, apparently, to the battle of Kanauj in 947 (1540), when the Moghuls were overwhelmed by the army of Shir Shah, Sur.

where the parrot is less common than the kite [*zaghan*]." Now, in this miracle there is a curious pun, for Humá Pádisháh did not throw his shadow in the country where the parrot is rarer than the kite. [Mauláná Muhammad] returned stupefied. . . .[1]

While I was in Láhur, Tahmásp Sháh, son of Sháh Ismáil, came from Irák, took Kandahár from the deputies of Kámrán Mirzá, and having given it over to some of his trusted officers, he returned. This caused Kámrán Mirzá intense grief, and he asked me to tell the Khwája of his misfortune. The next day, when I went to wait on the Khwája, he said to me: "I have seen his Holiness in a vision, and he asked me, 'Why are you sad?' I replied: 'On account of Kámrán Mirzá, for the Turkománs have taken Kandahár. What will come of it?' Then his Holiness advanced towards me and taking me by the hand said: 'Do not grieve; he will soon recover it.'" And thus, indeed, it came to pass, for Kámrán Mirzá marched against Kandahár, and the troops of Tahmásp Sháh gave up the city to him in peace. This is an especially strange thing to have occurred, since the Turkomán rulers are very severe with their subordinates. Be this as it may, the matter was terminated quite simply.

Khánzáda Begum, the Emperor's sister, who has been frequently mentioned in this book, fell ill in Kábul. She wrote a letter to the Khwája, and sent it by me, to ask him for a cure for her malady. Now as that letter was badly composed, I rewrote it correctly, and then took it to the Khwája. He, on my arrival, said to me: "I wish to make you partner in a secret," whereupon I stood up humbly. He continued: "Give me the letter that the Begum herself wrote." Now, as a fact, I had written my letter in secret, and no one knew anything about my having done so.

I witnessed many other wonders performed by him.

* * * * *[2]

[1] *Huma* is the name of a mythical bird, supposed to watch over, and throw its shadow upon, kings. By the land where the parrot is common, India is no doubt meant. The omission here consists of a miraculous tale concerning the fasting of the author.

[2] Here follows a Sufi letter by Khwája Nura, copied by the author into his text, but not translated.

CHAPTER LXXXVI.

THE END OF KHWÁJA NURÁ'S BIOGRAPHY.

Though I am not suited to the task, the context demands that I should give Khwája Nurá's line of descent in discipleship. . . .[1]

He was the disciple of his grandfather Khwája Násir-ud-Din Ubaidullah, the disciple of Mauláná Yákub Charkhi, the disciple of Khwája Bahá-ud-Din Nakshband, the disciple of Mir Kalál, the disciple of Khwája Muhammad Bábá-i-Samási, the disciple of Khwája Ali Rámatini, the disciple of Khwája Mahmud Anjir Faghravi, the disciple of Khwája Arif Rivgarvi, the disciple of Khwája Abdul Khálik Ghajdaváni. It were fitting that, in this place, I should speak of each of these holy men individually, but on consideration I do not think myself equal to the task. [Couplet]. . . .

I am fully aware that what I have already written is beyond my powers, but the requirements of the context have been the cause of my boldness, and I ask forgiveness for anything that be not pleasing to God or His Prophet, or the friends of God. [Verses]. . . .

After Khwája Nurá went to Hindustán, the Khán gave Amin Khwája Sultán (who had been brought from Aksu to Badakhshán) leave to go to India also. Although this step was necessitated by the affairs of the State, yet it did not cut the Khán off from his kin. However, Amin Khwája Sultán went to India, where he died a natural death. His eldest son, Masud Sultán, followed him into India. Khizir Khwája Sultán, Mahdi Sultán, and Isán Daulat Sultán, after this dispersion towards India, settled themselves in different places, but there is no object in entering into further details. Whatever God wills that should be said of them, will appear.

[1] Some Sufistic details are omitted here.—R.

CHAPTER LXXXVII.

CONCLUSION OF BÁBAR PÁDISHÁH'S HISTORY.

We have brought the Emperor's history down to the date contained in the words "*Fath-ba-daulat*" [930 = 1524]. So much treasure fell into his hands, that all the people of the world benefited by it. In short, I went to India and was employed in the direction of the affairs of that country, as will be mentioned. The Emperor took possession of all the dominions of Sultán Iskandar Aoghán. Raná Singá, one of the Rájas of Hindustán, came against Bábar Pádisháh with an army of several hundreds of thousands. The Emperor engaged him in battle, and defeated him; [1] and in his mandates took the title of *Ghází*. After this, he marched towards Chitur, where he won decisive victories over the infidels. Returning, he devoted himself to the settlement of the whole of Hindustán. In the course of the year 937 he fell a victim to a severe illness, which the efforts of the doctors were powerless to cure. [Two couplets] . . . . As his end approached, he entrusted all the Amirs and people of the world to Humáyun Mirzá (whom he had recalled from Badakhshán) and his own soul to the Creator of the world. As soon as Humáyun had mounted his father's throne, such persons as Muhammad Zamán Mirzá (son of Badi-uz-Zamán Mirzá, son of Mirzá Sultán Husain), who had been in Bábar Pádisháh's service, and was his son-in-law, together with others, began to raise the flag of revolt and sound the drums of sedition. But Humáyun quieted them all by his kindness. He conquered what little of Hind had been left unsubdued by his father, and went into Guzrát and captured it; but on account of discord among his brothers and the Amirs, he had to abandon it. The rest of his story will be told later.

[1] Raná Sánga, or Sánka, of Chitur—now Udaipur in Rajputana. The author appears to allude to the battle of Kanwa, in March, 1527, (Jamádi II., 933) when Baber defeated the Rána.

CHAPTER LXXXVIII.

INVASION OF TIBET BY THE KHÁN.

WHEN Khwája Nurá passed into Hindustán, and I withdrew from Aksu, Rashid Sultán also returned, as has been already mentioned. During the same winter Rashid Sultán went back, with his family, to Aksu. In the spring of that year, the Khán resolved to conduct a holy war against Tibet. Previous to this, [his] Amirs had frequently invaded and plundered that country, but on account of their ignorance and folly, Islám had made no progress, and there were still numberless infidels in Tibet, besides those whom the Amirs had subdued.[1]

The Khán had always been animated by a desire to carry on holy wars in the path of God, and especially so now that he had just assumed the saintly ways of the Khwájas. He was always ready to devote himself to the cause of the faith, and felt that the holy war was one of the surest roads to salvation and union with God. Prompted by such pious feelings as these, at the end of the year 938[2] he set out to invade Tibet.

Having reached this point in my narrative, it is necessary for me to give some account of the land of Tibet, for this country is so situated that only a few travellers have been able to visit it. On account of the difficulties of the route, which from every point of view is most dangerous—whether by reason of its hills and passes, or the coldness of the air, or the scarcity of water and fuel, or the shameless and lawless highwaymen, who know every inch of the roads and allow no travellers to pass—no one has ever brought back any information concerning this country. In such standard works as the *Muajjam ul Buldán*, the *Jám-i-Giti Numái*, and the Supplement to the *Surâh*, Tibet is not described as other countries are; they merely mention that there is such a region, and some few facts regarding it are given. I am therefore emboldened to furnish some details about the kingdom of Tibet which are to be found in no book.

[1] There appear to be no precise, or detailed, records of invasions of Ladak, from the side of Eastern Turkistan. From the allusions to them which Mirzá Haidar makes, they must have occurred pretty frequently during the early years of the sixteenth century, though previous to that period I know of no mention of them. Besides those incidentally referred to in this passage, it will be remembered that Abá Bakr's general, Mir Vali, overran Ladak, and afterwards one Mir Mazid, who, however, was killed there by a stone falling on his head. The date of Mir Vali's exploit can only be roughly placed towards the end of the fifteenth century. That of Mir Mazid must have been about the year 923 (1517). All were, no doubt, wanton plundering expeditions, hypocritically disguised as holy wars.

[2] 938 H. ended 2 August, 1532.

CHAPTER LXXXIX.

DESCRIPTION OF THE POSITION, MOUNTAINS, AND PLAINS OF TIBET, AND AN ACCOUNT OF THE CUSTOMS AND RELIGION OF THE INHABITANTS.

TIBET is a long [and narrow] country.[1] From *Rikan Báin*, which means "between the north and the west," towards *Bakani*,[2] which is "between the south and the east," is eight months' journey. Its breadth is [nowhere] more than one month's journey, nor less than ten days. Its frontier on the side of *Rikan Báin*, adjoins Baluristán (as was stated above, in the description of Balur); that on the *Bakani* side, touches Huchu Sálár, which is a dependency of [what is called] Kanjánfu[3] of Khitái. In the description of the

[1] The expression literally translated is "running lengthwise."

[2] These terms are not to be found in Persian or Turki dictionaries, and I am not aware what language they belong to. The first one especially is subject to many readings, and that adopted in the text is by no means certainly the right one. It may be *Rukn, Zikan*, etc., and *Baib, Payin*, etc., etc. *Bakani* may also be read in several ways. Fortunately, the author himself enlightens us as to the meaning.

[3] *Huchu*, properly *Hochou*, is a town of the Kansu province of China standing on a right tributary of the Yellow River, about 320 li (or some 80 miles) south-west of Lanchou. *Salar* consists of a large group of villages on the south bank of the Yellow River, to the north and north-west of *Hochou*. *Kanján-fu* represents the modern Si-Ngán-fu, the capital of the province of Shensi. The region does not fall within the limits of the map attached to this volume, but from a general map of China, it will be seen that, in reality, it lies more to the north-east of Tibet than to the south-east, as Mirza Haidar places it; but his statement of the general position he is indicating, is a remarkably clear one.

Si-Ngán-fu was known in the time of the Mongols as *Kenjan-fu*, or *Kan-zán-fu*, and it was so called by Marco Polo, who wrote: "And when you have travelled those eight days' journey, you come to that great city . . . . called Kenjan-fu. A very great and fine city it is, and the capital of the kingdom of Kenjan-fu, which in old times was a noble, rich, and powerful realm, and had many great and wealthy and puissant kings." Previous to the Mongol era it was the capital of several of the Chinese dynasties and bore, at different times, the names of *Chan-gan* and *King-chou-fu*. It is the latter which is believed to have been corrupted by the Mongols into Kenjan-fu. Thus its Mongol form seems to have survived among the nations of Turkistan, etc., down to the days of Mirza Haidar.

The *Hochou* and *Salar* district is chiefly known as the seat of a large and fanatical Musulman population, which has been settled there for at least four centuries. The region has lately been visited by Mr. W. W. Rockhill, who tells us that these Musulmans are of Turki extraction, and speak a language mixed with Turki words. They are divided into two sections called locally the "black capped" and the "white capped" Muhammadans. *Salar* is rather the name of the people than of a locality, though their chief town goes by the name of *Salar-pakun* (or *paken*). It is the *Salar* who are designated "Black Caps" by the Chinese. In an interesting note, Mr. Rockhill observes that the annals of the Ming dynasty make mention of the *Salar*, as the remnants of various Turki tribes who had settled in the *Ho-chou*, *Hwang-chou*, and other neighbouring districts, and had become a source of much trouble to the Empire. He concludes by pointing to the notice in the "Ming Shi," of the *Sali Uighur* (see note, p. 349), and inquires whether the *Salar* can be the same as the *Sari* (in Chinese *Sali*). The answer is that the two words can have no connection. *Sárigh Uighur* is the right term—*Sárigh* being the Turki for *yellow*, and Sali only its Chinese corrup-

mountains of Moghulistán and Káshghar, it was stated that the principal range in Moghulistán, from which all the other hills branch out, passes the north of Káshghar, runs towards the west, and continues to the south of Káshghar. It was also mentioned that the province of Farghána lies to the west of Káshghar, this range running between. [This part of the range] which lies between Káshghar and Farghána is called Alái.

Badakhshán is on the west of Yárkand. These countries are also divided by [a part of] this same range, which here takes the name of Pámir. The width of the Pámir, in some places, is eight days' journey. Passing onwards, one comes to some of the Yárkand mountains which adjoin Balur, such as Ráskám[1] and Tágh Dum Básh; proceeding yet further, one arrives in the land of Tibet. Badakhshán is in the direction of summer sunset (*tabistáni*) from Yárkand, as stated above, and Káshmir is in the direction of winter sunset (*zamistáni*) from Yárkand.[2] That same range runs between Yárkand and Káshmir, and is here called Bálti; this [district] belongs to the province of Tibet. There is, in these parts, a mountain[3] wider than the Alái or the Pámir. The width in Bálti is twenty days' journey.

The pass ascending from Yárkand is the pass of Sánju, and the pass descending on the side of Káshmir is the pass of Askárdu.[4] [From the Sánju pass to the Askárdu pass] is twenty days' journey. In the direction of winter sunset from Khotan, are some of the cities of Hind, such as Láhur, Sultánpur, and Bájwára,[5] and the

---

tion—while *Salar* is written in the Turki quite differently; it is a proper name and not an adjective.

It may be noted that it was among these turbulent Musulmans of Hochou and Salar, that the revolt broke out in 1862, which afterwards acquired the name of "the Tungani rebellion"—a movement which spread all over Shensi, Kansu, Eastern Turkistan, Zungaria, and some parts of Mongolia. (See Yule's *Marco Polo*, ii., pp. 18–23; Rockhill in *Land of the Lamas*, pp. 38–40; and in *J. R. A. S.*, 1892, p. 598).

[1] The Turki text spells *Rást-Kám*.

[2] The expressions used for indicating these directions are peculiar. They stand respectively, in the texts, *gharab i tabistáni* and *gharb i zamistáni* of Yárkand. The passage, however, falls within the brief extracts translated by the late Mr. R. B. Shaw in his paper entitled 'A Prince of Kashghar on the Geography of Eastern Turkistan,' and I have taken the rendering from him, knowing that he had the advantage, when using his *Tarikh-i-Rashidi*, of some excellent local instruction on such points. (See *J. R. G. S.*, 1876, p. 279.) The author's orientation is not particularly accurate, for Badakhshán lies nearly due west of Yarkand, and Kashmir between south and south-west.

[3] The meaning is a mountain mass, or mountainous region.

[4] Properly *Skardu*, or *Skardo*, written *Askardu* on account of the inability of Persian, Turki, and Hindustani-speaking peoples to pronounce an *s* immediately preceding a hard consonant at the beginning of a word. *Skardo* is a Tibetan name. From this reference to a pass behind Skardo it would appear that a road led over it in Mirza Haidar's time. The passes in that quarter are nowadays blocked by glaciers, and the road has become impracticable for travellers.

[5] The *Sultanpur* mentioned here, must be the chief town of Kulu in the valley of the upper Biás river. Just south of Sultanpur, and on the same side of the Biás, there is also a small place called *Bajáora*, which would appear, at first sight,

afore-mentioned mountain range lies between. Between Khotan and the towns of Hind above-named, are situated Arduk, Guga, and Aspati,[1] which belong to Tibet; and it must be supposed that those mountains extend into Khitái. On the west and south of the range lies Hindustán; while Bhira,[2] Lahur and Bangála are all on the skirts of it. All the rivers of Hind flow down from these hills, and their sources are in the country of Tibet.

On the north and east of Tibet lie Yárkand, Khotan, Chárchán, Lob, Katak and Sárigh Uighur. The rest is a sandy waste [*rigistan*], whose frontier adjoins Kanju and Sakju[3] of Khitái. All the streams which flow down from the mountains of Tibet, in a westerly and southerly direction, become rivers of Hind, such as the Niláb, the river of Bhira, the Chináb, the river of Lahur, the river of Sultánpur and the river of Bájwára, which are all rivers of Sind. The Jun and the Gang and others flow through Bangála into the ocean[4]; all the streams which flow in an easterly and northerly direction from the mountains of Tibet, such as the river of Yárkand, the Ak Kásh and the Kára Kásh, the Kirya, the Chárchán, and the rest, all empty themselves into the Kuk Naur,[5] which is a

---

to be the locality alluded to by our author; but Mr. Shaw notes: "I incline to think that *Bajwára* must be an old town of that name, not far from the Satlej, near Phillor, from its being mentioned afterwards in connection with that river." (*loc. cit.*, p. 279.) This is probably the correct view.

[1] These three names obviously stand for *Rudok*, *Gugeh*, and *Spiti*—the two first in Lassa-governed Tibet, the third within British territory.

[2] The *Bhira* here pointed to is, no doubt, the town of *Bhira* on the left bank of the Jhilam below Pind-Dádan-Khan. It was a place much in evidence in Mirza Haidar's time, and is often mentioned by Baber. Gen. A. Cunningham remarks that until it was supplanted by Pind-Dádan-Khan, *Bhira* was the principal town in that part of the country. He tells us also that on the opposite bank of the river, near Ahmadabad, there is a very extensive mound of ruins called *Old Bhira*, or *Jobnáthnagar*. (See Baber, pp. 253 *seqq.*; Elliot, ii., p. 392; and Cunningham, *Ancient Geog. Ind.*, p. 155.)

[3] Kan-chou and Su-chou in the province of Kansu.

[4] The *Niláb*, or Blue River, was the name almost always in use among the Musulman authors down to the seventeenth century (and perhaps later) for the *Ab-i-Sind*, or Indus; and must, from the sequence and the absence of any other mention of the Indus, be the river intended here. The "river of Bhira" is the Jhilam, and that of *Bájwára*, as we have just seen from Mr. Shaw's note, in all probability the Satlej. The *Jun* and the *Gang*, it is almost unnecessary to remark, stand for the Jamna and Ganges.

[5] The *Koko Nor*, or Blue Lake—the *Tsing-hai* of the Chinese. Though the author is remarkably correct regarding the rivers of India, he appears to have confused *Lob Nor* with *Koko Nor*. He could, with his excellent knowledge of the geography of Eastern Turkistan, have hardly been unaware of the fact that the *Kara Kásh* empties itself into *Lob Nor*. The river of *Kirya* he very probably regarded as a tributary of the *Yurung Kásh*, or of the united *Yurung* and *Kara Kásh*, though in reality, it loses itself in the sandy desert before reaching any great stream. The *Ak-Kásh* I cannot trace under that name, but I suspect, from the context, that he uses the term as another name for the *Yurung-Kásh*. Both, indeed, mean the same thing—*i.e.* 'white jade'; while Kara Kásh means 'black jade.' (See Rémusat, *Hist. de la ville de Khotan*, p. 151.) When, and immediately below, he writes that the *Kara Muran* (the Mongol name for the Yellow River of China) issues from *Koko Nor*, he is of course in error, but he would have been

lake in the aforesaid sand waste. I have heard some Moghuls say that one may travel round [the lake] in three months. From one end of it, issues a large river, which is called the Kará Murán of Khitái.

From these details it will be clear that Tibet is a very high-lying country, since its waters run in all directions. Any one wishing to enter Tibet, must first ascend lofty passes, which do not slope downward on the other side, for on the top the land is level; in a few cases only, the passes have slight declivities [on the far side]. On account [of the height] Tibet is excessively cold—so much so, that in most places nothing but turnips can be cultivated. The barley is generally of a kind that ripens in two months. In some parts of Tibet, the summer only lasts forty days, and even then the rivers are often frozen over after midnight. In all Tibet, in consequence of the severity of the cold, trees never reach any height; nor does the corn, for, being low on the ground, it is trodden down by the cattle.

Now the inhabitants of Tibet are divided into two sections. One is called the Yulpá—that is to say, 'dwellers in villages,' and the other the Champa, meaning 'dwellers in the desert.'[1] But these last are always subject to one of the provinces of Tibet. The inhabitants of the desert [nomads] of Tibet have certain strange practices, which are to be met with among no other people. Firstly, they eat their meat and all other foods in an absolutely raw state, having no knowledge of cooking. Again, they feed their horses on flesh instead of grain.[2] They also use sheep exclusively, as beasts of burden. Their sheep carry, perhaps, twelve statute *man*. They harness them with pack-saddles, halters, and girths; they place the load upon the sheep, and except when necessary, never take it off, so that summer and winter it remains on the animal's back.[3]

---

no more incorrect had he described it as issuing from *Lake Lob*. Indeed, the legend that the Yellow River flows by an underground channel from *Lake Lob*, is a very ancient one among the Chinese and some of their neighbours. The situation of the great lake in a sandy waste, would point far more accurately to *Lob Nor* than to *Koko Nor*.

[1] Probably *Yul-pá* is an abbreviation of *Yul-cho-pa*, from *Yul-cho*, or *Yul-che*, meaning a village. The *Cham-pa* are, as the author says, the dwellers in tents—the pastoral people, or nomads—of Tibet. But the ordinary meaning of *Yulpa*, Dr. Waddell tells me, is "native of the country."

[2] The first of these statements requires modification; the second is, of course, ludicrously wrong. In winter, when meat is frozen hard, the Champa, and indeed other Tibetans, have no objection to eat it raw, but they usually cook it after a fashion. In this respect their customs are the same as those of the Mongols, Kalmáks, and other similar tribes.

[3] Here too, the author mixes fact and fiction in a somewhat easy manner. The load-carrying sheep are, as far as I am aware, peculiar to Tibet and Tibetan regions, and are to the nomad tribesmen of those regions what the camel is to the Bedouin. They are of a large and handsome, though perhaps a rather leggy breed, and they carry a load of some 32 lbs. weight for a distance usually of about 7 or 8 miles a day. Gen. A. Cunningham gives 27 to 30 inches as their average

The Champa, or nomads, live in the following manner. In the winter they descend towards the western and southern slopes of the aforesaid mountains—that is to say, to Hindustán—taking with them wares of Khitái, salt, cloth of goats' hair [*tana-kâr*], zedoary,[1] kutás [*yaks*], gold, and shawls,[2] which are Tibetan goods. They trade in Hindustán and in the mountains of Hindustán, and in the spring they return from that country, bringing many of its products, such as cloths, sweets, rice, and grain, loaded upon their sheep. After feeding their flocks, they advance slowly but continuously into Khitái, which they reach in the winter. Having laid in a stock, during spring, of such Tibetan products as are in demand in Khitái, they dispose of the Indian and Tibetan goods there in the winter, and return to Tibet in the [following] spring, carrying with them Khitái wares. The next winter they again go on to India. The burdens which they load on the sheep in Hindustán are removed in Khitái, and those put on in Khitái are taken off in Hindustán. Thus they spend their winters alternately in Hindustán and Khitái.[3] This is the mode of life of all the Champa. A Champa will sometimes carry as many as 10,000 sheep-loads, and every sheep-load may be reckoned at twelve *man*. What an enormous quantity is this! That amount is loaded in one year, either in Hindustán or in Khitái. On every occasion,

---

height. As a rule, their burden consists of salt, soda, or borax when travelling towards India, and grain or flour when returning homeward. These products are sewn up in bags and, indeed, any other kind of load it would be almost impossible for them to carry. Col. J. Biddulph, when attached to Sir D. Forsyth's mission to Kashghar in 1873, made an interesting experiment with a flock of 30 sheep, carrying loads of grain and flour. He marched with them from Tankseh in Ladak, to Shahidulla on the Kara Kásh, a distance of 330 miles, by the Chang Chenmo road, in 31 days, but loaded only with 20 lbs. each. In his report he remarks: "The loads, secured by breast and breach ropes, ride well, sinking into the fleece and not being liable to shift. On fair ground, where they travelled with a broad front, they marched at the rate of 1¾ miles an hour; a large number would no doubt travel slower, and much must depend on the breadth of the road. . . . . On days when they had no grass, they had literally nothing to eat, for they refused grain, not being accustomed to it. . . . . On arrival in camp, they were unloaded, and turned out to shift for themselves till dark, when they were herded for the night." The Champa frequently march with several thousands of sheep, divided into flocks, which are driven separately, but within a few miles of each other, the whole forming one caravan. They usually camp about midday, turn the sheep loose, and stack the loads till the next morning. To leave them on their backs, as the author states, would soon make an end of both sheep and merchandise. When Mirza Haidar speaks of 12 statute *man*, he is probably alluding to the *man* of Andiján, which, as we have seen above (p. 327), weighed a fraction under 5 lbs., so that between 6 and 7 Andijáni *man* would be a more correct figure. (See, for Col. Biddulph's report, *Yarkand Mission Report*, p. 492, and Cunningham, *Ladak*, pp. 210–11.)

[1] *Zedoary*, or *jadwár*, is an aromatic root used in medicine by Orientals. (See Yule's *Glossary*, p. 74.)

[2] By 'shawls' the author probably means shawl-wool, for in this sense the word *shál* is frequently used in Kashmir and Ladak. Similarly the word *Kutás* or Yák is, I suspect, intended for 'Yak's wool.'

[3] This account of the mode of life led by the Champa sheep-traders, though correct in the main, is somewhat confused; it is, however, given literally, as the author states it.

wherever they go, they take all these loads with them, and are never caused fatigue or trouble by them. I have never heard of a similar practice among any other people. In fact, some do not even credit this story.

These Champa are a numerous race, inasmuch as one of their tribes, called Dulpa,[1] numbers more than 50,000 families. And

[1] The word *Dulpa* may be read in several different ways, such as *Dulia*, *Bulia*, *Pulba*, etc., etc. It seems also possible, as regards the text, that a *k* may be read for the *l*. I am inclined to think that the author intended a *k*, and that the word is meant either for *Dukpa* or *Pukpa*; though Dr. Waddell informs me that *Dolpa* (spelt *gol pa*) is the name of an aboriginal tribe in Tibet (analogous to the Chandals of India) to which the Tibetan butchers belong. From Jaeschke's dictionary, however, I infer that these Dolpa are more a caste than a tribe, and that they are persons dishonourably distinguished for taking animal life.

First, as to *Dukpa*. This word, or properly *Dogpa* in Western and Central Tibet, is a corruption all over the Tibetan provinces for *Drugpa*, *Drokpa*, or *Brokpa*. But if the author meant *Dokpa*, he could scarcely call them a tribe of the *Champa*, or nomads, though their habits are to some extent similar to those of the *Champa*; so much so, in some parts of Tibet, that Mr. Rockhill calls them "semi-nomadic herdsmen." The true definition of the word *Drok*, etc., is a mountain pasture used in summer only, or, as Mr. Shaw has happily translated it, "an Alp;" while both he and Mr. Drew render *Drokpa*, *Brokpa*, etc., by the term "highlander." In Ladak the *Drokpa* differs from the *Champa* in so far that he is only away in the *Drok* during summer; in winter he descends with his sheep, yaks, etc., to the settled villages and lives as an ordinary villager. The *Champa*, on the other hand, lives his whole life in tents made of yak hair, and merely moves between higher and lower grazing grounds, according to the seasons. In most villages in Ladak and the neighbouring provinces, there are a certain number of *Drokpa*, who take charge of the flocks and herds of their settled neighbours in summer, and drive them up to the *Droks* for pasture. Thus, judging by customs and mode of life, it appears doubtful if Mirza Haidar is alluding, here, to the *Drokpa* or *Dukpa*. It may be added that the term is often used to denote a strange, or foreign tribe, belonging to neighbouring hill countries, if of pastural, or semi-pastural, habits; such as the inhabitants of Bhutan and the hill tribes, mis-called *Dards*, living west of Baltistan.

Secondly, as to *Pukpa*. A little lower down (p. 411), Mirza Haidar tells us of gold mines worked by a branch of the *Dulpa* tribe, who live in caves, or holes in the ground near their mines. These gold mines and those who work them are described in almost exactly the same way by Pandit Nain Sing, who visited them on his journey from Ladak to Lassa in 1873. Speaking of the localities north of the Tsang-pu valley, he says, "the diggers mostly dwell in caves excavated in the earth. These habitations, which are locally termed, *Phukpa*, ... contain populations varying from five to twenty-five in each, according to the wealth of the proprietors," who live in them as a means of protection from robbers, the caves being easily defensible, while tents are peculiarly open to attack. These gold diggers the Pandit states to have been mostly *Champa*. Here the habitations, and not the inhabitants, are termed *Phukpa* (or, more probably, in Tibetan, Pugpa or Pukpa); but it is quite possible that the word may have been applied, by the Moghuls, to the diggers, and that Mirza Haidar came to know the latter as *Pukpa Champa*. It is also possible that he may have heard of both *Dukpa* and *Pukpa*, when in Tibet, and that when writing his history, some twelve years subsequently, may have confused the two strange words. In any case, he rightly describes the miners as *Champa*; while he would be scarcely correct in speaking of the *Drok* men as belonging to that class. The caste of Dogpa appear to have no special habitat, and it seems impossible that Mirza Haidar's narrative can apply to them, as it does to the *Pug-pa*, or cave-men. (See Rockhill, *J. R. A. S.*, 1890, pp. 56 and 128; Shaw, *J. A. S. B.*, XLVII., No. 1, 1878, p. 36; Drew, *Jummoo and Kashmir*, p. 434; and Pundit Nain Sing in *Rep. Trans-Himalayan Explorations*, 1873-5, p. 58; also Jaeschke's *Tib. Dict.* for meanings.)

there are many more tribes like this one. From some of the chiefs I have asked their numbers, but they have been unable to inform me. God knows best; and the responsibility be upon [those who have failed to inform me].

The dwellers in villages are called Yulpá; they inhabit many districts—such as Bálti, which is a province of Tibet; Bálti, in turn, comprises several [smaller] districts, such as Purik, Khápula, Ashigár, Askárdu, [Runk], and Ladaks, and each of these contains fortresses and villages. Wherever I went in Tibet, I either took the country by force or made peace, on the inhabitants paying tribute. Among these [places may be mentioned] Bálti, Zánskár, Máryul,[1] Rudok, Guga, Lu, Burás, Zunka, Minkáb [or Hinkáb], Zir-Sud-Kankar, Nisan, Ham, Alalai-Lutak, Tuk, Labug [or Lanuk], Astákbark [or Askábrak],[2] which is the limit of my

[1] The name of *Mar Yul*, though never used in Ladak nowadays, is not entirely forgotten there. It is said by Dr. Marx to include the upper and lower districts of Ladak proper, together with Nubra, Zangskar, etc.; General Cunningham speaks of it as applied to Ladak generally; while General Strachey gives it a much wider definition, and makes *Maryul* include the whole of Baltistan. I venture to think that Dr. Marx's definition is the one usually accepted by the natives of the province. On the meaning of the word too, our authorities are at variance. Dr. Marx, quoting a highly intelligent and well-instructed lama (my old acquaintance Táshi-Tanpel) says the word is derived from *me-ru*, meaning 'bare rocks;' General Cunningham translates 'red land;' Strachey and Csoma de Körös (cited by Cunningham), render it 'low country;' while Dr. Waddell agrees with the rendering of de Körös. There may, therefore, be still some uncertainty as to the meaning of the term. It may be thought that a country including no spot lower than about 9,500 ft. above sea-level, could scarcely gain the name of 'low,' but with reference to Gugeh, Rupchu, and the mountain tracts surrounding *Maryul*, the settled parts of the country, are, in fact, at a low elevation. The division between Upper and Lower Ladak is said, by Dr. Marx, to be the plateau dividing the village districts of Basgo and Saspola on the Indus. *Maryul*, however, must not be confounded with *Mang-yul*, or the "*Mang* country." *Mang*, as Dr. Waddell points out, is a specific name for the province lying between Ladak and Western Tibet, or Tsang; and is, in fact, another name for part of *Ngari*.

Mirza Haidar, when speaking of Ladak as a country, always applies to it the name of 'Tibet,' as is the custom at the present day among all natives of Eastern Turkistan, Badakhshán, etc. It is only on the south of the Karakorum and Hindu Kush that the name of 'Ladak' is heard; and in those regions it is applied to the chief town, Leh, as well as to the whole country, just as the name of 'Kashmir' is given to Srinagar, because it is the capital of Kashmir. 'Leh' and 'Srinagar' are rarely heard, among the natives, in Ladak and Kashmir. In the same way, when Mirza Haidar speaks of *Maryul*, he usually, if not always, denotes the capital and its immediate district—either the town of Leh, or else Sheh, in its near neighbourhood. The author is wrong in making Ladak a part of Baltistan in the sixteenth century.

The exact Tibetan spelling of the name *Ladak*, it may be added, is *Ladvags*, but in pronouncing these syllables, certain letters are dropped and others altered, so that the result arrived at is *Lá-dák*. The final *Kh*, so often seen in the name, is a Kashmiri and Hindustani corruption. (See Marx, *J. A. S. B.* as above, pp. 115, 116; Cunningham's *Ladak*, pp. 18, 19; and H. Strachey, *Phys. Geog. of West. Tibet*, p. 13.)

[2] These names, as far as 'Gugeh' inclusive, are easily recognised; for some attempts at identifying the remainder see lower down—Note 1, p. 456. As regards *Ursang*, which follows immediately, a reference to note 3, p. 136, in Part I., will show that *Lassa* is intended.

journey. From Askábrak to Bangála is twenty-four days' journey, and Ursáng is on the east, and Bangála on the south, of Askábrak. Ursáng is the Kibla and K'aba of all Khitái and Tibet, and has a vast idol-temple. As what I heard concerning this temple is incredible I have not written it. There are many false stories told of it. In short, it is the seat of learning and the city of the pious of Tibet and Khitái.

CHAPTER XC.

ACCOUNT OF THE CURIOSITIES OF TIBET.

THE nature of those portions of Tibet that I have visited, and of its inhabitants, is such that in spite of my strong wish to describe it I find it impossible. I will, however, on account of their strangeness, mention a few of the particulars which I have either seen myself or heard spoken of.

One of these is the gold-mines. In most of the Champa districts gold-mines are found. Among them are two strange mines; one is called by the Moghuls the *Altunji* [or Goldsmith] of Tibet, and it is worked by a branch of the above-mentioned tribe of Dulpa. On account of the extreme coldness of the atmosphere, they are not able to work more than forty days in the year. In the level ground are pits [or caves] large enough for a man to enter. There are numbers of these holes, and most of them terminate by running into one another. It is said that three hundred heads of families live permanently in those caves. They watch the Moghuls from afar, and when these come near, they all creep into their caves, where no one can find them. In the caves no oil burns except the oil made from sheep's milk [*sar-jush*] that has no fat in it.[1] Out of these caves they bring soil, which they wash, and (the responsibility be upon those who tell this story) it is said that in one sieve of soil from those mines, ten *mithkáls* of gold are sometimes found. One man digs the earth, carries it out and washes it by himself. Some days he sorts twenty sieves full. Although this may appear incredible, I have heard it confirmed all over Tibet, and for this reason I have written it down.

Again, Guga has two hundred forts and villages. It is three days' journey in length, and in it gold is everywhere to be found. Wherever they dig up the earth and spread it on a cloth, they find gold. The smallest pieces are about the size of a lentil [*adas*] or a pea [*másh*], and they say that sometimes [lumps] are found as large as a sheep's liver. At the time when I was settling the

[1] The translation of this passage, regarding the oil, is uncertain.

tribute upon Guga, the head men related to me that a man was lately digging a piece of ground, when his spade stuck fast in something, so that he could not, with all his efforts, draw it out. Having removed the earth, he saw that it was a stone, in the middle of which was gold; in this his spade had become fixed. Leaving the spade where it was, he went and informed the governor. A body of men went to the spot and extracted it, and having broken the stone, found in it 1,500 Tibetan *mithkáls* of pure [*mohri*] gold (a Tibetan *mithkál* is worth one-and-a-half ordinary *mithkáls*), and God has so created this soil that when the gold is taken from the ground it does not diminish [in bulk] however much they beat it out, bake it and stamp it; it is only fire that has any effect on it. This is all very wonderful, and is looked upon by assayers as very strange and curious. Nor is this peculiarity to be met with anywhere else in the world.[1] In the greater part of Tibet the merchandise of Khatai and India is to be found in about equal quantities.

Another peculiarity of Tibet is the *dam-giri*, which the Moghuls call *Yas*,[2] and which is common to the whole country, though less prevalent in the vicinity of forts and villages. The symptoms are a feeling of severe sickness [*nákhushi*], and in every case one's breath so seizes him that he becomes exhausted, just as if he had run up a steep hill with a heavy burden on his back. On account of the oppression [it causes] it is difficult to sleep. Should, however, sleep overtake one, the eyes are hardly closed before one is awoke with a start caused by oppression on the lungs and chest. And this is always the case with everybody. When overcome by this malady the patient becomes senseless, begins to talk nonsense, and sometimes the power of speech is lost, while the palms of the hands and soles of the feet become swollen. Often when this last symptom occurs, the patient dies between dawn and breakfast time; at other times he lingers on for several days. If, in the interval, his fate

[1] The existence of gold in the western provinces of Tibet is well known, but the quantities found are very small and usually confined to dust—nuggets being seldom heard of. The quality is said to be good, and most of it finds its way to Kashmir and India. The workings—in Ladak at any rate—are in the form of caves or pits, much as Mirza Haidar describes them. His mention of the miners watching for 'the Moghuls' is curious, but it is not quite clear whether he is alluding to his own expedition (presently to be described), when he may have seen the miners escape from his party by taking refuge underground, or whether he points to a general custom. If to the latter, it would imply that the Moghuls from Eastern Turkistan were in the habit of raiding on the gold diggers. In Chaps. XCII. and XCIV., we shall see that to plunder the Dulpa or Pukpa was, indeed, the chief object of the Khán's expedition to Tibet, though it was disguised as a holy war; and if this was the case in one instance, it is possible that former raids had been undertaken with the same end in view.

[2] The proper spelling of this word, according to Mr. Shaw would be *Iss*. There is no English word for *dam-giri* or "breath seizing," caused by the rarefied air at high altitudes. It is the French "mal de montagne," and the German "Passen-gift." (See note next page.)

has not been sealed, and he reach a village or a fort, it is probable that he may survive, otherwise he is sure to die. This malady only attacks strangers; the people of Tibet know nothing of it, nor do their doctors know why it attacks strangers. Nobody has ever been able to cure it. The colder the air, the more severe is the form of the malady. [Couplet] . . . . It is not peculiar to men, but attacks every animal that breathes, such as the horse, as will be presently instanced. One day, owing to the necessity of a foray, we had ridden faster than usual. On waking [next morning] I saw that there were very few horses in our camp, and [on inquiring] ascertained that more than 2000 had died in the night. Of my own stable there were twenty-four special [riding] horses, all of which were missing. Twenty-one of them had died during that night. Horses are very subject [*sarâyat*] to *dam-giri*. I have never heard of this disease outside Tibet. No remedy is known for it.[1]

[1] The effects of the rarefied atmosphere at high altitudes on respiration and circulation are, on the whole, well described, though the author had no idea of the cause of the symptoms. In some respects he is at fault, as when he says that the natives of Tibet do not suffer from it. Tibetans born and bred at an elevation of, say, 12,000 feet, will often suffer more severely from *dam-giri* (or *dam* as it is usually called) when they ascend to 17,000 or 18,000 feet, than natives of countries on about the level of the sea. The degree of suffering depends on the constitution of the individual, or on how far he has become accustomed to high altitudes. The cold too, so far from intensifying the symptoms, slightly mitigates them, as it modifies the pressure to some extent. This, however, is more a matter of theory than of experience. The only cure which modern science has suggested, is the use of salts which increase the supply of oxygen to the system, such as chlorate of potash; but no very marked result has, I believe, ever been attained from experiments of this kind. Dr. Bellew was of opinion that chlorate of potash "relieves the dreadful nausea and headache produced by the circulation of insufficiently oxygenated blood." Mirza Haidar, when he prescribes the removal of the patient to the neighbourhood of forts and villages, unconsciously proposes what is perhaps the only real cure—viz., a descent to a lower altitude, for it is only at comparatively low elevations, that villages or buildings of any kind are to be found. The natives of the Tibetan and Pamir regions have many nostrums, such as onions, dried apricots, aromatic herbs, etc., for mitigating the effects of attenuated air, which they almost invariably ascribe to poisonous exhalations from the ground, or to the presence of noxious weeds. Good accounts of the effects of "dam," or height sickness, in Central Asia, will be found in Wood's *Oxus*, pp. 236–238; Drew's *Jummoo and Kashmir*, pp. 290–2; Bellew's *Kashmir and Kashghar*, pp. 164, etc., and other works. Sir H. Yule (*Prelim: Essay* to Wood's *Oxus*, p. lxv.) says that the malady "is called by the Badakhshis and Wakhis *Tunk*, by the Turkis *Esh* [*Iss*?], signifying an odour or miasm, and by the Indian population of the Himalaya *Bish-kâ-hawa*, or poisonous air." In the Turki MS. employed for this translation the word used is *tutki*, which (Mr. Ross informs me) is "from the verb *tut-mak* to seize, as *gir* from *griftan*." The Tibetan words (as Dr. Waddell is good enough to note) are *Dug-ri*, or "poison of the mountain," and *La-dug*, or "pass poison." Other accounts of the malady are no doubt common in books dealing with the Alps, the Andes, etc.

CHAPTER XCI.

TIBET AND THE CUSTOMS OF ITS PEOPLE.

THEIR men of learning [*Ulama*] are, as a body, called Lámas. But they have different names, in proportion to the extent of their learning. Just as we say "Imám and Mujtahid," they say "Tunkana and Kahjavár."[1] I had much conversation with them with the help of an interpreter. But when it came to nice distinctions, the interpreter was at a loss both to understand and to explain, so that the conversation was incomplete. Of their tenets and rites, however, I was able to discover the following particulars. They say that the Most High God is from all eternity. At the beginning of creation, when He called the souls into being, He taught each one separately how to attain to the regions of the blessed (which was the path that leads to Paradise), and how to escape from hell. [This He taught them] without palate, or tongue, or any other [corporeal] medium. These souls He sent down at various times, as seemed fitting to Him, and mixed them with earth. And this is the origin of the power of vegetation of plants in the earth. When the soul has descended from the highest to the lowest degree, it is no longer pure, but unconsciousness and oblivion dominate it. In the process of time, it migrates to some vile body; and this migration, although it be into a base degree, is yet an advance upon the state of being mixed with earth. In every body [the soul] makes progress according to its conduct. If its conduct is perfect in that body, it enters into a better body; if, on the other hand, it errs, it enters a yet viler body; and if in this [last] body

[1] *Kahjavár* may also read *Kichuva.* On these terms Dr. Waddell has favoured me with the following remarks:—"The ordinary Tibetan degree of divinity, somewhat analogous to our B.D., carries with it the title of *Tung-Ba* (properly *Tung-ram-pa*—spelt *Drun-rams-pa*[1]) when the degree is conferred by the Tashi-lhunpo university; or *Ge-she* (spelt *dge-sés*) when conferred by the great universities of Central Tibet (viz., Depung, Serra and Gahldan). These may be the names here mentioned. The highest degree, however, which may be called the Doctorate, and held by very few Lamas, gives the title of *Kah-chan*, or *Kah-chu*, or *Kab-chu* (spelt *skabs-bchu*, or *skabs-s-tschu*[2]) when the degree is conferred by Tashi-lhunpo; but *Rab-byam-pa* when given by those of Central Tibet. *Khajavár* or *Kichuva* may thus be intended either for *Kah-chan* or *Ge-she*—the former more probably, though it is possibly meant for *Ku Shog*, a title given by courtesy to educated Tibetans, even amongst the laity, though in Ladak it seems restricted to the highest Lamas—those who pose as reincarnated hierarchs.

Nor does *Tunkana* probably mean *Tul-Ku*—the proper title of reincarnated Lamas—the *Khutuktu* of the Mongols. Taking the two titles together, I think they are probably intended for *Tung-ram-pa* and *Kah-Chu*, thus rendering it probable that the author was conversing with Lamas affiliated to Tashi-lhunpo which, in Northern Tibet and Mongolia, enjoys greater repute as a teaching centre than the universities of Lhasa ([1] *Cf.* Jaeschke's *Tibetan Dict.*, p. 263, and [2] Köppen, *Die Religion des Buddha*, ii., p. 253).—L. A. W."

it still does evil, it again becomes mixed with the earth, and again remains inanimate [*muattal*] for some time.

In this manner [the soul] migrates from one body to another, and progresses until it attains the human body. In the human body it first of all reaches the lowest degree, such as that of a peasant or a slave. It gradually rises in the scale of humanity, until it enters the body of a láma, in which state, if [the entity] conducts itself in a becoming manner, it attains a knowledge and insight into former states, and knows what it has done in each separate body, what has been the cause of its progress, and what the reason of its degradation. This knowledge and consciousness is the degree of saintliness. And in like manner, by means of much contemplation, people attain to the stage in which they recall what was taught them at the beginning of eternity; they remember everything that the Most High God communicated to them, without palate, tongue, or any other [physical] medium. This is the degree of prophecy. In it men learn what they have heard from God Almighty, and [on these revelations] are their religion and faith based. The soul which has attained to the degree of prophecy is no longer subject to death, but has eternal life. The being continues until his physical strength is quite broken, when his body perishes, and nothing remains but his spirituality. All who have spiritual force of this kind may see [the soul]; but otherwise it cannot be seen with the eye of the head, which is bodily vision.

Such are the tenets of the religion of Shaká Muni. All Khitái is of this faith, and they call it the religion of "Shakiá Muni"; while in Tibet it is called "Shaká Tu Bá,"[1] and "Shaká Muni." In histories it is written "Shaká Muni." In some histories, Shaká Muni is reckoned among the prophets of India, and some hold that he was a teacher [*hakim*]. Also, it is maintained that no one goes to Heaven by the mere acceptance of the faith and religion, but only in consequence of his works. If a Musulmán performs good acts, he goes to Heaven; if he do evil, he goes to Hell. This also applies to [these] infidels. They hold the Prophet in high esteem, but they do not consider it the incumbent duty of the whole of mankind to be of his religion. They say: "Your religion is true, and so is ours. In every religion one must conduct oneself well. Shaká Muni has said: After me there will arise 124,000 prophets, the last of whom will be called Jána Kasapa,[2] an orphan, without

[1] Dr. Waddell writes: "Sakya, Tu-Bá. *Tub-pa* is the Tibetan equivalent of the Sanscrit *Sákya*, and means, literally, 'the mighty one.' (*Cf.* Jaeschke's Dict., p. 234.)—L. A. W."

[2] This word is not badly transliterated. It should read, Professor Bendall informs me, *Jnána-Kásyapa*. Dr. Waddell notes on this subject: "*Kásyapa* was the last mythical human Buddha who preceded Sakya-Muni, and he is especially worshipped now by the *Bonpa* followers of the pre-Lamaist religion of Tibet. Compare Fa Hian's reference to the followers of the mystic cross in the regions about Ladak.—L. A. W."

father or mother. All the world will comprehend his religion. When he is sent, it will be necessary for the whole world to submit to him, and blessed will he be who hastens to adopt his faith. I bequeath my own religion in order that it may be handed down from generation to generation until the blessed time of his appearance. The semblance of this prophet will be in this wise"—and therewith he gave an image which the people were to remember, for in this form the prophet would appear. People should believe in him before all other men.

At the present time, the chief idol (which they place in the entrance of all the Idol Temples) besides all their fables,[1] have reference to him. This idol is the figure of Jána Kasapa. And they attribute most of those qualities to Jána Kasapa, which apply to our Prophet. I observed to them: "What Shaká Muni said refers to our Prophet." They replied: "Shaká Muni said he would come after 124,000 prophets, and after him would come no other prophet. Now of those 124,000, but few have appeared as yet." I insisted earnestly that they had all appeared, but they would not admit it, and so remained in their error.

At Zunka, which is the most famous [place] in Tibet, and one which produces zedoary [*máh farfin*], I saw another [interesting object], viz., an inscription of the Pádisháh of Khitái. It was written in the Khitái character, but in one corner it was in Tibetan writing, while in another corner was a clear Persian translation in the Naskhi hand. It ran as follows: "His Highness the king sends greeting to all his people, saying: It is more than 3,000 years ago now, that Shaká Muni introduced idol-worship and spoke words which are not intelligible to all. . . ." This much I have retained; the rest related to some orders for the repairing of the temple. I have quoted this to show that Shaká Muni lived 3,000 years previous to the date of the inscription,[2] which, however, not being [dated] in the Hajra, I could not understand. But judging from the extent to which the inscription was worn, not more than a hundred years could have elapsed since it was written. But God knows best. I was in Zunka in the month of Rabi ul Awal, 940 [October 1533].

Another [curiosity] is the wild *kutás*. This is a very wild and ferocious beast. In whatever manner it attacks one it proves fatal: whether it strike with its horns, or kick, or overthrow its

[1] The fables here alluded to, Prof. Bendall thinks, are probably the *Játakas*, or "Birth stories."

[2] The date usually assumed for the Nirvána of Sakya-Muni is about the middle of the fifth century, B.C.; thus Mirza Haidar's estimate would appear to be about 1,000 years too early, but Dr. Waddell informs me that, among the Tibetan Lamas, an antiquity of 3,000 years is often assigned to Sakya-Muni. Mirza Haidar, therefore, may have had authority for what he sets down here.

victim. If it has no opportunity of doing any of these things, it tosses its enemy with its tongue, twenty *gaz* into the air, and he is dead before reaching the ground. One male *kutás* is a load for twelve horses. One man cannot possibly raise a shoulder of the animal. In the days of my forays [*kazáki*] I killed a *kutás*, and divided it among seventy persons, when each had sufficient flesh for four days.[1] This animal is not to be met with outside the country of Tibet. The remaining particulars concerning Tibet will be given in the account of the campaign.

CHAPTER XCII.

THE KHÁN MAKES A HOLY WAR ON TIBET.

THE Holy War is the main support and fortifier of Islám—the most efficient ground-work for the foundations of the Faith . . . .[2] After the Khán's repentance, he had always awaited an opportunity for personally conducting a holy war [*ghazát*], nor could his hunger and thirst for this exploit be in any way satisfied by merely sending out a *ghazát* expedition, every year; so at length, in Zulhijja of the year 938 [July 1532] he set out to attack the infidels of Tibet.

As I mentioned above, Tibet is bounded on the north, where it is called Bálti, by Balur and Badakhshán; in the direction of winter sunrise[3] of that place is Yárkand, and on the west is Kashmir. Having bidden Iskandar Sultán accompany me, and having deputed me to that country, the Khán himself started (by way of Khotan) for the Altunji[4] of Tibet, which is another name for the Dulpa.

CHAPTER XCIII.

ARRIVAL OF THE AUTHOR IN TIBET, AND SUBSEQUENT EVENTS.

I SET out in Zulhijja of the aforesaid year, and in the beginning of Safar, reached Nubra, a dependent province of Tibet. I then sent a person all over that country to greet the people with a

[1] For the true dimensions of the *kutás*, or *yák*, see note, p. 302.

[2] Here ten lines of rhetoric on the virtues of the *Ghazát*, or holy war, are left untranslated.

[3] The expression is *Shark-i-Zamistáni*, and is translated, according to Mr. Shaw, "direction of winter sunrise," as in the cases mentioned in note 2, p. 405.

[4] See notes, pp. 409 and 412.

general invitation. [He was to say]: "This is a general invitation to the faith of Ahmad. Happy the man who comes to the Faith and obtains his portion." The greater number submitted; but not the chiefs of Nubra, who were refractory and rebellious, and retired to their castles and forts. A certain man named Bur Kápá, who was at the head of the chiefs of the infidels, strengthened himself within the castle of Mutadár,[1] which is the chief fort of that country. I laid siege to this fort, and was for some days employed in making ready the siege implements, such as catapults, shields [*turá*], etc. On the appointed day I approached the fort, and the talons of Islám, seizing the hands of infidelity, the enemy were thrown into disorder and routed. Having deserted the fort, they fled in confusion and dismay, while the Musulmáns gave them chase, as far as was possible, so that not one of these bewildered people escaped. Bur Kápá was slain together with all his men; their heads formed a lofty minaret—and the vapour from the brains of the infidels of that country ascended to the heavens.

Thenceforth no one dared offer resistance. Having thus reduced the whole province of Nubra, a garrison was placed in the fort and order established.

Thence we passed into Máryul, and there encamped. In Máryul there are two rulers. One called Lata Jughdán, and the other Táshikun.[2] They both hastened to wait [on me]. At that period

[1] This name may also read *Maut-dár*, but is probably intended for *Hundar*, near the junction of the Nubra and Shayok rivers. The chief village, and seat of the district officials in the Nubra Valley is, nowadays, *Tagár*—a name which bears a certain resemblance to a part of the word Mutadár. At one time *Charása*, on the opposite side of the river, was the chief place.

[2] The kings or rulers of Ladak are not easy to trace about this period. In the first place, the history of the country has not yet been completely worked out; in the second place, no dates are recorded (except one uncertain one) till the year 1580 A.D. is reached. We possess two lists of rulers previous to that date—one by the late Emil v. Schlagintweit, and the other by the late Dr. Karl Marx of the Moravian mission in Ladak. Both are taken from the same Tibetan work—the *Ladak Gyalrabs*—but they differ to some extent, and more especially about the period which embraces the transactions related by Mirza Haidar. On the whole, probably the later version of Dr. Marx is the one to be most trusted, as he collated several manuscripts of the *Ladak Gyalrabs*, and had the assistance of good local authorities on the history of the country. Had he only been able to supply dates for the reigns of the kings and for the events he mentions, his work would indeed have been valuable. The only way in which I have been able roughly to set up a reference mark for the dates, is to assume that the sixteenth king of the line, reigned not later than the early part of the fifteenth century, for it is during this king's time that an event is mentioned, showing that the famous religious reformer Tsong-Kapa was then alive, and the period of Tsong-Kapa's life is well known (from Chinese sources) to have been 1355 to 1417 A.D. Thus the sixteenth king of Ladak must have been ruling before 1417, while Mirza Haidar's invasion took place in the autumn of 1532 (Safar 939 H.), when the name of one of the rulers was Lata Jughdán, or Chogdan. Now the only ruler of the name of Chogdan (fully Lo-dos-chog-ldan) is the seventeenth, who was son of the sixteenth, and it would seem impossible that a man should be reigning in 1532 whose father was king some time previous to 1417. There is, therefore, some discrepancy here which I see no way of reconciling. The name of the other ruler, given by Mirza

Libra began to change. In the whole of Tibet during Libra, the cold is so intense that, compared with it, the winter of other countries is as the hottest days of summer. I then held a consultation with the Amirs, who were with me, as to which district of Tibet would be best suited to establish our winter quarters in, and where we might find grain and provender for the cattle during the winter. As no such place was to be found in those parts, Kashmir was decided upon for the winter quarters. If we could conquer it, well and good; if not, we could winter there and leave in the spring.

This matter having been settled, we left Máryul and the neighbouring districts, and taking the army of Tibet along with us, advanced towards Kashmir. At this juncture Abdál Kuli Yasávul, one of the Khán's trusty chamberlains, arrived with news that the Khán was making for this quarter [Máryul], that on the road he had been afflicted with *dam-giri* (which is the peculiarity of that infidel country), and [adding] that he wished to see me as soon as possible. That same hour I set out to [meet] him, leaving the army where it was.

Haidar as Táshikun, or Tashi-gon, may fit in somewhat better, for Dr. Marx's nineteenth king has the name of Ta-shis-nam-gyal. In reality this would be two very common Tibetan names, and the second *s* in *shis* would not be uttered; the whole would be pronounced *Táshi Namgyal.* It is related of this personage that he made himself master of the whole of the country from Purig (or Purik—lying between lower Ladak and Suru) in the west, to Do Shod, near the source of the Tsang-po (Brahmaputra) in the east; that "he fought against an invading force of Turks, and killed many Turks. He erected a temple (dedicated) to the (four) Lords . . . . and laid the corpses of the Turks under the feet of (the images of) the (four) Lords. Again, by building the temple to the (four) Lords, he obtained power over the demon that turns back hostile armies." Whether this invasion of "Turks" points to Mirza Haidar's exploit, can only be a matter of conjecture, and, indeed, it seems to me very doubtful if Táshi-Namgyal and Táshi-Kun can be regarded as one and the same person. Tashi is so common a name among the natives of Ladak, that it scarcely distinguishes one person from another. The Tashi-Kun named here is apparently the same chief who is mentioned later as having welcomed Mirza Haidar on returning from his expedition towards Lassa; while another person of the name seems to have been the head man of Nubra, and is recorded lower down to have been executed by the Moghuls. On the whole, nothing very distinct can be made out of the Ladak annals as we have them. (See, for Marx's translation, *J. A. S. B.*, Vol. LX., 1892, Part III., pp. 97 *seqq.*; and for Schlagintweit's tables in Stokvis' *Manuel d'Histoire, etc.*, i., pp. 242–3.)

CHAPTER XCIV.

ARRIVAL OF THE KHÁN IN TIBET, FOLLOWING THE AUTHOR. HIS ENTRANCE INTO BÁLTI. JOURNEY OF THE AUTHOR TO KASHMIR.

It was mentioned above that the Khán had decided to advance against the Dulpa, by way of Khotan, and had sent me forward to Bálti. At that time the Emperor of the firmament was in the sign of Leo; the Khán, having marched for one month, took up his summer quarters among the hill pastures of Khotan, until the end of the season of Virgo. Those who had had experience of that region then represented to the Khán: "It is now too late [in the season] to achieve anything: for very soon all the waters and rivers will be frozen over, so that no water will be obtainable: nor is there sufficient firewood to be found to melt the ice, for watering the cattle and horses. It will also be hardly possible to kill enough *kutás* to make a sufficient supply of soup. It is for these reasons that, on previous occasions, several armies have been dismounted [lost their horses] on this road." The Khán being convinced [of the impracticability of continuing by that route] said: "Were I to give up the holy war in Tibet, I should be disappointed of great recompense hereafter. If this route is too difficult, it will be best for me to follow in the steps of Mirzá Haidar, and complete the holy war in that quarter." So saying, he turned back from Khotan and advanced along the road which I had taken.[1]

On the way he was so severely attacked by *dam-giri*, that for some days he was quite insensible, and his life was reduced to a breath. The doctors applied suppositories [*shiyáf*] and used aperients, and whenever these took effect he became conscious for the moment, but soon again fainted away. To the nobles and courtiers he said: "Although my health is not strong enough to admit of my conducting a holy war, I shall not be wanting in intention. When I am deprived, as I certainly shall be, of the companionship of the living, it will only be to join the band of the departed. Perhaps I may die on the road. As long as there is a breath of life in me I will not abandon the war. When all life

[1] From this, it appears that the Khan had started from Khotan with the intention of crossing by one of the direct routes to Ngari-Khorsum, or the western province of what is now Lassa-governed Tibet—the region where the gold workings are to be found. These routes, whether by the upper Kárakásh, or by Polu, are so difficult and at such excessive altitudes, as to be practically impassable, except for light and well-equipped parties at the best season of the year. They are never used by traders or travellers and are very little known. Mirza Haidar's route (and the one the Khan afterwards followed) was the ordinary one over the Karakorum pass, as is evident from Nubra being mentioned as the first point reached on arriving in Ladak.

has gone out of me, you can do as you please." During this time he frequently asked after me, and used to say, with emotion and regret: "At the present moment I have no other desire than this [seeing the author], and I pray God that my life may be preserved until I meet him once more." He also repeated verses suited to his frame of mind: among them the following couplet. [Verses]. . . . He constantly uttered such sentiments during his intervals of consciousness.

It is strange that in spite of the severity of this malady, one never desires to stay in one place [for any length of time]. Indeed, so excessive is the cold, and so great the scarcity of water and corn, that supposing one to make a halt, it would only aggravate the disease. The cure is to do one's best to reach some place where *dam-giri* is less prevalent. Whenever the Khán reached such a place he recovered consciousness.

On the day that the Khán returned to his senses, I joined his camp. Having embraced me affectionately, he said: "Of all my friends or children, it is you who have been in my thoughts [the most], and I thank God for having been allowed to see you again." [Verses]. . . . From that hour he began to regain his usual health and strength, and by the time we reached Nubra he was entirely restored, so that he was able to enter that district on horseback. After this, all the Amirs assembled together in council and each gave his opinion on the best course to pursue. I suggested: "After careful investigation, I can discover no spot in these districts of Tibet, which can provide winter quarters for more than one thousand men. But with a thousand men, there will be no possibility of insubordination or revolt. There seems to be no place capable of supporting a large army in winter, except Kashmir. But on the road to Kashmir there are many passes, which the Khán's strength will not allow him to cross. If the Khán would issue the needful order, he might retain 1000 men in his own service and proceed to Bálti with them; for in Bálti there is no *dam-giri*, and no passes need be traversed [to reach it]. He might place me in command of the rest of the troops, when, having spent the winter in Kashmir, we could, on the return of spring, do whatever seemed wisest."

Of all the propositions this one pleased the Khán most, and thus it was decided. At the outset of his expedition [the Khán] knew that Tibet was no place for a large army. Five thousand men had been fixed [as the number]; 3,000 belonged to the Khán's army and 2,000 to mine. Of those 3,000 men, the Khán [now] retained 1,000 for his personal service and advanced towards Bálti, while I turned in the direction of Kashmir attended by 4,000 men, and also by several distinguished Amirs, such as Amir Dáim Ali, who was mentioned in the lists at Káshghar, Bábá Sárik Mirzá, and others.

CHAPTER XCV.

THE KHÁN'S EXPERIENCES IN BÁLTI.

At the end of Libra the Khán arrived in Bálti. Bahrám Chu, one of the head men of Bálti, submitted and waited on the Khán. All the other Chu[1] began to practise sedition and revolt, the natural outcome of infidelity. In the first place, under the guidance of Bahrám Chu, the Khán took the fort of Shigár[2] (which is the capital of all Bálti) at the first assault. All the men of the place were mown down by the blood-stained swords of the assailants, while the women and children, together with much property, fell a prey to the victorious army. Furthermore, wherever in that hill-country a hand was stretched out, it never missed its object; [and even the strongly fortified ravines and castles were trampled under foot by the horses of the Khán's army.][3]

On account of the snow, no news from Kashmir could reach the Khán during that winter, and the infidel insurgents, to serve their own vile purposes, spread many false reports, thereby causing the Khán, and all the army, to become distressed and anxious. At length, towards the end of winter, an express messenger who had been sent from Kashmir arrived, bearing news of our successes, whereupon the apprehension and distress of the Khán [and his troops] were changed to joy and gladness; and they recited the verse: "Thanks be to God who has put sorrow away from us."

At the beginning of spring they withdrew from Bálti. [At this juncture] the Khán entrusted to Amir Kambar Kukildásh, who was mentioned in the lists [muster roll] at Káshghar, the province

[1] *Chu* may also read *Ju*, which is a very common termination to the names of natives of the Kishtawár province of Kashmir, whether Hindus or Musulmáns. But this can hardly be the sense in which Mirza Haidar employs it, in this and many passages to come. He obviously means it to signify an official of some kind, and I believe it to be the word *Chho*, or *Chu*, of Gen. Cunningham. He writes (p. 260): "Among the Mahomedans of Ladak . . . . the petty chiefs are invariably called *Chho*"; while (p. 277) he gives *Chu-pon* as the equivalent of an inferior official—a "chief of ten," or sergeant. Moorcroft, too, (ii., pp. 29, 30, etc.) speaks of an inferior official by the style of *Chu-chu*. I do not know the word, in local use among modern officials in Ladak, but it may be current in Baltistan. Bahrám was, to judge by his name, a Musulmán, and it will be seen below, that it is with reference to Musulmán chiefs that Mirza Haidar always employs the word *Chu*.

[2] The right spelling; but written *Ashigár* at p. 410.

[3] The Persian texts make no apparent sense of this passage, so the Turki alone has been translated. The allusion is, I think, to the Tibetan method of defence, in barricading ravines by building walls of loose stones across them. The remains of defensive barricades of this kind, are found still, in many parts of Ladak. There are two, for instance, on the direct road to Yarkand, which were originally built to assist in keeping out the Moghuls.

of Nubra, which I had set in order and handed over to the Khán. But in consequence of the Amir's bad judgment and want of capacity, the country went to ruin and the inhabitants rose in revolt, each man betaking himself to some strong place. Utterly disregarding those weak men who had been placed over them, the people gave themselves up to robbery and every kind of crime. On this account [the Khán's officials] not deeming it safe to remain any longer in Nubra, came to Máryul.[1] Táshikun, for his neglect of duty, was deprived of his fortress and put to death.[2] It was here [in Máryul] that I found [the Khán's officers] encamped when I arrived from Kashmir, as shall be presently related.

CHAPTER XCVI.

THE AUTHOR'S ARRIVAL IN KASHMIR AND EVENTS CONNECTED THEREWITH.

I LEFT Nubra with the Amirs and the new army, which the Khán had sent with me, and joined my own forces in the district of Máryul; after which I set off, by forced marches, in the direction of Kashmir. On the road, all the chief men of Tibet submitted and, joining us, greatly increased the numbers of our army. Some of the Bálti Tibetans, who live in the valleys of Kashmir, acting as our guides, we reached that country at the beginning of the sign of Scorpio—Jamád II. 939—after crossing the pass of Kashmir, which is called Zuji. The chiefs of Kashmir had already heard of the approach of our army, and were occupying the narrow defile of Lár.[3] Having crossed the pass [of Zuji] I sent forward 400 men, chosen out of the whole army for their experience, under the command of Tumán Bahádar Kaluchi, who was one of those mentioned in the lists at Káshghar. When they reached the narrow defile, they found it occupied by the Kashmir army, a few of whom were stationed as outposts at its [upper] end. At dawn our soldiers made a charge on these pickets, who fled down the defile, followed by our men. When the main body perceived this, seeing no way of holding the road, they too turned and fled. Arriving [at

[1] Máryul is here differentiated from Nubra, and obviously stands for the district of the capital—at that time probably Sheh, near Leh. (See note, p. 410; also the first translated sentence of Chap. CV., where it is obviously used for the capital, and not for Ladak in general.)

[2] See note, pp. 418–19, regarding Tashikun.

[3] The *Sind* river (of our maps) flowing from the Zoji pass down towards the Jhilam, was called the *Lar*. The narrow and difficult defile mentioned immediately below, as the position defended by the Kashmiris, is most likely the defile of *Hang*, or *Hang Satu*, between the villages of Gangangir and Sonamarg —or about twenty miles below the western foot of the Zogi pass.

this moment] I gave them chase; thus easily did our whole force pass such a difficult place. On the second day after [this affair] we alighted in Kashmir. Having reached this point, it seems fitting, in order to render the subject clear and intelligible, to give some account of the country of Kashmir and its rulers.

CHAPTER XCVII.

DESCRIPTION OF KASHMIR.

KASHMIR is among the most famous countries of the world, and is celebrated both for its attractions and its wonders. In spite of its renown, no one knows anything about its present state, nor can any of its features or its history be learned from the books of former writers. At this present date of Moharram 950, [1543–4] now that I have subdued this beautiful country and seen all that is notable in it, whatever I shall write will be what I have witnessed.

The second time that I entered Kashmir, and when I had not reduced the whole of the country, I drew an omen [*fál*] from the Korán, with reference to its conquest and to my becoming established there. The verse that turned up was: "Eat of the daily bread from your Lord, and return your thanks to him in the shape of a fair city. The Lord is forgiving."

The plain [*julgá*] of Kashmir extends from the *Bakani* quarter, which means "between the south and the east," towards the *Rikan Bain* [or north-west]; it is a level expanse about a hundred *kruh* (equivalent to thirty *farsákhs*) in length. Its width is, at some parts, about twenty *kruh*, and in a few places ten *kruh*.[1] In this

[1] The word *Kruh* or *Kuroh* is the Persian form for the familiar *Kro* or *Kos* of India. As a measure of distance, it has varied so greatly with time, and still varies according to locality, that a better estimate could hardly be given than our author's, when he makes it 0·3 of a *farsákh*, or about 1⅓ mile. In Northern India and Kashmir, in our own times, the Kos is usually taken at about 1½ mile. The Emperor Akbar established the *Kos* on the basis of 5000 *Iláhi Gaz*, which produces an English equivalent of rather over 2½ miles: but it is probable that the value of the *Kos*, like that of the *Gaz*, had fallen very low previous to Akbar's reform, so that Mirza Haidar's *Kruh* may well have measured much less than the *Iláhi Kos*. Even later than Akbar's time, as General Cunningham shows, a Kos measuring much less than 2½ miles was in frequent use. On the whole, therefore, 1⅓ mile may be fairly assumed to have been the approximate length of Mirza Haidar's *Kruh*, and may be applied in all cases where he states distances in that measure. As a matter of fact, the length of the Kashmir valley is about 80 English miles, while its breadth varies so greatly that it is impossible to state it in figures. (For full and interesting discussions on the origin, etc., of the words *Kruh* and *Kos*, and the measurements they have represented at different periods, see Cunningham's *Anct. Geog. India*, Appendix B, and Yule's *Glossary*, p. 202.)

region all the land is divided into four kinds. The cultivation is: (1) by irrigation [*ábi*], (2) on land not needing artificial irrigation, (3) gardens, and (4) level ground, where the river banks abound in violets and many-coloured flowers. On the [level] ground, on account of the excessive moisture, the crops do not thrive, and for this reason the soil is not laboured, which constitutes one of its charms.[1] The heat in summer is so agreeable, that there is at no time any need of a fan. A soft and refreshing breeze is constantly blowing. . . .[2]

The climate in winter is also very temperate, notwithstanding the heavy snowfalls, so that no fur cloak [*pustin*] is necessary. In fact its coldness only serves to render the heat yet more agreeable. When the sun does not shine, the warmth of a fire is far from unpleasant. [Couplet]. . . .[3] In short I have neither seen nor heard of any country equal to Kashmir, for charm of climate during all the four seasons.

In the town there are many lofty buildings constructed of fresh cut pine. Most of these are at least five stories high and each story contains apartments, halls, galleries and towers. The beauty of their exterior defies description, and all who behold them for the first time, bite the finger of astonishment with the teeth of admiration. But the interiors are not equal to the exteriors.

The passages in the markets, and the streets of the city, are all paved with hewn stone. But the bazaars are not laid out as they are in other towns. In the streets of the markets, only drapers and retail dealers are to be found. Tradesmen do all their business in the seclusion of their own houses. Grocers, druggists, beer-sellers [*fukái*], and that class of provision vendors who usually frequent markets, do not do so here. The population of this city is equal to that of [other] large towns.

As for the fruits—pears, mulberries, [sweet] cherries and sour cherries are met with, but the apples are particularly good. There are other fruits in plenty, sufficient to make one break one's resolutions. Among the wonders of Kashmir are the quantities of mulberry trees, [cultivated] for their leaves, [from which] silk is obtained. The people make a practice of eating the fruit, but rather regard it as wrong. In the season, fruit is so plentiful that it is rarely bought and sold. The holder of a garden and the man that has no garden are alike; for the gardens have no walls and it is not usual to hinder anyone from taking the fruit.

[1] The whole of this passage, regarding the land, is obscure and the translation uncertain. The Turki MS. is clearer, but mentions only three categories of land: "One kind is land where agriculture is done with [river] water. Another where it is done with rain-water. Another is the level ground, where the river-banks abound in violets and many-coloured flowers; this land is too damp to cultivate."

[2] Some rhetorical sentences slightly abridged and a couplet omitted.—R.

[3] About half a folio of florid prose and verse, descriptive of the flowers, birds, etc., is omitted here.—R.

CHAPTER XCVIII.

FURTHER WONDERS.

FIRST and foremost among the wonders of Kashmir stand her idol temples. In and around Kashmir, there are more than one hundred and fifty temples which are built of blocks of hewn stone, fitted so accurately one upon the other, that there is absolutely no cement used. These stones have been so carefully placed in position, without plaster or mortar, that a sheet of paper could not be passed between the joints. The blocks are from three to twenty *gaz* in length, one *gaz* in depth, and one to five *gaz* in breadth. The marvel is how these stones were transported and erected. The temples are nearly all built on the same plan. There is a square enclosure which in some places reaches the height of thirty *gaz*, while each side is about three hundred *gaz* long. Inside this enclosure there are pillars, and on the top of the pillars there are square capitals; on the top of these again, are placed supports,[1] and most of these separate parts are made out of one block of stone. On the pillars are fixed the supports of the arches, and each arch is three or four *gaz* in width. Under the arch are a hall and a doorway. On the outside and inside of the arch are pillars of forty or fifty *gaz*[2] in height, having supports and capitals of one block of stone. On the top of this are placed four pillars of one or two pieces of stone.

The inside and the outside of the halls have the appearance of two porticos, and these are covered with one or two stones. The capitals, the ornamentation in relief, the cornices, the "dog tooth" work, the inside covering and the outside, are all crowded with pictures and paintings, which I am incapable of describing. Some represent laughing and weeping figures, which astound the beholder. In the middle is a lofty throne of hewn stone, and over that, a dome made entirely of stone, which I cannot describe. In the rest of the world there is not to be seen, or heard of, one building like this. How wonderful that there should [here] be a hundred and fifty of them![3]

[1] Literally, "small arm-pits."—R.

[2] Mirza Haidar's *gaz*, as we have already seen (note, pp. 58 and 256), was probably the same as that used by Baber, and therefore measured some 26 to 28 inches. But even if he is using, here, the smaller *gaz* of India—the ell, of 18 inches—it will be seen, in the note below, that his measurements are, out of all proportion, too great.

[3] There is nothing, in this account, to show which of the ruined temples of Kashmir the author is describing. When he gives one hundred and fifty as the number of them, he probably commits no great exaggeration, for even in Mr. Vigne's time (about 1834–8) the number was reckoned at not less than seventy to

Again, to the east of Kashmir there is a district called Barnág [Virnág]. Here there is a hill on the top of which is a ditch [*basti*] like a tank, and at the bottom of the tank is a hole. It

---

eighty. During the three intervening centuries, very many must have disappeared. Some are known to have been destroyed, and the stones they were made of used for various purposes. Others, again, have been built over, or otherwise hidden from sight; while some, no doubt, have been overgrown by the jungle. The five most remarkable ruins now known, are those at Martand, or Pandu Koru, about five miles east of Islámabád (the ancient capital of the valley, and now called, by the Hindus, Anant Nág), at Bhaniyar (near Uri), Avantipur, Pandrettan, and Páyech. The Martand temple is not only the largest of them all, but by far the finest, and as the late Mr. Fergusson observes, is the most typical example of the Kashmir style. It dates from about 750 A.D., and some of the others may be somewhat older; "but none," writes Mr. Fergusson, "can be carried farther back than the reign of Ránáditya—A.D. 578 to 594.[1] Nor can any be brought down below say 1200, which is probably the date of that of Páyech. . . . The style during these six centuries is so uniform that it may be taken as one, for the purposes of general history."

If we assume Mirza Haidar's description to refer to this, the largest of the temples, it may be interesting to compare Mr. Fergusson's account with it. He says: "The temple itself is a very small building, being only 60 feet in length, by 38 feet in width. The width of the facade, however, is eked out by two wings, or adjuncts, which make it 60 feet." He then cites General Cunningham, who estimated its height to be also 60 feet when complete, thus making each dimension 60 feet. Mr. Fergusson doubted if the temple ever had a roof. No fragments of a roof have been found in modern times on the floor of the temple, and judging from the tenuity of the walls, and the large voids they include, he doubted if they could have supported a stone roof. If, indeed, there was a roof he believed it must have been of wood. The courtyard that surrounds and encloses the temple, was regarded by Mr. Fergusson as a more remarkable object than the temple itself. Its internal dimensions he gives as 220 feet by 142 feet. On each face is a central cell which, if complete, would have reached to 30 feet in height, at the summit of its roof, while the pillars on each side of the cells are 9 feet high. No inscription has been found on the Martand ruin, and its date has been fixed from historical records only.

Mr. T. G. Vigne who published, in 1842, a narrative of his travels in Kashmir, had measurements made of the Martand temple, and records that the greatest length—that of the side walls—was about 270 feet, while that of the front was 168 feet. The height of the pillars, including foot and capital, he made barely 10 feet, and the huge blocks of limestone of which the temple was built, 6 to 9 feet in length, "of proportionate solidity, and cemented with an excellent mortar." His measurements of the side walls and front, evidently refer to the outer enclosure, and not to the temple itself. They are somewhat in excess of those given by Mr. Fergusson, but this discrepancy may be accounted for by Mr. Vigne having perhaps measured the outside of the walls, while Mr. Fergusson particularly mentions that his figures relate to the interior of the enclosure. But however this may be, the Brobdingnagian proportions of Mirza Haidar's account have to be considerably pared down in every instance, as is usually the case with statements made in figures by Asiatics. The chief interest that his description possesses is, that it is one of the oldest notices of the Kashmir ruins that have come down to us—perhaps the oldest from the pen of any Musulman, or foreign, writer.

As regards the question of the roof, if our author's account were otherwise exact, his particular mention of the existence of a dome would be important; but judging from the inaccuracy of his other statements, this one can scarcely deserve much consideration. (See Fergusson's *Hist. of Indian and Eastern Architecture*, 1876, pp. 279 *seqq.*; Vigne's *Travels in Kashmir*, i., pp. 385–6; also Moorcroft, ii., pp. 239 *seqq.*; and an interesting paper by Mr. W. Simpson, in the *Journal of the Inst. of Brit. Architects* for May, 1862.)

---

[1] Other authorities differ somewhat as to this date. (See Stokvis, i., p. 239.)

remains dry throughout the year, except during the season of Taurus, when water issues from it.[1] Two or three times a day it gushes out [with such force] that the tank is filled, and enough water flows down the side of the hill to drive one or even two mills. After this it subsides, so that no water remains except in the hole. When the season of Taurus is passed, it again becomes dry for a whole year. Though endeavours have been made to stop it up with lime and mortar, yet when the season has come, all this has been washed away, and it has never been found possible to stop its flow.

Further, in Nágám, a notable town of Kashmir,[2] there is a tree which is so high that if an arrow be shot at the top, it will probably not reach it. If anyone takes hold of one of the twigs and shakes it, the whole of this enormous tree is put in motion.

Again, Div Sar,[3] which is one of the most important districts of Kashmir, contains a spring twenty *gaz* square. On the sides of it are pleasant shady trees and soft herbage. One boils some rice, puts it in a bottle, closes up the mouth [of the bottle] tightly, and having written a name on it, throws it into the spring and then sits down [to wait]. Sometimes the bottle remains there five years; on other occasions it comes up again the same day: the time is uncertain. If, when it reappears, the rice is found to be warm, the circumstance is regarded as a good omen. Sometimes the rice has undergone a change, or earth and sand may have got inside it. The more [substances] that find their way into it, the more unfavourable is the omen considered.

Moreover, there is in Kashmir a lake called Ulur, the circumference of which is seven *farsákhs.* In the middle of this lake Sultán Zain-ul-Abidin, one of the Sultáns of Kashmir, erected a palace. First of all he emptied a quantity of stones into the lake, [at this spot] and on these constructed a foundation [or floor] of closely-fitting stones, measuring two hundred square *gaz* in extent,

[1] The spring of Virnág is one of the most famous in Kashmir, and is made much of by the Hindus. It is reputed to be the source of the Jhilam, but the real sources are in the hills at some distance to the south and east of Virnág. We read in Ince's *Kashmir Handbook*: "The water of the spring, which is very cold and of a deep bluish-green colour, is received into an octagonal stone basin, about 111 feet wide, 50 feet deep in the centre, and 10 feet deep at the sides, and filled with sacred fish; after flowing through the garden in stone-lined canals, it shortly joins the Saudrahán. Around the basin is an old building consisting of twenty-four arched alcoves, which were faced with large and elaborately carved stones, many of which still remain. . . ." The stone basin, the canals and other constructions are of a later date than Mirza Haidar: they are ascribed to the Emperor Jahángir, whose favourite resort was Virnág.

[2] Now a mere village. It lies one short march south of Srinagar.

[3] The name of *Div Sar*, or *Deo Sar*, does not appear to be in use nowadays. It was the district, however, of which Kolagám was the chief town or village, and Kolagám, or Kulgám, stands to the left of the upper Jhilam—to the south-west of Islámabád. (See Moorcroft, ii., p. 113; also the map in Cunningham's *Ladak.*)

and ten *gaz* in height. Hereupon he built a charming palace and planted pleasant groves of trees, so that there can be but few more agreeable places in the world.[1] Finally, this same Sultán Zain-ul-Abidin built himself a palace in the town, which in the dialect of Kashmir is called Rájdán. It has twelve stories, some of which contain fifty rooms, halls, and corridors. The whole of this lofty structure is built of wood.[2]

[Among] the vast kiosks of the world are :—in Tabriz, the Hasht Bihisht Kiosk of Sultán Yakub; in Herat the Bágh-i-Khán, the Bágh-i-Safid, and the Bágh-i-Shahr; and in Samarkand the Kuk

[1] The *Ular*, or *Wular* lake—the largest sheet of water in Kashmir. The author usually exaggerates measurements, but in giving 28 miles as the circumference of the Wular, he has somewhat understated the fact. It is about 12 miles by 10, but varies according to season. As regards the palace on the island of *Lanka*, its ruins are to be found still, and have often been explored by travellers since the days of Mirza Haidar. The island is near the entrance of the river Jhilam into the lake, and measures some 95 yards by 75. The French traveller, Bernier, visited Lanka in 1665, and speaks of the palace as "an hermitage . . . which it is pretended floats miraculously upon the water"; though he also explains that, according to tradition, "one of the ancient kings of Kachemire, out of mere fancy built it upon a number of thick beams fastened together." In 1821 Mr. Moorcroft landed on the island and found two ruined buildings: one of stone at its eastern extremity, around which were strewed several massive polygonal columns; the other merely an oblong house, with pitched roof and plastered walls, bearing fragments of blue enamel. The first of these he regarded as of undoubted Hindu construction, but he makes no mention of the origin of the other. The foundations of both, however, according to his native informants, had been made up of the stones derived from the ancient Hindu temples in other parts of Kashmir, which had been destroyed by the Musulmans. If this is the case it is possible that in constructing the mosque or palace itself, slabs, columns, etc., from the ancient temples may have been used; and this may have led Mr. Moorcroft to believe the ruin to be of Hindu origin, although he records having seen an inscription relating that the building had been erected by Sultan Zain-ul-Abidin, who reigned about 827 to 874 A.H. (1424 to 1469 A.D). There are many traditions connected with this island and its ruins, but all seem to point to an artificial foundation for the buildings that were erected there. In all probability there was a shoal rather than an island; or perhaps a shoal that appeared as an island above the surface of the lake, only during the low-water season. If this be the case, the spot would, no doubt, have been soft and muddy, and the foundation for any palace or temple put up there, would have had to be laid. However this may be, Mirza Haidar rightly ascribes the building to Sultan Zain-ul-Abidin, whose reign dates only about a hundred years previous to his own time. In 1874 Mr. A. Constable (Bernier's editor) saw there, like Mr. Moorcroft, a slab of black slate bearing a Persian inscription, dated 1443–4, which had been carved to commemorate the erection of the edifice by that Sultan—Bernier's "ancient king of Kachemire." The inscription is, I believe, still preserved.

The name of *Lanka* would seem to be of pre-Musulman origin, though Moorcroft heard that Zain-ul-Abidin had so named the place in ridicule of Hindu traditions. *Lanka*, or *Lanka-dipa*, is the ancient Hindu and Pali name for the island of Ceylon, and it is not improbable that this small island in the Wular, may have been named after the greater one, long before the days of the Musulman kings of Kashmir.

It may be remarked that it is with reference to this spot, that Moorcroft shows his acquaintance with our author. He writes: "The celebrated Mirza Haidar extols *Lanka* as a delightful spot for a party of pleasure"—but nothing more! (Constable's *Bernier*, pp. 416–17; Moorcroft, ii., pp. 223–5.)

[2] There appears to be no trace left of a palace bearing the name of *Rájdán*. That the building should have disappeared is not surprising, since it is reported to have been constructed of wood.

Sarái, the Ak Sarái, the Bágh-i-Dilkushái, and the Bágh-i-Buldi. Though [the Rájdán] is more lofty and contains more rooms than all these, yet it has not their elegance and style. It is, nevertheless, a more wonderful structure.

In the *Zafar-Náma*, Sharaf-ud-Din Ali Yazdi has stated a few facts with regard to Kashmir, but he is not quite consistent with reality. He had never been there himself, but derived his information from travellers, who had not a proper regard for accuracy; hence his statements are not always exact.

CHAPTER XCIX.

EXTRACT FROM THE "ZAFAR-NÁMA."

Though Kashmir is one of the most famous spots in the world, yet on account of its secluded position, it is seldom visited by any but those who make it the express object of a journey. I here give such details as I have been able to verify; having derived them from trustworthy sources and also from the natives. I have taken its position, size, and extent from geographical works.[1]

Kashmir lies near the middle of the fourth climate, for the beginning of the fourth climate is where the latitude is 33° 54′, and the latitude of Kashmir is 34° from the equator. Its longitude from the Jazáir-i-Sadá [2] is 105°. This country runs longitudinally, and is enclosed by mountains on every side; the southern range [lies] in the direction of Dahli [Delhi]; the northern [looks] towards Badakhshán and Khorasán; the west towards the county inhabited by the Ughani [Afghans] tribes; its eastern side terminates in the outlying districts of Tibet. The extent of its level plains from the eastern limits to the western, is about 40 *farsákhs*, and from south to north 20 *farsákhs*. In the heart of the level plain lying within this mountainous district, are 1000 inhabited villages, abounding in wholesome streams and vegetation. It is popularly believed that in the whole of the province—plains and mountains together—are comprised 100,000 villages. The land is thickly inhabited, and the soil is cultivated. The climate is very salubrious, while the beauty of the women of the country is proverbial. [Verses.] . . .

In the mountains and plains are to be found many kinds of fruit-trees, and the fruits are especially good and wholesome. But, since the temperature inclines to be cold and the snow falls in great abundance, those fruits which

[1] The remainder of the chapter is from the *Zafar-Náma*.

[2] The Arabic name for the *Insulæ Fortunatæ*, which the ancient geographers—Arabs as well as Greeks—took for their prime meridian, subsequent to the date of Ptolemy. The latitude given here, it may be observed, is remarkably correct, for Srinagar stands in 34° 7′ north lat.

require much warmth, such as dates, oranges and lemons, do not ripen there; these are imported from the neighbouring warm regions.

In the middle of the valley there is a town called Srinagar, which stretches eastward and westward for a *fursákh* in either direction. This is the residence of the governor of the country. Like at Baghdad, there flows through the middle of it a great river, which is even larger than the Tigris. The wonderful thing is that this mighty river comes from one spring, which rises within the limits of the country, and is called the spring of Vir [Virnág]. The people of the place have constructed across this river about thirty bridges of boats bound together by chains, through which they can open a way. Seven of these bridges are in the town of Srinagar, which is the capital of the province and the seat of the governors. After the river has passed the limits of Kashmir, it takes in one place the name of Dandána, in another that of Jumla;[1] it flows through the upper portion of Multán and joins the river Siyáb. The united streams empty themselves into the Sind near the [town of] Ucha, and the whole river thenceforth takes the name of Sind, which discharges itself into the sea of Oman at the extremity of the land of Tatta.[2]

[1] The two names, it will be remarked, are not Mirza Haidar's, but those of the author of the *Zafar-Náma*. Whether either, or both, are correctly given, or whether they are misrenderings copied from one history into another, it is not easy to conjecture, but my impression is that the *Jumla* of the text is a corruption of *Jamd*. Though Mirza Haidar professes to quote the *Zafar-Náma*, these passages by no means accord closely with the extracts on the same subject translated in Elliot's *Hist. of India*. They correspond far better with a part of the description of Kashmir contained in Abu Tálib Husaini's Persian version of the *Mulfazát-i-Timuri*, also reproduced in English by Elliot. It would not be unlikely that Mirza Haidar, possessed as he was of local knowledge, should amend the *Zafar-Náma* while copying it, but whether Sharaf-ud-Din copied from the original Turki of the *Mulfazát* (if there was one), or whether Abu Tálib (whose translation dates from 1620) copied from Sharaf-ud-Din, is by no means clear. The two accounts are, however, one and the same, small differences notwithstanding. The two names now in question for the Jhilam, are precisely the same in both, and Mirza Haidar has made no amendment in this instance. *Dandána* is mentioned, as far as I have been able to ascertain, nowhere else than in these passages of the *Zafar-Náma* and the *Mulfazát*; but *Jamd* (perhaps Jamad) occurs constantly in the latter work as the name of the Jhilam, not only in the neighbourhood of Kashmir, but throughout its course. The historian of Timur's campaigns seems to have deemed it the common name for the river. The *Tárikh-i-Háfiz Abru*, a work which dates from about the same period as the other two (the first half of the fifteenth century) describes the whole length of the Jhilam, from its source in Kashmir to its confluence with the Indus, under the name of *Jamd*; while the *Matla' us Sa'dain* (dating from about the middle of the fifteenth century) likewise speaks of the Jhilam as the *Jamd*. Somewhat less than a century later, however, we find Baber calling it the *Behat*—a name which has remained in use down to our own time, and is a form of the ancient *Bidasta* or *Vidasta*. Thus, at whatever period *Jamd* or *Jamad* may have first come into use, it seems to have been forgotten by Musulman writers since the fifteenth century. (See Elliot for *Zafar-Náma*, iii., p. 521; for *Mulfazát-i-Timuri*, iii., pp. 410–83; for *Tárikh-i-Háfiz Abru*, iv., p. 4; and for *Matla' us Sa'dain*, iv., p. 94; *Baber*, p. 294; also Major Raverty, *J. A. S. B.*, lxi., 1893, pt. i., pp. 290–1.) *Siyáb* is evidently *Chináb*, badly copied.

[2] The *Uch*, alluded to here, is no doubt the old town of that name, situated near the left bank of the Panjnad just below the Sutlej confluence. "In the time of Timur and Akbar," says General Cunningham, "the junction of the Chenab and Indus took place opposite *Uchh*, 60 miles above the present confluence at Mithankot. . . . But early in the present century the Indus gradually changed its course, and leaving the old channel at 20 miles above *Uchh*, continued its course to

This country [Kashmir] is protected naturally by its mountains on every side, so that the inhabitants, without the trouble of fortifying themselves, are safe from the attacks of enemies. Nor have they anything to fear from the revolutions worked by time, or by the rain or the wind.

There are three principal highways into Kashmir. The one leading to Khorásán is such a difficult route, that it is impossible for beasts of burden with loads to be driven along it; so the inhabitants, who are accustomed to such work, carry the loads upon their own shoulders for several days, until they reach a spot where it is possible to load a horse. The road to India offers the same difficulty. The route which leads to Tibet is easier than these two, but during several days one finds nothing but poisonous herbs, which make the transit inconvenient for travellers on horseback, since the horses perish.[1]

CHAPTER C.

THE CONVERSION OF KASHMIR TO ISLÁM, AND A SHORT ACCOUNT OF THE MUSULMÁN SULTANS OF KASHMIR.

THE conversion of Kashmir is a comparatively recent event. The people were all Hindus and professed the faith of Bráhma. A certain Sultán Shams-ud-Din came thither disguised as a kalandar. At that time there was a governor in every district of Kashmir. There was also a queen, into whose service Sultán Shams-ud-Din entered. After a short time the queen desired to marry Sultán Shams-ud-Din; and not long after this event, his power became absolute throughout Kashmir. He was succeeded by his son Alá-ud-Din, who was in turn succeeded by his son Kutb-ud-Din, during whose reign Amir Kabir Ali the Second, called Sayyid Ali Hamadáni,[2] appeared

---

the south-south-west, until it rejoined the old channel at Mithankot." At the time of Mirza Haidar, then, *Uch* must have been near the confluence of the greater rivers, and was, for this reason perhaps, a city of some importance. The name of *Uch* or *Uchcha* is common in Northern India; and one place so called, is to be found a short distance west of the junction of the Jhilam with the Chináb; while a third lies some 30 miles north of Jacobabad. (See Cunningham, *Ancient Geog.*, pp. 220–21 and 242 *seq.*)

Tatta, standing near the apex of the delta of the Indus, though a town of not much importance now, is a place of great antiquity, and at the period of the earlier Moghuls, seems to have given its name to the whole of Lower Sind. (See for a complete account of *Tatta*, Cunningham, pp. 288 *seq.*)

[1] The *Zafar-Náma* contains this passage about the poisonous herbs on the road from Kashmir to Ladak. Whoever originally wrote it, had remarkably accurate local information, and the statement holds good to the present day. Round about the spot called Báltal, at the western foot of the Zoji pass, there are poisonous weeds among the grass, which frequently prove fatal to horses if turned out to graze. Nowhere else in these regions (as far as I am aware) do similar poisonous herbs occur.

[2] This Sayyid Ali Hamadáni was a refugee from Hamadán in Persia, whence he and those of his order are said to have been expelled by Timur, about the

there. Kutb-ud-Din died in less than forty days,[1] and was succeeded by his son Sultán Iskandar, who established the Musulmán faith and destroyed all the idol-temples. His son Sultán Zain-ul-Abidin succeeded him, and reigned for fifty years.[2] He devoted

year 1380. Mr. Beale records that seven hundred Sayyids accompanied their leader in his flight to Kashmir in that year, while this large party was afterwards followed by another, of three hundred of the order, in the train of Sayyid Ali's son, Mir Muhammad. It is to these immigrations of Persian Sayyids, during the reign of Kutub-ud-Din, that the conversion of Kashmir to Islam is usually attributed. Sayyid Ali died in Pakhli about the year 1386, and the son seems to have left the country only some six years later. The name by which the father is usually known in Kashmir is "Sayyid Hamadáni," and he may be regarded as a sort of patron saint of the Musulmán section of the population. His descendants—or persons claiming this distinction—still exist, I believe, in Srinagar, while the mosque of Sháh-i-Hamadán is perhaps the most reverenced of any in the town. A recent writer in the *Times* tells us that the original Sayyid's "place of retreat and devotion" is still shown in the gloomy interior of the building, "where but little light breaks upon the pillars and ceiling and walls of stained deodar." The architecture he describes as peculiar to Kashmiri mosques, for neither cupola nor minaret exists, "but only a sloping four-sided roof, surmounted by a conical wooden steeple . . : from time to time the mosque of Shah-i-Hamadán is burned down, but is re-erected with faithful attention to the original model." (See Beale's *Orient. Biog. Dict.*, p. 238, and the *Times*, 7th November, 1894).

[1] This would appear to mean that the length of Kutub-ud-Din's reign was less than forty days, but a possible reading may be that he died less than forty days after the arrival, in Kashmir, of Sayyid Ali Hamadáni. The dates for Kutub-ud-Din's reign are uncertain, but they usually indicate for it a length of about fifteen years. (See the next note.)

[2] It would have been interesting and satisfactory to be able to accept Mirza Haidar as an original authority on the history of the kings of the country he ruled over so long; but his data are so entirely at variance with two of the best historians of India—Firishta and Abul Fazl—that it is impossible to place his brief remarks in the scale against their detailed accounts, and carefully elaborated tables. Firishta and Abul Fazl by no means agree in the dates they assign to the various Sultans, or in the length of their reigns; and even the different editions of Firishta vary to some extent among themselves. Mr. C. J. Rodgers has published a careful summary, from collated copies of Firishta, of the history of Kashmir, and has shown how uncertain some of the dates are; also how the coins in many cases give different results to the historical tables. It is possible, as he seems to think, that Firishta is a better authority than Abul Fazl; but as this note makes no pretension to investigate discrepancies, or to give a history of the Musulmán kings of Kashmir, I have only compiled a rough table, from Mr. Rodgers' translation, of those kings whose names a little more than cover the period which Mirza Haidar briefly touches on. Where the sign ? precedes a date, it means that I have merely taken an average figure among those Mr. Rodgers has found authority for, or one that appears to be preferable to the others:—

			A.H.		A.D.
1.	Shah Mir, or Shams-ud-Din . . .	began to reign	? 743	=	1342
2.	Jamshid	,, ,,	746	=	1345
3.	Ala-ud-Din	,, ,,	748	=	1347
4.	Shahāb-ud-Din	,, ,,	761	=	1360
5.	Kutub-ud-Din	,, ,,	781	=	1379
6.	Sikandar.	,, ,,	? 796	=	1394
7.	Ali Shir	,, ,,	819	=	1416
8.	Zain-ul-Abidin	,, ,,	? 827	=	1424
9.	Haidar Shah	,, ,,	? 874	=	1469
10.	Hasan Shah.	,, ,,	? 891	=	1486

After Hasan Shah there was much dissension, and those who followed him—

himself to embellishing Kashmir with buildings, and in order to humour all the nations of the world, he paid attention neither to Infidelity nor Islám. It was in his reign that Kashmir[1] became a city, which it has remained to this day.

In Kashmir one meets with all those arts and crafts which are, in most cities, uncommon, such as stone-polishing, stone-cutting, bottle-making, window-cutting [*tábdán-turásh*], gold-beating, etc. In the whole of Mávará-un-Nahr, except in Samarkand and Bokhárá, these are nowhere to be met with, while in Kashmir they are even abundant. This is all due to Sultán Zain-ul-Abidin. After him, the power of the Sultáns of Kashmir began to decline, and the Amirs became so strong that the Sultáns ruled in name only; insomuch that outward respect was no longer paid them. Those helpless Sultáns, therefore, in order to secure their own safety, had to flee the country and endure much adversity.

To Sultán Nazak, who is to-day my companion, I have shown far more respect than the former administrators of the kingdom ever showed [their contemporary Sultáns]. Since [the reign of] Zain-ul-Abidin a few of his offspring have borne the title of 'king,' but of authority they have had none.

CHAPTER CI.

ACCOUNT OF THE RELIGIOUS SECTS OF KASHMIR.

THE people were [formerly] all Hanifi, but in the reign of Fath Sháh, the father of this Sultán Nádir,[2] a man of the name of

---

Muhammad, Fath Shah, Ibrahim, Ismail, and Názuk—came to the throne and went down, time after time, until the date of Mirza Haidar's invasion of the country in 948 (= 1541). Názuk was the nominal Sultan during the Mirza's regency—*i.e.*, till 958 (= 1551). The date of the first of these Musulmán kings, Shams-ud-Din, is especially uncertain, for Mr. Rodgers appears to think that 747 is as likely a one as 743. In that case the whole of the above table would be inexact, as each date is usually based on the one that precedes it. This Shams-ud-Din, under the name of Shah Mirza, or Shah Mir, had been minister to the last Rajah of the preceding Hindu dynasty, Sinha Deva by name, and of his successors, and had served in that capacity for somewhere about thirty years, before he made himself king and married Sinha Deva's widow.

Abul Fazl's complete table of this Musulmán line of rulers will be found in vol. ii. (Colonel Jarrett's) of the *Ain-i-Akbari*, pp. 379–80. Briggs' *Firishta*, vol. iv., pp. 444 to 503, also contains their history, together with a genealogical tree. (See, for Mr. Rodgers' translation, *J. A. S. B.*, 1885, pt. i., pp. 98 *seq.*)

[1] Meaning, here, the town of Srinagar, usually called "Kashmir."

[2] By *Nádir*, the author probably means the same Sultan that he has just styled *Názak*. Mr. Rodgers shows that on the coins of Kashmir the name usually occurs as *Nádir*, though in histories it is more often met with in the form of *Názak*. (Rodgers *loc. cit.*)

Shams came from Tálish in Irák,[1] who gave himself out as a Nurbakhshi. He introduced a corrupt form of religion, giving it the name of Nurbakhshi' and practised many heresies. He wrote a book for these cowardly people called *Fikh-i-Ahwat*, which does not conform to the teachings of any of the sects, whether Sunni or Shia. [These sectaries] revile the companions of the Prophet and Áisha, as do the Shias, but contrary to the teaching of these latter, they look upon Amir Sayyid Muhammad Nur Bakhshi as the Lord of the Age and the promised Mahdi.

They do not believe in the saints and holy persons in whom the Shias believe, but regard all these as [appertaining to] Sunnis. [Shams] introduced many impious practices and infidel beliefs, and gave his heretical sect the name of 'Nurbakhshi.' I have seen many of the Nurbakhshi elders in Badakhshán and elsewhere. I discovered that outwardly they follow the precepts of the Prophet and hold with the Sunnis. One of the sons of this Amir Sayyid Muhammad Nurbakhshi showed me his tract. In it was written: "Sultáns, Amirs and fools [or the ignorant] maintain that worldly power cannot be combined with purity and piety. But this is absolutely false, for the great prophets and apostles, in spite of their missions, have exercised sovereignty, and have likewise striven diligently after those other matters [*i.e.*, purity and piety], as for example Joseph, Moses, David, Solomon and our Prophet."

Now this is opposed to the belief of the Nurbakhshi of Kashmir, and is in accordance with that of the Sunnis. That book, the *Fikh-i-Ahwat*, which is celebrated in Kashmir, I sent, complete, to the Ulamá of Hindustán, who repudiated it and wrote on the back of it a decree [*fatwá*] of remonstrance as follows: "In the name of God the Merciful. Oh! God, show unto us the truth in its reality, and the false, wherein it is void; also show us things as they are. After perusing this book and weighing its contents, it seemed clear [to us] that the author of it was of a false sect, who had gone against the Book and the Sunna, and did not belong to any denomination of the people of Truth. His pretension is that God hath commanded him to do away with all differences among the people; (Firstly) in the developments and ordinances of the Holy Law, and to make them as they were in his time, with neither increase nor diminution; and (Secondly) in the fundamental principles among all the peoples of the earth. [In this] he is certainly lying, and inclined to heresy and schism. It is the duty of such as have the power, to obliterate such a book, and a religious necessity for them to stamp out and extirpate this sect;

[1] *Tálish* appears to have been a name that was applied to the province of Gilán, though properly speaking, it was only that of a tribe which inhabited a part of Gilán. (See *Sádik Ispaháni*, p. 15.)

to prohibit persons from following it and acting according to its dogmas. If they persist in their belief and abandon not their false creed, it is necessary for the security of Musulmáns, from their evil example, to repulse them with chastisement and [even] death. If they repent and abandon the sect, they must be commanded to follow the teaching of Abu Hanifa."

At the present time in Kashmir, the Sufis have legitimatised so many heresies, that they know nothing of what is lawful or unlawful. They consider that piety and purity consist in night-watching and abstinence in food; yet they take and eat whatever they find, without ever considering what is forbidden or what is lawful. They give way to their lusts and desires in a manner not consistent with the law. They are for ever interpreting dreams, displaying miracles, and obtaining from the unseen, information regarding either the future or the past. They prostrate themselves before one another and, together with such disgraceful acts, observe the forty [days of retirement]. They blame and detest science and men of learning; consider the Holy Law second in importance to the True 'Way,' and that in consequence the people of the 'Way' have nothing to do with the Holy Law. In short, nowhere else is such a band of heretics to be found. May the Most High God defend all the people of Islám from such misfortunes and calamities as this, and turn them all into the true path of righteousness.

Thanks be to God that, at the present time, no one in Kashmir dares openly profess this faith; but all deny it, and give themselves out as good Sunnis. They are aware of my severity towards them, and know that if any one of the sect appears, he will not escape the punishment of death. I hope and trust that through the intervention of God and by my own efforts, the land will gradually be entirely delivered of this misfortune, and that all will become, as they now profess to be, Musulmáns from the bottom of their hearts. Amen! Oh Lord of the two worlds!

There was also a sect of infidels who were Sun-worshippers, called Shammási. Their creed is as follows: "The phenomenon of luminosity of the sun is due to the purity of our faith: and our being is derived from the sun's luminosity. If we defile the purity of our creed the sun would no longer have any existence, and if the sun withdraw its bounty from us, we should no longer have any being. We are dependent on it for our existence, and it on us. Without us it has no existence, without it we have none. As long as the sun is visible, our actions are visible to it, and nothing but uprightness is lawful. When night falls, it does not see us or know us." Since the sun is not aware of what passes in the night, they cannot be called to account for what they do in the night season. This sect used to be called Shammási. . . . .

When this Mir Shams appeared in Kashmir and corrupted its people, he bore the title of Shams-ud-Din [Sun of the Faith]. All titles descend from heaven, and the real one must have been Shammás-ud-Din. It has been misunderstood by the Kashmiris, or else they called him Shams-ud-Din by way of reproach. For this reason they called him Mir Shams.

CHAPTER CII.

RETURN TO THE MAIN NARRATIVE.

BEFORE entering upon the description of Kashmir, I had brought the thread of my story down to the point where, after passing the defile of Lár without difficulty, we entered the city. The army of Kashmir was dispersed, and the townspeople, forsaking their city and homes, fled towards the hills and glens, leaving their property in their dwellings. I took up my quarters in the Rájdán, which has been mentioned, and entrenched my men within its walls. During many days no trace of any one was visible. For twenty-four days we remained there, by which time the horses and cattle had quite recovered their strength. The army of Kashmir was stationed in the middle of some swamps [*lái*] at about two *farsákhs* to the south of the city, where they could be seen. Wise men were of opinion that we ought not to remain within the city, but thought that we should march out and watch for an opportunity to give them battle. For, though the enemy were far stronger than we, both in arms and numbers, we might yet defeat them by strategy. [Couplet] . . . . So, sallying forth from the city, we passed, in line, in sight of the enemy, and went and encamped at a place called Baklata [1] on the east side of Kashmir.

In a word, from that date of Jamád II. till Shabán—that is to say, from the end of autumn till the spring—we avoided the army of Kashmir, who on this account became elated, and grew so bold that, at first, every time we marched on, they halted for some days, finding some strong position from which to oppose us. In the first place they would fortify the position secretly, by every means in their power, and then, advancing in the night, would take up a defensive station in the place [where they halted]. At

[1] Or *Bakláná*, or *Nakláná*, etc. It is not traceable on existing maps. By the "east side of Kashmir," the author probably means "to the eastward of Srinagar."

length they became so [confident] that they would follow after us on the same day that we made a move, without taking any precautions. Finally, in a village called Bágh Navin,[1] after they had advanced fearlessly and had hastened over some level ground, having drawn up my men, I turned and faced them. It would be tedious to enter here into details, but, to be brief, in the twinkling of an eye, the wind of victory began to blow and the enemy were scattered and discomfited . . . .[2] The chief Malik of Kashmir, Malik Ali, together with several other eminent Maliks who were generals and commanders, perished.[3] Those who escaped the sword, fled to the tops of the mountains. Many were wounded, while such as remained unhurt had their hearts broken in two from fear. That night they resolved on flight, lest on the morrow it should be impossible. Their generals were alarmed and stupefied.

By the ordering of Providence, the following noteworthy incident occurred to me: I discovered the devilry and base nature of Mirzá Ali Taghái, who for devilish designs is more famous than Satan himself. [Couplet] . . . . In short, Mirzá Ali Taghái came to me and offered his advice, saying: "If our army had fled, it would have been utterly broken. When the [enemy] reach the hills, it is clear that they will there take up a strong position, and it will not be prudent for us to advance into the hills to attack them. It is foolish to risk a disgrace. The way to destroy the enemy at this juncture, is for us to descend with all speed to the lowlands of Kashmir, and attack their families; it will then be impossible that they should remain where they are; they will perforce come down to defend their families. Those that have their households with them in the hills will not want to descend, while those whose families are on the lowlands, will make for the hill-tops. A certain number will remain where they are. Being once separated in this manner, they will find no possibility of reuniting, and no further fighting will be necessary."

I allowed myself to be deceived by these devilish promptings and lying suggestions, and decided that on the following morning we should descend with all baste. [Couplet] . . . . At dawn [next day] we started on the downward road. Mir Dáim Ali came to me and said with much severity: "What bitterness have we swallowed that matters should have come to this pass? Now that we have scattered the enemy and have driven him into these hills, you would leave him? Where are you going?" I then hesitated and halted, when Mirzá Ali Taghái, who had marched forward, came back and asked why I had stopped. Mir Dáim Ali then

[1] The variants might be *Banin*, *Baun*, etc. It does not appear on modern maps.
[2] Two lines of rhetoric and a couplet omitted.—R.
[3] This sentence is somewhat abridged.—R.

repeated to him what he had said to me. Mirzá Ali Taghái, turning towards me his double-faced countenance, said: "It is childish to alter one's decisions; I maintain my opinion still" [Couplet] .... But I, setting aside the wise counsel of the provident Mir Dáim Ali, followed the evil advice of that worthless wretch ....[1]

In short, we set out and came to the district of Nágám. Mirzá Ali Taghái went in advance. At the second stage we learnt that lower down there was no road, or if there were one, it was not suitable for the passage of an army. Chased from one place, and stopping in another, we finally halted at a spot called Jarura. The army of Kashmir, overjoyed with this march of ours, began again to collect their scattered forces from all sides, and descending from the hills, stationed themselves in a strong position, round which they threw a stockade [*shákh*]. [Couplet] .... This happened on the 4th of Shabán, 939. (An ingenious person found the date in *Ruz-i-chahárum az mah-i-Shabán*). When Shabán was over and the season of Taurus had come to an end, the snows of mid-winter (that is, the season of Capricorn) were melted from the passes by the heat of the summer sun.

Mirzá Ali Taghái, continuing his intrigues, began to point out, and enlarge upon, the enormous difficulties which the conquest of Kashmir would involve. He thus turned the hearts of the whole army from a desire to conquer Kashmir. The only exception was Mir Dáim Ali, upon whom these base reasonings had no effect. All the leaders of the army of the Moghuls ...[2] who had been scattered about, and were now re-united, came to Mir Dáim Ali, and with one mind and one accord said, amid much noise and commotion: "Tell a certain person" (by which they meant me) "that we are Moghuls, and we have been continually occupied with the affairs of Moghulistán. The natural solace and joy of the Moghul *Ulus* is the desert, in which there is no cultivation [*ábádáni*]. The screeching of the owl in the wilderness is sweeter, to our ear, than the song of the nightingale in the grove. We have never made a cultivated land our home. Our companions have been the ravenous beasts of the mountains, and our associates the wild boars of the desert. Our favourite haunts and our most agreeable dwellings have been the caves in the mountain tops; our clothing the skins of dogs and wild animals, our food the flesh of birds and wild beasts. How can men of our race associate with this besotted band of infidels of Kashmir, which is the garden of Aram—nay more, a specimen of Paradise? It has been said: The idolaters shall not enter Paradise. Moreover, from Kashmir to Káshghar is a long

[1] A quatrain and a play on words are omitted here.—R.

[2] The passage left out here is, *balka jamhur-i-zaráil-i-chaghulán*. I can make nothing of it.—R.

journey, and not only is the distance great, but the difficulties of the road are well nigh insurmountable. There are [to be considered] our families, our baggage, and our flocks and herds. Without flocks we must despair of our lives: separated from our herds we shall have to give up existence, and resign ourselves to death. Therefore, it is better that having ruined the army of Kashmir, we should return to the Khán. If the Khán kills us, our bodies will at least be buried by our own people. If he does not kill us, we will certainly never again draw our bridles towards any other place than Moghulistán." [Couplet] . . . .

Mir Dáim Ali came to me and reported what had been said. I was astounded at the men's behaviour. [Verse] . . . It is related that a certain sweeper [*kannás*] was passing a perfumer's shop, and when the scent got into his head, he fainted away. A doctor, who happened to be present, cried: "Apply some filth to his nose;" and the man immediately came to his senses. [Two couplets] . . . . . Finally, I said to Mir Dáim Ali: "[If I make an attempt to complete the conquest of Kashmir], these cowardly men will be eager to do something to shatter the foundations of sovereignty." Mir Dáim Ali replied: "On our departure, the Khán told us that Mirzá Ali Taghái, in all affairs of the State, considered in the first place, his own advantage, and generally neglected the rest. By this rule he abides, so that in considering his own personal gain, he entirely ignores the necessities of the State . . . . .[1]

"Let us put the Khán's proposal into practice, so that henceforth no one will dare to show signs of insolence or insubordination; perfect concord will ensue, and thus the kingdom of Kashmir, which has never yet been subdued by a Moghul Khákán, will fall into your hands. You will earn a great name for all time, and the gratitude of the race of Moghul Kháns. For this country has never been conquered by any one [of them]."

To this I replied: "It is now ten years since the affairs of the Khán's army have been placed under my direction, and suitable Amirs have always been associated with me. I thank God that hitherto all has gone well with me, and that nothing has ever occurred to cause the finger of reproach or blame to be pointed at me. If this [execution] should take place, all the blame will be laid at my door, and all these Amirs, whose minds are full of devilish promptings, will be convinced that he [Mirzá Ali Taghái] was sent with the army in order that I might carry out the orders of the king of death. He would doubtless make every effort to save his

[1] In this place there follows a passage of which I have been able to make but little sense. The substance seems to be that the Khán had frequently overlooked the misdeeds of Mirzá Ali Taghái; but desired that if he were found to be laying plots, such as winning over Sultán Iskandar to his side, there should be no delay in putting him to death. This is the end of what the Khán told Dáim Ali, who continues to Mirza Haidar as follows in the text.—R.

own life, and every one will imagine that in accompanying me, his own life is in danger. Moreover, it would not be acting like a good Musulmán."

After much reflection, I saw that there were only two courses open to me to pursue. On the one hand, to kill Mirzá Ali Taghái and subdue Kashmir; on the other, to spare him and retire from the country. I finally decided upon the latter course, and sent messages of truce to the Maliks of Kashmir. Thus did I disregard the dictates of wisdom, and my action has caused me much suffering. I have seen what I have seen. As has been said: 'He that hath his enemy before him, if he do not kill him, he is his own enemy.' [Couplet] . . .

CHAPTER CIII.

RETREAT FROM KASHMIR AND SUBSEQUENT EVENTS.

THE government of Kashmir was, at that time, conducted in the name of Muhammad Sháh. Among the Maliks of Kashmir, after Ali Mir, who was killed [in an engagement with us], there were Abdál Makri, Kájichak, Láhur Makri and Yakchak. When terms of peace were proposed, they were very thankful, but they did not credit [our good faith], wondering how people who had once conquered such a beautiful country, could be so senseless as to give it up.

In a word the *Khutba* was read and coins were struck in the exalted name of the Khán. The revenue of Kashmir, which was due to the Moghuls, we took. One of Muhammad Sháh's daughters was wedded to Iskandar Sultán. And everyone, according to his rank, formed a connection [*mulákát*] with one of the Sultáns or Maliks of Kashmir. I, for example, became connected with Muhammad Sháh, and in accordance with the Moghul practice we called each other "friend." Similar [relations] were established between Mir Dáim Ali and Abdul Makri; Mirzá Ali Taghái and Láhur Makri; Bábá Sárik Mirzá and Kájichak; my uncle's son Mahmud Mirzá (who will be mentioned below) and Yakchak. Numerous presents and offerings were interchanged.[1]

[1] It may be worth while to transcribe in this place Firishta's account of Mirza Haidar's campaign in Kashmir, as translated by Mr. C. J. Rodgers. "In 939," he says, "the Sultan of Kashghar, Said Shah, sent his son, Sikandar Khan, together with Mirza Haidar and 12,000 soldiers, by the way of Tibet and Lar, to invade Kashmir. The inhabitants, fearing the hardy valour of the Central Asians, fled from their homes in all directions, and took refuge in the mountains.

At the end of Shawál we set out again by way of Lár, as we had come. On reaching the frontiers of Tibet many of the inhabitants hastened out to receive us, bringing presents and flocks. But Karsa,[1] which is a district of Tibet, contains a valley, which is as narrow as a miser's heart, and in it is a very deep ravine, forming a lofty rampart wall, which seemed beyond the realms of possibility to pass. So narrow indeed was the road, that on the brightest day the darkness of night prevailed there. Trusting to this valley, which they considered no human being could take, they were refractory and refused to pay the tribute [demanded of them]. We encamped there at the noontide prayer-hour. During the night all were engaged in making preparations for an assault. At dawn next day[2] all the warriors raised a shout, and made ready to fight. In short, fierce fighting ensued. More than once the Musulmán forces were driven back by blows, or by rocks which were rolled [down the sides of the ravine], but each time they again made fast the skirt of valour in the girdle of endeavour, and kept a firm footing on the hill-side of holy war! Finally the infidels were routed and most of them perished;[3] those who escaped the edge of the sword fled like chaff before the wind. All their women, children and families fell a portion to the victorious army. The rest of the infidels were filled with the utmost alarm.

To save their own lives and those of their children, they came and delivered up whatever they possessed. All the property of the province of Purik, which is one of the most important in Tibet, was collected together and distributed among the Amirs and soldiers of our army. Having selected a few curiosities and rarities for the Khán, we set out for Máryul.

The invaders, finding everything open before them, destroyed the palaces of the olden kings and levelled them with the dust. The city was burnt. The treasury and the buried treasures were plundered, and the whole army of invaders was laden with goods and gold. Wherever the Kashmiris were found hidden, they were pursued and slain or imprisoned. This state of things lasted six months." A great battle then took place, and is described in detail; but Firishta does not assign the victory to either side. He continues: "In the evening the prisoners were numbered on both sides and were liberated, and both armies were ready to accept peace, the Kashghar party taking with them presents of wool, hawks, and precious things, went to Muhammad Shah (the king then reigning) and asked his daughter in marriage to Sikandar Khan, and desired that the women whom the Moghuls had in their hands should there remain. Peace being thus concluded the Central Asians returned to their homes, and peace once more reigned in Kashmir." (*J. A. S. B.*, 1885, pt. i., p. 115.) Mr. Rodgers does not indicate what the term is which he translates "Central Asian."

[1] Probably *Kártse* is intended by *Kársa*. It is a district and village between Kargil and Suru. But it is also possible that *Kálsa*, or *Kálsi*, may be meant—a village on the Indus, on the main road to Ladak, and near the foot of an extraordinarily deep and narrow gorge.

[2] and [3] These two passages are slightly abridged.—R.

CHAPTER CIV.

RETURN OF THE KHÁN FROM MÁRYUL TO HIS CAPITAL, YÁRKAND; AND THE AUTHOR'S MISSION TO URSANG.

On my return from the war, I was most affectionately welcomed by the Khán, who embraced me and showed his abundant regard for me in every way.[1] After these demonstrations, the Khán questioned me concerning the particulars of the campaign. I told him what I have herein written down. When I arrived at the end of my recital, the Khán said: "Hitherto no one of the conquering Khákáns, from the time of Chingiz Khán to the present day, has laid the hand of dominion upon the collar of Kashmir. But now, by your laudable and strenuous efforts, the pulpits of Kashmir have been decorated with the titles of the Moghul Khákáns. The Sultáns of Kashmir, who in former times owed allegiance to none, and the governors who were dependent on them alone, are now subject to the Moghul Kháns. For this mighty achievement, not only I, but all the Moghul Khákáns owe you a debt of gratitude, as do also my nobles, and especially my own children, for whom such a glorious name has been won."

By order of the Khán, I left the army and entered his [personal] service. On the next day, the rest of the Amirs and Iskandar Sultán had the honour of waiting on the Khán. I laid before the Khán, as offerings, some valuables from Kashmir and some coins both silver and gold, which had been struck in his name, together with other treasures which I had brought back from the various countries. All of these he graciously deigned to accept, and, according to the custom, distributed them [among his men].

These formalities being terminated, he summoned a council of all the great Amirs and nobles. Each one spoke as his feelings prompted him. Having listened to these speeches, the Khán pondered for a while and then said to me: "You well know that it has always been my ardent desire and earnest intention to conduct the holy wars in person. I am resolved on the destruction of the idol-temple of Ursang, which is the point of adoration of the whole of Khitái. Now, this has never been achieved by any Musulmán king; not one of them, indeed, has ever been near the place. My health will not withstand such an undertaking.[2] I

[1] The chapter opens with a few lines of rhetoric and verse, concerning separation and union, which are omitted, while this sentence is much abridged.—R.

[2] In the Turki version this sentence stands: It is a pity that, having made such a resolution, my health should have failed me.—R.

have come to the end of my strength, and since I have this feeling of weakness, which is apparent from my exterior, I desire you to commend me to the protection of God, and full of earnestness and religious fervour, to hasten to destroy that temple. I will meanwhile return to my loved home, leaving the whole of the administration in your hands. Let me and your uncle, who have both grown old, retire to the corner of devotion, which is a haven of repose, while you take upon yourself the affairs of the State. We will help you with our prayers for your welfare; you will benefit us by your good actions."

After this lengthy speech, he issued a mandate of the following purport, viz.: "Mirzá Haidar had been elected. He may take with him whomsoever he chooses. Those who accompany him are subject to his commands and not to mine."[1] When this mandate had been promulgated, I gave the great Amirs leave to return home. I then chose to accompany me, my brother Abdullah Mirzá and my uncle's son Mahmud Mirzá. I set in command of the army Janaka Mirzá and Bahrika Mirzá, who were both mentioned in the lists [muster roll] at Káshghar. From the rest of the soldiers I selected 2000 men. I then turned my attention to this matter [the invasion of Ursang], and before the [preparations] were completed, six days of Zulhijja were past. This was the extent of my attendance [on the Khán].

On the day of leave-taking, the Khán sent for me privately, and bestowed on me, as gifts, all the royal clothing he had at hand, besides some horses. In addition he gave me a belt and a sheath containing several knives, both of which he had devised himself. He gave these to me with his own hands, saying: "These I have acquired myself, I entrust them to you as a keepsake. If you return in safety, and find me still among the living, you can return them to me. They are a deposit. But if anything should occur which should separate us for ever, you can keep them as a remembrance of me." I thanked him greatly for his kindness; but the reins of self-control fell from my hands, and my extreme grief and sorrow caused the humidity, which lay in the recesses of my heart, to pour forth by way of my eyes: I was much affected. The Khán, in his kindness of heart, began to comfort me, and after he had in a measure succeeded in quieting my mind, I said to him: "What heart would be strong enough to be consoled after hearing such words as yours? Allow me to accompany you as far as your capital, Yárkand. When I have seen you seated on your happy throne, I will then return to my own duties; in the meanwhile the rest of the army can pasture their cattle in one of the grazing grounds of Tibet."

[1] This sentence is somewhat obscure in the text, and I have not been literal.—R.

But the Khán replied: "It is not wise to despise difficult undertakings. You have misunderstood what I said to you. [My meaning was that there is no living person who does not doubt whether he will remain in the world, or whether he will not taste of the wine of death]; nor is this dependent on an illness. I am not exempt from the hand of fate. Even though I reach Yárkand in safety, I am not secure from death. Since our separation is likely to be of long duration, and since no man can hear what is said, I have taken this opportunity of speaking to you. What I have said to you I have said, and I do not think that your accompanying me and then returning, is compatible with what I have arranged.[1] In every circumstance one must look to God. Everything must be entrusted to Him. I consign you to God, and I hope that we may meet again in Yárkand. Be strong of heart and energetic! The great name you have won by the conquest of Kashmir will be magnified by this expedition." Having uttered these words he allowed me to depart, and himself set out on the return journey.

CHAPTER CV.

THE DEATH OF THE KHÁN AND AN EPITOME OF HIS LIFE.

* * * * * *[2]

In short the Khán, having finally arranged the above-mentioned affairs, set out from Máryul in Tibet, for Yárkand. I attended him on his first stage, and then, with evil forebodings, took a touching and melancholy leave of him. [Two couplets]. . . . Four days later I received a letter in the Khán's own handwriting, stating that he had crossed the pass of Sákri,[3] and that the feelings of weakness which he apprehended, had not come over him. He had reached Nubra in safety and was camped there, intending to proceed towards Yárkand after the festival of the Sacrifice.

[1] In these passages, the Persian texts being very corrupt, I have partially followed the Turki.—R.

[2] This chapter opens with half a folio of verse and rhetoric on the mortality of man, the whole of which is passed over.

[3] By the *Sákri*, probably the Kardung pass is indicated. It leads across the range immediately north of the town of Leh, and is about 17,800 feet in height. If not the Kardung, the pass within a few miles east of it, called the Digar, and of about the same height, may be meant. The local names for these passes vary considerably among the people of the country; but as these are the only practicable ones that lead into Nubra in about three marches, the Khan must have followed one or the other, if news of his arrival there was received in Leh four days after his departure.

[Turkish quatrain.] The last letter sent me from the Khán's [camp] was to the following effect:—Having celebrated the Festival of the Sacrifice, they set forth on their homeward road with all speed. When they had crossed the ice passes [*muzájat*][1] a grave change for the worse took place in the Khán's condition, from the effects of that hell-tainted air. From that place to a region where there was no *dam-giri*, was eight days' journey. (I have already explained the symptoms of this malady, in my account of Tibet.) All the Amirs were agreed that both hurry and delay were to be feared. Still, they considered that a place where there was no *dam-giri* should be reached as quickly as possible, hoping that the Khán's natural strength would enable him to combat the violence of the malady, until such a spot should be attained. If they delayed any longer in a neighbourhood where *dam-giri* prevailed, his strength might not hold out. [Couplet] . . .

But the ill-advised nobles, foremost among whom was Mirzá Ali Taghái, mounted the Khán, in his weak condition, upon his horse, and then started with all speed, supporting him on every side. As it is dangerous [with this malady] to remain in an upright position, it would have been proper to construct a litter. But these Amirs excused themselves for not making one, on the ground that it could not be carried over the passes. [Verse]. . . . They made eight days' journey in four, and at eventide prayers they arrived within three *farsákhs* of a stage where *dam-giri* is less prevalent. There, suddenly, the Khán's strength gave way before the violence of his malady, and his nature became utterly exhausted by that hell-tainted climate.[2] Thus did the pure soul of that noble-minded and just ruler hasten to the regions of the blessed. [Three couplets]. . . . This awful and heartrending event happened on the 16th of Zulhijja in the year 939 [9 July, 1533]. After this calamity many terrible and strange things came about, of which I shall speak presently.

The life of the Khán, his noble character and worthy qualities have already been fully described in these pages: but although an account of the whole of his life is contained in this history, the context has rendered it necessary to give the facts in a somewhat disjointed and scattered manner. I will therefore add here a brief recapitulation. His genealogy is as follows: Abul Fath

[1] Meaning the 'glacier pass,' or Sasser, which consists of a series of glaciers. The elevation of the highest point is about 17,700 feet.

[2] The eighth stage on the road to Yarkand, from the east foot of the Sasser pass, is in the Suget ravine, which leads from the Suget pass down to the Karakásh river, a little above Sháhidulla. Three *farsákhs* short of the Suget halting-place would mean some spot on the pass of that name, which is, as nearly as possible, 18,000 feet in altitude. It is a locality noted for height-sickness, and no doubt it was on this pass that Sultan Said succumbed. The twelve miles which he failed to accomplish, would have carried him to a level nearly 6000 feet lower.

Sultán Said Khán Gházi, was son of Sultán Ahmad Khán, son of Yunus Khán, son of Shir Ali Khán,[1] son of Muhammad Khán, son of Khizir Khwája Khán, son of Tughluk Timur Khán. The descent of Tughluk Timur Khán from Japhet, the son of Noah, is traced in both the *Mujma ut Tavárikh* and in the Prolegomena to the *Zafar-Náma*, and God willing, the details shall be given in the first part [of this history]; I will therefore avoid repeating it [in this place].

He was born in Moghulistán in the year 892 [1487]. He received his name from his distinguished grandfather, Yunus Khán. Up to the age of fourteen he remained in Moghulistán, under the care and guidance of his father. But when Sultán Ahmad Khán went to Táshkand to meet his brother Sultán Mahmud Khán, he took the [young] Khán with him. On the occasion when the battle took place between Sháhi Beg Khán and the two brothers, at Akhsi, in which the Kháns were defeated, the [young] Khán being wounded, fell into the hands of Shaikh Báyazid, who was Governor of Akhsi. As was shown above, there was but an insincere alliance between Shaikh Báyazid and Sháhi Beg Khán. [Shaikh Báyazid] detained the Khán in prison one year, but the following year Sháhi Beg Khán came and put Shaikh Báyazid, and his brother Tambal, to death, and conquered the province of Farghána. He next released the Khán from his confinement in Akhsi, and took him with him on the expedition which resulted in the capture of Hisár and Kunduz. On his return from that expedition, [Sháhi Beg] set out to attack the Khwárizin.

The Khán, who was then sixteen years of age, having, together with seventeen other persons, escaped from Samarkand, went and joined his uncle, Sultán Mahmud Khán, in Moghulistán. Finally, fleeing after one of the contests in Moghulistán, he repaired to Andiján, where the governor, who was subject to Sháhi Beg Khán, threw him into prison, with the intention of putting him to death; but escaping thence, he took refuge with his cousin, Bábar Pádisháh, in Kábul. When the Emperor marched again upon Hisár, with the purpose of subduing Mávará-un-Nahr, he sent the Khán to Andiján. On reaching this place, it was given up to him by my uncle, who entered his service. When the Uzbeg a second time became masters of Mávará-un-Nahr, the Khán abandoned Andiján and went to Káshghar, which he took by force of arms, and there he reigned absolute during twenty years. At the end [of his reign] he undertook a holy war against Tibet, where, in the year 939, he died of *dam-giri* at the age of forty-seven.

He was a Hanifi by descent. In his youth he was addicted to forbidden pleasures, and little inclined towards laudable and

[1] The author has omitted Vais Khan, who was father of Yunus: see pp. 73 and 120.

becoming pursuits. On attaining the age of thirty-seven, he renounced all unlawful enjoyments and betook himself to a religious life, under the guidance of Hazrat Makhdumi Khwája Shaháb-ul-Millat wa ud-Din, better known as Khwája Khávand Mahmud. He devoted all his attention and thought to this noble course, fasting by day and watching by night.[1] In all his private gatherings little else was discussed but religious matters, and by these conferences he was much influenced. Justice had a strong hold over his mind, and in all his affairs he conformed with the Holy Law, never tiring of its observances, but rather delighting in them. He referred most questions to the spiritual courts [*dár ush-shar*] for settlement.

He had the greatest reverence for the Ulama. For this he was much blamed by the Sultáns of the day; but he answered them saying: "It is fitting to honour and exalt those of my own rank: these people, considering their station in life, cannot claim equality with the humblest of my servants, but I reverence them on account of their knowledge. Whether they are great or whether they are humble [in station, makes no difference], I regard only their learning. No reproach can be levelled at me for this. Those who honour the man for his learning, and not the learning [for its own sake] commit an act of folly."[2] He treated Sufis and pious men as brothers, and they never overstepped the bounds of propriety with him [though there was no ceremony between him and them]. Thoughts of sovereignty and royal dignity never entered his head. He was equally polite to all; and although he upheld the dignity of the royal state, he observed an attitude of affability beyond all conception.

I was twenty-four years in his service, and do not remember ever having heard him use abusive or obscene language to an inferior. If any of the slaves in his attendance committed an offence worthy of punishment or reproof, he would frown, but keep his temper and say very little. If he did speak and wished to use abusive language, he never went beyond calling any one "unclean" or "carrion," and if he spoke in Turki he said much the same.

[1] That is, observing the hours for night prayers.—R.

[2] This passage is not an exact rendering. In order to make sense, the translation has, of necessity, been somewhat freely dealt with.

CHAPTER CVI.

EVENTS IN KÁSHGHAR AFTER THE KHÁN'S DEATH.

* * * * *[1]

In short, after the Khán had resigned his life into the hands of the angel of death, Mirzá Ali Tagháí (that Shaikh of Satans) and Khwája Sháh Muhammad Diván (mother of Satans, in whose eyes for years past, the ophthalmia of envy had filled the place of light) having conspired together, sent Yádgár Muhammad, son-in-law of Mirzá Ali, to Rashid Sultán in Aksu, with a letter issued in the Khán's name and made up of impertinences and falsehoods. They declared it to be the Khán's last testament, and that he, before dying, had said: "I did not wish to make the holy war in Tibet. It was Sayyid Muhammad Mirzá and Mirzá Haidar who forced me to take the step. I shall never be satisfied with my son Abdur Rashid, if he does not put these men to death. Their death will be in retaliation for mine. Moreover, as long as they exist, the sovereignty will not be his." Having devised such infamous lies as these—the outcome of that devilry which for so many years had held possession of their brains—they sent [the letter] off. At the same time, they sent another messenger to my uncle, relating the manner of the Khán's death, asking what was to be done, and adding that any instructions should be carried out in full. These lies were confirmed by the most solemn oaths.

When this message reached my uncle, he was filled with emotion and alarm. He performed the proper ceremonies of mourning, and set out from Káshghar for Yarkand. As it was the season of Asad and the heat was excessive, the Khán's remains were brought in and buried, as quickly as possible, in a chamber of the palace [*Diván-khána*]. In the meanwhile, my uncle arrived from Káshghar. Having paid a visit of condolence to the ladies of [the late Khán's] haram, he performed similar duties with respect to the rest of the household. All the Amirs who were on the spot, came and begged my uncle for a compact or treaty. First of all, in the presence of this body of grandees, Ulama and Amirs, he promised that their interests should be attended to even better than they had been in the lifetime of the late Khán. They, on their part, professed their allegiance to him by means of the strongest and most solemn oaths. "We too," [they said] "will, even more than in times past, show our loyalty and singleness of purpose." In

[1] This chapter opens with about ten lines, chiefly of verse, regretting the severity of the Fates in cutting off the Khán's life.—R.

particular, Mirzá Ali Tagháí was profuse in his protestations of devotion and sincerity.

Having satisfied their minds on these points, they turned their attention to the raising up of Abdur Rashid Sultán as the new Khán, and plans were suggested for his installation. These having been settled in the most satisfactory manner, they only awaited the arrival of Rashid Sultán. It was the last day of Zul-hijja when news of his arrival was received. My uncle sent forward the grandees to meet him, and made every preparation for a royal and dignified reception. "But," he said, "it is not proper that he should make his entry on the last day of the month and of the year, and on a Wednesday. To-night he had better remain in the suburbs, and to-morrow, Thursday, the first of Moharram, and the beginning of the year 940, he should enter the town." This plan was decided upon and the Amirs went forward.

But Mirzá Ali Tagháí went privately, and said to [Rashid Sultán]:—"As the Khán's honour is in my keeping, I feel it my duty to tell him of a scheme now being laid, which was proposed to myself and the Amirs by Sayyid Muhammad Mirzá. I would lay it before you now, in order that timely measures may be taken to check it. The promise he exacted from us was, that as soon as Rashid Sultán arrived, we should lay him by his father's side, and that we should set upon the throne of the Khánate, Iskandar Sultán, who is in Tibet.." Such lies as these he not only invented, but impressed in such a way [on Rashid Sultán] that [the latter] saw no good reason for doubting him. On the morning of Thursday, the first of Moharram 940, Rashid Sultán set out towards his father's tomb. My uncle, clothed in mourning, [two couplets] . . . was seated by the [late] Khán's grave. As Rashid Sultán rode up to the door of the house, my uncle came forward, his vest rent open, his beard torn, his black turban thrown upon the ground, and on his shoulders black felt [two couplets], . . . uttering moans and laments. Rashid Sultán [immediately] ordered his men to seize him, which they did from either side, and let fall upon his Musulmán neck, a non-Musulmán sword—severing his head from his body. Ali Sayyid, likewise, who has been mentioned in several places, attained the degree of martyr.

Having murdered these two unfortunates, he dismounted and advanced to the head of his father's tomb. Thence, he went and paid a visit of condolence to the ladies of the haram. Meanwhile, he sent Mirzá Ali Tagháí to Káshghar to put to death my uncle's children, Husain Mansur, son of Sayyid Muhammad Mirzá, and Sultán Muhammad Mirzá, son of Mirzá Abá Bakr, and also the son of Sayyid Mahmud; none of these three had attained the age of twenty. He spared no act of insult or violence [towards those who were left alive—namely, the wives and families of my uncle]. Thus were my uncle's faithful and devoted services to Rashid Sultán, rewarded with murder and violence, and those solemn oaths and binding compacts which they had mutually sworn to, consumed like blood-money.[1] [Couplet]. . . It is a practice among [some] nations to do honour to their dead, by sacrificing the choicest of their flocks and the best of their cattle. Rashid Sultán, on his father's demise, put to death my uncle, his children and Ali Sayyid: that is to say, he sacrificed them. [Two couplets]. . .

After he had killed my uncle, and had ill-treated [his family], he went on to offer such insults and indignities to the haram of his noble father, as modesty prevents me from describing. Mauláná Sharaf-ud-Din Ali Yazdi, in the *Zafar-Náma*, describes the misdeeds of Sultán Khalil Mirzá, one of the grandsons of Amir Timur, who succeeded his grandfather on the throne of Samarkand. This passage I have copied exactly into this place. Certainly, with the exception of Sultán Khalil Mirzá, no one but Rashid Sultán has practised such tyranny and wrong. These matters being somewhat delicate to relate, I have copied out the passage in order to give some idea of this lamentable affair. The evident intention of Sharaf-ud-Din Ali Yazdi, in mentioning these hideous deeds, was that his readers and men of note might be warned to avoid criminal acts, and practise works of righteousness.[2]

Rashid Sultán did not stop here, but also subjected to every kind of harsh treatment and insult, his aunts, who were members of my haram, and the mother of the children of Sháh Muhammad Sultán, who have been mentioned above on various occasions, and will be spoken of again in their proper place. The mother of the children of Sháh Muhammad Sultán is Khadija Sultán, a full sister to the late Khán. Though she was suffering from hectic fever and dropsy, and confined to her bed, he banished her and her children into Badakhshán, but ere she could arrive, she died on the road, after undergoing a thousand trials and hardships. Her children, Ismail Sultán, Ishák Sultán, Yakub Sultán, and Muhtarima Khánim—some in infancy, some still at the breast, desolate and friendless exiles—were sent to Kábul, where they were received with fatherly kindness by Timur Sultán, who has been mentioned as being in Hind, in the service of Kámrán Mirzá. He undertook the entire charge of his sister's sons.

Ismail Sultán perished in the wars in Hindustán. Yakub Sultán died a natural death. Muhtarima Khánim was, by my agency, married to Kámrán Mirza, as will be related; Ishák Sultán, also through my influence, is still with Kámrán.

[1] This is nearly a literal translation of the sentence *Chun Khunbahá-i-ishán áshámid*, which, however, has no meaning in English.—R.

[2] Here is omitted a short extract from the *Zafar-Náma* consisting of about a dozen lines of mere rhetoric and some verses.—R.

CHAPTER CVII.

ACCOUNT OF MUHAMMADI BARLÁS WHO WAS[1] AMIR-UL-UMARÁ TO RASHID KHÁN—OR RATHER HIS REASONING SOUL.

He was son of Ali Mirák, son of Darvish Husain Barlás. During the Khán's sojourn in the province of Farghána, on the occasion of the release of Rashid Sultán from the captivity of the Uzbeg, and when he rejoined his father, the latter appointed Ghuri Barlás, Muhammadi's uncle, to be [Rashid's] Atá Beg. But about the same time, Ghuri Barlás died a natural death. The office of Atá Beg was then, quite properly, conferred upon Ali Mirák Barlás. A few years after the reduction of Káshghar, Ali Mirák Barlás went on a holy war to Tibet, and the office of Atá Beg to Rashid Sultán, descended by inheritance, to Muhammadi. Soon after this, Rashid Sultán was brought into Moghulistán. The Amirship over all, was given to Mirzá Ali Taghái, while the affairs of the Kirghiz were placed under the control of Muhammad Kirghiz. Muhammadi was likewise in the service of Rashid Sultán, as has been explained.

Ali Mirák Barlás was my uncle's maternal uncle, by reason of which connection, my uncle and I used every effort to further his interests. But Mirzá Ali Taghái was not friendly towards him. Without showing it, he was afraid that my uncle's intentions were evil and his devotion insincere. On [Muhammadi's] account, Mirzá Ali Taghái's dislike for my uncle increased, while Muhammadi, on every occasion, sought to defend my uncle. At length, Sháh Muhammad Sultán was killed by [Muhammadi]. It has been mentioned above, how the Khánims and the heirs of the dead man, were bent on retaliating by the death of Muhammadi, and how my uncle and I rescued him from that calamity. This produced bitterness against me on the part of my maternal aunts, their children and my other relations. All this [hostility] was encountered for the sake of Muhammadi.

The atrocities which took place after the death of the Khán, the murders, the violence, all [seemed to be the working of Mirzá Ali Taghái]. Though Mirzá Ali Taghái used all his influence, yet without the sanction of [Muhammadi], Rashid Sultán would never have committed such scandalous acts. In fact [Muhammadi's] influence for evil was greater [than Mirzá Ali Taghái's], and his control over Rashid Sultán's mind was so great, that the latter

[1] A word occurs here signifying apparently some other office, but it is illegible in the text.—R.

did whatever he told him, however "infidel" the action might be. All these lying tales and unrighteous deeds were for the sake of [Muhammadi]. The ladies of the Khán's haram—Rashid Sultán's [step-] mothers—were pressed to marry Muhammadi, and those who did not yield, he went so far, in his resentment, as to plunder and expel. But he did not see fit that the mates of the *humá* should become the co-mates of the crows.

His own sister Badi-ul-Jamál Khánim had been engaged to Báush Sultán, son of Adik Sultán, the Uzbeg Kazák. When he [Rashid Sultán], in alliance with the Uzbeg Shaibán, routed the Uzbeg Kazák, Báush Sultán, because of his position as son-in-law, and relying on this [for safety], came forward to meet Rashid Sultán, who threatened to put him to death if he did not at once divorce Badi-ul-Jamál Khánim. Having taken her from this chief, who was worthy of the alliance, he gave her to Muhammadi, whose ancestors had never attained to a dignity nearly so great. This act was a complete breach of propriety: for a peasant was treated as of equal rank with a prince. But Rashid Sultán disregarded everything, and brought disgrace upon his own house. He could not distinguish a man endowed with reason, from a brute beast. Still the most infamous thing of all, was taking her from a worthy man and giving her to an unworthy one. Such a deed is quite unheard of.

[Muhammadi's] influence over Rashid Sultán was without limit, but the reason for it was never apparent. It did not lie in the merit of past services, nor in his intelligence and sagacity as an Amir; nor yet in eloquence in council, nor in affable manners or good breeding, nor in vivacious humour at feasts, nor in courage in battle, nor in grace or charm of bearing. [Verses] . . . All that he said and did, was tainted with falsehood and evil. In short, all the unworthy deeds of Rashid Sultán are to be traced to him. We have nothing further to blame Rashid Sultán for, than that he allowed himself, on every occasion, to be guided by Muhammadi. There has lately come a report that Muhammadi has bidden this life farewell. If it is true, it is not unlikely that Rashid Sultán will grasp the reins of rectitude, and renouncing his evil ways, will repent him fully. Amen. Oh Lord of the two worlds!

CHAPTER CVIII.

MARCH OF THE AUTHOR TOWARDS URSANG. THE SLAYING OF HIS BROTHER ABDULLAH MIRZÁ. DETAILS OF THE EXPEDITION.

When the Khán set out for Yarkand, I took leave of him, and in the first ten days[1] of Zulhijja of the year 939, after keeping the feast of the Sacrifice in Máryul, I set out to destroy the idol-temple of Ursang. After marching for twenty days in that part of Tibet, we found no signs of infidels, except a few fortresses. These were so strongly situated and fortified, that they could only have been taken with great difficulty, and the gain was not worth the pain. Leaving behind Iskandar Sultán, my brother Abdullah Mirzá and my cousin Mahmud Mirza, together with the heavy baggage and the tired beasts of burden, I took the strongest and freshest of the horses with me, and started in all haste.

On the first of Safar we reached a place called Bármáng. Here we found some of the Chámpa people of Tibet, whom we plundered; nearly 300,000 sheep fell to the lot of our victorious army, besides prisoners, horses and goods, in proportion. For the completion of our desires, and the satisfaction of our necessities, we halted in a suitable pasture land, to rest and refresh our horses; by this means we afforded Iskandar Sultán, Abdullah Mirzá and Mahmud Mirzá, time to overtake and rejoin us. But while I had hastened forward, they had followed leisurely, and on the first of Moharram 940, they had approached one of the above-mentioned fortresses, which was called Kárdun.

The despicable men [in the fortress] being reduced to extremities, applied for aid to one of the Rai of Hindustán, who sent 3,000 Hindu *Katará-dar* infantry[2] [men armed with short swords]. [Couplet . . .]. Iskandar Sultán and my brothers advanced with 200 men, to give them battle, but they pushed

[1] This sentence should perhaps read, "on the eleventh day of . . ."—R.

[2] The Rai, or Raja, of Hindustán would appear rather to have been one of the rulers of Nipál, for the events described in this passage, took place in the near neighbourhood of the Nipál frontier. The circumstance that the men sent by the Rai, to help the Tibetans, were armed with "katara," or short swords, would also point to inhabitants of Nipál—of one tribe or another—armed with their national weapon, the kukri. The katára is, in fact, not the same as the kukri; it is an Indian weapon, of which the handle consists of two parallel bars with a cross-piece joining them; but it is short, and its name would probably be a sufficiently accurate description of the kukri, for a writer who may not have known the name of "kukri." At the date in question, the ruling dynasty in Nipál was that of the Malla, a line of reputed Rajput origin, like that of the Ghurkas, or Ghurkháli, who succeeded them, but the particular Rai or Raja who was reigning in 1533 does not appear to be known.

forward so rapidly that only a few of the 200 kept up with them. My brother, Abdullah Mirzá, was a daring youth, and had already distinguished himself in the Khán's service in Balti, where having gained the *juldu*, he was respected by all the army. Elated and animated by this distinction, and without reflection, he neglected to await the main body, but advancing with only three men, threw himself into the middle of the 3,000. He was dismounted, but at this juncture my cousin Mahmud Mirzá came up with four men. Seeing his brother [cousin ?] in this plight, he too made a daring charge, and saved his brother from imminent danger; whereupon the latter again returned to the charge, only to be a second time dismounted. At this moment five of the bravest warriors arrived on the scene, and seeing the two brothers so hard pressed, they charged the enemy; but by this time my brother, Abdullah, had been cut in pieces—so completely that each separate part of his cuirass and coat was in the possession of some infidel. [Four couplets] . . . . I repeated the verse, "Verily unto God do we return."

I halted for some days in that pasture-ground, until the beasts were rested and refreshed. I then sent back all the booty that had fallen into our hands, and having chosen out 900 men from the army, set forth with them for Ursang. From Máryul of Tibet to that place is two months' journey. After one month's journey, one comes to a spot where a lake is situated; it is forty *farsákhs* in circumference, and on its shores there is a castle, which is called Luk-u-Labuk. We halted there for the night; the next morning we found all our horses had died, except a few that were half dead—groaning and writhing [with pain]. Thus of my own twenty-seven horses, only one was, on that morning, in a sound condition, two others were dying, and the remaining twenty-four were dead. The cause [of their death] was the *dam-giri*, which has been described above.

When we left that place, [only] a fifth part of the army were mounted, all the rest proceeded on foot. On the second day we plundered the province of Ham [or Hari]. The people of that place assert that it is twenty-four days' journey into Bangála. Many captives were taken by us. Those of our army who were mounted on serviceable horses, only numbered ninety men. With these ninety, I advanced and plundered a place called Askábrak. About 100,000 sheep, 20,000 *kutás* and a proportionate number of prisoners and horses, fell into our hands. There remained eight days' journey from Askábrak to Ursang. However, the horses of our party being entirely broken down, we were obliged to turn back. Six days later, we reunited and set out on our return. This took place on the 8th of Rabi II. On the last day of Jamád II. we overtook the party that had been sent back with the booty and plunder, at a place called Támlik, which is twenty days' journey from Máryul.[1]

The Guga people came and represented to us that Guga was the chief district of Tibet; they were willing to pay any capitation

[1] Mirza Haidar's expedition into Tibet, though one of his most remarkable exploits, is related with tantalising brevity and with an absence of explicitness, as to localities and dates, that renders his record of it unsatisfactory in the extreme. It would be interesting to be able to trace his route from the borders of Ladak, to the point where he had to turn back, and give up his designs on Lassa. If indeed, this one point, the name of which he writes *Astákbark*, or *Askábrak*, could be identified, the extent of his incursion might be determined, and a clue would be obtained to the whereabouts of the other places he mentions. But I am unable to trace the name *Askábrak*, on any map or in any account of Tibet known to me. It appears from his narrative that he started from Maryul (Leh, or its immediate neighbourhood), and passed, on his line of march to *Askábrak*, four places, the first of which he names *Barmang* (or *Yarmang*, or *Bartang*, etc.—the variants would be numerous); the second *Kardun;* the third *Luk Liuk* (or *Tuk u Labuk*, or *Luk Lanuk*, etc.), on a large lake, and halfway from Leh to Lassa; the fourth *Ham* (or *Hari*), two marches farther on; and finally arrived at *Askábrak*, which he puts at eight days' journey from Lassa. Here he stayed six days, and then took eighty days to return to a place which he writes *Támlik*. This last was two days' short of *Gugeh* (the chief village of the Gugeh district may be assumed) and twenty days from *Maryul*, or Leh.

The distance from Leh to Lassa is actually reckoned at sixty ordinary marches, just as Mirza Haidar has it; and about halfway on this journey—or one month, as he also puts it—the great lakes of Mansarowar (the Tso Lanak and Tso Mapham) are passed. Thus we seem here, to have a referring point; for no other lake that he could estimate at 40 farsakhs (160 miles) in circumference, is to be found anywhere near the halfway point between Leh and Lassa.

According to the itinerary compiled by the Indian Survey Pundit in 1866, the post-station called *Barkha*, close to the north shore of the Lanak Lake, is the twentieth from Lassa, while each post-stage would, on the average, be 35½ miles in length—total, 710 miles. The ordinary marches shown by the Pundit's table, average something under 14 miles each, but these are traders' stages, intended only for loaded animals. If we take ordinary marches for travellers without caravans, at an average of about 23½ miles, the estimate for thirty days' journey would bring the distance tolthe same—or, nearly 710 miles. Mirza Haidar is speaking everywhere, apparently, of ordinary marches for mounted travellers, but he may have obtained his information of the distance between *Askábrak* and Lassa, in post-stages, or in either kind of ordinary, or road, march. If the first be reckoned, *Askábrak* should be looked for about 284 miles from Lassa; if the last, only some 102 miles. The name of the eighth post-station from Lassa, in the Pundit's list, is *Jang Lache;* the name of the eighth traders' halting-place is *Gobzi;* while the eighth stage, at about 23½ miles, would be *Pena-jong.* Of these names, not one has any resemblance to *Askábrak* or *Astákbark.*

But there is reason to believe that *Askábrak* was much more than eight marches, or indeed, than eight post-stages, distant from Lassa, and that the Mirza was not so near his goal as he imagined. The only one point that is certain, on the route from Ladak, is the great lake; even the name of the "castle," or fort, which stood near it (though it may contain the word "Lanak") cannot be located exactly. The Pundit shows a place he calls *Long-gong* near the northern shore of the Lanak, which bears a faint likeness to *Luk-Liuk*, but not sufficient to hazard an identification. However, Mirza Haidar tells us that he marched only two days from this "castle" to the province of *Ham* (or *Hari*), whence it required twenty-four days' journey to reach Bengal. After proceeding for an undefined distance towards Lassa, and on arriving at *Askábrak*, he records that from that place also, the journey to Bengal was twenty-four days. If the same distance to Bengal was reckoned from both these places, the probability is that they were not far apart. Moreover, it was at the castle near the great lake that the disastrous loss of horses occurred; it was from here that the Mirza set out with only ninety mounted men, while four times that number

tax which I might impose, in accordance with the extent and wealth of the country; I therefore proceeded to Guga, where I arrived in two marches from Támlik. I was received by the people in the most respectful, obedient, and hospitable way. After

went on foot. Thus it is scarcely likely that with his force in this condition, and with winter setting in (for it was towards the end of October), he would have pushed forward to any great distance.

Again, the dates given in the narrative are too imperfect to afford any sure basis for an estimate of distances or halts. We find scarcely more than that the expedition left Leh, on or about the 4th July, 1533; that it reached *Askábrak* on the 22nd October; started thence on its retreat 28th October; and arrived at *Támlik* on the border of *Gugeh* on the 10th January, 1534. This *Támlik* was two days from the chief place in *Gugeh* (possibly *Tsaprang* or *Dankar*), and twenty days from Maryul or Leh. Of the other places the author mentions on this expedition, *Barmang* (or *Barkang*, etc.) should probably be looked for in the districts of either *Gugeh* or *Chumurti*, in order to accord with the estimate of twenty days from Leh; while *Kardun* may be the *Kardam*, or *Kardung*, marked on the maps of Tibet at about twelve miles south of the *Lanak* lake.

The names detailed at p. 410, are, from that of *Gugeh* onwards, fully as puzzling as those on the line of march towards Lassa. Indeed, most of them appear to refer to places visited in the course of that march. For the position of the place written *Zunka* in the text, a vague clue might be obtained from the passage at p. 416, if the author can be credited with a mistake of a month in the dates. He records, there, that he was at *Zunka* in the month of Rabi I., 940. He also says (1) that he reached *Barmang* on the 1st Safar, and (2) that that place was only twenty days from Maryul, while he marched rapidly from one to the other. From the date of leaving Maryul, twenty days would bring the date to 1st Muharam, while fifty days would be needed to attain the 1st Safar. But at the same time, the author implies that he was at, or near, *Kardun* on the 1st Muharam, and halted there for some days. *Kardun* (if *Kardum*) is a good distance farther removed from Maryul than is *Barmang*, or than any point twenty days from Leh; but the author places himself at the former spot one month earlier than at the latter. Thus, in all probability, the dates in the text should read, 1st Muharam at Barmang, and 1st Safar at Kardun—that is, twenty days from Maryul to the former, and fifty days to the latter. And, if so, *Zunka* would have to lie (according to the dates) between *Kardun* (or the great lake) and *Askábrak*. This correction is the more reasonable, as the author states that he went on rapidly from Maryul to *Barmang*, and that his relations followed leisurely till the two parties met near *Kardun*. If such an amendment is admissible, the clue to Zunka would be as above.

Now, an itinerary obtained by Captain H. Strachey in 1846, gives a place called *Samku* as the fourteenth post-stage from Lassa, which would locate it at *Sarka* of the Pundit's and other maps, and in this position *Zunka* (if *Samku*) might fall within Mirza Haidar's location for the month of Rabi I. In this case *Ham* (or *Hari*) and *Askábrak* could not, with regard to dates, have been far off, and it is just possible that if *Hari* be the right reading, that place may be represented by the *Ari dsong* shown on D'Anville's map, as standing near an unnamed lake to the south of the great river, but intended obviously for the lake *Palgu*, or *Palu*, of later maps. Yet, strangely enough, the position of D'Anville's *Ari-dsong* is occupied, on more modern maps, by a spot called *Jongku*—a word bearing a curious resemblance to *Zun-ka*. However, the *Samku* of Strachey's itinerary is not far off, and is the preferable of the two names, as a possible identification of *Zunka*. If not a corruption of the same word, *Samku* may be another name for *Sarka*. Captain Strachey gives no particulars of the place, but the Pundit describes it as "a large village containing numerous houses," while Mirza Haidar says it was the most famous place in Tibet. The result, in any case, is that Mirza Haidar's farthest point towards Lassa could not (on these assumptions) have been beyond the Palgu, or Palu lake, situated about the 86th degree of E. long., or some 350 miles, at least, from Lassa.

Still, all this is based on more or less of speculation, for very little can be certainly established. The Tibetan names are, in all probability fairly well

staying there three days, and fixing the levy at 3,000 Tibetan *mithkáls* (one of which is equal to one and a half statute *mithkál*) I returned, and on the road heard of the dispersion [*virán*] of my army, which I will speak of immediately.

represented in Mirza Haidar's Persian, since in the list of places at p. 410, those that are known in Ladak and Baltistan, are transliterated with remarkable accuracy, and it is only when we come to localities which are (almost certainly) in the imperfectly known regions of Tibet proper, that difficulties occur. The explanation probably is, that we know too little of this region to be aware of the names of places ordinarily in use. Most of those on our maps reach us from foreign sources—the Chinese of the last century, and the Indian Survey Pundits—and are, therefore, as likely to be distorted as those in Mirza Haidar's text. The narratives of more modern travellers, moreover, do not help us. Even that of Ippolito Desideri, the Jesuit missionary of the first quarter of the last century, contains scarcely the name of a place between Ladak and Lassa, or so much as a glance at the geography of the country. Yet he travelled, it seems, over almost exactly the same route as Mirza Haidar. The same must, as we have seen, be said of the Pundit's narrative.

It may be added here, that Dr. Waddell informs me the meaning of Stak-brak is *Tiger Rock*, which would be a very likely name to occur in Tibet. In Western and Central Tibet these syllables would be pronounced *Ta Dak*, or *Ta Da*; but even in this form I cannot trace the name. (See for Strachey, *Journey . . . in Tibet*, Extr., *J. A. S. B.*, 1848: and *Physical Geography of Tibet*, *J. R. G. S.*, 1854; the Pundit in *Report of Trans. Himalayan Explorations*, 1865–7; D'Anville's map in *Duhalde*, iv., pl., p. 458; and Desideri in *MS.* belonging to Hakluyt Society.)

The likeness that Mirza Haidar's expedition bears to that of the Dogras under Zoráwar Sing, just 300 years later, is remarkable. Goláb Sing, the Dogra Rajah of Kashmir, having subdued Ladak without much difficulty, thought it also an easy matter to extend his conquests to Lassa territory. In the spring of the year 1841, a force commanded by Zoráwar Sing was pushed forward into the Tibetan province of Nari Khorsum, in three columns—one advancing by Tankse, one by the Indus valley, and the third over the Rupshu table-land. At first no resistance was offered by the Tibetans, and the Dogras made easy progress; but after passing to the south-eastward of the Mansarowar lakes, and while in a region some 15,000 feet above the level of the sea, the winter set in. The cold was intense; supplies and shelter were alike wanting, and the sepoys are recorded to have burned their arrows and gunstocks for fuel. The Tibetans, having awaited their opportunity, sent up a large force from the eastern provinces, and attacked the invaders while hard pressed by cold and hunger, or, as the Dogra chronicler puts it, "by the army of the season." The Dogras were defeated about the middle of December, in a battle which took place between Kardung and Purang.

Though Mirza Haidar's expedition ended in a somewhat less disastrous way, the similarity with that of Zoráwar Sing extends to the circumstance of the Nipalis becoming alarmed at the presence of an invading army so near their frontier. Their Government sent envoys to demand explanations of the Dogra commander, and apparently they received satisfaction, for no hostilities are recorded to have occurred with Nipal, while, after the disaster near Kardung, the fugitive sepoys were permitted to take refuge in the Ghurka Raja's territory.

(An account of this expedition will be found in the *Guláb-Náma* of Diwán Kirpa Rám of Kashmir: a Persian history of the Dogras in Kashmir, some extracts from which I translated some years ago.)

It may be added that the Government of India, believing Nari Khorsum to belong to China, decided, on hearing of the invasion, that the Dogras should evacuate the territory they had seized, in order to avoid complications with the Chinese Government, and the 10th December, 1841, was fixed for the surrender. A British officer, Captain J. Davey Cunningham, R.E., was sent to see that the decision was carried out, and Zoráwar Sing was accordingly recalled. But before the order could reach him, the disaster above related, had overtaken his force. (See J. D. Cunningham's *Hist. of the Sikhs*, pp. 256–8.)

CHAPTER CIX.

SUFFERINGS IN TIBET, AND THE DEATH OF THE AUTHOR'S COUSIN, MAHMUD MIRZÁ.

* * * * * *[1]

As soon as Rashid Sultán had made an end of murdering and insulting my uncle and others of his near relations, he sent a messenger into Tibet bearing divers mandates. One of these was for his brother Iskandar Sultán, and ran thus: "We have conferred upon you the country of Tibet. [We desire] Mirzá Haidar and Mahmud Mirzá also to remain there." Another was addressed to the whole army as follows: "The wives and families of all those who are in Tibet will be sold. Immediately upon the arrival of this, you are ordered to disperse and set out for Yárkand." When these unwelcome orders arrived, I had gone to Guga, as has been said. No sooner did the soldiers learn the purport of the message than, seizing their opportunity, they set out for Yárkand; but Iskandar Sultán and my cousin Mahmud, with a handful of men, having got away [from the rest], remained behind. Two days later, I reached the stage where the men had disbanded [*virán shuda*]. Iskandar Sultán and my cousin Mahmud pointed out that we had better remain there that night, as many of the soldiers had fled unwillingly, and were probably only watching for an occasion to rejoin us.

There yet remained with me more than a hundred men; these were all brave soldiers or commanders of battalions, whose service was hereditary, who had often distinguished themselves in battle, and had won *juldus*; each one also had been born to the title of Amir. Some of them were my [foster]-brothers, and were called [by me] *Kukildásh*; from these I had no reason to expect opposition. But on the morrow I discovered that all my trusted men had disappeared, like the stars at dawn.

After the sun had lit up the earth's dark surface, Ján Ahmad Ataka, who has been already mentioned as my foster-brother, came to me with a certain Sháh Muhammad, a *Kukildásh*, and one of the most distinguished of that band. With them they brought five followers. Thus was the fear of loneliness dispelled. After a while, Iskandar Sultán and my cousin Mahmud came back, and having collected about fifty men we proceeded towards Máryul.

[1] The chapter opens with some high-flown passages and many verses concerning bad news, misfortunes, and the like. The author then says that, for the information of the reader, he will venture to record, briefly but truly, some of the terrible events which immediately succeeded upon the death of the Khán.—R.

It was the beginning of the season of Capricorn, and the commencement of winter-time. [Couplet]. . . The cold was so intense that were I to describe it, I should be accused of word-painting. Out of those fifty men, more than forty had either hands or feet, or nose or ears, taken off by the cold [frost-bitten]. Sustaining such fatigues and sufferings as these, at the end of twenty-five days we reached Máryul. The *Chui* of Máryul, named Táshikun and Lata Jughdán, who have been mentioned in a few places already, hastened out to wait upon us. Since we had [on a former occasion] treated them with violence, both plundering and killing [their people], I was inwardly in great fear of them. But contrary to my apprehensions, they showed their willingness to assist us in every way, and even proffered excuses, saying: "For four hundred years, from father to son, we have been the subjects and you the king; we the slave, you the master; if in the days of your glory and greatness we were alarmed and trangressed, we met with our due retribution at your hands. At that time the *Chui* of Tibet submitted to and obeyed you, solely from fear. But now we offer our services, out of attachment to you, and in all sincerity." [Verses.]

They gave us the castle of Shaya, which is the capital of Máryul.[1] In Shaya we took the opportunity to recover [from our fatigues], and here, some of the army who had stayed behind, now rejoined us. Among them was Maulána Darvish Muhammad Kará Tágh, one of the attendants of Khwája Muhammad Yusuf, who has been mentioned above. This Mauláná Darvish Muhammad was a pious and devoted Musulmán. He knew the Tibetan language remarkably well, and enjoyed the entire confidence of all the *Chui* of Tibet. He was thus able to settle all our affairs with them in a satisfactory way.

From Kashmir there came a certain man named Háji, who attached himself to my service; he will be mentioned frequently hereinafter; our party now numbered more than sixty persons.

But the disbanded army, as it advanced, began to suffer from

[1] *Shaya*, ordinarily called *Sheh*, or *Shay*, but properly written *Shel* in Tibetan, is a village about eight miles south-east of Leh, on the right bank of the Indus. On a high rock above the village, stands one of the old residences of the Ladak Kings, who, at various times, have made it their headquarters. This may have been the case in Mirza Haidar's time, and for this reason, probably, he calls *Sheh* the capital of Ladak. The period when Leh became the capital is nowhere recorded that I am aware of, but the Ladak Chronicle, translated by Dr. Marx, states that the 19th King (the Táshi Namgyal mentioned in note 2, p. 418) was the builder of the old fort at Leh, the ruins of which are still to be seen on a pinnacle overlooking the town. As the Leh "palace," which stands on the same hill, but a little lower down, is not mentioned in the Chronicle, I infer that it was built somewhat later, though it is generally said to date from over three hundred years ago. It was at Sheh that Moorcroft, in 1821, found settled one Khwája Shah Niáz, whom he describes as a descendant of "a branch of the same family as the Emperor Baber." (See Marx, *J. A. S. B.*, lx., pt. iii., 1891, pp. 123-4: and Moorcroft, i., p. 241.)

the change in the season; so much so, that most of the men were unable to proceed, while those who attempted to go on, lost all their effects. Nearly one hundred and fifty men died from exposure to the cold. The rest arrived in a half-dead state at Yárkand. Another party, turning back, reached Máryul in a helpless condition. Thus a body numbering five hundred men was again assembled, together with about 10,000 sheep. [For a time] we enjoyed a complete rest.

Before reaching Máryul, I sent forward Ján Ahmad Ataka and Sháh Muhammad Kukildásh, to Rashid Sultán in Yárkand, with many gifts from the spoil we had taken in our last expedition. I also wrote him a few lines, reminding him of our ancient bonds of friendship, and sent him as proof thereof, some old tokens we had interchanged. A dark coloured Arab *pustin*, and a steel *báluka*, both of which Rashid Sultán had given me, I now sent back to him, just as they were [*ba-jins*]. [Verses] . . .

Towards the close of that winter Rashid Sultán sent Bidakan, son of my foster-brother Ján Ahmad Ataka, accompanied by Hasan Diváná, to bear to me messages of apology and expressions of repentance. His past behaviour [he admitted] had been due to his ignorance, and was a cause for shame in this world and the next. He now frankly begged the forgiveness of his dear friend. He had sent Mauláná Kudásh with two hundred men, for my service. All those of my following who had gone over to him, might now return to me; no one should hinder them. He also sent me some horses and other gifts. I was not a little encouraged by these messages, and most of Tibet submitted.

In the meanwhile Mauláná Kudásh arrived, bringing with him some of my chief retainers. Being reinforced by this band, we marched for Bálti, which touches the confines of Kashmir. All Bálti paid the appointed tax in kind, without hesitation or delay. Suru is a department of Bálti, and its chief defence and stronghold. Mauláná Kudásh asked permission from me to go and impose a levy upon Suru, but I would not consent to this, knowing that those infidels would not be willing to let any one visit their districts and valleys.[1] [Indeed the people of Suru] begged that [no one might come]. "Whatever amount is due," [they said], "that we will ourselves bring to the camp where you now are; there is no need for you to come [to us]." However, when the fowler of destiny places the grain of earthly desire in the net of fate, not even a bird of wisdom can escape from that net. [Couplet]. . . . But Kudásh, not accepting my refusal, was so

[1] It is remarkable that, even in our own times, the people of Suru have the reputation for being contumacious; they have a strong dislike to foreigners visiting their district, and throw whatever obstacles they are able, in the traveller's way. The invasion of the Dogras, in the present century, was resisted by them with much determination.

importunate in his demands that I at last sanctioned his going, and he set forth. The people of Suru put him to death in a narrow pass, together with twenty-four worthy men who were with him; they were subjected to a hundred ignominies, and were unable to strike a blow. Although our force numbered some seven hundred men, yet, on account of our poverty and want of arms, we were unable to avenge him. [Three couplets]. . . .

Leaving Bálti, we set out towards a province in Tibet called Zangskar. The crops had, as yet, attained no height; harvest time was not yet come, when we arrived. While we were waiting for the harvest, that we might divide the crops, one of the *Chui* of Bálti, named Tangi Sakáb, who had in the past rendered us useful services, came and told us that the time had come to go and attack the murderers of Kudásh, that is to say, the people of Suru. "You can go and pillage their country," [he said], "carry off their women and take vengeance on their men."

Some of those who had lost their strength, were at once despatched to Máryul, in order that the strong men among us might proceed with all speed. I sent my cousin to escort the party [going to Máryul], as one day's march of that journey was very dangerous. He was to see them [safely] through this part of the road. At night he encamped there. As the place was dangerous, he kept his horse by him all through the night. During his sleep, the horse, while grazing, kicked him so hard on the forehead as to fracture his skull [making a wound] the size of the hoof. On the next day he came to me and showed me his wound. According to the practice of Moghul surgeons, I broke the bone [again], and seizing the edge of it, applied remedies. I then sent to tell Tangi Sakáb what I had done. He sent back answer: "Since your coming would involve no little difficulty, [you had better] send me a small contingent to take Suru. We will send you a fifth part of all that falls into our hands. This also would be an acceptable service."

Between Zangskar, where I was dwelling, and Sut,[1] the home of Tangi Sakáb, is five days' journey. I sent [to Tangi Sakáb], seventy men under the command of Mauláná Darvish Muhammad Kará Tágh, who enjoyed the entire confidence of the *Chui* of Tibet, and Nur Ali Divána, one of the most promising young soldiers, and who had turned back to rejoin me. Nearly two months were passed in exchange of messages before a decision was arrived at. Mahmud Mirzá's wound had opened afresh, and it became quite impossible for him to remain in Zangskar, on account of the severity of the weather. So I was obliged to send him back to Máryul,

[1] *Sut* or *Sot* is a name not often seen on modern maps. It will be found, however, on Moorcroft's map, spelled *Soth*. It is one of the group of villages usually known as *Kargil*. It may, indeed, have been another name for Kargil.

while I remained in Zangskar, in order that, as soon as he had reached Máryul in safety, I might myself proceed to Suru, where I hoped to find some means of existence. When Mahmud reached the spot where he had received the kick from his horse, he halted for the night, and on the morrow, as he was about to mount, he exposed his head to apply the dressing. The cold got into the wound and, fainting away, he became insensible. At noontide prayers a person came and informed me of his condition. I at once set out in all haste to see him. I arrived at midnight and found him unconscious. On the following day he came to himself and entirely recovered consciousness. The next day also, he was conscious, but on the third day he began to talk incoherently, and two nights later he died.[1]

Meanwhile a messenger arrived from the party which I had despatched against Suru, saying that Nur Ali Divána, in company with his companions and Mauláná Kará Tágh, had gone to attack Bághán, who was a *Chui* of the provinces of Tibet. Mauláná Darvish Muhammad having enticed him into a place [apart], they exchanged blows, and at length Bághán, being mortally wounded, they made a present of that infidel to the Musulmáns, and taking leave, proceeded to Yárkand.[2] That infidel killed the Mauláná by transfixing him with a stick. Thus the Suru expedition came to nothing. Having conveyed Mahmud's body to Máryul, I sent it on thence to Káshghar [to be buried in the tomb] of his forefathers. These events happened in the beginning of the season of Scorpio. It was at the commencement of the cold season of Tibet, that we went to Máryul. That winter, until spring came round, we passed in such a manner that, were I to describe our sufferings, I should be suspected of exaggeration.

On the return of spring, seventy persons were sent with the horses, to a place called Utluk—a ravine [*mughára*] famous in all Tibet for the richness of its crops. I spent the interim in hunting the wild ass and the wild *kutás*, and then returned. On my departure, I had left Iskandar Sultán in Máryul with a body of men. When we had once again reassembled, the horses had grown fat and strong, but our men, unable to support the pressure of misfortune and trial, all at once dispersed and went off to Yárkand; only fifty of them stayed behind, the rest all fled. At this juncture Ján Ahmad Ataka, whom, two years previously (on my return

[1] Half a folio of verse and florid passages is omitted here. The author complains of the grief he has suffered from the loss of his uncle and other relatives. His troubles, he says, reached their climax when he was past thirty years of age and not yet forty.—R.

[2] This passage is obscure, and makes little sense. It would appear that Bághán killed the Mauláná, and was afterwards made over to the Musulmans of the district, as a slave, by the Mauláná's companions, who then went on to Yárkand.

from the Ursang expedition) I had sent to Rashid Sultán (as was mentioned), came back from Yárkand, bringing the orders that we were to stay no longer in Tibet. Hitherto my reason for lingering in Tibet had been, that if of my own choice I moved to some other place, I should be accused of breaking my engagement. He [Rashid Sultán], however, while outwardly pretending to be upright, had broken this engagement, which he had sworn to with the most solemn oaths, and now, disregarding every [honourable] consideration, ordered me to take flight. [Verses]. . . . No sooner had Ján Ahmad Ataka delivered his message, than I set out for Badakhshán.

CHAPTER CX.

THE AUTHOR CROSSES FROM TIBET TO BADAKHSHÁN.

I MENTIONED above that out of my force of 700 men, only fifty remained with me. The rest all got away to Yárkand, as best they could. It has also been already observed, that the difficulties of travelling in Tibet are due to the scarcity of provender and the terrible severity of the cold, while the roughness of the paths is almost beyond conception. We were without a proper supply of clothing and food, and more particularly of horse-shoes, which are above all things indispensable on those roads; our horses were few, and were in a broken condition. To remain in Tibet, therefore, became impossible; while to leave it was difficult. However, if to stay and to go were both attended by obstacles, there was at least hope in the latter course; to it we might look for a termination of our troubles, but we could foresee none if we determined to stay. [Verse]. . . . [The routes] to Kashmir, Káshghar, Turfán, and Hindustán were all equally impossible. The road to Badakhshán was the only one that offered any hope of safety.

No one of us had ever travelled from Tibet to Badakhshán, excepting by way of Káshghar. But among those who had deserted and fled to Yárkand, was a certain man named Jahán Sháh. He once related that he had heard from the people of the mountain districts of Yárkand, that from a place called Tágh Nák,[1]

[1] Mirza Haidar's spelling of this name is probably the right one. It appears on our latest maps as *Tokanak*, and is a spot on the Yárkand river just below Kulan-uldi, where the track to Kugiar and Yárkand leaves the valley of that river. Mirza Haidar's party (it will be seen by the map) branched of from the direct route to Yárkand at Ak-Tágh, then followed down the Yárkand river past Kulan-uldi, *Tágh-nák*, etc., first into the district known as Ráskám and eventually on to the Pamir of Taghdumbásh. The route is an exceedingly difficult one, on account of the river crossings, and is seldom or never followed by traders or travellers.

there was a bye-path leading to the Pamirs of Badakhshán. I had inquired the particulars of him. By that unknown road we now advanced. "Can one travel by a road one has never seen and knows not?" Of the fifty persons who had remained with me many, from want of strength, stayed behind in Tibet.

I moved off finally, with twenty-seven men. [We suffered much] from want of supplies for the journey—from the weakness of the beasts of burden, from the difficulties of the road and from the cold. For although it was now the season of Virgo, the cold was so severe, that at a place we came to called Kara Kuram, as the sun sank, the river (which is a large one) froze over so completely, that wherever one might break the ice, not a drop of water was forthcoming.[1] We continued our efforts [to obtain water] until bed-time prayers. The horses that had travelled all day over *dam-giri* ground, arriving at a stage where there was neither water nor grass, refused to eat the little barley that was left (and which we now gave them) because they had not drunk. Ján Ahmad Ataka said: "I remember once noticing a spring at about half a *farsákh's* distance from here." He indicated a spot in the middle of the ice, where we had to cut a hole; this time there was water, and we gave the horses to drink. There was one mare [*hajr*] among them, the strongest of all the beasts, whose teeth, from want of water, became so tightly locked together, that in spite of every exertion she could not drink, and therefore died.[2] The baggage which she had carried was thus left behind. This will give some idea of the intensity of the cold. [Verse.] . . .

When, after much hardship, we reached the spot where the untried road to Badakhshán branched off, Iskandar Sultán came to ask my permission to make his way to Rashid Sultán, saying: "Perhaps his brotherly affection will induce him to take pity on me, and cause him to heal the wounds which have hitherto cut him off from his relations." I replied: "Your brother is certainly not a man of his word, as his actions testify. Good faith is the first duty of a Musulmán; but he is so entirely under the evil influence of Muhammadi, that you need never expect mercy at his hands." [Quatrain] . . . With such words did I attempt to dissuade him, but

[1] The meaning is that the river was flowing till the sun set, and then suddenly froze over—not an uncommon circumstance, in clear weather, at great altitudes.

[2] Neither is it uncommon to find that horses refuse their ration of grain, when they have been some days without grass or chopped straw, or when suffering from height-sickness. When food is refused for these reasons, usually no great harm results to the animal, but when he declines it on account of thirst, he generally succumbs within a short time. Lockjaw is, as the author rightly implies, caused by the cold and not by the rarefied air, as is often supposed. It occurs even at low altitudes during severe cold. It may be observed here, that though the word "horse" is always used in this translation, the more correct term would be "pony;" for in none of the regions east of Afghanistan and Western Turkistan are the horses more than about 13 hands, as a rule. In some places they are seldom above 12 or 12½ hands.

he, being worn out with the sufferings of the journey and the misfortunes in Tibet, shut his eyes to the path of reason, and was so persistent in his demands, that at last I gave him leave to go, sending four men to accompany him.

My party of twenty-seven, by the loss of these five, was thus reduced to twenty-two, and with these I went forward upon this [strange] road. A few of our horses had become useless from want of shoes. On the same day that we parted from Iskandar Sultán, towards midday prayer-time, we killed a wild *kutás*. With its skin we made coverings for the feet of our disabled horses: of its flesh we carried away as much as we were able, and even then there remained what would have been sufficient for a day or two. This was a favour bestowed upon us by the Giver of daily bread. We carried away as much as our beasts could bear, which amounted to about five days' provisions for the party. I suppose about a quarter of the *kutás* was lost: that is to say about that quantity remained behind. The crows and ravens, by their screams, gave a general invitation to the beasts of prey of the neighbourhood, and they celebrated a feast in company.[1]

We proceeded in this manner, guessing [our way]. On the next day we killed another *kutás*, of a very large breed. [Couplet.] . . .

From the information I had gathered from Jahán Sháh, I reckoned that it would be another six days, before we should come to a cultivated region; but on the third day after our separation from Iskandar Sultán, at about breakfast-time, we met with some men with their families, some of whom came out to receive us with great cordiality, and asked us whence we had come and whither we were going. They told us that this valley was called Rás Kám, and that from here to [the] Pamir was five days' journey. When we arrived at this place [Rás Kám], all of us took a rest, after the trials of so many years.

The people took over all our broken horses and gave us strong ones in their stead. They also supplied us, in the most hospitable manner, with such meat and drink as they had to give. When they saw me, they all began to weep and cried, in their own language: "Thanks be [to God] that there still remains a prince of the dynasty that has ruled over us for four hundred years: we are your faithful and devoted servants." They then attached themselves, with their wives and families, to me. I was powerless to hinder them. At every place we came to, I was joined by all the men, women and children of the district. For the space

[1] It may be noticed that the wild yák, or kutás, is not found nowadays so far west as the valley of the Yarkand river. Its most westerly limits are the head-waters of the Karakásh and the Chang Chenmo valley, in the extreme east of Ladak.

of seven days they lavished every attention and honour upon us, brought us to the Pamir, and induced us to proceed to Badakhshán. (Sulaimán Sháh Mirzá, the son of Mirzá Khán, the son of my maternal aunt, has been mentioned in several places above. When I came to his [abode] he hastened out to receive me, showing me honour, by every means at his disposal.)[1] We then offered up a thousand thanks to God Almighty, who had delivered us from such great dangers, and had brought us into safety; [verse] . . . . and from a land of Infidels to one of true Believers. [Three couplets.] . . .

When we reached Wákhán, which is the frontier [*sar-hadd*] of Badakhshán, there came to me one of Rashid Sultán's followers, who was there on some business. I gave him some Turki verses, which I had composed, to deliver over to his master. . . .[2]

If I were to detail the acts of violence and unkindness of Rashid Sultán, a separate chapter would be necessary. God willing an account of his life will be given in the First Part; repetition would not be pleasing.

To be brief, at this time my wife, who was Rashid Sultán's paternal aunt, was banished [*ikhráj*] in a kindly way, with Iskandar Sultán to accompany her. Another act of kindness was that she was not robbed, or deprived of anything; all that she had at hand was sent with her. She reached Badakhshán, however, in a pitiable and destitute condition. About ten persons were allowed, by Rashid's favour, to accompany her, and these took with them all their cattle.[3]

That winter I passed in Badakhshán in perfect comfort, and the spring I spent in the plains and hills of that country; in the summer I went to Kábul. Soon after my arrival, there came together, in Kábul, some of my connections who had been banished [by Rashid Sultán]: namely, the Khán's wife, Zainab Sultán Khánim, who was his cousin, with her children Ibráhim Sultán (the Khán's favourite child), Muhassan Sultán and Mahmud Yusuf.

[Afterwards] I passed on into Hindustán. When I reached Láhur I found Kámrán Mirzá, son of Bábar Pádisháh, there. He came out to meet me with every mark of respect, and bestowed honours on me. From the depths of distress and hardship, I found myself raised to honour and dignity. [Verses.] . . . The princely patronage and attention [of Kámrán Mirzá]

[1] The two sentences enclosed within parentheses are obviously out of place here. They anticipate the narrative, for it could not have been till after passing through Wakhán and arriving in Badakhshán, that the author was received by Sulaimán Sháh.

[2] Three couplets in Turki omitted. They contain reproaches addressed to Rashid Sultan for his bad faith.—R.

[3] The translation of this passage is uncertain.

acted as an antidote to the numerous sufferings and griefs, which had made the sweetness of life bitter on the palate of my soul. [Verses.] . . .

At this period, one of the sons of Sháh Ismáil marched upon Kandahar, and captured it. It came about thus: Sám Mirzá, one of Sháh Ismáil's sons, fleeing with a body of men from his brother Sháh Tahmásp, reached the territory of Sistán. Thence he turned towards Kandahár, where was Mir Khwája Kilán. This Mir Khwája Kilán was the son of Mauláná Muhammad Sadr, one of the pillars of religion and state to Mirzá Amar Shaikh, son of Mirzá Sultán Abu Said. His [Mauláná Sadr's] children, after the death of Mirzá Amar Shaikh, entered, by hereditary succession, the service of Bábar Pádisháh, for whom they achieved great things. In that family their reputation stands high, for six brothers were killed in battle on separate occasions, and this one, Mir Khwája Kilán, alone survived.

He was a brave and learned man, and by his sound judgment was able to regulate most of the Emperor's affairs of State. It was owing to his exertions that, under the divine decree, the Emperor achieved the conquest of Hindustán.[1] In short, he defended the fort of Kandahár in such a way, that Sám Mirzá, after besieging it vigorously and persistently for eight months, was unable to take it. At the end of eight months, Kámrán Mirzá arrived from Hindustán and engaged [Sám Mirzá] in battle, at the very gates of the fort of Kandahár. Through the gallantry and energy of Mir Khwája Kilán, victory declared for Kámrán Mirzá after a hard fought combat, and Sám Mirzá, humbled and discomfited, fell back on Irák,[2] while Kámrán Mirzá returned to Láhur. It was at that time that I arrived at Láhur.

That winter passed over, and in the following spring, Sháh Tahmásp marched against Kandahár to avenge his brother. It was this Sháh Tahmásp who, whenever he made war upon Khorásán, met with such determined opposition from the Uzbeg under Ubaid Ullah Khán, and such overpowering resistance from their numerous forces, that he was always compelled to retreat. [Couplet]. . . . Mir Khwája Kilán was not able to put the fort in a state to withstand a siege, on account of the numbers and the strength of Sháh Tahmásp's army, and also because, having the year before sustained a siege of eight months, his ammunition and other necessaries were exhausted. Moreover, he entertained

[1] This Mir, or Amir, Khwája Kilán is frequently mentioned by Baber. He was one of the Emperor's best generals and most trusted followers. At one time he held the governorship of Bajaur, and at another was in charge of Ghazni and Kabul; but during the later part of Baber's career, was always entrusted with some important command. (See *Memoirs*, pp. 248, 293, 335, etc.)

[2] The date of this victory is given by Erskine, as 25th January, 1536. (*Hist.*, ii., p. 101.)

no hope of Kámrán Mirzá coming to his relief. Under these conditions, he abandoned Kandahár and retired to Ucha and Tatta, whence he passed on to Láhur.

When this news reached the ears of Kámrán Mirzá, he resolved to march [at once] for Kandahár. Leaving the whole of Hindustán and its dependencies in my charge, and giving me entire authority over all his officials and nobles—setting me, in fact, over the whole of the affairs of his kingdom—he proceeded to Kandahár. On reaching this place, the emissaries of Sháh Tahmásp gave the fort up to him peacefully, and returned to Irák. This journey [of Kámrán Mirzá] lasted rather more than a year, during which period I did all that was possible to discharge my duties, in the administration of the State. I attended carefully to collecting taxes, suppressing revolt, protecting the frontiers and establishing Islám, so that when Kámrán Mirzá returned, in the full glow of victory, to his capital Láhur, he raised my salary from fifteen to fifty *laks*, and distinguished me among my peers, by his favours. One *lak* of Hindustán is worth twenty thousand *sháhrukhis*. A current *sháhrukhi* is worth one *mithkál* of silver.[1]

CHAPTER CXI.

HUMÁYUN PÁDISHÁH, SON OF BÁBAR PÁDISHÁH, AND HIS DOWNFALL.

HUMÁYUN PÁDISHÁH was the eldest, greatest, and most renowned of Bábar's sons. I have seen few persons possessed of so much natural talent and excellence as he, but in consequence of frequent intercourse with the sensual and profligate men who served him, such as Mauláná Muhammad Parghari in particular, and others like him, he had contracted some bad habits; among these was his addiction to opium. All the evil that has been set down to the Emperor, and has become the common talk of the people, is attributable to this vice. Nevertheless he was endowed with excellent qualities, being brave in battle, gay in feast and very generous. [Couplet.] . . . In short, he was a dignified, stately and regal sovereign, who observed much state and pomp. When, for example, I entered his service at Agra, as shall be mentioned, it was after his defeats, and when people said that compared with

[1] Thus, one *sháhrukhi* was equal to five of some coin of India then current, and contained 71·18 grains of silver—for this, as we have seen, was the true weight of the *mithkal*. Its value is estimated, as already noted, at about 9½ pence; at which rate the Indian current coin or money of account would have been worth something under two pence. But see Erskine, *Hist.* i. App. E.

what it had been, there was nothing left of his pomp and magnificence. Yet when his army was arrayed for the Ganges campaign (in which the whole direction devolved upon me) there were still 17,000 menials [*shagird pisha*] in his retinue, from which circumstance an estimate may be formed of the rest of his establishment.

To be brief; when Kámrán Mirzá went the first time to Kandahár, the Emperor invaded Gujrát and conquered it. But on account of the insubordination and discord that prevailed among the Amirs, he was obliged to abandon the country, and return empty handed. To repair this disappointment—being still at the height of his power—he turned to attack Bangála, which he also conquered, and where he made a protracted stay.

Hindál Mirzá, his youngest brother, was in Agra. [Hearing that] Shir Khán was coming from Barkunda and Ruhtás, against Agra, [Hindál] put to death Shaikh Pul who has been mentioned as the Emperor's spiritual guide, and caused the *Khutba* to be read in his own name. He began openly to sound the drums of sovereignty. As the proverb says: "Whenever sedition arises, prosperity gets up [to go]." [1] When this news reached Bangála, the Emperor at once set out for Agra, leaving Bangála in charge of Jahángir Kuli, son of Ibrahim Begjik, the Moghul, supported by 5000 men. But when Hindál read the *Khutba* in his own name, none of the Emperor's Amirs who were in the surrounding cities, would acknowledge him. With his lack of good sense—and this was the cause of his misfortunes—he left Shir Khán behind, and turned to conquering the Emperor's dominions. As has been said: "Do the work of your friends, that your enemy may do his own work." In the first place he marched against Dehli, the capital of the whole of Hindustán. But the governors of Dehli, who were Amirs of the Emperor, would not give up the town, and a fierce encounter ensued between the two parties, each filling its enemy with fear, and its friends with courage.

While Hindál Mirzá was thus engaged, Humáyun came from Bangála to Jusa and Páik. Shir Khán, seizing his opportunity, cut off his progress.[2] The Emperor had lost all his horses in Bangála, and the strength of his army was wasted; the rainy season too, had come on. He remained for three months encamped opposite to Shir Khán. Repeated messengers came [from the

[1] This is really a play on the Persian verbs *khást* and *bar-khást*.—R.

[2] The allusion here is to the defeat which Humayun suffered at Chausa (the *Jusa* of the text) near Buxar on 27th June, 1539, while marching northward from Bengal. Shir Khán, after coming to an understanding with the Emperor, treacherously attacked his camp on the banks of the Karamnása, and afterwards endeavoured to cut off his road to Kalpi and Agra. In most histories, the surprise of Humayun's camp is said to have occurred at Chapa Ghát on the Ganges—a spot not far from Chausa. The name written *Paik*, or *Baik*, in the text does not appear in any other account of these events that I am acquainted with.

Emperor] saying that Shir Khán was at the bottom of all the confusion in Hindustán, that he was now face to face with him, and that his brothers should come quickly, as it was necessary to make an end of Shir Khán. [The letters arrived, but] the brothers were engaged in hostilities, so the enemy remained at his ease.

When news of these events reached Kámrán Mirzá, he at once led his army against Dehli. [On his approach] Hindál Mirzá fled, and the Emperor's Amirs came out to meet him. His arrival filled the breasts of the people with fresh courage, so that the veterans exerted themselves in affording assistance to the Emperor in Jusa. But some perverse advisers offered different counsel, saying: "To go to Jusa would release the Emperor, destroy the enemy and ensnare us." Kámrán Mirzá, in his ignorance and childlike folly, mistook this bad advice for wisdom, and delayed in setting forth. But men of experience said: "Since he is putting off his departure, we had better return, lest the equipment of the army be spoiled. Let every one go back to his own home and make fitting preparations for an active campaign. If Shir Khán defeat the Emperor, we shall be equipped and ready [to meet him]. If, on the other hand, the Emperor destroys Shir Khán, well and good."

But this did not quite satisfy [the discontented]. They argued: "If the Emperor destroy Shir Khán, he will be enraged against us. We must contrive some means to procure the forgiveness of the offended Emperor." In short they returned to Agra. After they had been there a little more than a month, the Emperor arrived, defeated and crestfallen. In the middle of the rains [*pashkál*] the brothers came together. This occurred in Safar of the year 946.[1]

CHAPTER CXII.

THE BATTLE OF THE GANGES.[2]

When all the brothers were assembled, they conferred together upon the state of affairs. The discussion was protracted, but no profitable decision was arrived at; in fact, nothing was proposed that was worthy of the occasion, for as it is said: "When fortune's adverse, minds are perverse." Kámrán Mirzá was very anxious to return, but Humáyun, conceding all other representations, disregarded his request on this point. Seven months were wasted

[1] The month of Safar 946 H., fell 18th June to 17th July, 1539.
[2] Throughout this chapter the word *Gang* has been rendered *Ganges*.

in weary indecision, until the opportunity was lost, and Shir Khán was on the Ganges, ready for war. [Verses]. . . . In the midst of this discussion and argument, Kámrán Mirzá became very ill. The climate of Hindustán had brought on some serious disorders.[1] When he had thus suffered for two or three months, he lost the use of his hands and feet. [Verses]. . . . As no medicine or treatment relieved him, he became more desirous of departing to Láhur. At length his maladies so increased, that he made up his mind to return thither.

This departure of Kámrán Mirzá was the turning-point in the rise of Shir Khán, and in the downfall of the Chaghatái power. The Emperor strongly urged him to leave some of his officers and forces as auxiliaries, but Kámrán Mirzá, on the contrary, did all he could to induce those who were at Agra to go away with him, and strenuously rejected the proposal to leave his own army behind. Mir Khwája Kilán, who was his prime minister (and a slight allusion to whose character has been made above), exerted himself to the same purpose. Kámrán Mirzá sent him on in advance, and then followed in person.

While this was passing, Shir Khán advanced to the banks of the Ganges and crossed his army over. Kutb Khán, his son, marched towards Atáva [Etáwa] and Kálpi. These territories were the fiefs [*ikta*] of Husain Sultán, who was one of the Uzbeg Sultáns,[2] and Yádgár Násir Mirzá, son of Sultán Násir Mirzá, the brother of the Emperor Bábar, whose story has been told above. Part of Kálpi had been given to Kámrán Mirzá and he had sent to that district Iskandar Sultán, as his representative. These three persons advanced against Kutb Khán, who was slain in the battle, and they gained a complete victory. The Emperor now marched from Agra towards the Ganges against Shir Khán.

Kámrán Mirzá, having placed the entire management of his own affairs in my hands, strongly urged me to return to Láhur. He represented as follows: "You left Kashghár on account of the unworthy treatment of your own people, whom you had served faithfully all your life: the result is evident. When you came to me, I treated you, in consideration of our relationship, like a brother—nay, even better: I entrusted the conduct of all my affairs to you and gave you full authority to appoint and displace, and generally to administer [my dominion]. If in these matters I have been guilty of any shortcoming, you must point it out to me, that I may make reparation. But do not, on the other hand, at such a crisis as this, when the enemy has the upper hand in my kingdom and disease in my body, withdraw the hand of brotherly

[1] The various complications are specified, but omitted in translation.

[2] One Persian MS. has here: "The Uzbeg and Kirim Sultans" "Crimean."

compassion from acts of kindness; rather save me from these two imminent dangers, and accompany me to Láhur."

Now the Emperor and myself had become friends, after the Moghul fashion, and he had given me the name of *dust* [friend]. In council he never addressed me by any other name, and on the *firmáns* it was written in this manner. No one of my brothers or the Sultáns of the time, who had been in the Emperor's service, had ever been honoured in such a way as was I, Muhammad Haidar Kurkán, who being the approved friend of such a prince as the Emperor, was called not merely 'brother' but was chosen as *dust.*

Although I was already in the service of Kámrán Mirzá [the Emperor] acted upon my advice in all his affairs. He said: "What Kámrán Mirzá asks of you, with regard to escorting him [to Láhur], in consequence of the aggravated symptoms of his malady, which prevent his full comprehension of things as they are, is not an affair of yours. His going does not depend upon your accompanying him, nor are you in any way bound to go to Láhur. If he gives his illness as a reason, you are not a physician, nor have you any remedies. If he urges you on the ground of kinship, your relationship descends from the [late] Emperor, and therefore your connection with me and with Kámrán Mirzá is exactly equal. Consider, for the sake of justice, the truth of what I am saying to you! On the issue of this battle between myself and Shir Khán, depends the fate of all India and all the house of Bábar Pádisháh. If, with such a conflict about to take place, you betake yourself to Láhur on account of Kámrán Mirzá's sickness, two things will ensue. Firstly, having escaped from the yawning abyss, you will save your own head, and by means of Kámrán Mirzá's feigned illness, will regain safety. All the rest will die, but you will be safe! Secondly, you being the cousin of Bábar Pádisháh, your relationship [to his sons] is equal, and it is fitting that you should show your sympathy with the whole of the Emperor's race. In such a flight as you meditate, you will bear nobody's sorrow.[1] Escaping in safety to Láhur, you will thence proceed to whatever place you consider secure. If you think this conformable with the conduct of a 'friend' and a 'brother,' you may act accordingly: but know, for a certainty, that you will encounter the opposition of the people. Instead of their saying: 'In spite of Kámrán Mirzá's illness, he did not escort him to Láhur, but with sound judgment, took part in the Ganges campaign with the army:' they will say that you left me alone to undertake a combat, on the result of which hung the fate of the house to whom your loyalty is owing. [They will add] that giving as an excuse the illness of Kámrán Mirzá, you found for yourself

[1] Or "you will be showing sympathy with none."—R.

a place of security. Besides, it is a fact that if we lose the day here, Láhur too will quickly fall."

These arguments quite convinced me, and being unable to obtain Kámrán Mirzá's permission, I remained behind without it.[1]

Kámrán Mirzá himself, shamefully leaving only Iskandar Sultán with about one thousand men as auxiliaries, went off to Láhur, taking with him all the men from Agra whom he could carry with him, thus giving strength to the enemy and preparing defeat for his friends.

The Imperial army reached the banks of the Ganges in the best way that it could. There it encamped and lay for about a month, the Emperor being on one side of the river, and Shir Khán on the other, facing each other. The armies may have amounted to more than 200,000 men. Muhammad Sultán Mirzá, a descendant of Ulugh Mirzá and Sháh Mirzá (who were of the house of Timur) and grandson (by a daughter) of Sultán Husain Mirzá (of Khorásán), had come to India to wait upon the Emperor Bábar, and had been received with every mark of kindness and royal favour. After Bábar's death, he had several times revolted against Humáyun; but being unsuccessful, he had sought forgiveness, and had been pardoned. Now having colluded with Shir Khán, he deserted. A new way was thus opened. Everybody began to desert, and the most surprising part of it was, that many of those who deserted did not go over to Shir Khán, and so could expect no favour from him. An excited feeling ran through the army and the cry was, "Let us go and rest in our homes." A number of Kámrán's auxiliary forces also abandoned him and fled to Láhur.

Among the equipments which were in the train of the Emperor were 700 carriages (*gardun*), each drawn by four pairs of bullocks, and carrying a swivel (*zarb-zan*), which discharged a ball (*kalola*) of 500 *mithkáls* weight. I, myself, saw several times that from the top of an eminence they unfailingly (*bi-khatá*) struck horsemen who slightly and unsuspectingly exposed themselves. And there were twenty-one carriages, each drawn by eight pairs of bullocks. Stone balls were of no use in these, but the shots were of molten brass weighing 5000 *mithkáls*, and the cost of each was 200 *mithkáls* of silver. They would strike anything that was visible at the distance of a *parasang*.

As the army had taken to desert, it was judged better to risk a battle, than to see it go to ruin without fighting. If the result were unfavourable, we could not, at least, be accused of having

[1] Firishta, according to Briggs' translation, disposes of this subject in one short sentence:—"Mirza Haidar Doghlat, disgusted with his [Kamrán's] conduct, abandoned his standard and joined Hoomayoon, to whom he was afterwards of great service." And the translator adds in a footnote:—"This person ascended the throne of Kashmir, and is the author of the most authentic history of that interesting principality." Would that it were so! (Briggs, ii., p. 89.)

abandoned an empire like Hindustán, without striking a blow. Another consideration was, that if we passed the river, desertion would no longer be possible. We therefore crossed over.

Both armies entrenched themselves. Everyday skirmishes occurred between the adventurous, swaggering spirits of both sides. These proceedings were put an end to by the monsoon rains, which came on and flooded the ground, rendering it unfit for a camp. To move was indispensable. Opinions were expressed that another such a deluge would sink the whole army in the abyss of despair, and it was proposed to move to some rising ground which the inundation could not reach, and which lay in front of the enemy. I went to reconnoitre, and found a place suitable for the purpose.

I said that we would, on the morrow, try the enemy on the touchstone of experience; for he ought not to attack while we were on the march, but if he should do so, it would be wrong to attempt a pitched battle while moving. The morrow would be the 10th of Moharram, and we must keep our forces well under control, until we should see if the enemy came out of his trenches and advanced against us. Then, at last, a regular pitched battle would be fought between us. The proper plan would be for us to place the mortars and swivels in front: and the gunners, nearly 5000 in number, must be stationed with the guns. If he should come out to attack us, there would be no time or place more suitable than the present, for battle. If he should not come out of his entrenchments, we must remain drawn up till about midday, and then return to our position. Next day we must act in just the same way. Then the baggage must move to the new position, and we must follow and occupy the place. This scheme of mine met with general approbation.

On the 10th Moharram, 947, we mounted to carry the plan into effect, and made our dispositions. As had been determined, the carriages and mortars and small guns were placed in the centre. The command of the guns was given to Muhammad Khán Rumi, to the sons of Ustád Ali Kuli, to Ustád Ahmad Rumi and Husain Khalifa. They placed the carriages and mortars in their proper positions, and stretched chains between them. In other divisions there were Amirs of no repute—men who were Amirs [nobles] only in name. They had got possession of the country, but they had not a tincture of prudence or knowledge, or energy or emulation, or dignity of mind or generosity—qualities from which nobility draws its name.

The Emperor had posted the author of this work upon his left, so that his right flank should be on the Emperor's left. In the same position he had placed a force of chosen troops. On my left all my retainers were stationed. I had 400 chosen men, inured to warfare and familiar with battle, fifty of whom were mounted on horses accoutred with armour. Between me and the river (*jui-bár*) there was a force of twenty-seven Amirs, all of whom carried the *tugh* [banner]. In this position also, were the other components of the left wing, and they must be judged of by the others. On the day of battle, when Shir Khán, having formed his divisions, marched out, of all these twenty-seven banners not one was to be seen, for the great nobles had hidden them, in the apprehension that the enemy might advance upon them. The soldiership and bravery of the Amirs may be conceived from this exhibition of courage.

Shir Khán came out in five divisions of 1000 men each, and in advance of him were 3000 men. I estimated the whole as being less than 15,000, but I calculated the Chaghatái force at about 40,000, all mounted on *tipchák* horses, and clad in iron armour. They surged like the waves of the sea, but the courage of the Amirs and officers of the army was such as I have described. When Shir Khán's army came out of its entrenchments, two divisions (*jauk*) which seemed to be equal to four divisions, drew up in that place, and three divisions advanced against their opponents. On our side I was leading the centre, to take up the position which I had selected; but when we reached the ground, we were unable to occupy it, for every Amir and Vazir in the Chaghatái army, whether he be rich or poor, has his camp-followers [*ghulam*]. An Amir of note, with his 100 retainers and followers, has 500 servants and *ghulams*, who on the day of battle render no assistance to their masters and have no control over themselves. So in whatever place there was a conflict, the *ghulams* were entirely ungovernable. When they lost their masters, they were seized with panic and blindly rushed about in terror. In short, it was impossible to hold our ground. They so pressed us in the rear, that they drove the centre upon the chains stretched between the chariots, and they and the soldiers dashed each other upon them. Those who were behind, so pressed upon those who were in front, that they broke through the chains. The men who were posted by the chains were driven beyond them, and the few who remained behind were broken, so that all formation was destroyed.[1]

[1] The Indian historian, Jauher, refers to this episode of breaking through the chains of the gun-carriages. He implies that the chains were loosened by order of Humayun, and attributes the order to bad advice given by Mirza Haidar. He writes: "Mirza Haidar represented that, in order to let the fugitives pass, it was requisite to loose the chains of the carriages which formed a barricade in front of the centre; His Majesty unfortunately complied with this advice, and the chains, being unloosed, the runaways passed through the line of carriages in files." There appears, however, to be no reason to doubt Mirza Haidar's version of the affair. He took an active part in the battle, and was an eye-witness of what occurred. (For Jauher, see *Elliot*, v., p. 143; or C. Stewart's *Mem. of Humayun*, p. 21.)

Such was the state of the centre. On the right Shir Khán advanced in battle array; but before an arrow was discharged, the camp followers fled like chaff before the wind, and breaking the line, they all pressed towards the centre. The *ghulams* whom the commanders had sent to the front, rushed to the lines of chariots, and the whole array was broken: the Mir was separated from his men, and the men from the Mir. While the centre was thus thrown into disorder, all the fugitives from the right bore down upon it. So before the enemy had discharged an arrow, the whole army was scattered and defeated. I had estimated the Chaghatái army as numbering 40,000 men, excluding the camp-followers [*ghulam*] and workmen [*shágird pisha*]. They fled before 10,000 men, and Shir Khán gained a victory, while the Chaghatái were defeated on this battle-field, where not a man, either friend or foe, was wounded. Not a gun was fired and the chariots [*gardun*] were useless.

When the Chaghatái took to flight, the distance between their position and the Ganges might be nearly a *farsákh*. All the Amirs and braves [*báhadurán*] fled for safety to the river, without a man of them having received a wound. The enemy pursued them, and the Chaghatái, having no time to throw off their armour and coats, plunged into the water. The breadth of the river might be about five bowshots. Many illustrious Amirs were drowned, and each one remained or went on, at his will. When we came out of the river, His Majesty, who at midday had a retinue of 17,000 in attendance upon his court, was mounted upon a horse which had been given to him by Tardi Beg, and had nothing on his head or feet. "Permanence is from God and dominion is from God." Out of 1000 retainers eight persons came out of the river; the rest had perished in the water. The total loss may be estimated from this fact. When we reached Agra, we made no tarry, but, broken and dispirited, in a state heart-rending to relate, we went on to Láhur.

CHAPTER CXIII.

FLIGHT OF THE CHAGHATÁI FROM HINDUSTÁN TO LÁHUR.

On the 1st of Rabi I. 947, all the Sultáns, Amirs and people assembled together. So great was the crowd of people that there was but little space for moving about, while it was difficult to find a lodging. High and low, each had his own ends to serve, and each made suggestions; every man of noble birth had his scheme, and all those of low parentage their ideas. Among them were Muhammad Sultán Mirzá and Ulugh Mirzá, who had deserted on the banks of the Gang, on the eve of the battle. Not finding any place in which they could remain, they came in a most pitiable condition to Láhur. They kept apart [from the others] and were still boasting hostility. [These two] made themselves the heads, or rather the donkeys'-heads, of a rabble of ruffians and senseless Hindus. Hindál Mirzá and Yádgár Násir Mirzá likewise entered into baseless and idle plans, [saying]: We will go to Bakar and take it from Sháh Husain Arghun, and with his forces will subdue Gujrát. Kámrán Mirzá was engrossed with devising some plan for dispersing all this assemblage, while he should repair, alone, to Kábul.

Humáyun Pádisháh for a time thought of reunion, but seeing difficulties in the way, he abandoned all hope of this, and was at a loss what to do next. [Reunion], however, was his object. At this time repeated meetings were held, out of mere hypocrisy. Union was discussed, but they had only disunion at heart; they called in the magnates and leading men, to be witnesses that no one opposed or deviated from the resolutions agreed to. Thus were summoned Khwája Khánd Máhmud,[1] his younger brother Khwája Abdul Hakk and Mir Abul-baká, who were all noted for their learning and esteemed for their piety, together with many other great men, whose names it would take too long to mention individually. The Sultáns, Amirs and many others were present. At first they assented to reunion and drew up a written engagement, upon the margin of which the magnates signed their names as witnesses. They then embarked upon the discussion.

First of all the Emperor, pointing to me, said: "You must tell us what you consider the most suitable line of action to pursue at this moment." I represented: "When Sultán Husain Mirzá of Khorásán departed this life, his seventeen sons, in consequence of their disunion, abandoned Khorásán to Sháhi Beg Khán, so that to the present day they are objects of reproach to the people, and rejected of all mankind. To add to this disgrace they have all been extinguished; insomuch that within the space of one year, excepting Badi-uz-Zamán who went to Rum, not one remains alive. The late Emperor, Bábar, conquered this far-stretching land of Hindustán with much exertion and toil, and on leaving this world, transmitted [the empire] to you. Would you suffer a country like Hindustán to be seized by such a man as Shir Khán? Consider what a difference there is between Hindustán with all its revenues, and Khorásán; and how inferior is Shir Khán to Sháhi Beg Khán! Also remember the degree of censure you will

[1] Three lines of titles of the Khwája are omitted.—R.

incur from mankind! Now is the moment for you to consider your condition, and having removed your head from the collar of envy, to place it in the pocket of meditation, that you may acquire the esteem of the people. Formerly, when matters could have been arranged with ease, you put obstacles in the way, by your want of constancy and of purpose. At present it is impossible to achieve anything, without encountering untold difficulties.

"I will now lay before you what seems to me your wisest course. It involves great hardships, but it is you who have made hard what was once easy. And moreover, if you do not bear patiently your present troubles, they will become yet more onerous. My advice is as follows: Shir Khán will still take four months to reach Láhur. During these four months, the mountain slopes of Hindustán should be given to the Sultáns, and each one, in proportion to his share, should be made to pledge his allegiance.

"Let every man attend to the particular business to which he has been appointed. Let me, for instance, be appointed to the task of subduing Kashmir, and I engage that within two months I will accomplish it. As soon as you hear of my arrival in Kashmir, let every one send his family and baggage thither, while he betakes himself to the mountains, and forms a strong position on the slopes—from the hills of Sarind to those [occupied by] Sarang.[1]

[1] As this passage has been differently translated in two published works—those of Mr. Erskine and Major Price—a few words of explanation are necessary, to account for the alteration I have made in the text. The *Tárikh-i-Rashidi* reads (and Mr. Ross translated the sentence in this way) just as Erskine has it, *i.e.*, "the skirts of the hill-country between Sirhind and Sárang"; but no indication is afforded of the meaning of *Sárang*. It appears to be intended for the name of a place or district, but no such place-name occurs in the part of India in question. Price's translation is not from the *Tárikh-i-Rashidi*, but from the *Akbar-Náma*, though the author of that work evidently copied from Mirza Haidar. The passage stands thus, as Price gives it: "they should . . . occupy the acclivities of the hills all the way from Sehrind to Saurung, that is, all across the sources of the Kuggar, Sareswaty, and Jumna rivers, from Sehrind to Sauhaurungpour." The last sentence is, apparently, an insertion by the author of the *Akbar-Náma*, added by way of explanation.

In the next chapter but one of the *Tárikh-i-Rashidi*, it will be seen that the name *Sárang* appears again, and this time is applied to a person and not to a place. But Sárang is then described as: "One of the Sultans of the slopes of the hills of Hind." From this indication, it is, I think, clear that the personage alluded to, can be no other than Sultan Sárang of the tribe of Gakars, and that the region which Mirza Haidar advised should be occupied by the Chaghatai princes and army, was that of the lower or outer hills, extending from Sirhind to the Salt Range—for it was in and about the Salt Range, that the Gakar country was situated. Therefore, in making the passage read as it now does in the text, the only intelligible meaning has been given to it.

Sultan Sárang, as chief of the Gakars and the ally of the Chaghatais, in the early half of the sixteenth century, is a character fairly well known in Indian history, and the tract of country which was occupied by the Gakar tribe, was then very much the same as now. Nizám-ud-Din Ahmad, in the *Tabákát-i-Akbari* says: "The country of the Gakars lies upon the banks of the river Sind, well-known as the Niláb. This territory, from the Siwalik hills to the borders of Kashmir, has been, from all time, the possession of the Gakars." By the Siwalik hills he means, apparently, the Salt Range. Though Sádik

The mortars [*dig*] and swivels [*zarb-zan*] of Shir Khán are the mainstay of his fighting power. It is impossible to bring gun-carriages into the hills, and he will not hazard a battle without them. His army, from stress of numbers, will perish for want of grain, and must perforce retreat."

Ispaháni, it may be mentioned, speaks of Jammu as "a territory in the Kuhistan of *Suválik*" (p. 86)—thus the skirts of the Pir Panjal range. Abul Fazl, in the *Akbar-Náma*, more briefly locates it "between the Sind and the Behat," that is, between the Indus and the Jhilam. What little is to be found about the Gakars in the two authors above-named, in the *Tarikh-i-Daudi*, and the *Tarikh-i-Jahán Khán Lodi*, differs very considerably, while dates are very sparingly furnished in any of the extracts from these works, as published by Elliot. It appears, however, that the Gakar country belonged to Kashmir in the first half of the fifteenth century, but during the reign of the Kashmir Sultan, Zain-ul-Abidin (1423–69 according to Firishta, and 1422–72 according to others), one Malik Kad, Amir of Ghazni, invaded the territory and wrested it from the Kashmiris. Malik Kad was succeeded by his son, Malik Kilán, as chief of the tribe, and the latter by his son, Malik Pir. After the reign of Malik Pir, and shortly before the year 1519, the Gakars seem to have been divided into two factions. One, Hati Khan, possessed the higher and more inaccessible country, while a certain Tátár Khan held the lower tracts. When Baber was about to return from Bhira to Kabul in 1519, Hati Gakar had made war on Tátár, had defeated and slain him, and seized his territory. Baber planned an expedition against Perhálah (or Pharwala), which had been the capital of Tátár, and took it, together with the whole country. Shortly afterwards Hati Khan, who had escaped from Perhálah, tendered his submission, and from that time forward his family became the staunch allies of the Chaghatais.

At his death, which appears to have taken place about 1525, he left two sons named Sárang and Adam respectively; the former succeeded to the chief-ship, and at once gave in his allegiance to Baber. After the disasters experienced by Humayun in 1540, and his flight across the Indus, Sárang maintained himself bravely against the Afghans, under Shir Shah, but was at last, after several years of hostilities, taken prisoner and flayed alive. The date of his death I find nowhere stated with certainty, and moreover, the native authors disagree as to the name of the Afghan king of Hindustan who committed this act of barbarity. Niámat Ullah and Nizám-ud-Din Ahmad ascribe it to Shir Shah, and in this case it must have occurred before the year 1545, when the latter's death took place. Shir Shah was succeeded by his son Salim, in May of that year, and two years later marched to attack the Gakars. It is to this prince that Abdulla, the author of the *Tarikh-i-Daudi,* attributes the death of Sárang, and, if his story is the correct one, the date would be 1547 or 1548. At any rate the authorities appear to be so far agreed, as to make Sultan Adam, Sárang's brother, the reigning chief of the Gakars, when Salim prevailed over them in 1548. In the closing chapters of his book, which relate to Kashmir, Mirza Haidar gives few particulars, but by a comparison of the events of that period, as recounted by Firishta, Abul Fazl and others, it would appear that the end of Sárang's career must have occurred about the date estimated above.

However this may be, it is evident that *Sárang* was not a place-name, but that of a Gakar chief, who was an ally of Humayun and the house of Chaghatai, and who was alive in 1540; while nothing is more consistent with the narrative than that Mirza Haidar should have advised his master, after the defeat at Kanauj, to take up a position that included Sárang's territory as a support. A subsequent allusion to Adam, Sultan of the Gakars, occurs in Firishta, when he is represented as having met Mirza Haidar at "the fortress of Dibal" [Deobal?] in 1549, for the purpose of mediating between the refugee Maliks of Kashmir. (See Erskine, *Hist.*, i., pp. 414–15; ii., pp. 425–27 and 465–6. Also *Baber*, pp. 259–62; *Abul Fazl* in Price's *Muham. Hist.*, iii., pp. 787–8; *Tarikh-i-Daudi* in Elliot, iv., p. 493; *Tarikh-i-Jáhán Khán Lodi*, *ib.*, p. 114; *Tabákát-i-Akbari*, *ib.*, v., pp. 278–80; Firishta (Briggs), iv., p. 501, and *ib.* (Rodgers), *J. A. S. B.*, 1855, pt. i., p. 118.)

Kámrán Mirzá, frowning at these words, said: "Although what you recommend is plausible enough, it involves difficulties too great." I replied: "When I began, I represented, in excuse for myself, that the business was a difficult one. All easy methods are now out of question. Nothing but difficulties remain. If any one can suggest an easier solution, let him speak." Kámrán Mirzá said: "We have now with us nearly 200,000 householders [*khána-vár mardum*]. Should the advice just offered be acted upon, and the attempt fail, it is probable that all this multitude will be destroyed. It is, therefore, better that the Emperor and the Mirzás should go unencumbered, either to the hills or to Kashmir, leaving their families to be conducted to Kábul by me. Having safely disposed of the families, I will return to join the army."

All were bewildered by this suggestion and asked themselves, "What has now become of our oath of union? What are these sentiments? Who would think of sending his family to Kábul and himself remaining without baggage? Between Láhur and Kábul there are rivers, highway robbers, and mountains. The Mirzá's scheme is quite impracticable." Although much discussion followed, Kámrán Mirzá did not carry a single point. Thus [ostensible] desires for union were shown to be hypocrisy, and the meeting broke up. But time passed, and meanwhile Shir Khán had reached the banks of the river of Sultánpur.[1] Every man chose a place of retreat for himself. The Emperor consulted with me in this exigency, and I again respectfully represented that I still held by the Kashmir plan. "At any rate," I continued, "if you allow me to go in advance, the rest can follow after, and I guarantee that I will conquer Kashmir." The Emperor then gave me leave to depart, furnishing me with what help he was able; so that with four hundred freed men and slaves, I set out for Kashmir.

CHAPTER CXIV.

ORIGIN OF THE AUTHOR'S EXPEDITION TO KASHMIR.

It has been observed above, that the Sultáns of Kashmir had fallen under the power of their worthless Amirs, every one of whom acted in whatever way he saw fit. At the time when Kámrán Mirzá went to Kandahár to fight the son of Sháh Ismail, as was mentioned, the chiefs [*maliks*] of Kashmir were engaged in mutual

[1] The Biás.

hostilities. Káchi Chak, Abdál Makri and Zangi Chak had been turned out of Kashmir and, having taken up their abode at the foot of the mountains of Hind, they appealed to me for help.[1] Háji, who was mentioned in the relation of events in Tibet, acted as intermediary. Frequently, and with insistence, had I tried to convince Kámrán Mirzá on the subject of Kashmir. At the time of [Kámrán Mirzá's] march on Dehli, an army was mustered in Agra, and a certain Bábá Chuchak was placed at the head of it. Háji came from Agra to Láhur with Bábá Chuchak, to join in the expedition against Kashmir. But Bábá Chuchak, being weak-minded and incapable, could not manage this business, and delayed in setting out till the news of the defeat on the Gang arrived. The soldiers stood fast, and Bábá Chuchak was released from [the duty of] conducting the Kashmir expedition.

At the time when the general assemblage took place in Láhur, Háji carried many messages to and fro, between myself on the one hand, and Abdál Makri on the other, in furtherance of my plan. All terminated in a most desirable way, and I was thus able to impress it strongly on the Emperor. I showed him the letter which had been sent me, and he became convinced that Kashmir would be conquered as soon as I should appear there.

[1] It may be noted here, that there had existed in Kashmir, since the days of the first Musulman Sultan, Shah Mir, about the middle of the fourteenth century, two great families, or houses, known as the *Chak* and the *Makri*. Their rivalry seems to have been the cause of most of the disorder and confusion, from which the State suffered for the greater part of the sixteenth century. They contended with one another perpetually, for the office of chief minister under the dynastic princes, whose power was merely nominal, and who were, apparently, incapable either of administering their dominions, or suppressing the ambitions of these two influential houses. The names of the *Chak* and *Makri* are very variously spelled by Mirza Haidar, Firishta, Abul Fazl, and other writers, but they may generally be identified one with another. One, Malik Achi, Káchi, or Ajhi, of the *Chak* family, appears to have been the minister in power, under a prince called Názuk Shah (or sometimes Nádir Shah) when Mirza Haidar invaded the country.

A detailed account of the affairs of Kashmir during Mirza Haidar's regency, will be found in Appendix A. It consists of an extract from Mr. C. J. Rodgers' able paper on "The Coins of the Sultans of Kashmir," which is based chiefly on translations made by him from collated copies of Firishta. (See *J. A. S. B.*, liv., pt. i., 1885, pp. 92, *seq.*)

CHAPTER CXV.

THE AUTHOR CONQUERS KASHMIR. ADVENTURES OF THE CHAGHATÁI AFTER THEIR DEPARTURE FROM HINDUSTÁN.

I HAD arranged with the Emperor that I should, in the first place, proceed with a small number of men to Nau Shahr,[1] and that as soon as the Maliks of Kashmir should have joined me, Iskandar Tupchi should overtake me there. When I should have reached the pass, Mir Khwája Kilán, in praise of whom I have spoken above, was to enter Nau Shahr. On my descending into Kashmir Mir Khwája Kilán was to advance to the foot of the pass of Kashmir, while the Emperor would pitch his camp at Nau Shahr. Matters having been thus arranged, Kámrán Mirzá and the rest were allowed to go wherever they pleased.

All being settled, I set out, and in Nau Shahr was joined by all the Maliks of Kashmir. Iskandar Tupchi was one day's journey from Nau Shahr. Mir Khwája Kilán was in Siálkut. On the same day that I despatched a messenger to Iskandar Tupchi, news reached me that all our people had evacuated Láhur. I started in all haste: when I arrived at the foot of the pass [leading to] Kashmir, Káchi Chak ascended by one road, and we by another, and without further contention or discussion we [all] arrived at [Kashmir].

Now when Iskandar Tupchi and Mir Khwája Kilán heard of the evacuation of Láhur, the former sought a refuge with Sárang, who was one of the Sultáns of the slopes of the hills [*kuh páya*] of Hind, while the latter, leaving Siálkut, went and joined the fugitives [from Láhur]. In spite of the Emperor's endeavours to reach Kashmir, he could induce no one to accompany him. Some foolish imbeciles, namely, Hindál Mirzá, Yádgár Násir Mirzá and others beside, carried him off to Tatta and Bakar, to attack [*basar*] Mirzá Sháh Husain the son of Sháh Beg Arghun (son of Zulnun Arghun). This Mirzá Sháh Husain is the same personage who was spoken of above. When Bábar Pádisháh wrested Kandahár from Sháh Beg, the latter retired to Ucha and Tatta and subdued the whole of the surrounding country. He was succeeded on his death by his son Mirzá Sháh Husain, who busied himself for some time in strengthening his forts and settling his country; for he was, in truth, a methodical and prudent man.[2] Against him it

[1] A village in the lower hills of Rajaori.

[2] Shah Beg seems to be usually known in history as Shah Shujá Beg, while his son is as often called Shah Hasan, as Shah Husain. The former's conquest of Tatta (or Sind), here alluded to, took place in 1521. He died in 1524, when his dominions in Sind passed to his son Husain or Hasan, who, after two years

was that this blundering band marched. But being able to achieve nothing, Hindál Mirzá went to Kandahár, whose governor came out to receive him. He began to boast of empire, [whereupon] Kámrán Mirzá marched against him, from Kábul. After some unfortunate occurrences, and being reduced to extremities, he begged Kámrán Mirzá to spare his life, promising that he would enter his service. Not long after this, Yádgár Násir Mirzá and Kásim Husain Sultán also fled from the Emperor and joined Kámrán Mirzá. The Emperor, after endless hardships and incalculable misfortunes, passed on to Irák, but up to the present time it is not known what has become of him. As for Kámrán Mirzá, he is at Kábul and in despair from the buffetings of fortune.

My trust is in the most glorious and merciful God, that He will again raise to the throne of sovereignty Humáyun Pádisháh, than whom there have been few greater Sultáns. He has endured such suffering and misery as have fallen to the lot of few Emperors. May he make the people prosperous and contented under his benevolent shadow. It is thus written in the "Sunna": that when the affairs of a great ruler go to ruin, he is himself the cause. If, as is rarely the case, the ruler be spared these calamities, his escape must be certainly attributable to his good sense.

It is related, in the earlier portion of this book, that his [Humáyun's] father, Bábar Pádisháh, on several occasions mounted the throne of Samarkand, but as often suffered ruinous defeats. In those defeats his own head was kept safe, and finally God raised him to such power, that all the world felt his influence, while his name remains among the [immortal] Sultáns. May God, having delivered Humáyun Pádisháh from these perils and dangers, grant him similar well-being and wisdom!

CHAPTER CXVI.

PARTING OF THE AUTHOR FROM HUMÁYUN PÁDISHÁH. HIS MARCH AGAINST, AND CONQUEST OF KASHMIR. CONTEMPORANEOUS EVENTS, AND CONCLUSION OF THE "TÁRIKH-I-RÁSHIDI."

AFTER a settlement of some kind had been arrived at among the Mirzás, I obtained, by the grace of Providence, the permission of Humáyun to depart, and for the reasons above stated, started from

---

of hard struggles, possessed himself of Uch and Multan. He lost the latter province to Baber in 1527, but eventually recovered it from Humayun. He was the third and last of the Arghun line, while his rule continued till 1554. (See Erskine, *Hist.*, i., chap. vi., secs. 1 and 2; and Stokvis, i., p. 253.)

Láhur in the direction of Kashmir. I have explained that on the 22nd of Rajab, I crossed the pass of Kashmir. This date I discovered in the words "*Julus-i-dár-ul-mulk-i-Kashmir*," [ascending the throne of Kashmir]. It was the season of Sagittarius. I had scarce ascended the throne of triumph, when the snow began to fall and the face of the earth became white, while the eyes of the enemy turned dark. By the divine favour, that winter passed in quiet.

Now Káchi Chak had been forced, thrice previously, to disconnect himself from the government of Kashmir. His own wife and children had not seen him, for he had left them in the care of Malik Abdál and Zangi Chak, and had gone off, thinking that, as on former occasions, his resignation and resumption of power would not be settled within a year. [Verse] . . . All the [chief] men of Kashmir, believing this too, went with him, ignoring that God gives to whomsoever He will, and takes away from whomsoever He will. [Two couplets]. . . . Káchi Chak, vainly imagining that Shir Khán, by force of arms, could change the decree of the Most High God, appealed to him for aid.

In the beginning of spring . . . . [1] having obtained auxiliaries from Shir Khán, he again moved forward with a large force. Just at this juncture, and when this news was confirmed, Malik Abdál [Makri] who was the mainstay of the whole scheme, was attacked by paralysis, and migrated to the Eternal abode, so that the brunt of the affair fell on Zangi Chak. In a word, after various difficulties had been surmounted, which it would be tedious to relate in detail, we left our families in the fort of Andarkul [2] and went out to meet and oppose [the enemy], with a vacillating band. [Two couplets] . . . During three months we attacked their strongholds and met them in the field; till at length, Káchi Chak, having formed a junction with the auxiliaries of Shir Khán, marched boldly out of the hill district [*Báládast*] which he had fortified, and took up a position on a spot that was a halting stage. At this place the army of Kashmir, who from their outward appearance looked as if they must disperse in flight, held their ground. [On our side] [only] the Moghul army kept its position. No one expected a battle that day; most had gone off in different directions to attend to their own affairs; so that only about 250 men were present, together with a few Kashmiris who had joined the Moghuls, making in all about 300. These advanced and attacked a force comprising 5000 cavalry, two elephants, and a body of infantry more numerous than the cavalry. Falling upon their rear, [our army]

[1] The omission here consists of a few lines descriptive of spring.—R.

[2] Firishta makes this name (according to both Rodgers and Briggs) *Indrakot*, a form which would be thoroughly Kashmiri, and more likely to be correct than *Andarkul*. I cannot identify the place, but infer from the context in Firishta (see App. A., p. 489) that it must have been near the modern Báràmula.

began by plundering their baggage and stores. The battle was so desperate, that should I enter into the particulars, the reader would imagine I was exaggerating. Therefore, avoiding details, I will content myself with a summary account. To resume, at noonday prayers on Monday, the 8 Rabi II. 948,[1] we routed an army of 5000 cavalry, and several thousand foot, with a body of only 300 men. [Verses] . . . The preacher [*Khatib*] of Kashmir, Mauláná Yusuf, found the date in *Fath-i-Mukarrar* [The repeated victory], for I had already once entered Kashmir and gained a victory there, as has been related.

[Here follows a prayer, ending with an apology to the reader for the faults and shortcomings of the "Epitome."]

[1] 2nd August, 1541 A.D.

THE END.

APPENDIX A.

EXTRACT from a paper entitled: *The Square Silver Coins of the Sultáns of Kashmir*, by Mr. C. J. Rodgers, M.R.A.S., &c., in the *Journ. Asiat. Socy. Bengal*, Vol. LIV. Pt. I., No. 2, 1885, pp. 92 to 139 (see pp. 116–21).

In Notes 2, p. 433—1, p. 441—1, p. 482, and in Sec. I of the *Introduction*, reference has been made to Mr. C. J. Rodgers' translations from Firishta's History contained in the able and interesting paper cited above. As Mirza Haidar closes his narrative somewhat abruptly, at the time of his conquest of Kashmir, I believe that a summary of the affairs of the country during his regency, will be found useful to the reader, and therefore transcribe here, that portion of Mr. Rodgers' published paper which deals with the period in question. It comprises the last ten years of Mirza Haidar's life, and is also, no doubt, the best account that exists of a little known phase of Indian history.

Názuk Sháh. 2nd Time.—After his father, Názuk sat on the throne of the kingdom. (His father we are told was Ibrahim Sháh. There is confusion again here.) He had not, however, reigned more than five or six months when Mirzá Haidar Turk, having obtained a firm footing in Kashmir ruled it. In his time the Khutba was read and coins were struck in the name of *Násir-ud-Din Muhammad Humáyun Bádsháh.* (The coins of Humáyun struck in Kashmir are exceedingly rare. They are exactly of the same type as those of the preceding kings. There are some small differences in the inscriptions in the arrangements of the letters. One coin has a *ha* in the field to the right, which I consider to be the first letter of Haidar's name. The dates of the coins fall within the period during which Mirzá Haidar ruled Kashmir nominally in his master's name. But all these ten years poor Humáyun was a fugitive in Sind and Persia and Affghánistán and he never derived any benefit from the fact that prayers were used in Kashmir with his name in them, and coins current with his name on them.)

In the year 948 A.H.[1] when Humáyun, flying before Sher Sháh Suri, reached Lahore, Malik Abdál Mákari, Zangi Chakk and other petitioners wrote about Humáyun's taking Kashmir and sent the letter by the hands of Mirzá Haidar. The emperor dismissed the Mirzá in the direction of Kashmir and gave it out as his intention to follow shortly himself. When the Mirzá arrived at Bhir he was met by Abdál Mákari and Zangi Chakk. The Mirzá had with him only three or four thousand horsemen, but when he arrived at Rájáori, Malik Gáji Chakk who was the ruler of Kashmir, arrived at Khabal Kartal (it is called Karmal by Erskine) and entrenched himself with from three to four thousand horsemen and 50,000 infantry. Mirzá Haidar therefore changed his route and went by Pabhaj (the Panuj of Erskine) which Gáji Chakk in his pride had forgotten to defend. The Mirzá crossed the mountains and descending into the plain of Kashmir took possession at once of Srinagar. Abdál Mákari and Zangi Chakk finding themselves strong, busied themselves with the affairs of the kingdom, and they gave several pergunnahs to the Mirzá. But just at this time Abdál Mákari, died after recommending his sons to the care of the Mirzá.

After the arrival of Mirzá Haidar in Kashmir, Malik Gáji Chakk went to Sher Sháh Afghán for assistance. He obtained five thousand horsemen, over whom were Husain Sharváni and Adil Khán; and two elephants. Mirzá Haidar met him between Danahdyár and Káwah, and the zephyr of victory blowing in favour of the Mirzá, the Malik and his Affghán allies fled from the field and took possession of Bahrámgalla.

In the year 950 A.H. Mirzá Haidar settled himself in the fort of Indarkot. Zangi Chakk being suspected by him fled to Gáji Chakk and in 951 A.H. the two set out, in the direction of Srinagar, determined to root out Mirzá Haidar. Bahrám Chakk, son of Zangi Chakk arrived first at Srinagar, but he was easily put to flight by two of the Mirzá's generals, and his disorganised troops falling back on the main army Zangi Chakk and Gáji Chakk also fled and returned to Bahrámgalla. After this the Mirzá employed his army in invading Tibet. He took Lansur and many other large forts.

In 952 A.H. Gáji Chakk and his son Muhammad Chakk died of fever and ague. This year the Mirzá spent in ease.

In 953 A.H. Zangi Chakk fighting with Mirzá Haidar was killed. His head with the head of his son Gázi Khán were presented to Haidar.

In 954 A.H. ambassadors came to the Mirzá from Káshgar and he went with many nobles as far as Lár to meet them. In Lár the head of Khwája Ujh son of Masaud Chakk was brought to him. This man had for the space of seven years been fighting in Kamráj, but at last he had desired peace. Mirzá Mirak, swearing that all should be right, asked him to attend on him to make a treaty. But when Ujh came into the assembly he was stabbed by Mirak and he fled to the jungle pursued by Mirak who took his head off and sent it to Mirzá Haidar. Ide Ziná was far from pleased at seeing it, and, standing up in anger said, that after an oath and covenant had been made the slaughter of one man was not necessary. Haidar replied that he was not privy to the circumstances of the death.

After this Mirzá Haidar turned his attention to Kishtwár. Bandagán Kukah, Muhammad Mákari and Yahi Ziná led the van. The Mirzá took up his abode at Jhapur near Kishtwár. The van, doing three days' journey in one descended on Dahlot, where the river winds, and they were not able to ford it, for the enemy too opposed them. The next day the army of Haidar made a diversion to the right in hopes of reaching Kishtwár, but when they reached the town of Dhár, gusts of cold air laden with dust came down upon them, the day became dark and the people of the town made an attack on them. Bandagán Kukah with five other men was slain. The rest of the army with a thousand exertions at last joined themselves with Haidar. The Mirzá was not successful: he was obliged to retrace his steps ingloriously.

In 955 he turned his attention to Tibet. Taking Rájáori he gave it to Muhammad Nazir and Nasir Ali. Pakli[1] he gave to Mulla Abdullah and Little Tibet[2] he gave to Mullah Qásim. Conquering Great Tibet,[3] he appointed Mulla Hasan its governor.

In 956 he took the fort of Danel. At this time Adam Ghakkar came before the Mirzá and asked him to pardon Daulat Chakk. He agreed to do so and Adam called Daulat into the tent. The Mirzá, on his coming in, showed him no honour. For this reason Daulat became very angry, and taking away the elephant he had brought as a present, he went away. The courtiers wished to pursue him but the Mirzá forbade them. After some time Haidar returned to Kashmir. Daulat Chakk and Gázi Khán and Jai Chakk went to Haidar Khán who had fled from Islám Sháh to Rájáori. When Islám Sháh who was pursuing the Niyázis arrived at the town of Madawár from Naoshahra, Haibat Khán Niyázi sent Sayyid Khán to him. Sayyid Khán making propositions of peace gave up the mother and son of Haibat Khán Niyázi to Islám Sháh who turning back went to the town of Bán near Siálkot and agreed to the conditions. The three Kashmiris above-mentioned then took Haibat Khán to Bárámula and wished to take him to Kashmir, and carry away Haidar. As Haibat did not see his way to doing this he sent a Bráhman to Haidar with conditions of peace. When he had received a promise from Haidar he went to live at Hir (Nir in MS. No. 6571 opening 190 in British Museum) in Jammu and the Kashmiris went to Islám Sháh. Gházi Khán Chakk, however, went to Mirzá Haidar. (It is evident that at this time the Kashmiris were tired of Haidar. They wished Islám Sháh to be king. We do not read that Islám ever went so far as Kashmir. The nobles, however, must have struck coins in his name, using the formula ***struck in Kashmir*** on the reverse. I have seen two coins of Islám Sháh of this time. It was a common practice to strike coins anticipating events which did *not* come to pass. The date on this coin is 957 A.H. It may have been struck by Haidar as a compliment to Islám Sháh.)

In the year 957 A.H. Mirzá Haidar being at peace with his neighbours sent presents of saffron to Islám Sháh by the hands of Khwájah Shams Mughal. In the following year Islám Sháh sent the ambassadors back with presents of silk cloth and goods accompanied by Yásin (Básin in above MS.) as envoy. Mirzá Haidar sent back Yásin laden with shawls and saffron to Islám Sháh.

Mirzá Qarrá Bahádur was appointed governor of Bhirpul (or Bharmal) and along with him were sent from amongst the Kashmiris Idi Ziná and Názuk Sháh, Husain Mákari and Khwájah Háji. The whole of these with Mirzá Qarrá came back to Indarkot and went thence to Bárámula and became rebellious. The reason of this rebellion was that the Mughals (the forces of Mirzá Haidar) were not acceptable to them. When the Mughals informed the Mirzá of this he told them they were no less ready than the Kashmiris to rebel. Husain Mákari sent his brother Ali Mákari to Mirzá Haidar to make excuse for the Kashmiris and to call again the army. Haidar was not aware

[1] The western province of Kashmir. See Pakhli on map.—[ED.].
[2] Baltistan.—[ED.].
[3] Ladak.—[ED.].

of the condition of things, and told them that the Kashmiris were powerless and that there was no use in calling the army.

On the 27th of Ramzán a great fire burst out in Indarkot. Mirzá Qarrá and his following sent word that their houses were destroyed, and asked for orders saying that if convenient they would rebuild their houses and next year go to Bhirpul. Mirzá Haidar was displeased at this conduct. Nevertheless whether he would or not the army went towards Bhirpul. At night time, however, Idi Ziná and the rest of the Kashmiris left the Mughals and came to the pass of Bhirpul and took with them Husain Mákari, Ali Mákari and others in order that they might not be slain by the Mughals. When it was morning the men of Bhirpul fought with the Mughals who were fastened in the mountains. Sayyid Mirzá fled and went into the fort of Bhirpul. About 80 Mughals, men of note were slain in this affair. Muhammad Nazir and Mirzá Qarrá Bahádur were captured. The rest of the army came to Bahrámgalla. When Mirzá Haidar heard of this he was sorely vexed and ordered all the silver vessels to be broken and the coin now current in Kashmir was struck from them. Jahángir Mákari at this time got into favour and the estates of Husain Mákari were bestowed upon him. Tradespeople had horses and outfits given to them and were made soldiers. After this news came that Mulla Abdullah, hearing of the exodus of the Kashmiris, was coming to Kashmir. When he got near to Bárámula the Kashmiris crowded on him and slew him. Khwájah Qásim was slain in Little Tibet. Muhammad Nazir was imprisoned in Rájáori. The Kashmiris leaving Bahrámgalla came to Hambarapur. Mirzá Haidar was thus forced to fight them and he came to Indarkot. He had with him only a thousand men. With him were Mughal nobles who had 700 men more. The whole took up a position in Shaháb-ud-Dinpur. Daulat Chakk and Gházi Khán Chakk went to Hambarapur to help Idi Ziná and coming from that place assembled in Khánpur. Mirzá Haidar took up his position in the plain of Khálidgarh near Srinagar. Fath Chakk, whose father had been slain by the Mughals, Khwájah Bahrám brought, with 3,000 men to Indarkot to revenge his father's death. They burned all the palaces of Mirzá Haidar in the Safá gardens. When Mirzá Haidar heard of this he said, "I have not brought this from Káshgar that I might by the grace of God, again build it." Jai Ali in revenge burnt the palaces of Zain-ul-Abidin in Suryápur, but this did not please Mirzá Haidar and the army burnt the palaces of Idi Ziná and Nauroz Chakk in Srinagar. Mirzá Haidar himself took up a position in Khánpur in which place was a willow tree under which 22 horsemen could stand. If one branch of this tree were shaken the whole tree was moved. At last the Kashmiris came from Khánpur and took up a position at Adnipur and not more than a distance of two kos remained between the two armies. Mirzá Haidar determined to make a night attack on the enemy. He first of all made his own younger brother Mirzá Abdur Rahmán his heir-apparent and inaugurated him, then getting his men into order he prepared for the night attack. It so happened that the night was very cloudy and when he got to the tent of Khwájah Háji who was the soul of the rebellion and the agent of the Mirzá, the darkness hid everything. Sháh Nazar a cuirassier of Mirzá Haidar said, "When I shot an arrow the voice of the Mirzá fell on my ear, saying, 'you are at fault.' I then knew that the arrow had accidentally struck the Mirzá." It is also said that a butcher shot him in the thigh with an arrow. In another tradition it is stated that Kamál Kuka killed him with a sword. But except an arrow-wound in his heart no other thing was visible. In reality this is the sum of the traditions. When morning dawned it became noised abroad amongst the Kashmiris that a Mughal was lying slain in their camp. When Khwájah Háji came to view the corpse, he said it was that of Haidar. He held up the head from the earth but nothing but the last breath remained. He moved his eyes and gave up the ghost. After this the Mughals fled to Indarkot and the Kashmiris buried the corpse of Haidar and then pursued the Mughals. They took refuge in Indarkot and for three days defended themselves. On the fourth day Muhammad Rumi loaded the cannon with copper coins and fired them on the enemy. Every one who was struck with them died. At last, however, Khánmai, the widow of Mirzá Haidar, and her sister Khánji spoke to the Mughals and said, 'Inasmuch as Mirzá Haidar has departed from our midst, it would be better to make peace with the Kashmiris." The Mughals agreed to this and sent Amir Khán, builder, to the Kashmiris to ask for peace. The Kashmiris were pleased at this and wrote a letter with oath and covenant that they would not persecute the Mughals any more. The government of Haidar Turk lasted for ten years.

Názuk Sháh. 3rd Time.—When the doors of the fort were opened, the Kashmiris went into the treasury of Mirzá Haidar and plundered it, taking away the beautiful and delicate garments it contained. The family of the Mirzá was taken to Srinagar and placed in the hands of Manujá. The Kashmiri chiefs then divided Kashmir between themselves. Daulat Chakk got the parganah of Deosar, Ghází Khán the parganah of Wáhi; Yusuf Chakk and Bahrám Chakk obtained Kamráj. Khwájah Háji the wakil of the Mirzá took a lákh of shawls and the whole of the nobles of Kashmir, but especially Idi Ziná, took the government of the province into their hands. Názuk Sháh as a kind of shadow of a king was upheld in name. In truth Idi Ziná was king.

APPENDIX B.

THE KARAWANAS.

Some inquiries regarding the Karáwánás, which were very kindly made for me in Khorasán by Mr. Maula Bakhsh, K.B., Attaché at the Meshed Consulate General, have resulted, it would seem, in tracing some of the posterity of the Karáwánás. Mr. Maula Bakhsh writes from near Asterabad :—" Only the other day, while passing through the Mána district of Bujnurd, I heard of a village called Samandarra or Kárnás. This excited my curiosity and, on inquiry, I found that the village derived its name from its Kárnás inhabitants, about thirty families of whom (the total population of the village) are settled there. In the Gurgán country again, which extends from Dáhana-i-Gurgán on the east, to the Gunbad-i-Kábus (or Káus) on the west, on both banks of the Gurgán river, and is occupied by the Goklán Turkomans, I found about fifty families of Kárnás, and was told that there were some families in Khiva also.

" These people speak Turki now, and are considered part of the Goklán Turkomans. They, however, say they are Chingiz-Kháni Moghuls, and are no doubt the descendants of the same Kárnás, or Karávanás, who took such a prominent part in the Moghul victories in Persia.

"The word Kárnás, I was told by a learned Goklan Mullah, means *Tirandáz*, or *Shikári* (*i.e.*, Archer or Hunter) and was applied to this tribe of Moghuls on account of their professional skill in shooting, which apparently secured them an important place in the army. In Turki the word Kárnás means *Shikam-parast*—literally 'belly worshippers,' which implies avarice. This term is in use at present, and I was told, by a Kázi of Bujnurd, that it is sometimes used by way of reproach . . . . The Kárnás people in Mána and Gurgán say it is the name of their tribe, and they can give no other explanation."

Although the modern name has become curiously abbreviated, there appears to be little reason to doubt that these Kárnás, or "shooters," represent, at any rate, the "artillerists" of Wassáf (see pp. 76, 77, *Introduction*).

APPENDIX C.

CHRONOLOGICAL TABLE OF EVENTS.

ENGLAND.	CONTINENTAL EUROPE.
1327. Edward II. deposed and murdered.	1328. Valois dynasty founded in France.
1338. Edward III. invaded France.	1358. Turks first cross the Hellespont.
1346. Battle of Creçy.	1378. The Papacy restored in Rome.
1356. Battle of Poictiers.	1385. Independence of Portugal.
1371. Stuart dynasty established in Scotland.	1396. Crusade in Hungary against the Turks.
1377. Accession of Richard II.	1403. Sultan Báyazid defeated by Timur.
1399. Deposition of Richard II.	1428. Joan of Arc delivers Orleans.
1403. Battle of Shrewsbury.	1436. Supposed date of invention of printing.
1413. Accession of Henry V.	1453. Constantinople taken by the Turks.
1415. Battle of Agincourt.	1462. Ivan III. becomes Prince of Muscovy.
1422. Henry VI. proclaimed king of France.	1467. Bombs and mortars invented in Italy.
1461. Edward IV. becomes king.	1478. Khans of Crimea submit to Turks.
1485. Battle of Bosworth Field. Tudor dynasty founded.	1482. Ivan III. becomes first Tsar of Muscovy.
1509. Death of Henry VII.	1483. Cape of Good Hope discovered. (Portugal).
1512. Henry VIII. invades France.	
1520. Field of the Cloth of Gold.	
1534. Papal authority abolished.	
1547. Accession of Edward VI.	
1553. Accession of Mary.	
1558. Accession of Elizabeth.	

1492. Discovery of America. (Spain).
1501. Naples subdued by France.
1516. Charles V. ascends the throne of Spain.
1517. Egypt conquered by Turks.
1523. Gustavus Wasa becomes king of Sweden.
1529. Vienna besieged by the Turks.
1533. Ivan IV. (the Terrible) succeeds as Tsar.
1545. Council of Trent assembles.
1552. Treaty of Passau.
1584. Death of Ivan the Terrible.

INDIA.

1325. Death of Mahom. Tughluk, founder of Tughluk dynasty of Delhi.
1398. Timur invades India.
1450. Lodi dynasty of Afghans.
1498. Arrival of Vasco de Gama at Malabar.
1509. Albuquerque becomes viceroy of Portuguese India (d. 1519).
1526. Baber founds Moghul (Chaghatai) Empire.
1530. Humayun succeeds.
1538. Turkish attack on Portuguese at Diu.
1540. Humayun defeated by Shir Khan at Kanauj.
1540. Rule of Afghan Sur dynasty begins.
1555. Return of Humayun to India.
1556. Accession of Akbar.

CHINA.

1333. Accession of Ching-tsung (or Tohan Timur), last Emperor of Mongol dynasty.
1368. Ming dynasty established. Emperor Hung Wu. Capital at Nanking.
1403. Yung Loh, 2nd Ming Emperor, changes capital to Peking.
1536. Macao granted to the Portuguese.
1580. (abt.) Jesuit missions first established.
1644. Ming dynasty ends.

PERSIA.

1380 Invaded by Timur.
1399. " "
1468. Conquered by Turkomans.
1501. Sufavi dynasty founded by Shah Ismail.
1519. Ismail conquers Georgia.
1525. Accession of Shah Tahmasp.
1576. Ismail II. succeeds.

INDEX.

(ABBREVIATIONS: * denotes 'Introduction'; and *n.* signifies 'footnote.')

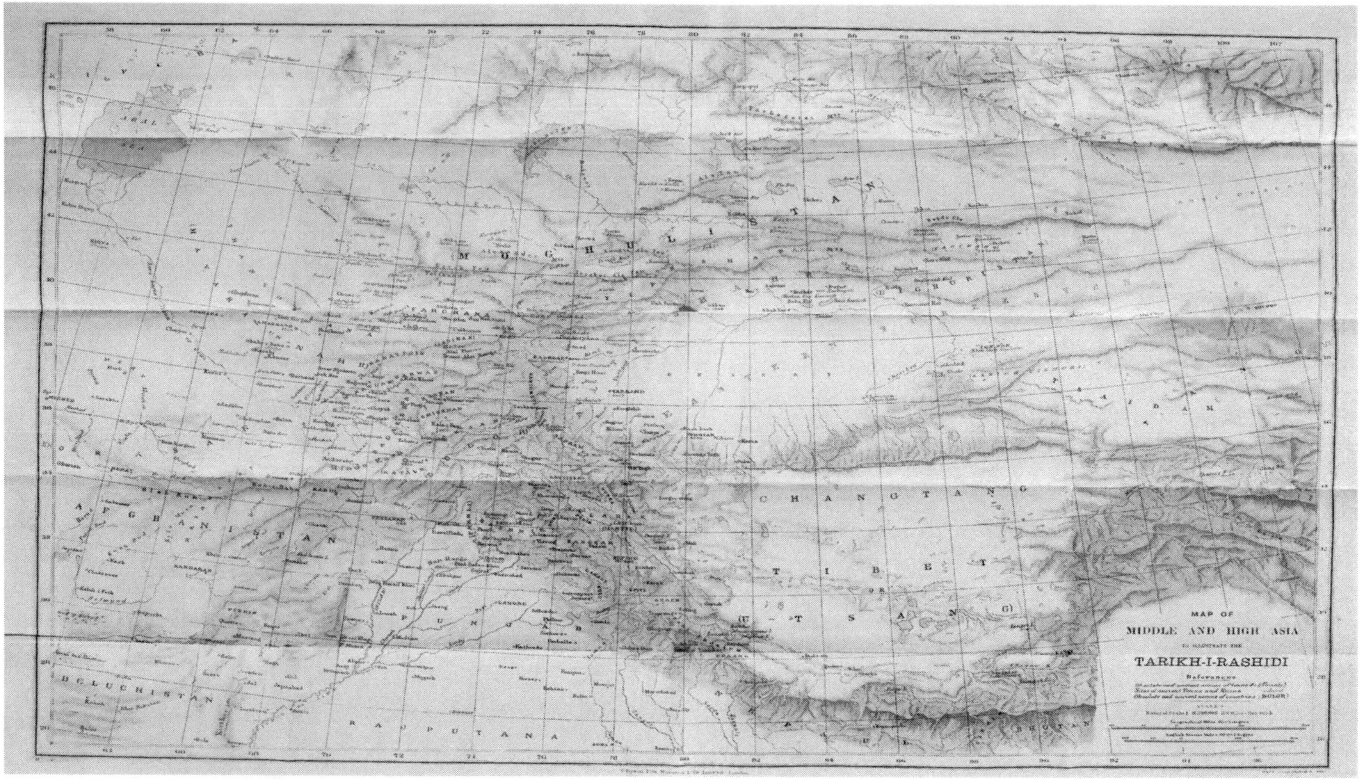
MAP OF
MIDDLE AND HIGH ASIA
TO ILLUSTRATE THE
TARIKH-I-RASHIDI
MOGHULISTAN
FARGHANA
AFGHANISTAN
BELUCHISTAN
RAJPUTANA
CHANGTANG
TIBET
BHOTAN
ARAL SEA